Avionics:
Fundamentals of Aircraft Electronics
The Guide to Aviation Electronics Technician Certification

Scott Kenney

Production Staff

Designer/Photographer Dustin Blyer
Production Manager Holly Bonos
Designer/Production Coordinator Roberta Byerly
Lead Illustrator Amy Siever

© Copyright 2013 by
Avotek Information Resources, LLC.
All Rights Reserved

International Standard Book Number 1-933189-28-2
ISBN 13: 978-1-933189-28-4
Order # T-AVFUN-0101

For Sale by: Avotek
A Select Aerospace Industries company

Mail to:
P.O. Box 219
Weyers Cave, Virginia 24486
USA

Ship to:
200 Packaging Drive
Weyers Cave, Virginia 24486
USA

Toll Free: 1-800-828-6835
Telephone: 1-540-234-9090
Fax: 1-540-234-9399

First Printing
Printed in the USA

www.avotek.com

Preface

This textbook is intended for those individuals who are working toward their National Center for Aerospace and Transportation Technologies (NCATT) certification and want to pursue a career in avionics. This book provides the student with the basic knowledge needed to begin working as an entry level avionics technician as well as preparing the student to take the NCATT Aircraft Electronics Technician (AET) certification test. It also covers basic electronic material that Aircraft Maintenance Technicians (AMTs) will find helpful in furthering their careers in maintaining modern aircraft with computerized and electronic systems.

Avionics: Fundamentals of Aircraft Electronics, the first book in Avotek's avionics series, covers the basic building blocks needed to understand electronics. These include direct current, alternating current, electronic components, electricity generation and digital theory. The volume presents this material in an aviation context and also covers basic aircraft information including aircraft terminology, aerodynamics, corrosion control and shop safety.

Today's aircraft contain a diverse blend of systems. This text explains both new technology and, what some may consider, legacy technology. The extreme reliability of aircraft and their systems serves to keep avionics in operation for many years. A competent technician must have a broad knowledge of these technologies.

A student study guide is available for this book that provides a variety of questions presented in assignment format. Each page is designed so the assignment can be turned in individually.

Textbooks, by nature, must be general in their overall coverage of a subject area. As always, the aircraft manufacturer is the sole source of operation, maintenance, repair and overhaul information. Their manuals are approved by the FAA and must always be followed. No material presented in this or any other textbook may be used as a manual for actual operation, maintenance or repairs.

The author has, to the best of his abilities, tried to provide accurate, honest and pertinent material in this textbook. However, as with all human endeavors, errors and omissions can show up in the most unexpected places. If any exist, they are unintentional. Please bring them to our attention.

Email us at comments@avotek.com for comments or suggestions.

Avotek® Aircraft Maintenance Series
Introduction to Aircraft Maintenance
Aircraft Structural Maintenance
Aircraft System Maintenance
Aircraft Powerplant Maintenance

Avotek® Aircraft Avionics Series
Avionics: Fundamentals of Aircraft Electronics
Avionics: Beyond the AET
Avionics: Systems and Troubleshooting

Other Books by Avotek®
Aircraft Corrosion Control Guide
Aircraft Structural Technician
Aircraft Turbine Engines
Aircraft Wiring & Electrical Installation
AMT Reference Handbook
Avotek Aeronautical Dictionary
Fundamentals of Modern Aviation
Light Sport Aircraft Inspection Procedures
Structural Composites: Advanced Composites in Aviation

Acknowledgements

Brian Stoltzfus — *Priority Air Charter*

Classic Aviation Services

David Jones — *Aviation Institute of Maintenance*

Greg Campbell, Sherman Showalter, Stacey Smith — *Shenandoah Valley Regional Airport*

Harry Moyer, Virgil Gottfried — *Samaritan's Purse*

Jeremy Nafziger

Lufthansa

Karl Stoltzfus, Sr., Michael Stoltzfus, Aaron Lorson and Staff — *Dynamic Aviation Group, Inc.*

Lori Johnson, Larry Bartlett — *Duncan Aviation*

Mark Stoltzfus — *Preferred Airparts*

NASA Langley Research Center

National Business Aviation Association

Pat Colgan — *Capital Aviation*

Select Aerospace Industries, Inc.

Select Airparts

Steve Hanson, Jeff Ellis, Tim Travis — *Beechcraft*

Snap-on Tools

U.S. Industrial Tools

Contents

Preface iii

Acknowledgements iv

1 Fundamentals of Direct Current

1-2	The Atom: Matter, Energy and Electricity	1-25	DC Calculations
		1-30	Series DC Circuits
1-10	Magnetism	1-34	Parallel DC Circuits
1-17	Electrical Characteristics		

2 Basic Components

2-1	Circuit Control Devices	2-28	Electrical Resistors
2-16	Circuit Protection Devices		

3 Concepts of Alternating Current

3-1	Alternating Current	3-35	AC Calculations
3-12	Inductance	3-50	Transformers
3-22	Capacitance		

4 Generation and Storage of Electricity

4-1	The Battery	4-16	Alternators
4-7	Generators		

5 Introduction to Solid-State Components

5-1	Introduction to Solid-State Devices	5-18	Introduction to Transistors
5-11	Semiconductor Diodes	5-43	Electrostatic Discharge Sensitive Components

6 Advanced Solid-State Components

6-1	Special Diodes	6-16	Advanced Transistors

7 Frequency Generation

7-1	Amplifiers	7-15	Filters
7-7	Oscillators	7-31	Waves and Wave Shaping

8 Digital Theory

| 8-1 | Numbering Systems | 8-24 | Logic Functions |

9 Fundamentals of Flight

9-1	Theory of Flight	9-15	Aircraft Control
9-6	Airfoils	9-19	Transport Aircraft Control Surfaces
9-9	Thrust and Drag		
9-11	Aircraft Stability	9-27	Control Systems

10 Corrosion Control

| 10-1 | Corrosion Prevention and Control |

11 Aircraft Manuals and Drawings

| 11-1 | Manufacturers' Maintenance Manuals | 11-5 | Purpose and Function of Aircraft Drawings |

12 Aircraft Safety

| 12-1 | Shop Safety | 12-15 | Safety on the Flightline |
| 12-9 | Fire Protection | | |

13 Tools and Test Equipment

13-1	Tool Procedures and Practices	13-26	Power Tools
13-3	Measuring Tools	13-30	Soldering Tools
13-7	General Purpose Tools	13-38	Conductor Termination
13-15	Cutting Tools	13-42	Special Tools and Test Equipment

Index — I-1

1

Fundamentals of Direct Current

Aviation electronics, commonly known as *avionics*, are an integral part of modern aircraft. The term was first used in the early years of aviation and frequently referred to a very basic navigation and/or communication radio installed in the instrument panel. Since the development of the transistor and integrated circuit, electronics have found their way into many areas of the aircraft.

In modern production aircraft, electronics are integrated throughout the airframe and powerplant areas. The separation of avionics from the rest of the aircraft is not as clear as it was in the past. In today's world, the avionics technician frequently works alongside the aviation maintenance technician in troubleshooting and repairing these integrated systems.

Aviation maintenance industry professionals also see the opportunities presented by broadening technicians' education to include an understanding of electronics. Many aircraft components that previously were mechanical in nature or used basic electrical circuits, are now operated by advanced electronic controls.

This volume is designed to give the student a principal understanding of electronics and the aviation environment that the avionics technician operates in. The student will learn basic electricity and electronics theory as well as the common components that are the building blocks of operational circuits. Aviation fundamentals are also presented. Additional volumes in the series detail specific avionics applications and further prepare an individual for a fulfilling career in aviation.

We start with the basic concepts of matter and electricity and then show how these can be controlled and directed.

Learning Objective

DESCRIBE
- electron theory
- the six methods of producing a voltage

EXPLAIN
- the difference between a conductor, an insulator and a semiconductor

APPLY
- use Ohm's Law to calculate the relationship between power, resistance, voltage, and current
- use Kirchhoff's Laws to calculate series, parallel, and complex circuits

Left. Most corporate aircraft are equipped with a 28 volt direct current electrical system. This is often powered by a direct current generator.

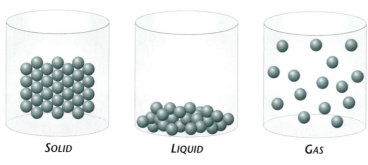

Figure 1-1-1. The three states of matter

Section 1

The Atom: Matter, Energy and Electricity

If there are roots to western science, they no doubt lie under the rubble that was once ancient Greece. With the exception of the Greeks, ancient people had little interest in the structure of materials. They accepted a solid as being just that—a continuous, uninterrupted substance. One Greek school of thought believed that if a piece of matter, such as copper, were subdivided, it could be done indefinitely and still only that material would be found. Others reasoned that there must be a limit to the number of subdivisions that could be made and have the material still retain its original characteristics. They held fast to the idea that there must be a basic particle upon which all substances are built. Modern experiments have revealed that there are, indeed, several basic particles, or building blocks within all substances.

Matter

Matter is defined as anything that occupies space and has weight; that is, the weight and dimensions of matter can be measured. Examples of matter are air, water, automobiles, clothing and even the human body. Thus, it can be said that matter may be found in any one of three states:

1. Solid
2. Liquid
3. Gas

Elements and Compounds

An *element* is a substance that cannot be reduced to a simpler substance by chemical means. Examples of elements that are encountered in everyday life are iron, gold, silver, copper and oxygen. There are now more than 100 known elements. All the different known substances are composed of one or more elements. When two or more elements are chemically combined, the resulting substance is called a compound

A compound is a chemical combination of elements that can be separated by chemical means but not by physical means. Examples of common compounds are water, which consists of hydrogen and oxygen, and table salt, which consists of sodium and chlorine. A mixture, on the other hand, is a combination of elements and compounds, not chemically combined, that can be separated by physical means. Examples of mixtures are air, which is made up of nitrogen, oxygen, carbon dioxide, small amounts of several rare gases, and sea water, which consists chiefly of salt and water.

Molecules

A *molecule* is a chemical combination of two or more atoms. In a compound the molecule is the smallest particle that has all the characteristics of the compound. Consider water, for example. Water is matter, since it occupies space and has weight. Depending on the temperature, it may exist as a liquid (water), a solid (ice) or a gas (steam), as seen in Figure 1-1-1. Regardless of the temperature, it will still have the same composition. Start with a quantity of water, divide this and pour out one half and continue this process a sufficient number of times, and eventually the remaining quantity of water cannot be further divided without ceasing to be water. This quantity is called a molecule of water. If this molecule of water divided, instead of two parts of water, there will be one part of oxygen and two parts of hydrogen (H_2O) as seen in Figure 1-1-2.

Atoms

Molecules are made up of smaller particles called *atoms*. An atom is the smallest particle of an element that retains the characteristics of that element. The atoms of one element, however, differ from the atoms of all other elements. Since there are over 100 known elements, there must be over 100 different atoms, or a different atom for each element. Just as thousands of words can be made

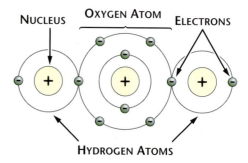

Figure 1-1-2. A water molecule

by combining the proper letters of the alphabet, so thousands of different materials can be made by chemically combining the proper atoms. Any particle that is a chemical combination of two or more atoms is called a molecule

The oxygen molecule consists of two atoms of oxygen, and the hydrogen molecule consists of two atoms of hydrogen. Sugar, on the other hand, is a compound composed of atoms of carbon, hydrogen and oxygen (Figure 1-1-3). These atoms are combined into sugar molecules. Since the sugar molecules can be broken down by chemical means into smaller and simpler units, sugar atoms cannot exist.

The atoms of each element are made up of *electrons*, *protons* and, in most cases, *neutrons*, which are collectively called subatomic particles (Figure 1-1-4). Furthermore, the electrons, protons and neutrons of one element are identical to those of any other element. The reason that there are different kinds of elements is that the number and the arrangement of electrons and protons within the atom are different for the different elements. The electron is considered to be a small negative charge of electricity. The proton has a positive charge of electricity equal and opposite to the charge of the electron.

Scientists have measured the mass and size of the electron and proton, and they know how much charge each possesses. The electron and proton each have the same quantity of charge, although the mass of the proton is approximately 1,837 times that of the electron. All atoms except hydrogen have at least one neutral particle called a neutron. The neutron has a mass approximately equal to that of a proton, but it has no electrical charge. According to a popular theory, the electrons, protons and neutrons of the atoms are thought to be arranged in a manner similar to a miniature solar system. The protons and neutrons form a heavy nucleus with a positive charge, around which the very light electrons revolve.

Energy Levels

Since an electron in an atom has both mass and motion, it contains two types of energy. By virtue of its motion the electron contains *kinetic energy*. Due to its position it also contains *potential energy*. The total energy contained by an electron (kinetic plus potential) is the factor that determines the radius of the electron orbit. In order for an electron to remain in this orbit, it must neither gain nor lose energy. It is well known that light is a form of energy, but the physical form in which this energy exists is not known

Accepted theory proposes the existence of light as tiny packets of energy called *photons*. Photons can contain various quantities of energy. The amount

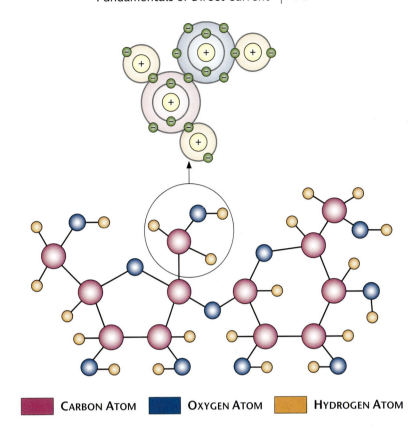

Figure 1-1-3. A sugar molecule

depends upon the color of the light involved. Should a photon of sufficient energy collide with an orbital electron, the electron will absorb the photon's energy. The electron, which now has a greater-than-normal amount of energy, will jump to a new orbit farther from the nucleus. The first new orbit to which the electron can jump has a radius four times as large as the radius of the original orbit. Had the electron received a greater amount of energy, the next possible orbit to which it could jump would have a radius nine times the original. Thus, each orbit may be considered to

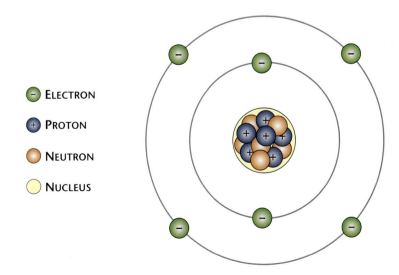

Figure 1-1-4. Atomic model showing the basic structure of a carbon atom

1-4 | Fundamentals of Direct Current

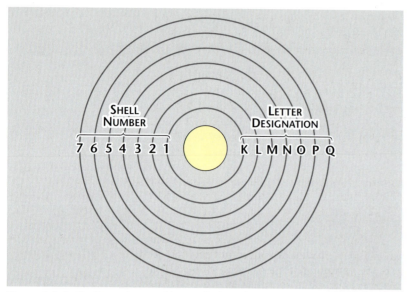

Figure 1-1-5. Shell number and letter designation

represent one of a large number of energy levels that the electron may attain.

It must be emphasized that the electron cannot jump to just any orbit. The electron will remain in its lowest orbit until a sufficient amount of energy is available, at which time the electron will accept the energy and jump to one of a series of permissible orbits. An electron cannot exist in the space between energy levels. This indicates that the electron will not accept a photon of energy unless it contains enough energy to elevate it to one of the higher energy levels. Heat energy and collisions with other particles can also cause the electron to jump orbits.

Once the electron has been elevated to an energy level higher than the lowest possible energy level, the atom is said to be in an excited state. The electron will not remain in this excited condition for more than a fraction of a second before it will radiate the excess energy and return to a lower energy orbit. To illustrate this principle, assume that a normal electron has just received a photon of energy sufficient to raise it from the first to the third energy level. In a short period of time the electron may jump back to the first level, emitting a new photon identical to the one it received.

A second alternative would be for the electron to return to the lower level in two jumps; from the third to the second, and then from the second to the first. In this case the electron would emit two photons, one for each jump. Each of these photons would have less energy than the original photon that excited the electron.

This principle is used in the fluorescent light, where ultraviolet light photons, which are not visible to the human eye, bombard a phosphor coating on the inside of a glass tube. The electrons in the coating, in returning to their normal orbits, emit visible photons. By using the proper chemicals for the phosphor coating, any color of light may be obtained, including white. This same principle is also used in lighting up the screen of a television picture tube.

The basic principles just developed apply equally well to the atoms of more complex elements. In atoms containing two or more electrons, the electrons interact with each other and the exact path of any one electron is very difficult to predict. However, each electron lies in a specific energy band and the orbits will be considered as an average of the electron's position.

Shells and Subshells

The difference between the atoms, insofar as their chemical activity and stability are concerned, is dependent upon the number and position of the electrons included within the atom. How are these electrons positioned within the atom? In general, the electrons reside in groups of orbits called shells.

These shells are elliptically shaped and are assumed to be located at fixed intervals. Thus, the shells are arranged in steps that correspond to fixed energy levels. The shells, and the number of electrons required to fill them, may be predicted by the employment of Pauli's exclusion principle. Simply stated, this principle specifies that each shell will contain a maximum of $2n^2$ electrons, where n is the shell number starting with the one closest to the nucleus. By this principle, the second shell, for example, would contain $2(2)^2$ or 8 electrons when full.

In addition to being numbered, the shells are also given letter designations (Figure 1-1-5). Starting with the shell closest to the nucleus and progressing outward, the shells are labeled K, L, M, N, O, P and Q, respectively. The shells are considered to be full, or complete, when they contain the following quantities of electrons: 2 in the K shell, 8 in the L shell, 18 in the M shell, and so on, in accordance with the exclusion principle. Each of these shells is a major shell and can be divided into subshells, of which there are four, labeled s, p, d and f. Like the major shells, the subshells are also limited as to the number of electrons which they can contain. Thus, the s subshell is complete when it contains 2 electrons, the p subshell when it contains 6, the d subshell when it contains 10, and the f subshell when it contains 14 electrons.

Valence

The number of electrons in the outermost shell determines the *valence* of an atom. For this reason, the outer shell of an atom is called the valence shell; and the electrons contained in this shell are called valence electrons. The valence of an atom determines its ability to gain or lose an electron, which in turn determines the chemical and electrical properties of the atom. An atom that is lacking only one or two electrons from its outer shell will easily gain electrons to complete its shell, but a large amount of energy is required to free any of its electrons. An atom having a relatively small number of electrons in its outer shell in comparison to the number of electrons required to fill the shell will easily lose these valence electrons. The valence shell always refers to the outermost shell.

Ionization

When the atom loses electrons or gains electrons in this process of electron exchange, it is said to be *ionized*. For ionization to take place, there must be a transfer of energy, which results in a change in the internal energy of the atom. An atom having more than its normal amount of electrons acquires a negative charge, and is called a negative ion. The atom that gives up some of its normal electrons is left with fewer negative charges than positive charges and is called a positive ion. Thus, ionization is the process by which an atom loses or gains electrons.

Prefixes

In any system of measurements, a single set of units is usually not sufficient for all the computations involved in electrical repair and maintenance. Small distances, for example, can usually be measured in inches, but larger distances are more meaningfully expressed in feet, yards or miles.

Because electrical values often vary from numbers that are a millionth part of a basic unit of measurement to very large values, it is often necessary to use a wide range of numbers to represent the values of such units as volts, amperes or ohms. A series of prefixes which appear with the name of the unit have been devised for the various multiples or submultiples of the basic units. There are 12 of these prefixes, which are also known as conversion factors. Six of the most commonly used prefixes with a short definition of each are as follows:

Mega — one million (1,000,000)

Kilo — one thousand (1,000)

Centi — one-hundredth (1/100)

Milli — one-thousandth (1/1,000)

Micro — one-millionth (1/1,000,000)

Pico — one-millionth-millionth (1/1,000,000,000,000)

One of the most extensively used conversion factors, kilo, can be used to explain the use of prefixes with basic units of measurement.

Kilo means 1,000, and when used with volts is expressed as kilovolt, meaning 1,000 volts. The symbol for kilo is the letter k. Thus, 1,000 volts is one kilovolt or 1 kV. Conversely, 1 volt would equal one-thousandth of a kV, or 1/1000 kV. This could also be written 0.001 kV.

Similarly, the word milli means one-thousandth; thus, 1 millivolt equals one-thousandth (1/1,000) of a volt.

These prefixes may be used with all electrical units. They provide a convenient method for writing extremely large or small values. Most electrical formulas require the use of values expressed in basic units. Therefore, all values must usually be converted before computation can be made.

Table 1-1-1 contains a conversion table, which lists a number of the most commonly used electrical values.

CONVERSION TABLE
1 ampere = 1,000,000 microamperes
1 ampere = 1,000 milliamperes
1 farad = 1,000,000,000,000 picofarads
1 farad = 1,000,000 microfarads
1 farad = 1,000 millifarads
1 Henry = 1,000,000 microhenrys
1 Henry = 1,000 millihenrys
1 kilovolt = 1,000 volts
1 kilowatt = 1,000 watts
1 megohm = 1,000,000 ohms
1 microampere = 0.000001 ampere
1 microfarad = 0.000001 farad
1 microhm = 0.000001 ohm
1 microvolt = 0.000001 volt
1 microwatt = 0.000001 watt
1 picofarad = 0.000000000001 farad
1 milliampere = 0.001 ampere
1 millihenry = 0.001 henry
1 millisiemens = 0.001 siemens
1 milliohm = 0.001 ohm
1 millivolt = 0.001 volt
1 milliwatt = 0.001 watt
1 volt = 1,000,000 microvolts
1 volt = 1,000 millivolts
1 watt = 1,000 milliwatts
1 watt = 0.001 kilowatt

Table 1-1-1. Conversion table

1-6 | Fundamentals of Direct Current

NUMBER	PREFIX	SYMBOL
1,000,000,000,000	tera	T
1,000,000,000	giga	G
1,000,000	mega	M
1,000	kilo	k
100	hecto	h
10	deka	da
0.1	deci	d
0.01	centi	c
0.001	milli	m
0.000001	micro	µ
0.000000001	nano	n
0.000000000001	pico	p

Table 1-1-2. Prefixes and symbols for multiples of basic quantities

Table 1-1-2 contains a complete list of the multiples used to express electrical quantities, together with the prefixes and symbols used to represent each number.

Conductors, Semiconductors, and Insulators

In this study of electricity and electronics, the association of matter and electricity is important. Since every electronic device is constructed of parts made from ordinary matter, the effects of electricity on matter must be well understood. As a means of accomplishing this, all elements of which matter is made may be placed into one of three categories:

1. Conductors (Figure 1-1-6). Elements that readily conduct electricity

2. Insulators (Figure 1-1-7). Elements that do not conduct electricity readily

3. Semiconductors (Figure 1-1-8). All matter between these two extremes

The electron theory states that all matter is composed of atoms and the atoms are composed of smaller particles called protons, electrons and neutrons. The electrons orbit the nucleus, which contains the protons and neutrons. It is the valence electrons that are the most important in electricity. These are the electrons that are easiest to break loose from their parent atom. Normally, conductors have three or fewer valence electrons; insulators have five or more valence electrons; and semiconductors usually have four valence electrons.

The electrical conductivity of matter is dependent upon the atomic structure of the material from which the conductor is made. In any solid material, such as copper, the atoms that make up the molecular structure are bound firmly together. At room temperature, copper will contain a considerable amount of heat energy. Since heat energy is one method of removing electrons from their orbits, copper will contain many free electrons that can move from atom to atom. When not under the influence of an external force, these electrons move in a haphazard manner within the conductor. This movement is equal in all directions so that electrons are not lost or gained by any part of the conductor. When controlled by an external force, the electrons move generally in the same direction. The effect of this movement is felt almost instantly from one end of the conductor to the other. This electron movement is called an electric current.

Some metals are better conductors of electricity than others. Silver, copper, gold and aluminum are materials with many free electrons

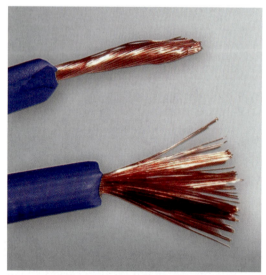

Figure 1-1-6. Copper wire is an example of a conductor.

Figure 1-1-7. Electrical tape is an example of an insulator.

and make good conductors. Silver is the best conductor, followed by copper, gold and aluminum. Copper is used more often than silver because of cost. Aluminum is used where weight is a major consideration, such as in high-tension power lines, with long spans between supports (Figure 1-1-9). Gold is used where oxidation or corrosion is a consideration and good conductivity is required. An example of gold tip connectors are pictured in Figure 1-1-10. The ability of a conductor to handle current also depends upon its physical dimensions.

Conductors are usually found in the form of wire, but may be in the form of bars, tubes or sheets.

Nonconductors have few free electrons. These materials are called insulators. Some examples of these materials are rubber, plastic, enamel, glass, dry wood and mica. Just as there is no perfect conductor, neither is there a perfect insulator.

Some materials are neither good conductors nor good insulators, since their electrical characteristics fall between those of conductors and insulators. These in-between materials are classified as semiconductors. Germanium and silicon are two common semiconductors used in solid-state devices.

Electrostatics

Electrostatics (electricity at rest) is a subject with which most people entering the field of electricity and electronics are somewhat familiar. For example, the way a person's hair stands on end after a vigorous rubbing is an effect of electrostatics. The student studying electrostatics, will gain a better understanding of this common occurrence. Of even greater significance, the study of electrostatics will provide the student with important background knowledge and concepts that are essential to the understanding of electricity and electronics.

Interest in the subject of static electricity can be traced back to the Greeks. Thales of Miletus, a Greek philosopher and mathematician born in the sixth century B.C., discovered that when an amber rod is rubbed with fur, the rod has the amazing characteristic of attracting some very light objects such as feathers and shavings of wood.

About 1600, William Gilbert, an English scientist, made a study of other substances that had been found to possess qualities of attraction similar to amber. Among these were glass, when rubbed with silk, and ebonite, when rubbed with fur. Gilbert classified all the substances that possessed properties similar to

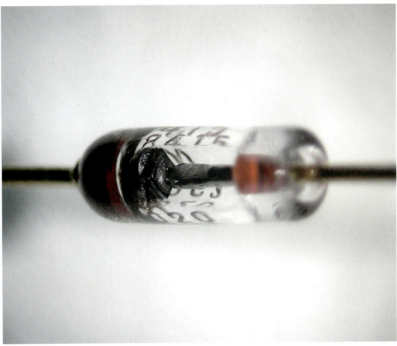

Figure 1-1-8. A silicon diode is an example of a semiconductor.

those of amber as "electrics," a word of Greek origin meaning amber.

Because of Gilbert's work with electrics, a substance such as amber or glass when given a vigorous rubbing was recognized as being electrified, or charged with electricity.

In 1733, Charles du Fay, a French chemist, made an important discovery about electrification. He found that when a glass was rubbed with fur, both the glass rod and the fur became electrified. This realization came when he systematically placed the glass rod and the fur near

Figure 1-1-9. High-tension power lines

Figure 1-1-10. Gold electrical connectors and jumper plug with gold pins

other electrified substances and found that certain substances that were attracted to the glass rod were repelled by the fur, and vice versa. From experiments such as this, he concluded that there must be two exactly opposite kinds of electricity.

Benjamin Franklin, American statesman, inventor and philosopher, is credited with first using the terms positive and negative to describe the two opposite kinds of electricity. The charge produced on a glass rod when it is rubbed with silk, Franklin labeled "positive." He attached the term "negative" to the charge produced on the silk. Those bodies that were not electrified or charged, he called neutral.

Static Electricity

In a natural, or neutral state, each atom in a body of matter will have the proper number of electrons in orbit around it. Consequently, the whole body of matter composed of the neutral atoms will also be electrically neutral. In this state, it is said to have a "zero charge." Electrons will neither leave nor enter the neutrally charged body should it come in contact with other neutral bodies. If, however, any number of electrons are removed from the atoms of a body of matter, there will remain more protons than electrons and the whole body of matter will become electrically positive.

Should the positively charged body come in contact with another body having a normal charge or having a negative (too many electrons) charge, an electric current will flow between them. Electrons will leave the more negative body and enter the positive body. This electron flow will continue until both bodies have equal charges. When two bodies of matter have unequal charges and are near one another, an electric force is exerted between them because of their unequal charges. However, since they are not in contact, their charges cannot equalize. The existence of such an electric force, where current cannot flow, is referred to as *static electricity*. Static in this instance means not moving. It is also referred to as an *electrostatic force*.

One of the easiest ways to create a static charge is by friction. When two pieces of matter are rubbed together, electrons can be "wiped off" one material onto the other. If the materials used are good conductors, it is quite difficult to obtain a detectable charge on either, since equalizing currents can flow easily between the conducting materials. These currents equalize the charges almost as fast as they are created.

A static charge is more easily created between nonconducting materials. When a hard rubber rod is rubbed with fur, the rod will accumulate electrons given up by the fur (Figure 1-1-11). Since both materials are poor conductors, very little equalizing current can flow and an electrostatic charge builds up. When the charge becomes great enough, current will flow regardless of the poor conductivity of the materials. These currents will cause visible sparks and produce a crackling sound, as shown in Figure 1-1-12.

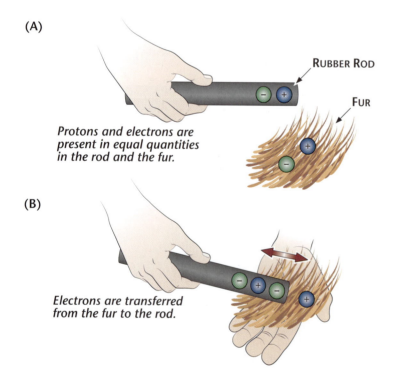

Figure 1-1-11. Producing static electricity by friction

Nature of Charges

When in a natural, or neutral state, an atom has an equal number of electrons and protons. The net negative charge of the electrons in orbit is exactly balanced by the net positive charge of the protons in the nucleus, making the atom electrically neutral.

An atom becomes a positive ion whenever it loses an electron and has an overall positive charge. Conversely, whenever an atom acquires an extra electron, it becomes a negative ion and has a negative charge.

Due to normal molecular activity, there are always ions present in any material. If the number of positive ions and negative ions is equal, the material is electrically neutral. When the number of positive ions exceeds the number of negative ions, the material is positively charged. The material is negatively charged whenever the negative ions outnumber the positive ions.

Since ions are actually atoms without their normal number of electrons, it is the excess or lack of electrons in a substance that determines its charge. In most solids, the transfer of charges is by movement of electrons rather than ions. The transfer of charges by ions will become more significant when electrical activity in liquids and gases is considered. At this time, the electrical behavior in terms of electron movement will be discussed.

Charged Bodies

One of the fundamental laws of electricity is that "like charges repel each other and unlike charges attract each other" (Figure 1-1-13). A positive charge and negative charge, being unlike, tend to move toward each other. In the atom, the negative electrons are drawn toward the positive protons in the nucleus. This attractive force is balanced by the electron's centrifugal force, which is caused by its rotation about the nucleus. As a result, the electrons remain in orbit and are not drawn into the nucleus. Electrons repel each other because of their like negative charges, and protons repel each other because of their like positive charges (Figure 1-1-14).

Coulomb's Law of Charges

The relationship between attracting or repelling charged bodies was first discovered and written about by a French scientist named Charles-Augustin de Coulomb. Coulomb's Law states that "charged bodies attract or repel each other with a force that is directly proportional to the product of their individual charges, and is inversely pro-

Figure 1-1-12. Result of electrostatic charge build

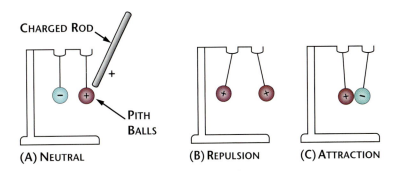

Figure 1-1-13. Reaction of like and unlike charges

portional to the square of the distance between them." The amount of attracting or repelling force that acts between two electrically charged bodies in free space depends on two things:

- Their charges
- The distance between them

Electric Fields

The space between and around charged bodies in which their influence is felt is called an electric *field of force*. It can exist in air, glass, paper or a vacuum. Electrostatic fields and dielectric fields are other names used to refer to this region of force.

Fields of force spread out in the space surrounding their point of origin and, in general,

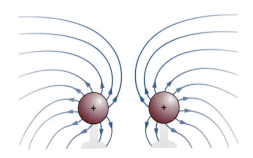

Figure 1-1-14. Field around two positively charged bodies

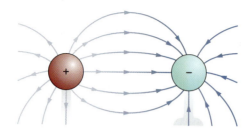

Figure 1-1-15. Direction of electric field around positive and negative charges

diminish in proportion to the square of the distance from their source.

The field about a charged body is generally represented by lines that are referred to as electrostatic lines of force. These lines are imaginary and are used merely to represent the direction and strength of the field. To avoid confusion, the lines of force exerted by a positive charge are always shown leaving the charge, and for a negative charge they are shown entering (Figure 1-1-15).

Section 2

Magnetism

In order to properly understand the principles of electricity, it is necessary to study magnetism and the effects of magnetism on electrical equipment. Magnetism and electricity are so closely related that the study of either subject would be incomplete without at least a basic knowledge of the other.

Much of today's modern electrical and electronic equipment (Figure 1-2-1) could not function without magnetism. Magnetic storage media, primarily computer hard drives, are widely used to store data as well as audio and video files. High-fidelity speakers use magnets to convert amplifier outputs into audible sound. Electrical motors use magnets to convert electrical energy into mechanical motion; generators use magnets to convert mechanical motion into electrical energy.

Magnetic Materials

Magnetism is generally defined as that property of a material that enables it to attract pieces of iron. A material possessing this property is known as a magnet. The word originated with the ancient Greeks, who found stones possessing this characteristic. Materials that are attracted by a magnet, such as iron, steel, nickel and cobalt, have the ability to become magnetized. These are called magnetic materials. Materials such as paper, wood, glass or tin that are not attracted by magnets, are considered nonmagnetic. Nonmagnetic materials are not able to become magnetized.

Ferromagnetic Materials

The most important group of materials connected with electricity and electronics are the ferromagnetic materials. Ferromagnetic materials are those that are relatively easy to magnetize, such as iron, steel, cobalt and the alloys alnico and permalloy. (An *alloy* is made from combining two or more elements, one of which must be a metal.) These new alloys can be very strongly magnetized, and are capable of obtaining a magnetic strength great enough to lift 500 times their own weight.

Natural Magnets

Magnetic stones such as those found by the ancient Greeks are considered to be natural magnets. These stones had the ability to attract small pieces of iron in a manner similar to the magnets that are common today. However, the magnetic properties attributed to the stones were products of nature and not the result of the efforts of man. The Greeks called these substances magnetite.

The Chinese are said to have been aware of some of the effects of magnetism as early as 2600 B.C. They observed that stones similar to magnetite, when freely suspended, had a tendency

Figure 1-2-1. Computer with hi-fidelity speakers

to assume a nearly north-and-south direction (Figure 1-2-2). Because of the directional quality of these stones, they were later referred to as lodestones or leading stones. An example of a lodestone is pictures in Figure 1-2-3.

Natural magnets, which presently can be found in the United States, Norway and Sweden, no longer have any practical use, for it is now possible to easily produce more powerful magnets.

Artificial Magnets

Magnets produced from magnetic materials are called artificial magnets. They can be made in a variety of shapes and sizes and are used extensively in electrical apparatus. Artificial magnets are generally made from special iron or steel alloys that are usually magnetized electrically. The material to be magnetized is inserted into a coil of insulated wire and a heavy flow of electrons is passed through the wire. Magnets can also be produced by stroking a magnetic material with magnetite or with an artificial magnet. The forces causing magnetization are represented by magnetic lines of force, very similar in nature to electrostatic lines of force.

Artificial magnets are usually classified as *permanent* or *temporary*, depending on their ability to retain their magnetic properties after the magnetizing force has been removed. Magnets made from substances such as hardened steel and certain alloys that retain a great deal of their magnetism are called permanent magnets. These materials are relatively difficult to magnetize because of the opposition offered to the magnetic lines of force as the lines of force try to distribute themselves throughout the material. The opposition that a material offers to the magnetic lines of force is called *reluctance*. All permanent magnets are produced from materials having a high reluctance.

A material with a low reluctance, such as soft iron or annealed silicon steel, is relatively easy to magnetize but will retain only a small part of its magnetism once the magnetizing force is removed. Materials of this type that easily lose most of their magnetic strength are called temporary magnets. The amount of magnetism that remains in a temporary magnet is referred to as its residual magnetism. The ability of a material to retain an amount of residual magnetism is called the *retentivity* of the material.

The difference between a permanent and a temporary magnet has been indicated in terms of reluctance, a permanent magnet having a high reluctance and a temporary magnet having a low reluctance. Magnets are also described in terms of the permeability of their materials, or the ease with which magnetic lines of force distribute themselves throughout the material. A permanent magnet, which is produced from a material with a high reluctance, has a low permeability. A temporary magnet, produced from a material with a low reluctance, would have a high permeability.

Magnetic Poles

The magnetic force surrounding a magnet is not uniform. There exists a great concentration of force at each end of the magnet and a very weak force at the center. Proof of this fact can be obtained by dipping a magnet into iron filing. It is found that many filings will cling to the ends of the magnet while very few adhere to the center. The two ends, which are the regions of concentrated lines of force, are called

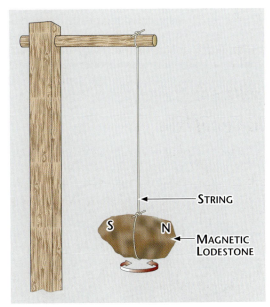

Figure 1-2-2. When suspended on a string, a lodestone oscillates until its north-south axis aligns with the magnetic field of the earth.

Figure 1-2-3. Lodestone

the poles of the magnet (Figure 1-2-4). Magnets have two magnetic poles and both poles have equal magnetic strength.

Law of Magnetic Poles

If a bar magnet is suspended freely on a string it will align itself in a north-and-south direction. When this experiment is repeated, it is found that the same pole of the magnet will always swing toward the north magnetic pole of the earth. Therefore, it is called the north-seeking pole or simply the north pole. The other pole of the magnet is the south-seeking pole or the south pole.

A practical use of the directional characteristic of the magnet is the compass, a device in which a freely rotating magnetized needle indicator points toward the North Pole (Figure 1-2-5). The realization that the poles of a suspended magnet always move to a definite position gives an indication that the opposite poles of a magnet have opposite magnetic polarity.

The law previously stated regarding the attraction and repulsion of charged bodies may also be applied to magnetism if the pole is considered as a charge. The north pole of a magnet will always be attracted to the south pole of another magnet and will show repulsion to a north pole. The law for magnetic poles is: Like poles repel, unlike poles attract.

The Earth's Magnetic Poles

The fact that a compass needle always aligns itself in a particular direction, regardless of its location on earth, indicates that the earth is a huge natural magnet. The distribution of the magnetic force about the earth is the same as that which might be produced by a giant bar magnet running through the center of the earth (Figure 1-2-6). The magnetic axis of the earth is located about 15° from its geographical axis, meaning that the magnetic poles are some distance from the geographical poles. The ability of the north pole of the compass needle to point toward the north geographical pole is due to the presence of the magnetic pole nearby. This magnetic pole is named the magnetic North Pole. However, in actuality, it must have the polarity of a south magnetic pole since it attracts the north pole of a compass needle. The reason for this conflict in terminology can be traced to the early users of the compass. Knowing little about magnetic effects, they called the end of the compass needle that pointed towards the geographical North Pole, the north pole of a compass. It is now known that the north pole of a compass needle (a small bar magnet) can be attracted only by an unlike magnetic pole, that is, a pole of south magnetic polarity.

Weber's Theory of Magnetism

Weber's theory of magnetism considers the molecular alignment of the material. This theory assumes that all magnetic substances are composed of tiny molecular magnets. Any unmagnetized material has the magnetic forces of its molecular magnets neutralized by adjacent molecular magnets, thereby eliminating any magnetic effect. A magnetized material will have most of its molecular magnets lined up so that the north pole of each molecule points in one direction, and the south pole faces the opposite direction (Figure 1-2-7). A material with its molecules thus aligned will then have one effective north pole and one effective south pole.

Domain Theory

A more modern theory of magnetism is based on the electron spin principle. From the study of atomic structure it is known that all matter is composed of vast quantities of atoms, each atom containing one or more orbital electrons. The electrons are considered to orbit in various shells and subshells depending upon their distance from the nucleus. The structure of the atom has

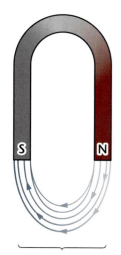

LINES OF FORCE

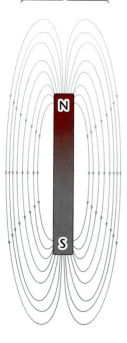

Figure 1-2-4. Magnetic field around a magnet

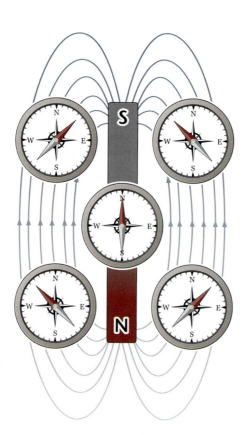

Figure 1-2-5. Bar magnet used as a compass

previously been compared to the solar system, wherein the electrons orbiting the nucleus correspond to the planets orbiting the sun.

Along with its orbital motion about the sun, each planet also revolves on its axis. It is believed that the electron also revolves on its axis as it orbits the nucleus of an atom. It has been experimentally proven that an electron has a magnetic field about it along with an electric field. The effectiveness of the magnetic field of an atom is determined by the number of electrons spinning in each direction. If an atom has equal numbers of electrons spinning in opposite directions, the magnetic fields surrounding the electrons cancel one another, and the atom is unmagnetized. However, if more electrons spin in one direction than another, the atom is magnetized. An atom with an atomic number of 26, such as iron, has 26 protons in the nucleus and 26 revolving electrons orbiting its nucleus. If 13 electrons are spinning in a clockwise direction and 13 electrons are spinning counterclockwise, the opposing magnetic fields will be neutralized. When more than 13 electrons spin in either direction, the atom is magnetized.

Magnetic Fields

The space surrounding a magnet where magnetic forces act is known as the magnetic field.

A pattern of this directional force can be obtained by performing an experiment with iron filings (Figure 1-2-8). A piece of glass is placed over a bar magnet and the iron filings are then sprinkled on the surface of the glass. The magnetizing force of the magnet will be felt through the glass and each iron filing becomes a temporary magnet. If the glass is now tapped gently, the iron particles will align themselves with the magnetic field surrounding the magnet (Figure 1-2-9) just as the compass needle did previously. The filings form a definite pattern, which is a visible representation of the forces comprising the magnetic field. It is also apparent that the magnetic field extends from one pole to the other, constituting a loop about the magnet.

Lines of Force

To further describe and work with magnet phenomena, lines are used to represent the force in the area surrounding a magnet. These lines, called magnetic lines of force, do not actually exist but are imaginary lines used to illustrate and describe the pattern of the magnetic field. The magnetic lines of force are assumed to emanate from the north pole of a magnet, pass through surrounding space, and enter the south pole. The lines of force then travel inside the magnet from the south pole to the north pole, thus completing a closed loop.

When two magnetic poles are brought close together, the mutual attraction or repulsion of the poles produces a more complicated pattern than that of a single magnet. These magnetic

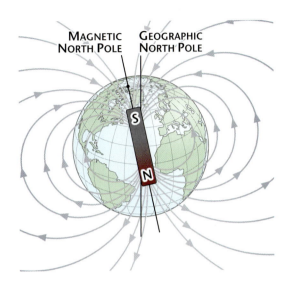

Figure 1-2-6. Earth's magnetic field

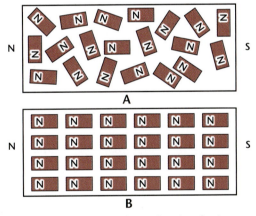

Figure 1-2-7. Arrangements of molecules in a piece of magnetic material

Figure 1-2-8. Iron filings

1-14 | Fundamentals of Direct Current

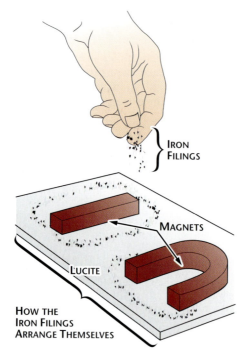

Figure 1-2-9. Tracing out a magnetic field with iron filings

lines of force can be plotted by placing a compass at various points throughout the magnetic field, or they can be roughly illustrated, as before, by the use of iron filings..

Although magnetic lines of force are imaginary, a simplified version of many magnetic phenomena can be explained by assuming the magnetic lines to have certain real properties. The lines of force can be compared to rubber bands that stretch outward when a force is exerted upon them and contract when the force is removed. The characteristics of magnetic lines of force can be described as follows:

- Magnetic lines of force are continuous and will always form closed loops.
- Magnetic lines of force will never cross one another.
- Parallel magnetic lines of force traveling in the same direction repel one another (Figure 1-2-10). Parallel magnetic lines of force traveling in opposite directions tend to unite with each other and form into single lines traveling in a direction determined by the magnetic poles creating the lines of force.
- Magnetic lines of force tend to shorten themselves. Therefore, the magnetic lines of force existing between two unlike poles cause the poles to be pulled together (Figure 1-2-11).
- Magnetic lines of force pass through all materials, both magnetic and nonmagnetic.
- Magnetic lines of force always enter or leave a magnetic material at right angles to the surface.

Magnetic Effects

There are three types of magnetic effects:

1. Magnetic flux – the total number of magnetic lines of force leaving or entering the pole of a magnet is called magnetic flux. The number of flux lines per unit area is known as flux density.

2. Field intensity – the intensity of a magnetic field is directly related to the magnetic force exerted by the field.

3. Attraction/Repulsion – the intensity of attraction or repulsion between magnetic poles may be described by a law almost identical to Coulomb's Law of Charged Bodies. The force between two poles is directly proportional to the product of the pole strengths and inversely proportional to the square of the distance between the poles.

Magnetic Induction

It has been previously stated that all substances that are attracted by a magnet are capable of becoming magnetized. The fact that a material is attracted by a magnet indicates the material must itself be a magnet at the time of attraction.

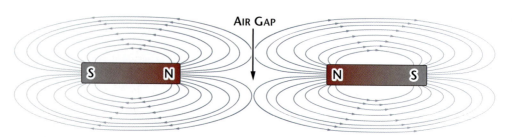

Figure 1-2-10. Like poles repel.

With the knowledge of magnetic fields and magnetic lines of force developed up to this point, it is simple to understand the manner in which a material becomes magnetized when brought near a magnet as demonstrated in Figure 1-2-12. As an iron nail is brought close to a bar magnet, some flux lines emanating from the north pole of the magnet pass through the iron nail in completing their magnetic path. Since magnetic lines of force travel inside a magnet from the south pole to the north pole, the nail will be magnetized in such a polarity that its south pole will be adjacent to the north pole of the bar magnet. There is now an attraction between the two magnets.

If another nail is brought in contact with the end of the first nail, it would be magnetized by induction. This process could be repeated until the strength of the magnetic flux weakens as distance from the bar magnet increases. However, as soon as the first iron nail is pulled away from the bar magnet, all the nails will fall. The reason being that each nail becomes a temporary magnet, and as soon as the magnetizing force is removed, their domains once again assume a random distribution.

Magnetic induction will always produce a pole polarity on the material being magnetized opposite that of the adjacent pole of the magnetizing force. It is sometimes possible to bring a weak north pole of a magnet near a strong magnet's north pole and see attraction between the poles. The weak magnet, when placed within the magnetic field of the strong magnet, has its magnetic polarity reversed by the field of the stronger magnet. Therefore, it is attracted to the opposite pole. For this reason, a very weak magnet, such as a compass needle, must be kept away from a strong magnet.

Magnetism can be induced in a magnetic material by several means. The magnetic material may be placed in the magnetic field (Figure 1-2-13), brought into contact with a magnet, or stroked by a magnet. Stroking and contact both indicate actual contact with the material but are considered in magnetic studies as magnetizing by induction.

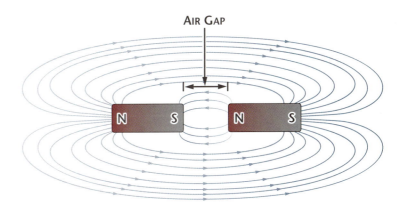

Figure 1-2-11. Unlike poles attract.

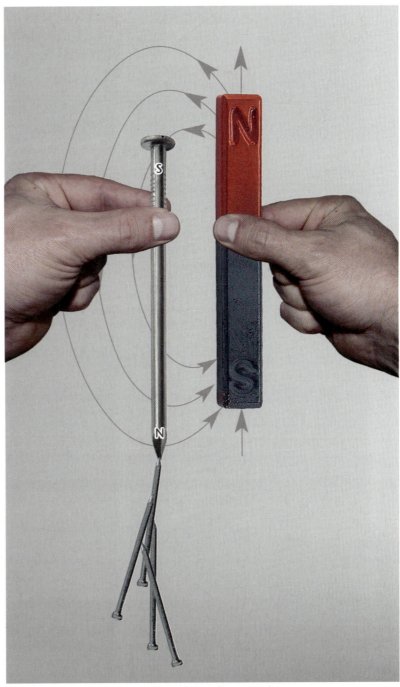

Figure 1-2-12. Magnetized nail (unlike poles attract)

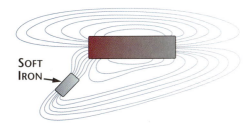

Figure 1-2-13. Effect of a magnetic substance in a magnetic field

Magnetic Shielding

There is no known insulator for magnetic flux. If a nonmagnetic material is placed in a magnetic field, there is no appreciable change in flux—that is, the flux penetrates the nonmagnetic material. For example, a glass plate placed between the poles of a horseshoe magnet will have no appreciable effect on the field, although glass itself is a good insulator in an electric circuit. If a magnetic material (for example, soft iron) is placed in a magnetic field, the flux may be redirected to take advantage of the greater permeability of the magnetic material. Permeability, as discussed earlier, is the quality of a substance that determines the ease with which it can be magnetized.

The sensitive mechanisms of electric instruments and meters can be influenced by stray magnetic fields that will cause errors in their readings. Because instrument mechanisms cannot be insulated against magnetic flux, it is necessary to employ some means of directing the flux around the instrument.

This is accomplished by placing a soft-iron case, called a magnetic screen or shield, about the instrument. Because the flux is established more readily through the iron (even though the path is longer) than through the air inside the case, the instrument is effectively shielded, as seen in Figure 1-2-14.

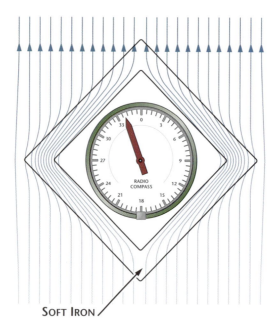

Figure 1-2-14. Magnetic shield around an instrument

Magnetic Shapes

Because of the many uses of magnets, they are found in various shapes and sizes. However, magnets usually come under one of three general classifications: bar magnets, horseshoe magnets or ring magnets (Figure 1-2-15).

The bar magnet is most often used in schools and laboratories for studying the properties and effects of magnetism. In the preceding material, the bar magnet proved very helpful in demonstrating magnetic effects.

Another type of magnet is the ring magnet, which is used for computer memory cores. A common application for a temporary ring magnet would be the shielding of electrical instruments.

The shape of the magnet most frequently used in electrical and electronic equipment is called the horseshoe magnet. A horseshoe magnet is similar to a bar magnet but is bent in the shape of a horseshoe. The horseshoe magnet provides much more magnetic strength than a bar magnet of the same size and material because of the closeness of the magnetic poles. The magnetic strength from one pole to the other is greatly increased due to the concentration of the magnetic field in a smaller area. Electrical measuring devices quite frequently use horseshoe-type magnets.

Care of Magnets

A piece of steel that has been magnetized can lose much of its magnetism by improper handling. If it is jarred or heated, there will be a disalignment of its domains resulting in the loss of some of its effective magnetism. Had this piece of steel formed the horseshoe magnet of a meter, the meter would no longer be

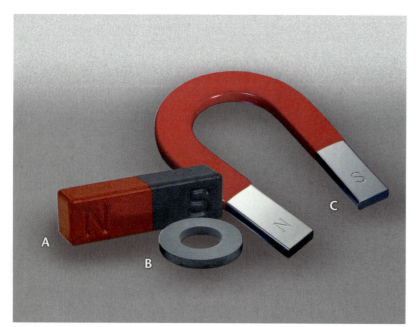

Figure 1-2-15. (A) Bar magnet, (B) Ring magnet, (C) Horseshoe magnet

operable or would give inaccurate readings. Therefore, care must be exercised when handling instruments containing magnets. Severe jarring or subjecting the instrument to high temperatures will damage the device.

A magnet may also become weakened from loss of flux. Thus when storing magnets, one should always try to avoid excess leakage of magnetic flux. A horseshoe magnet should always be stored with a keeper, a soft iron bar used to join the magnetic poles (Figure 1-2-16B). By using the keeper while the magnet is being stored, the magnetic flux will continuously circulate through the magnet and not leak off into space, as seen in Figure 1-2-16A.

When bar magnets are stored, the same principle must be remembered. Therefore, bar magnets should always be stored in pairs with a north pole and a south pole placed together (Figure 1-2-17). This provides a complete path for the magnetic flux without any flux leakage.

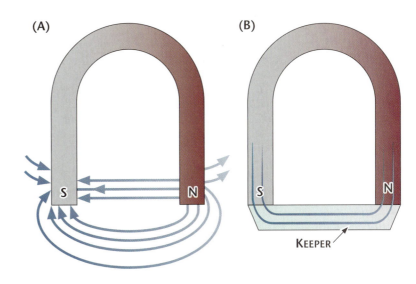

Figure 1-2-16. Proper storage of a horseshoe magnet

Section 3
Electrical Characteristics

Electrical Charges

The previous study of electrostatics discussed that a field of force exists in the space surrounding any electrical charge. The strength of the field is directly dependent on the force of the charge.

The charge of one electron might be used as a unit of electrical charge, since charges are created by displacement of electrons; but the charge of one electron is so small that it is impractical to use. The practical unit adopted for measuring charges is the *coulomb* (C), named after the scientist Charles Coulomb. One coulomb is equal to the charge of approximately 6,240,000,000,000,000,000 (six quintillion two hundred and forty quadrillion) or (6.24×10^{18}) electrons.

When a charge of one coulomb exists between two bodies, one unit of electrical potential energy exists, which is called the difference of potential between the two bodies. This is referred to as *electromotive force* or *voltage,* and the unit of measure is the volt (V).

Electrical charges are created by the displacement of electrons, so that there exists an excess of electrons at one point and a deficiency at another point. Consequently, a charge must always have either a negative or positive polarity. A body with an excess of electrons is considered to be negative, whereas a body with a deficiency of electrons is positive.

A difference of potential can exist between two points, or bodies, only if they have different charges. In other words, there is no difference in potential between two bodies if both have a deficiency of electrons to the same degree. If, however, one body is deficient of 6 coulombs (representing 6 V), and the other is deficient by 12 coulombs (representing 12 V), there is a difference of potential of 6 V. The body with the greater deficiency is positive with respect to the other.

In most electrical circuits only the difference of potential between two points is of importance and the absolute potentials of the points are of little concern. Very often it is convenient to use one standard reference for all of

Figure 1-2-17. Proper storage of a bar magnet

the various potentials throughout a piece of equipment. For this reason, the potentials at various points in a circuit are generally measured with respect to the metal chassis on which all parts of the circuit are mounted. The chassis is considered to be at zero potential and all other potentials are either positive or negative with respect to the chassis. When used as the reference point, the chassis is said to be at *ground potential*.

Occasionally, rather large values of voltage may be encountered, in which case the volt becomes too small a unit for convenience. In a situation of this nature, the kilovolt (kV), meaning 1,000 V, is frequently used. As an example, 20,000 volts would be written as 20 kV. In other cases, the volt may be too large a unit, as when dealing with very small voltages. For this purpose the millivolt (mV), meaning one-thousandth of a volt, and the microvolt (μV), meaning one-millionth of a volt, are used. For example, 0.001 volt would be written as 1 mV, and 0.000025 volt would be written as 25 μV.

When a difference in potential exists between two charged bodies that are connected by a conductor, electrons will flow along the conductor. This flow is from the negatively charged body to the positively charged body, until the two charges are equalized and the potential difference no longer exists.

Electron movement through an electric circuit is directly proportional to the difference in potential or electromotive force (emf), across the circuit, just as the flow of water through the pipe in Figure 1-3-1 is directly proportional to the difference in water level in the two tanks.

A fundamental law of electricity is that the electron flow is directly proportional to the applied voltage. If the voltage is increased, the flow is increased. If the voltage is decreased, the flow is decreased.

How Voltage Is Produced

It has been demonstrated that a charge can be produced by rubbing a rubber rod with fur. Because of the friction involved, the rod acquires electrons from the fur, making it negatively charged; the fur becomes positively charged due to the loss of electrons. These quantities of charge constitute a difference of potential between the rod and the fur. The electrons that make up this difference of potential are capable of doing work if a discharge is allowed to occur.

To be a practical source of voltage, the potential difference must not be allowed to dissipate, but must be maintained continuously. As one electron leaves the concentration of negative charge, another must be immediately provided to take

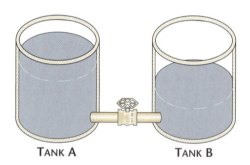

Figure 1-3-1. Water analogy of electric differences of potential

METHOD	DESCRIPTION
Friction	voltage produced by rubbing certain materials together
Pressure (Piezoelectricity)	voltage produced by squeezing crystals of certain substances
Heat (Thermoelectricity)	voltage produced by heating the joint (junction) where two unlike metals are joined
Light (Photoelectricity)	voltage produced by light striking photosensitive (light-sensitive) substances
Chemical Action	voltage produced by chemical reaction in a battery cell
Magnetism	voltage produced in a conductor when the conductor moves through a magnetic field, or a magnetic field moves around the conductor in such a manner as to cut the magnetic lines of force of the field

Table 1-3-1. Six known methods of producing voltage

its place or the charge will eventually diminish to the point where no further work can be accomplished. A *voltage source*, therefore, is a device which is capable of supplying and maintaining voltage while some type of electrical apparatus is connected to its terminals. The internal action of the source is such that electrons are continuously removed from one terminal, keeping it positive, and simultaneously supplied to the second terminal, which maintains a negative charge.

Presently, there are six known methods for producing a voltage or emf. Some of these methods are more widely used than others, and some are used mostly for specific applications. Table 1-3-1 lists the six known methods of producing a voltage.

Voltage Produced by Friction

The first method discovered for creating a voltage was generation by friction. The development of charges by rubbing a rod with fur is a prime example of this. Because of the nature of the materials with which this voltage is generated, it cannot be conveniently used or maintained. For this reason, very little practical use has been found for voltages generated by this method.

In the search for methods to produce a voltage of a larger amplitude and of a more practical nature, machines were developed in which charges were transferred from one terminal to another by means of rotating glass discs or moving belts. The most notable of these machines is the Van de Graaff generator. It is used today to produce potentials in the order of millions of volts for nuclear research. These machines have little value outside the field of research.

Voltage Produced by Pressure

One specialized method of generating an emf utilizes the characteristics of certain ionic crystals such as quartz, Rochelle salts and tourmaline. These crystals have the remarkable ability to generate a voltage whenever stresses are applied to their surfaces. Thus, if a quartz crystal is squeezed, charges of opposite polarity will appear on two opposite surfaces of the crystal (Figure 1-3-2). If the force is reversed and the crystal is stretched, charges will again appear, but will be of the opposite polarity from those produced by squeezing. If a crystal of this type is given a vibratory motion, it will produce a voltage of reversing polarity between two of its sides. Quartz or similar crystals can thus be used to convert mechanical energy into electrical energy. This phenomenon is called the *piezoelectric effect* (Figure 1-3-3). "Piezo" is derived from the Greek word for "squeeze" or "press."

Some of the common devices that have piezoelectric crystals are microphones (Figure 1-3-4), oscillators used in non solid-state radio transmitters, radio receivers and sonar equipment. This method of generating an emf is not suitable for applications having large voltage or power requirements, but is widely used in sound and communications systems where small signal voltages can be effectively used.

Crystals of this type also possess another interesting property, the *converse piezoelectric effect*. That is, they have the capability to convert elec-

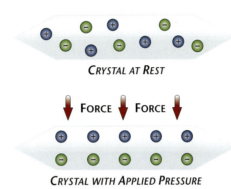

Figure 1-3-2. Result of pressure being applied to quartz crystal

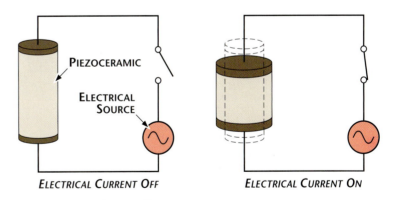

Figure 1-3-3. Piezoelectric effect

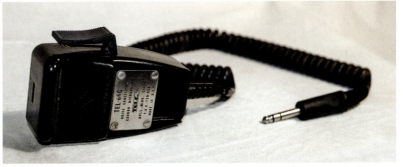

Figure 1-3-4. Example of a microphone that uses piezoelectric crystal

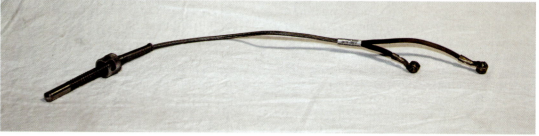

Figure 1-3-5. Aircraft thermocouple

trical energy into mechanical energy. A voltage impressed across the proper surfaces of the crystal will cause it to expand or contract its surfaces in response to the voltage applied.

Voltage Produced by Heat

When a length of metal, such as copper, is heated at one end, electrons tend to move away from the hot end toward the cooler end. This is true of most metals. However, in some metals, such as iron, the opposite takes place and electrons tend to move toward the hot end. This device is generally referred to as a *thermocouple* (Figure 1-3-5).

Thermocouples have somewhat greater power capacities than crystals, but their capacity is still very small compared to some other sources. The thermoelectric voltage in a thermocouple depends mainly on the difference in temperature between the hot and cold junctions. Consequently, they are widely used to measure temperature and as heat-sensing devices in automatic temperature control equipment. Thermocouples generally can be subjected to much greater temperatures than ordinary mercury or alcohol thermometers.

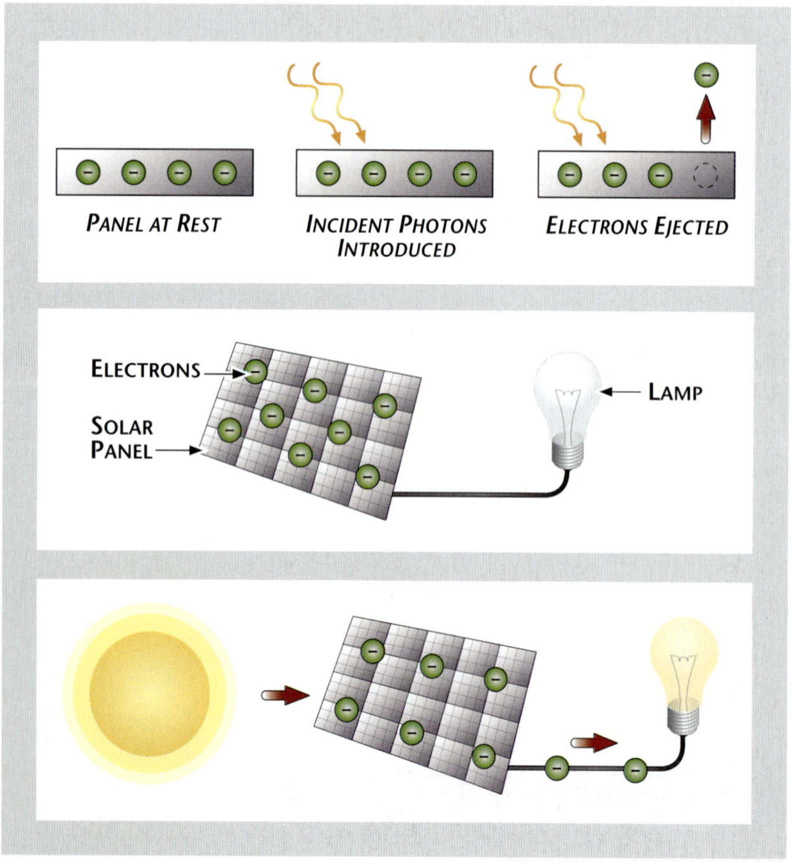

Voltage Produced by Light

When light strikes the surface of a substance, it may dislodge electrons from their orbits around the surface atoms of the substance. This occurs because light has energy, the same as any moving force.

Some substances, mostly metallic ones, are far more sensitive to light than others. That is, more electrons will be dislodged and emitted from the surface of a highly sensitive metal by a given amount of light, than will be emitted from a less sensitive substance. Upon losing electrons, the *photosensitive* (light-sensitive) metal becomes positively charged and an electric force is created. Voltage produced in this manner is referred to as a *photoelectric voltage*.

The photosensitive materials most commonly used to produce a photoelectric voltage are various compounds of silver oxide or copper oxide. A complete device that operates on the photoelectric principle is referred to as a photoelectric cell. There are many different sizes and types of photoelectric cells in use, and each serves the special purpose for which it is designed. Nearly all, however, have some of the basic features of the photoelectric cells.

The cell has a curved, light-sensitive surface focused on the central anode. When light strikes the sensitive surface, it emits electrons toward the anode. The more intense the light, the greater the number of electrons emitted. When a wire is connected between the filament and the back or dark side of the cell, the accumulated electrons will flow to the dark side. These electrons will eventually pass through the metal of the reflector and replace the electrons leaving the light-sensitive surface. Thus, light energy is converted to a flow of electrons, and a usable current is developed.

Figure 1-3-6. Photoelectric principle

The cell is constructed in layers. A base plate of pure copper is coated with light-sensitive copper oxide. An extremely thin, semitransparent layer of metal is placed over the copper oxide. This additional layer permits the penetration of light to the copper oxide and collects the electrons emitted by the copper oxide.

An externally connected wire completes the electron path, the same as in the reflector-type cell. The photocell's voltage is used as needed by connecting the external wires to some other device, which amplifies (enlarges) it to a usable level.

The power capacity of a photocell is very small. However, it reacts to variations in the intensity of light in an extremely short time. This characteristic makes the photocell very useful in detecting or accurately controlling a great number of operations. For instance, the photoelectric cell, or some form of the photoelectric principle (Figure 1-3-6), is used in television cameras, automatic manufacturing process controls, door openers, burglar alarms and solar panels (Figure 1-3-7).

Figure 1-3-7. Solar panels

Voltage Produced by Chemical Action

Voltage may be produced chemically when certain substances are exposed to chemical action.

If two dissimilar substances (usually metals or metallic materials) are immersed in a solution that produces a greater chemical action on one substance than on the other, a difference of potential will exist between the two. If a conductor is then connected between them, electrons will flow through the conductor to equalize the charge. This arrangement is called a *primary cell*. The two metallic pieces are called *electrodes* and the solution is called the *electrolyte*. The difference of potential results from the fact that material from one or both of the electrodes goes into solution in the electrolyte, and in the process, ions form in the vicinity of the electrodes. Due to the electric field associated with the charged ions, the electrodes acquire charges.

Figure 1-3-8. Lead acid battery

The amount of difference in potential between the electrodes depends principally on the metals used. The type of electrolyte and the size of the cell have little or no effect on the potential difference produced.

There are two types of primary cells, the wet cell and the dry cell. In a *wet cell* the electrolyte is a liquid. A cell with a liquid electrolyte must remain in an upright position and is not readily transportable. An automotive battery is an example of this type of cell (Figure 1-3-8). The *dry cell* (Figure 1-3-9), much more commonly

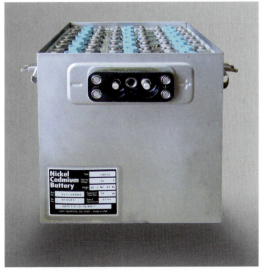

Figure 1-3-9. Nickel-cadmium battery

1-22 | Fundamentals of Direct Current

Figure 1-3-10. Generator cutaway

used than the wet cell, is not actually dry, but contains an electrolyte mixed with other materials to form a paste. Flashlights and portable radios are commonly powered by dry cells.

Batteries are formed when several cells are connected together to increase electrical output.

Voltage Produced by Magnetism

Magnets or magnetic devices are used for thousands of different jobs. One of the most useful and widely employed applications of magnets is in the production of vast quantities of electric power from mechanical sources. The mechanical power may be provided by a number of different sources, such as gasoline or diesel engines, or water or steam turbines. However, the final conversion of these source energies to electricity is done by generators (Figure 1-3-10) employing the principle of electromagnetic induction. These generators are discussed in a later chapter of this text. The important subject to be discussed here is the fundamental operating principle of all such electromagnetic-induction generators.

To begin with, there are three fundamental conditions that must exist before a voltage can be produced by magnetism.

1. There must be a conductor in which the voltage will be produced.
2. There must be a magnetic field in the conductor's vicinity.
3. There must be relative motion between the field and conductor. The conductor must be moved so as to cut across the magnetic lines of force, or the field must be moved so that the lines of force are cut by the conductor.

In accordance with these conditions, when a conductor or conductors move across a magnetic field so as to cut the lines of force, electrons within the conductor are propelled in one direction or another. Thus, an electric force, or voltage, is created.

Electric Current

It has been proven that electrons (negative charges) move through a conductor in response to an electric field. "Electron current flow" will be used throughout this explanation. *Electron current* is defined as the directed flow of electrons. The direction of electron movement is from a region of negative potential to a region of positive potential (Figure 1-3-11A). Therefore electric current can be said to flow from negative to positive. The direction of current flow in a material is determined by the polarity of the applied voltage. In some electrical/electronic communities, the direction of current flow is recognized as being from positive to negative as illustrated in Figure (Figure 1-3-11B).

Magnitude of Current Flow

Electric current has been defined as the directed movement of electrons. Directed drift, therefore, is current and the terms can be used interchangeably. The expression "directed drift" is particularly helpful in differentiating between the random and directed motion of electrons. However, current flow is the terminology most

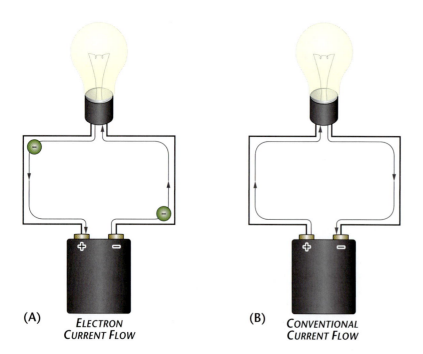

(A) ELECTRON CURRENT FLOW (B) CONVENTIONAL CURRENT FLOW

Figure 1-3-11. Conventional and electron current flow

commonly used in indicating a directed movement of electrons.

The magnitude of current flow is directly related to the amount of energy that passes through a conductor as a result of the drift action. An increase in the number of energy carriers (the mobile electrons) or an increase in the energy of the existing mobile electrons would provide an increase in current flow. When an electric potential is impressed across a conductor, there is an increase in the velocity of the mobile electrons, causing an increase in the energy of the carriers. There is also the generation of an increased number of electrons providing added carriers of energy. The additional number of free electrons is relatively small, hence the magnitude of current flow is primarily dependent on the velocity of the existing mobile electrons.

The magnitude of current flow is affected by the difference of potential in the following manner. Initially, mobile electrons are given additional energy because of the repelling and attracting electrostatic field. If the potential difference is increased, the electric field will be stronger, the amount of energy imparted to a mobile electron will be greater, and the current will be increased. If the potential difference is decreased, the strength of the field is reduced, the energy supplied to the electron is diminished, and the current is decreased.

Measurement of Current

The magnitude of current is measured in *amperes* (A). A current of one ampere is said to flow when one coulomb of charge passes a point in one second. Remember, one coulomb is equal to the charge of 6.24×10^{18} electrons.

Electrical Resistance

It is known that the directed movement of electrons constitutes a current flow. It is also known that the electrons do not move freely through a conductor's crystalline structure. Some materials offer little opposition to current flow, while others greatly oppose current flow. This opposition to current flow is known as *resistance* (R), and the unit of measure is the *ohm*. The standard of measure for one ohm is the resistance provided at 0°C by a column of mercury having a cross-sectional area of 1 mm^2 and a length of 106.3 cm. A conductor has one ohm of resistance when an applied potential of one volt produces a current of one ampere. The symbol used to represent the ohm is the Greek letter omega (Ω).

Resistance, although an electrical property, is determined by the physical structure of a material. The resistance of a material is governed by many of the same factors that control current flow. Therefore, in a subsequent discussion, the factors that affect current flow will be used to assist in the explanation of the factors affecting resistance.

Factors That Affect Resistance

The magnitude of resistance is determined in part by the number of free electrons available within the material. Since a decrease in the number of free electrons will decrease the current flow, it can be said that the opposition to current flow (resistance) is greater in a material with fewer free electrons. Thus, the resistance of a material is determined by the number of free electrons available in a material. A knowledge of the conditions that limit current flow and, therefore, affect resistance can now be used to consider how the type of material, physical dimensions and temperature will affect the resistance of a conductor.

Type of material. Depending upon their atomic structure, different materials will have different quantities of free electrons. Therefore, the various conductors used in electrical applications have different values of resistance.

Consider a simple metallic substance. Most metals are crystalline in structure and consist of atoms that are tightly bound in the lattice network. The atoms of such elements are so close together that the electrons in the outer shell of the atom are associated with one atom as much as with its neighbor. As a result, the force of attachment of an outer electron with an individual atom is practically zero. Depending on the metal, at least one electron, sometimes two, and in a few cases, three electrons per atom exist in this state. In such a case, a relatively small amount of additional energy would free the outer electrons from the attraction of the nucleus. At normal room temperature materials of this type have many free electrons and are good conductors. Good conductors will have a low resistance.

If the atoms of a material are farther apart, the electrons in the outer shells will not be equally attached to several atoms as they orbit the nucleus. They will be attracted by the nucleus of the parent atom only. Therefore, a greater amount of energy is required to free any of these electrons. Materials of this type are poor conductors and therefore have a high resistance.

Silver, gold and aluminum are good conductors. Therefore, materials composed of their atoms would have a low resistance.

Copper is the conductor most widely used throughout electrical applications. Silver has a lower resistance than copper but its cost limits its usage to circuits where a high conductivity is demanded. Aluminum, which is considerably lighter than copper, is used as a conductor when weight is a major factor.

Effect of cross-sectional area. Cross-sectional area greatly affects the magnitude of resistance. If the cross-sectional area of a conductor is increased, greater quantities of electrons are available for movement through the conductor. Therefore, a larger current will flow for a given amount of applied voltage. An increase in current indicates that when the cross-sectional area of a conductor is increased, the resistance must have decreased. If the cross-sectional area of a conductor is decreased, the number of available electrons decreases and, for a given applied voltage, the current through the conductor decreases. A decrease in current flow indicates that when the cross-sectional area of a conductor is decreased, the resistance must have increased. Thus, the resistance of a conductor is inversely proportional to its cross-sectional area.

The diameter of conductors used in electronics is often only a fraction of an inch; therefore, the diameter is expressed in *mils* (thousandths of an inch). It is also standard practice to assign the unit circular mil to the cross-sectional area of the conductor. The circular mil is found by squaring the diameter when the diameter is expressed in mils. Thus, if the diameter is 35 mils (0.035 in.), the circular mil area is equal to 35^2 or 1,225 circular mils.

Effect of conductor length. The length of a conductor is also a factor that determines the resistance of a conductor. If the length of a conductor is increased, the amount of energy given up is also increased (Figure 1-3-12). As free electrons move from atom to atom, some energy is given off as heat. The longer a conductor, the more energy is lost to heat. The additional energy loss subtracts from the energy being transferred through the conductor, resulting in a decrease in current flow for a given applied voltage. A decrease in current flow indicates an increase in resistance, since voltage was held constant. Therefore, if the length of a conductor is increased, the resistance increases. The resistance of a conductor is directly proportional to its length.

Effect of temperature. Temperature changes affect the resistance of materials in different ways (Table 1-3-2). In some materials an increase in temperature causes an increase in resistance, whereas in others, an increase in temperature causes a decrease in resistance. The amount of change of resistance per unit

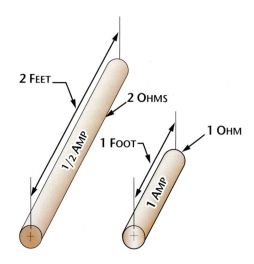

Figure 1-3-12. Resistance varies with length of conductors

change in temperature is known as the *temperature coefficient*. If for an increase in temperature the resistance of a material increases, it is said to have a positive temperature coefficient. A material whose resistance decreases with an increase in temperature has a negative temperature coefficient. Most conductors used in electronic applications have a positive temperature coefficient. However, carbon, a frequently used material, has a negative temperature coefficient. Several materials, such as the alloys constantan and Manganin, are considered to have a zero temperature coefficient because their resistance remains relatively constant over changes in temperature.

Conductance

Electricity is a study that is frequently explained in terms of opposites. The opposite of resistance is *conductance*. Conductance is the ability of a material to pass electrons. The factors that affect

INITIAL TEMP. °C	INCREASE IN RESISTANCE PER °C	
	COPPER	ALUMINUM
0	0.00427	0.00439
5	0.00418	0.00429
10	0.00409	0.00420
15	0.00401	0.00411
20	0.00393	0.00403
25	0.00385	0.00396
30	0.00378	0.00388
40	0.00364	0.00373
50	0.00352	0.00360

Table 1-3-2. Temperature resistance coefficients

the magnitude of resistance are exactly the same for conductance, but they affect conductance in the opposite manner. Therefore, conductance is directly proportional to area and inversely proportional to the length of the material. The temperature of the material is definitely a factor, but assuming a constant temperature, the conductance of a material can be calculated.

The unit of conductance is the *mho* (G), which is ohm spelled backwards. Recently the term mho has been redesignated *siemens* (S). Whereas the symbol used to represent resistance (R) is the Greek letter omega (Ω), the symbol is used to represent conductance (G) is (S). The relationship that exists between resistance (R) and conductance (G) is a reciprocal one. A reciprocal of a number is one divided by that number. In terms of resistance and conductance:

$G = 1/R$

Section 4
DC Calculations

Ohm's Law

In the early part of the 19th century, Georg Simon Ohm (Figure 1-4-1) proved by experiment that a precise relationship exists between current, voltage and resistance. This relationship is called Ohm's law and is stated as follows: The current in a circuit is directly proportional to the applied voltage and inversely proportional to the circuit resistance. Ohm's law may be expressed as an equation:

$I = E/R$

Where: E = Voltage in volts

I = Current in amperes

R = Resistance in ohms

As stated in Ohm's law, current is inversely proportional to resistance. This means, as the resistance in a circuit increases, the current decreases proportionately.

In the equation, $I = E/R$, if any two quantities are known, the third one can be determined. If the battery supplies a voltage of 1.5 V, and a lamp has a resistance of 5Ω, then the current in the circuit can be determined. Using this equation and substituting values:

$I = 1.5 \text{ V}/5Ω$

$I = 0.3 \text{ A}$

If there were two cells instead of one, there would be twice the voltage, or 3 V, applied to the circuit. Using this voltage in the equation:

$I = 3 \text{ V}/5Ω$

$I = 0.6 \text{ A}$

The current has doubled as the voltage has doubled. This demonstrates that the current is directly proportional to the applied voltage. If the value of resistance of the lamp is doubled, the equation will be:

$I = 3 \text{ V}/10Ω$

$I = 0.3 \text{ A}$

The current has been reduced to one half of the value of the previous equation, or 0.3 A. This demonstrates that the current is inversely proportional to the resistance. Doubling the value of the resistance of the load reduces circuit current value to one half of its former value.

Application of Ohm's Law

By using Ohm's law, it is possible to find the resistance of a circuit if only the voltage and the current in the circuit are known.

In any equation, if all the variables (parameters) are known except one, that unknown can be found. For example, using Ohm's law, if current (I) and voltage (E) are known, resistance (R) the only parameter not known, can be determined:

$R = E/I$

If the unknown parameter is the voltage (E), use the equation:

$E = I \times R$

The Ohm's law equation and its various forms may be obtained readily with the aid of the

Figure 1-4-1. Georg Simon Ohm

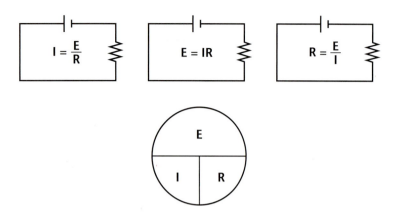

Figure 1-4-2. Ohm's law in diagram form

power circle, shown in Figure 1-4-2. The circle containing E, I and R is divided into two parts, with E above the line and with I and R below the line. To determine the unknown quantity, cover that quantity with a finger. The position of the uncovered letters in the circle will indicate the mathematical operation to be performed. For example, to find I, cover I with a finger. The uncovered letters indicate that E is to be divided by R.

Do not to rely wholly on the use of this diagram when transposing the Ohm's law formulas. The diagram should be used only as supplement knowledge for the algebraic method. Algebra is a basic tool in the solution of electrical problems.

Graphical Analysis of the Basic Circuit

One of the most valuable methods of analyzing a circuit is by constructing a graph. No other method provides a more convenient or more rapid way to observe the characteristics of an electrical device.

The first step in constructing a graph is to obtain a table of data. The information in the table can be obtained by taking measurements on the circuit under examination, or can be obtained theoretically through a series of Ohm's law computations. The latter method is used here.

Since there are three variables (E, I and R) to be analyzed, there are three distinct graphs that may be constructed.

To construct any graph of electrical quantities, it is standard practice to vary one quantity in a specified way and note the changes that occur in a second quantity. The quantity that is intentionally varied is called the independent variable and is plotted on the horizontal axis. The horizontal axis is known as the *x-axis*. The second quantity, which varies as a result of changes in the first quantity, is called the dependent variable and is plotted on the vertical, or *y-axis*. Other quantities involved are held constant.

For example, in the circuit shown in Figure 1-4-3, if the resistance were held at 10Ω and the voltage were varied, the resulting changes in current could then be graphed. The resistance is the constant, the voltage is the independent variable, and the current is the dependent variable. An example of a basic circuit is pictured in Figure 1-4-4.

Figure 1-4-5 shows the graph and a table of values. This table shows R held constant at 10Ω as E is varied from 0 to 20 V in 5 V steps. Through the use of Ohm's law, the value of current (I) for each value of voltage (E) shown in the table can be calculated. When the table is complete, the information it contains can be used to construct the graph shown in Figure 1-4-5. For example, when the voltage applied to the 10Ω resistor is 10 V, the current is 1 A. These values of current and voltage determine a point on the graph. When all five points have been plotted, a smooth curve (a line in this case) is drawn through the points.

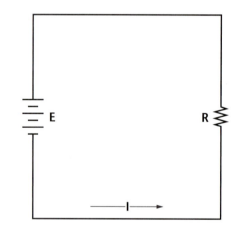

Figure 1-4-3. Three variables in a basic circuit

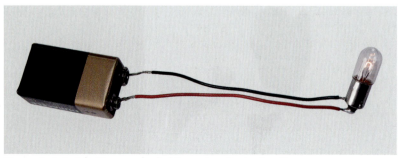

Figure 1-4-4. A battery and a light create a basic circuit

Through the use of this curve, the value of current through the resistor can be quickly determined for any value of voltage between 0 and 20 V.

Since the curve is a straight line, it shows that equal changes of voltage across the resistor produce equal changes in current through the resistor. This fact illustrates an important characteristic of the basic law—the current varies directly with the applied voltage when the resistance is held constant.

When the voltage across a load is held constant, the current depends solely upon the resistance of the load. For example, Figure 1-4-6 shows a graph with the voltage held constant at 12 V. The independent variable is the resistance, which is varied from 2 to 12Ω. The current is the dependent variable. Values for current can be calculated as:

Given:

$E = 12$ V

$R = 2Ω$ to $12Ω$

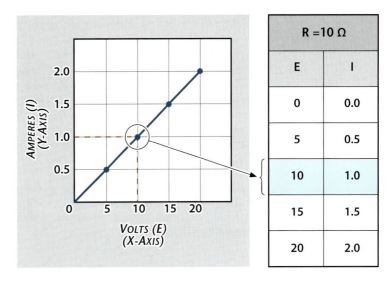

Figure 1-4-5. Volt-ampere characteristic

Solution:

$I = E \div R$

$I = 12$ V $\div 12Ω = 1$ A

$I = 12$ V $\div 10Ω = 1.2$ A

$I = 12$ V $\div 8Ω = 1.5$ A

$I = 12$ V $\div 6Ω = 2$ A

This process can be continued for any value of resistance. It is apparent that as the resistance is halved, the current is doubled; when the resistance is doubled, the current is halved.

This illustrates another important characteristic of Ohm's law—current varies inversely with resistance when the applied voltage is held constant.

Power

Power, whether electrical or mechanical, pertains to the rate at which work is being done. Work is done whenever a force causes motion. When a mechanical force is used to lift or move a weight, work is done. However, force exerted without causing motion, such as the force of a compressed spring acting between two fixed objects, does not constitute work.

Previously, it was shown that voltage is an electrical force, and that voltage forces current to flow in a closed circuit. However, when voltage exists but current does not flow because the circuit is open, no work is done. This is similar to the spring under tension that produced no motion. When voltage causes electrons to move, work is done. The instantaneous rate at

which this work is done is called the *electric power rate*, and is measured in *watts* (W).

A total amount of work may be done in different lengths of time. For example, a given number of electrons may be moved from one point to another in 1 second or in 1 hour, depending on the rate at which they are moved. In both cases, the total work done is the same. However, when the work is done in a short time, the wattage, or *instantaneous power rate*, is greater than when the same amount of work is done over a longer period of time.

As stated, the basic unit of power is the watt. *Power* in watts is equal to the voltage across a circuit multiplied by current through the circuit. This represents the rate at any given instant at which work is being done. The symbol P indicates electrical power. Thus, the basic power formula is $P = E \times I$, where E is voltage

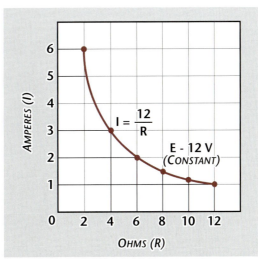

Figure 1-4-6. Relationship between current and resistance

and I is current in the circuit. The amount of power changes when either voltage or current, or both voltage and current, change.

In practice, the only factors that can be changed are voltage and resistance. In explaining the different forms that formulas may take, current is sometimes presented as a quantity that is changed. Remember, if current is changed, it is because either voltage or resistance has been changed.

Figure 1-4-7 shows a basic circuit using a source of power that can be varied from 0 to 8 V and a graph that indicates the relationship between voltage and power.

The resistance of this circuit is 2Ω; this value does not change. Voltage (E) is increased (by increasing the voltage source), in steps of 1 V, from 0 to 8 V. By applying Ohm's law, the current (I) is determined for each step of voltage. For instance, when E is 1 volt, the current is:

I = 1 V ÷ 2Ω

I = .5 A

Power (P), in watts, is determined by applying the basic power formula:

P = E x I

P = 1 V x 0.5 A

P = 0.5 W

When E is increased to 2 V:

I = E ÷ R

I = 2 V ÷ 2Ω

I = 1 A

and

P = E x I

P = 2 V x 1 A

P = 2 W

When E is increased to 3 V:

I = E ÷ R

I = 3 V ÷ 2Ω

I = 1.5 A

and

P = E x I

P = 3 V x 1.5 A

P = 4.5 W

Notice that when the voltage was increased to 2 V, the power increased from 0.5 W to 2 W, or four times. When the voltage increased to 3 V, the power increased to 4.5 W, or nine times. This shows that if the resistance in a circuit is held constant, the power varies directly with the square of the voltage.

For all equations, refer to another power wheel, the Ohm's law wheel seen in Figure 1-4-8. The equations that were already discussed for power, voltage, resistance and amperage can be seen in this power wheel. More equations that have not been discussed can also be seen. In total there are 12 equations that a technician will need to know, and all of them are labeled on the power wheel.

Another unit of work was created by and named for the English physicist James Prescott Joule. The Joule is defined as one watt of work done in one second. One joule is the equivalent of 0.7376 ft. lb. To see how much work in joules is done to lift 1,000 lbs. to a height of 25 feet, multiple 1,000 x 25 to get 25,000 ft. lbs. The next step is to divide 25,000 ft. lbs. by 0.7376, resulting in a solution of 33,893.71 joules (J) of work performed.

Understanding the joule makes it easier for the technician to convert other units of work, such as the British thermal unit (BTU), watt-hour (Wh), and foot-pound, since the joule is a metric measurement.

Power Rating

Electrical components are often given a power rating. The power rating, in watts, indicates the rate at which the device converts electrical energy into another form of energy such as light, heat or motion. An example of such a rating is noted when comparing a 150 W lamp to a 100 W lamp. The higher wattage rating of the 150 W lamp indicates that it is capable of converting more electrical energy into light energy than the lamp of the lower rating. Other common examples of devices with power ratings are soldering irons and small electric motors.

In some electrical devices the wattage rating indicates the maximum power the device is designed to use rather than the normal operating power. A 150 W lamp, for example, uses 150 W when operated at the voltage printed on the bulb. In contrast, a device such as a resistor is not normally given a voltage or a current rating. A resistor is given a power rating in watts and can be operated at any combination of voltage and current as long as the power rating is not exceeded. In most circuits, the actual power used by a resistor is considerably less than the power rating of the resistor because a 50 percent safety factor is used. For example, if a resistor normally used 2 watts of power, a resistor with a power rating of 3 watts would be used.

Resistors of the same resistance value are available in different wattage values. Carbon resistors, for example, are commonly made in wattage ratings of $1/8$, $1/4$, $1/2$, 1 and 2 W. The larger the physical size of a carbon resistor, the higher the wattage rating. This is true because a larger surface area of material radiates a greater amount of heat more easily.

When resistors with wattage ratings greater than 5 W are needed, wire-wound resistors are used. Wire-wound resistors are made in values between 5 and 200 W. Special types of wire-wound resistors are used for power in excess of 200 W.

As with other electrical quantities, prefixes may be attached to the word watt when expressing very large or very small amounts of power. Some of the more common of these are the kilowatt (1,000 W), the megawatt (1,000,000 W), and the milliwatt (1/1,000 W).

Power Conversion and Efficiency

The term *power consumption* is common in the electrical field. It is applied to the use of power in the same sense that gasoline consumption is applied to the use of fuel in an automobile.

Another common term is *power conversion*. Power is used by electrical devices and is converted from one form of energy to another (Figure 1-4-9). An electrical motor converts electrical energy to mechanical energy. An electric light bulb converts electrical energy into light energy, and an electric range converts electrical energy into heat energy. Power used by electrical devices is measured in energy. This practical unit of electrical energy is equal to 1 watt of power used continuously for 1 hour. The term *kilowatt-hour* (kWh) is used more extensively on a daily basis and is equal to 1,000 watt-hours.

The *efficiency* of an electrical device is the ratio of power converted to useful energy divided by the power consumed by the device. This number will always be less than one because of the losses in any electrical device. If a device has an efficiency rating of 0.95, it effectively transforms 95 W into useful energy for every 100 W of input power. The other 5 W are lost to heat or other losses that cannot be used.

Calculating the amount of power converted by an electrical device is a simple matter. The length of time the device is operated and the input power or *horsepower rating* must be

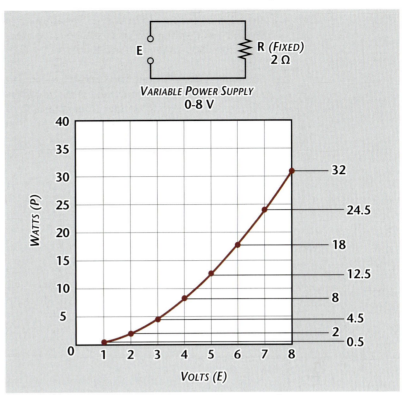

Figure 1-4-7. Graph of power related to changing voltage

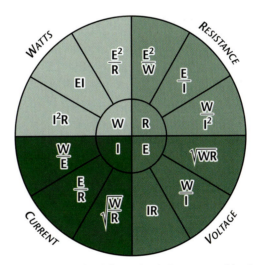

Figure 1-4-8. Ohm's law wheel: Summary of basic equations using the volt, ampere, ohm and watt.

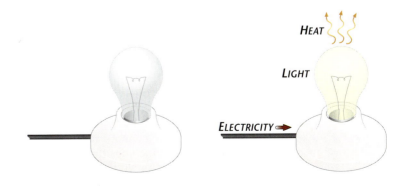

Figure 1-4-9. Power conversion

known. Horsepower, a unit of work, is often found as a rating on electrical motors. One horsepower (hp) is equal to 746 W.

Example: A 3/4-hp motor operates 8 hours a day. How much power is converted by the motor per month? How many kWh does this represent?

Given:

T = 8 hrs x 30 days
P = 3/4 hp

Solution: Convert horsepower to watts

P = hp x 746 watts
P = 3/4 x 746 watts
P = 560 watts

Convert watts to watt-hours

P = work x time
P = 560 watts x 8 x 30
P = 134,400 watt-hours per month

To convert to kWh

P = Power in watt-hours ÷ 1000
P = 134,400 ÷ 1000
P = 134 kWh

If the motor actually uses 137 kWh per month, what is the efficiency of the motor?

Given: Power converted = 134 kWh per month

Power used = 137 kWh per month

Solution:

Efficiency = Power converted ÷ Power used
Efficiency = 134 kWh per month ÷ 137 kWh per month
Efficiency = 0.978 (rounded to three figures)

Section 5

Series DC Circuits

When two unequal charges are connected by a conductor, a complete pathway for current exists. An electric circuit is a complete conducting pathway. It consists not only of the conductor, but also includes the path through the voltage source. Inside the voltage source, current flows from the positive terminal, through the source, emerging at the negative terminal. A *series circuit* is defined as a circuit that contains only one path for current flow (Figure 1-5-1).

Series Circuit Characteristics

Resistance in a Series Circuit

The current in a series circuit must flow through each resistor to complete the electrical path in the circuit. Each additional load offers added resistance. In a series circuit, the *total circuit resistance* (R_T) is equal to the sum of the individual resistances. As an equation:

$$R_T = R_1 + R_2 + R_3 + \ldots R_n$$

The subscript n denotes any number of additional resistances that might be in the equation.

For Example, a series circuit consisting of three resistors: one of 10Ω, one of 15Ω, and one of 30Ω. A voltage source provides 110 V. What is the total resistance?

$$R_T = 10\Omega + 15\Omega + 30\Omega$$
$$R_T = 55\Omega$$

In some circuit applications, the total resistance is known and the value of one of the circuit resistors has to be determined. The equation $R_T = R_1 + R_2 + R_3$ can be transposed to solve for the value of the unknown resistance.

A second example shows the total resistance of a circuit containing three resistors is 40Ω. Two of the circuit resistors are 10Ω each. Calculate the value of the third resistor (R_3).

$$40\Omega = 10\Omega + 10\Omega + R_3$$
$$40\Omega - 10\Omega - 10\Omega = R_3$$
$$20\Omega = R_3$$

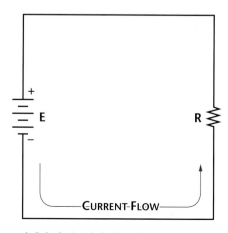

Figure 1-5-1. Series DC Circuit

Current in a Series Circuit

Since there is only one path for current in a series circuit, the same current must flow through each component of the circuit. To determine the current in a series circuit, the current through only one of the components need be known.

The fact that the same current flows through each component of a series circuit can be verified by inserting meters into the circuit at various points. If this were done, each meter would indicate the same value of current.

Voltage in a Series Circuit

The voltage dropped across the resistor in a circuit consisting of a single resistor and a voltage source is the total voltage across the circuit and is equal to the applied voltage. The total voltage across a series circuit that consists of more than one resistor is also equal to the applied voltage, but consists of the sum of the individual resistor voltage drops. In any series circuit, the sum of the resistor voltage drops must equal the source voltage. This statement can be proven by an examination of this example. In this circuit a source potential (E_T) of 20 V is dropped across a series circuit consisting of two 5Ω resistors. The total resistance of the circuit (R_T) is equal to the sum of the two individual resistances, or 10Ω. Using Ohm's law the circuit current may be calculated as follows:

Given:

$E_T = 20$ V
$R_T = 10Ω$

Solution:

$I_T = 20$ V/10Ω
$I_T = 2$ A

Since the value of the resistors is known to be 5Ω each, and the current through the resistors is known to be 2 A, the voltage drops across the resistors can be calculated. The voltage (E_1) across R_1 is therefore:

Given:

$I_1 = 2$ A
$R_1 = 5Ω$

Solution:

$E_1 = I_1 \times R_1$
$E_1 = 2$ A $\times$ 5Ω
$E_1 = 10$ V

R_2 has the same ohmic value as R_1 and carries the same current. The voltage drop across R_2 is therefore also equal to 10 V. Adding these two 10 V drops together gives a total drop of 20 V, exactly equal to the applied voltage. For a series circuit then:

$E_T = E_1 + E_2 + E_3 = \ldots E_n$

Example: A series circuit consists of three resistors having values of 20Ω, 30Ω, and 50Ω, respectively. Find the applied voltage if the current through the 30Ω resistor is 2 A.

Given:

$R_1 = 20Ω$
$R_2 = 30Ω$
$R_3 = 50Ω$
$I = 2$ A

Solution:

$E_T = E_1 + E_2 + E_3$
$E_1 = R_1 \times I_1$ (I_1 = The current through resistor R_1)
$E_2 = R_2 \times I_2$
$E_3 = R_3 \times I_3$

Substituting:

$E_T = (R_1 \times I_1) + (R_2 \times I_2) + (R_3 \times I_3)$
$E_T = (20Ω \times 2$ A$) + (30Ω \times 2$ A$) + (50Ω \times 2$ A$)$
$E_T = 40$ V $+ 60$ V $+ 100$ V
$E_T = 200$ V

When Ohm's law is used, the quantities for the equation must be taken from the same part of the circuit. In the above example the voltage across R_2 was computed using the current through R_2 and the resistance of R_2.

The value of the voltage dropped by a resistor is determined by the applied voltage and is in proportion to the circuit resistances. The voltage drops that occur in a series circuit are in direct proportion to the resistances. This is the result of having the same current flow through each resistor—the larger the ohmic value of the resistor, the larger the voltage drop across it.

Power in a Series Circuit

Each of the resistors in a series circuit consumes power, which is dissipated in the form of heat. Since this power must come from the source, the total power must be equal to the power consumed by the circuit resistances. In a series circuit the total power is equal to the sum of the power dissipated by the individual resistors. Total power (P_T) is equal to:

$P_T = P_1 + P_2 + P_3 \ldots P_n$

Figure 1-5-2. Gustav Robert Kirchhoff

Example: A series circuit consists of three resistors having values of 5Ω, 10Ω and 15Ω. Find the total power when 120 V is applied to the circuit.

Given:

$R_1 = 5\Omega$
$R_2 = 10\Omega$
$R_3 = 15\Omega$
$E_T = 120\text{ V}$

Solution: First, figure total resistance.

$R_T = R_1 + R_2 + R_3$
$R_T = 5\Omega + 10\Omega + 15\Omega$
$R_T = 30\Omega$

By using the total resistance and the applied voltage, the circuit current is calculated.

$I = E_T \div R_T$
$I = 120\text{ V} \div 30\Omega$
$I = 4\text{ A}$

By means of the power formulas, the power can be calculated for each resistor:

$R_1: P_1 = I^2 \times R_1$
$P_1 = 4\text{ A}^2 \times 5\Omega$
$P_1 = 80\text{ W}$
$R_2: P_2 = I^2 \times R_2$
$P_2 = 4\text{ A}^2 \times 10\Omega$
$P_2 = 160\text{ W}$
$R_3: P_3 = I^2 \times R_3$
$P_3 = 4\text{ A}^2 \times 15\Omega$
$P_3 = 240\text{ W}$

Total power can now be calculated:

$P_T = P_1 + P_2 + P_3$
$P_T = 80\text{ W} + 160\text{ W} + 240\text{ W}$
$P_T = 480\text{ W}$

To check the answer, the total power delivered by the source can be calculated:

$P_T = E_T \times I_T$
$P_T = 120\text{ V} \times 4\text{ A}$
$P_T = 480\text{ W}$

The total power is equal to the sum of the power used by the individual resistors.

Rules for Series DC Circuits

The important factors governing the operation of a series circuit are listed below. These factors have been set up as a group of rules so that they may be easily studied. These rules must be completely understood before the study of more advanced circuit theory is undertaken.

- The same current flows through each part of a series circuit.
- The total resistance of a series circuit is equal to the sum of the individual resistances.
- The total voltage across a series circuit is equal to the sum of the individual voltage drops.
- The voltage drop across a resistor in a series circuit is proportional to the ohmic value of the resistor.
- The total power in a series circuit is equal to the sum of the individual powers used by each circuit component.

Kirchhoff's Voltage Law

In 1847, G. R. Kirchhoff (Figure 1-5-2) extended the use of Ohm's law by developing a simple concept concerning the voltages contained in a series circuit loop. Kirchhoff's voltage law states: "The algebraic sum of the voltage drops in any closed path in a circuit and the electromotive forces in that path is equal to zero."

To state Kirchhoff's law another way, the voltage drops and voltage sources in a circuit are equal at any given moment in time. If the voltage sources are assumed to have one sign (positive or negative) at that instant and the voltage drops are assumed to have the opposite sign, the result of adding the voltage sources and voltage drops will be zero.

The terms electromotive force and emf are used when explaining Kirchhoff's law because Kirchhoff's law is used in alternating current circuits (covered in Chapter 3). In applying Kirchhoff's law to direct current circuits, the terms electromotive force and emf apply to voltage sources such as batteries or power supplies. Through the use of Kirchhoff's law, circuit problems can be solved that would be difficult, and often impossible, with knowledge of Ohm's law alone. When Kirchhoff's law is properly applied, an equation can be set up for a closed loop and the unknown circuit values can be calculated.

Polarity of Voltage

To apply Kirchhoff's voltage law, the meaning of voltage polarity must be understood.

In the circuit shown in Figure 1-5-3, the current is shown flowing in a counterclockwise direction. Notice that the end of resistor R_1, into which the current flows, is marked negative (-). The end of R_1 from which the current leaves is marked positive (+). These polarity markings are used to show that the end of R_1 into which the current flows is at a higher negative potential than the end of the resistor at which the current leaves. Point A is more negative than point B.

Point C, which is at the same potential as point B, is labeled negative. This is to indicate that point C is more negative than point D. To say a point is positive (or negative) without stating what the polarity is based upon has no meaning. In working with Kirchhoff's law, positive and negative polarities are assigned in the direction of current flow.

Application of Kirchhoff's Voltage Law

Kirchhoff's voltage law can be written as an equation, as shown below:

$E_a + E_b + E_c + \ldots E_n = 0$

Where E_a, E_b, etc., signify a voltage drop or an emf around any closed circuit loop. To set up the equation for an actual circuit, the following procedure is used.

1. Assume a direction of current through the circuit. (The correct direction is desirable but not necessary.)
2. Using the assumed direction of current, assign polarities to all resistors through which the current flows.
3. Place the correct polarities on any sources included in the circuit.
4. Starting at any point in the circuit, trace around the circuit, writing down the amount and polarity of the voltage across each component in succession. The polarity used is the sign *after* the assumed current has passed through the component. Stop when the point at which the trace was started is reached.
5. Place these voltages, with their polarities, into the equation and solve for the desired quantity.

For example, three resistors are connected across a 50 V source. What is the voltage across the third resistor if the voltage drops across the first two resistors are 25 V and 15 V?

To solve the problem, first, a diagram is drawn. Next, a direction of current is assumed. Using this current, the polarity markings are placed at each end of each resistor and also on the terminals of the source. Starting at point A, trace around the circuit in the direction of current flow, recording the voltage and polarity of each component. Starting at point A and using the components from the circuit:

$(+E_X) + (+E_2) + (+E_1) + (-E_A) = 0$

Substituting values from the circuit:

$E_X + 15\,V + 25\,V - 50\,V = 0$
$E_X - 10 = 0$
$E_X = 10$

Using the same idea as above, a problem in which the current is the unknown quantity can be solved.

Another example shows a circuit having a source voltage of 60 V contains three resistors of 5Ω, 10Ω and 15Ω. Find the circuit current.

To solve the problem, draw and label the circuit. Establish a direction of current flow and assign polarities. Next, starting at any point—point A will be used in this example—write out the loop equation.

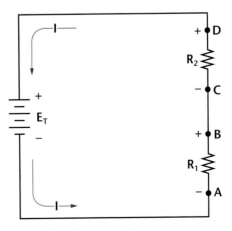

Figure 1-5-3. Voltage polarities

Basic Equation:

$$E_2 + E_1 + E_A + E_3 = 0$$

Since E=IR, substitute:

$$(I \times R_2) + (I \times R_1) + E_A + (I \times R_3) = 0$$

Substituting values:

$$(I \times 10\Omega) + (I \times 5\Omega) + (-60\text{ V}) + (I \times 15\Omega) = 0$$

Combine like terms:

$$(I \times 30\Omega) + (-60\text{ V}) = 0$$
$$(I \times 30\Omega) = 60\text{ V}$$
$$I = 60\text{ V} \div 30\Omega$$
$$I = 2\text{ A}$$

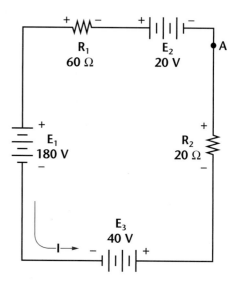

Figure 1-5-4. Solving for circuit current using Kirchhoff's voltage equation

Since the current obtained in the above calculations is a positive 2 A, the assumed direction of current was correct. To show what happens if the incorrect direction of current is assumed, the problem will be solved as before, but with the opposite direction of current. The circuit is redrawn showing the new direction of current and new polarities. Starting at point A the loop equation is:

$$E_3 + E_A + E_1 + E_2 = 0$$
$$(I \times R_3) + E_A + (I \times R_1) + (I \times R_2) = 0$$

Substitute values:

$$(I \times 15\Omega) + 60\text{ V} + (I \times 5\Omega) + (I \times 10\Omega) = 0$$

Combine like terms:

$$(I \times 30\Omega) + 60\text{ V} = 0$$
$$I \times 30\Omega = -60\text{ V}$$
$$I = -60\text{ V} \div 30\Omega$$
$$I = -2\text{ A}$$

Notice that the amount of current is the same as before. The polarity, however, is negative. The negative polarity simply indicates the wrong direction of current was assumed. Should it be necessary to use this current in further calculations on the circuit using Kirchhoff's law, the negative polarity should be retained in the calculations.

Series Aiding and Opposing Sources

In many practical applications a circuit may contain more than one source of emf. Sources of emf that cause current to flow in the same direction are considered to be *series aiding* and the voltages are added. Sources of emf that would tend to force current in opposite directions are said to be *series* *opposing*, and the effective source voltage is the difference between the opposing voltages. When two opposing sources are inserted into a circuit, current flow will be in a direction determined by the larger source.

A simple solution may be obtained for a multiple-source circuit through the use of Kirchhoff's voltage law. In applying this method, the same procedure is used for the multiple-source circuit as was used above for the single-source circuit. This is demonstrated in the following example.

Example: Using Kirchhoff's voltage equation, find the amount of current in the circuit shown in Figure 1-5-4.

Solution: As before, a direction of current flow is assumed and polarity signs are placed on the drawing. The loop equation will start at point A.

$$E_2 + E_{R1} + E_1 + E_3 + E_{R2} = 0$$
$$20\text{ V} + (I \times 60\Omega) + (-180\text{ V}) + 40\text{ V} + (I \times 20\Omega) = 0$$
$$20\text{ V} - 180\text{ V} + 40\text{ V} + (I \times 60\Omega) + (I \times 20\Omega) = 0$$
$$-120\text{ V} + (I \times 80\Omega) = 0$$
$$I \times 80\Omega = 120\text{ V}$$
$$I = 120\text{ V} \div 80\Omega$$
$$I = 1.5\text{ A}$$

Section 6

Parallel DC Circuits

The discussion of electrical circuits presented to this point has been concerned with series circuits in which there is only one path for current. There is another basic type of circuit known as the parallel circuit with which a technician must become familiar. Where the series circuit has only one path for current, the parallel circuit has more than one path for current.

Ohm's law and Kirchhoff's law apply to all electrical circuits, but the characteristics of a parallel DC circuit are different than those of a series DC circuit.

Parallel Circuit Characteristics

A *parallel circuit* is defined as one having more than one current path connected to a common voltage source (Figure 1-6-1). Parallel circuits, therefore, must contain two or more resistances that are not connected in series. An example of a basic parallel circuit is shown in Figure 1-6-2.

Start at the voltage source (E_S) and trace counterclockwise around the circuit. Two complete and separate paths can be identified in which current can flow. One path is traced from the source, through resistance R_1, and back to the source. The other path is from the source, through resistance R_2, and back to the source.

Voltage in a Parallel Circuit

It has been shown that the source voltage in a series circuit divides proportionately across each resistor in the circuit. In a parallel circuit, the same voltage is present in each branch. (A *branch* is a section of a circuit that has a complete path for current.) In Figure 1-6-2 this voltage is equal to the applied voltage (E_S). This can be expressed in equation form as:

$E_S = E_{R1} = E_{R2}$

Example: Assume that the current through a resistor of a parallel circuit is known to be 4.5 milliamperes (4.5 mA) and the value of the resistor is 30,000Ω (30 kΩ). Determine the source voltage.

Given:

$R_2 = 30$ kΩ

$I_{R2} = 4.5$ mA

Solution:

$E = IR$

$E_{R2} = 4.5$ mA $\times$ 30 kΩ

$E_{R2} = 0.0045$ A $\times$ 30,000Ω

$E_{R2} = 135$ V

Since the source voltage is equal to the voltage of a branch: $E_S = 135$ V

Current in a Parallel Circuit

Ohm's law states that the current in a circuit is inversely proportional to the circuit resistance. This fact is true in both series and parallel circuits.

There is a single path for current in a series circuit. The amount of current is determined by the total resistance of the circuit and the applied voltage. In a parallel circuit the source current divides among the available paths.

The behavior of current in parallel circuits will be shown by a series of illustrations using example circuits with different values of resistance for a given value of applied voltage.

Figure 1-6-3 shows two resistors (R_1 and R_2) of equal value connected in parallel across the voltage source. The following shows how to calculate the current.

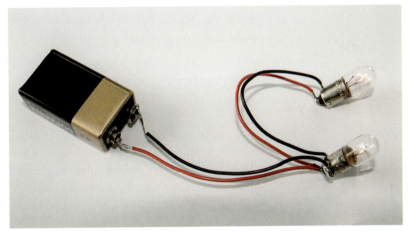

Figure 1-6-1. Example of basic parallel circuit

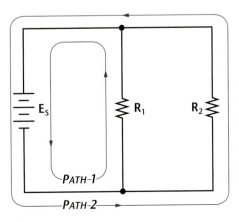

Figure 1-6-2. Basic parallel circuit

1-36 | Fundamentals of Direct Current

Given:

$$E_S = 50 \text{ V}$$
$$R_1 = 10\Omega$$
$$R_2 = 10\Omega$$

Solution:

$$I = E \div R$$
$$E_S = E_{R1} = E_{R2}$$
$$I_{R1} = E_{R1} \div R_1$$
$$I_{R1} = 50 \text{ V} \div 10\Omega$$
$$I_{R1} = 5 \text{ A}$$

Since the resistance and voltage for R_1 is the same as R_2, it is safe to say that the current of R_2 is also 5 amps. If there is 5 amps of current through each of the two resistors, there must be a total current of 10 amps drawn from the source. The total current of 10 amps, as illustrated in Figure 1-6-3B, leaves the negative terminal of the battery and flows to point A. Since point A is a connecting point for the two resistors, it is called a *junction*. At junction A, the total current divides into two currents of 5 amps each. These two currents flow through their respective resistors and rejoin at junction B. The total current then flows from junction B back to the positive terminal of the source. The source supplies a total current of 10 amps and each of the two equal resistors carries one-half the total current.

Each individual current path in the circuit of Figure 1-6-3 is referred to as a branch. Each branch carries a current that is a portion of the total current. Two or more branches form a *network*.

From the previous explanation, the characteristics of current in a parallel circuit can be expressed in terms of the following general equation:

$$I_T = I_1 + I_2 + \ldots I_n$$

Compare Figure 1-6-4A with the circuit in Figure 1-6-3. Notice that doubling the value of the second branch resistor (R_2) has no effect on the current in the first branch (I_{R1}), but does reduce the second branch current (I_{R2}) to one-half its original value. The total circuit current drops to a value equal to the sum of the branch currents. These facts are verified by the following equations.

Given:

$$E_S = 50 \text{ V}$$
$$R_1 = 10\Omega$$
$$R_2 = 20\Omega$$

Solution:

$$I = E \div R$$
$$E_S = E_{R1} = E_{R2}$$
$$I = E_{R1} \div R_1$$
$$I = 50 \text{ V} \div 10\Omega$$
$$I_{R1} = 5 \text{ A}$$
$$I_{R2} = E_{R2} \div R_2$$
$$I_{R2} = 50 \text{ V} \div 20\Omega$$
$$I_{R2} = 2.5 \text{ A}$$
$$I_T = I_{R1} + I_{R2}$$
$$I_T = 5 \text{ A} + 2.5 \text{ A}$$
$$I_T = 7 \text{ A}$$

The amount of current flow in the branch circuits and the total current in the circuit shown in Figure 1-6-4B are determined by the following computations.

Given:

$$E_S = 50 \text{ V}$$
$$R_1 = 10\Omega$$
$$R_2 = 10\Omega$$
$$R_3 = 10\Omega$$

(A)
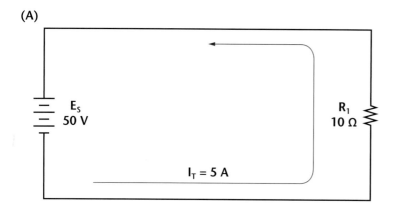

(B)
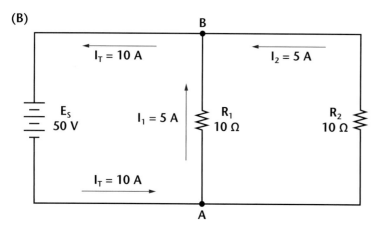

Figure 1-6-3. Current analysis in parallel circuit

Solution:

$I = E \div R$

$E_S = E_{R1} = E_{R2} = E_{R3}$

$I_{R1} = E_{R1} \div R_1$

$I_{R1} = 50\,V \div 10\,\Omega$

$I_{R1} = 5\,A$

$I_{R2} = E_{R2} \div R_2$

$I_{R2} = 50\,V \div 10\,\Omega$

$I_{R2} = 5\,A$

$I_{R3} = E_{R3} \div R_3$

$I_{R3} = 50\,V \div 10\,\Omega$

$I_{R3} = 5\,A$

$I_T = I_{R1} + I_{R2} + I_{R3}$

$I_T = 5\,A + 5\,A + 5\,A$

$I_T = 15\,A$

Notice that the sum of the ohmic values in each circuit shown in Figure 1-6-4 is equal (30Ω), and that the applied voltage is the same (50 V). However, the total current in Figure 1-6-4B is twice the amount in Figure 1-6-4A. It is apparent, therefore, that the manner in which resistors are connected in a circuit, as well as their actual ohmic values, affect the total current.

The division of current in a parallel network follows a definite pattern. This pattern is described by Kirchhoff's current law, which states: "The algebraic sum of the currents entering and leaving any junction of conductors is equal to zero."

This law can be stated mathematically as:

$I_a + I_b + \ldots I_n = 0$

where: I_a, I_b, etc., are the currents entering and leaving the junction. Currents entering the junction are considered to be positive and currents leaving the junction are considered to be negative. When solving a problem using Kirchhoff's current law, the currents must be placed into the equation with the proper polarity signs attached.

Example: Solve for the value of I_3 in Figure 1-6-5.

Given:

$I_1 = 10\,A$

$I_2 = 5\,A$

$I_4 = 5\,A$

$I_a + I_b + \ldots I_n = 0$

Solution:

$I_a + I_b + \ldots I_a + 0$

(A)

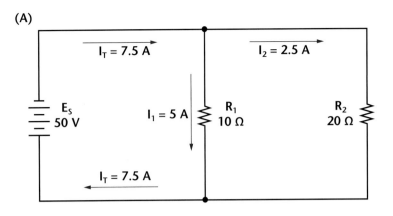

(B)

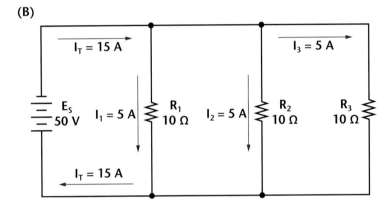

Figure 1-6-4. Current behavior in parallel circuits

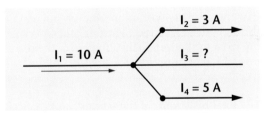

Figure 1-6-5. Circuit for example problem

The currents are placed into the equation with the proper signs.

$I_1 + I_2 + I_3 + I_4 = 0$

$10\,A + (-3\,A) + I_3 + (-5\,A) = 0$

$I_3 + 2\,A = 0$

$I_3 = -2\,A$

I_3 has a value of 2 A, and the negative sign shows it to be a current leaving the junction.

Example: Using Figure 1-6-6, solve for the magnitude and direction of I_3.

Given:

$I_1 = 6\,A$

$I_2 = 3\,A$

$I_4 = 5\,A$

Solution:

$I_a + I_b + \ldots I_n = 0$

$I_1 + I_2 + I_3 + I_4 = 0$

$6\,A + (-3\,A) + I_3 + (-5\,A) = 0$

$I_3 + (-2\,A) = 0$

$I_3 = -2\,A$

I_3 is 2 A and its positive sign shows it to be a current entering the junction.

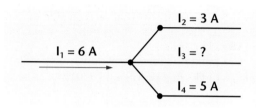

Figure 1-6-6. Circuit for example problem

Resistance in a Parallel Circuit

In the example diagram, Figure 1-6-7, there are two resistors connected in parallel across a 5 V battery. Each has a resistance value of 10Ω. A complete circuit consisting of two parallel paths is formed and current flows as shown.

Computing the individual currents shows that there is one-half of an ampere of current through each resistance. The total current flowing from the battery to the junction of the resistors and returning from the resistors to the battery is equal to 1 A.

The total resistance of the circuit can be calculated by using the values of total voltage (E_T) and total current (I_T).

Given:

$E_T = 5\,V$

$I_T = 1\,A$

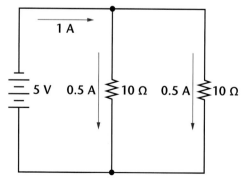

Figure 1-6-7. Two equal resistors connected in parallel

Solution:

$R = E \div I$

$R_T = E_T \div I_T$

$R_T = 5\,V \div 1\,A$

$R_T = 5\,\Omega$

This computation shows the total resistance to be 5Ω; one-half the value of either of the two resistors.

Since the total resistance of a parallel circuit is smaller than any of the individual resistors, total resistance of a parallel circuit is *not* the sum of the individual resistor values as was the case in a series circuit. The total resistance of resistors in parallel is also referred to as *equivalent resistance* (R_{eq}). The terms *total resistance* and *equivalent resistance* are used interchangeably.

There are several methods used to determine the equivalent resistance of parallel circuits. The best method for a given circuit depends on the number and value of the resistors.

For the circuit described above, where all resistors have the same value, the following simple equation is used:

$R_{eq} = R \div N$

R_{eq} = equivalent parallel resistance

R = ohmic value of one resistor

N = number of resistors

This equation is valid for any number of parallel resistors of equal value.

Example: Four 40Ω resistors are connected in parallel. What is their equivalent resistance?

Given:

$R_1 + R_2 + R_3 + R_4$

$R_1 = 40\,\Omega$

Solution:

$R_{eq} = R \div N$

$R_{eq} = 40\,\Omega \div 4$

$R_{eq} = 10\,\Omega$

Figure 1-6-8 shows two resistors of unequal value in parallel. Since the total current is shown, the equivalent resistance can be calculated.

The equivalent resistance of the circuit shown in Figure 1-6-8 is smaller than either of the two resistors (R_1, R_2). An important point to remember is that the equivalent resistance of a parallel circuit is always less than the resistance of any branch.

Equivalent resistance can be found if the individual resistance values and the source voltage are known. By calculating each branch current, adding the branch currents to calculate total current, and dividing the source voltage by the total current, the total can be found. This method, while effective, is somewhat lengthy. A quicker method of finding equivalent resistance is to use the general formula for resistors in parallel:

$$1 \div R_{eq} = (1 \div R_1) + (1 \div R_2) + (1 \div R_3) + \ldots (1 \div R_n)$$

If the general formula to the circuit shown in Figure 1-6-8 is applied, the same value for equivalent resistance (2Ω) will be obtained as was achieved in the previous calculation that used source voltage and total current.

Given:

$R_1 = 3\Omega$

$R_2 = 6\Omega$

Solution:

$1 \div R_{eq} = (1 \div R_1) + (1 \div R_2)$
$1 \div R_{eq} = (1 \div 3\Omega) + (1 \div 6\Omega)$

Convert the fractions to a common denominator.

$1 \div R_{eq} = (2 \div 6\Omega) + (1 \div 6\Omega)$
$1 \div R_{eq} = (3 \div 6\Omega)$
$1 \div R_{eq} = 1 \div 2\Omega$

Since both sides are reciprocals (divided into one), disregard the reciprocal function.

$R_{eq} = 2\Omega$

The formula supplied for equal resistors in parallel is a simplification of the general formula for resistors in parallel.

$$1 \div R_{eq} = (1 \div R_1) + (1 \div R_2) + (1 \div R_3) + \ldots (1 \div R_n)$$

There are other simplifications of the general formula for resistors in parallel that can be used to calculate the total or equivalent resistance in a parallel circuit.

Reciprocal method. This method is based upon taking the reciprocal of each side of the equation. This presents the general formula for resistors in parallel as:

$$R_{eq} = 1 \div (1 \div R_1 + 1 \div R_2 + \ldots 1 \div R_n)$$

This formula is used to solve for the equivalent resistance of a number of unequal parallel resistors. The lowest common denominator must be found in solving these problems.

Example: Three resistors are connected in parallel as shown in Figure 1-6-9. The resistor values are: $R_1 = 20\Omega$, $R_2 = 30\Omega$, $R_3 = 40\Omega$. What is the equivalent resistance? (Use the reciprocal method.)

Given:

$R_1 = 20\Omega$

$R_2 = 30\Omega$

$R_3 = 40\Omega$

Solution:

$R_{eq} = 1 \div (1 \div R_1 + 1 \div R_2 + 1 \div R_3)$
$R_{eq} = 1 \div (1 \div 20\Omega + 1 \div 30\Omega + 1 \div 40\Omega)$
$R_{eq} = 1 \div (6 \div 120\Omega + 4 \div 120\Omega + 3 \div 120\Omega)$
$R_{eq} = 1 \div (13\Omega \div 120\Omega)$
$R_{eq} = 120\Omega \div 13\Omega$
$R_{eq} = 9.23\Omega$

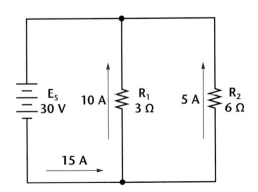

Figure 1-6-8. Circuit with unequal parallel resistors

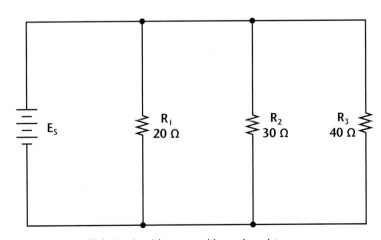

Figure 1-6-9. Parallel circuit with unequal branch resistors

Product over the sum method. A convenient method for finding the equivalent, or total, resistance of two parallel resistors is by using the following formula.

$$R_{eq} = (R_1 \times R_2) \div (R_1 + R_2)$$

This equation, called the product over the sum formula, is used so frequently it should be committed to memory.

Example: What is the equivalent resistance of a 20Ω and a 30Ω resistor connected in parallel, as seen in Figure 1-6-10?

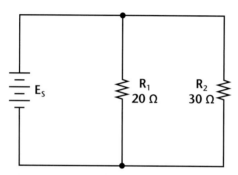

Figure 1-6-10. Parallel circuit with two unequal resistors

Given:

$R_1 = 20\Omega$
$R_2 = 30\Omega$

Solution:

$R_{eq} = (R_1 \times R_2) \div (R_1 + R_2)$
$R_{eq} = (20\Omega \times 30\Omega) \div (20\Omega + 30\Omega)$
$R_{eq} = 600\Omega \div 50\Omega$
$R_{eq} = 12\Omega$

Power in a Parallel Circuit

Power computations in a parallel circuit are essentially the same as those used for the series circuit. Since power dissipation in resistors consists of heat loss, power dissipations are additive regardless of how the resistors are connected in the circuit. The total power is equal to the sum of the power dissipated by the individual resistors. Like the series circuit, the total power consumed by the parallel circuit is:

$$P_T = P_1 + P_2 + \ldots P_n$$

Example: Find the total power consumed by the circuit in Figure 1-6-11.

Given:

$R_1 = 10\Omega$
$I_{R1} = 5\text{ A}$
$R_2 = 25\Omega$
$I_{R2} = 2\text{ A}$
$R_3 = 50\Omega$
$I_{R3} = 1\text{ A}$

Solution:

$P = I^2 R$
$P_{R1} = (I_{R1})^2 \times R_1$
$P_{R1} = (5\text{ A})^2 \times 10\Omega$
$P_{R1} = 250\text{ W}$
$P_{R2} = (I_{R2})^2 \times R_2$
$P_{R2} = (2\text{ A})^2 \times 25\Omega$
$P_{R2} = 100\text{ W}$
$P_{R3} = (I_{R3})^2 \times R_3$
$P_{R3} = (1\text{ A})^2 \times 50\Omega$
$P_{R3} = 50\text{ W}$
$P_T = P_{R1} + P_{R2} + P_{R3}$
$P_T = 250\text{ W} + 100\text{ W} + 50\text{ W}$
$P_T = 400\text{ W}$

Since the total current and source voltage are known, the total power can also be computed by:

Given:

$E_S = 50\text{ V}$
$I_T = 8\text{ A}$

Solution:

$P_T = E_S \times I_T$
$P_T = 50\text{ V} \times 8\text{ A}$
$P_T = 400\text{W}$

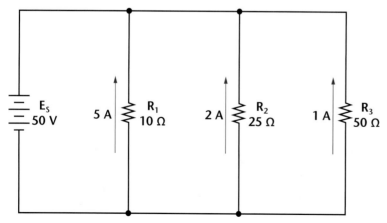

Figure 1-6-11. Parallel circuit

Rules for Parallel DC Circuits

1. The same voltage exists across each branch of a parallel circuit and is equal to the source voltage.
2. The current through a branch of a parallel network is inversely proportional to the amount of resistance of the branch.
3. The total current of a parallel circuit is equal to the sum of the individual branch currents of the circuit.
4. The total resistance of a parallel circuit is found by the general formula:

$$1 \div R_{eq} = (1 \div R_1) + (1 \div R_2) + \ldots (1 \div R_n)$$

or one of the formulas derived from this general formula.

5. The total power consumed in a parallel circuit is equal to the sum of the power consumptions of the individual resistances.

Series-Parallel DC Circuits

In the preceding discussions, series and parallel DC circuits have been considered separately. The technician will encounter circuits consisting of both series and parallel elements. A circuit of this type is referred to as a *combination circuit*. Solving for the quantities and elements in a combination circuit is simply a matter of applying the laws and rules discussed up to this point.

Solving Combination Circuit Problems

The basic technique used for solving DC combination circuit problems is the use of equivalent circuits. To simplify a complex circuit to a simple circuit containing only one load, equivalent circuits are substituted (on paper) for the complex circuit they represent. To demonstrate the method used to solve combination circuit problems, the network shown in Figure 1-6-12A will be used to calculate circuit quantities such as resistance, current, voltage and power.

Examination of the circuit shows that the only quantity that can be computed with the given information is the equivalent resistance of R_2 and R_3.

Given:

$R_2 = 20\Omega$
$R_3 = 30\Omega$

Solution:

$R_{eq1} = (R_2 \times R_3) \div (R_2 + R_3)$ (Product over the sum)
$R_{eq1} = (20\Omega \times 30\Omega) \div (20\Omega + 30\Omega)$
$R_{eq1} = 600\Omega \div 50\Omega$
$R_{eq1} = 12\Omega$

Now that the equivalent resistance for R_2 and R_3 has been calculated, the circuit can be redrawn as a series circuit, as shown in Figure 1-6-12B.

The equivalent resistance of this circuit (total resistance) can now be calculated.

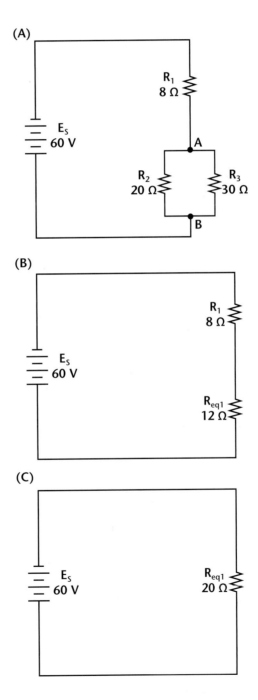

Figure 1-6-12. Combination circuit

Given:

$R_1 = 8\Omega$ (Resistors in series)

$R_{eq1} = 12\Omega$

Solution:

$R_{eq} = R_1 + R_{eq1}$

$R_{eq} = 8\Omega + 12\Omega$

$R_{eq} = 20\Omega$ or $R_T = 20\Omega$

The original circuit can be redrawn with a single resistor that represents the equivalent resistance of the entire circuit as shown in Figure 1-6-12C.

To find total current in the circuit:

Given:

$E_S = 60$ V

$R_T = 20\Omega$

Solution:

$I_T = E_S \div R_T$

$I_T = 60$ V $\div 20\Omega$ (Ohm's Law)

$I_T = 3$ A

To find total power in the circuit:

Given:

$E_S = 60$ V

$I_T = 3$ A

Solution:

$P_T = E_S \times I_T$

$P_T = 60$ V $\times 3$ A

$P_T = 180$ W

To find the voltage dropped across R_1, R_2 and R_3, refer to Figure 1-6-12B. R_{eq1} represents the parallel network of R_2 and R_3. Since the voltage across each branch of a parallel circuit is equal, the voltage across R_{eq1} (E_{eq1}) will be equal to the voltage across R_2 (E_{R2}) and also be equal to the voltage across R_3 (E_{R3}).

Given:

$I_T = 3$ A (Current through each part

$R_1 = 8\Omega$ of a series circuit is equal

$R_{eq1} = 12\Omega$ to total current)

Solution:

$E_{R1} = I_1 \times R_1$

$E_{R1} = 3$ A $\times 8\Omega$

$E_{R1} = 24$ V

$E_{R2} = E_{R3} = E_{eq1}$

$E_{eq1} = I_T \times R_{eq1}$

$E_{eq1} = 3$ A $\times 12\Omega$

$E_{eq1} = 36$ V

$E_{R2} = 36$ V

$E_{R3} = 36$ V

To find power used by R_1:

Given:

$E_{R1} = 24$ V

$I_T = 3$ A

Solution:

$P_{R1} = E_{R1} \times I_T$

$P_{R1} = 24$ V $\times 3$ A

$P_{R1} = 72$ W

To find the current through R_2 and R_3, refer to the original circuit, Figure 1-6-12A. In previous calculations, E_{R2} and E_{R3} were given.

Given:

$E_{R2} = 36$ V

$E_{R3} = 36$ V

$R_2 = 20\Omega$

$R_2 = 30\Omega$

Solution:

$I_{R2} = E_{R2} \div R_2$ (Ohm's Law)

$I_{R2} = 36$ V $\div 20\Omega$

$I_{R2} = 1.8$ A

$I_{R3} = E_{R3} \div R_3$

$I_{R3} = 36$ V $\div 30\Omega$

$I_{R3} = 1.2$ A

To find power used by R_2 and R_3, using values from previous calculations:

Given:

$E_{R2} = 36$ V

$E_{R3} = 36$ V

$I_{R2} = 1.8$ A

$I_{R2} = 1.2$ A

Solution:

$P_{R2} = E_{R2} \times I_{R2}$
$P_{R2} = 36\,V \times 1.8\,A$
$P_{R2} = 64.8\,W$
$P_{R3} = E_{R3} \times I_{R3}$
$P_{R3} = 36\,V \times 1.2\,A$
$P_{R3} = 43.2\,W$

Now that the solution for the unknown quantities in this circuit has been found, apply what has been learned to any series, parallel or combination circuit. It is important to remember to first look at the circuit and from observation make a determination of the type of circuit, what is known and what is unknown. A minute spent in this manner may save many unnecessary calculations.

Having computed all the currents and voltages of Figure 1-6-12, a complete description of the operation of the circuit can be made. The total current of 3 A leaves the negative terminal of the battery and flows through the 8Ω resistor (R_1). In so doing, a voltage drop of 24 V occurs across resistor R_1. At point A, this 3-A current divides into two currents. Of the total current, 1.8 A flows through the 20Ω resistor. The remaining current of 1.2 A flows from point A, down through the 30Ω resistor to point B. This current produces a voltage drop of 36 V across the 30Ω resistor. (Notice that the voltage drops across the 20 and 30Ω resistors are the same.) The two branch currents of 1.8 and 1.2 A combine at junction B and the total current of 3 A flows back to the source. The action of the circuit has been completely described with the exception of power consumed, which could be described using the values previously computed.

It should be pointed out that the combination circuit is not difficult to solve. The key to its solution lies in knowing the order in which the steps of the solution must be accomplished.

Section 7

Bridge Circuits

There are some circuits that contain two delta formations and share a common middle resistor. These types of circuits are called bridge circuits, as seen in Figure 1-7-1. The formulas used up to this point for solving resistance will not work to solve these. Fortunately there is a mathematical method to solve these types of circuits. In essence, the technician converts the delta circuits into a Y circuit, as seen in Figure 1-7-2.

To get started, convert one side of the delta into a Y (R_1, R_4, and R_5). To do this use the following equations

$$R_A = \frac{R_1 \times R_2}{R_1 + R_2 + R_3}$$

$$R_B = \frac{R_1 \times R_3}{R_1 + R_2 + R_3}$$

$$R_C = \frac{R_2 \times R_3}{R_1 + R_2 + R_3}$$

Next, plug in the numbers and convert the circuit into a Y circuit.

$$R_A = \frac{12\Omega \times 18\Omega}{12\Omega + 18\Omega + 6\Omega} = \frac{216}{36} = 6\Omega$$

$$R_B = \frac{12\Omega \times 6\Omega}{12\Omega + 18\Omega + 6\Omega} = \frac{72}{36} = 2\Omega$$

$$R_C = \frac{18\Omega \times 6\Omega}{12\Omega + 18\Omega + 6\Omega} = \frac{108}{36} = 3\Omega$$

Now that the two deltas are converted into the Y formation, the circuit is shown as a series-parallel circuit. All the formulas learned up

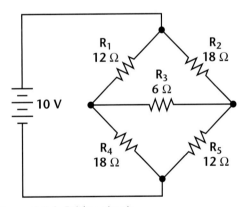

Figure 1-7-1. Bridge circuit

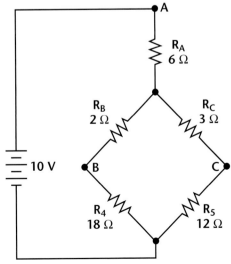

Figure 1-7-2. Converting delta circuits into a Y circuit

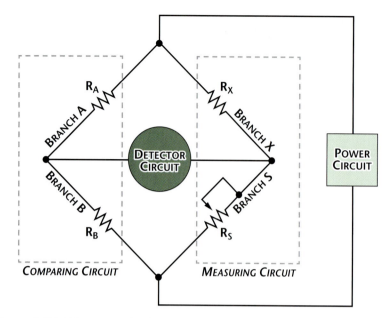

Figure 1-7-3. Wheatstone bridge circuit

to this point can now be used to solve for total resistance.

$R_{C5} = 3\Omega + 12\Omega$ $R_{B4} = 2\Omega + 18\Omega$
$R_{C5} = 15\Omega$ $R_{B4} = 20\Omega$

$R_{BC45} = \dfrac{15\Omega \times 20\Omega}{15\Omega + 20\Omega} = \dfrac{300}{35} = 8.75\Omega$

$R_T = 8.57 + 6\Omega$
$R_T = 14.57\Omega$

Bridge circuits have many purposes in aviation. Some of the uses can be seen in temperature detection circuits, such as the wheatstone bridge, in warning systems, and in precision measurement equipment. Figure 1-7-3 is an example of a of the wheatstone bridge.

Section 8

Circuit Analysis and Troubleshooting

Principles of Troubleshooting

One of the most important facets of an aircraft maintenance technician's job is troubleshooting. The technician must be able to analyze circuit problems and determine probable causes of malfunctions with minimal time and effort.

Troubleshooting is the process of locating causes for malfunctions or trouble in a circuit. The following are definitions of key terms.:

Short circuit. A low resistance path. It can be across the power source or between the sides of a circuit. It usually creates high current flow, which will burn out or cause damage to the circuit conductor or components.

Open circuit. A circuit that is not complete or continuous.

Continuity. The state of being continuous, or connected together; said of a circuit that is not broken or does not have an open.

Discontinuity. The opposite of continuity, indicating that a circuit is broken or not continuous.

Open Circuits

The open circuits shown in Figure 1-8-1 can often be located by visual inspection, but many circuit opens cannot be seen. In such cases, a meter must be used.

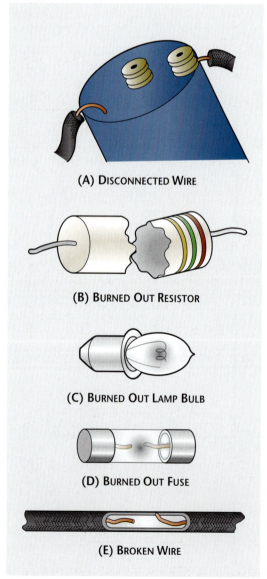

Figure 1-8-1. Common causes of open circuits

Some common sources of open circuits (commonly called *opens* or *an open*) are shown in Figure 1-8-1. A loose connection or no connection is a frequent cause of an open circuit.

In Figure 1-8-1A, the end of a conductor has separated from the battery terminal. This type of malfunction opens a circuit and stops the flow of current.

Another type of malfunction that will cause an open circuit is a burned-out resistor, shown in Figure 1-8-1B. When a resistor overheats, its resistance value changes, and, if the current flow through it is great enough, it can burn and open the circuit.

Illustrations C, D and E of Figure 1-8-1 show three more common causes of opens.

The circuit shown in Figure 1-8-2 is designed to cause current to flow through a lamp, but because of the open resistor, the lamp will not light. To locate this open, a voltmeter or an ohmmeter can be used.

If a voltmeter is connected across the lamp, as shown in Figure 1-8-3, the voltmeter will read zero. Since no current can flow in the circuit because of the open resistor, there is no voltage drop across the lamp. This illustrates an important troubleshooting rule: When a voltmeter is connected across a good (not defective) component in an open circuit, the voltmeter will read zero.

Next, the voltmeter is connected across the open resistor, as shown in Figure 1-8-4. The voltmeter has closed the circuit by shunting (paralleling) the burned-out resistor, allowing current to flow.

Current will flow from the negative terminal of the battery, through the switch, through the voltmeter and the lamp, back to the positive terminal of the battery. However, the resistance of the voltmeter is so high that only a very small current flows in the circuit.

The current is too small to light the lamp, but the voltmeter will read the battery voltage, illustrating another troubleshooting rule. When a voltmeter is placed across an open component in a series circuit, it will read the battery, or applied voltage.

This type of open circuit malfunction can also be traced by using an ohmmeter. When an ohmmeter is used, the circuit component to be tested must be isolated and the power source removed from the circuit.

In the example shown in Figure 1-8-5, these requirements can be met by opening the circuit switch. The ohmmeter is zeroed and placed across (in parallel with) the lamp.

In this circuit, some value of resistance is read. This illustrates another important troubleshooting rule: When an ohmmeter is properly connected across a circuit component and a resistance reading is obtained, the component has continuity and is not open.

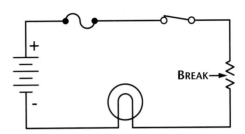

Figure 1-8-2. An open circuit

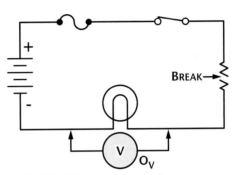

Figure 1-8-3. Voltmeter across a lamp in an open circuit

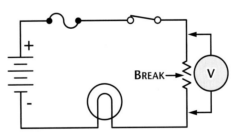

Figure 1-8-4. Using a voltmeter to check a circuit component

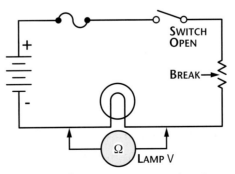

Figure 1-8-5. Ohmmeter across a resistor in an open circuit

When the ohmmeter is connected across the open resistor, as shown in Figure 1-8-6, it indicates infinite resistance, or a discontinuity. Thus, the circuit open has been located with both a voltmeter and an ohmmeter.

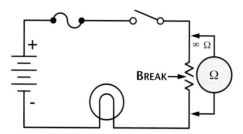

Figure 1-8-6. Using an ohmmeter to check an open in a circuit component

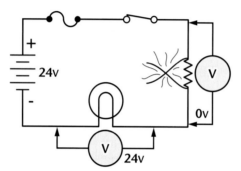

Figure 1-8-7. A shorted resistor

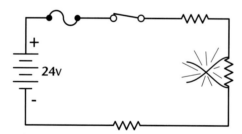

Figure 1-8-8. A short that does not open the circuit

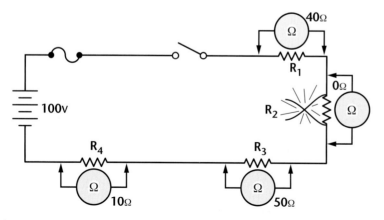

Figure 1-8-9. Using an ohmmeter to locate a shorted resistor

Short Circuits

An open in a series circuit will cause the current flow to stop. A short circuit, or short, will cause the opposite effect. A short across a series circuit produces a greater-than-normal current flow. A short can be caused by two bare wires in a circuit that are touching each other, two terminals of a resistor connected together, etc. Thus, a short can be described as a connection of two conductors of a circuit through a very low resistance.

A circuit designed to light a lamp is shown in Figure 1-8-7. A resistor is connected in the circuit to limit current flow. If the resistor is shorted, as shown in the illustration, the current flow will increase and the lamp will become brighter. If the applied voltage were high enough, the lamp would burn out, but in this case the fuse would protect the lamp by opening first.

Usually a short circuit will produce an open circuit by either blowing (opening) the fuse, or burning out a circuit component. But in some circuits, such as the one illustrated in Figure 1-8-8, there may be additional resistors which will not allow one shorted resistor to increase the current flow enough to blow the fuse or burn out a component. Thus, with one resistor shorted out, the circuit will still function since the power dissipated by the other resistors does not exceed the rating of the fuse.

To locate the shorted resistor while the circuit is functioning, a voltmeter could be used. When it is connected across any of the unshorted resistors, a portion of the applied voltage will be indicated on the voltmeter scale. When it is connected across the shorted resistor, the voltmeter will read zero.

The shorted resistor shown in Figure 1-8-9 can be located with an ohmmeter. First the switch is opened to isolate the circuit components. In Figure 1-8-9, this circuit is shown with an ohmmeter connected across each of the resistors. Only the ohmmeter connected across the shorted resistor shows a zero reading, indicating that this resistor is shorted.

Troubleshooting a Parallel Circuit

The procedures used in troubleshooting a parallel circuit are sometimes different from those used in a series circuit. Unlike a series circuit, a parallel circuit has more than one path in which current flows. A voltmeter cannot be used, since, when it is placed across an open resistor, it will read the voltage drop in a parallel branch. But an ammeter or the modified use of an ohmmeter can be employed to detect an open branch in a parallel circuit.

If the open resistor shown in Figure 1-8-10 was not visually apparent, the circuit would appear to be functioning properly, since current would continue to flow in the other two branches of the circuit.

To determine that the circuit is not operating properly, the total resistance, total current and the branch currents of the circuit should be calculated as if there were no open path in the circuit:

$$R_T = \frac{R}{N}$$

$$= \frac{30}{3}$$

$$= 10 \, \Omega \text{ total resistance}$$

Since the voltage applied to the branches is the same and the value of each branch resistance is known,

$$I = \frac{E_1}{R_1} \qquad I_3 = \frac{E_3}{R_3}$$

$$= \frac{30 \, V}{30 \, \Omega} \qquad = \frac{30 \, V}{30 \, \Omega}$$

$$= 1 \text{ ampere} \qquad = 1 \text{ ampere}$$

$$I_2 = \frac{E_2}{R_2} \qquad I_T = \frac{E_T}{R_T}$$

$$= \frac{30 \, V}{30 \, \Omega} \qquad = \frac{30 \, V}{30 \, \Omega}$$

$$= 1 \text{ ampere} \qquad = 3 \text{ amperes (total current)}$$

An ammeter placed in the circuit to read total current would show 2 amperes instead of the calculated 3 amperes. Since 1 ampere of current should be flowing through each branch, it is obvious that one branch is open. If the ammeter is connected into the branches, one after another, the open branch will be located by a zero ammeter reading.

A modified use of the ohmmeter can also locate this type of open.

If the ohmmeter is connected across the open resistor, as shown in Figure 1-8-11, an erroneous reading of continuity would be obtained. Even though the circuit switch is open, the open resistor is still in parallel with R_1 and R_2, and the ohmmeter would indicate the open resistor had a resistance of 15 ohms, the equivalent resistance of the parallel combination of R_1 and R_2.

It is necessary to open the circuit as shown in Figure 1-8-12 in order to check the resistance of R_3. In this way the resistor is not shunted (paralleled) and the reading on the ohmmeter will indicate infinite resistance. On the other hand, if an open should occur in this circuit (Figure 1-8-12) between the battery and point A, or between the battery and point B, current would not flow in the circuit.

As in a series circuit, a short in a parallel circuit will usually cause an open circuit by blowing the fuse. But, unlike a series circuit, one shorted component in a parallel circuit will stop current flow by causing the fuse to open. This can be seen by referring to the circuit in Figure 1-8-13.

If resistor R_3 is shorted, a path of almost zero resistance will be offered the current, and all the circuit current will flow through the branch containing the shorted resistor. Since this is practically the same as connecting a wire between the

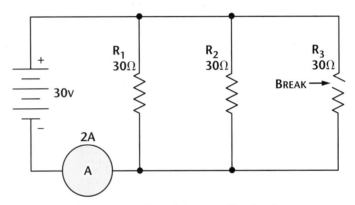

Figure 1-8-10. Finding an open branch in a parallel circuit

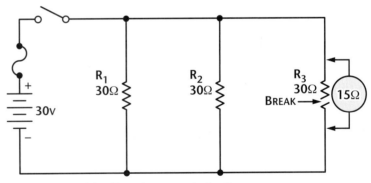

Figure 1-8-11. A misleading ohmmeter indication

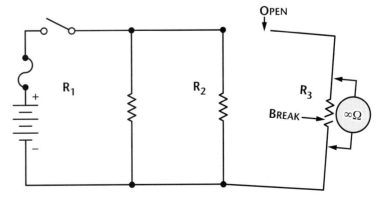

Figure 1-8-12. Opening a branch circuit to obtain an accurate ohmmeter reading

terminals of the battery, the current will rise to an excessive value and the fuse will open.

Since the fuse opens almost as soon as a resistor shorts out, there is no time to perform a current or voltage check. Therefore, troubleshooting a parallel DC circuit for a shorted component should be accomplished with an ohmmeter. But, as in the case of checking for an open resistor in a parallel circuit, a shorted resistor can be detected with an ohmmeter only if one end of the shorted resistor is disconnected.

Troubleshooting a series-parallel resistive circuit involves locating malfunctions similar to those found in a series or a parallel circuit.

An open has occurred in the circuit shown in Figure 1-8-14, in the series portion of the circuit. When an open occurs anywhere in the series portion of a series-parallel circuit, current flow in the entire circuit will stop. In this case, the circuit will not function, and the lamp, L_1, will not be lit.

If an open occurs in the parallel portion of a series-parallel circuit, as shown in Figure 1-8-15, part of the circuit will continue to function. In this case, the lamp will continue to burn, but its brightness will increase, since the total resistance of the circuit has increased and the total current has decreased.

If a break occurs in the branch containing the lamp, as shown in Figure 1-8-16, the circuit will continue to function with increased resistance and decreased current, but the lamp will not burn.

To explain how the voltmeter and ohmmeter can be used to troubleshoot series-parallel circuits, the circuit shown in Figure 1-8-17 has been labeled at various points.

By connecting a voltmeter between points A and D, the battery and fuse can be checked for opens. By connecting the voltmeter between points A and B, the voltage drop across R_1 can be checked along with the switch. This voltage drop is a portion of the applied voltage.

The conductor between the negative terminal of the battery and point E can be checked for continuity by connecting the voltmeter between points A and E. If the conductor or fuse is open, the voltmeter will read zero.

If the lamp is burning, it is obvious that no open exists in the branch containing the lamp, and the voltmeter could be used to detect an open in the branch containing R_2 by removing lamp, L_1, from the circuit.

Troubleshooting the series portion of a series-parallel circuit presents no difficulties, but in the parallel portion of the circuit, misleading readings can be obtained.

An ohmmeter can be used to troubleshoot this same circuit.

With the switch open, the series portion of the circuit can be checked by placing the ohmmeter leads between this switch and point B. If R_1 or the conductor is open, the ohmmeter will read infinity; if not, the value of the resistor will be indicated on the ohmmeter.

Between points D and E, the conductor can be checked for continuity, but in the parallel portion of the circuit, care must be exercised, since misleading ohmmeter indications can be obtained.

To check between points B and E, the branch must be disconnected at one of these points and, while one of these points and the switch are open, the branch containing the lamp can be checked with the ohmmeter.

A short in the series part of a series-parallel circuit will cause a decrease in total resistance, which will cause total current to increase.

In the circuit shown in Figure 1-8-18, the total resistance is 100 ohms and the total current is 2 amperes. If R_1 became shorted, total resistance would become 50 ohms, and the total current would double to 4 amperes.

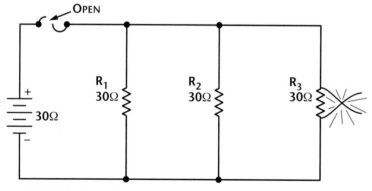

Figure 1-8-13. A shorted component causes the fuse to open

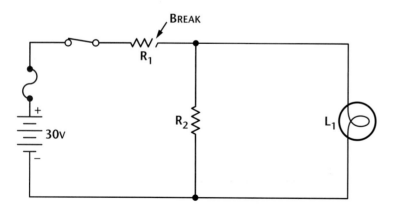

Figure 1-8-14. An open in the series portion of a series-parallel circuit

In the circuit shown, this would cause the 3-amp fuse to blow, but with a 5-amp fuse the circuit would continue to function. The result would be the same if R_2 or R_3 were to become shorted. The total resistance in either case would drop to 50 ohms.

When a short occurs in a series-parallel circuit, as has been seen, the total resistance will decrease and the total current will increase. A short will normally cause an open circuit by either blowing the fuse or burning out a circuit component. And, as in the case of an open, a short in a series-parallel circuit can be detected with either an ohmmeter or a voltmeter.

System Troubleshooting

Much of the technician's time is spent troubleshooting systems. Many of the systems aboard modern aircraft are complex and difficult to troubleshoot. The troubleshooter's job can be simplified if the following steps are considered:

- Determine what constitutes normal operation for the system being tested.

- Analyze the symptom of the problem.

- Detect and isolate the problem.

- Make repairs as necessary to correct the problem.

- Perform an operational test to verify that the repairs corrected the problem.

The aviation maintenance technician cannot possibly hope to effectively analyze problems in systems in which normal operating parameters are not known.

Consult aircraft or system manuals to determine what the minimum performance standards are before attempting to analyze the problem.

Once system operating parameters have been established, the most likely cause for the problem can be determined.

The history of the malfunctioning system may need to be checked as part of the troubleshooting process. If maintenance has recently been performed, clues may be present as to what is causing the current problem. The technician should also check for interrelated problems. For example, if a voltage control unit has recently been replaced and is again malfunctioning after working normally for a short time, perhaps an electrical connector was not tightened properly when the original component was replaced.

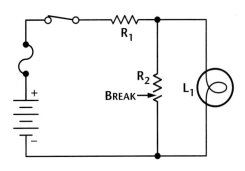

Figure 1-8-15. An open in the parallel portion of the series-parallel circuit

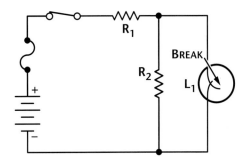

Figure 1-8-16. An open lamp in a series-parallel circuit

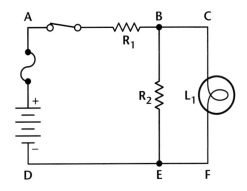

Figure 1-8-17. Using the voltmeter to troubleshoot a series-parallel circuit

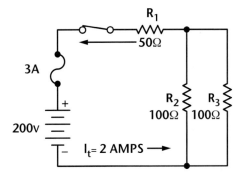

Figure 1-8-18. Finding a short in a series-parallel circuit

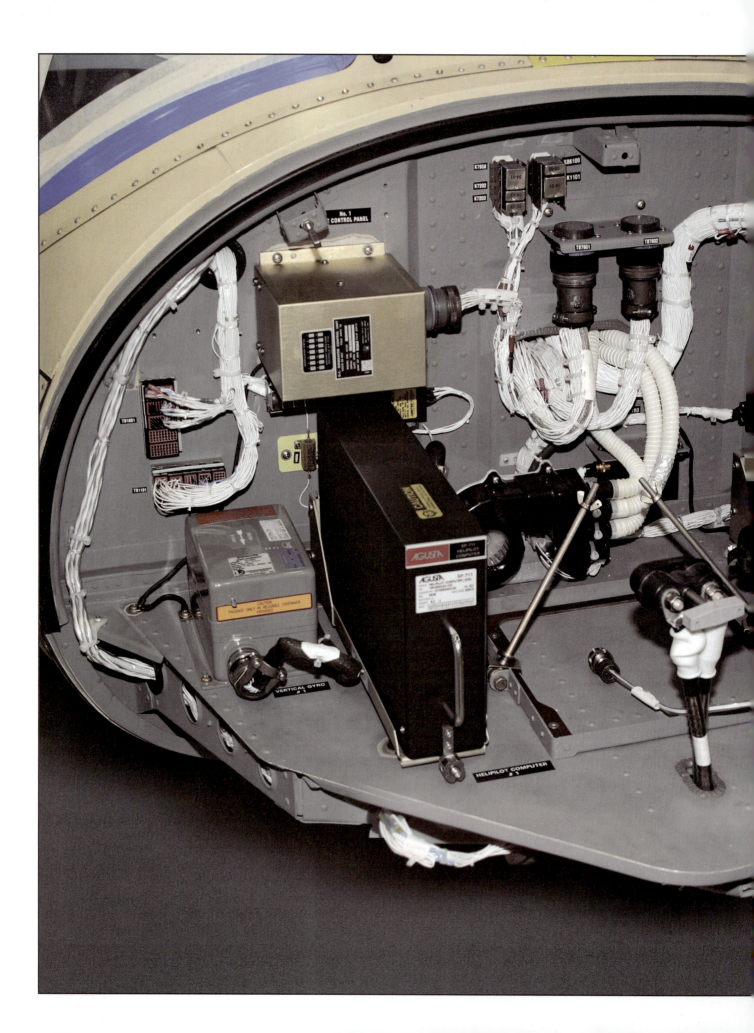

2

Basic Components

Section 1

Circuit Control Devices

Circuit control devices are used everywhere that electrical or electronic circuits are used. They are found in aircraft, helicopters, submarines, computers, televisions, ships, space vehicles, medical instruments and many other places. This chapter covers what circuit control devices are, how they are used, and some of their characteristics.

Introduction

Electricity existed well before the beginning of recorded history. Lightning was a known and feared force to early man, but the practical uses of electricity were not recognized until the late 18th century. The early experimenters in electricity controlled power to their experiments by disconnecting a wire from a battery or by the use of a clutch between a generator and a steam engine. As practical uses were found for electricity, a convenient means for turning power on and off was needed.

Telegraph systems, tried as early as the late 1700s and perfected by Morse in the 1830s, used a mechanically operated contact lever for opening and closing the signal circuit. This was later replaced by the hand-operated contact lever or "key."

Early power switches were simple hinged beams, arranged to close or open a circuit. The blade-and-jaw knife switch, with a wooden, slate, or porcelain base and an insulated handle, was developed a short time later. This was the beginning of circuit control devices.

Learning Objective

DESCRIBE
- the different types of toggle switches

EXPLAIN
- the difference between a relay and a solenoid
- the difference between a rheostat and a potentiometer

APPLY
- resistor color chart to determine the value of a resistor
- the ability to troubleshoot a switch
- the ability to troubleshoot a fuse or circuit breaker
- the ability to troubleshoot a resistor

Left. The avionics bay on a A119 Koala helicopter is filled with many different circuit control devices.

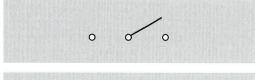

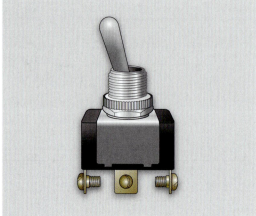

Figure 2-1-1. Toggle switch and schematic symbol

Modern circuit control devices can change their resistance from a few milliohms (when closed) to well over 100,000 megaohms (when open) in a couple of milliseconds. In some circuit control devices, the movement necessary to cause the device to open or close is only 0.001 in. (0.025 mm). Computer chips have some of the smallest circuit control devices within them.

Need for Circuit Control

Circuit control, in its simplest form, is the application and removal of power. This can also be expressed as turning a circuit "off and on" or "opening and closing" a circuit. Before discussing the types of circuit control devices, it is important to understand why circuit control is needed.

If a circuit develops problems that could damage the equipment or endanger personnel, it should be possible to remove the power from that circuit. Circuit protection devices will remove power automatically if current or temperature increase enough to cause the circuit protection device to act. Even with this protection, a manual means of control is needed to allow the user to remove power from the circuit before the protection device acts.

When working on a circuit, the technician often needs to remove power from it to connect test equipment or to remove and replace components. When removing power from a circuit so that it can be worked on, be sure to "tag out" the switch. This ensures that power is not applied to the circuit while the technician is working.

When work has been completed, power must be restored to the circuit. This will allow the technician to check the proper operation of the circuit and place it back in service. After the circuit has been checked for proper operation, remove the tag from the power switch.

Many electrical devices are used some of the time and not needed at other times. Circuit control devices allow the user to turn the device on when it is needed and off when it is not needed.

Some devices, like multimeters or televisions, require the selection of a specific function or circuit. A circuit control device makes possible the selection of the particular circuit the user desires to use.

Types of Circuit Control Devices

Circuit control devices have many different shapes and sizes, but most circuit control devices are *switches*, *solenoids* or *relays*.

Figure 2-1-1 is a simple toggle switch and the schematic symbol for this switch is shown above it. Figure 2-1-2 is a cutaway view of a solenoid. The schematic symbol above the solenoid is one of the schematic symbols used for this solenoid.

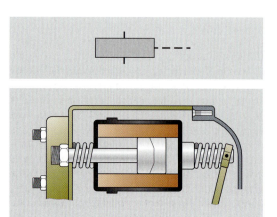

Figure 2-1-2. Solenoid and schematic symbol

Figure 2-1-3. Solenoid

An example of a solenoid is pictured in Figure 2-1-3. Figure 2-1-4 shows a simple relay. One of the schematic symbols for this relay is shown above to the relay. An example of a relay coil terminal is pictured in Figure 2-1-5.

Switch Types

There are thousands and thousands of switch applications found in home, industry and in aviation. Hundreds of electrical switches are used everyday to perform functions that many take for granted. Some switches operate by the touch of a finger and many others are operated automatically.

Switches are used in the home to turn off the alarm clock; to control the stove; to turn on the refrigerator light; to turn on and control radios and televisions, hair dryers, dishwashers, garbage disposals, washers and dryers; as well as to control heating and air conditioning. A modern luxury automobile with power seats and windows may have hundreds of switches.

Industry uses switches in a wide variety of ways. They are found in the business office on computers, copy machines, fax machines, printers and other equipment. A factory or shop may use thousands of switches and they are found on almost every piece of machinery. Switches are used on woodworking machinery, metal working machinery, conveyors, automation devices, elevators, hoists and lift trucks as well as throughout aircraft.

Switches are designed to work in many different environments from extreme high pressure, as in a submarine, to extreme low pressure, as in a spacecraft. Other environmental conditions to consider are high or low temperature, rapid temperature changes, humidity, liquid splashing or immersion, ice, corrosion, sand or dust, fungus, shock or vibration, and an explosive atmosphere.

It would not be possible to describe all the different switches used. This chapter will describe the most common types of switches.

Manual Switches

A *manual switch* is a switch that is controlled by a person. In other words, a manual switch is a switch that someone turns on or off. Examples of common manual switches are a light switch, the ignition switch on a motor vehicle, the speed control on a fan and buttons on a video game controller. A fan speed control is probably not the first thing one thinks of when referring to a switch, but that is what it does. The speed control turns on the proper circuit for the fan speed that the user desires.

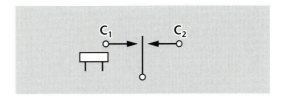

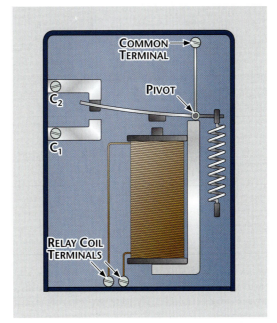

Figure 2-1-4. Relay and schematic symbol

Figure 2-1-5. Relay coil terminal

Automatic Switch

An *automatic switch* is a switch that is controlled by a mechanical or electrical device. Someone does not have to turn an automatic switch on or off. Two examples of automatic switches are a temperature thermostat and the distributor in a motor vehicle. The thermostat will turn a furnace or air conditioner on or off by responding to the temperature in a room. The distributor electrically turns on the spark plug circuit at the proper time by responding to the mechanical rotation of a shaft. Older vehicles were entirely mechanical. Newer vehicles have electronics that monitor the shaft rotation and activate the spark plug circuit using automatic switches. Even the switch that

2-4 | Basic Components

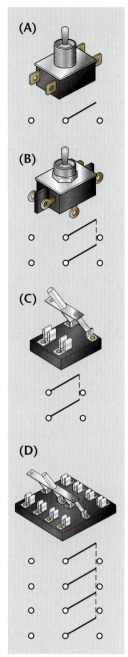

Figure 2-1-7. Multi-contact switches and schematic symbols

Figure 2-1-6. Multi-contact switch

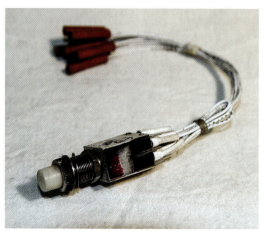

Figure 2-1-9. Double-break pushbutton switch

turns on the light in a refrigerator when the door is opened is an automatic switch.

Automatic switches are not always as simple as the examples given above. Limit switches, which sense some limit such as fluid level, mechanical movement, pressure (altitude or depth under water), or an electrical quantity, are automatic switches. Computers use and control automatic switches that are sometimes quite complicated.

Basically, any switch that will turn a circuit on or off without human action is an automatic switch.

Multi-contact Switches

Switches are sometimes used to control more than one circuit or to select one of several possible circuits. An example of a switch controlling more than one circuit is the AM/FM selector on a radio. This switch enables the user to control either the AM or FM portion of the radio with a single switch. An example of a switch that selects one of several circuits is the speed control on a fan.

These switches are called *multi-contact switches* because they have more than one contact, or multi(ple) contacts. An example of a multi-contact switch is pictured in Figure 2-1-6.

Number of poles and number of throws. Multi-contact switches (other than rotary switches, which will be covered later) are usually classified by the number of poles and number of throws. *Poles* are shown in schematics as those contacts through which current enters the switch; they are connected to the movable contacts. Each pole may be connected to another part of the circuit through the switch by "throwing" the switch (movable contacts) to another position. This action provides an individual conduction path through the switch for each pole connection.

The number of *throws* indicates the number of different circuits that can be controlled by each pole. Count the number of points where current enters the switch (from the schematic symbol or the switch itself), to determine the number of poles. By counting the number of different points each pole can connect with, the number of throws is determined.

Figure 2-1-7 shows a single-pole, double-throw switch. The illustration shows three terminals (connections) on this switch. The schematic symbol for the switch is also shown.

The center connection of the schematic symbol represents the point at which current enters the switch. The left and right connections represent the two different points to which this current can be switched. From the schematic symbol, it is easy to determine that this is a single-pole, double-throw switch.

Now look at Figure 2-1-7B. The switch is shown with its schematic symbol. The schematic symbol has two points at which current can enter the switch, so this is a double-pole switch. Each of the poles is mechanically connected (still electrically separate) to one point, so this is a single-throw switch. Only one throw is required to route two separate circuit paths through the switch.

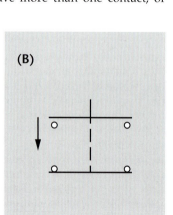

Figure 2-1-8. Double-break pushbutton switch and schematic

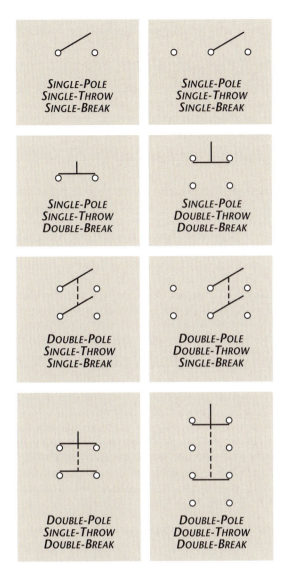

Figure 2-1-10. Schematic symbols for different switch configurations

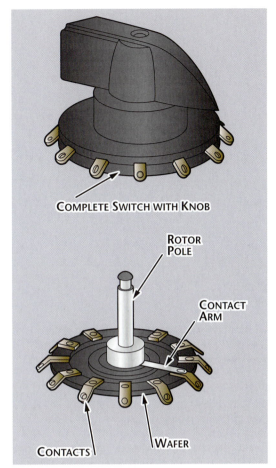

Figure 2-1-11. Rotary switch

Figure 2-1-7C shows a double-pole, double-throw switch and its schematic symbol. Figure 2-1-7D shows a four-pole, double-throw switch and its schematic symbol.

It might help to think of switches with more than one pole as several switches connected together mechanically. For example, the knife switch shown in Figure 2-1-7D could be thought of as four single-pole, double-throw switches mechanically connected together.

Single-break and double-break switches. Switches can also be classified as single-break or double-break switches. This refers to the number of places in which the switch opens or breaks the circuit. All of the switches shown so far have been single-break switches. A *double-break switch* is shown in Figure 2-1-8A.

The schematic symbol shown in Figure 2-1-8B shows that this switch breaks the circuit in two places (i.e., at both terminals). The upper part of the schematic symbol indicates that these contacts are in the open position and the circuit will close when the switch is acted upon (manually or automatically). The lower symbol shows closed contacts. These contacts will open the circuit when the switch is acted upon.

An example of a pushbutton switch is pictured in Figure 2-1-9. This switch is called a *pushbutton switch* because it has a button that must be pushed to change the switch contact connections. Notice that the switch in Figure 2-1-8A has four terminals. The schematic symbol in Figure 2-1-8B shows that when one set of contacts is open, the other set of contacts is closed. This switch is a double-pole, single-throw, double-break switch.

The number of poles in a switch is independent of the number of throws and whether it is a single- or double-break switch. The number of throws in a switch is independent of the number of poles and whether it is a single- or double-break switch. In other words, each characteristic of a switch (poles, throws, breaks) is not determined by either of the other characteristics. Figure 2-1-10 shows the schematic symbols for several different switch configurations.

Rotary switches. A rotary switch (Figure 2-1-11) is a mid-contact switch with the contacts

Figure 2-1-12. Rotary switch

vehicle, and the channel selector on some older television sets are rotary switches. An example of a rotary switch is pictured in Figure 2-1-12.

A pre-electronic automobile distributor cap and rotor are an example of the simplest form of an automatic rotary switch. Figure 2-1-13 shows a portion of a simple, pre-electronic automobile ignition system with the distributor cap and rotor shown.

The rotor is the portion of this switch that moves (rotates) and selects the circuit (spark plug). The rotor does not actually touch the contacts going to the spark plugs, but the signal (spark) jumps the gap between the rotor and the contacts. This switch has one input (the rotor) and six positions (one for each spark plug). A schematic diagram for this rotary switch overlies the illustration of the distributor cap below. Modern automobiles add electronics to adjust the spark timing depending on the engine speed and other factors.

The rotor in the distributor rotates continually (when in use) in one direction and makes a complete circle. This is not true for all rotary switches. The ignition switch in an automobile is also a rotary switch. It usually has four positions (accessory, off, on, start). Unlike the rotor, it does not rotate continually when in use, can be turned in either direction, and does not move through a complete circle.

arranged in a full or partial circle. Instead of a pushbutton or toggle, the mechanism used to select the contact moves in a circular motion and must be turned. Rotary switches can be manual or automatic switches. An automobile distributor, the ignition switch on a motor

Some rotary switches are made with several layers or levels. The arrangement makes possible the control of several circuits with a single switch. Each layer has a selector and 20 contacts. As this switch is rotated, both layers select a single circuit (contact) of the 20.

The channel selector on analog aircraft communication radios is typically a multi-layer rotary switch. It is also called a *wafer switch*, and each layer is known as a wafer. The schematic of the wafer is always drawn to represent the wafer as it would look if viewed from opposite the operating handle or mechanism. If the wafer has contacts on both sides, two drawings are used to show the two sides of the wafer. The two drawings are labeled "front" and "rear." The drawing labeled "front" represents the side of the wafer closest to the operating mechanism.

Figure 2-1-14A shows one wafer of a wafer switch and its schematic symbol. Contact 1 is the point at which current enters the wafer. It is always connected to the movable portion of the wafer. With the wafer in the position shown, contact 1 is connected to both contact 5 and 6 through the movable portion. If the movable portion was rotated slightly clockwise, contact 1 would only be connected to contact 5. This arrangement is known as "make before break"

Figure 2-1-13. Rotary switch in an automobile ignition

Basic Components | 2-7

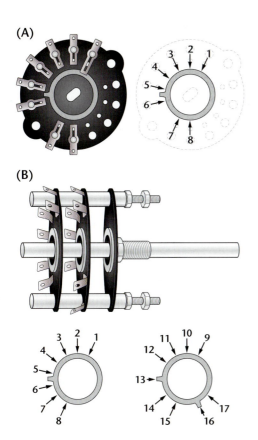

Figure 2-1-14. Wafer switch and schematic symbol

Figure 2-1-15. Rotary wafer switches are commonly found in the tuning selector circuits of analog communication radios.

because the switch makes a contact before breaking the old contact.

Figure 2-1-14B is an illustration of the entire switch and its schematic symbol. Since the switch has two wafers mechanically connected by the shaft of the switch, the shaft rotates the movable portion of both wafers at the same time. This is represented on the schematic symbol by the dotted line connecting the two wafers.

The upper wafer of the schematic symbol is the wafer closest to the control mechanism, and is identical to the wafer shown in Figure 2-1-14A. When switches have more than one wafer, the first wafer shown is always the wafer closest to the operating mechanism. The lower wafer on the schematic diagram is the wafer farthest away from the operating mechanism. Contact 9 of this wafer is connected to the movable portion and is the point at which current enters the wafer. In the position shown, contact 9 is connected to both contact 13 and 16. If the switch is rotated slightly clockwise, contact 9 would no longer be connected to contact 13. A further clockwise movement would connect contact 9 to contact 12. This arrangement is called "break before make." Contact 9 will also be connected to contact 15 at the same time as it is connected to contact 12. An example of a wafer switch, and it's application, is pictured in Figure 2-1-15.

Other Types of Switches

Switches are classified by the number of poles, throws and breaks. There are other factors used to describe a switch such as the type of actuator and the number of positions. In addition, switches are classified by whether the switch has momentary contacts or is locked into or out of position and whether or not the switch is snap-acting.

Type of actuator. In addition to the pushbutton, toggle and knife-actuated switches already described, switches can have other actuators. There are rocker switches, paddle switches, keyboard switches and mercury switches (in which a small amount of mercury makes the electrical contact between two conductors).

Number of positions. Switches are also classified by the number of positions of the actuating device. Figure 2-1-16 shows three toggle switches, the toggle positions and schematic diagrams of the switch. Figure 2-1-16A is a single-pole, single-throw, two-position switch. The switch is marked to indicate the on position (when the switch is closed) and the off position (when the switch is open). Figure 2-1-16B is a single-pole, double-throw, three-position switch. The switch markings show two on positions and an off position.

When this switch is off, no connection is made between any of the terminals. In either of the on positions, the center terminal is connected to one of the outside terminals. This also means that that the outside terminals are not connected together in any position of the switch. Figure 2-1-16C is a single-pole, double-throw, two-position switch. There is no off position. In either position of this switch, the center terminal is connected to one of the outside terminals.

2-8 | Basic Components

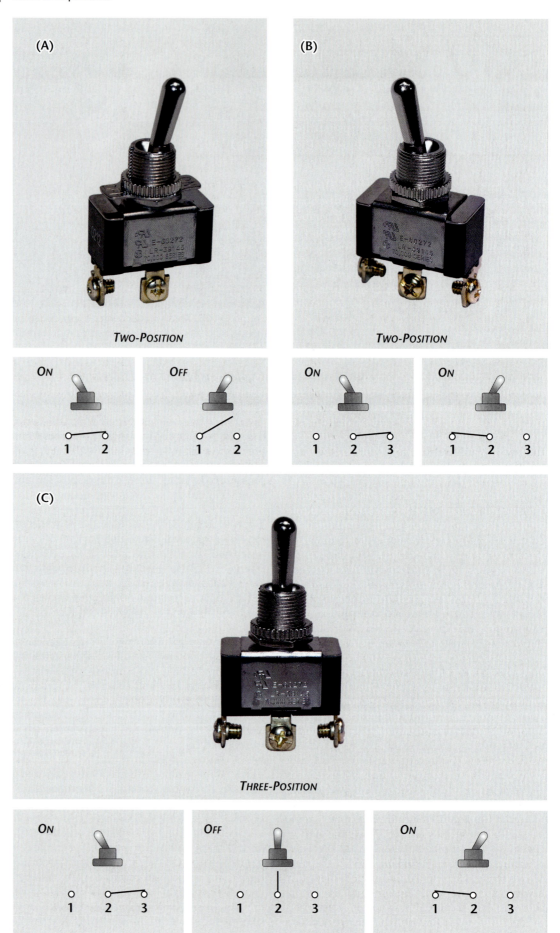

Figure 2-1-16. Two- and three-position switches

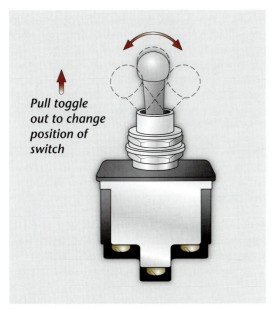

Figure 2-1-17. Three-position locking switch

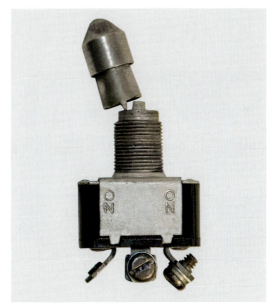

Figure 2-1-18. Two-position locking switch

Momentary and locked position switches. In some switches, one or more of the switch positions are *momentary*. This means that the switch will only remain in the momentary position as long as the actuator is held in that position. As soon as the actuator is released, the switch will return to a non-momentary position. The starter switch on an automobile is an example of a momentary switch. As soon as the key in the switch is released, the switch no longer applies power to the starter.

Another type of switch can be locked in or out of some of the switch positions. Figure 2-1-17 shows a three-position locking switch. This locking prevents the accidental movement of the switch. If a switch has locked-in positions, the switch cannot be moved from those positions accidentally, such as by the switch being bumped or mistaken for an unlocked switch. If the switch has locked-out positions, the switch cannot be moved into those positions accidentally. An example of a two-position locking switch is pictured in Figure 2-1-18.

Snap-acting switches. A *snap-acting* switch is a switch in which the movement of the switch mechanism (contacts) is relatively independent of the activating mechanism movement. In other words, in a toggle switch, no matter how fast or slow the toggle is moved, the actual switching of the circuit takes place at a fixed speed. The snap-acting switch is constructed by making the switch mechanism a leaf spring so that it "snaps" between positions. A snap-acting switch will always be in one of the positions designed for that switch. The switch cannot be "between" positions. A two-position, single-pole, double-throw, snap-acting switch could not be left in an off position.

Accurate snap-acting switches. An accurate snap-acting switch is a snap-acting switch in which the operating point is pre-set and very accurately known. The operating point is the point at which the plunger causes the switch to "switch." The accurate snap-acting switch is commonly called a *microswitch*. Two types of microswitches are shown in Figure 2-1-19 and Figure 2-1-20.

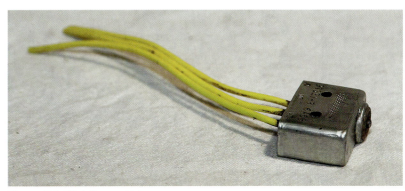

Figure 2-1-19. Microswitch

Figure 2-1-20. Microswitch

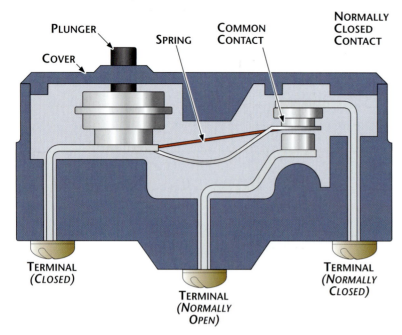

Figure 2-1-21. Accurate snap-acting microswitch

The full description of the microswitch shown in Figure 2-1-21 is a two-position, single-pole, double-throw, single-break, momentary-contact, accurate, snap-acting switch. Notice the terminals marked C, NO, and NC. These letters stand for "common," "normally open," and "normally closed." The common terminal is connected to the normally closed terminal until the plunger is depressed. When the plunger is depressed, the spring will "snap" into the momentary position and the common terminal will be connected to the normally open terminal. As soon as the plunger is released, the spring will "snap" back to the original condition.

This basic accurate snap-acting switch is used in many applications as an automatic switch. Several different methods are used to actuate this type of switch.

Proximity switch. A proximity switch, or proximity sensor, is a type of switch that can be activated without physical contact (see Figure 2-1-22). These units are typically semiconductive devices that produce a magnetic field. When an object penetrates this magnetic field, it causes a fluctuation in the field. The switch senses this fluctuation and turns on or off, depending on the wiring to the switch.

Proximity switches have many uses in the world of aviation, one of which is in the landing gear circuit. In this circuit these switches are used as limit switches to let the system and the pilot know if the landing gear is all the way up or down. Another common application is as a vibration sensing switch

Selecting a Switch

When selecting a switch for an aircraft, the technician should use caution. Selection of a switch involves more than just finding one that looks the same as the one that was removed. All switches have a rating associated with them, and if a technician chooses the wrong switch, it will not last very long. To assist the technician there is a derating factor for switches (Table 2-1-1).

To use this table, first identify on what voltage the aircraft operates, then determine what kind of system is being operated. As an example, start with a 28 V motor that requires 10 A to operate. Refer to the table and find that the derating factor is 3. Multiply the continuous amperage rating by the derating factor to get the nominal switch rating. Select a switch with at least this rating.

By using the derating chart in switch selection, the technician will not have to worry about the switch malfunctioning, and ensures that the switch being installed will operate efficiently.

Switch Ratings

Switches are rated according to their electrical characteristics. The rating of a switch is deter-

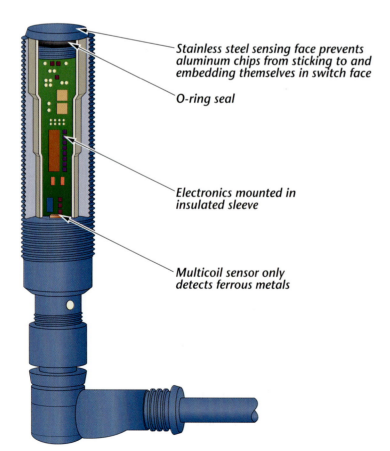

Figure 2-1-22. Proximity switch

mined by such factors as contact size, contact material and contact spacing. There are two basic parts to a switch rating—the current and voltage rating. For example, a switch may be rated at 250 V DC, 10 A. Some switches have more than one rating. An example would be a single switch may be rated at 250 V DC, 10 A; 500 V AC, 10 A; and 28 V DC, 20 A. This rating indicates a current rating that depends upon the voltage applied.

Current rating of a switch. The current rating of a switch refers to the maximum current the switch is designed to carry. This rating is dependent on the voltage of the circuit in which the switch is used. This is shown in the example given above. The current rating of a switch should never be exceeded because the contacts may "weld" together, making it impossible to open the circuit.

Voltage rating of a switch. The voltage rating of a switch refers to the maximum voltage allowable in the circuit in which the switch is used. The voltage rating may be given as an AC voltage, a DC voltage or both. The voltage rating of a switch should never be exceeded because the voltage may be able to "jump" the open contacts of the switch. This would make it impossible to control the circuit in which the switch was used.

Maintenance and Replacement of Switches

Switches are usually a very reliable electrical component. This means they don't fail very often. Most switches are designed to operate 100,000 times or more without failure if the voltage and current ratings are not exceeded. Even so, switches do fail. The following information will help you in maintaining and changing switches.

NOMINAL SYSTEM VOLTAGE	TYPE OF LOAD	DERATING FACTOR
28 VDC	Lamp	8
28 VDC	Inductive (Relay Solenoid)	4
28 VDC	Resistive (Heater)	2
28 VDC	Motor	3
12 VDC	Lamp	5
12 VDC	Inductive (Relay Solenoid)	2
12 VDC	Resistive (Heater)	1
12 VDC	Motor	2

NOTES:
1. *To find the nominal rating of a switch required to operate a given device, multiply the continuous current rating of the device by the derating factor corresponding to the voltage and type of load.*
2. *To find the continuous rating that a switch of a given nominal rating will handle efficiently, divide the switch nominal rating by the derating factor corresponding to the voltage and type of load.*

Table 2-1-1. Switch derating factors

Checking Switches

There are two basic methods used to check a switch. An ohmmeter or a voltmeter are the two tools used (Figure 2-1-23). Each of these methods will be explained using a single-pole, double-throw, single-break, three-position, snap-acting toggle switch.

Figure 2-1-23. Checking a switch with a multimeter

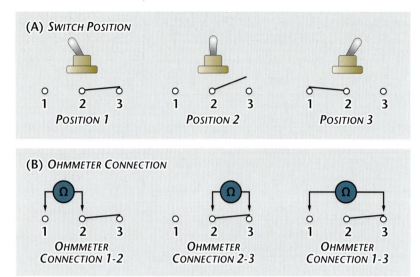

Figure 2-1-24. Switch position and ohmmeter positions

SWITCH POSITION	OHMMETER CONNECTION	CORRECT READING
1	1-2	∞
1	2-3	0
1	1-3	∞
2	1-2	∞
2	2-3	∞
2	1-3	∞
3	1-2	0
3	2-3	∞
3	1-3	∞

Table 2-1-2. Correct readings for switch position and ohmmeter positions

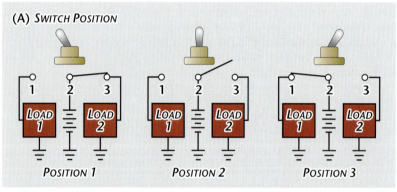

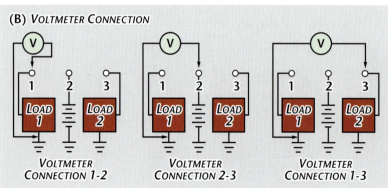

Figure 2-1-25. Switch position and voltmeter connection

Figure 2-1-24 is used to explain the method of using an ohmmeter to check a switch. Figure 2-1-24A shows the toggle positions and schematic diagrams for the three switch positions. Figure 2-1-24B shows the ohmmeter connections used to check the switch while the toggle is in position 1. Table 2-1-2 shows the switch position, ohmmeter connection and correct ohmmeter reading for those conditions.

With the switch in position 1 and the ohmmeter connected to terminals 1 and 2 of the switch, the ohmmeter should indicate (∞). When the ohmmeter is moved to terminals 2 and 3, the ohmmeter should indicate zero ohms. With the ohmmeter connected to terminals 1 and 3, the indication should be (∞).

Power must be removed from the circuit and the component being checked should be isolated from the circuit. The best way to isolate the switch is to remove it from the circuit completely. This is not always practical, and it is sometimes necessary to check a switch while there is power applied to it. In these cases, an ohmmeter will not be able to check the switch, but the switch can be checked with a voltmeter.

Figure 2-1-25A shows a switch connected between a power source (battery) and two loads. In Figure 2-1-25B, a voltmeter is shown connected between ground and each of the three switch terminals while the switch is in position 1. Table 2-1-3 shows the switch position, voltmeter connection and the correct voltmeter reading.

With the switch in position 1 and the voltmeter connected between ground and terminal 1, the voltmeter should indicate no voltage (0 V). When the voltmeter is connected to terminal 2, the voltmeter should indicate the source voltage. With the voltmeter connected to terminal 3, the source voltage should also be indicated. Table 2-1-3 shows you the correct readings with the switch in position 2 or 3.

Replacement of Switches

When a switch is faulty, it must be replaced. The technical manual for the equipment will specify the exact replacement switch. If it is necessary to use a substitute switch, the following guidelines should be used. The substitute switch must have all of the following characteristics.

- At least the same number of poles
- At least the same number of throws
- The same number of breaks

- At least the same number of positions
- The same configuration in regard to momentary or locked positions
- A voltage rating equal to or higher than the original switch
- A current rating equal to or higher than the original switch
- A physical size compatible with the mounting

In addition, the type of actuator (toggle, push-button, rocker, etc.) should be the same as the original switch. This is desirable but not necessary. For example, a toggle switch could be used to replace a rocker switch if it were acceptable in all other ways.

The number of poles and throws of a switch can be determined from markings on the switch itself. The switch case will be marked with a schematic diagram of the switch or letters such as "SPST" for single-pole, single-throw. The voltage and current ratings will also be marked on the switch. The number of breaks can be determined from the schematic marked on the switch or by counting the terminals after determining the number of poles and throws. The type of actuator, number of positions, and the momentary and locked positions of the switch can all be determined by looking at the switch and switching it to all the positions.

Preventive Maintenance of Switches

As already mentioned, switches do not fail very often. However, there is a need for preventive maintenance of switches. Periodically switches should be checked for corrosion at the terminals, smooth and correct operation and physical damage. Any problems found during inspection should be corrected immediately. Most switches can be inspected visually for corrosion or damage. The operation of the switch may be checked by moving the actuator. When the actuator is moved, the technician can feel whether the switch operation is smooth or seems to have a great deal of friction. To check the actual switching, observe the operation of the equipment or check the switch with a meter.

Solenoids

A *solenoid* is a control device that uses electromagnetism to convert electrical energy into mechanical motion. The movement of the solenoid may be used to close a set of electrical contacts, cause the movement of a mechanical device, or both at the same time.

SWITCH POSITION	VOLTMETER CONNECTION	CORRECT READING
1	1	0 V
1	2	voltage
1	3	voltage
2	1	0 V
2	2	voltage
2	3	0 V
3	1	voltage
3	2	voltage
3	3	0 V

Table 2-1-3. Correct readings for switch position and ohmmeter positions

Figure 2-1-26 is a cutaway view of a solenoid showing the solenoid action. A solenoid is an electromagnet formed by a conductor wound in a series of loops in the shape of a spiral. Inserted within this coil is a soft-iron core and a movable plunger. The soft-iron core is pinned or held in an immovable position. The movable plunger (also soft iron) is held away from the core by a spring when the solenoid is de-energized.

When current flows through the conductor, it produces a magnetic field. The magnetic flux produced by the coil results in establishing north and south poles in both the core and the plunger. The plunger is attracted along the lines of force to a position at the center of the coil. As shown in Figure 2-1-26, the de-energized position of the plunger is partially out of the coil due to the action of the spring. When voltage is applied, the current

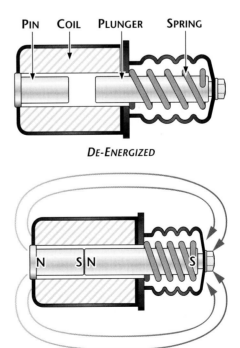

Figure 2-1-26. Solenoid action

through the coil produces a magnetic field. This magnetic field draws the plunger within the coil, resulting in mechanical motion. When the coil is de-energized, the plunger returns to its normal position because of spring action. The effective strength of the magnetic field on the plunger varies according to the distance between the plunger and the core. For short distances, the strength of the field is strong; as distances increase, the strength of the field drops off quite rapidly.

While a solenoid is a control device, the solenoid itself is energized by some other control device such as a switch or a relay. One of the distinct advantages in the use of solenoids is that a mechanical movement can be accomplished at a considerable distance from the control device. The only link necessary between the control device and the solenoid is the electrical wiring for the coil current. The solenoid can have large contacts for the control of high current. Therefore, the solenoid also provides a means of controlling high current with a low-current switch. For example, the ignition switch on an automobile controls the large current of a starter motor by the use of a solenoid. Figure 2-1-27 shows a cutaway view of a starter motor-solenoid combination and a section of the wiring for the solenoid. Notice that the solenoid provides all electrical contact for current to the starter motor as well as a mechanical movement of the shift lever.

Maintenance of Solenoids

If a solenoid is believed to have failed, the first step in troubleshooting it is a good visual inspection. Check the connections for poor soldering, loose connections or broken wires. The plunger should be checked for cleanliness, binding, mechanical failure and proper alignment. The mechanism that the solenoid is connected to (i.e., that it actuates) should also be checked for proper operation.

The second step is to check the energizing voltage with a voltmeter. If the voltage is too low, the result is less current flowing through the coil and a weak magnetic field. A weak magnetic field can result in slow or poor operation. Low voltage could also result in chatter or no operation at all. If the energizing voltage is too high, it could damage the solenoid by causing overheating or arcing. In either case, the voltage should be reset to the proper value so that further damage or failure of the solenoid will not result.

The solenoid coil should then be checked for opens, shorts, and proper resistance with an ohmmeter. If the solenoid coil is open, current cannot flow through it and the magnetic field is lost. A short results in fewer turns and higher current in the coil. The net result of a short is a weak magnetic field. A high-resistance coil will reduce coil current and also result in a weak magnetic field. A weak magnetic field will cause less attraction between the plunger and the core of the coil. This will result in improper operation similar to that caused by low voltage. If the coil is open, shorted, or has changed in resistance, the solenoid should be replaced.

Finally, check the solenoid to determine if the coil is shorted to ground. If a short to ground is found, the short should be removed to restore the solenoid to proper operation.

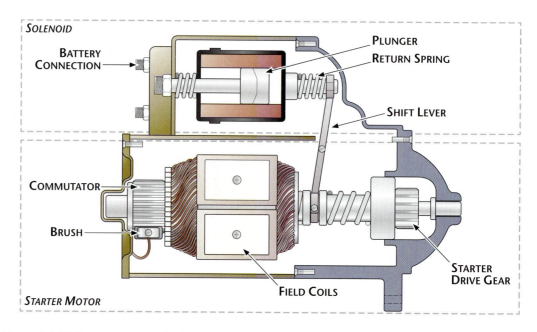

Figure 2-1-27. Starter motor and solenoid

Relays

The *relay* is a device that acts upon the same fundamental principle as the solenoid. The difference between a relay and a solenoid is that a relay does not have a movable core (plunger) while the solenoid does. Where multi-pole relays are used, several circuits may be controlled at once.

Relays are electrically operated control switches, and are classified according to their use as *power relays* or *control relays*. Power relays are called *contactors*; control relays are usually known simply as relays.

The function of a contactor is to use a relatively small amount of electrical power to control the switching of a large amount of power. The contactor permits power to be controlled at other locations in the equipment, and the heavy power cables need be run only through the power relay contacts.

Only lightweight control wires are connected from the control switches to the relay coil. Safety is also an important reason for using power relays, since high power circuits can be switched remotely without danger to the operator.

Control relays, as their name implies, are frequently used in the control of low-power circuits or other relays, although they also have many other uses. In automatic relay circuits, a small electric signal may set off a chain reaction of successively acting relays, which then perform various functions.

In general, a relay consists of a magnetic core and its associated coil, contacts, springs, armature and the mounting. Figure 2-1-28 illustrates the construction of a relay. When the coil is energized, the flow of current through the coil creates a strong magnetic field that pulls the armature downward to contact C1, completing the circuit from the common terminal to C1. At the same time, the circuit to contact C2 is opened.

A relay can have many different types of contacts. The relay shown in Figure 2-1-28 has contacts known as "break-make" contacts because they break one circuit and make another when the relay is energized.

Some equipment requires a warm-up period between the application of power and some other action. For example, vacuum tubes are a type of device that require a delay between the application of filament power and high voltage. A time-delay relay will provide this required delay.

A thermal time-delay relay (Figure 2-1-29) is constructed to produce a delayed action when energized. Its operation depends on the

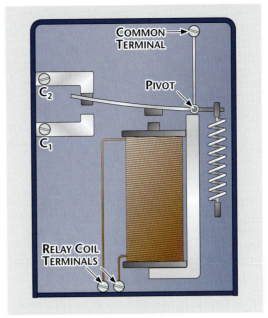

Figure 2-1-28. Relay construction

Figure 2-1-29. Thermal time-delay relay

Figure 2-1-30. Open relay

Figure 2-1-31. Semi-sealed relay

Figure 2-1-32. Sealed relay

thermal action of a bimetallic element similar to that used in a thermal circuit breaker. A heater is mounted around or near the element. The movable contact is mounted on the element itself. As the heat causes the element to bend (because of the different thermal expansion rates), the contacts close.

Relays can be described by the method of packaging; open, semi-sealed and sealed. Figure 2-1-30, Figure 2-1-31 and Figure 2-1-32 show several different relays and illustrate these three types of packaging.

Figure 2-1-30 is an example of an open relay. The mechanical motion of the contacts can be observed and the relays are easily available for maintenance. These types of relays are no longer used, but the function of a relay is visible and helps understand modern sealed relays. Figure 2-1-31 is an example of a semi-sealed relay. The covers provide protection from dust, moisture and other foreign material, but can be removed for maintenance.

The clear plastic or glass covers provide a means of observing the operation of the relay without removal of the cover. Figure 2-1-32 is an example of a hermetically sealed relay. These relays are protected from temperature or humidity changes as well as dust and other foreign material. Since the covers cannot be removed, the relays are also considered to be tamper-proof. With metal or other opaque covers, the operation of the relay can be felt by placing a finger on the cover and activating the relay.

Troubleshooting Relays

Relays can be easy to troubleshoot. On a simple relay there are two sets of contacts, one set for the coil and the other for the circuit power being controlled. If using a multimeter, continuity between the contacts for the coil should normally be read. Without current applied to the coil, the contacts should read infinite ohms. If current is directed to the coil, but not the contacts, continuity can be read across the contacts.

Sometimes a relay fault can be difficult to troubleshoot. On some relay circuits a diode (diodes are discussed in a later chapter) is used to reduce line noise. Sometimes this diode is the actual faulty component and not the relay itself.

Section 2

Circuit Protection Devices

Electricity, like fire, can be either helpful or harmful to those who use it. A fire can keep people warm and comfortable when it is confined in a campfire or a furnace. It can be dangerous and destructive if it is on the loose and uncontrolled in the woods or in a building. Electricity can provide people with the light to read by or, in a blinding flash, destroy their eyesight. It can help save people's lives, or it can kill them. While we take advantage of the tremendous benefits electricity can provide, we must be careful to protect the people and systems that use it.

It is necessary then that the mighty force of electricity be kept under control at all times. If for some reason it should get out of control, there must be a method of protecting people and equipment. Devices have been developed to protect people and electrical circuits from currents and voltages outside their normal operating ranges.

Introduction

An electrical unit is built with great care to ensure that each separate electrical circuit is fully insulated from all the others. This is done so that the current in a circuit will follow its intended path. Once the unit is placed into service, however, many things can happen to alter the original circuitry. Some of the changes can cause serious problems if they are not detected and corrected. While circuit protection devices cannot correct an abnormal current condition, they can indicate that an abnormal condition exists and protect personnel and circuits from that condition. The following material explains what circuit conditions require protection devices and the types of protection devices used.

Circuit Conditions Requiring Protection Devices

Some of the changes in circuits can cause conditions that are dangerous to the circuit itself or to people living or working near the circuits. These potentially dangerous conditions require circuit protection. The conditions that require circuit protection are direct shorts, excessive current and excessive heat.

Direct short. One of the most serious troubles that can occur in a circuit is a *direct short*. Another term used to describe this condition is a *short circuit*. The two terms mean the same thing and, in this chapter, the term "direct short" will be used. A direct short is a situation in which some point in the circuit, where full system voltage is present, comes in direct contact with the ground or return side of the circuit (Figure 2-2-1). This establishes a path for current flow that contains only the very small resistance present in the wires carrying the current.

According to Ohm's law, if the resistance in a circuit is extremely small, the current will be extremely large. Therefore, when a direct short occurs, there will be a very large current through the wires. Suppose, for instance, that the two leads from a battery to a motor came in contact with each other. If the leads were bare at the point of contact, there would be a direct short. The motor would stop running because all the current would be flowing through the short and none through the motor. The battery would become discharged quickly (perhaps ruined) and there could be a fire or explosion.

The battery cables in our example would be large wires capable of carrying heavy currents. Most wires used in electrical circuits are smaller and their current carrying capacity is limited. The size of wire used in any given circuit is determined by space considerations, cost factors, and the amount of current the wire is expected to carry under normal operating conditions. Any current flow greatly in excess of normal, such as there would be in the case of a direct short, would cause a rapid generation of heat in the wire.

If the excessive current flow caused by the direct short is left unchecked, the heat in the wire will continue to increase until some portion of the circuit burns. Perhaps a portion of the wire will melt and open the circuit so that nothing is damaged other than the wire involved. The possibility exists, however, that much greater damage will result. The heat in the wire can char and burn the insulation of the wire and that of other wires bundled with it, which can cause more shorts. If a fuel or oil leak is near any of the hot wires, a disastrous fire might be started.

Excessive current. It is possible for the circuit current to increase without a direct short. If a resistor, capacitor or inductor changes value, the total circuit impedance will also change in value. If a resistor decreases in ohmic value, the total circuit resistance decreases. If a capacitor has a dielectric leakage, the capacitive reactance decreases. If an inductor has a partial short of its winding, inductive reactance decreases. Any of these conditions will cause an increase in circuit current. Since the circuit wiring and components are designed to withstand normal circuit current, an increase in current would cause overheating (just as in the case of a direct short). Therefore, excessive current without a direct short will cause the same problems as a direct short.

Excessive heat. Most of the problems associated with a direct short or excessive current concern

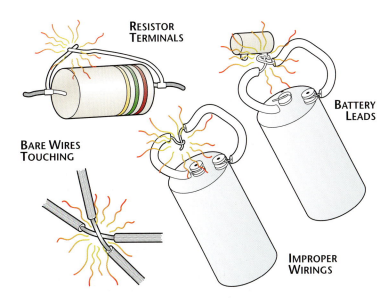

Figure 2-2-1. Common causes of short circuits

the heat generated by the higher current. The damage to circuit components, the possibility of fire, and the possibility of hazardous fumes being given off from electrical components are consequences of excessive heat.

It is possible for excessive heat to occur without a direct short or excessive current. If the bearings on a motor or generator were to fail, the motor or generator would overheat. If the temperature around an electrical or electronic circuit were to rise (through failure of a cooling system for example), excessive heat would be a problem. No matter what the cause, if excessive heat is present in a circuit, the possibility of damage, fire, and hazardous fumes exists.

Circuit Protection Devices

All of the conditions mentioned are potentially dangerous and require the use of circuit protection devices. Circuit protection devices are used to stop current flow or open the circuit. To do this, a circuit protection device must always be connected in series with the circuit it is protecting. If the protection device is connected in parallel, current will simply flow around the protection device and continue in the circuit.

A circuit protection device operates by opening and interrupting current to the circuit. The opening of a protection device shows that something is wrong in the circuit and should be corrected before the current is restored. When a problem exists and the protection device opens, the device should isolate the faulty circuit from the other unaffected circuits, and should respond in time to protect unaffected components in the faulty circuit. The protection device should not open during normal circuit operation.

The two types of circuit protection devices discussed in this chapter are fuses and circuit breakers. Circuit breakers are by far the most common type of circuit protection device in aviation. They can be reset once a fault is isolated. Fuses, however, must be replaced, which can be difficult while the plane is in flight.

Fuses are common in household and automotive applications. They have limited uses in modern aircraft. The avionics technician will most often see fuses in test equipment and other tools that are available in the shop.

Fuses. A *fuse* is the simplest circuit protection device. It derives its name from the Latin word "fusus," meaning "to melt." Fuses have been used almost from the beginning of the use of electricity. The earliest type of fuse was simply a bare wire between two connections. The wire was smaller than the conductor it was protecting and, therefore, would melt before the conductor it was protecting was harmed. Some "copper fuse link" types are still in use, but most fuses no longer use copper as the fuse element (the part of the fuse that melts). After the change from copper to other metals, tubes or enclosures were developed to hold the melting metal. The enclosed fuse made possible the addition of filler material, which helps to contain the arc that occurs when the element melts.

For many low-power uses, the finer material is not required. A simple glass tube is used. A glass tube shows when a fuse is open. Fuses of this type are commonly found in automobile lighting circuits. Figure 2-2-2 shows several fuses and the symbols used on schematics.

The copper fuse link shown in the center right of Figure 2-2-2 is the most common type in aviation. It is often referred to as a fuseable link. This style of fuse is frequently used to provide protection between the busses of a split buss electrical system on multi-engine aircraft.

Circuit breakers. While a fuse protects a circuit, it is destroyed in the process of opening the circuit. Once the problem that caused the increased current or heat is corrected, a new fuse must be placed in the circuit. A circuit protection device that can be used more than once solves the problems of replacement fuses. Such a device is safe, reliable and tamper proof. It is also resettable, so it can be reused without replacing any parts. This device is called a *circuit breaker* (Figure 2-2-3) because it breaks (opens) the circuit.

The first compact, workable circuit breaker was developed in 1923. It took four years to design

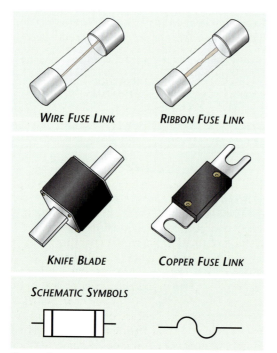

Figure 2-2-2. Fuses and schematic symbols

a device that would interrupt circuits of 5,000 A at 120 V AC or DC. In 1928, the first circuit breaker was placed on the market.

Fuse Types

Fuses are manufactured in many shapes and sizes in addition to the copper fuse link already described. While the variety of fuses may seem confusing, there are basically only two types of fuses: plug-type fuses and cartridge fuses. Both types use either a single wire or a ribbon as the fuse element. The condition (good or bad) of some fuses can be determined by visual inspection. The condition of other fuses can only be determined with a meter. Both methods are discussed.

Plug-type fuse. The plug-type fuse is constructed so that it can be screwed into a socket mounted on a control panel or electrical distribution center. The fuse link is enclosed in an insulated housing of porcelain or glass, but visible through a window of mica or glass.

The plug-type fuse is used primarily in low-voltage, low-current circuits. The operating range is usually up to 150 V and from 0.5 to 30 A. This type of fuse is found in older circuit protection devices and has been replaced by the circuit breaker. An example of a plug-type fuse is pictured in Figure 2-2-4.

Cartridge fuse. The cartridge fuse (Figure 2-2-5) operates exactly like the plug-type fuse. In the cartridge fuse, the fuse link is enclosed in a tube of insulating material with metal ferrules at each end (for contact with the fuse holder). Some common insulating materials are glass, bakelite or a fiber tube filled with insulating powder.

Cartridge fuses are available in a variety of physical sizes and are used in many different circuit applications. They can be rated at voltages up to 10,000 V and have current ratings of from 1/500 (0.002) to 800 A.

Fuse Ratings

The physical size and type of a fuse is determined by looking at it, but additional information is required to use it properly. Fuses are rated by current, voltage and time-delay characteristics. To select the proper fuse, the meaning of each of the fuse ratings must be understood.

Current rating. The current rating of a fuse is a value expressed in amperes that represents the current the fuse will allow without opening. The current rating is always indicated on the fuse.

Figure 2-2-3. Circuit Breaker

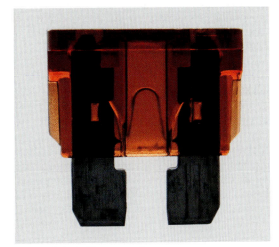

Figure 2-2-4. Plug-type fuse

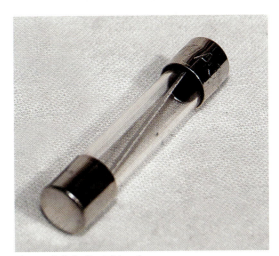

Figure 2-2-5. Cartridge fuse

The normal operating current of the circuit must be known in order to select the proper fuse. To protect the circuit from overloads (excessive current), select a fuse rated at 125 percent of the normal circuit current. In other words, if a circuit has a normal current of 10 A, a 12.5-A fuse will provide overload protection. To protect against direct shorts only, select a fuse rated at 150 percent of the normal circuit current. In the case of a circuit with 10 A of current, a 15-A fuse will protect against direct shorts, but will not be adequate protection against excessive current.

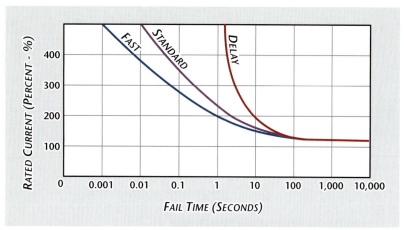

Figure 2-2-6. Time required for fuse to open

Voltage rating. The voltage rating of a fuse is *not* an indication of the voltage the fuse is designed to withstand while carrying current. The voltage rating indicates the ability of the fuse to quickly extinguish the arc after the fuse element melts and the maximum voltage the open fuse will block. In other words, once the fuse has opened, any voltage less than the voltage rating of the fuse will not be able to "jump" the gap of the fuse. Because of the way the voltage rating is used, it is a maximum root mean square voltage value. Always select a fuse with a voltage rating equal to or higher than the voltage in the circuit that is being protected.

Time-delay rating. There are many kinds of electrical and electronic circuits that require protection. In some of these circuits, it is important to protect against temporary or transient current increases. Sometimes the device being protected is very sensitive to current and cannot withstand an increase in current. In these cases, a fuse must open very quickly if the current increases.

Some other circuits and devices have a large current for short periods and a normal (smaller) current most of the time. An electric motor, for instance, will draw a large current when the motor starts, but normal operating current for the motor will be much smaller. A fuse used to protect a motor would have to allow for this large temporary current, but would open if the large current were to continue.

Fuses are time-delay rated to indicate the relationship between the current through the fuse and the time it takes for the fuse to open. The three time delay ratings are delay, standard and fast.

A *delay*, or slow-blowing, fuse has a built-in delay that is activated when the current through the fuse is greater than the current rating of the fuse. This fuse will allow temporary increases (surges) in current without opening. Some delay fuses have two elements; this allows a very long delay. If the overcurrent condition continues, a delay fuse will open, but it will take longer to open than a standard or a fast fuse. Delay fuses are used for circuits with high surge or starting currents, such as motors, solenoids and transformers.

Standard fuses have no built-in time delay. Also, they are not designed to be very fast acting. Standard fuses are sometimes used to protect against direct shorts only. They may be wired in series with a delay fuse to provide faster direct short protection. For example, in a circuit with a 1-A delay fuse, a 5-A standard fuse may be used in addition to provide faster protection against a direct short.

A standard fuse can be used in any circuit where surge currents are not expected and a very fast opening of the fuse is not needed. A standard fuse opens faster than a delay fuse, but slower than a fast fuse. Standard fuses can be used for automobiles, lighting circuits or electrical power circuits.

Fast fuses are designed to open very quickly when the current through the fuse exceeds the current rating of the fuse. Fast fuses are used to protect devices that are very sensitive to increased current. A fast fuse will open faster than a delay or standard fuse. Fast fuses can be used to protect delicate instruments or semiconductor devices.

Figure 2-2-6 illustrates the differences between delay, standard and fast fuses. Figure 2-2-6 shows that, if a 1-A rated fuse had 2 A of current through it (i.e., 200 percent of the rated value), a fast fuse would open in about 0.7 seconds, a standard fuse would open in about 1.5 seconds, and a delay fuse would open in about 10 seconds. Notice that in each of the fuses, the time required to open the fuse decreases as the rated current increases.

Identification of Fuses

Fuses have identifications printed on them. The printing on the fuse identifies the physical size, the type of fuse and the fuse ratings. There are four different systems used to identify fuses: the old commercial designation, the new commercial designation, the old military designation and the new military designation. Both commercial designation systems are presented here.

An open fuse that is identified by one system may need to be replaced with a good fuse that is identified by another system. The designation systems are fairly simple to understand and cross-reference.

Old commercial designation. Figure 2-2-7A shows the old commercial designation for a fuse. The first part of the designation is a combination of three letters and numbers that indicates the style and time-delay characteristics.

The catalog will list the physical size, the material from which the fuse is constructed, and the time-delay rating of the fuse. A 3AG fuse is a glass-bodied fuse, 0.25 in. by 1.25 in. (6.35 mm by 31.8 mm) and has a standard time-delay rating.

Following the style designation is a number that is the current rating of the fuse (1). This could be a whole number, a fraction, a whole number and a fraction, a decimal, or a whole number and a decimal. Following the current rating is the voltage rating, which, in turn, is followed by the letter "V," which stands for "volts or less" (250 V).

New commercial designation. Figure 2-2-7B shows the new commercial designation for fuses. It is the same as the old commercial designation except for the style portion of the coding. In the old commercial system, the style was a combination of letters and numbers. In the new commercial system, only letters are used. In the example shown, 3AG in the old system becomes AGC in the new system. Since "C" is the third letter of the alphabet, it is used instead of the "3" in the old system. Once again, the only way to find out the time-delay rating is to look up this code in the manufacturer's catalog or to use a cross-reference listing. The remainder of the new commercial designation is exactly the same as the old commercial designation.

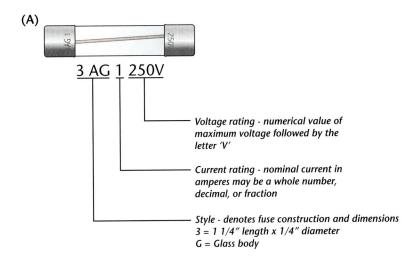

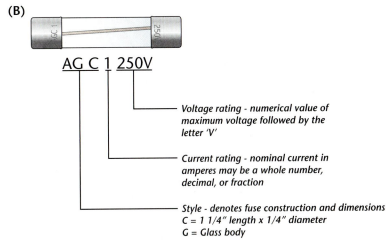

Figure 2-2-7. Commercial designations for fuses: (A) old commercial designations (B) new commercial designations

Fuse Holders

For a fuse to be useful, it must be connected to the circuit it will protect. Some fuses are "wired in" or soldered to the wiring of circuits, but most circuits make use of *fuse holders*. A fuse holder is a device that is wired into the circuit and allows easy replacement of the fuse. Fuse holders are made in many shapes and sizes, but most are either clip-type or post-type. Figure 2-2-8 shows typical clip-type and post-type fuse holders.

Clip-type fuse holder. The clip-type fuse holder is used for cartridge fuses. The ferrules or knife blade of the fuse are held by the spring tension of the clips. These clips provide the electrical connection between the fuse and the circuit. If a glass-bodied fuse is used, the fuse can be inspected visually for an open without removing the fuse from the fuse holder. Clip-type fuse holders are made in several sizes to hold the many styles of fuses. The clips may be made for ferrules or knife-blade car-

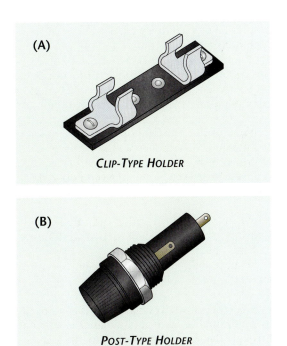

Figure 2-2-8. Typical fuse holders

tridge fuses. While the base of a clip-type fuse holder is made from insulating material, the clips themselves are conductors. The current through the fuse goes through the clips and care must be taken to not touch the clips while power is applied, as a severe shock or a short circuit will occur.

Post-type fuse holders. Post-type fuse holders, pictured in Figure 2-2-9, are made for cartridge fuses. The post-type fuse holder is much safer because the fuse and fuse connections are covered with insulating material. The disadvantage of the post-type fuse holder is that the fuse must be removed to visually check for an open. The post-type fuse holder has a cap that screws onto the body of the fuse holder. The fuse is held in this cap by a spring-type connector and, as the cap is screwed on, the fuse makes contact with the body of the fuse holder. When the cap and fuse are removed from the body of the fuse holder, the fuse is removed from the circuit and there is no danger of shock or short circuit from touching the fuse.

Post-type fuse holders are usually mounted on the chassis of the equipment in which they are used. After wires are connected to the fuse holder, insulating sleeves are placed over the connections to reduce the possibility of a short circuit. Notice the two connections on the post-type fuse holder in Figure 2-2-8B. The connection on the right is called the center connector. The other connector is the outside connector. The outside connector will be closer to the equipment chassis. The threads and nut shown are used to fasten the fuse holder to the chassis. The possibility of the outside connector coming in contact with the chassis (causing a short circuit) is much higher than the possibility of the center conductor contacting the chassis. The power source should always be connected to the center connector so the fuse will open if the outside connector contacts the chassis. If the power source were connected to the outside connector, and the outside connector contacted the chassis, there would be a direct short, but the fuse would not open.

Checking and Replacement of Fuses

A fuse, if properly used, should not open unless something is wrong in the circuit the fuse is protecting. When a fuse is found to be open, the reason it is open must be determined. Replacing the fuse is not enough.

Figure 2-2-9. Post-type fuse holder

Checking for an Open Fuse

There are several ways of checking for an open fuse. Some fuses and fuse holders have indicators built in. A multimeter can also be used to check fuses. The simplest way to check glass-bodied fuses is visual inspection.

Visual inspection. An open glass-bodied fuse can usually be found by visual inspection. Figure 2-2-10 shows how a glass-bodied cartridge fuse looks. If the fuse element is not complete, or if the element has been melted onto the glass tube, the fuse is open.

It is not always possible to tell whether a fuse is open by visual inspection. Fuses with low current ratings have elements that are so small, it is sometimes not possible to know if the fuse link is complete simply by looking at it. If the fuse is not glass-bodied, it is not possible to check the fuse visually. Also, sometimes a fuse will look good, but will, in fact, be open. Therefore, while it is sometimes possible to know if a fuse is open by visual inspection, it is not possible to be sure a fuse is good just by looking at it.

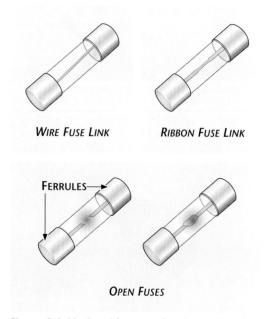

Figure 2-2-10. Cartridge-type fuse inspection chart

Fuse indicators. Some fuses and fuse holders have built-in indicators to show when a fuse is open. Examples of these open-fuse indicators are shown in Figure 2-2-11. Figure 2-2-11A shows a cartridge fuse with an open-fuse indicator. The indicator is spring loaded and held by the fuse link. If the fuse link opens, the spring forces the indicator out. Some manufacturers color the indicator so it is easier to see in the open-fuse position.

Figure 2-2-11B shows a plug-type fuse holder with an indicating lamp in the fuse cap. If the fuse opens, the lamp in the fuse cap will light. Figure 2-2-11C shows a clip-type fuse holder with an indicating lamp.

Just as in visual checking, the indicator can show an open fuse. Since the indicator may not always work, that fact that the indicator has not tripped does not necessarily mean the fuse is still good.

Checking fuses with a meter. The only sure method of determining whether a fuse is open is to use a meter (Figure 2-2-12). An ohmmeter can be used to check for an open fuse by removing the fuse from the circuit and checking for continuity through the fuse (0Ω). If the fuse is not removed from the circuit, and the fuse is open, the ohmmeter may measure the circuit resistance. This resistance reading might imply that the fuse is good. This may be an incorrect assumption, particularly when using an ohmmeter to check fuses with small current ratings (1/32 A or less).

The current from the ohmmeter may be larger than the current rating of the fuse. For most practical uses, a small current capacity fuse can be checked out of the circuit through the use of a resistor. The ohmic value of the resistor is first measured and then placed in series with the fuse. The continuity reading on the ohmmeter should be of the same value, or close to it, as the original value of the resistor. This method provides protection for the fuse by dropping the voltage across the resistor. This in turn decreases the power in the form of heat at the fuse. Remember, it is heat that melts the fuse element.

A voltmeter can also be used to check for an open fuse. The measurement is taken between each end of the fuse and the common, or ground, side of the line. If voltage is present on both sides of the fuse, from the voltage source and to the load, the fuse is not open. Another method commonly used is to measure across the fuse with the voltmeter. If no voltage is indicated on the meter, the fuse is good.

Remember there is no voltage drop across a straight piece of wire. Some plug-type fuse holders have test points built in to allow a technician to check the voltage. To check for voltage on a clip-type fuse holder, check each of the clips. The advantage of using a voltmeter to check for an open fuse is that the circuit does not have to be de-energized and the fuse does not have to be removed.

WARNING: *Personnel may be exposed to hazardous voltage.*

Safety precautions when checking a fuse. Since a fuse has current through it, care must be exercised when checking for an open fuse

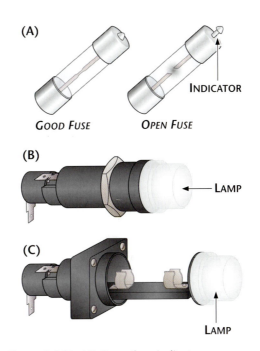

Figure 2-2-11. (A) Open fuse indicators
(B) Post-type fuse holder with an indicating lamp
(C) Clip-type fuse holder with an indicating lamp

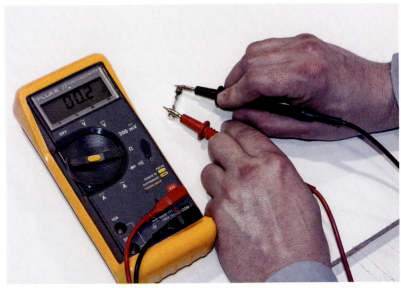

Figure 2-2-12. Checking a fuse with an ohmmeter

to avoid being shocked or damaging the circuit. The following safety precautions will protect the technician and the equipment being used.

- Turn the power off and discharge the circuit before removing a fuse.
- Use a fuse puller (an insulated tool) when removing a fuse from a clip-type fuse holder (Figure 2-2-13).
- When checking a fuse with a voltmeter, be careful to avoid shocks and short circuits.
- When using an ohmmeter to check fuses with low current ratings, be careful to avoid opening the fuse by excessive current from the ohmmeter.

Replacement of Fuses

After an open fuse is found and the trouble that caused the fuse to open has been corrected, the fuse must be replaced. Before replacing the fuse, verify that the replacement fuse is the proper type and fits correctly.

Proper type of replacement fuse. To be certain a fuse is the proper type, check the technical manual for the equipment. The parts list will show the proper fuse identification for a replacement fuse. Obtain the exact fuse specified, if possible, and check the identification number of the replacement fuse against the parts list. If a direct replacement is not available, use the following guidelines:

- Never use a fuse with a higher current rating, a lower voltage rating, or a slower time-delay rating than the specified fuse.
- The best substitution fuse is a fuse with the same current and time-delay ratings and a higher voltage rating.
- If a lower current rating or a faster time-delay rating is used, the fuse may open under normal circuit conditions.
- Substitute fuses must have the same style (physical dimensions) as the specified fuse.

Proper fit of replacement fuses. When the proper replacement fuse has been obtained, make certain it will fit correctly in the fuse holder. If the fuse holder is corroded, the fuse will not fit properly. In addition, the corrosion can cause increased resistance or heating. Clean corroded terminals with fine sandpaper so that all corrosion is removed. Do *not* lubricate the terminals. If the terminals are badly pitted, replace the fuse holder. Be certain the replacement fuse holder is the correct size and type by checking the parts list in the technical manual for the equipment.

After checking for and correcting any corrosion problems, be certain the fuse fits tightly in the fuse holder. When inserting the fuse in the cap of a plug-type fuse holder, the fuse should fit tightly. A small amount of pressure should be needed to insert the fuse and cap into the fuse holder body.

In clip-type fuse holders, the clips can be easily bent out of shape. This causes an incorrect fit, which in time could cause an equipment malfunction. Figure 2-2-14 shows examples of correct and incorrect fuse contacts for clip-type fuse holders used with knife-blade and ferrule cartridge fuses. The clips shown in the left picture of each row have the correct contact. The three pictures on the right of each row show incorrect contact. Notice how the clips are not contacting completely with the knife blade or ferrules. This incomplete contact can cause corrosion at the contacts, which in turn can create a high resistance and drop some of the circuit voltage at this point.

If the fuse clips do not make complete contact with the fuse, try to bend the clips back into shape. If the clips cannot be repaired by bending, replace the fuse holder or use clip clamps. Clip clamps are shown in Figure 2-2-15.

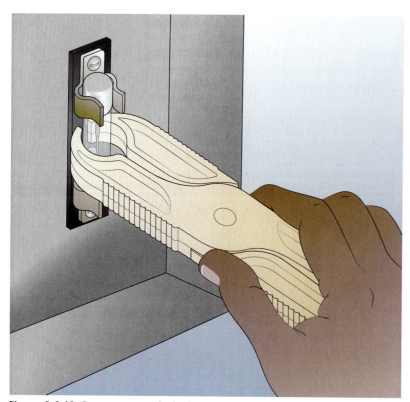

Figure 2-2-13. Proper removal of a fuse

Safety precautions when replacing fuses. The following safety precautions will prevent injury to personnel and damage to equipment. These are the *minimum* safety precautions for replacing fuses.

- Be sure the power is off in the circuit and the circuit is discharged before replacing a fuse.
- Use an identical replacement fuse if possible.
- Remove any corrosion from the fuse holder before replacing the fuse.
- Be certain the fuse properly fits the fuse holder.

Preventive Maintenance of Fuses

Preventive maintenance of fuses consists of checking for the following conditions and correcting any discrepancies.

- **Improper Fuse**. Check the fuse installed against that recommended in the technical manual for the equipment. If an incorrect fuse is installed, replace it with the correct fuse.
- **Corrosion**. Check for corrosion on the fuse holder terminals or the fuse itself. If corrosion is present, remove it with fine sandpaper.
- **Improper Fit**. Check for contact between the fuse and fuse holder. If a piece of paper will fit between the fuse and the clips on a clip-type fuse holder, there is improper contact. If the fuse is not held in the cap of a plug-type fuse holder, the contacts are too loose.
- **Open Fuses**. Check fuses for opens. If any fuse is open, repair the trouble that caused the open fuse and replace the fuse.

Circuit Breakers

A circuit breaker is a circuit protection device that, like a fuse, will stop current in the circuit if there is a direct short, excessive current or excessive heat. Unlike a fuse, a circuit breaker is reusable. The circuit breaker does not have to be replaced after it has opened or broken the circuit. Instead of replacing the circuit breaker, it can be reset.

Circuit breakers can also be used as circuit control devices. By manually opening and closing the contacts of a circuit breaker, power can be switched on and off. Circuit control devices will be covered in more detail in the next chapter.

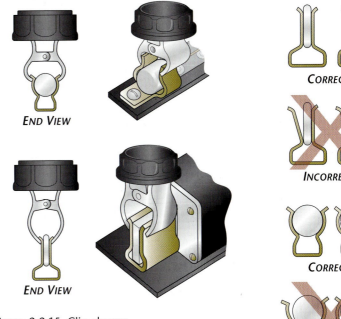

Figure 2-2-15. Clip clamps

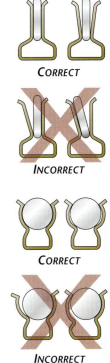

Figure 2-2-14. Contact between clips & fuses

Circuit breakers are available in a great variety of sizes and types. It would not be possible to describe every type of circuit breaker in use today, but this chapter will describe the basic types of circuit breakers and their operational principles.

Circuit breakers have five main components, as shown in Figure 2-2-16. The components are the frame, the operating mechanism, the contacts, the terminal connectors and the trip elements.

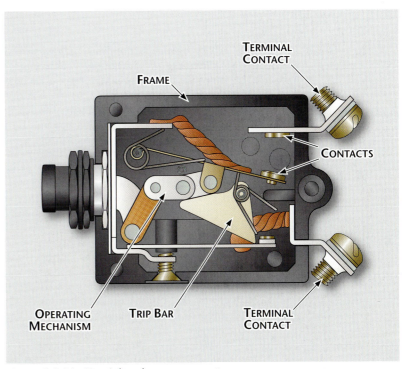

Figure 2-2-16. Circuit breaker components

Figure 2-2-17 Arc extinguisher action

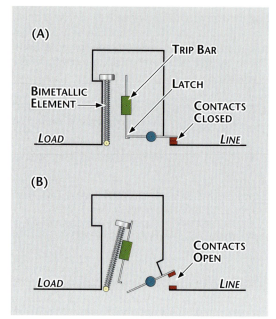

Figure 2-2-18. Thermal trip element action;
(A) Trip element with normal current
(B) Contacts open

The *frame* provides an insulated housing and is used to mount the circuit breaker components (Figure 2-2-16). The frame determines the physical size of the circuit breaker and the maximum allowable voltage and current.

The *operating mechanism* provides a means of opening and closing the breaker contacts (i.e., turning the circuit on and off). The toggle mechanism shown in Figure 2-2-16 is the quick-make, quick-break type, which means the contacts snap open or closed quickly regardless of how fast the handle is moved. In addition to indicating whether the breaker is on or off, the operating mechanism handle indicates when the breaker has opened automatically (tripped) by moving to a position between on and off. To reset the circuit breaker, the handle must first be moved to the off position, and then to the on position.

The *arc extinguisher* confines, divides and extinguishes the arc drawn between contacts each time the circuit breaker interrupts current. The arc extinguisher is actually a series of contacts that open gradually, dividing the arc and making it easier to confine and extinguish. This is shown in Figure 2-2-17. Arc extinguishers are generally used in circuit breakers that control a large amount of power, such as those found in power distribution panels. Small-power circuit breakers (such as those found in lighting panels) may not have arc extinguishers.

Terminal connectors are used to connect the circuit breaker to the power source and the load. They are electrically connected to the contacts of the circuit breaker and provide the means of connecting the circuit breaker to the circuit.

The *trip element* is the part of the circuit breaker that senses the overload condition and causes the circuit breaker to trip or break the circuit. This chapter will cover the thermal, magnetic and thermal-magnetic trip units used by most circuit breakers. Some circuit breakers make use of solid-state trip units using current transformers and solid-state circuitry.

Thermal Trip Element

A thermal trip element circuit breaker uses a bimetallic element that is heated by the load current. This style is frequently seen in aviation applications. The bimetallic element is made from strips of two different metals bonded together. The metals expand at different rates as they are heated. This causes the bimetallic element to bend as it is heated by the current going to the load. Figure 2-2-18 shows how this can be used to trip the circuit breaker.

Figure 2-2-18A shows the trip element with normal current. The bimetallic element is not heated excessively and does not bend. If the current increases (or the temperature around the circuit breaker increases), the bimetallic element bends, pushes against the trip bar and releases the latch. Then, the contacts open, as shown in Figure 2-2-18B.

The amount of time it takes for the bimetallic element to bend and trip the circuit breaker depends on the amount the element is heated. A large overload will heat the element quickly. A small overload will require a longer time to trip the circuit breaker.

Magnetic Trip Element

A magnetic trip element circuit breaker uses an electromagnet in series with the circuit load, as shown in Figure 2-2-19. With normal current, the electromagnet will not have enough attraction to the trip bar to move it, and the contacts will remain closed, as shown in Figure 2-2-19A. The strength of the magnetic field of the electromagnet increases as current through the coil increases. As soon as the current in the circuit becomes large enough, the trip bar is pulled toward the magnetic element (electromagnet), the contacts are opened, and the current stops, as shown in Figure 2-2-19B.

The amount of current needed to trip the circuit breaker depends on the size of the gap between the trip bar and the magnetic element. On some circuit breakers, this gap (and therefore the trip current) is adjustable.

Thermal-Magnetic Trip Element

The thermal trip element circuit breaker, like a delay fuse, will protect a circuit against a small overload that continues for a long time. The larger the overload, the faster the circuit breaker will trip. The thermal element will also protect the circuit against temperature increases. A magnetic circuit breaker will trip instantly when the preset current is present. In some applications, both types of protection are desired. Rather than use two separate circuit breakers, a single trip element combining thermal and magnetic trip elements is used. A thermal-magnetic trip element is shown in Figure 2-2-20.

In the thermal-magnetic trip element circuit breaker, a magnetic element is connected in series with the circuit load, and a bimetallic element is heated by the load current. With normal circuit current, the bimetallic element does not bend, and the magnetic element does not attract the trip bar, as shown in Figure 2-2-20A.

If the temperature or current increases over a sustained period of time, the bimetallic element will bend, push the trip bar and release the latch. The circuit breaker will trip as shown in Figure 2-2-20B.

If the current suddenly or rapidly increases enough, the magnetic element will attract the trip bar, release the latch, and the circuit breaker will trip, as shown in Figure 2-2-20C. This circuit breaker has tripped even though the thermal element has not had time to react to the increased current.

Trip-Free/Nontrip-Free Circuit Breakers

Circuit breakers are classified as being trip-free or nontrip-free. A trip-free circuit breaker is a circuit breaker that will trip even if the operating mechanism (the on-off switch) is

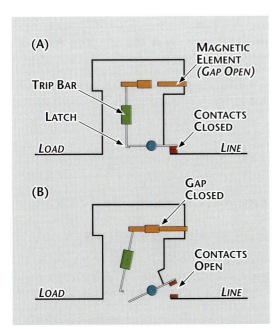

Figure 2-2-19. Magnetic trip element action

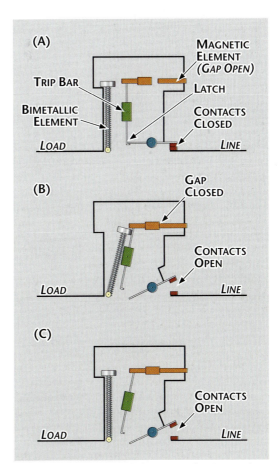

Figure 2-2-20. Thermal-magnetic element action

held in the on position. A nontrip-free circuit breaker can be reset and/or held on even if an overload or excessive heat condition is present. In other words, a nontrip-free circuit breaker can be bypassed by holding the operating mechanism on.

Trip-free circuit breakers are used on circuits that cannot tolerate overloads and on nonemergency circuits. Examples of these are precision or current-sensitive circuits, nonemergency lighting circuits and nonessential equipment circuits. Nontrip-free circuit breakers are used for circuits that are essential for operations. Examples of these circuits are emergency lighting, required control circuits and essential equipment circuits.

Time-Delay Ratings

Circuit breakers, like fuses, are rated by the amount of time delay. In circuit breakers the ratings are instantaneous, short, and long. The delay times of circuit breakers can be used to provide for selective tripping.

Selective tripping is used to cause the circuit breaker closest to the faulty circuit to trip. This will remove power from the faulty circuit without affecting other, non-faulty circuits.

Figure 2-2-21 shows a power distribution system using circuit breakers for protection. Circuit breaker 1 (CB1) has the entire current for all seven loads through it. CB2 feeds loads 1, 2, 3 and 4 (through CB4, CB5, CB6 and CB7), and CB3 feeds loads 5, 6 and 7 (through CB8, CB9 and CB10). If all the circuit breakers were rated with the same time delay, an overload on load 5 could cause CB1, CB3 and CB8 to trip. This would remove power from all seven loads, even though load 5 was the only circuit with an overload.

Selective tripping would have CB1 rated as long time-delay, CB2 and CB3 rated as short time-delay, and CB4 through CB10 rated as instantaneous. With this arrangement, if load 5 had an overload, only CB8 would trip. CB8 would remove the power from load 5 before CB1 or CB3 could react to the overload. In this way, only load 5 would be affected and the other circuits would continue to operate.

Circuit Breaker Maintenance

Before attempting to work on circuit breakers, check the applicable technical manual carefully. Be certain to remove all power to the circuit breaker before work begins. Tag the switch that removes the power to the circuit breaker to ensure that power is not applied while someone is working.

Once approval has been obtained, the incoming power has been removed, the switch tagged and the applicable technical manual has been consulted, check the circuit breaker. Manually operate the circuit breaker several times to be sure the operating mechanism works smoothly.

Check the connections at the terminals to be certain the terminals and wiring are tight and free from corrosion. Check all mounting hardware for tightness and wear. Check all components for wear. Clean the circuit breaker completely.

When finished working on the circuit breaker, restore power and remove the tag from the switch that applies power to the circuit.

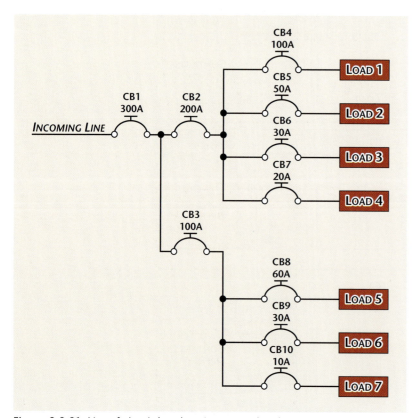

Figure 2-2-21. Use of circuit breakers in power distribution system

Section 3

Electrical Resistors

Resistance is a property of every electrical component. At times, its effects will be undesirable. However, resistance is used in many varied ways. *Resistors* are components manufactured to possess specific values of resistance. They are manufactured in many types and sizes. When drawn using its schematic representation, a resistor is shown as a series of jagged lines, as illustrated in Figure 2-3-1.

Composition of Resistors

In the past, one of the most common types of resistors was the molded composition style, usually referred to as the carbon resistor. These resistors are manufactured in a variety of sizes and shapes. The chemical composition of the resistor determines its ohmic value and is accurately controlled by the manufacturer in the development process. They are made in ohmic values that range from one ohm to millions of ohms. The physical size of the resistor is related to its wattage rating, which is the ability of the resistor to dissipate heat caused by the resistance.

Carbon resistors have as their principal ingredient the element carbon. In the manufacture of carbon resistors, fillers or binders are added to the carbon to obtain various resistor values.

Examples of these fillers are clay, bakelite, rubber and talc. These fillers are doping agents and cause the overall conduction characteristics to change.

Carbon resistors are no longer the most common resistors. Their prime disadvantage is that they have a tendency to change value as they age. Another disadvantage of carbon resistors is their limited power handling capacity.

The disadvantage of carbon resistors can be overcome by the use of wire-wound resistors (Figure 2-3-1A and Figure 2-3-1B). Wire-wound resistors have very accurate values and possess a higher current handling capability than carbon resistors. The material that is frequently used to manufacture wire-wound resistors is

TYPICAL RESISTOR	TYPE	SYMBOL
(A) 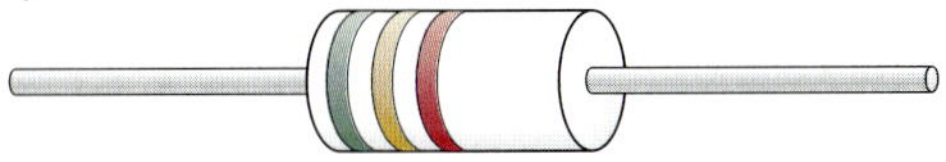	Fixed Carbon	
(B) 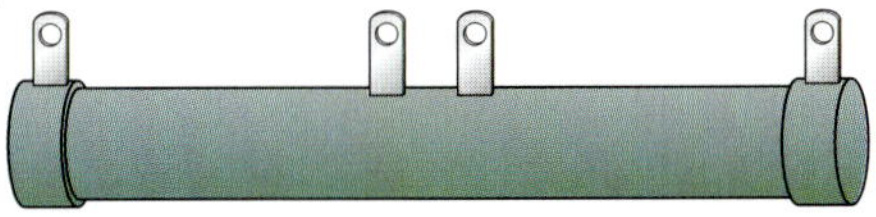	Fixed Wire-Wound (Tapped)	
(C) 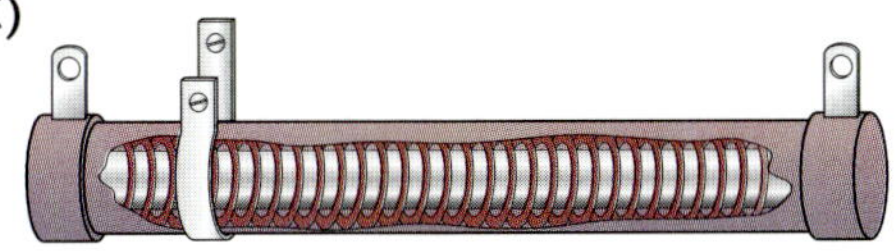	Adjustable Wire-Wound	
(D) 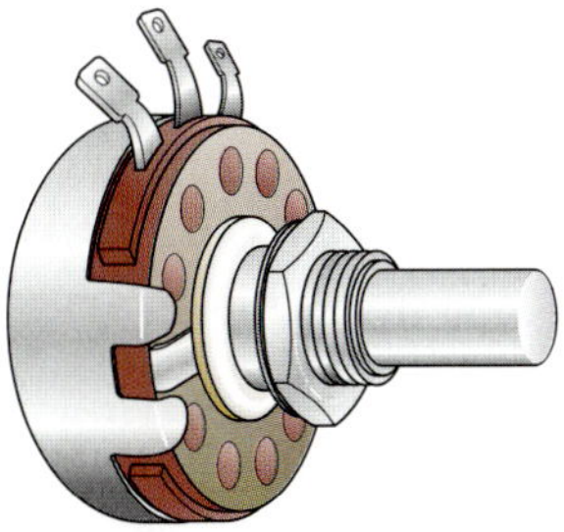	Potentiometer	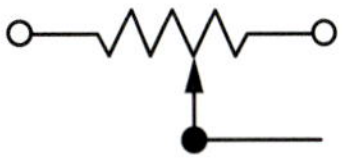
(E) 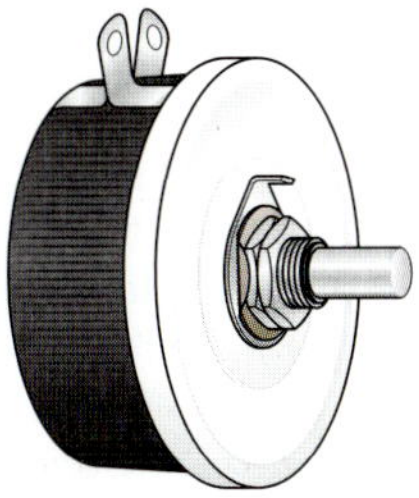	Rheostat	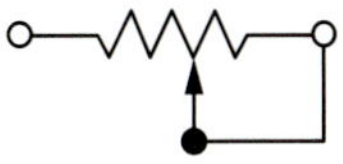

Figure 2-3-1. Types of resistors

Figure 2-3-2. Fixed carbon resistor

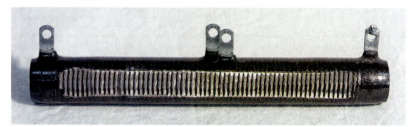

Figure 2-3-3. Fixed wire-wound resistor

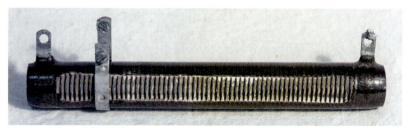

Figure 2-3-4. Adjustable wire-wound resistor

German silver, which is composed of copper, nickel and zinc. The qualities and quantities of these elements present in the wire determine the resistivity of the wire. (The *resistivity* of the wire is the measure or ability of the wire to resist current. Usually the percent of nickel in the wire determines the resistivity.) One disadvantage of the wire-wound resistor is that it takes a large amount of wire to manufacture a resistor of high ohmic value, thereby increasing the cost. A variation of the wire-wound resistor provides an exposed surface to the resistance wire on one side. An adjustable tap is attached to this side. Such resistors, sometimes with two or more adjustable taps, are used as voltage dividers in power supplies and other applications where a specific voltage is desired to be "tapped" off.

Another type of resistor is the film resistor. Actually the term film resistor is very broad. There are many types of film resistors.

- Metal film resistor
- Carbon film resistor
- Metal oxide film fesistor
- Cermet resistor

These resistors are made by depositing pure metals into a ceramic rod or substrate. Some of the pure metals used are nickel or an oxide film. The resistance of the resistor can be controlled by making the resistor thicker or thinner. This gives them the nickname of thick-film or thin-film resistors.

Metal film resistors have better temperature stability than carbon film resistors. Metal oxide resistors have better high-surge current capability with an even higher temperature rating than the metal film resistor. Carbon film resistors are a low noise filter and therefore are better for radio frequency operations.

The cermet resistor is a special design. The name cermet is a combination of ceramic and metal. The substrate is made of an alumina ceramic. These resistors have good voltage ratings, good temperature stability, low noise, but low surge current properties.

Fixed and Variable Resistors

There are two kinds of resistors: fixed and variable. The *fixed resistor* (Figure 2-3-1A) will have one value and will never change (other than through temperature, age, etc.). The resistor pictured in Figure 2-3-2 is classed as a fixed resistor. The *tapped resistor* in Figure 2-3-1B has several fixed taps and makes more than one resistance value available. An example of a fixed wire-wound resistor is pictured in Figure 2-3-3. The sliding contact resistor shown in Figure 2-3-1C has an adjustable collar that can be moved to tap off any resistance within the ohmic value range of the resistor. An example of an adjustable wire-wound resistor is pictured in Figure 2-3-4.

Figure 2-3-5. Potentiometer

There are two types of *variable resistors*, one called a potentiometer (Figure 2-3-5) and the other a rheostat (Figure 2-3-6). An example of the *potentiometer* is the volume control on in a radio, and an example of the *rheostat* is the dimmer control for the dash lights in an automobile. There is a slight difference between them. Rheostats usually have two connections, one fixed and the other moveable. Any variable resistor can properly be called a rheostat. The potentiometer always has three connections, two fixed and one moveable. Generally, the rheostat has a limited range of values and a high current handling capability. The potentiometer has a wide range of values, but it usually has a limited current handling capability.

Figure 2-3-6. Rheostat

Wattage Rating

When a current is passed through a resistor, heat is developed within the resistor. The resistor must be capable of dissipating this heat into the surrounding air; otherwise, the temperature of the resistor rises, causing a change in resistance or possibly causing the resistor to burn out.

The ability of the resistor to dissipate heat depends upon the design of the resistor itself. This ability to dissipate heat varies with the amount of surface area that is exposed to the air. A resistor designed to dissipate a large amount of heat must therefore have a large physical size. The heat dissipating capability of a resistor is measured in watts (W). Some of the more common wattage ratings of carbon resistors are: $1/8$ W, $1/4$ W, $1/2$ W, 1 W, and 2 W. In some of the newer state-of-the-art circuits, much smaller wattage resistors are used. The higher the wattage rating of the resistor, the larger is the physical size. Resistors that dissipate very large amounts of power are usually wire-wound resistors. Wire-wound resistors with ratings up to 50 W are not uncommon.

Standard Color Code System

In the standard color code system, four bands are painted on the resistor.

The color of the first band indicates the value of the first significant digit. The color of the second band indicates the value of the second significant digit. The third color band represents a decimal by which the first two digits must be multiplied to obtain the resistance value of the resistor. The colors for the bands and their corresponding values are shown in Table 2-3-1.

COLOR	SIGNIFICANT FIGURE	DECIMAL MULTIPLIER	TOLERANCE PERCENT	RELIABILITY LEVEL PER 1,000 HOURS (%)
Black	0	1	–	1.0
Brown	1	10	1	0.1
Red	2	100	2	0.01
Orange	3	1,000	–	0.001
Yellow	4	10,000	–	–
Green	5	100,000	–	–
Blue	6	1,000,000	–	–
Violet	7	10,000,000	–	–
Gray	8	100,000,000	–	–
White	9	1,000,000,000	–	–
Gold	–	0.1	5	–
Silver	–	0.01	10	–
No Color	–	–	20	–

Table 2-3-1. Standard color code for resistors

Use the example colors shown in Figure 2-3-7. Since red is the color of the first band, the first significant digit is 2. The second band is green; therefore the second significant digit is 5. The third band is yellow, which indicates that the number formed as a result of reading the first two bands is multiplied by 10,000. In this case 25 x 10,000 = 270,000Ω.

The last band on the resistor indicates the tolerance; that is the manufacturer's allowable ohmic deviation as a percentage above and below the numerical value indicated by the resistor's color code. The example illustration has no band, indicating a 20% tolerance rating.

When measuring resistors, there are situations in which the quantities to be measured may be extremely large, and the resulting number using the basic unit, the ohm, may prove too cumbersome. Therefore, a metric system prefix is usually attached to the basic unit of measurement to provide a more manageable unit. Two of the most commonly used prefixes are kilo- and mega-. Kilo- represents thousand and is abbreviated k. Mega- represents million and is abbreviated M.

Simplifying the Color Code

Resistors are the most common components used in electronics. The technician must identify, select, check, remove and replace resistors. Resistors and resistor circuits are usually the easiest branches of electronics to understand.

Black, brown, red, orange, yellow, green, blue, violet, gray, white—this is the order of colors a technician should know automatically. There is a memory aid to help remember the code in its proper order: "Bad Boys Run Over Yellow Gardenias Behind Victory Garden Walls." Each word starts with the first letter of the colors. Match it up with the color code to help remember the correct sequence and code:

- **Black**—Bad
- **Brown**—Boys
- **Red**—Run
- **Orange**—Over
- **Yellow**—Yellow
- **Green**—Gardenias
- **Blue**—Behind
- **Violet**—Victory
- **Gray**—Garden
- **White**—Walls

There are a number of other memory aid sentences that experienced technicians use. If one of them is easier to remember, use it.

When working from memory, mistakes on a resistor's color band can happen. Most technicians do at one time or another. If a mistake is made on the first two significant colors, it usually is not too serious. If a make a mistake is made on the third band, it is much more significant, because the value is going to be at least 10 times too high or too low. Some important points to remember about the third band are:

When the third band is:

- **Black**—the resistor's value is less than 100 ohms.
- **Brown**—the resistor's value is in hundreds of ohms.
- **Red**—the resistor's value is in thousands of ohms.
- **Orange**—the resistor's value is in tens of thousands of ohms.
- **Yellow**—the resistor's value is in hundreds of thousands of ohms.
- **Green**—the resistor's value is in megaohms.
- **Blue**—the resistor's value is in tens of megaohms or more.

Although any of the above colors may be present in the third band, red, orange and yellow are the most common. In some cases, the third band will be silver or gold. Multiply the first two bands by 0.01 if it is silver, and 0.1 if it is gold.

The fourth band, the tolerance band, usually does not present a problem. If there is no fourth band, the resistor has a 20 percent tolerance; silver indicates a 10 percent tolerance; and gold indicates a 5 percent tolerance.

Resistors that conform to military specifications have a fifth band. The fifth band indicates the reliability level per 1,000 hours of operation as follows:

- **Brown**—1.0 percent
- **Red**—0.1 percent
- **Orange**—0.01 percent
- **Yellow**—0.001 percent

For a resistor whose fifth band is colored brown, the resistor's chance of failure will not exceed 1 percent for every 1,000 hours of operation.

Some resistors, both wire-wound and composition, do not use the resistor color code. These resistors will have the ohmic value and tolerance imprinted on the resistor itself.

Troubleshooting Resistors

Resistors are very reliable and have a low failure rate. In fact, their failure rate is lower than that of semiconductors. Most faults in resistors are caused by overheating. This is usually caused by an excess of power being sent through the resistor. Many times this type of fault is due to an external circuit or another component. Never install a resistor into a circuit with a power requirement too close to its power rating. By doing this, the life span of the resistor can be reduced.

Although not commonly seen in metal film and wire wound resistors, over heating in carbon film can cause a decrease or an increase in its resistance.

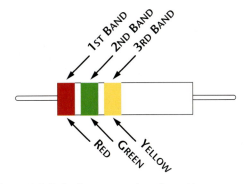

Figure 2-3-7. End-to-center band marking

Testing resistors is a simple task; all that is needed is an ohmmeter. If a resistor fails open when measuring the resistance, the meter will read infinite. If a reading shows on the ohmmeter, make sure that the value displayed matches the color code and is within tolerance according to the color code marked on the resistor.

3
Concepts of Alternating Current

A coil rotating in a magnetic field generates a current that regularly changes direction. This current is called alternating current or AC.

Section 1

Alternating Current

Alternating current is current that constantly changes in amplitude and that reverses direction at regular intervals. Chapter one discussed that direct current (DC) flows only in one direction, and that the amplitude of current is determined by the number of electrons flowing past a point in a circuit in one second. If, for example, a coulomb of electrons moves past a point in a wire in one second and all of the electrons are moving in the same direction, the amplitude of direct current in the wire is one ampere. Similarly, if half a coulomb of electrons moves in one direction past a point in the wire in half a second, then reverses direction and moves past the same point in the opposite direction during the next half-second, a total of one coulomb of electrons passes the point in one second. The amplitude of the alternating current is one ampere.

Disadvantages of DC Compared to AC

When commercial use of electricity became widespread in the United States, certain disadvantages in using DC in the home became apparent. If a commercial DC system is used, voltage must be generated at the level (amplitude or value) required by the load. To properly light a 240-V lamp, for example, the DC generator must deliver 240 V. If a 120-V lamp is to be

Learning Objective

DESCRIBE
- the effect that a capacitor or inductor has on a circuit

EXPLAIN
- the difference between apparent and true power
- the difference between a step up and step down transformer

APPLY
- use the formulas presented to calculate all aspects of an AC circuit
- determine the voltage and current rise or fall in a transformer
- determine the phase condition of an AC circuit

Left. Alternating current is used to power many airliner and corporate aircraft systems.

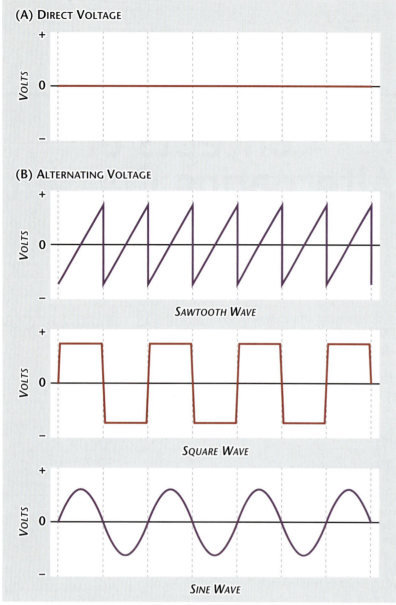

Figure 3-1-1. Voltage waveforms

Unlike direct voltages, alternating voltages can be stepped up or down in amplitude by a device called a transformer. Use of the transformer permits efficient transmission of electrical power over long-distance lines. At the electrical power station, the transformer output power is at high voltage and low current levels. At the consumer end of the transmission lines, the voltage is stepped down by a transformer to the value required by the load. Due to its inherent advantages and versatility, AC has replaced DC in all but a few commercial power distribution systems.

Voltage Waveforms

There are two types of current and voltage—direct current and voltage, and alternating current and voltage. Figure 3-1-1A shows the amplitude of a DC voltage across the terminals of a battery over time. Note that the DC voltage has a constant amplitude. Some voltages go through periodic changes in amplitude like those shown in Figure 3-1-1B. A *waveform* is a pattern of changes in amplitude over time. Figure 3-1-1B shows some of the common electrical waveforms. Of those illustrated, the sine wave will be most frequently encountered.

Electromagnetism

The sine wave illustrated in Figure 3-1-1B is a plot of a current that changes amplitude and direction. Although there are several ways of producing this current, the method based on the principles of electromagnetic induction is by far the easiest and most common method in use.

Fundamental theories concerning simple magnets and magnetism were discussed in Chapter 1, but how magnetism can be used to produce electricity was only briefly mentioned. This chapter gives a more in-depth study of magnetism. The main points that will be explained are how magnetism is affected by an electric current and, conversely, how electricity is affected by magnetism. This general subject area is referred to as *electromagnetism*. To properly understand electricity, it is important to first become familiar with the relationships between magnetism and electricity. The following are important things to know:

- An electric current always produces some form of magnetism.

- The most commonly used means for producing or using electricity involves magnetism.

- The peculiar behavior of electricity under certain conditions is caused by magnetic influences.

supplied power from the 240-V generator, a resistor or another 120-V lamp must be placed in series with the 120-V lamp to drop the extra 120 V. When the resistor is used to reduce the voltage, an amount of power equal to that consumed by the lamp is wasted.

Another disadvantage of the DC system becomes evident when the DC (I) from the generating station must be transmitted a long distance over wires to the consumer: a large amount of power is lost due to the resistance (R) of the wire. The power loss is equal to I^2R. This loss can be greatly reduced if the power is transmitted at a very high voltage level and a low current level. However, this is not a practical solution to the power loss since the load would then have to be operated at a dangerously high voltage. Because of the disadvantages related to transmitting and using DC, practically all modern commercial electric power companies generate and distribute AC.

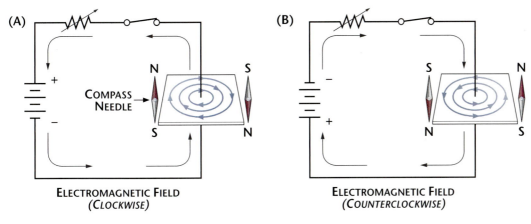

Figure 3-1-2. Magnetic field around a current-carrying conductor

Magnetic Fields

In 1819, Hans Christian Oersted, a Danish physicist, found that a definite relationship exists between magnetism and electricity. He discovered that an electric current is always accompanied by certain magnetic effects and that these effects obey definite laws.

Magnetic Field Around a Current-Carrying Conductor

If a compass is placed in the vicinity of a current-carrying conductor, the compass needle will align itself at right angles to the conductor, indicating the presence of a magnetic force. The presence of this force is demonstrated by using the arrangement illustrated in Figure 3-1-2. In both views, current flows in a vertical conductor through a horizontal piece of cardboard. To determine the direction of the magnetic force produced by the current, place a compass at various points on the cardboard and note the compass needle deflection. The direction of the magnetic force is assumed to be the direction in which the north pole of the compass points.

In Figure 3-1-2A, the needle deflections show that a magnetic field exists in circular form around the conductor. When the current flows upward, the direction of the field is clockwise, as viewed from the top. However, if the polarity of the battery is reversed so that the current flows downward (Figure 3-1-2B), the direction of the field will reverse itself in the counterclockwise direction.

The relation between the direction of the magnetic lines of force around a conductor and the direction of electron current flow in the conductor may be determined by means of the *left-hand rule for a conductor*:

> **RULE:** *If the conductor is held in the left hand with the thumb extended in the direction of the electron flow (current, negative to positive), the holder's fingers will point in the direction of the magnetic lines of force.*

Now apply this rule to Figure 3-1-2. Note that the holder's fingers point in the direction that the north pole of the compass points when it is placed in the magnetic field surrounding the wire. An arrow is generally used in electrical diagrams to denote the direction of current in a length of wire (see Figure 3-1-3A, for example). Where a cross-section of a wire is shown,

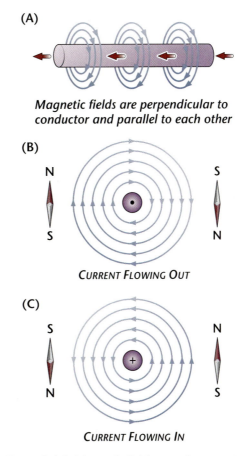

Figure 3-1-3. Magnetic field around a current-carrying conductor (detailed view)

3-4 | Concepts of Alternating Current

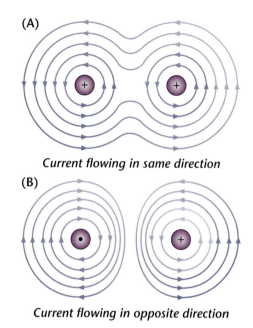

Figure 3-1-4. Magnetic field around two parallel conductors

an end view of the arrow is used. A cross-sectional view of a conductor that is carrying current toward the observer is illustrated in Figure 3-1-3B. Notice that the direction of current is indicated by a dot, representing the head of the arrow. A conductor that is carrying current away from the observer is illustrated in Figure 3-1-3C. Note that the direction of current is indicated by a cross, representing the tail of the arrow. Also note that the magnetic field around a current-carrying conductor is perpendicular to the conductor, and that the magnetic lines of force are equal along all parts of the conductor.

When two parallel conductors are carrying current in the same direction, the magnetic lines of force combine and increase the strength of the field around the conductors as shown in Figure 3-1-4A. Two parallel conductors carrying currents in opposite directions are shown in Figure 3-1-4B. Note that the field around one conductor is opposite in direction to the field around the other conductor. The resulting lines of force oppose each other in the space between the wires, thus deforming the field around each conductor. This means that if two parallel and adjacent conductors are carrying currents in the same direction, the fields about the two conductors aid each other. Conversely, if the two conductors are carrying currents in opposite directions, the fields about the conductors repel each other.

Magnetic Field of a Coil

Figure 3-1-3A illustrates that the magnetic field around a current-carrying wire exists at all points along the wire. Figure 3-1-5 illustrates that when a straight wire is wound around a core, it forms a coil and that the magnetic field about the core assumes a different shape. Figure 3-1-5A is actually a partial cutaway view showing the construction of a simple coil. Figure 3-1-5B shows a cross-sectional view of the same coil. Notice that the two ends of the coil are identified as X and Y.

When current is passed through the coil, the magnetic field about each turn of wire links with the fields of the adjacent turns (Figure 3-1-4A). The combined influence of all the turns produces a two-pole field similar to that of a simple bar magnet. One end of the coil is a north pole and the other end is a south pole.

Polarity of an electromagnetic coil. Figure 3-1-2 shows that the direction of the magnetic field around a straight wire depends on the direction of current in that wire. Thus, a reversal of current in a wire causes a reversal in the direction of the magnetic field. It follows that a reversal of the current in a coil also causes a reversal of the two-pole magnetic field about the coil.

When the direction of the current in a coil is known, it is possible to determine the magnetic polarity of the coil by using the left-hand rule for coils. This rule, illustrated in Figure 3-1-6, is stated as follows:

> **RULE:** *Grasp the coil in your left hand, with your fingers "wrapped around" in the direction of the electron current flow. Your thumb will point toward the north pole of the coil.*

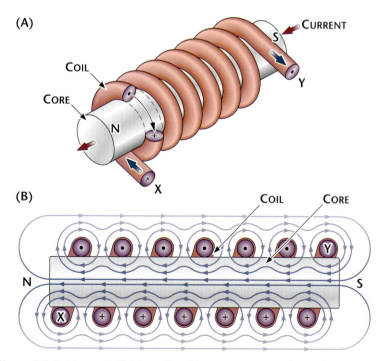

Figure 3-1-5. Magnetic field produced by a current-carrying coil

Strength of an electromagnetic field. The strength or intensity of a coil's magnetic field depends on a number of factors. The main ones are listed below and will be discussed later.

- The number of turns of wire in the coil
- The amount of current flowing in the coil
- The ratio of the coil length to the coil width
- The type of material in the core

Losses in an electromagnetic field. When current flows in a conductor, the atoms in the conductor all line up in a definite direction, producing a magnetic field. When the direction of the current changes, the direction of the atoms' alignment also changes, causing the magnetic field to change direction. To reverse all the atoms requires that power be expended, and this power is lost. This loss of power (in the form of heat) is called *hysteresis loss*. Hysteresis loss is common to all AC equipment; however, it causes few problems except in motors, generators and transformers. When these devices are discussed later in this chapter, hysteresis loss will be covered in more detail.

Basic AC Generation

The previous section illustrated that a current-carrying conductor produces a magnetic field around itself. In an earlier chapter, the text covered how a changing magnetic field produces an electromotive force (emf) in a conductor. That is, if a conductor is placed in a magnetic field, and either the field or the conductor moves, an emf is induced in the conductor. This effect is called *electromagnetic induction*.

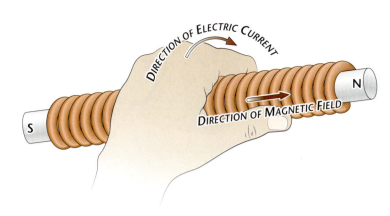

Figure 3-1-6. Left-hand rule for coils

Cycle

Figure 3-1-7 shows a suspended loop of wire (conductor) being rotated in a clockwise direction through the magnetic field between the poles of a permanent magnet. For ease of explanation, the loop has been divided into a dark half and light half. Notice in Figure 3-1-7A that

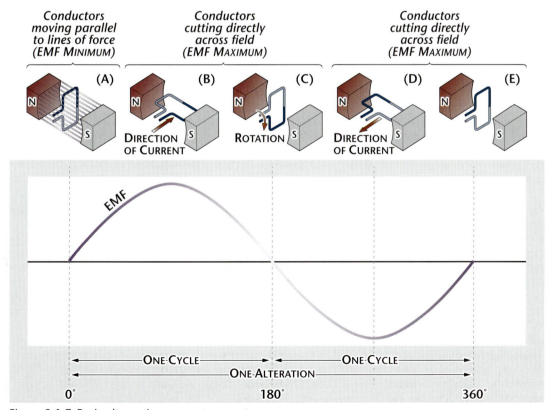

Figure 3-1-7. Basic alternating-current generator

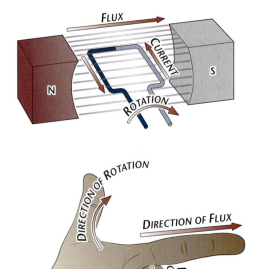

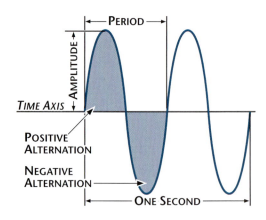

Figure 3-1-9. Period of a sine wave

Figure 3-1-7. Notice the only difference is in the polarity of the induced voltage. Where previously the polarity was positive, it is now negative.

The sine curve shows the value of induced voltage at each instant of time during rotation of the loop. Notice that this curve contains 360°, or two alternations. Two alternations represent one complete cycle of rotation.

Assuming a closed path is provided across the ends of the conductor loop, it is possible to determine the direction of current in the loop by using the left-hand rule for generators (Figure 3-1-8). The left-hand rule is applied as follows: First, place the left hand on the illustration with the fingers as shown. The thumb will now point in the direction of rotation (relative movement of the wire to the magnetic field); the forefinger will point in the direction of magnetic flux (north to south); and the middle finger (pointing out of the paper) will point in the direction of electron current flow.

By applying the left-hand rule to the dark half of the loop in Figure 3-1-7B, the technician will find that the current flows in the direction indicated by the heavy arrow. Similarly, by using the left-hand rule on the light half of the loop, the technician will find that current in that loop flows in the opposite direction. The two induced voltages in the loop add together to form one total emf. It is this emf that causes the current in the loop.

When the loop rotates to the position shown in Figure 3-1-7D, the action reverses. The dark half is moving up instead of down, and the light half is moving down instead of up. By applying the left-hand rule once again, see that the total induced emf and its resulting current have reversed direction. The voltage builds up to maximum in this new direction, as shown by the sine curve in Figure 3-1-7. The loop finally returns to its original position (Figure 3-1-7E), at which point voltage is again zero. The sine curve represents one complete

Figure 3-1-8. Left-hand rule for generators

the dark half is moving along (parallel to) the lines of force. Consequently, it is not cutting any lines of force. The same is true of the light half, which is moving in the opposite direction. Since the conductors are cutting no lines of force, no emf is induced. As the loop rotates toward the position shown in Figure 3-1-7B, it cuts more and more lines of force per second (inducing an ever-increasing voltage) because it is cutting more directly across the field. In Figure 3-1-7B, the conductor is shown completing one-quarter of a complete revolution, or 90° of a complete circle. Because the conductor is now cutting directly across the field, the voltage induced in the conductor is at its maximum. When the value of induced voltage at various points during the rotation from Figure 3-1-7A to Figure 3-1-7B is plotted on a graph (and the points connected), a curve appears as shown.

As the loop continues to be rotated toward the position shown in Figure 3-1-7C, it cuts fewer and fewer lines of force. The induced voltage decreases from its peak value. Eventually, the loop is once again moving in a plane parallel to the magnetic field, and no emf is induced in the conductor.

The loop has now been rotated through half a circle (180°). If the preceding quarter-cycle is plotted, it appears as shown on the graph in Figure 3-1-7.

When the same procedure is applied to the second half of rotation (180° through 360°), the curve on the graph changes as seen in

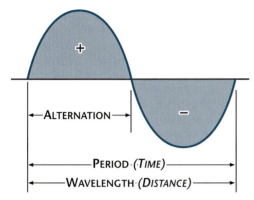

Figure 3-1-10. Wavelength

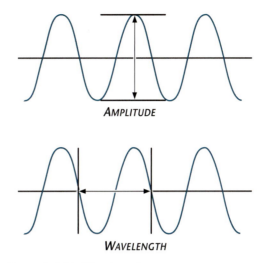

Figure 3-1-11. Wavelength measurement

cycle of voltage generated by the rotating loop. All the illustrations used in this chapter show the wire loop moving in a clockwise direction. In actual practice, the loop can be moved clockwise or counterclockwise. Regardless of the direction of movement, the left hand rule applies.

If the loop is rotated through 360° at a steady rate, and if the strength of the magnetic field is uniform, the voltage produced is a sine wave of voltage, as indicated in Figure 3-1-9. Continuous rotation of the loop will produce a series of sine-wave voltage cycles or, in other words, an AC voltage.

As mentioned previously, the cycle consists of two complete alternations in a period of time. The measure of hertz (Hz) was given to indicate one cycle per second. If one cycle per second is 1 Hz, then 100 cycles per second are 100 Hz, and so on. Throughout this text the term *cycle* will be used when no specific time element is involved, and the term *hertz* (Hz) will be used when the time element is measured in seconds.

Frequency. If the loop in Figure 3-1-7A makes one complete revolution each second, the generator will produce one complete cycle of AC during each second (1 Hz). Increasing the number of revolutions to two per second will produce two complete cycles per second (2 Hz). The number of complete cycles of alternating current or voltage completed each second is referred to as frequency. Frequency is always measured and expressed in hertz.

Alternating current frequency is an important term to understand since most AC electrical equipment requires a specific frequency for proper operation.

Period. A cycle of any sine wave represents a definite amount of time. Notice that Figure 3-1-9 shows two cycles of a sine wave that has a frequency of 2 Hz. Since two cycles occur each second, one cycle must require half of a second. The time required to complete one cycle of a waveform is called the *period* of the wave. In Figure 3-1-9, the period is one-half second. The relationship between time (t) and frequency (f) is indicated by the formulas:

$$t = \frac{1}{f} \text{ and } f = \frac{1}{t}$$

Where:

t = period in seconds and

f = frequency in hertz

Amplitude. Each cycle of the sine wave shown in Figure 3-1-9 consists of two identically shaped variations in voltage. The variation that occurs during the time the voltage is positive is called the *positive alternation*, while the variation that occurs during the time the voltage is negative is called the *negative alternation*. In a sine wave, these two alternations are identical in size and shape, but opposite in polarity.

The distance from zero to the maximum value of each alternation is called the *amplitude*. The amplitude of the positive alternation and the amplitude of the negative alternation are the same.

Wavelength. The time it takes for a sine wave to complete one cycle is defined as the period of the waveform. The distance traveled by the sine wave during this period is referred to as the *wavelength*. Wavelength, indicated by the symbol λ (Greek lambda), is the distance along the waveform from one point to the same point on the next cycle. This relationship can be observed by examining Figure 3-1-10. The point on the waveform that measurement of wavelength begins is not important as long as the distance is measured to the same point on the next cycle. See Figure 3-1-11.

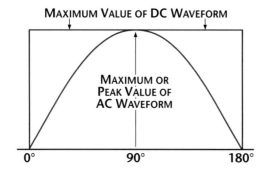

Figure 3-1-12. Maximum or peak value

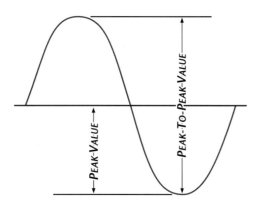

Figure 3-1-13. Peak and peak-to-peak values

Alternating Current Values

In discussing alternating current and voltage, it is often necessary to express the current and voltage in terms of maximum or peak values, peak-to-peak values, effective values, average values or instantaneous values. Each of these values has a different meaning and is used to describe a different amount of current or voltage.

Peak and Peak-to-Peak Values

Notice that Figure 3-1-12 shows the positive alternation of a sine wave (a half-cycle of AC) and a DC waveform that occur simultaneously. Note that the DC starts and stops at the same moment as the positive alternation, and that both waveforms rise to the same maximum value. However, the DC values are greater than the corresponding AC values at all points except the point at which the positive alternation passes through its maximum value. At this point the DC and AC values are equal. This point on the sine wave is referred to as the maximum or *peak value*.

During each complete cycle of AC there are always two maximum or peak values, one for the positive half-cycle and the other for the negative half-cycle. The difference between the peak positive value and the peak negative value is called the *peak-to-peak value* of the sine wave. This value is twice the maximum or peak value of the sine wave and is sometimes used for measurement of AC voltages. Note the difference between peak and peak-to-peak values in Figure 3-1-13. Usually alternating voltage and current are expressed in effective values (a term that will be studied later) rather than in peak-to-peak values.

Instantaneous Value

The *instantaneous value* of an alternating voltage or current is the value of voltage or current at one particular instant. The value may be zero if the particular instant is the point in the cycle at which the polarity of the voltage is changing. It may also be the same as the peak value, if the selected instant is the point in the cycle at which the voltage or current stops increasing and starts decreasing. There are actually an infinite number of instantaneous values between zero and the peak value.

Average Value

The *average value* of an alternating current or voltage is the average of all the instantaneous values during one alternation. Since the voltage increases from zero to peak value and decreases back to zero during one alternation, the average value must be some value between those two limits. It is possible to determine the average value by adding together a series of instantaneous values of the alternation (between 0° and 180°), and then dividing the sum by the number of instantaneous values used. The computation would show that one alternation of a sine wave has an average value equal to 0.636 times the peak value. The formula for average voltage is:

$$E_{avg} = 0.636 \times E_{max}$$

Where E_{avg} is the average voltage of one alternation, and E_{max} is the maximum or peak voltage. Similarly, the formula for average current is:

$$I_{avg} = 0.636 \times I_{max}$$

Where I_{avg} is the average current in one alternation, and I_{max} is the maximum or peak current.

Do not confuse the above definition of an average value with that of the average value of a complete cycle. Because the voltage is positive during one alternation and negative during the other alternation, the average value of the voltage values occurring during the complete cycle is zero.

Effective Value of a Sine Wave

E_{max}, E_{avg}, I_{max} and I_{avg} are values used in AC measurements. Another value used is the *effective value* of AC. This is the value of alternating voltage or current that will have the same effect on a resistance as a comparable value of direct voltage or current will have on the same resistance.

In an earlier discussion it was stated that when current flows in a resistance, heat is produced. When direct current flows in a resistance, the amount of electrical power converted into heat equals I^2R watts. However, since an alternating current having a maximum value of 1 ampere (A) does not maintain a constant value, the alternating current will not produce as much heat in the resistance as will a direct current of 1 A.

Figure 3-1-14 compares the heating effect of 1 A of DC to the heating effect of 1 A of AC.

Examine Figure 3-1-14A and Figure 3-1-14B and notice that the heat (159.26° F, or 70.7° C) produced by 1 A of alternating current is less than 71 percent of the heat produced by 1 A of direct current (212°F, or 100° C). This can be shown mathematically by the following formula:

$$\frac{\text{The heating effect of 1 maximum AC ampere}}{\text{The heating effect of 1 maximum DC ampere}} = \frac{70.7°C}{100°C} = 0.707$$

Therefore, for effective value of AC (I_{eff}) = 0.707 x I_{max}.

The rate at which heat is produced in a resistance forms a convenient basis for establishing an effective value of alternating current, and is known as the *heating effect* method. An alternating current is said to have an effective value of 1 A when it produces heat on a given resistance at the same rate as does 1 A of direct current.

The effective value of a sine wave of current can be computed to a fair degree of accuracy by taking equally spaced instantaneous values of current along the curve and extracting the square root of the average sum of the squared values.

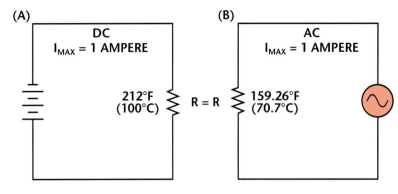

Figure 3-1-14. Heating effect of AC and DC

For this reason the effective value is often called the root-mean-square (RMS) value. Thus,

$$I_{eff} = \sqrt{\text{Average of the sum of the squares of } I_{inst}}$$

Stated another way, the effective or RMS value (I_{eff}) of a sine wave of current is .707 times the maximum value of current (I_{max}). Thus, I_{eff} = 0.707 x I_{max}. When I_{eff} is known, the technician can find the maximum current by using the formula I_{max} = 1.414 x I_{eff}. A common question at this point is, "Where did the constant 1.414 come from?" To find out, examine Figure 3-1-14 again and read the following explanation. Assume that the DC in Figure 3-1-14A is maintained at 1 A and the resistor temperature is 212°F (100° C). Also assume that the AC in Figure 3-1-14B is increased until the temperature of the resistor is 212°F (100° C). At this point it is found that a maximum AC value of 1.414 A is required in order to have the same heating effect as direct current. Therefore, in the AC circuit the maximum current required is 1.414 times the effective current. It is important to remember the above relationship and that the effective value (I_{eff}) of any sine wave of current is always .707 times the maximum value (I_{max}).

Since alternating current is caused by an alternating voltage, the ratio of the effective value of voltage to the maximum value of voltage is the same as the ratio of the effective value of current to the maximum value of current. Stated in another way, the effective or RMS value (E_{eff}) of a sine wave of voltage is 0.707 times the maximum value of voltage (E_{max}).

When an alternating current or voltage value is specified in any text (book or diagram), the value is an effective value unless otherwise stated. Also remember that all meters, unless marked to the contrary, are calibrated to indicate effective values of current and voltage

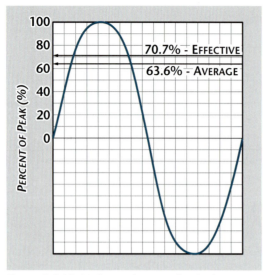

Figure 3-1-15. Various values used to indicate sine-wave amplitude

Figure 3-1-15 shows the relationship between the various values used to indicate sine wave amplitude. Review the values to ensure a full understanding of what each value indicated.

Sine Waves in Phase

When a sine wave of voltage is applied to a resistance, the resulting current is also a sine wave. This follows Ohm's law, which states that current is directly proportional to the applied voltage. Now examine Figure 3-1-16. Notice that the sine wave of voltage and the resulting sine wave of current are plotted on the same time axis. Notice also that as the voltage increases in a positive direction, the current increases along with it, and that when the voltage reverses direction, the current also reverses direction. When two sine waves, such as those represented in Figure 3-1-16, are precisely in step with one another, they are said to be *in phase*. To be in phase, the two sine waves must go through their maximum and minimum points at the same time and in the same direction.

In some circuits, several sine waves can be in phase with each other. Thus, it is possible to have two or more voltage drops in phase with each other and also be in phase with the circuit current.

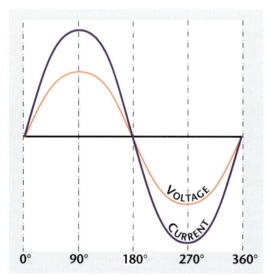

Figure 3-1-16. In-phase condition of current and voltage

Sine Waves out of Phase

Figure 3-1-17 shows voltage wave E_1, which is considered to start at 0° (Time 1). As E_1 reaches its positive peak, voltage wave E_2 starts its rise (Time 2). Since these voltage waves do not go through their maximum and minimum points at the same instant, a phase difference exists between the two waves. The two waves are said to be *out of phase*. For the two waves in Figure 3-1-17 the phase difference is 90°.

To further describe the phase relationship between two sine waves, the terms *lead* and *lag* are used. The amount by which one sine wave leads or lags another sine wave is measured in degrees. Refer again to Figure 3-1-17. Observe that wave E_2 starts 90° later in time than wave E_1. This relationship can be described by saying that wave E_1 leads wave E_2 by 90°, or that wave E_2 lags wave E_1 by 90°. Either statement is correct; it is the phase relationship between the two sine waves that is important.

It is possible for one sine wave to lead or lag another sine wave by any number of degrees, except 0° or 360°. When the latter condition exists, the two waves are said to be in phase. Thus, two sine waves that differ in phase by 450° are actually out of phase with each other, whereas two sine waves that differ in phase by 3600° are considered to be in phase.

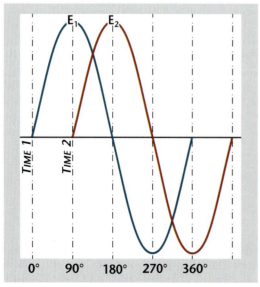

Figure 3-1-17. Voltage waves 90° out of phase

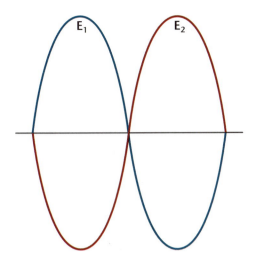

Figure 3-1-18. Voltage waves 180° out of phase

A phase relationship that is quite common is shown in Figure 3-1-18. Notice that the two waves illustrated differ in phase by 180°. Notice also that although the waves pass through their maximum and minimum values at the same time, their instantaneous voltages are always of opposite polarity. If two such waves exist across the same component, and the waves are of equal amplitude, they cancel each other. When they have different amplitudes, the resultant wave has the same polarity as the larger wave and has an amplitude equal to the difference between the amplitudes of the two waves.

To determine the phase difference between two sine waves, locate the points on the time axis where the two waves cross the time axis traveling in the same direction. The number of degrees between the crossing points is the phase difference. The wave that crosses the axis at the later time (to the right on the time axis) is said to lag the other wave.

Ohm's Law in AC Circuits

Many AC circuits contain resistance only. The rules for these circuits are the same rules that apply to DC circuits. Resistors, lamps and heating elements are examples of resistive elements. When an AC circuit contains only resistance, Ohm's law, Kirchhoff's law, and the various rules that apply to voltage, current and power in a DC circuit also apply to the AC circuit. The Ohm's law formula for an AC circuit can be stated as:

$$I_{eff} = \frac{E_{eff}}{R} \quad \text{or} \quad I = \frac{E}{R}$$

Remember, unless otherwise stated, all AC voltage and current values are given as effective values. The formula for Ohm's law can also be stated as:

$$I_{avg} = \frac{E_{avg}}{R} \quad \text{or} \quad I_{max} = \frac{E_{max}}{R}$$

$$I_{peak\text{-}to\text{-}peak} = \frac{E_{peak\text{-}to\text{-}peak}}{R}$$

The important thing to keep in mind is: do not mix AC values. When solving for effective values, all values used in the formula must be effective values. Similarly, when solving for average values, all values used must be average values. This point should be clearer after working the following problem: A series circuit consists of two resistors—$R_1 = 5$ ohms (Ω) and $R_2 = 15\Omega$—and an alternating voltage source of 120 V. What is I_{avg}?

Given:

$R_1 = 5\Omega$
$R_2 = 15\Omega$
$E_s = 120$ V

Solution: First solve for total resistance R_T

$R_T = R_1 + R_2$
$R_T = 5\Omega + 15\Omega$
$R_T = 20\Omega$

The alternating voltage is assumed to be an effective value (since it is not specified to be otherwise). Apply the Ohm's law formula.

$$I_{eff} = \frac{E_{eff}}{R}$$

$$I_{eff} = \frac{120 \text{ V}}{20\Omega}$$

$$I_{eff} = 6 \text{ A}$$

The problem, however, asked for the average value of current (I_{avg}). To convert the effective value of current to the average value of current, first determine the peak or maximum value of current, I_{max}.

$I_{max} = 1.414 \times I_{eff}$
$I_{max} = 1.414 \times 6$ A
$I_{max} = 8.484$ A

Now find I_{avg}. Just substitute 8.484 A in the I_{avg} formula and solve for I_{avg}.

$I_{avg} = 0.636 \times I_{max}$
$I_{avg} = 0.636 \times 8.484$ A
$I_{avg} = 5.4$ A (rounded off to one decimal place)

Remember, the Ohm's law formulas can be used to solve any purely resistive AC circuit problem. Use the formulas in the same manner as used when solving a DC circuit problem.

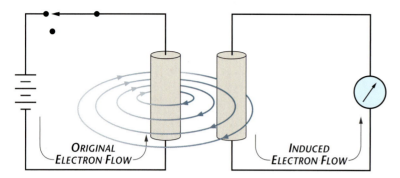

Figure 3-2-1. Generation of an emf in an electrical conductor

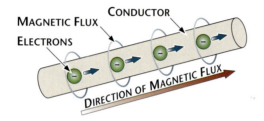

Figure 3-2-2. Movement of magnetic lines of flux

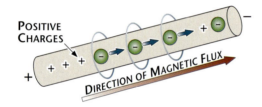

Figure 3-2-3. Electron movement in a conductor

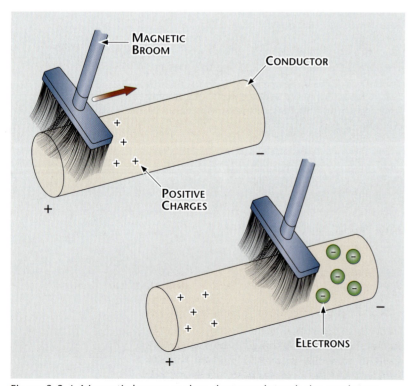

Figure 3-2-4. Magnetic broom pushes electrons through the conductor

Section 2:
Inductance

The study of inductance presents a very challenging but rewarding segment of electricity. It is challenging in the sense that, at first, it will seem that new concepts are being introduced. Realize however, that these "new concepts" are merely extensions and enlargements of fundamental principles that were previously learned in the study of magnetism and electron physics. The study of inductance is rewarding in the sense that a thorough understanding of it will enable the student to acquire a working knowledge of electrical circuits more rapidly.

Characteristics of Inductance

Inductance is the characteristic of an electrical circuit that opposes the starting, stopping or a change in value of current. The above statement is of such importance to the study of inductance that it bears repeating: Inductance is the characteristic of an electrical conductor that opposes a change in current. The symbol for inductance is L and the basic unit of inductance is the henry (H). One henry is equal to the inductance required to induce 1 V in an inductor by a change of current of 1 A per second.

It is not necessary to look far to find a physical analogy of inductance. Anyone who has ever had to push a heavy load (say, a wheelbarrow or a car) is aware that it takes more work to start the load moving than it does to keep it moving. Once the load is moving, it is easier to keep the load moving than to stop it again. This is because the load possesses the property of *inertia*. Inertia is the characteristic of mass that opposes a change in velocity. Inductance has the same effect on current in an electrical circuit as inertia has on the movement of a mechanical object. It requires more energy to start or stop current than it does to keep it flowing.

Electromotive Force (emf)

This text has discussed that an electromotive force is developed whenever there is relative motion between a magnetic field and a conductor.

Electromotive force is a difference of potential or voltage that exists between two points in an electrical circuit. In generators and inductors, the emf is developed by the action between the magnetic field and the electrons in a conductor. This is shown in Figure 3-2-1.

When a magnetic field moves through a stationary metallic conductor, electrons are dislodged from their orbits. The electrons move in a direction determined by the movement of the magnetic lines of flux (Figure 3-2-2).

The electrons move from one area of the conductor into another area. The area that the electrons moved from has fewer negative charges (electrons) and becomes positively charged. The area the electrons move into becomes negatively charged (Figure 3-2-3).

The difference between the charges in the conductor is equal to a difference of potential (or voltage). This voltage caused by the moving magnetic field is called electromotive force (emf).

In simple terms, the action of a moving magnetic field on a conductor can be compared to the action of a broom. Consider the moving magnetic field to be a moving broom. As the magnetic broom moves along (through) the conductor, it gathers up and pushes electrons before it, as shown in Figure 3-2-4.

The area from which electrons are moved becomes positively charged, while the area into which electrons are moved becomes negatively charged. The potential difference between these two areas is the emf.

Self-Inductance

Even a perfectly straight length of conductor has some inductance. As shown previously, current in a conductor produces a magnetic field surrounding the conductor. When the current changes, the magnetic field changes. This causes relative motion between the magnetic field and the conductor, and an emf is induced in the conductor. This emf is called a *self-induced emf* because it is induced in the conductor carrying the current. The emf produced by this moving magnetic field is also referred to as *counter electromotive force (cemf)*. The polarity of the cemf is in the opposite direction to the applied voltage of the conductor. The overall effect will be to oppose a change in current magnitude. This effect is summarized by Lenz's law: The induced emf in any circuit is always in a direction to oppose the effect that produces it.

If the shape of the conductor is changed to form a loop, then the electromagnetic field around each portion of the conductor cuts across some other portion of the same conductor. This is shown in its simplest form in Figure 3-2-5. A length of conductor is looped so that two portions of the conductor lie next to each other. These portions are labeled conductor 1 and conductor 2. When the switch

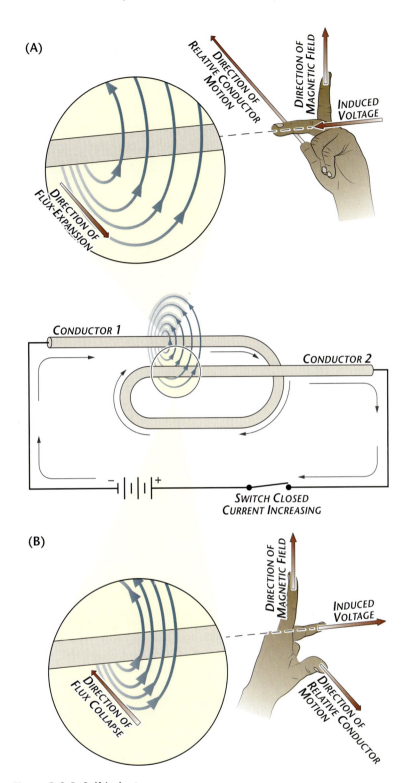

Figure 3-2-5. Self-inductance

is closed, current (electron flow) in the conductor produces a magnetic field around all portions of the conductor. For simplicity, the magnetic field (expanding lines of flux) is shown in a single plane perpendicular to both conductors. Although the expanding field of flux originates at the same time in both conductors, it is considered as originating in conductor 1 and its effect on conductor

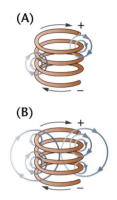

Figure 3-2-6. Inductance

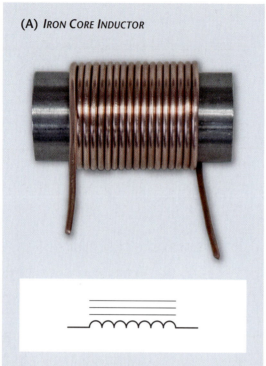

(A) IRON CORE INDUCTOR

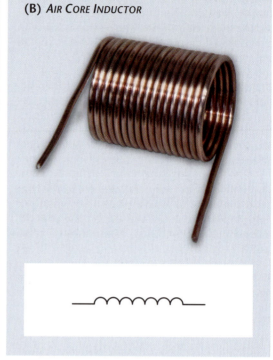

(B) AIR CORE INDUCTOR

Figure 3-2-7. Inductor types and schematic symbols

2 will be explained. With increasing current, the flux field expands outward from conductor 1, cutting across a portion of conductor 2. This results in an induced emf in conductor 2, as shown by the dashed arrow. Note that the induced emf is in the opposite direction to (in opposition to) the battery current and voltage, as stated in Lenz's law.

The direction of this induced voltage may be determined by applying the left-hand rule for generators. This rule is applied to a portion of conductor 2 that is "lifted" and enlarged for this purpose in Figure 3-2-5A. This rule states that if the user points the thumb of the left hand in the direction of relative motion of the conductor and the index finger in the direction of the magnetic field, the middle finger, extended as shown, will now indicate the direction of the induced current, which will generate the induced voltage (cemf) as shown.

In Figure 3-2-5B, the same section of conductor 2 is shown after the switch has been opened. The flux field is collapsing. Applying the left-hand rule in this case shows that the reversal of flux movement has caused a reversal in the direction of the induced voltage. The induced voltage is now in the same direction as the battery voltage. The most important thing to note is that the self-induced voltage opposes both changes in current. That is, when the switch is closed, this voltage delays the initial buildup of current by opposing the battery voltage. When the switch is opened, it keeps the current flowing in the same direction by aiding the battery voltage.

From the above explanation, it can be seen that when a current is building up it produces an expanding magnetic field. This field induces an emf in the direction opposite to the actual flow of current. This induced emf opposes the growth of the current and the growth of the magnetic field. If the increasing current had not set up a magnetic field, there would have been no opposition to its growth. The whole reaction, or opposition, is caused by the creation or collapse of the magnetic field, the lines of which as they expand or contract cut across the conductor and develop the cemf.

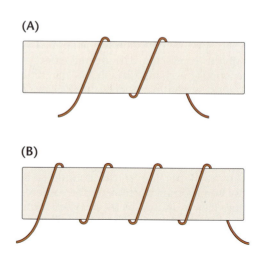

Figure 3-2-8. Inductance factor (turns)

Since all circuits have conductors in them, it can be assumed that all circuits have inductance. However, inductance has its greatest effect only when there is a change in current. Inductance does *not* oppose current, only a *change* in current. Where current is constantly changing as in an AC circuit, inductance has more effect.

To increase the property of inductance, the conductor can be formed into a loop or coil. A coil is also called an *inductor*. Figure 3-2-6 shows a conductor formed into a coil. Current through one loop produces a magnetic field that encircles the loop in the direction, as shown in Figure 3-2-6A. As current increases, the magnetic field expands and cuts all the loops, as shown in Figure 3-2-6B. The current in one loop affects all other loops. The field cutting the other loop has the effect of increasing the opposition to a current change.

Inductors are classified according to core type. The *core* is the center of the inductor just as the core of an apple is the center of an apple. The inductor is made by forming a coil of wire around a core. The core material is normally one of two basic types: soft-iron or air. An iron-core inductor and its schematic symbol (which has lines across the top of it to indicate the presence of an iron core) are shown in Figure 3-2-7A. The air-core inductor may be nothing more than a coil of wire, but it is usually a coil formed around a hollow form of some nonmagnetic material such as cardboard. This material serves no purpose other than to hold the shape of the coil. An air-core inductor and its schematic symbol are shown in Figure 3-2-7B.

Factors Affecting Coil Inductance

There are several physical factors that affect the inductance of a coil. They include the number of turns in the coil, the diameter of the coil, the coil length, the type of material used in the core, and the number of layers of winding in the coils.

Inductance depends entirely upon the physical construction of the circuit, and can only be measured with special laboratory instruments. Of the factors mentioned, consider first how the number of turns affects the inductance of a coil. Figure 3-2-8 shows two coils. Coil A has two turns and coil B has four turns. In A, the flux field set up by one loop cuts one other loop. In B, the flux field set up by one loop cuts three other loops. Doubling the number of turns in the coil produces a field twice as strong, if the same current is used. A field twice as strong, cutting twice

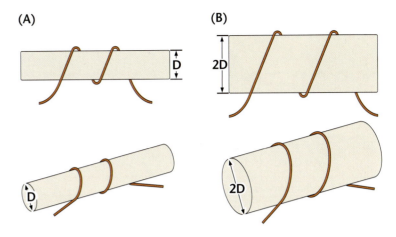

Figure 3-2-9. Inductance factor (diameter)

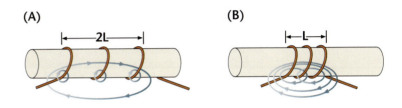

Figure 3-2-10. Inductance factor (coil length) closely wound

the number of turns, will induce four times the voltage. Therefore, it can be said that the inductance varies as the square of the number of turns.

The second factor is the coil diameter. Notice that the coil in Figure 3-2-9B has twice the diameter of the coil in Figure 3-2-9A. Physically, it requires more wire to construct a coil of large diameter than one of small diameter with an equal number of turns. Therefore, more lines of force exist to induce a cemf in the coil with the larger diameter. Actually, the inductance of a coil increases directly as the cross-sectional area of the core increases. Recall the formula for the area of a circle: $A = \pi r^2$. Doubling the radius of a coil increases the inductance by a factor of four.

The third factor that affects the inductance of a coil is the length of the coil. Figure 3-2-10 shows two examples of coil spacing. Coil A has three turns, rather widely spaced, making a relatively long coil. A coil of this type has few flux linkages due to the greater distance between each turn. Therefore, coil A has a relatively low inductance. Coil B has closely spaced turns, making a relatively short coil. This close spacing increases the flux linkage, increasing the inductance of the coil. Doubling the length of a coil while keeping the same number of turns halves the value of inductance.

(A) AIR CORE

(B) SOFT IRON CORE

Figure 3-2-11. Inductance factor (core material)

The fourth physical factor is the type of core material used with the coil. Figure 3-2-11 shows two coils: coil A has an air core, and coil B has a soft-iron core. The magnetic core of coil B is a better path for magnetic lines of force than is the nonmagnetic core of coil A. The soft-iron magnetic core's high permeability has less reluctance to the magnetic flux, resulting in more magnetic lines of force. This increase in the magnetic lines of force increases the number of lines of force cutting each loop of the coil, thus increasing the inductance of the coil. It should now be apparent that the inductance of a coil increases directly as the permeability of the core material increases.

Another way of increasing the inductance is to wind the coil in layers. Figure 3-2-12 shows three cores with different amounts of layering. The coil in Figure 3-2-12A is a poor inductor compared to the others in the figure because its turns are widely spaced and there is no layering. The flux movement, indicated by the red arrows, does not link effectively because there is only one layer of turns. A more inductive coil is shown in Figure 3-2-12B. The turns are closely spaced and the wire has been wound in two layers. The two layers link each other with a greater number of flux loops during all flux movements. Note that nearly all the turns, such as X, are next to four other turns (shaded green). This causes the flux linkage to be increased.

A coil can be made still more inductive by winding it in three layers, as shown in Figure 3-2-12C. The increased number of layers (cross-sectional area) improves flux linkage even more. Note that some turns, such as Y, lie directly next to six other turns (shaded green). In actual practice, layering can continue on through many more layers. The important fact to remember, however, is that the inductance of the coil increases with each layer added.

As shown, several factors affect the inductance of a coil, and all of these factors are variable. Many differently constructed coils can have the same inductance. The important information to remember, however, is that inductance is dependent upon the degree of linkage between the wire conductors and the electromagnetic field. In a straight length of conductor, there is very little flux linkage between one part of the conductor and another. Therefore, its inductance is extremely small. It was shown that conductors become much more inductive when they are wound into coils. This is true because there is maximum flux linkage between the conductor turns, which lie side by side in the coil.

Unit of Inductance

As stated before, the basic unit of inductance (L) is the *henry* (H), named after Joseph Henry, the co-discoverer with Faraday of the principle of electromagnetic induction. An inductor has an inductance of 1 H if an emf of 1 V is induced in the inductor when the current through the inductor is changing at the rate of 1 A per second. The relationship between the induced voltage, the inductance, and the rate of change of current with respect to time is stated mathematically as:

$$E_{ind} = L \frac{\Delta I}{\Delta t}$$

Where E_{ind} is the induced emf in volts; L is the inductance in henrys; and ΔI is the change in current in amperes occurring in Δt seconds. The symbol Δ (Greek delta), means "a change in ....". The henry is a large unit of inductance and is used with relatively large inductors. With small inductors, the millihenry (mH) is used. (A millihenry is equal to 1×10^{-3} H, and 1 H is equal to 1,000 mH.) For still smaller inductors,

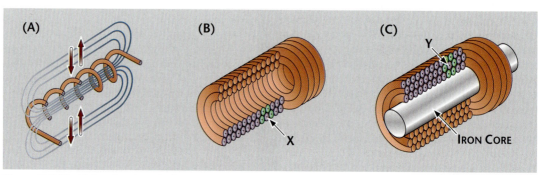

Figure 3-2-12. Coils of various inductances

the unit of inductance is the microhenry (μH). (A microhenry is equal to 1×10^{-6} H, and 1 H is equal to 1,000,000 μH.)

Growth and Decay of Current in an LR Series Circuit

When a battery is connected across a "pure" inductance, the current builds up to its final value at a rate determined by the battery voltage and the internal resistance of the battery. The current buildup is gradual because of the cemf generated by the self-inductance of the coil. When the current starts to flow, the magnetic lines of force move outward from the coil. These lines cut the turns of wire on the inductor and build up a cemf that opposes the emf of the battery. This opposition causes a delay in the time it takes the current to build up to a steady value. When the battery is disconnected, the lines of force collapse. Again these lines cut the turns of the inductor and build up an emf that tends to prolong the flow of current.

A voltage divider containing resistance and inductance may be connected in a circuit by means of a special switch, as shown in Figure 3-2-13A. Such a series arrangement is called an LR series circuit.

When switch S_1 is closed (as shown), a voltage (E_S) appears across the voltage divider. At this instant the current will attempt to increase to its maximum value. However, this instantaneous current change causes coil L to produce a back emf (cemf), which is opposite in polarity and almost equal to the emf of the source. This cemf opposes the rapid current change. Figure 3-2-13B shows that at the instant switch S_1 is closed, there is no measurable growth current (i_g), a minimum voltage drop is across resistor R, and maximum voltage exists across inductor L.

As current starts to flow, a voltage (e_R) appears across R, and the voltage across the inductor is reduced by the same amount. The fact that the voltage across the inductor (L) is reduced means that the growth current (i_g) is increased and consequently e_R is increased. Figure 3-2-13B shows that the voltage across the inductor (e_L) finally becomes zero when the growth current (i_g) stops increasing, while the voltage across the resistor (e_R) builds up to a value equal to the source voltage (E_S).

Electrical inductance is like mechanical inertia, and the growth of current in an inductive circuit can be likened to the acceleration of a boat on the surface of the water. The boat does not move at the instant a constant force is applied to it. At this instant all the applied force is used to overcome the inertia of the boat. Once the inertia is overcome the boat will start to move. After a while, the speed of the boat reaches its maximum value and the applied force is used up in overcoming the friction of the water against the hull.

When the battery switch (S_1) in the LR circuit of Figure 3-2-13A is closed, the rate of the current increase is maximum in the inductive circuit. At this instant all the battery voltage is used in overcoming the emf of self-induction, which is a maximum because the rate of change of current is maximum. Thus the battery voltage is equal to the drop across the inductor and the voltage across the resistor is zero. As time goes on more of the battery voltage appears across the resistor and less across the inductor. The rate of

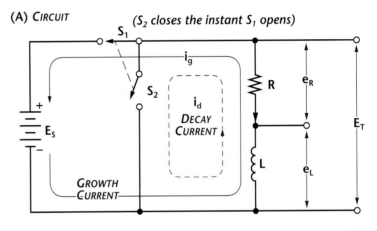

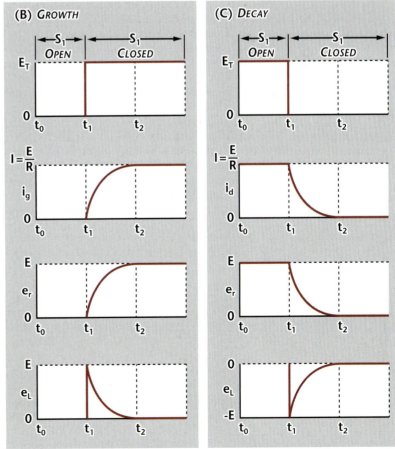

Figure 3-2-13. Growth and decay of current in an LR series circuit

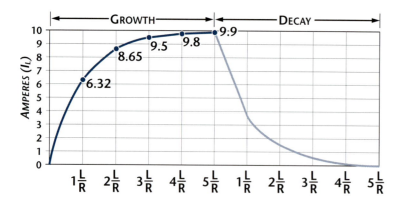

Figure 3-2-14. L/R time constant

change of current is less and the induced emf is less. As the steady-state condition of the current is approached, the drop across the inductor approaches zero and all of the battery voltage is "dropped" across the resistance of the circuit.

Thus the voltages across the inductor and the resistor change in magnitude during the period of growth of current the same way the force applied to the boat divides itself between the effects of inertia and friction. In both examples, the force is developed first across the inertia/inductive effect and finally across the friction/resistive effect.

Figure 3-2-13C shows that when switch S_2 is closed (i.e., source voltage E_S is removed from the circuit), the flux that has been established around the inductor (L) collapses through the windings. This induces a voltage e_L in the inductor that has a polarity opposite to E_S and is essentially equal to E_S in magnitude. The induced voltage causes decay current (i_d) to flow in resistor R in the same direction in which current was flowing originally (when S_1 was closed). A voltage (e_R) that is initially equal to the source voltage (E_S) is developed across R. The voltage across the resistor (e_R) rapidly falls to zero as the voltage across the inductor (e_L) falls to zero due to the collapsing flux.

Just as the example of the boat was used to explain the growth of current in a circuit, it can also be used to explain the decay of current in a circuit. When the force applied to the boat is removed, the boat still continues to move through the water for a while, eventually coming to a stop. This is because energy was being stored in the inertia of the moving boat. After a period of time the friction of the water overcomes the inertia of the boat, and the boat stops moving. Just as inertia of the boat stored energy, the magnetic field of an inductor stores energy. Because of this, even when the power source is removed, the stored energy of the magnetic field of the inductor tends to keep current flowing in the circuit until the magnetic field collapse.

L/R Time Constant

The L/R time constant is a valuable tool for use in determining the time required for current in an inductor to reach a specific value. As shown in Figure 3-2-14, one L/R time constant is the time required for the current in an inductor to increase to 63 percent (actually 63.2 percent) of the maximum current. Each time constant is equal to the time required for the current to increase by 63.2 percent of the difference in value between the current flowing in the inductor and the maximum current. Maximum current flows in the inductor after five L/R time constants are completed. The following example should clear up any confusion about time constants. Assume that maximum current in an LR circuit is 10 A. As covered previously, when the circuit is energized, it takes time for the current to go from zero to 10 A. When the first time constant is completed, the current in the circuit is equal to 63.2 percent of 10 A. Thus the amplitude of current at the end of one time constant is 6.32 A.

During the second time constant, current again increases by 63.2 percent (0.632) of the difference in value between the current flowing in the inductor and the maximum current. This difference is 10 A minus 6.32 A, or 3.68 A; 63.2 percent of 3.68 A is 2.32 A. This increase in current during the second time constant is added to that of the first time constant. Thus, upon completion of the second time constant, the amount of current in the LR circuit is 6.32 A plus 2.32 A, or 8.64 A.

During the third constant, current again increases:

10 A - 8.64 A = 1.36 A

1.36 A x 0.632 = 0.860 A

8.64 A + 0.860 A = 9.50 A

During the fourth time constant, current again increases:

10 A - 9.50 A = 0.5 A

0.5 A x 0.632 = 0.316 A

9.50 A + 0.316 A = 9.82 A

During the fifth constant, current increases as before:

10 A - 9.82 A = 0.18 A

0.18 A x 0.632 = 0.114 A

9.82 A + 0.114 A = 9.93 A

Thus, the current at the end of the fifth time constant is almost equal to 10 A, the maximum current. For all practical purposes the slight difference in value can be ignored.

When an LR circuit is de-energized, the circuit current decreases (decays) to zero in five time constants at the same rate that it previously increased. If the growth and decay of current in an LR circuit are plotted on a graph, the curve appears as shown in Figure 3-2-14. Notice that current increases and decays at the same rate in five time constants.

The value of the time constant in seconds is equal to the inductance in henrys divided by the circuit resistance in ohms.

The formula used to calculate one L/R time constant is:

$$\text{Time Constant (TC) in seconds} = \frac{L \text{ (in henrys)}}{R \text{ (in ohms)}}$$

Power Loss in an Inductor

Since an inductor (coil) consists of a number of turns of wire, and since all wire has some resistance, every inductor has a certain amount of resistance. Normally this resistance is small. It is usually neglected in solving various types of AC circuit problems because the reactance of the inductor (the opposition to alternating current, which will be discussed later) is so much greater than the resistance that the resistance has a negligible effect on the current.

However, since some inductors are designed to carry relatively large amounts of current, considerable power can be dissipated in the inductor even though the amount of resistance in the inductor is small. This power is wasted power and is called *copper loss*. The copper loss of an inductor can be calculated by multiplying the square of the current in the inductor by the resistance of the winding (I^2R).

In addition to copper loss, an iron-core coil (inductor) has two iron losses. These are called hysteresis loss and eddy-current loss. *Hysteresis loss* is due to power that is consumed in reversing the magnetic field of the inductor core each time the direction of current in the inductor changes. *Eddy-current loss* is due to heating of the core by circulating currents that are induced in the iron core by the magnetic field around the turns of the coil. These currents are called eddy currents and circulate within the iron core only.

All these losses dissipate power in the form of heat. Since this power cannot be returned to the electrical circuit, it is lost power.

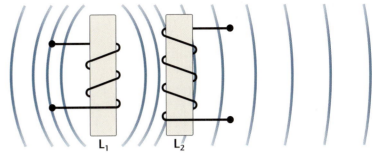
INDUCTORS CLOSE (LARGE MUTUAL INDUCTANCE)

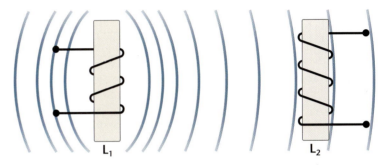
INDUCTORS FAR APART (SMALL MUTUAL INDUCTANCE)

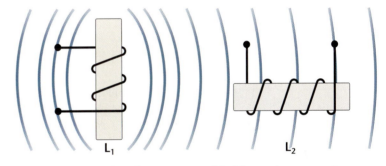
INDUCTOR AXES PERPENDICULAR (NO MUTUAL INDUCTANCE)

Figure 3-2-15. The effect of position of coils on mutual inductance (M)

Mutual Inductance

Whenever two coils are located so that the flux from one coil links with the turns of the other coil, a change of flux in one coil causes an emf to be induced in the other coil. This allows the energy from one coil to be transferred or coupled to the other coil. The two coils are said to be coupled or linked by the property of *mutual inductance* (M). The amount of mutual inductance depends on the relative positions of the two coils. This is shown in Figure 3-2-15. If the coils are separated a considerable distance, the amount of flux common to both coils is small and the mutual inductance is low. Conversely, if the coils are close together so that nearly all the flux of one coil links the turns of the other, the mutual inductance is high. The mutual inductance can be increased greatly by mounting the coils on a common iron core.

3-20 | Concepts of Alternating Current

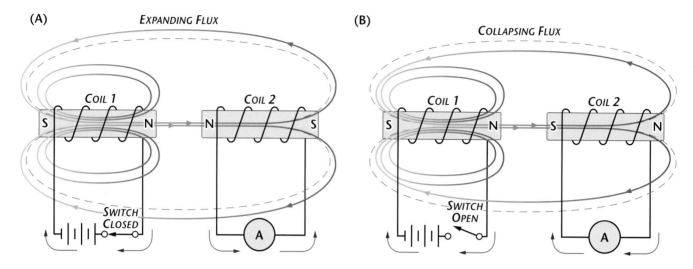

Figure 3-2-16. Mutual inductance

Two coils are placed close together as shown in Figure 3-2-16. Coil 1 is connected to a battery through switch S, and coil 2 is connected to an ammeter (A). When S is closed, as in Figure 3-2-16A, the current that flows in coil 1 sets up a magnetic field that links with coil 2, causing an induced voltage in coil 2 and a momentary deflection of the ammeter. When the current in coil 1 reaches a steady value, the ammeter returns to zero. If S is now opened, as in Figure 3-2-16B, the ammeter deflects momentarily in the opposite direction, indicating a momentary flow of current in the opposite direction in coil 2. This current in coil 2 is produced by the collapsing magnetic field of coil 1.

Factors Affecting Mutual Inductance

The mutual inductance of two adjacent coils is dependent upon the physical dimensions of the two coils, the number of turns in each coil, the distance between the two coils, the relative positions of the axes of the two coils, and the permeability of the cores.

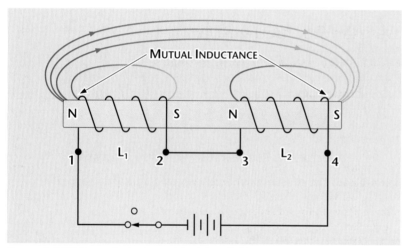

Figure 3-2-17. Series inductors with aiding fields

The coefficient of coupling between two coils is equal to the ratio of the flux cutting one coil to the flux originated in the other coil. If the two coils are so positioned with respect to each other so that all of the flux of one coil cuts all of the turns of the other, the coils are said to have a *unity coefficient of coupling*. It is never exactly equal to unity (1), but it approaches this value in certain types of coupling devices. If all of the flux produced by one coil cuts only half the turns of the other coil, the coefficient of coupling is 0.5. The coefficient of coupling is designated by the letter K.

The mutual inductance between two coils, L_1 and L_2, is expressed in terms of the inductance of each coil and the coefficient of coupling K. As a formula:

$$M = K\sqrt{L_1 L_2}$$

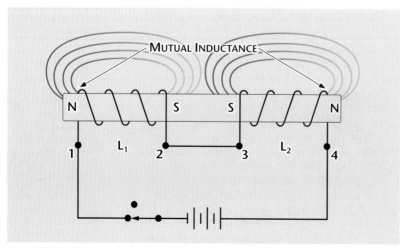

Figure 3-2-18. Series inductors with opposing fields

Where:

M = Mutual inductance in henrys
K = Coefficient of coupling
L_1, L_2 = Inductance of coil in henrys

EXAMPLE: One 10-H coil and one 20-H coil are connected in series and are physically close enough to each other so that their coefficient of coupling is 0.5. What is the mutual inductance between the coils?

Use the formula:

$M = K\sqrt{L_1 L_2}$
$M = 0.5\sqrt{(10H)(20H)}$
$M = 0.5\sqrt{200H}$
$M = .05 \times 14.14H$
$M = 7.07H$

Series Inductors Without Magnetic Coupling

When inductors are well shielded or are located far enough from one another, the effect of mutual inductance is negligible. If there is no mutual inductance (magnetic coupling) and the inductors are connected in series, the total inductance is equal to the sum of the individual inductances. As a formula:

$L_T = L_1 + L_2 + L_3 + ..L_n$

Where L_T is the total inductance; L_1, L_2 and L_3 are the inductances of L_1, L_2 and L_3; and L_n means that any number (n) of inductors may be used. The inductances of inductors in series are added together like the resistances of resistors in series.

Series Inductors with Magnetic Coupling

When two inductors in series are so arranged that the field of one links to the other, the combined inductance is determined as follows:

$L_T = L_1 + L_2 \pm 2M$
L_T = The total inductance
L_1, L_2 = The inductances of L_1, L_2
M = The mutual inductance between the two inductors

The plus sign is used with M when the magnetic fields of the two inductors are aiding each other, as shown in Figure 3-2-17. The minus sign is used with M when the magnetic field of the two inductors oppose each other, as shown in Figure 3-2-18. The factor 2M accounts for the influence of L_1 on L_2 and L_2 on L_1.

EXAMPLE: A 10-H coil is connected in series with a 5-H coil so the fields aid each other. Their mutual inductance is 7 H. What is the combined inductance of the coils?

Use the formula:

$L_T = L_1 + L_2 + 2M$
$L_T = 10H + 5H + 2(7H)$
$L_T = 29H$

Parallel Inductors Without Coupling

The total inductance (L_T) of inductors in parallel is calculated in the same manner that the total resistance of resistors in parallel is calculated, provided the coefficient of coupling between the coils is zero. Expressed mathematically:

$\frac{1}{L_T} = \frac{1}{L_1} + \frac{1}{L_2} + \frac{1}{L_3} .... + \frac{1}{L_n}$

Inductor Troubleshooting

In inductors there are only three possible faults:

- Open windings
- Short in the windings
- Short to the core

One thing to remember is that an inductor, in essence, is a conductor in a winding. A normal working inductor, when tested with an ohmmeter, shows a low resistance of around 2 to 3 Ω. If the windings are open, an infinite reading on the ohmmeter will result (Figure 3-2-19).

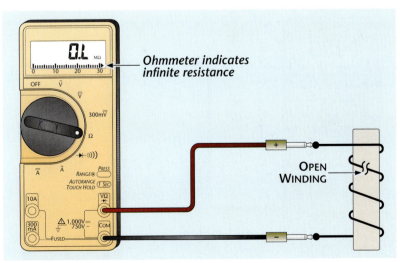

Figure 3-2-19. Ohmmeter showing infinite resistance

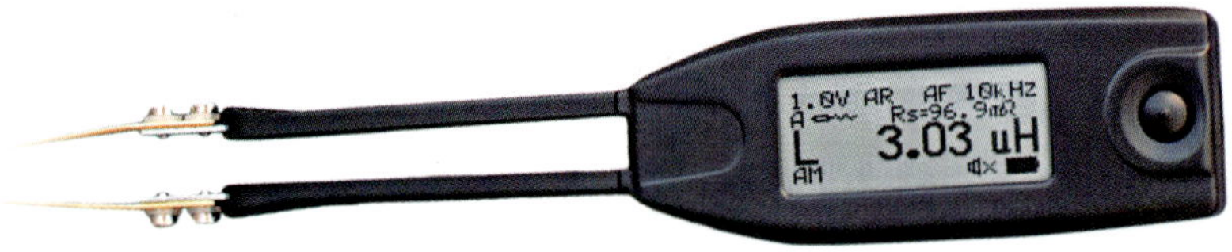

Figure 3-2-20. Digital inductance meter

The next possible problem is a short in the windings themselves. In this scenario, one winding could be shorted to another. Using an ohmmeter to measure the inductor, the reading will be lower than the normal reading of 2 to 3 Ω. Because the normal voltage is low to begin with, it may be difficult to detect. Another method to measure the inductor is to use a meter designed to detect inductance. (Figure 3-2-20) A shorted inductor can sometimes be caused by a breakdown in the inductor itself where the windings melt together.

The last possible issue is a short to the core. Like the short in windings, these can be caused by the melting of wire, but instead of melting together, they melt to the core. A multimeter can be used to determine if there is a short. Normally the core and coils are separate from each other and, therefore, read infinite resistance on the multimeter. If there is a short to the coil, the multimeter will indicate a very low reading of resistance (Figure 3-2-21).

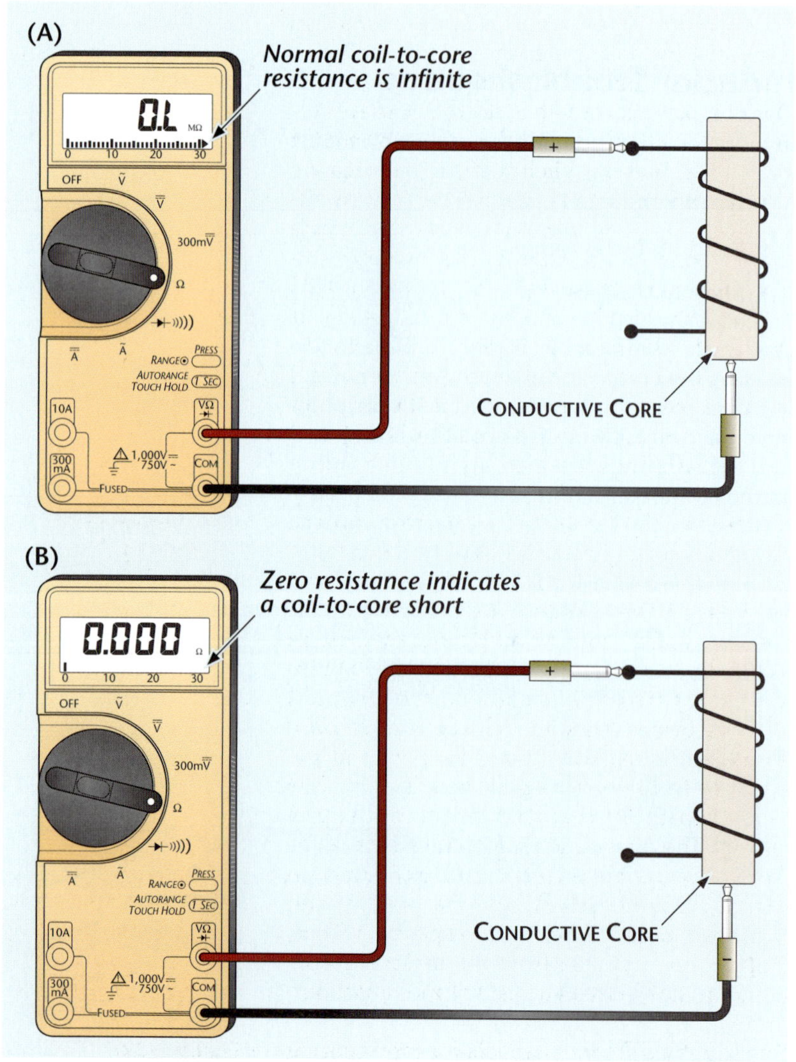

Section 3

Capacitance

In the previous section the text discussed that inductance is the property of a coil that causes electrical energy to be stored in a magnetic field about the coil. The energy is stored in such a way as to oppose any change in current. *Capacitance* is similar to inductance because it also causes storage of energy. A capacitor is a device that stores electrical energy in an electrostatic field. The energy is stored in such a way as to oppose any change in voltage. Just how capacitance opposes a change in voltage is explained below. However, it is first necessary to explain the principles of an electrostatic field as it is applied to capacitance.

The Electrostatic Field

As previously discussed, opposite electrical charges attract each other while like electrical charges repel each other. The reason for this is

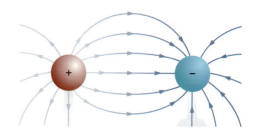

Figure 3-3-1. Direction of electric field around positive and negative charges

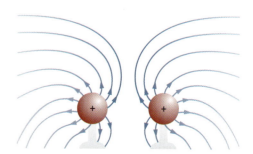

Figure 3-3-2. Field around two positively charged bodies

Figure 3-2-21. Resistance readings on a multimeter; (A) Normal, (B) Zero

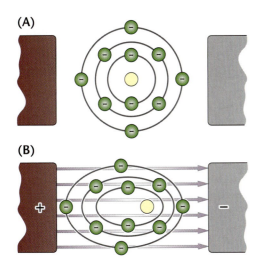

Figure 3-3-3. Distortion of electron orbital paths due to electrostatic force

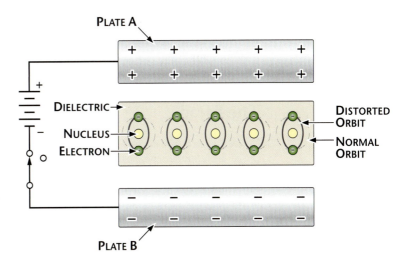

Figure 3-3-4. Distortion of electron orbits in a dielectric

the existence of an *electrostatic field*. Any charged particle is surrounded by invisible lines of force, called *electrostatic lines of force*. These lines of force have some interesting characteristics:

- They are polarized from positive to negative.
- They radiate from a charged particle in straight lines and do not form closed loops.
- They have the ability to pass through any known material.
- They have the ability to distort the orbits of tightly bound electrons.

Look at Figure 3-3-1. It represents two unlike charges surrounded by their electrostatic field. Because an electrostatic field is polarized positive to negative, arrows are shown radiating away from the positive charge and toward the negative charge. Stated another way, the field from the positive charge is pushing, while the field from the negative charge is pulling. The effect of the field is to push and pull the unlike charges together.

In Figure 3-3-2, two like charges are shown with their surrounding electrostatic field. The effect of the electrostatic field is to push the charges apart.

If two unlike charges are placed on opposite sides of an atom whose outermost electrons cannot escape their orbits, the orbits of the electrons are distorted, as shown in Figure 3-3-3. Figure 3-3-3A shows the normal orbit. Figure 3-3-3B shows the same orbit in the presence of charged particles. Since the electron is a negative charge, the positive charge attracts the electrons, pulling the electrons closer to the positive charge. The negative charge repels the electrons, pushing them further from the negative charge. It is this ability of an electrostatic field to attract and to repel charges that allows the capacitor to store energy.

The Simple Capacitor

A simple capacitor consists of two metal plates separated by an insulating material called a *dielectric*, as illustrated in Figure 3-3-4. Note that one plate is connected to the positive terminal of a battery; the other plate is connected through a closed switch (S_1) to the negative terminal of the battery. Remember, an insulator is a material whose electrons cannot easily escape their orbits. Due to the battery voltage, plate A is charged positively and plate B is charged negatively. (How this happens is explained later in this chapter.) Thus an electrostatic field is set up between the positive and negative plates. The electrons on the negative plate (B) are attracted to the positive charges on the positive plate (A).

Notice that the orbits of the electrons in the dielectric material are distorted by the electrostatic field. The distortion occurs because the electrons in the dielectric are attracted to the top plate while being repelled from the bottom plate. When switch S_1 is opened, the battery is removed from the circuit and the charge is retained by the capacitor. This occurs because the dielectric material is an insulator, and the electrons in the bottom plate (negative charge) have no path to reach the top plate (positive charge). The distorted orbits of the atoms of the dielectric plus the electrostatic force of attraction between the two plates hold the positive and negative charges in their original position. Thus, the energy that came from the battery is now stored in the electrostatic field of the capacitor.

Two slightly different symbols for representing a capacitor are shown in Figure 3-3-5. Notice

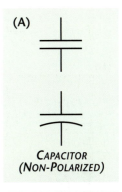

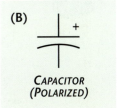

Figure 3-3-5. Capacitor symbols

that each symbol is composed of two plates separated by a space that represents the dielectric. The curved plate in Figure 3-3-5B indicates that the plate should be connected to a negative polarity.

The Farad

Capacitance is measured in units called *farads* (F). A 1-F capacitor stores 1 coulomb (a unit of charge (Q) equal to 6.28×10^{18} electrons) when a potential of 1 V is applied across the terminals of the capacitor. This can be expressed by the formula:

$$C \text{ (farads)} = \frac{Q \text{ (coulombs)}}{E \text{ (volts)}}$$

The farad is a very large unit of measurement of capacitance. For convenience, the microfarad or the picofarad is used. One microfarad (μF) is equal to 0.000001 farad (1×10^{-6} F), and 1 picofarad (pF) is equal to 0.000000000001 farad (1.0×10^{-12} F). Capacitance is a physical property of the capacitor and does not depend on circuit characteristics of voltage, current and resistance. A given capacitor always has the same value of capacitance in one circuit as in any other circuit.

Factors Affecting the Value of Capacitance

The value of capacitance of a capacitor depends on three factors:

- Plate area. The area of the plates affects the value of capacitance in the same manner that the size of a container affects the amount of water that can be held by the container. A capacitor with a large plate area can store more charges than a capacitor with a small plate area. Simply stated, the larger the plate area, the larger the capacitance.

- Between the plates. Electrostatic lines of force are strongest when the charged particles that create them are close together. When the charged particles are moved further apart, the lines of force weaken, and the ability to store a charge decreases.

- Dielectric constant. The dielectric constant applies to the insulating material between the plates of a capacitor. The various insulating materials used as the dielectric in a capacitor differ in their ability to respond to (pass) electrostatic lines of force. A dielectric material, or insulator, is rated as to its ability to respond to electrostatic lines of force in terms of a figure called the dielectric constant. A dielectric material with a high dielectric constant is a better insulator than a dielectric material with a low dielectric constant. Dielectric constants for some common materials are given in Table 3-3-1.

Notice the dielectric constant for a vacuum. Since a vacuum is the standard of reference, it is assigned a constant of 1. The dielectric constants of all materials are compared to that of a vacuum. Since the dielectric constant of air has been determined to be approximately the same as that of a vacuum, the dielectric constant of air is also considered to be equal to 1.

The formula used to compute the value of capacitance is:

$$C = 0.2249 \left(\frac{KA}{d}\right)$$

Where:

C = capacitance in picofarads
A = area of one plate, in square inches
d = distance between the plates, in inches
K = dielectric constant of the insulating material
0.2249 = a constant resulting from conversion from metric to English units.

EXAMPLE: Find the capacitance of a parallel plate capacitor with paraffin paper as the dielectric.

Given:

K = 3.5
d = 0.05 inch
A = 12 square inches

MATERIAL	CONSTANT
Vacuum	1.0000
Air	1.0006
Paraffin	3.5
Glass	5 to 10
Mica	3 to 6
Rubber	2.5 to 35
Wood	2.5 to 8
Glycerine (15°C)	56
Petrolem	2
Pure Water	81

Table 3-3-1. Dielectric constants for common materials

SOLUTION:

$$C = 0.2249 \left(\frac{KA}{d}\right)$$

$$C = 0.2249 \left(\frac{3.5 \times 12}{0.05}\right)$$

$$C = 189 \text{ picofarads}$$

By examining the above formula, it can be seen that capacitance varies directly as the dielectric constant and the area of the capacitor plates, and inversely as the distance between the plates.

Voltage Rating of Capacitors

In selecting or substituting a capacitor for use, consideration must be given to the value of capacitance desired and the amount of voltage to be applied across the capacitor. If the voltage applied across the capacitor is too great, the dielectric will break down and arcing will occur between the capacitor plates. When this happens the capacitor becomes a short-circuit and the flow of direct current through it can cause damage to other electronic parts. Each capacitor has a voltage rating (a working voltage) that should not be exceeded.

The working voltage of the capacitor is the maximum voltage that can be steadily applied without danger of breaking down the dielectric. The working voltage depends on the type of material used as the dielectric and on the thickness of the dialectic. (A high-voltage capacitor that has a thick dielectric must have a relatively large plate area in order to have the same capacitance as a similar low-voltage capacitor with a thin dielectric.) The working voltage also depends on the applied frequency because the losses, and the resultant heating effect, increase as the frequency increases.

A capacitor with a voltage rating of 500 V DC cannot be safely subjected to an alternating voltage or a pulsating direct voltage having an effective value of 500 V. Since an alternating voltage of 500 R (RMS) has a peak value of 707 V, a capacitor to which it is applied should have a working voltage of at least 750 V. In practice, a capacitor should be selected so that its working voltage is at least 50 percent greater than the highest effective voltage to be applied to it.

Capacitor Losses

Power loss in a capacitor may be attributed to dielectric hysteresis and dielectric leakage. *Dielectric hysteresis* may be defined as an effect in a dielectric material similar to the hysteresis found in a magnetic material. It is the result of changes in orientation of electron orbits in the

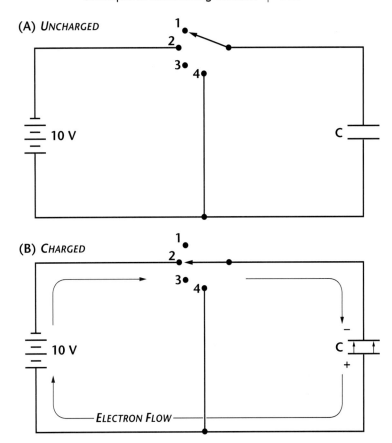

Figure 3-3-6. Charging a capacitor

dielectric because of the rapid reversals of the polarity of the line voltage. The amount of power loss due to dielectric hysteresis depends upon the type of dielectric used. A vacuum dielectric has the smallest power loss.

Dielectric leakage occurs in a capacitor as the result of leakage current through the dielectric. Normally it is assumed that the dielectric will effectively prevent the flow of current through the capacitor. Although the resistance of the dielectric is extremely high, a minute amount of current does flow. Ordinarily this current is so small that for all practical purposes it is ignored. However, if the leakage through the dielectric is abnormally high, there will be a rapid loss of charge and an overheating of the capacitor.

The power loss of a capacitor is determined by loss in the dielectric. If the loss is negligible and the capacitor returns the total charge to the circuit, it is considered to be a perfect capacitor with a power loss of zero.

Charging a Capacitor

To better understand the action of a capacitor in conjunction with other components, the charge and discharge actions of a purely capacitive circuit are analyzed first. Assume the capacitor and voltage source shown in Figure 3-3-6 are assumed to be perfect (no internal resistance), although this is impossible in practice.

In Figure 3-3-6A, an uncharged capacitor is shown connected to a four-position switch. With the switch in position 1 the circuit is open and no voltage is applied to the capacitor. Initially each plate of the capacitor is a neutral body and until a difference of potential is impressed across the capacitor, no electrostatic field can exist between the plates.

To charge the capacitor, the switch must be thrown to position 2, which places the capacitor across the terminals of the battery. Under the assumed perfect conditions, the capacitor would reach full charge instantaneously. However, the charging action is spread out over a period of time in the following discussion so that a step-by-step analysis can be made.

At the instant the switch is thrown to position 2 (Figure 3-3-6B), a displacement of electrons occurs simultaneously in all parts of the circuit. This electron displacement is directed away from the negative terminal and toward the positive terminal of the source (the battery). A brief surge of current will flow as the capacitor charges.

If it were possible to analyze the motion of the individual electrons in this surge of charging current, the following action (Figure 3-3-7) would be observed.

At the instant the switch is closed, the positive terminal of the battery extracts an electron from the bottom conductor. The negative terminal of the battery forces an electron into the top conductor. At this same instant an electron is forced into the top plate of the capacitor and another is pulled from the bottom plate. Thus, in every part of the circuit a clockwise displacement of electrons occurs simultaneously.

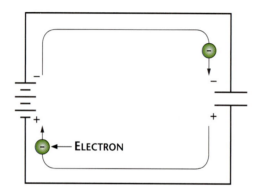

Figure 3-3-7. Electron motion during charge

As electrons accumulate on the top plate of the capacitor and others depart from the bottom plate, a difference of potential develops across the capacitor. Each electron forced onto the top plate makes that plate more negative, while each electron removed from the bottom causes the bottom plate to become more positive. Notice that the polarity of the voltage that builds up across the capacitor is such as to oppose the source voltage. The source voltage (emf) forces current around the circuit in Figure 3-3-7 in a clockwise direction. The emf developed across the capacitor, however, has a tendency to force the current in a counterclockwise direction, opposing the source emf. As the capacitor continues to charge, the voltage across the capacitor rises until it is equal to the source voltage. Once the capacitor voltage equals the source voltage, the two voltages balance one another and current ceases to flow in the circuit.

In studying the charging process of a capacitor, be aware that no current flows through the capacitor. The material between the plates of the capacitor must be an insulator. However, to an observer stationed at the source or along one of the circuit conductors, the action has all the appearances of a true flow of current, even though the insulating material between the plates of the capacitor prevents the current from having a complete path. The current that appears to flow through a capacitor is called displacement current.

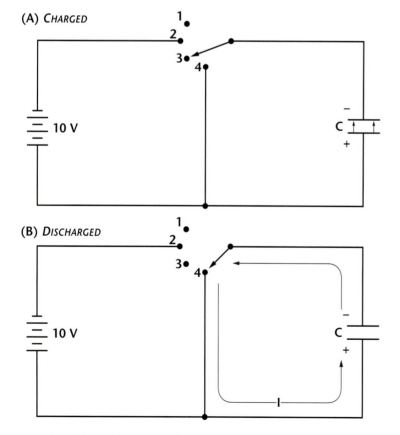

Figure 3-3-8. Discharging a capacitor

When a capacitor is fully charged and the source voltage is equaled by the counter electromotive force (cemf) across the capacitor, the electrostatic field between the plates of the capacitor is maximum. (Look again at Figure 3-3-4) Since the electrostatic field is maximum the energy stored in the dielectric is also maximum.

If the switch is now opened as shown in Figure 3-3-8A, the electrons on the upper plate are isolated. The electrons on the top plate are attracted to the charged bottom plate. Because the dielectric is an insulator, the electrons cannot cross it to the bottom plate. The charges on both plates will be effectively trapped by the electrostatic field and the capacitor will remain charged indefinitely. Note that at this point the insulating dielectric material in a practical capacitor is not perfect and a small leakage current will flow through the dielectric. This current will eventually dissipate the charge. However, a high-quality capacitor may hold its charge for a month or more.

To review briefly, when a capacitor is connected across a voltage source, a surge of charging current flows. This charging current develops a cemf across the capacitor that opposes the applied voltage. When the capacitor is fully charged, the cemf is equal to the applied voltage and charging current ceases. At full charge, the electrostatic field between the plates is at maximum intensity and the energy stored in the dielectric is maximum. If the charged capacitor is disconnected from the source, the charge will be retained for some period of time. The length of time the charge is retained depends on the amount of leakage current present. Since electrical energy is stored in the capacitor, a charged capacitor can act as a source emf.

Discharging a Capacitor

To discharge a capacitor, the charges on the two plates must be neutralized. This is accomplished by providing a conducting path between the two plates as shown in Figure 3-3-8B. With the switch in position 4, the excess electrons on the negative plate can flow to the positive plate and neutralize its charge. When the capacitor is discharged, the distorted orbits of the electrons in the dielectric return to their normal positions and the stored energy is returned to the circuit. It is important to note that a capacitor does *not* consume power. The energy the capacitor draws from the source is recovered when the capacitor is discharged.

Charge and Discharge of an RC Series Circuit

Ohm's law states that the voltage across a resistance is equal to the current through the resistance times the value of the resistance. This means that a voltage is developed across a resistance only when current flows through the resistance.

A capacitor is capable of storing or holding a charge of electrons. When uncharged, both plates of the capacitor contain essentially the same number of free electrons. When charged, one plate contains more free electrons than the other plate. The difference in the number of electrons is a measure of the charge on the capacitor. The accumulation of this charge builds up a voltage across the terminals of the capacitor, and the charge continues to increase until this voltage equals the applied voltage. The charge in a capacitor is related to the capacitance and voltage as follows:

$$Q = CE$$

Where Q is the charge in coulombs, C the capacitance in farads, and E is the emf across the capacitor in volts.

Charge Cycle

A voltage divider containing resistance and capacitance is connected in a circuit by means of a switch, as shown in Figure 3-3-9A. Such a series arrangement is called an RC series circuit.

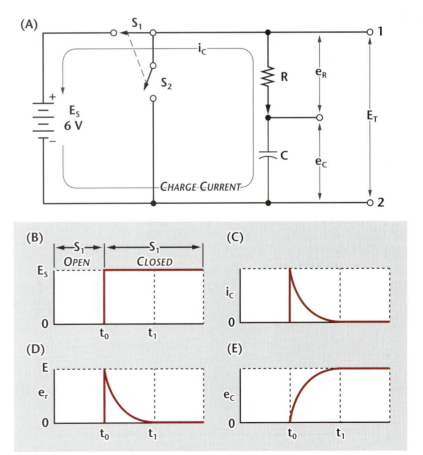

Figure 3-3-9. Charge of an RC series circuit

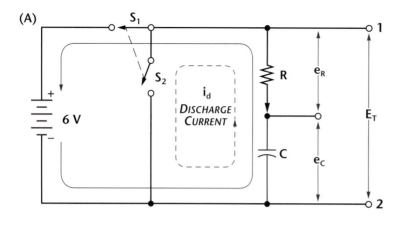

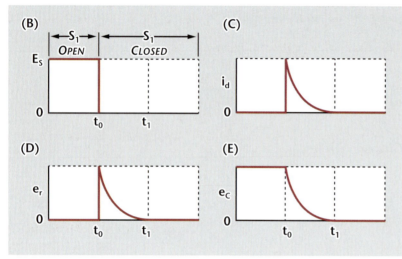

Figure 3-3-10. Discharge of an RC series circuit

capacitor. At time t_0 the current flowing to the capacitor is maximum. Thus, the voltage drop across the resistor is maximum (E = IR). As time progresses toward time t_1, the current flowing to the capacitor steadily decreases and causes the voltage developed across the resistor (R) to steadily decrease. When time t_1 is reached, current flowing to the capacitor is stopped and the voltage developed across the resistor has decreased to zero.

Remember that capacitance opposes a change in voltage. This is shown by comparing graph B to graph E. In graph B the voltage changed instantly from 0 to 6 V across the circuit, while the voltage developed across the capacitor in graph E took the entire time interval from time t_0 to time t_1 to reach 6 V. The reason for this is that in the first instant at time t_0, maximum current flows through R and the entire circuit voltage is dropped across the resistor. The voltage impressed across the capacitor at t_0 is 0 Vs. As time progresses toward t_1, the decreasing current causes progressively less voltage to be dropped across the resistor (R), and more voltage builds up across the capacitor. At time t_1, the voltage felt across the capacitor is equal to the source voltage (6 V), and the voltage dropped across the resistor (R) is zero. This is the complete charge cycle of the capacitor.

As may have been noticed, the processes that take place in the time interval t_0 to t_1 in a series RC circuit are exactly opposite to those in a series LR circuit.

For comparison, the important points of the charge cycle of RC and LR circuits are summarized in Table 3-3-2.

Discharge Cycle

In Figure 3-3-10 at time t_0, the capacitor is fully charged. When S_1 is open and S_2 closes, the capacitor discharge cycle starts. At the first instant, circuit voltage attempts to go from source potential (6 V) to zero volts, as shown in graph B. Remember, though, the capacitor during the charge cycle has stored energy in an electrostatic field.

Because S_2 is closed at the same time S_1 is open, the stored energy of the capacitor now has a path for current to flow. At t_0, discharge current (i_d) from the bottom plate of the capacitor through the resistor (R) to the top plate of the capacitor (C) is maximum. As time progresses toward t_1, the discharge current steadily decreases until at time t_1 it reaches zero, as shown in graph C.

The discharge causes a corresponding voltage drop across the resistor as shown in graph D.

In explaining the charge and discharge cycles of an RC series circuit, the time interval from time t_0 (when the switch is first closed) to time t_1 (when the capacitor reaches full charge or discharge potential) will be used. (Note that switches S_1 and S_2 move at the same time and can never both be closed at the same time.)

When switch S_1 of the circuit in Figure 3-3-9 is closed at t_0, the source voltage (E_S) is instantly felt across the entire circuit. Graph B of the figure shows an instantaneous rise at time t_0 from zero to source voltage (E_S = 6 V). The total voltage can be measured across the circuit between points 1 and 2. Now look at graph C, which represents the charging current in the capacitor (i_c). At time t_0, charging current is maximum. As time elapses toward time t_1, there is a continuous decrease in current flowing into the capacitor. The decreasing flow is caused by the voltage buildup across the capacitor. At time t_1, current flowing in the capacitor stops. At this time, the capacitor has reached full charge and has stored maximum energy in its electrostatic field. Graph D represents the voltage drop (e) across the resistor (R). The value of e_r is determined by the amount of current flowing through the resistor on its way to the

At time t_0, the current through the resistor is maximum and the voltage drop (e_r) across the resistor is maximum. As the current through the resistor decreases, the voltage drop across the resistor decreases until at t_1 it has reached a value of zero. Graph E shows the voltage across the capacitor (e_c) during the discharge cycle. At time t_0 the voltage is maximum and as time progresses toward time t1, the energy stored in the capacitor is depleted. At the same time the voltage across the resistor is decreasing, the voltage (e) across the capacitor is decreasing until at time t_1 the voltage (e_c) reaches zero.

By comparing graph B with graph E of Figure 3-3-10, one can see the effect that capacitance has on a change in voltage. If the circuit had not contained a capacitor, the voltage would have ceased at the instant S_1 was opened (time t_0). Because the capacitor is in the circuit, voltage is applied to the circuit until the capacitor has discharged completely at t_1. The effect of capacitance has been to oppose this change in voltage.

RC Time Constant

The time required to charge a capacitor to 63 percent (actually 63.2 percent) of full charge or to discharge it to 37 percent (actually 36.8 percent) of its initial voltage is known as the time constant (TC) of the circuit. The charge and discharge curves of a capacitor are shown in Figure 3-3-11. Note that the charge curve is like the curve in Figure 3-3-9E, and the discharge curve is like the curve in Figure 3-3-9C.

The value of the time constant in seconds is equal to the product of the circuit resistance in ohms and the circuit capacitance in farads. The value of one time constant is expressed mathe-

		TIME ZERO (t_0)	TIME BETWEEN (t_0 and t_1)	TIME ONE (t_1)
Circuit Current	(capacitor)	Maximum	Decreasing	Zero
	(inductor)	Zero	Increasing	Maximum
Voltage Developed Across the Resistor	(capacitor)	Maximum	Decreasing	Zero
	(inductor)	Zero	Increasing	Maximum
Voltage Developed Across Capacitor/ Inductor	(capacitor)	Zero	Increasing	Maximum
	(inductor)	Maximum	Decreasing	Zero

Table 3-3-2. Summary of capacitive and inductive characteristics

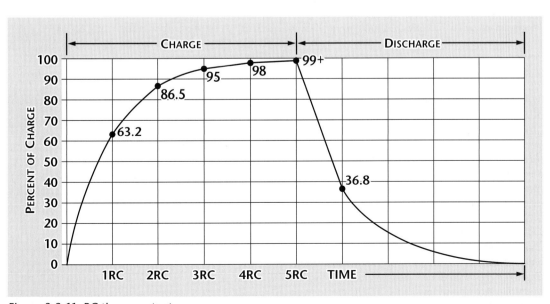

Figure 3-3-11. RC time constant

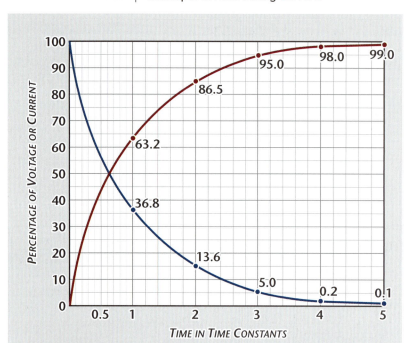

CURVE	RC CIRCUIT	RL CIRCUIT
A	Capacitor voltage on charge	Inductor current or resistor voltage on buildup
B	Capacitor voltage on discharge	Inductor current or resistor voltage on decay
B	Resistor voltage or capacitor current on charge or discharge	Inductor voltage on buildup or decay

Figure 3-3-12. Universal time constant chart for RC and RL circuit

The time scale (horizontal scale) is graduated in terms of the RC or L/R time constants so that the curves may be used for any value of R and C or L and R. The voltage and current scales (vertical scales) are graduated in terms of percentage of the maximum voltage or current so that the curves may be used for any value of voltage or current. If the time constant and the initial or final voltage for the circuit in question are known, the voltages across the various parts of the circuit can be obtained from the curves for any time after the switch is closed, either on charge or discharge. The same reasoning is true of the current in the circuit.

The following problem illustrates how the universal time constant chart may be used.

EXAMPLE: An RC circuit is to be designed in which a capacitor (C) must charge to 20 percent (0.20) of the maximum charging voltage in 100 microseconds (0.0001 second). Because of other considerations, the resistor (R) must have a value of 20,000Ω. What value of capacitance is needed?

Given:

Percent of charge = 20% (.20)

t = 100 μs

R = 20,000Ω

Find the capacitance of capacitor C.

SOLUTION: Because the only values given are in units of time and resistance, a variation of the formula to find RC time is used:

RC = R x C

Where:

1 RC time constant = R x C and R is known

Transpose the formula to:

$$C = \frac{RC}{R}$$

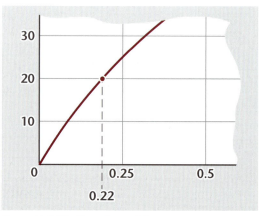

0.22

Figure 3-3-13. Sample problem

matically as t = RC. Some forms of this formula used in calculating RC time constants are:

t (in seconds) = R (in ohms) x C (in farads)

t (in seconds) = R (in megohms) x C (in microfarads)

t (in microseconds) = R (in ohms) x C (in microfarads)

t (in microseconds) = R (in megohms) X C (In picofarads)

Universal Time Constant Chart

Because the impressed voltage and the values of R and C or R and L in a circuit are usually known, a universal time constant chart (Figure 3-3-12) can be used to find the time constant of the circuit. Curve A is a plot of both capacitor voltage during charge and inductor current during growth. Curve B is a plot of both capacitor voltage during discharge and inductor current during decay.

Find the value of RC by referring to the universal time constant chart in Figure 3-3-12 and proceed as follows:

1. Locate the 20 percent point on the vertical scale at the left side of the chart.
2. Follow the horizontal line from this point to intersect curve A.
3. Follow an imaginary vertical line from the point of intersection on curve A downward to cross the RC scale at the bottom of the chart.

Note that the vertical line crosses the horizontal scale at about 0.22 RC, as illustrated in Figure 3-3-13.

The value selected from the graph means that a capacitor (including the one the equation is solving for) will reach 20 percent of full charge in 22 hundredths (0.22) of one RC time constant. Remember that it takes 100 µs for the capacitor to reach 20 percent of full charge. Since 100 µs is equal to 0.22 RC, then the time required to reach one RC time constant must be equal to:

$$0.22 RC = 100 \text{ µs}$$

$$RC = \frac{1}{22} \times 100 \text{ µs}$$

$$RC = \frac{100 \text{ µs}}{.22}$$

$$RC = 454.54 \text{ µs (rounded to 455 µs)}$$

$$RC = 455 \text{ µs}$$

Now use the following formula to find C:

$$C = \frac{RC}{R}$$

$$C = \frac{455 \text{ µs}}{20,000 \Omega}$$

$$C = 0.0227 \text{ µF}$$

$$C = 0.023 \text{ µF}$$

The graphs shown in Figure 3-3-11 and Figure 3-3-12 are not entirely complete. That is, the charge or discharge (or the growth or decay) is not quite complete in 5 RC or 5 L/R time constants. However, when the values reach 0.99 of the maximum (corresponding to 5 RC or 5 L/R), the graphs may be considered accurate enough for all practical purposes.

Capacitors in Series

The overall effect of connecting capacitors in series is to move the plates of the capacitors further apart. This is shown in Figure 3-3-14. Notice that the junction between C_1 and C_2

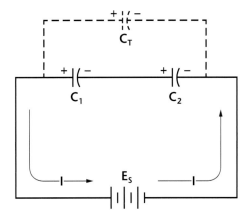

Figure 3-3-14. Capacitors in series

has both a negative and a positive charge. This causes the junction to be essentially neutral. The total capacitance of the circuit is developed between the left plate of C_1 and the right plate of C_2. Because these plates are farther apart, the total value of the capacitance in the circuit is decreased. Solving for the total capacitance (C_T) of capacitors connected in series is similar to solving for the total resistance (R_T) of resistors connected in parallel.

Note the similarity between the formulas for R_T and C_T:

$$R_T = \frac{1}{\frac{1}{R_1} + \frac{1}{R_2} + ... \frac{1}{R_n}}$$

$$C_T = \frac{1}{\frac{1}{C_1} + \frac{1}{C_2} + ... \frac{1}{C_n}}$$

If the circuit contains more than two capacitors, use the formula above. If the circuit contains only two capacitors, use this formula:

$$C_T = \frac{C_1 \times C_2}{C_1 + C_2}$$

Note that all values for C_T, C_1, C_2, C_3,... C_n should be in farads. It should be evident from the above formulas that the total capacitance of capacitors in series is less than the capacitance of any of the individual capacitors.

EXAMPLE: Determine the total capacitance of a series circuit containing three capacitors whose values are 0.01 µF, 0.25 µF and 50,000 pF, respectively.

Given:

$C_1 = 0.01$ µs
$C_2 = 0.25$ µs
$C_3 = 50,000$ pF

SOLUTION:

$$C_T = \frac{1}{\frac{1}{C_1} + \frac{1}{C_2} + \frac{1}{C_3}}$$

$$C_T = \frac{1}{\frac{1}{.01\ \mu F} + \frac{1}{.25\ \mu F} + \frac{1}{50,000\ pF}}$$

$$C_T = \frac{1}{\frac{1}{1 \times 10^{-8}} + \frac{1}{25 \times 10^{-8}} + \frac{1}{5 \times 10^{-8}}} F$$

$$C_T = \frac{1}{100 \times 10^6 + 4 \times 10^6 + 20 \times 10^6} F$$

$$C_T = \frac{1}{124 \times 10^6} F$$

$$C_T = 0.008\ \mu F$$

The total capacitance of $0.008\mu F$ is slightly smaller than the smallest capacitor $(0.01\mu F)$.

Capacitors in Parallel

When capacitors are connected in parallel, one plate of each capacitor is connected directly to one terminal of the source, while the other plate of each capacitor is connected to the other terminal of the source. Figure 3-3-15 shows all the negative plates of the capacitors connected together and all the positive plates connected together. C_T, therefore, appears as a capacitor with a plate area equal to the sum of all the individual plate areas. As previously mentioned, capacitance is a direct function of plate area. Connecting capacitors in parallel effectively increases plate area and thereby increases total capacitance.

For capacitors connected in parallel the total capacitance is the sum of all the individual capacitances. The total capacitance of the circuit may by calculated using the formula:

$$C_T = C_1 + C_2 + C_3 \ldots\ldots C_n$$

Where: all capacitances are in the same units.

EXAMPLE: Determine the total capacitance in a parallel capacitive circuit containing three capacitors whose values are 0.03 μF, 2.0 μF and 0.25 μF, respectively.

Given:

$C_1 = 0.03\ \mu F$

$C_2 = 2\ \mu F$

$C_3 = 0.25\ \mu F$

SOLUTION:

$C_T = C_1 + C_2 + C_3$

$C_{T2} = 0.03\ \mu F + 2.0\ \mu F + 0.25\ \mu F$

$C_{T3} = 2.28\ \mu F$

Fixed Capacitor

A fixed capacitor is constructed in such manner that it possesses a fixed value of capacitance that cannot be adjusted. A fixed capacitor is classified according to the type of material used as its dielectric, such as paper, oil, mica or electrolyte.

A paper capacitor is made of flat, thin strips of metal foil conductors that are separated by waxed paper (the dielectric material). Paper capacitors usually range in value from about 300 pF to about 4 μF. The working voltage of a paper capacitor rarely exceeds 600 V. Paper capacitors are sealed with wax to prevent the harmful effects of moisture and to prevent corrosion and leakage.

Many kinds of outer covering are used on paper capacitors, the simplest being a tubular cardboard covering. Some types of paper capacitors are encased in very hard plastic. These types are very rugged and can be used over a much wider tem-

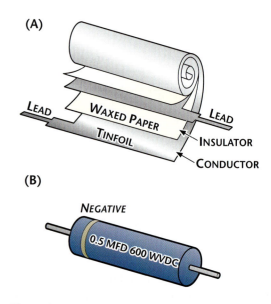

Figure 3-3-16. Paper capacitor

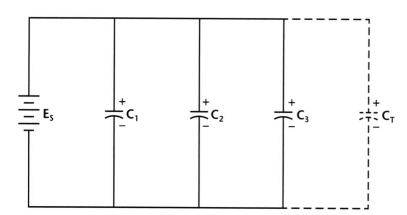

Figure 3-3-15. Capacitors in series

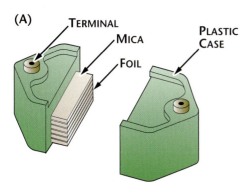 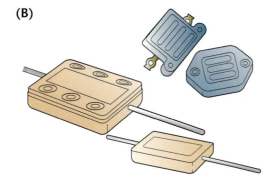

Figure 3-3-17. Mica capacitors

perature range than can the tubular cardboard type. Figure 3-3-16A shows the construction of a tubular paper capacitor; Figure 3-3-16B shows a completed cardboard-encased capacitor.

A mica capacitor is made of metal foil plates that are separated by sheets of mica (the dielectric). The whole assembly is encased in molded plastic. Figure 3-3-17A shows a cut-away view of a mica capacitor. Because the capacitor parts are molded into a plastic case, corrosion and damage to the plates and dielectric are prevented. In addition, the molded plastic case makes the capacitor mechanically stronger. Various types of terminals are used on mica capacitors to connect them into circuits. These terminals are also molded into the plastic case.

Mica is an excellent dielectric and can withstand a higher voltage than can a paper dielectric of the same thickness. Common values of mica capacitors range from approximately 50 pF to 0.02 µF. Some different shapes of mica capacitors are shown in Figure 3-3-17B.

A ceramic capacitor is so named because it contains a ceramic dielectric. One type of ceramic capacitor uses a hollow ceramic cylinder as both the form on which to construct the capacitor and as the dielectric material. The plates consist of thin films of metal deposited on the ceramic cylinder.

A second type of ceramic capacitor is manufactured in the shape of a disk. After leads are attached to each side of the capacitor, the capacitor is completely covered with an insulating moisture-proof coating. Ceramic capacitors usually range in value from 1 pF to 0.01 µF and may be used with voltages as high as 30,000 V. Some different shapes of ceramic capacitors are shown in Figure 3-3-18.

An electrolytic capacitor (Figure 3-3-19) is used where a large amount of capacitance is required. As the name implies, an electrolytic capacitor contains an electrolyte. This electrolyte can be in the form of a liquid, but this type of wet electrolytic capacitor is no longer in popular use due to the care needed to prevent spilling of the electrolyte.

A dry electrolytic capacitor consists essentially of two metal plates separated by the electro-

Figure 3-3-18. Ceramic capacitors

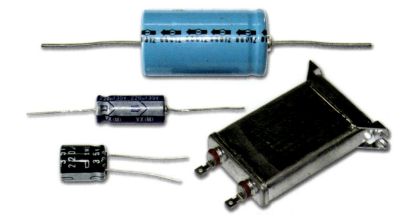

Figure 3-3-19. Electrolytic capacitors

lyte. In most cases the capacitor is housed in a cylindrical aluminum container that acts as the negative terminal of the capacitor (Figure 3-3-20). The positive terminal (or terminals, if the capacitor is of the multisection type) is a lug on the bottom end of the container. The capacitance value and the voltage rating of the capacitor are generally printed on the side of the aluminum case.

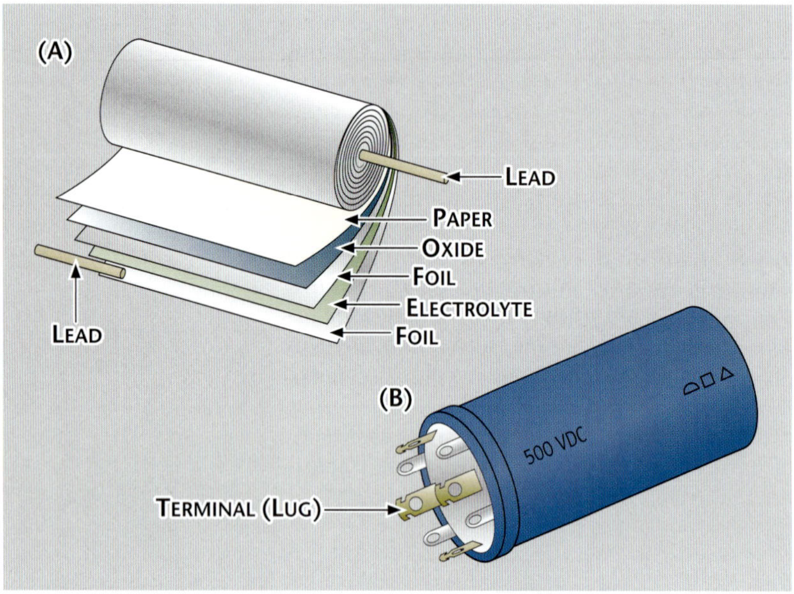

An example of a multiple-section electrolytic capacitor is shown in Figure 3-3-20B. The four lugs at the end of the cylindrical aluminum container indicates that four electrolytic capacitors are enclosed in the can. Each section of the capacitor is electrically independent of the other sections. It is possible for one section to be defective while the other sections are still good. The can is the common negative connection to the four capacitors. Separate terminals are provided for the positive plates of the capacitors. Each capacitor is identified by an embossed mark adjacent to the lugs. Note the identifying marks used on the electrolytic capacitor are the half moon, the triangle, the square and no embossed mark. By looking at the bottom of the container and the identifying sheet pasted to the side of the container, it is possible to identify the value of each section.

Internally, the electrolytic capacitor is constructed similarly to the paper capacitor. The positive plate consists of aluminum foil covered with an extremely thin film of oxide. This thin oxide film (which is formed by an electrochemical process) acts as the dielectric of the capacitor. Next to and in contact with the oxide is a strip of paper or gauze that has been impregnated with a paste-like electrolyte. The electrolyte acts as the negative plate of the capacitor. A second strip of aluminum foil is then placed against the electrolyte to provide electrical contact to the negative electrode (the electrolyte). When the three layers are in place they are rolled nto a cylinder as shown in Figure 3-3-20A.

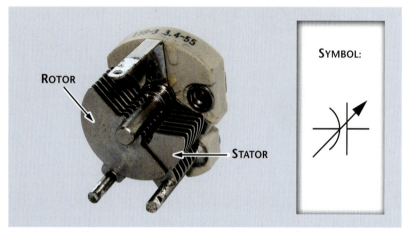

Figure 3-3-20. Construction of an electrolytic capacitor

An electrolytic capacitor has two primary disadvantages compared to a paper capacitor in that the electrolytic type is polarized and has a low leakage resistance. This means that should the positive plate be accidentally connected to the negative terminal of the source, the thin oxide film dielectric will dissolve and the capacitor will become a conductor (i.e., it will short). The polarity of the terminals is normally marked on the case of the capacitor. Since an electrolytic capacitor is polarity sensitive, its use is ordinarily restricted to a DC circuit or to a circuit where a small AC voltage is superimposed on a DC voltage. Special electrolytic capacitors are available for certain AC applications, such as a motor starting capacitor. Dry electrolytic capacitors vary in size from about 4 μF to several thousand microfarads and have a working voltage of approximately 500 V.

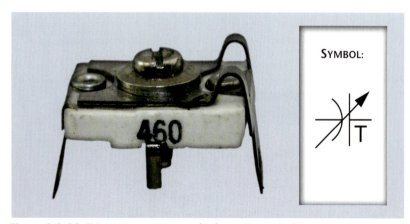

Figure 3-3-21. Rotor-stator type variable capacitor and schematic symbol

Figure 3-3-22. Trimmer capacitor and schematic symbol

The type of dielectric used and its thickness govern the amount of voltage that can safely be applied to the electrolytic capacitor. If the voltage applied to the capacitor is high enough to cause the atoms of the dielectric material to become ionized, arcing between the plates will occur. In most other types of capacitors, arcing will destroy the capacitor. However, an electrolytic capacitor has the ability to be self-healing. If the arcing is small, the electrolytic will regenerate itself. If the arcing is too large, the capacitor will not self-heal and will become defective.

Oil capacitors are often used in high-power electronic equipment. An oil-filled capacitor is nothing more than a paper capacitor that is immersed in oil. Since oil-impregnated paper has a high dielectric constant, it can be used in the production of high-value capacitors. Many capacitors use oil with another dielectric material to prevent arcing between the plates. If arcing should occur between the plates of an oil-filled capacitor, the oil tends to reseal the hole caused by the arcing. Such a capacitor is referred to as a *self-healing capacitor.*

Variable Capacitor

A variable capacitor is constructed in such manner that its value of capacitance can be varied. A typical variable, or adjustable, capacitor is the *rotor-stator type*. It consists of two sets of metal plates arranged so that the rotor plates move between the stator plates. Air is the dielectric. As the position of the rotor is changed, the capacitance value is likewise changed. This type of capacitor is used for tuning most radio receivers. It and its symbol are shown in Figure 3-3-21.

Another type of variable capacitor—a trimmer capacitor—and its symbol are shown in Figure 3-3-22. This capacitor consists of two plates separated by a sheet of mica. A screw adjustment is used to vary the distance between the plates, thereby changing the capacitance.

Capacitor Troubleshooting

Capacitors are often a source of trouble in some circuits, such as power supplies. Capacitors may be checked with a tester specifically designed to test capacitance values, or they may be given a quick check with an ohmmeter.

To test capacitors with a capacitance tester, follow the instructions given by the tester manufacturer. The instructions will vary somewhat depending on the type of tester being used.

To test a capacitor with an ohmmeter, first discharge the capacitor and remove it (at least one lead) from the circuit where it is connected. Set the ohmmeter to a mid-resistance scale and connect it to the capacitor and observe the meter scale for *capacitor action*. (Note: An analog meter with a needle pointer works best for this test.)

Capacitor action is observed when the meter needle moves upscale, toward zero ohms, and then slowly moves downscale toward infinite ohms. The needle action is due to the ohmmeter internal voltage source (battery) charging the capacitor. It may be necessary to try more than one resistance scale before observing any significant capacitor action. Remember to discharge the capacitor after every attempt to observe capacitor action.

A continuous low reading indicates a shorted capacitor, and a continuous high reading denotes an open capacitor. Ohmmeter checks of capacitors are not always accurate, and any suspicious capacitors may need to be tested with a capacitor analyzer.

Section 4:
AC Calculations

Previous sections of this text have covered how inductance and capacitance individually behave in a DC circuit. This section shows how inductance, capacitance and resistance affect alternating current.

Inductance and Alternating Current

This might be a good place to recall what was learned about phase. When two things are in step, going through a cycle together, falling together and rising together, they are in phase. When they are out of phase, the angle of lead or lag—the number of electrical degrees by which one of the values leads or lags the other—is a measure of the amount they are out of step. The time it takes the current in an inductor to build up to maximum and to fall to zero is important for another reason. It helps illustrate a very useful characteristic of inductive circuits—the current through the inductor always lags the voltage across the inductor.

A circuit having pure resistance (if such a thing were possible) would have the alternating current through it and the voltage across it rising and failing together. This is illustrated in Figure 3-4-1A, which shows the sine waves for current and voltage in a purely resistive AC circuit. The current and voltage do not have the same amplitude, but they are in phase.

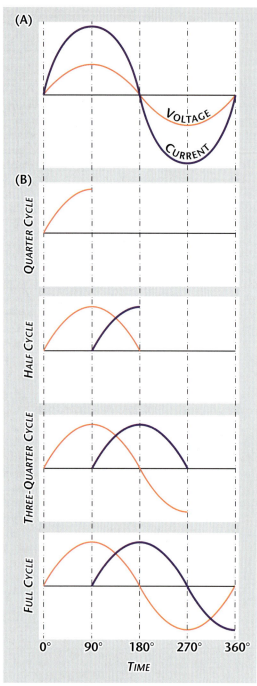

Figure 3-4-1. Voltage and current waveforms in an inductive circuit

In the case of a circuit having inductance, the opposing force of the cemf would be enough to keep the current from remaining in phase with the applied voltage. Remember that in a DC circuit containing pure inductance, the current took time to rise to maximum even though the full applied voltage was immediately at maximum. Figure 3-4-1B shows the waveforms for a purely inductive AC circuit in steps of quarter-cycles.

With an AC voltage, in the first quarter-cycle (0° to 90°) the applied AC voltage is continually increasing. If there were no inductance in the circuit, the current would also increase during this first quarter-cycle. This circuit does have inductance. Since inductance opposes any change in current flow, no current flows during the first quarter-cycle. In the next quarter-cycle (90° to 180°) the voltage decreases back to zero; current begins to flow in the circuit and reaches a maximum value at the same instant the voltage reaches zero. The applied voltage now begins to build up to maximum in the other direction, to be followed by the resulting current. When the voltage again reaches its maximum at the end of the third quarter-cycle (270°) all values are exactly opposite to what they were during the first half-cycle. The applied voltage leads the resulting current by one quarter-cycle or 90°. To complete the full 360°-cycle of the voltage, the voltage again decreases to zero and the current builds to a maximum value.

Do not get the idea that any of these values stops cold at a particular instant. Until the applied voltage is removed, both current and voltage are always changing in amplitude and direction.

As previously discussed, the sine wave can be compared to a circle. Just as a circle can be marked off into 360°, the time of one cycle of a sine wave can be marked off into 360 electrical degrees. This relationship is shown in Figure 3-4-2. This figure shows why the current is said to lag the voltage, in a purely inductive circuit, by 90°. Furthermore, Figure 3-4-2 and Figure 3-4-1A show why the current and voltage are said to be in phase in a purely resistive circuit. In a circuit having both resistance and inductance then, as expected, the current lags the voltage by an amount somewhere between 0 and 90°.

The word ELI is a simple reminder of the relationship of voltage and current in an inductive circuit. Since E is the symbol for voltage, L is the symbol for inductance, and I is the symbol for current; the word ELI demonstrates that current comes after (lags) voltage in an inductor.

Inductive Reactance

When the current flowing through an inductor continuously reverses itself, as in an AC source, the inertia effect of the cemf is greater than with DC. The greater the amount of inductance (L), the greater the opposition from this inertia effect. Also, the faster the reversal of current, the greater this inertial opposition. This opposing force that an inductor presents to the flow of alternating current cannot be called resistance since it is not the result of friction within a conductor. The name given to it is *inductive reactance* because it is the "reaction" of the inductor to the changing value of alternating current. Inductive reactance is measured in ohms and its symbol is X_L.

As discussed, the induced voltage in a conductor is proportional to the rate at which magnetic lines of force cut the conductor. The greater the rate (the higher the frequency), the greater the cemf. Also, the induced voltage increases with an increase in inductance; the more ampere-turns, the greater the cemf. Reactance, then, increases with an increase of frequency and with an increase of inductance. The formula for inductive reactance is as follows:

$X_L = 2\pi f L$

Where:

X_L = inductive reactance in ohms
2π = a constant in which the Greek letter π, called "pi," represents 3.1416 and $2 \times \pi = 6.28$ approximately
f = a frequency of the alternating current in Hz
L = inductance in henrys

The following example problem illustrates the computation of X_L.

Given:

F = 60 Hz
L = 20 H

SOLUTION:

$X_L = 2\pi f L$
$X_L = 6.28 \times 60 \text{ Hz} \times 20 \text{H}$
$X_L = 7{,}536 \Omega$

Capacitors and Alternating Current

The four parts of Figure 3-4-3 show the variation of the alternating voltage and current in a capacitive circuit, for each quarter-cycle. The solid line represents the voltage across the capacitor, and the dotted line represents the current. The line running through the center is the zero, or reference point, for both the voltage and the current. The bottom line marks off the time of the cycle in terms of electrical degrees. Assume that the AC voltage has been acting on the capacitor for some time before the time represented by the starting point of the sine wave in the figure.

At the beginning of the first quarter-cycle (0° to 90°) the voltage has just passed through zero and is increasing in the positive direction. Since the passage through the zero point is the steepest part of the sine wave, the voltage is changing at its greatest rate. The charge on a capacitor varies directly with the voltage, and therefore the charge on the capacitor is also changing at its greatest rate at the beginning of the first quarter-cycle. In other words, the greatest number of electrons is moving off one plate and onto the other plate. Thus the capacitor current is at its maximum value, as part A of the figure shows.

As the voltage proceeds toward maximum at 90°, its rate of change becomes less and less, and the current must decrease toward zero. At 90° the voltage across the capacitor is maximum, the capacitor is fully charged, and there is no further movement of electrons from plate to plate. That is why the current at 90° is zero.

At the end of this first quarter-cycle the alternating voltage stops increasing and starts to decrease. It is still a positive voltage, but to the capacitor the decrease in voltage means that the plate that has just accumulated an excess of electrons must lose some electrons. The current flow, therefore, must reverse its direction. Figure 3-4-3B shows the current curve to be below the zero line (negative current direction) during the second quarter-cycle (90° to 180°).

At 180° the voltage has dropped to zero. This means that for a brief instant the electrons are equally distributed between the two plates; the current is maximum because the rate of change of voltage is maximum. Just after 180° the voltage has reversed polarity

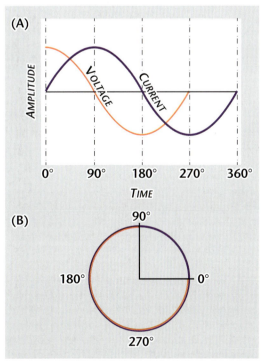

Figure 3-4-2. Comparison of sine wave and circle in an inductive circuit

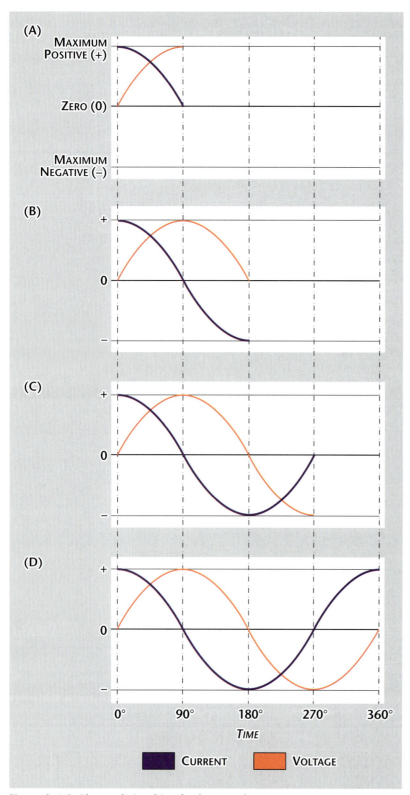

Figure 3-4-3. Phase relationship of voltage and current in a capacitive circuit

fully charged there is no further exchange of electrons; therefore, the current flow is zero at this point. The conditions are exactly the same as at the end of the first quarter-cycle (90°) but the polarity is reversed.

Just after 270° the impressed voltage once again starts to decrease, and the capacitor must lose electrons from the negative plate. It must discharge, starting at a minimum rate of flow and rising to a maximum. This discharging action continues through the last quarter-cycle (270° to 360°) until the impressed voltage has reached zero. At 360°, everything starts over again at the beginning of the cycle.

Examine the complete voltage and current curves in Figure 3-4-3D. This shows that the current always arrives at a certain point in the cycle 90° ahead of the voltage because of the charging and discharging action. This time and place relationship between the current and voltage is called the phase relationship. The voltage-current phase relationship in a capacitive circuit is exactly opposite to that in an inductive circuit. The current of a capacitor leads the voltage across the capacitor by 90°.

Realize that the current and voltage are both going through their individual cycles at the same time during the period the AC voltage is impressed. The current does not go through part of its cycle (charging or discharging), stop, and wait for the voltage to catch up. The amplitude and polarity of the voltage and the amplitude and direction of the current are continually changing. Their positions with respect to each other and to the zero line at any electrical instant—any point between 0° and 360°—can be seen by reading upwards from the time-degree line. The current swing from the positive peak at 0° to the negative peak at 180° is not a measure of the number of electrons or the charge on the plates. It is a picture of the direction and strength of the current in relation to the polarity and strength of the voltage appearing across the plates.

At times it is convenient to use the word "ICE" to recall to mind the phase relationship of the current and voltage in capacitive circuits. I is the symbol for current, and in the word ICE it leads, or comes before, the symbol for voltage, E. C, of course, stands for capacitor. This memory aid is similar to the "ELI" used to remember the current and voltage relationship in an inductor. The phrase "ELI the ICE man" is helpful in remembering the phase relationship in both the inductor and capacitor.

Since the plates of the capacitor are changing polarity at the same rate as the AC voltage, the capacitor seems to pass an alternating current.

and starts building up its maximum negative peak, which is reached at the end of the third quarter-cycle (180° to 270°). During this third quarter-cycle, the rate of voltage change gradually decreases as the charge builds to a maximum at 270°. At this point the capacitor is fully charged and it carries the full impressed voltage. Because the capacitor is

Actually, the electrons do not pass through the dielectric, but their rushing back and forth from plate to plate causes a current flow in the circuit. It is convenient, however, to say that the alternating current flows "through" the capacitor. This is not technically correct, but the expression avoids a lot of trouble when speaking of current flow in a circuit containing a capacitor. By the same short cut, it can be said that the capacitor does not pass a direct current: If both plates are connected to a DC source, current will flow only long enough to charge the capacitor. With a capacitor type of hookup in a circuit containing both AC and DC, only the AC will be "passed on" to another circuit.

At this point there are two things to remember about a capacitor: A capacitor will appear to conduct an alternating current and a capacitor will not conduct a direct current.

Capacitive Reactance

So far the capacitor has been treated as a device that passes AC and in which the only opposition to the alternating current has been the normal circuit resistance present in any conductor. However, capacitors themselves offer a very real opposition to current flow. This opposition arises from the fact that, at a given voltage and frequency, the number of electrons that go back and forth from plate to plate is limited by the storage ability—that is, the capacitance—of the capacitor. As the capacitance increases, a greater number of electrons change plates every cycle, and (since current is a measure of the number of electrons passing a given point in a given time) the current increases.

Increasing the frequency will also decrease the opposition offered by a capacitor. This occurs because the number of electrons the capacitor is capable of handling at a given voltage will change plates more often. As a result, more electrons will pass a given point in a given time (i.e., current flow will be greater). The opposition a capacitor offers to AC is therefore inversely proportional to frequency and to capacitance. This opposition is called *capacitive reactance*. It can be said that capacitive reactance decreases with increasing frequency or, for a given frequency, the capacitive reactance decreases with increasing capacitance. The symbol for capacitive reactance is X_C.

This gives an understanding of why it is said that the X_C varies inversely with the product of the frequency and capacitance. The formula is:

$$X_C = \frac{1}{2\pi f C}$$

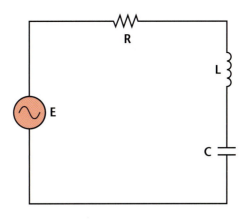

Figure 3-4-4. Series RLC circuit

Where:

X_C = capacitive reactance in ohms
f = frequency in Hertz
C = capacitance in farads
π = is 6.28 (2 × 3.1416)

The following example problem illustrates the computation of X_C.

Given:

F = 100 Hz
C = 50 μF

Solution:

$$X_C = \frac{1}{2\pi f C}$$

$$X_C = \frac{1}{6.28 \times 100 \text{ Hz} \times 50 \text{ μF}}$$

$$X_C = \frac{1}{.0314} \Omega$$

X_C = 31.8Ω or 32Ω

Reactance, Impedance and Power Relationships in AC Circuits

Up to this point inductance and capacitance have been explained individually in AC circuits. The rest of this chapter will concern the combination of inductance, capacitance and resistance in AC circuits.

To explain the various properties that exist within AC circuits, the series RLC circuit will be used. Figure 3-4-4 is the schematic diagram of the series RLC circuit. In that diagram, the symbol marked E is the general symbol used to indicate an AC voltage source.

Reactance

The effect of inductive reactance is to cause the current to lag the voltage, while that of capacitive reactance is to cause the current to lead the voltage. Therefore, since inductive reactance and capacitive reactance are exactly opposite in their effects, what will be the result when the two are combined? It is not hard to see that the net effect is a tendency to cancel each other, leaving the combined effect equal to the difference between their values. This resultant is called *reactance*. Reactance is represented by the symbol X and expressed by the equation $X = X_L - X_C$ or $X = X_C - X_L$. Thus, if a circuit contains 50 Ω of inductive reactance and 25Ω of capacitive reactance in series, the net reactance, or X, is 50Ω - 25Ω, or 25Ω of inductive reactance.

EXAMPLE: suppose that a circuit is present containing an inductor of 100 μH in series with a capacitor of 0.001 μF, and operating at a frequency of 4 MHz. What is the value of net reactance, or X?

Given:

f = 4 MHz
L = 100 μH
C = 0.001 μF

SOLUTION:

$X_L = 2\pi f L$
$X_L = 6.28 \times 4$ MHz $\times 100$ μH
$X_L = 2512 \Omega$

$X_C = \dfrac{1}{2\pi f C}$

$X_C = \dfrac{1}{6.28 \times 4 \text{ MHz} \times 0.001 \text{ μF}}$

$X_C = \dfrac{1}{0.02512} \Omega$

$X_C = 39.8 \Omega$
$X = X_L - X_C$
$X = 2512\Omega - 39.8\Omega$
$X = 2472.2\Omega$ (inductive)

EXAMPLE: Now assume that there is a circuit containing an inductor of 100 μH in series with a 0.0002-μF capacitor, and operating at a frequency of 1 MHz. What is the value of the resultant reactance in this case?

Given:

f = 1 MHz
L = 100 μH
C = 0.0002 μF

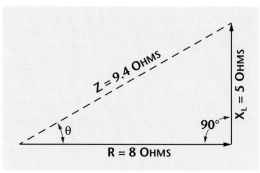

Figure 3-4-5. Relationship of resistance, inductive reactance, and impedance in a series circuit

SOLUTION:

$X_L = 2\pi f L$
$X_L = 6.28 \times 1$ MHz $\times 100$ μH
$X_L = 628 \Omega$

$X_C = \dfrac{1}{2\pi f C}$

$X_C = \dfrac{1}{6.28 \times 1 \text{ MHz} \times .0002 \text{ μF}}$

$X_C = \dfrac{1}{.001256} \Omega$

$X_C = 796\Omega$
$X = X_C - X_L$
$X = 796\Omega - 628\Omega$
$X = 168\Omega$ (capacitive)

Notice that in this case the inductive reactance is smaller than the capacitive reactance and is therefore subtracted from the capacitive reactance.

These two examples serve to illustrate an important point: when capacitive and inductive reactances are combined in series, the smaller is always subtracted from the larger and the resultant reactance always takes the characteristics of the larger.

Impedance

From the study of inductance and capacitance it is known how inductive reactance and capacitive reactance act to oppose the flow of current in an AC circuit. However, there is another factor—the resistance—that also opposes the flow of the current. Since in practice AC circuits containing reactance also contain resistance, the two combine to oppose the flow of current. This combined opposition is called the *impedance*, and it is represented by the symbol Z.

Since the values of resistance and reactance are both given in ohms, it might at first

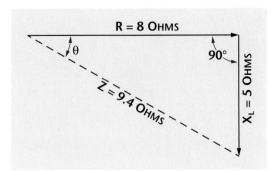

Figure 3-4-6. Relationship of resistance, capacitive reactance, and impedance in a series circuit

seem possible to determine the value of the impedance by simply adding them. It cannot be done so easily, however. it is known that in an AC circuit that contains only resistance, the current and the voltage will be in step (that is, in phase) and will reach their maximum values at the same instant. it is also known that in an AC circuit containing only reactance the current will either lead or lag the voltage by one-quarter cycle or 90°. Therefore, the voltage in a purely reactive circuit will differ in phase by 90° from that in a purely resistive circuit and for this reason reactance and resistance cannot simply be combined by adding them.

When reactance and resistance are combined, the value of the impedance will be greater than either. It is also true that the current will not be in step with the voltage nor will it differ in phase by exactly 90° from the voltage, but it will be somewhere between the in-step and the 90° out-of-step conditions. The larger the reactance compared with the resistance, the more nearly the phase difference will approach 90°. The larger the resistance compared to the reactance, the more nearly the phase difference will approach 0°.

If the value of resistance and reactance cannot simply be added together to find the impedance, or Z, how is it determined? Because the current through a resistor is in step with the voltage across it and the current in a reactance differs by 90° from the voltage across it, the two are at right angles to each other. They can therefore be combined by means of the same method used in the construction of a right angle triangle.

To find the impedance of a series combination of 8Ω resistance and 5Ω inductive reactance, start by drawing a horizontal line, R, representing 8Ω resistance, as the base of the triangle. Then, since the effect of the reactance is always at a right angle, or 90°, to that of the resistance, draw the line X_L representing 5° inductive reactance, as the altitude of the triangle (with the two line segments meeting at an end point of line R). This is shown in Figure 3-4-5. Now, complete the hypotenuse (longest side) of the triangle. The hypotenuse represents the impedance of the circuit.

One of the properties of a right triangle is:

$(hypotenuse)^2 = (base)^2 + (altitude)^2$ or,

$hypotenuse = \sqrt{(base)^2 + (altitude)^2}$

Applied to impedance, this becomes,

$(impedance)^2 = (resistance)^2 + (reactance)^2$ or,

$impedance = \sqrt{(resistance)^2 + (reactance)^2}$ or,

$Z = \sqrt{R^2 + X^2}$

EXAMPLE: Now apply this equation to check the results in the previous example.

Given:

$R = 8Ω$
$X_L = 5Ω$

SOLUTION:

$Z = \sqrt{R^2 + X_L^2}$

$Z = \sqrt{(8Ω)^2 + (5Ω)^2}$

$Z = \sqrt{64 + 25Ω}$

$Z = \sqrt{89Ω}$

$Z = 9.4Ω$

When working with a capacitive reactance instead of with an inductive reactance as in the previous example, it is customary to draw the line representing the capacitive reactance in a downward direction. This is shown in Figure 3-4-6. The line is drawn downward for capacitive reactance to indicate that it acts in a direction opposite to inductive reactance (which is drawn upward). In a series circuit containing capacitive reactance the equation for finding the impedance becomes:

$Z = \sqrt{R^2 + X_C^2}$

In many series circuits the technician will find resistance combined with both inductive reactance and capacitive reactance. Since it is known that the value of the reactance, X, is equal to the difference between the values of the inductive reactance, X_L, and the capacitive reactance, X_C, the equation for the impedance in a series circuit containing R, X_L and X_C then becomes:

$Z = \sqrt{R^2 + (X_L - X_L)^2}$ or,

$Z = \sqrt{R^2 + X^2}$

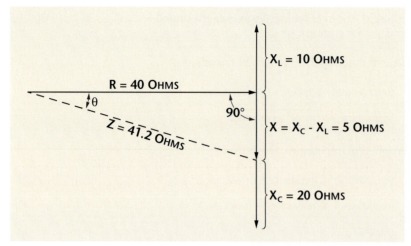

Figure 3-4-7. Relationship of resistance, reactance and impedance in a series circuit

NOTE: *The following formulas can be used to calculate Z only if the resistance and reactance are connected in series.*

$$Z = \sqrt{R^2 + X_L^2}$$
$$Z = \sqrt{R^2 + X_C^2}$$
$$Z = \sqrt{R^2 + X^2}$$

Figure 3-4-7 illustrates a method that may be used to determine the impedance in a series circuit consisting of resistance, inductance and capacitance.

Assume that 10Ω inductive reactance and 20Ω capacitive reactance are connected in series with 40Ω resistance. Let the horizontal line represent the resistance R. The line drawn upward from the end of R represents the inductive reactance, X_L. Represent the capacitive reactance by a line drawn downward at a right angle from the same end of R. The resultant of X_L and X_C is found by subtracting X_L from X_C. This resultant represents the value of X.

Therefore:

$$X = X_C - X_L$$
$$X = 10Ω$$

The line, Z, will represent the resultant of R and X. The value of Z can be calculated as follows:

EXAMPLE:

Given:

$X_L = 10Ω$
$X_C = 20Ω$
$R = 40Ω$

SOLUTION:

$X = X_C - X_L$
$X = 20Ω - 10Ω$
$X = 10Ω$

$Z = \sqrt{R^2 + X^2}$
$Z = \sqrt{(40Ω)^2 + (10Ω)^2}$
$Z = \sqrt{1600 + 100Ω}$
$Z = \sqrt{1700Ω}$
$Z = 41.2Ω$

Ohm's Law for AC Circuits

In general, Ohm's law cannot be applied to alternating-current circuits since it does not consider the reactance that is always present in such circuits. However, by a modification of Ohm's law that does take into consideration the effect of reactance we obtain a general law applicable to AC circuits. Because the impedance, Z, represents the combined opposition of all the reactance and resistances, this general law for AC is,

$$I = \frac{E}{Z}$$

This general modification applies to alternating current flowing in any circuit, and any one of the values may be found from the equation if the others are known.

EXAMPLE: Suppose a series circuit contains an inductor having 5Ω resistance and 25Ω inductive reactance in series with a capacitor having 15Ω capacitive reactance. If the voltage is 50 V, what is the current? This circuit can be drawn as shown in Figure 3-4-8.

Given:

$R = 5Ω$
$X_L = 25Ω$
$X_C = 15Ω$
$E = 50$ V

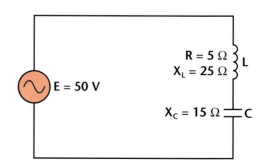

Figure 3-4-8. Series LC circuit

SOLUTION:

$X = X_L - X_C$
$X = 25Ω - 15Ω$
$X = 10Ω$

$Z = \sqrt{R^2 + X^2}$
$Z = \sqrt{(5Ω)^2 + (10Ω)^2}$
$Z = \sqrt{25 + 100}Ω$
$Z = \sqrt{125}Ω$
$Z = 11.2Ω$

$I = \dfrac{E}{Z}$

$I = \dfrac{50\text{ V}}{11.2Ω}$

$I = 4.46\text{ A}$

EXAMPLE: Now suppose the circuit contains an inductor having 5Ω resistance and 15Ω inductive reactance in series with a capacitor having 10Ω capacitive reactance. If the current is 5 A, what is the voltage?

Given:

$R = 5Ω$
$X_L = 15Ω$
$X_C = 10Ω$
$I = 5\text{ A}$

SOLUTION:

$X = X_L - X_C$
$X = 15Ω - 10Ω$
$X = 5Ω$

$Z = \sqrt{R^2 + X^2}$
$Z = \sqrt{(5Ω)^2 + (5Ω)^2}$
$Z = \sqrt{25 + 25}Ω$
$Z = \sqrt{50}Ω$
$Z = 7.07Ω$

$E = IZ$
$E = 5A \times 7.07Ω$
$E = 35.35\text{ V}$

Power in AC Circuits

As covered previously, in a DC circuit the power is equal to the voltage times the current, or $P = E \times I$. If 100 V applied to a circuit produces a current of 10 A, the power is 1,000 W. This is also true in an AC circuit when the current and voltage are in phase—that is, when the circuit

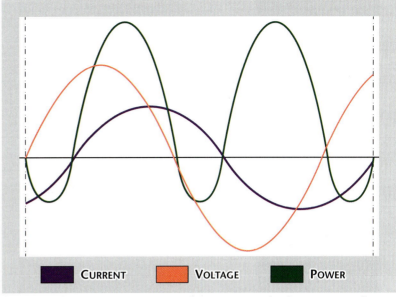

Figure 3-4-9. Instantaneous power when current and voltage are out of phase

is effectively resistive. But, if the AC circuit contains reactance, the current will lead or lag the voltage by a certain amount (the phase angle). When the current is out of phase with the voltage, the power indicated by the product of the applied voltage and the total current gives only what is known as the *apparent power*. The true power depends upon the phase angle between the current and voltage. The symbol for phase angle is the Greek letter *theta*, θ.

When an alternating voltage is impressed across a capacitor, power is taken from the source and stored in the capacitor as the voltage increases from zero to its maximum value. Then, as the impressed voltage decreases, the capacitor discharges and returns the power to the source. Likewise, as the current through an inductor increases from zero to its maximum value, the field around the inductor builds up to a maximum, and when the current decreases the field collapses and returns the power to the source. This means that no power is used up in either case, since the power alternately flows to and from the source. This power that is returned to the source by the reactive components in the circuit is called *reactive power*.

In a purely resistive circuit, all of the power is consumed and none is returned to the source. In a purely reactive circuit, no power is consumed and all of the power is returned to the source. It follows that in a circuit that contains both resistance and reactance, there must be some power dissipated in the resistance as well as some returned to the source by the reactance.

Figure 3-4-9 shows the relationship between the voltage, the current and the power in such a circuit. The part of the power curve that is below the horizontal reference line is the result of multiplying a positive instantaneous value of current by a negative instantaneous value of the voltage, or vice versa. As discussed earlier, multiplying a positive value by a negative value results in a negative value. Therefore the power at that instant must be considered as negative power. In other words, during this time the reactance was returning power to the source.

The instantaneous power in the circuit is equal to the product of the applied voltage and current through the circuit. When the voltage and current are of the same polarity, they are acting together and taking power from the source. When the polarities are unlike, they are acting in opposition and power is being returned to the source. Briefly then, in an AC circuit that contains reactance as well as resistance, the apparent power is reduced by the power returned to the source, so that in such a circuit the net power, or true power, is always less than the apparent power.

Calculating true power in AC circuits. As mentioned before, the *true power* of a circuit is the power actually used in the circuit. This power, measured in watts, is the power associated with the total resistance in the circuit. To calculate true power, the voltage and current associated with the resistance must be used. Since the voltage drop across the resistance is equal to the resistance multiplied by the current through the resistance, true power can be calculated by the formula:

True Power = $(I_R)^2 \times R$

Where:

True Power (measured in watts)
I_R = resistive current in amperes
R = resistance in ohms

EXAMPLE: find the true power of the circuit shown in Figure 3-4-10.

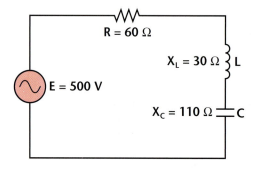

Figure 3-4-10. Example circuit for determining power

Given:

$R = 60\Omega$
$X_L = 30\Omega$
$X_C = 110\Omega$
$E = 500$ V

SOLUTION:

$X = X_C - X_L$
$X = 110\Omega - 30\Omega$
$X = 80\Omega$

$Z = \sqrt{R^2 + X^2}$
$Z = \sqrt{(60\Omega)^2 + (80\Omega)^2}$
$Z = \sqrt{3600 + 6400\Omega}$
$Z = \sqrt{10,000\Omega}$
$Z = 100\Omega$

$I = \dfrac{E}{Z}$

$I = \dfrac{500 \text{ V}}{100\Omega}$

$I = 5$ A

Since the current in a series circuit is the same in all parts of the circuit:

True Power = $(I_R)^2 \times R$
True Power = $(5 \text{ A})^2 \times 60\Omega$
True Power = 1,500 W

Calculating reactive power in AC circuits. The *reactive power* is the power returned to the source by the reactive components of the circuit. This type of power is measured in volt-amperes-reactive, abbreviated var.

Reactive power is calculated by using the voltage and current associated with the circuit reactance. Since the voltage of the reactance is equal to the reactance multiplied by the reactive current, reactive power can be calculated by the formula:

Reactive power = $(I_X)^2 X$

Where:

Reactive power is measured in volt – ampere – reactive
I_X is reactive current in amperes
X is total reactance in ohms

Another way to calculate reactive power is to calculate the inductive power and capacitive power and subtract the smaller from the larger.

Reactive power = $(I_L)^2 X_L - (I_C)^2 X_C$ or,
$(I_C)^2 X_C - (I_L)^2 X_L$

Where:

Reactive power is measured in volt – ampere – reactive

I_C is capacitive current in amperes

X_C is capacitive reactance in ohms

I_L is inductive current in amperes

X_L is inductive reactance in ohms

EXAMPLE: Either one of these formulas will work. The formula used depends upon the values that are given in a circuit. Find the reactive power of the circuit shown in Figure 3-4-10.

Given:

$X_L = 30\Omega$

$X_C = 110\Omega$

$X = 80\Omega$

$I = 5 A$

SOLUTION:

Reactive power = $(I_X)^2 X$

Reactive power = $(5 A)^2 \times 80\Omega$

Reactive power = 2,000 var

Since this is a series circuit, current (I) is the same in all parts of the circuit. To prove the second formula also works, see below:

Reactive power = $(I_C)^2 X_C - (I_L)^2 X_L$

Reactive power = $(5 A)^2 \times 110\Omega - (5 A)^2 \times 30\Omega$

Reactive power = 2,750 var – 750 var

Reactive power = 2,000 var

Calculating apparent power in AC circuits. *Apparent power* is the power that appears to the source because of the circuit impedance. Since the impedance is the total opposition to AC, the apparent power is that power the voltage source "sees." Apparent power is the combination of true power and reactive power. Apparent power is not found by simply adding true power and reactive power just as impedance is not found by adding resistance and reactance.

To calculate apparent power, use either of the following formulas:

Apparent power = $(I_Z)^2 Z$

Where:

Apparent power is measured in VA (volt – amperes)

I_Z = impedance current in amperes

Z = impedance in ohms

or,

Apparent power = $\sqrt{(\text{True power})^2 + (\text{reactive power})^2}$

EXAMPLE: find the apparent power for the circuit shown in Figure 3-4-10.

Given:

$Z = 100\Omega$

$I = 5 A$

Recall that current in a series circuit is the same in all parts of the circuit.

SOLUTION:

Apparent power = $(I_Z)^2 Z$

Apparent power = $(5 A)^2 \times 100\Omega$

Apparent power = 2,500 VA   or,

Given:

True power = 1,500 W

Reactive power = 2,000 var

Apparent power = $\sqrt{(\text{True power})^2 + (\text{reactive power})^2}$

Apparent power = $\sqrt{(1,500 W)^2 + (2,000 var)^2}$

Apparent power = $\sqrt{625 \times 10^4}$ VA

Apparent power = 2,500 VA

Power factor. The power factor is a number (represented as a decimal or a percentage) that represents the portion of the apparent power dissipated in a circuit.

If the technician is familiar with trigonometry, the easiest way to find the power factor is to find the cosine of the phase angle (θ). The cosine of the phase angle is equal to the power factor.

It is not necessary to use trigonometry to find the power factor. Since the power dissipated in a circuit is true power, then:

Apparent power x PF = True power

Therefore:

$PF = \dfrac{\text{True power}}{\text{Apparent power}}$

If true power and apparent power are known, use the formula shown above.

Going one step further, another formula for power factor can be developed. By substituting the equations for true power and apparent power in the formula for power factor, the following formula is derived:

$PF = \dfrac{(I_R)^2 R}{(I_Z)^2 Z}$

Since current in a series circuit is the same in all parts of the circuit, IR equals I_Z. Therefore, in a series circuit:

$$PF = \frac{R}{Z}$$

EXAMPLE: to compute the power factor for the series circuit shown in Figure 3-4-10, any of the above methods may be used.

Given:

True power = 1,500 V
Reactive power = 2,500 VA

SOLUTION:

$$PF = \frac{\text{True power}}{\text{Apparent power}}$$

$$PF = \frac{1,500 \text{ W}}{2,500 \text{ VA}}$$

$$PF = 0.6$$

Another method:

Given:

$R = 60\Omega$
$Z = 100\Omega$

SOLUTION:

$$PF = \frac{R}{Z}$$

$$PF = \frac{60\Omega}{100\Omega}$$

$$PF = 0.6$$

If the technician is familiar with trigonometry, then it can be used to solve for angle θ and the power factor.

Given:

$R = 60\Omega$
$X = 80\Omega$

SOLUTION:

$$\tan \theta = \frac{X}{R}$$

$$\tan \theta = \frac{80\Omega}{60\Omega}$$

$$\tan \theta = 1.333$$

$$\theta = 53.1°$$

$$PF = \cos \theta$$

$$PF = 0.6$$

Power factor correction. The apparent power in an AC circuit has been described as the power the source "sees." As far as the source is concerned the apparent power is the power that must be provided to the circuit. Remember that the true power is the power actually used in the circuit. The difference between apparent power and true power is wasted because, in reality, only true power is consumed. The ideal situation would be for apparent power and true power to be equal. If this were the case the power factor would be 1 (unity), or 100 percent. There are two ways this condition can exist:

- The circuit is purely resistive, or
- The circuit "appears" purely resistive to the source.

To make the circuit appear purely resistive, there must be no reactance. To have no reactance in the circuit, the inductive reactance (X_L) and capacitive reactance (X_C) must be equal.

$$X = X_L - X_C$$

Therefore, when:

$$X_L = X_C, \text{ then } X = 0$$

The expression "correcting the power factor" refers to reducing the reactance in a circuit.

The ideal situation is to have no reactance in the circuit. This is accomplished by adding capacitive reactance to a circuit that is inductive and inductive reactance to a circuit that is capacitive. For example, the circuit shown in Figure 3-4-10 has a total reactance of 80Ω capacitive and the power factor is 0.6, or 60 percent. If 80Ω of inductive reactance were added to this circuit (by adding another inductor) the circuit would have a total reactance of 0Ω and a power factor of 1, or 100 percent. The apparent and true power of this circuit would then be equal.

Parallel RLC Circuits

When dealing with a parallel AC circuit, the technician will find that the concepts presented in this section for series AC circuits still apply. There is one major difference between a series circuit and a parallel circuit that must be considered: Current is the same in all parts of a series circuit, whereas voltage is the same across all branches of a parallel circuit. Because of this difference, the total impedance of a parallel circuit must be computed on the basis of the current in the circuit.

Remember that in the series RLC circuit the following three formulas were used to find reactance, impedance and power factor:

$$X = X_L - X_C \text{ or } X = X_C - X_L$$
$$Z = \sqrt{(I_R)^2 + X^2}$$
$$PF = \frac{R}{Z}$$

When working with a parallel circuit the following formulas must be used instead:

$$I_X = I_L - I_C \text{ or } I_X = I_C - I_L$$
$$I_Z = \sqrt{(I_R)^2 + (I_X)^2}$$
$$PF = \frac{I_R}{I_Z}$$

The impedance of a parallel circuit is found by the formula:

$$Z = \frac{E}{I_Z}$$

NOTE: *If no value for E is given in a circuit, any value of E can be assumed to find the values of I_L, I_C, I_X, I_R and I_Z. The same value of voltage is then used to find impedance.*

EXAMPLE: Find the value of Z in the circuit shown in Figure 3-4-11.

Given:

$$E = 300 \text{ V}$$
$$R = 100 \Omega$$
$$X_L = 50 \Omega$$
$$X_C = 150 \Omega$$

The first step in solving for Z is to calculate the individual branch currents.

SOLUTION:

$$I_R = \frac{E}{R}$$
$$I_R = \frac{300 \text{ V}}{100 \Omega}$$
$$I_R = 3 \text{ A}$$

$$I_L = \frac{E}{X_L}$$
$$I_L = \frac{300 \text{ V}}{50 \Omega}$$
$$I_L = 6 \text{ A}$$

$$I_C = \frac{E}{X_C}$$
$$I_C = \frac{300 \text{ V}}{150 \Omega}$$
$$I_C = 2 \text{ A}$$

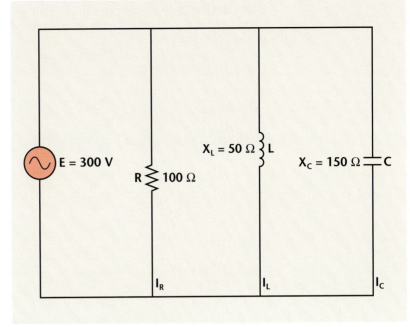

Figure 3-4-11. Parallel RLC circuit

Using the values for I_R, I_L and I_C, solve for I_X and I_Z.

$$I_X = I_L - I_C$$
$$I_X = 6 \text{ A} - 2 \text{ A}$$
$$I_X = 4 \text{ A (inductive)}$$
$$I_Z = \sqrt{(I_R)^2 + (I_X)^2}$$
$$I_Z = \sqrt{(3 \text{ A})^2 + (4 \text{ A})^2}$$
$$I_Z = \sqrt{25} \text{ A}$$
$$I_Z = 5 \text{ A}$$

Using this value of I_Z, solve for Z.

$$Z = \frac{E}{I_Z}$$
$$Z = \frac{300 \text{ V}}{5 \text{ A}}$$
$$Z = 60 \Omega$$

If the value for E was not given and it is necessary to solve for Z, any value of E could be assumed. If, in the example problem above, it is assigned a value of 50 V for E, the solution would be:

Given:

$$R = 100 \Omega$$
$$X_L = 50 \Omega$$
$$X_C = 150 \Omega$$
$$E = 50 \text{ V (assumed)}$$

First solve for the values of current in the same manner as before.

SOLUTION:

$$I_R = \frac{E}{R}$$

$$I_R = \frac{50 \text{ V}}{100 \Omega}$$

$$I_R = 0.5 \text{ A}$$

$$I_L = \frac{E}{X_L}$$

$$I_L = \frac{50 \text{ V}}{50 \Omega}$$

$$I_L = 1 \text{ A}$$

$$I_C = \frac{E}{X_C}$$

$$I_C = \frac{50 \text{ V}}{150 \Omega}$$

$$I_C = 0.33 \text{ A}$$

Solve for I_X and I_Z.

$$I_X = I_L - I_C$$
$$I_X = 1 \text{ A} - 0.33 \text{ A}$$
$$I_X = 0.67 \text{ A (inductive)}$$
$$I_Z = \sqrt{(I_R)^2 + (I_X)^2}$$
$$I_Z = \sqrt{(0.5 \text{ A})^2 + (0.67 \text{ A})^2}$$
$$I_Z = \sqrt{0.6989} \text{ A}$$
$$I_Z = 0.836 \text{ A}$$

Solve for Z.

$$Z = \frac{E}{I_Z}$$

$$Z = \frac{50 \text{ V}}{0.836 \text{ A}}$$

$$Z = 60 \Omega \text{ (rounded off)}$$

When the voltage is given, the technician can use the values of I_R, I_X and I_Z to calculate for the true power, reactive power, apparent power and power factor. For the circuit shown in Figure 3-4-11, the calculations would be as follows:

To find true power:

Given:

R = 100Ω
I_R = 3 A

SOLUTION:

True power = $(I_R)^2 X$
True power = $(3 \text{ A})^2 \times 75 \Omega$
True power = 900 W

To find reactive power, first find the value of reactance (X).

Given:

E = 300 V
I_X = 4 A (inductive)

SOLUTION:

$$X = \frac{E}{I_X}$$

$$X = \frac{300 \text{ V}}{4 \text{ A}}$$

$$X = 75 \Omega$$

Reactive power = $(I_X)^2 X$
Reactive power = $(4 \text{ A})^2 \times 75 \Omega$
Reactive power = 1,200 var

To find apparent power:

Given:

Z = 60Ω
I_Z = 5 A

SOLUTION:

Apparent power = $(I_Z)^2 Z$
Apparent power = $(5 \text{ A})^2 \times 60 \Omega$
Apparent power = 1,500 VA

The power factor in a parallel circuit is found by either of the following methods.

Given:

True power = 900 W
Apparent power = 900 W

SOLUTION:

$$PF = \frac{\text{True power}}{\text{Apparent power}}$$

$$PF = \frac{900 \text{ W}}{1,500 \text{ VA}}$$

PF = 0.6 or,

Given:

I_R = 3 A
I_Z = 5 A

SOLUTION:

$$PF = \frac{I_R}{I_Z}$$

$$PF = \frac{3 \text{ A}}{5 \text{ A}}$$

PF = 0.6

Resonance in Alternating Current Circuits

Series resonant circuit. It has been shown that both inductive reactance ($X_L = 2\pi fL$) and capacitive reactance ($X_C = 1/2\pi fC$) are functions of an AC frequency. Decreasing the frequency decreases the ohmic value of the inductive reactance, but a decrease in frequency increases the capacitive reactance.

At some particular frequency, known as the resonant frequency, the reactive effects of a capacitor and an inductor will be equal. Since these effects are the opposite of one another, they will cancel, leaving only the ohmic value of the resistance to oppose current flow in a circuit. If the value of resistance is small or consists only of the resistance in the conductors, the value of current flow can become very high.

In a circuit where the inductor and capacitor are in series and the frequency is the resonant frequency, or frequency of resonance, the circuit is said to be *in resonance* and is referred to as a series resonant circuit. The symbol for resonant frequency is F_R.

If, at the frequency of resonance, the inductive reactance is equal to the capacitive reactance, then:

$$X_L = X_C, \text{ or}$$

$$2\pi fL = \frac{1}{2\pi fC}$$

Dividing both sides by 2fL,

$$F_R^2 = \frac{1}{(2\pi)^2 LC}$$

Extracting the square root of both sides gives:

$$F_R = \frac{1}{2\pi \sqrt{LC}}$$

Where F_R is the resonant frequency in hertz, C is the capacitance in farads and L is the inductance in henrys. With this formula the frequency at which a capacitor and inductor will be resonant can be determined.

To find the inductive reactance of a circuit use

$$XL = 2(\pi)fL$$

Parallel resonant circuit. The impedance formula used in a series AC circuit must be modified to fit a parallel circuit.

$$Z = \frac{R_{XL}}{\sqrt{R^2 - XL^2}}$$

To find the parallel networks of inductance and capacitive reactors, use:

$$X = \frac{X_L X_C}{\sqrt{X_L + X_C}}$$

To find the parallel networks with resistance capacitive and inductance, use:

$$Z = \frac{R X_L X_C}{\sqrt{X_L^2 + X_C^2 + (RX_L - RX_C)^2}}$$

Since at the resonant frequency X_L cancels X_C, the current can become very high, depending on the amount of resistance. In such cases, the voltage drop across the inductor or capacitor will often be higher than the applied voltage.

In a parallel resonant circuit (Figure 3-4-12), the reactances are equal and equal currents will flow through the coil and the capacitor.

Since the inductive reactance causes the current through the coil to lag the voltage by 90°, and the capacitive reactance causes the current through the capacitor to lead the voltage by 90°, the two currents are 180° out of phase.

The canceling effect of such currents would mean that no current would flow from the generator and the parallel combination of the inductor and the capacitor would appear as an infinite impedance.

In practice, no such circuit is possible, since some value of resistance is always present, and the parallel circuit (sometimes called a tank circuit) acts as a very high impedance. It is also called an anti-resonant circuit, since its effect in a circuit is opposite to that of a series-resonant circuit, in which the impedance is very low.

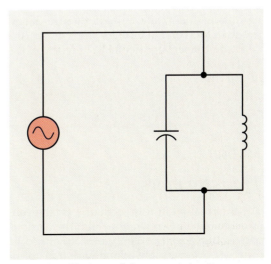

Figure 3-4-12. A parallel resonant circuit

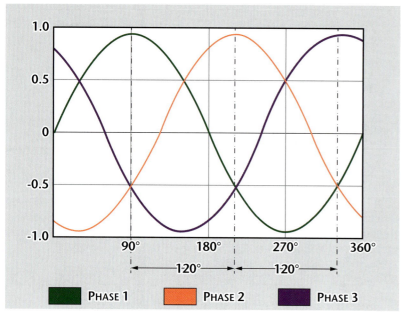

Figure 3-4-13. Example of a three-phase circuit

Three Phase

Up to this point, a single phase circuit, meaning that there is one sine wave being generated, has been discussed. Aircraft produce three-phase electric power, also known as polyphase. Each phase is separated by 120°. This is done by two different types of windings: a delta winding and a wye winding.

The delta winding as seen in Figure 3-4-13 is in the shape of the Greek letter delta, while the wye winding is in the shape of a Y. In a wye winding configuration, it is possible to extract two separate voltages from the three phases. For instance, such an arrangement could provide both 230 V and 400 V. The 230 V is supplied from the neutral and any one of the three windings, while the other two windings produce 400 V. In the delta configuration, only one voltage is possible, however this configuration does have a higher redundancy. If one of the three windings were to fail, the delta could operate at about 57.7 percent of the total capacity.

Section 5

Transformers

The information in this section is on the construction, theory, operation and the various uses of transformers. Safety precautions to be observed by a person working with transformers are also discussed.

A *transformer* is a device that transfers electrical energy from one circuit to another by electromagnetic induction (transformer action). The electrical energy is always transferred without a change in frequency, but may involve changes in magnitudes of voltage and current. Because a transformer works on the principle of electromagnetic induction, it must be used with an input source voltage that varies in amplitude. There are many types of power that fit this description; for ease of explanation and understanding, transformer action will be explained using an AC voltage as the input source.

In a previous section it was discussed that alternating current has certain advantages over direct current. One important advantage is that when AC is used, the voltage and current levels can be increased or decreased by means of a transformer.

As discussed, the amount of power used by the load of an electrical circuit is equal to the current in the load times the voltage across the load, or P = EI. If, for example, the load in an electrical circuit requires an input of 2 A at 10 V (20 W) and the source is capable of delivering only 1 A at 20 V, the circuit could not normally be used with this particular source. However, if a transformer is connected between the source and the load, the voltage can be decreased (stepped down) to 10 V and the current increased (stepped up) to 2 A. Notice in the above case that the power remains the same. That is, 20 V times 1 A equals the same power as 10 V times 2 A.

Basic Operation of a Transformer

In its most basic form a transformer is comprised of:

- A primary coil or winding
- A secondary coil or winding
- A core that supports the coils or windings

Refer to the transformer circuit in Figure 3-5-1 while reading this explanation. The primary winding is connected to a 60-Hz AC voltage source. The magnetic field (flux) builds up (expands) and collapses (contracts) about the primary winding. The expanding and contracting magnetic field around the primary winding cuts the secondary winding and induces an alternating voltage into the winding. This voltage causes alternating current to flow through the load. The voltage may be stepped up or stepped down depending on the design of the primary and secondary windings.

The Components of a Transformer

Two coils of wire (called windings) are wound on some type of core material. In some cases the coils of wire are wound on a cylindrical or rectangular cardboard form. In effect, the core material is air and the transformer is called an air-core transformer. Transformers used at low frequencies, such as 60 Hz and 400 Hz, require a core of low-reluctance magnetic material, usually iron. This type of transformer is called an iron-core transformer. Most power transformers are of the iron-core type. The principle parts of a transformer and their functions are:

- The core, which provides a path for the magnetic lines of flux
- The primary winding, which receives energy from the AC source
- The secondary winding, which receives energy from the primary winding and delivers it to the load
- The enclosure, which protects the above components from dirt, moisture and mechanical damage

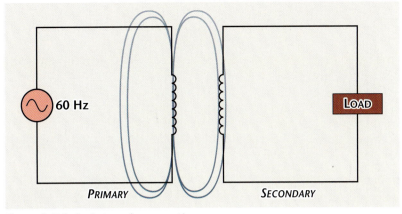

Figure 3-5-1. Basic transformer action

Core Characteristics

The composition of a transformer core depends on such factors as voltage, current and frequency. Size limitations and construction costs are also factors to be considered. Commonly used core materials are air, soft iron and steel. Each of these materials is suitable for particular applications and unsuitable for others. Generally, air-core transformers are used when the voltage source has a high frequency (above 20 kHz). Iron-core transformers are usually used when the source frequency is low (below 20 kHz). A soft-iron-core transformer is very useful where the transformer must be physically small, yet efficient. The iron-core transformer provides better power transfer than does the air-core transformer. A transformer whose core is constructed of laminated sheets of steel dissipates heat readily; thus it provides for the efficient transfer of power.

These steel laminations (Figure 3-5-2) are insulated with a nonconducting material, such as varnish, and then formed into a core. It takes about 50 laminations to make a core one inch thick. The purpose of the laminations is to reduce certain losses that will be discussed later in this chapter. An important point to remember is that the most efficient transformer core is one that offers the best path for the most lines of flux with the least loss in magnetic and electrical energy.

Hollow-core transformers. There are two main shapes of cores used in laminated-steel-

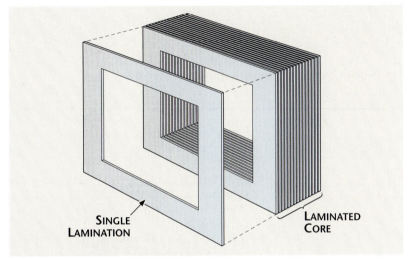

Figure 3-5-2. Hollow-core construction

core transformers. One is the hollow core, so named because the core is shaped with a hollow square through the center. Figure 3-5-2 illustrates this shape of core. Notice that the core is made up of many laminations of steel. Figure 3-5-3 illustrates how the transformer windings are wrapped around both sides of the core.

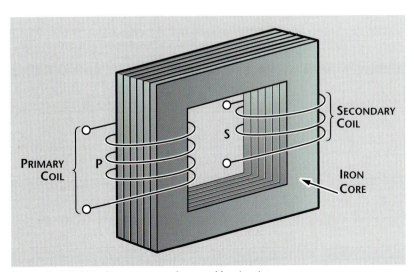

Figure 3-5-3. Windings wrapped around laminations

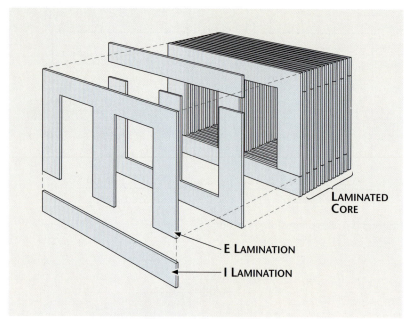

Figure 3-5-4. Shell-type core construction

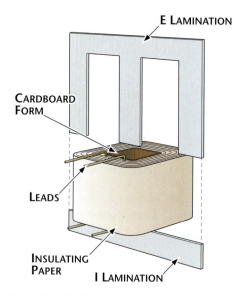

Figure 3-5-5. Shell-type transformer construction

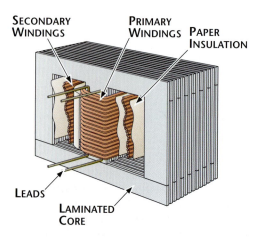

Figure 3-5-6. Cutaway view of shell-type core with windings

Shell-core transformers. The most popular and efficient transformer core is the shell core, as illustrated in Figure 3-5-4. As shown, each layer of the core consists of E- and I-shaped sections of metal. These sections are butted together to form the laminations. The laminations are insulated from each other and then pressed together to form the core.

Transformer Windings

As stated above, the transformer consists of two coils, called *windings*, that are wrapped around a core. The transformer operates when a source of AC voltage is connected to one of the windings and a load device is connected to the other.

The winding that is connected to the source is called the primary winding. The winding that is connected to the load is called the secondary winding. (Note: In this chapter the terms "primary winding" and "primary" are used interchangeably, as are "secondary winding" and "secondary.")

Figure 3-5-5 shows an exploded view of a shell-type transformer. The primary is wound in layers directly on a rectangular cardboard form.

In the transformer shown in the cutaway view in Figure 3-5-6, the primary consists of many turns of relatively small wire. The wire is coated with varnish so that each turn of the winding is insulated from every other turn. In a transformer designed for high-voltage applications, sheets of insulating material, such as paper, are placed between the layers of windings to provide additional insulation.

When the primary winding is completely wound, it is wrapped in insulating paper or cloth. The secondary winding is then wound on top of the primary winding. After the secondary winding is complete, it too is covered with insulating paper. Next, the E and I sections of the iron core are inserted into and around the windings as shown.

The leads from the windings are normally brought out through a hole in the enclosure of the transformer. Sometimes, terminals may be provided on the enclosure for connections to the windings. The figure shows four leads, two from the primary and two from the secondary. These leads are to be connected to the source and load, respectively.

Schematic Symbols for Transformers

Figure 3-5-7 shows typical schematic symbols for transformers. The symbol for an air-core transformer is shown in view A. Views B and C show iron-core transformers. The bars between the coils are used to indicate an iron core. Frequently, additional connections are made to the transformer windings at points other than the ends of the windings. These additional connections are called *taps*. When a tap is connected to the center of the winding, it is called a *center tap*. View C shows the schematic of a center-tapped iron-core transformer. A ferrite core schematic is seen in View D.

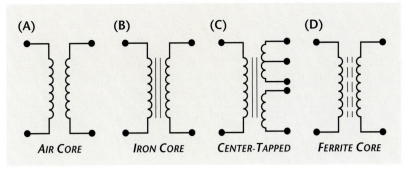

Figure 3-5-7. Schematic symbols for various types of transformers

No-Load Condition

As covered in an earlier section, a transformer is capable of supplying voltages which are usually higher or lower than the source voltage. This is accomplished through mutual induction, which takes place when the changing magnetic field produced by the primary voltage cuts the secondary winding.

A no-load condition is said to exist when a voltage is applied to the primary, but no load is connected to the secondary, as illustrated by Figure 3-5-8. Because of the open switch, there is no current flowing in the secondary winding. With the switch open and an AC voltage applied to the primary, there is, however, a very small amount of current, called *exciting current*, flowing in the primary. Essentially, what the exciting current does is "excite" the coil of the primary to create a magnetic field. The amount of exciting current is determined by three factors:

- The amount of voltage applied (E_a)
- The resistance (R) of the primary coil's wire and core losses
- The X_L, which is dependent on the frequency of the exciting current

These last two factors are controlled by transformer design.

This very small amount of exciting current serves two functions:

- Most of the exciting energy is used to maintain the magnetic field of the primary.
- A small amount of energy is used to overcome the resistance of the wire and core losses that are dissipated in the form of heat (power loss).

Exciting current will flow in the primary winding at all times to maintain this magnetic field, but no transfer of energy will take place as long as the secondary circuit is open.

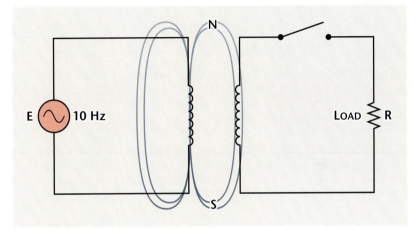

Figure 3-5-8. Transformer under no-load conditions

Producing a Counter emf

When an alternating current flows through a primary winding, a magnetic field is established around the winding. As the lines of flux expand outward, relative motion is present, and a counter emf is induced in the winding. This is the same cemf that was discussed in the section about inductors. Flux leaves the primary at the north pole and enters the primary at the south pole. The cemf induced in the primary has a polarity that opposes the applied voltage, thus opposing the flow of current in the primary. It is the cemf that limits exciting current to a very low value.

Inducing a Voltage in the Secondary

To visualize how a voltage is induced into the secondary winding of a transformer, again refer to Figure 3-5-8. As the exciting current flows through the primary, magnetic lines of force are generated. While current is increasing in the primary, magnetic lines of force expand outward from the primary and cut the secondary. Recall that a voltage is induced into a coil when magnetic lines cut across it. Therefore, the voltage across the primary causes a voltage to be induced across the secondary.

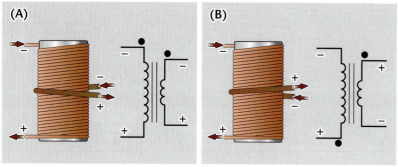

Figure 3-5-9. Instantaneous polarity depends on direction of winding

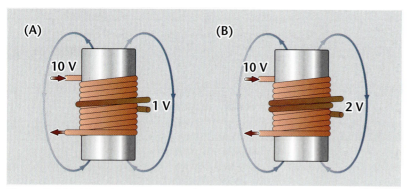

Figure 3-5-10. Transformer turns and voltage ratios

Primary and Secondary Phase Relationship

The secondary voltage of a simple transformer may be either in phase or out of phase with the primary voltage. This depends on the direction in which the windings are wound and the arrangement of the connections to the external circuit (load). Simply, this means that the two voltages may rise and fall together or one may rise while the other is falling.

Transformers in which the secondary voltage is in phase with the primary are referred to as *like-wound transformers*, while those in which the voltages are 180° out of phase are called *unlike-wound transformers*.

Dots are used to indicate points on a transformer schematic symbol that have the same instantaneous polarity (points that are in phase).

The use of phase-indicating dots is illustrated in Figure 3-5-9. In Figure 3-5-9A, both the primary and secondary windings are wound from top to bottom in a clockwise direction, as viewed from above the windings. When constructed in this manner, the top lead of the primary and the top lead of the secondary have the same polarity. This is indicated by the dots on the transformer symbol. A lack of phasing dots indicates a reversal of polarity.

Figure 3-5-9B illustrates a transformer in which the primary and secondary are wound in opposite directions. As viewed from above the windings, the primary is wound in a clockwise direction from top to bottom, while the secondary is wound counterclockwise. Notice that the top leads of the primary and secondary have opposite polarities. This is indicated by the dots being placed on opposite ends of the transformer symbol. Thus, the polarity of the voltage at the terminals of the secondary of a transformer depends on the direction in which the secondary is wound with respect to the primary.

Coefficient of Coupling

The coefficient of coupling of a transformer is dependent on the portion of the total flux lines that cuts both primary and secondary windings. Ideally, all the flux lines generated by the primary should cut the secondary, and all the lines of the flux generated by the secondary should cut the primary. The coefficient of coupling would then be one (unity), and maximum energy would be transferred from the primary to the secondary. Practical power transformers use high-permeability silicon-steel cores and close spacing between the windings to provide a high coefficient of coupling.

Lines of flux generated by one winding that do not link with the other winding are called *leakage flux*. Since leakage flux generated by the primary does not cut the secondary, it cannot induce a voltage into the secondary. The voltage induced into the secondary is therefore less than it would have been if the leakage flux did not exist. Since the effect of leakage flux is to lower the voltage induced into the secondary, the effect can be duplicated by assuming an inductor to be connected in series with the primary. This series leakage inductance is assumed to drop part of the applied voltage, leaving less voltage across the primary.

Turns and Voltage Ratios

The total voltage induced into the secondary winding of a transformer is determined mainly by the ratio of the number of turns in the primary to the number of turns in the secondary, and by the amount of voltage applied to the primary. Figure 3-5-10A shows a transformer whose primary consists of 10 turns of wire and whose secondary consists of a single turn of wire. As lines of flux generated by the primary expand and collapse, they cut both the 10 turns of the primary and the single turn of the secondary. Since the length of the wire in the secondary is approximately the same as the length of the wire in each turn in the primary, emf induced into the secondary will be the same as the emf induced into each turn in the primary. This means that if the voltage applied to the primary winding is 10 V, the cemf in the primary is almost 10 V. Thus, each turn in the primary will have an induced cemf of approximately one-tenth of the total applied voltage, or 1 V. Since the same flux lines cut the turns in both the secondary and the primary, each turn will have an emf of 1 V induced into it. The transformer in Figure 3-5-10A has only one turn in the secondary; thus, the emf across the secondary is 1 V.

The transformer represented in Figure 3-5-10B has a 10-turn primary and a 2-turn secondary. Since the flux induces 1 V per turn, the total voltage across the secondary is 2 V. Notice that the volts per turn are the same for both primary and secondary windings. Since the cemf in the primary is equal (or almost) to the applied voltage, a proportion may be set up to express the value of the voltage induced in terms of the voltage applied to the primary and the number of turns in each winding. This proportion also shows the relationship between the number of turns in each winding and the voltage across each winding. This proportion is expressed by the equation:

$$\frac{E_S}{E_P} = \frac{N_S}{N_P}$$

Where:

N_P = number of turns in the primary
E_P = voltage applied to the primary
E_S = voltage induced in the secondary
N_S = number of turns in the secondary

Notice the equation shows that the ratio of secondary voltage to primary voltage is equal to the ratio of secondary turns to primary turns. The equation can be written as:

$$E_P N_S = E_S N_P$$

The following formulas are derived from the above equation:

Transposing for E_S:

$$E_S = \frac{E_P N_S}{N_P}$$

Transposing for E_P:

$$E_P = \frac{E_S N_P}{N_S}$$

EXAMPLE: If any three of the quantities in the above formulas are known, the fourth quantity can be calculated. A transformer has 200 turns in the primary, 50 turns in the secondary, and 120 V applied to the primary (E_P). What is the voltage across the secondary (E_S)?

Given:

N_P = 200 turns
N_S = 50 turns
E_P = 120 V
E_S = ? V

SOLUTION:

$$E_S = \frac{E_P N_S}{N_P}$$

Substitution:

$$E_S = \frac{120 \text{ V} \times 50 \text{ turns}}{200 \text{ turns}}$$

$$E_S = 30 \text{ V}$$

EXAMPLE: There are 400 turns of wire in an iron-core coil. If this coil is to be used as the primary of a transformer, how many turns must be wound on the coil to form the secondary winding of the transformer to have a secondary voltage of 1 V if the primary voltage is 5 V?

Given:

N_P = 400 turns
E_P = 5 V
E_S = 1 V
N_S = ? turns

SOLUTION:

$$E_P N_S = E_S N_P$$

Transposing for N_S:

$$N_S = \frac{E_S N_P}{E_P}$$

Substitution:

$$N_S = \frac{1 \text{ V} \times 400 \text{ turns}}{5 \text{ V}}$$

$$N_S = 80 \text{ turns}$$

NOTE: *The ratio of the voltage (5:1) is equal to the ratio of the turns (400:80). Sometimes, instead of specific values, a turns or voltage ratio is given. In this case, assume any value for one of the voltages (or turns) and compute the other value from the ratio. For example, if a turn ratio is given as 6:1, then assume a number of turns for the primary and compute the secondary number of turns (60:10, 36:6, 30:5, etc.).*

The transformer in each of the above problems has fewer turns in the secondary than in the primary. As a result, there is less voltage across the secondary than across the primary.

A transformer in which the voltage across the secondary is less than the voltage across the primary is called a *step-down transformer*. The ratio of a four-to-one step-down transformer is written as 4: 1. A transformer that has fewer turns in the primary than in the secondary will produce a greater voltage across the secondary than the voltage applied to the primary. This is called a *step-up transformer*. The ratio of a one-to-four step-up transformer is written as 1:4. Notice in the two ratios that the value of the primary winding is always stated first.

Effect of a Load

When a load device is connected across the secondary winding of a transformer, current flows through the secondary and the load. The magnetic field produced by the current in the secondary interacts with the magnetic field produced by the current in the primary. This interaction results from the mutual inductance between the primary and secondary windings.

Mutual Flux

The total flux in the core of the transformer is common to both the primary and secondary windings. It is also the means by which energy is transferred from the primary winding to the secondary winding. Since this flux links both windings, it is called *mutual flux*. The inductance that produces this flux is also common to both windings and is called *mutual inductance*.

Figure 3-5-11 shows the flux produced by the currents in the primary and secondary windings of a transformer when source current is flowing in the primary winding.

When a load resistance is connected to the secondary winding, the voltage induced into the secondary winding causes current to flow in the secondary winding. This current produces a flux field about the secondary (shown in green) that is in opposition to the flux field about the primary (Lenz's law). Thus, the flux about the secondary cancels some of the flux about the primary. With less flux surrounding the primary, the cemf is reduced and more current is drawn from the source. The additional current in the primary generates more lines of flux, nearly reestablishing the original number of total flux lines.

Turns and Current Ratios

The number of flux lines developed in a core is proportional to the magnetizing force (in ampere-turns) of the primary and secondary windings. The ampere-turn ($I \times N$) is a measure of *magneto motive force*; it is defined as the magneto motive force developed by one ampere of current flowing in a coil of one turn. The flux that exists in the core of a transformer surrounds both the primary and secondary windings. Since the flux is the same for both windings, the ampere-turns in both the primary and secondary windings must be the same.

Therefore:

$$I_P N_P = I_S N_S$$

Where:

$I_P N_P$ = ampere – turns in the primary winding

$I_S N_S$ = ampere – turns in the secondary winding

By dividing both sides of the equation by $I_P N_S$, obtain the following:

$$\frac{N_P}{N_S} = \frac{I_S}{I_P}$$

Since:

$$\frac{E_S}{E_P} = \frac{N_S}{N_P}$$

Then:

$$\frac{E_P}{E_S} = \frac{N_P}{N_S}$$

And:

$$\frac{E_P}{E_S} = \frac{I_S}{I_P}$$

Where:

E_P = voltage applied to the primary in volts

E_S = voltage across the secondary in volts

I_P = current in the primary in amperes

I_S = current in the secondary in amperes

Notice the equations show the current ratio to be the inverse of the turn ratio and the voltage ratio. This means a transformer having fewer turns in the secondary than in the primary would step down the voltage, but would step up the current.

EXAMPLE: A transformer has a 6:1 voltage ratio. Find the current in the secondary if the current in the primary is 200 mA.

Given:

E_P = 6 V (assumed)

E_S = 1 V

I_P = 200 mA or 0.2 A

I_S = ?

SOLUTION:

$$\frac{E_P}{E_S} = \frac{I_S}{I_P}$$

Transposing for I_S:

$$I_S = \frac{E_P I_P}{E_S}$$

Substitution:

$$I_S = \frac{6\,V \times 0.2\,A}{E_S}$$

$$I_S = 1.2\,A$$

The above example points out that although the voltage across the secondary is one-sixth the voltage across the primary, the current in the secondary is six times the current in the primary.

The above equations can be looked at from another point of view. The expression below is called the transformer turn ratio and may be expressed as a single factor.

$$\frac{N_P}{N_S}$$

Remember, the turn ratio indicates the amount by which the transformer increases or decreases the voltage applied to the primary. For example, if the secondary of a transformer has two times as many turns as the primary, the voltage induced into the secondary will be two times the voltage across the primary. If the secondary has one-half as many turns as the primary, the voltage across the secondary will be one-half the voltage across the primary. However, the turn ratio and the current ratio of a transformer have an inverse relationship. Thus, a 1:2 step-up transformer will have one-half the current in the secondary as in the primary. A 2:1 step-down transformer will have twice the current in the secondary as in the primary.

EXAMPLE: A transformer with a turn ratio of 1:12 has 3 A of current in the secondary. What is the value of current in the primary?

Given:

N_P = 1 turn (assumed)
E_S = 12 turns
I_S = 3 A
I_P = ?

SOLUTION:

$$\frac{N_P}{N_S} = \frac{I_S}{I_P}$$

Transposing for I_P:

$$I_P = \frac{N_S I_S}{N_P}$$

Substitution:

$$I_P = \frac{12\,\text{turns} \times 3\,A}{1\,\text{turn}}$$

$$I_P = 36\,A$$

Power Relationship Between Primary and Secondary Windings

As just explained, the turn ratio of a transformer affects current as well as voltage. If voltage is doubled in the secondary, current is halved in the secondary. Conversely, if voltage is halved in the secondary, current is doubled in the secondary. In this manner, all the power delivered to the primary by the source is also delivered to the load by the secondary (minus whatever power is consumed by the transformer in the form of losses). Refer again to the transformer illustrated in Figure 3-5-11. The turn ratio is 20:1. If the input to the primary is 0.1 A at 300 V, the power in the primary is P = E x I = 30 W. If the transformer has no losses, 30 W is delivered to the secondary. The secondary steps down the voltage to 15 V and steps up the current to 2 A. Thus, the power delivered to the load by the secondary is P = E x I = 15 V x 2 A = 30 W.

The reason for this is that when the number of turns in the secondary is decreased, the opposition to the flow of the current is also decreased. Hence, more current will flow in the secondary. If the turn ratio of the transformer is increased to 1:2, the number of turns on the secondary is twice the number of turns on the primary. This means the opposition to current is doubled. Thus, voltage is doubled, but current is halved due to the increased opposition to current in the secondary. The important thing to remember is that with the exception of the power consumed within the transformer, all power delivered to the primary by the source will be delivered to

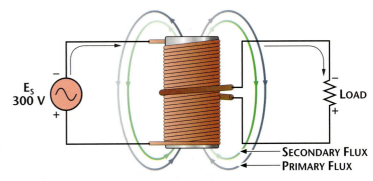

Figure 3-5-11. Transformer indicating primary- and secondary-winding flux relationship

the load. The form of the power may change, but the power in the secondary almost equals the power in the primary.

As a formula:

$P_S = P_P - P_L$

Where:

P_S = power delivered to the load by the secondary
P_P = power delivered to the primary by the source
P_L = power losses in the transformer

Transformer Losses

Practical power transformers, although highly efficient, are not perfect devices. Small power transformers used in electrical equipment have an 80 to 90 percent efficiency range, while large, commercial powerline transformers may have efficiencies exceeding 98 percent.

The total power loss in a transformer is a combination of three types of losses. One loss is due to the DC resistance in the primary and secondary windings. This loss is called *copper loss* or I^2R loss. The two other losses are due to eddy current and to hysteresis in the core of the transformer. Copper loss, eddy-current loss and hysteresis loss result in undesirable conversion of electrical energy into heat energy.

Copper Loss

Whenever current flows in a conductor, power is dissipated in the resistance of the conductor in the form of heat. The amount of power dissipated by the conductor is directly proportional to the resistance of the wire and to the square of the current through it. The greater the value of resistance or current, the greater is the power dissipated. The primary and secondary windings of a transformer are usually made of low-resistance copper wire. The resistance of a given winding is a function of the diameter and length of the wire. Using the proper diameter wire minimizes copper loss. Large-diameter wire is required for high-current windings, whereas small-diameter wire can be used for low-current windings.

Eddy-Current Loss

The core of a transformer is usually constructed of some type of ferromagnetic material because it is a good conductor of magnetic lines of flux.

Whenever the primary of an iron-core transformer is energized by an AC source, a fluctuating magnetic field is produced. This magnetic field cuts the conducting core material and induces a voltage into it. The induced voltage causes random currents to flow through the core, which dissipates power in the form of heat. These undesirable currents are called *eddy currents*.

To minimize the loss resulting from eddy currents, transformer cores are laminated. Since the thin, insulated laminations do not provide an easy path for current, eddy-current losses are greatly reduced.

Hysteresis Loss

When a magnetic field is passed through a core, the core material becomes magnetized. To become magnetized, the domains within the core must align themselves with the external field. If the direction of the field is reversed, the domains must turn so that their poles are aligned with the new direction of the external field.

Power transformers normally operate from 60-Hz or 400-Hz alternating current. Each tiny domain must realign itself twice during each cycle, or a total of 120 times a second when 60-Hz alternating current is used. The energy used to turn each domain is dissipated as heat within the iron core. This loss, called *hysteresis loss*, can be thought of as resulting from molecular friction. Hysteresis loss can be held to a small value by proper choice of core materials.

Transformer Efficiency

To compute the efficiency of a transformer, the input power to and the output power from the transformer must be known. The input power is equal to the product of the voltage applied to the primary and the current in the primary. The output power is equal to the product of the voltage across the secondary and the current in the secondary. The difference between the input power and the output power represents a power loss. The technician can calculate the percentage of efficiency of a transformer by using the standard efficiency formula shown here:

$$\text{Efficiency (in \%)} = \frac{P_{out}}{P_{in}} \times 100$$

Where:

P_{out} = total output power delivered to the load
P_{in} = total input power

EXAMPLE. If the input power to a transformer is 650 W and the output power is 610 W, what is the efficiency?

SOLUTION:

$$\text{Efficiency} = \frac{P_{out}}{P_{in}} \times 100$$

$$\text{Efficiency} = \frac{610 \text{ W}}{650 \text{ W}} \times 100$$

$$\text{Efficiency} = 93.8\%$$

Hence, the efficiency is approximately 93.8 percent, with approximately 40 W being wasted due to heat losses.

Transformer Ratings

When a transformer is to be used in a circuit, more than just the turn ratio must be considered. The voltage, current and power-handling capabilities of the primary and secondary windings must also be considered.

The maximum voltage that can safely be applied to any winding is determined by the type and thickness of the insulation used. When a better (and thicker) insulation is used between the windings, a higher maximum voltage can be applied.

The maximum current that can be carried by a transformer winding is determined by the diameter of the wire used for the winding. If current is excessive in a winding, a higher than ordinary amount of power will be dissipated in the form of heat. This heat may be sufficiently high to cause the insulation around the wire to break down. If this happens, the transformer may be permanently damaged.

The power handling capacity of a transformer is dependent upon its ability to dissipate heat. If heat can safely be removed, the power handling capacity of the transformer can be increased. This is sometimes accomplished by immersing the transformer in oil, or by the use of cooling fins. The power handling capacity of a transformer is measured in either the volt-ampere unit or the watt unit.

Two common power generator frequencies (60 Hz and 400 Hz) have been mentioned, but the effect of varying frequency has not been discussed. If the frequency applied to a transformer is increased, the inductive reactance of the windings is increased, causing a greater AC voltage drop across the windings and a lesser voltage drop across the load. However, an increase in the frequency applied to a transformer should not damage it. But, if the frequency applied to the transformer is decreased, the reactance of the windings is decreased and the current through the transformer winding is increased. If the decrease in frequency is enough, the resulting increase in current will damage the transformer. For this reason a transformer may be used at frequencies above its normal operating frequency, but not below that frequency.

Types and Applications of Transformers

The transformer has many useful applications in an electrical circuit. A brief discussion of some of these applications will help the technician recognize the importance of the transformer in electricity and electronics.

Power Transformers

Power transformers are used to supply voltages to the circuits in electrical equipment. These transformers have two or more windings on a laminated iron core. The number of windings and the turns per winding depend upon the voltages that the transformer is to supply. Their coefficient of coupling is 0.95 or more.

The technician can usually distinguish between the high-voltage and low-voltage windings in a power transformer by measuring the resistance. The low-voltage winding usually carries the higher current and, therefore, has the larger diameter wire. This means that its resistance is less than the resistance of the high-voltage winding, which normally carries less current and, therefore, may be constructed of smaller diameter wire.

So far the discussion has covered transformers that have but one secondary winding. The typical power transformer has several secondary windings, each providing a different voltage. The schematic symbol for a typical power-supply transformer is shown in Figure 3-5-12.

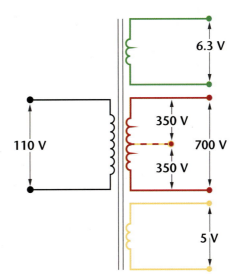

Figure 3-5-12. Schematic diagram of a typical power transformer

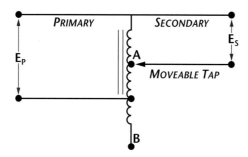

Figure 3-5-13. Schematic diagram of an autotransformer

For any given voltage across the primary, the voltage across each of the secondary windings is determined by the number of turns in each secondary. A winding may be center-tapped like the secondary 350-V winding shown in the figure. To center tap a winding means to connect a wire to the center of the coil, so that between this center tap and either terminal of the winding there appears one-half of the voltage developed across the entire winding. Most power transformers have colored leads so that it is easy to distinguish between the various windings to which they are connected. Figure 3-5-12 also illustrates the color codes for a typical power transformer. Usually, red is used to indicate the high-voltage leads, but it is possible for a manufacturer to use some other color.

There are many types of power transformers. They range in size from huge transformers weighing several tons (used in power substations of commercial power companies) to very small ones weighing as little as a few ounces (used in electronic equipment).

Autotransformers

It is not necessary in a transformer for the primary and secondary to be separate and distinct windings. Figure 3-5-13 is a schematic diagram of what is known as an *autotransformer*. Note that a single coil of wire is "tapped" to produce what is electrically a primary and secondary winding. The voltage across the secondary winding has the same relationship to the voltage across the primary that it would have if they were two distinct windings. The movable tap in the secondary is used to select a value of output voltage, either higher or lower than E_P, within the range of the transformer. That is, when the tap is at point A, E_S is less than E_P; when the tap is at point B, E_S is greater than E_P.

Audio-Frequency Transformers

Audio-frequency (AT) transformers are used in audio-frequency circuits as coupling devices.

Audio-frequency transformers are designed to operate at frequencies in the audio-frequency spectrum (generally considered to be 15 Hz to 20 kHz). They consist of a primary and a secondary winding wound on a laminated iron or steel core. Because these transformers are subjected to higher frequencies than are power transformers, special grades of steel such as silicon steel or special alloys of iron that have a very low hysteresis loss must be used for core material. These transformers usually have a greater number of turns in the secondary than in the primary; common step-up ratios being 1:2 or 1:4. With audio-frequency transformers, the impedance of the primary and secondary windings is as important as the ratio of turns, since the transformer selected should have its impedance match the circuits to which it is connected.

Radio-Frequency Transformers

Radio-frequency (RF) transformers are used to couple circuits to which frequencies above 20,000 Hz are applied. The windings are wound on a tube of nonmagnetic material, have a special powdered-iron core, or contain only air as the core material. In standard broadcast radio receivers, they operate in a frequency range of from 530 kHz to 1,550 kHz. In a short-wave receiver, RF transformers are subjected to frequencies up to about 20 MHz; in radar, up to and even above 200 MHz.

Impedance-Matching Transformers

For maximum or optimum transfer of power between two circuits, it is necessary for the impedance of one circuit to be matched to that of the other circuit. One common impedance-matching device is the transformer. To obtain proper matching, the technician must use a transformer having the correct turn ratio. The number of turns on the primary and secondary windings and the impedance of the transformer have the following mathematical relationship:

$$\frac{N_P}{N_S} = \sqrt{\frac{Z_P}{Z_S}}$$

Because of this ability to match impedances, the impedance-matching transformer is widely used in electronic equipment.

Transformer Troubleshooting

There are occasions when a transformer must be checked for opens or shorts, and it is often necessary to determine whether a transformer is a step-up or step-down transformer.

An open winding in a transformer can be located by connecting an ohmmeter as shown in Figure 3-5-14. Connected as shown, the ohmmeter would read infinity. If there were no open in the coil, the ohmmeter would indicate the resistance of wire in the coil. Both primary and secondary can be checked in the same manner.

The ohmmeter may also be used to check for shorted windings, as shown in Figure 3-5-15; however, this method is not always accurate. If, for example, the transformer had 500 turns and a resistance of 2 ohms, and 5 turns were shorted out, the resistance would be reduced to approximately 1.98 ohms, which is not enough of a change to be read on the ohmmeter. In this case, the rated input voltage can be applied to the primary to permit measurement of the secondary output voltage.

If the secondary voltage is low, it can be assumed that the transformer has some shorted windings, and the transformer should be replaced.

If the output voltage is normal after replacement, the original transformer can be considered defective.

An ohmmeter can be used to determine whether a transformer is a step-up or step-down transformer. In a step-down transformer, the resistance of the secondary will be less than that of the primary, and the opposite will be true in the case of a step-up transformer. Another method involves applying a voltage to the primary and measuring the secondary output. The voltages used should not exceed the rated input voltage of the primary.

If a winding is completely shorted, it usually becomes overheated because of the high value of current flow. In many cases, the high heat will melt the wax in the transformer, and this can be detected by the resulting odor. Additionally, a voltmeter reading across the secondary will read zero. If the circuit contains a fuse, the heavy current may cause the fuse to blow before the transformer is heavily damaged.

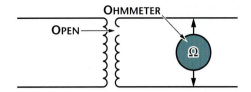

Figure 3-5-14. Checking for an open in a transformer winding

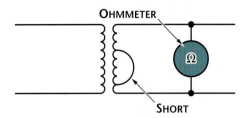

Figure 3-5-15. Checking for shorted transformer winding

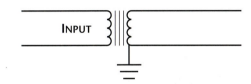

Figure 3-5-16. Part of a transformer winding grounded

One point on a transformer winding is shown connected to ground in Figure 3-5-16. If the external circuit of the transformer circuit is grounded, a part of the winding is effectively shorted. A high-resistance reading ohmmeter connected between one side of the winding and the transformer case (ground) will verify this condition with a low or zero reading. In such a case, the transformer must be replaced.

4

Generation and Storage of Electricity

Aircraft include a multitude of different systems, from complex autopilot systems to the simplest operation of a light bulb. But one thing that all these systems need is a source of energy. And now with the changing of the times the need for more efficient and effective ways to produce that energy is being looked at.

An aircraft relies on three sources of energy: batteries, generators and alternators. Alternators and generators produce their energy from electromagnetic induction, while the battery produces its energy through chemical reactions.

In this section, each of these three sources of energy, as well as basic maintenance techniques that may be required in the field, will be covered. The operation and composition of these power sources will also be discussed.

Section 1

The Battery

To understand how a battery works, first look at a battery cell. In this section different types of batteries are covered as well as the physical make-up of the battery, and the chemical reaction that produces electricity. Proper maintenance, care and safety measures used with batteries are also detailed. For the purpose of this section, only the secondary type of battery will be talked about in detail.

The Cell

A cell is where the chemical reaction that transforms chemical energy into electrical

Learning Objective

DESCRIBE
- the different types of voltage regulators
- how the voltage regulator controls a generator or alternator

EXPLAIN
- clean up procedures for different types of batteries
- the difference between a primary and secondary battery
- the different battery charging methods
- the difference between an alternator and a generator

APPLY
- determine the state of a lead acid battery
- charge a battery
- perform inspections on generators
- troubleshoot batteries
- troubleshoot generators and alternators

Left. An aircraft's many systems all rely on an energy source to operate.

Figure 4-1-1. The voltaic pile, invented by Alessandro Volta in 1800, was the first electric battery.

energy takes place. The earliest battery was constructed by Alessandro Volta (Figure 4-1-1). By using the theory of animal electricity produced by Luigi Galvani, Volta in the year 1800 produced what he called the voltaic pile.

The *voltaic pile* was simply a zinc bar and a carbon bar suspended in a tank of water and sulfuric acid. Zinc is a negatively charged metal (*cathode*), while carbon is a positively charged metal (*anode*). These metal pieces are called electrodes. The water and sulfuric acid act as an *electrolyte*. This laid the ground work for the modern battery.

There are two different types of battery cells on the market today, primary and secondary cells. The primary cell is a onetime-use cell (Figure 4-1-2). As the cell is used, one of the electrodes (typically the negative one) is eaten away by the chemical reaction. When this happens the electrode must be replaced to restore the electrical potential of the battery. It is always easier and cheaper to just replace the battery as a whole. The other type of cell, secondary, is rechargeable. Instead of the electrode being eaten away, the electrode and electrolyte is altered by the chemical reaction. By applying an electrical current back into the cell, the electrode and electrolyte are restored to their normal states.

Chemical Reaction

The chemical reaction that converts chemical energy into electrical energy inside a battery is called *electrochemical action*. When the two electrodes are connected by a piece of wire and a load (completing the circuit), an electrical pressure is produced, causing electrons to travel from the anode to the cathode. Once the electrons reach the cathode, they are sent out to the load, providing it with a voltage and a current. Lastly the electrons will travel back to the cathode, starting the process all over.

The amount of voltage and current are dependent on a multitude of factors. For voltage, look at the material that the electrodes are made of and the composition of the electrolyte. The current will depend on the internal resistance of the cell, as well as the total resistance of the circuit. To determine the internal resistance of the cell, look at the size of the electrodes, the distance between them in the electrolyte, and the resistance of the electrolyte. In general the larger the electrodes and the closer they are, the lower the internal resistance will be.

Secondary Cells

There are many types of secondary cell batteries. In aircraft, the only types of batteries that are used are lead-acid and nickel-cadmium (Figure 4-1-3).

Lead-Acid Batteries

In the lead-acid battery, the cathode is made of a sponge lead, while the anode is lead peroxide. The electrolyte used is a mixture of sulfuric acid and water. As discussed previously, the electrodes in secondary cells are chemically altered as the charge of the battery is decreased. In a lead-acid battery the lead peroxide is changed into lead sulfate by the sulfuric acid. When completely discharged, the lead sulfate is at a maximum while the sulfuric acid is at a minimum. This will cause no chemical action to occur.

As discussed earlier, secondary cells can be recharged by connecting another power source to the battery in reverse (i.e., negative to positive and positive to negative). During the recharge process the lead sulfate is chemically changed

Figure 4-1-2. A variety of standard size primary cell batteries; from left, D battery, 9V battery, AA battery, and AAA battery

back to lead sponge in the cathode, lead peroxide in the anode, and sulfuric acid in the electrolyte.

Nickel-Cadmium Batteries

Nickel-cadmium cells has many advancements compared to lead-acid cells. The five main advantages are as follows:

- Less maintenance—electrolyte does not need to be added.
- Shorter time for charging.
- The battery can stay in an idle state longer and can keep charge while stored.
- The battery can be charged and discharged many times without any appreciable damage.
- The battery stays at a full voltage state until the battery is completely depleted.

Like the lead-acid battery, the Nickel-cadmium still contains two electrodes and an electrolyte. Where they start to differ is in the material and chemicals used inside the battery. The positive plate (electrode) is made of a porous plaque that has nickel hydroxide deposited onto it. The negative plate will have a similar plaque of cadmium hydroxide deposits. The porous plaques on the positive and negative plates are obtained by sintering nickel powder to a fine-wire screen. *Sintering* is the process that fuses together extremely small granules of powder at a high temperature. The electrolyte is a 30 percent solution of potassium hydroxide in distilled water.

During the charging process, the negative plates lose oxygen and form metallic cadmium, and the positive plates become highly oxidized. This continues until the charging process is completed. At the end of the charging cycle the cell emits a gas. This gas occurs because of the breakdown of the water in the electrolyte (hydrogen at the negative plates, and oxygen at the positive plate).

The chemical action is reversed during the discharge process. Oxygen is lost by the positive plate and regained by the negative plate. Also during discharge, the electrolyte is absorbed into the plates, but will be released during charge. For this reason the electrolyte will be highest at a full charge. Water should only be added for servicing when the battery is fully charged.

Combining Cells

In most cases, one battery is not enough to supply full power to the equipment it is meant to power. The batteries used to power an aircraft are made up of multiple cells, typically in series, though they can be wired in parallel. If the batteries are

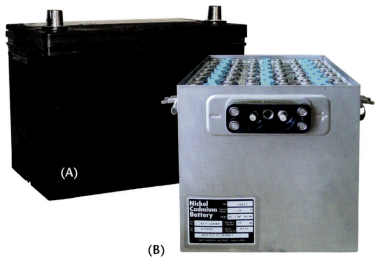

Figure 4-1-3. (A) Lead-acid and, (B) Nickel-cadmium batteries

connected in series, a higher voltage will be present for the circuit. Wiring in parallel provides a higher current. The last possible combination is in series-parallel. This configuration provides adequate power when voltage and current requirements are higher then what one cell can supply.

Series-Connected Cells

It is possible to have a circuit that may require 6 V and only $1/8$ A. The downfall is that most cells only have a voltage of 1.5 V a piece. To obtain the necessary 6 V, connect four cells in series (Figure 4-1-4). The process is very easy; each battery is

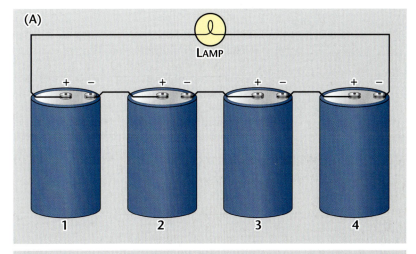

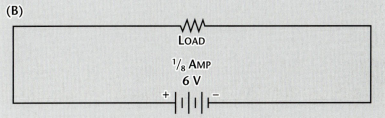

Figure 4-1-4. Series-connected; (A) Cells and, (B) Schematic

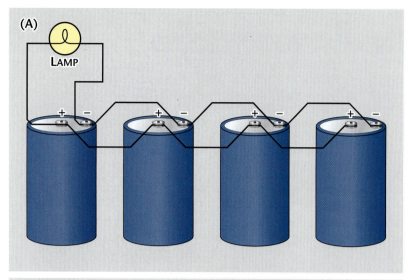

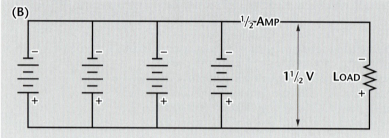

Figure 4-1-5. Parallel-connected; (A) Cells and, (B) Schematic

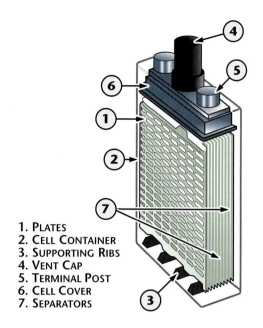

1. Plates
2. Cell Container
3. Supporting Ribs
4. Vent Cap
5. Terminal Post
6. Cell Cover
7. Separators

Figure 4-1-7. Lead-acid cell construction

connected from negative to positive. Since this is a series circuit the voltage will be added to reach 6 volts, and throughout the circuit is equal to the current of a single cell, $1/8$ A. As a note of caution, make sure to not connect the last two terminals together because there is the possibility for some types of cells to explode.

Parallel-Connected Cells

There are other situations where a low voltage, but a high current might be needed. If only 1.5 V is required, but $1/2$ A. To do this use the same four batteries as in the series example, but instead connect them in parallel (Figure 4-1-5). This is accomplished by simply connecting all the positive terminals and all the negative terminals. With this procedure, the voltage stays constant at 1.5 V, but the current of each battery is added together and reaches $1/2$ A.

Series-Parallel-Connected Cells

The last scenario is where a higher voltage as well as a higher current are needed. This is done by wiring the batteries in a series-parallel circuit (Figure 4-1-6). The downfall to this is that more batteries will be required. Say, for example, that 4.5 V and $1/2$ A are required. First make four sets of three batteries wired in series. Then wire those four sets in parallel. The three batteries will add up their voltage to the 4.5 V, while the four sets of the batteries in parallel will add up the current to the $1/2$ A.

Battery Construction

Batteries are constructed of multiple cells. The individual cell has been covered, but not how the complete battery is constructed.

Lead-Acid Construction

In a lead acid battery, the container houses many separate cells (Figure 4-1-7). The number of cells depends on the amount of voltage that is needed. If the aircraft requires 12 V, there will be six cells. If the aircraft requires 24 V, there will be 12 cells.

The container is made up of rubber, plastic or some other type of material that is resistant to the electrolyte and mechanical shock. A

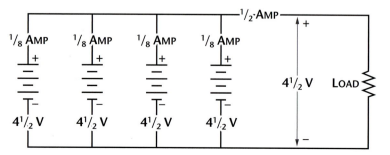

Figure 4-1-6. Schematic of series-parallel connected cells.

container must be able to resist extreme temperature. The case has a vent plug that will allow the gasses from the cells to escape.

Earlier discussions covered the cathode and anode, which are the plates. Physically the plates are interlaced with the terminal, which is attached to each plate group. The terminals of each cell are connected by link connectors in series. On the two end cells, one of the cells will have its positive terminal as the positive terminal for the battery, while the other will have its negative terminal as the negative terminal for the battery.

The terminals of the lead acid battery are identified by the size of the terminal or by the markings on the terminal. The positive terminal is marked with a (+) symbol, and the color of the terminal is sometimes red. The negative terminal will have a (–) symbol and is physically larger.

The cells inside the lead-acid battery are not replaceable. When a single cell fails, the whole battery must be replaced.

Nickel-cadmium Construction

The internal construction of the Nickel-cadmium battery is very similar to the construction of the lead-acid battery. Where they differ is that the cells inside of the battery are replaceable. The case is usually made of metal, unlike the lead-acid battery. Inside the case, all the cells are connected to each other by metal plates that can be removed to facilitate the removal of the individual cell (Figure 4-1-8). The outside terminal also differs in the fact that a special plug connects the battery to the rest of the system.

Battery Maintenance

The following is some of the maintenance that may have to be done on lead-acid or Nickel-cadmium batteries. Always refer to the technical manual for the specific battery prior to performing maintenance.

Lead-Acid Battery Maintenance

At times the technician may be required to service a lead-acid battery. Listed below are items to look for and their fixes.

- Any leaking electrolyte—Clean with soda bicarbonate (baking soda) and water and determine whether the case cracked or the electrolyte overflowed out of the battery.

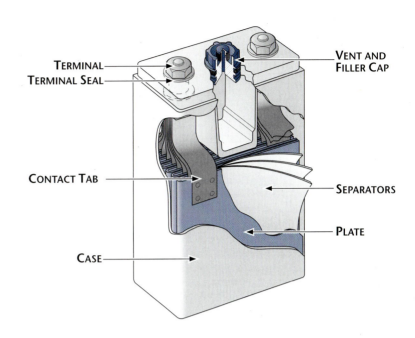

Figure 4-1-8. Nickel-cadmium cell construction

- Loose or missing hold-down fittings—Tighten or replace fittings.
- Broken or loose terminal—Tighten or replace terminal.
- Loose or missing vent caps—Tighten or replace vent cap.
- Low electrolyte levels—Fill to appropriate level with distilled water.
- Vent lines with kinks, cuts or blockage—Replace vent lines.

Another item to look at during an inspection of a lead-acid battery is the specific gravity. *Specific gravity* is a comparison between the weight of a fluid compared to water. To check this, use a hydrometer (Figure 4-1-9). The denser the electrolyte, the higher the float in the hydrometer will rise, as illustrated in

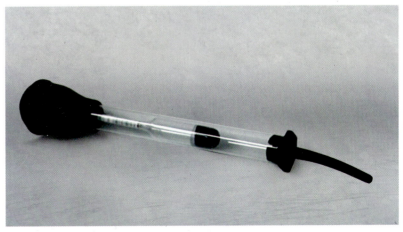

Figure 4-1-9. Hydrometer

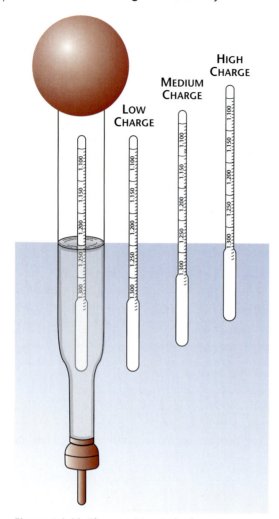

Figure 4-1-10. Float position in hydrometer

Figure 4-1-10. This reading helps in determining what the charge of the battery is. Typically a brand new battery will have a specific gravity of 1.3, but as time goes on the specific gravity will drop, indicating a lower charge of the battery.

Proper cleanliness of lead-acid batteries is also essential to a long lifespan. If a battery is not kept clean it can be prone to self discharge. The chemical powder that is produced by lead-acid batteries is corrosive and conductive. To clean off the battery use a nonconductive brush to loosen any powder that may be stuck onto the battery then use soda bicarbonate and water to wash the battery off.

Nickel-cadmium Maintenance

There is not as much maintenance to be done on a Nickel-cadmium battery as on a lead-acid battery. There are a few guidelines to follow to keep the battery up and running.

In the Nickel-cadmium battery there will be no appreciable change in the electrolyte during charging and discharging of the battery. Because of this, a hydrometer cannot be used since the specific gravity of the electrolyte will not change until the battery is completely depleted.

The one thing that must be maintained is the electrolyte, which must be just above the plates. To maintain the proper level of the electrolyte, wait three to four hours after a charge has been completed to prevent a spill. In the case of a spill, use boric acid or vinegar to clean the mess. When refilling the electrolyte, potassium hydroxide is added to the distilled water.

One thing that is a bother in Nickel-cadmium batteries is *thermal runaway*. Thermal runaway is a condition where the battery is trying to pull too much current to the point where the temperature melts the individual cells. The only way to correct this condition is to replace the cell.

The formation of potassium carbonate is an indication that the battery maybe overcharged. This is never a desirable condition. Clean off the potassium carbonate and ensure that no other damage has occurred to the battery. Personal protective equipment (PPE) such as goggles, rubber gloves and rubber aprons should be used when servicing Nickel-cadmium batteries. Potassium hydroxide used in the electrolyte is extremely corrosive.

Other Maintenance

There are a few things to consider when doing maintenance on both of these types of batteries. Some of these techniques are:

- Nickel-cadmium and lead-acid batteries should always be stored in separate areas to prevent cross-contamination.
- All tools used for the servicing of the batteries should also remain separate.
- When finished with tools, clean them off or rinse them out to prevent damage to them.
- Personal Protective Equipment (PPE) should be used when servicing Ni-Cad, such as goggles, rubber gloves, and rubber aprons. Potassium hydroxide used in the electrolyte is extremely corrosive
- A suitable washing facility should be provided in the case of a spill.
- Use of a wire brush to clean the battery can produce arcing, and vent plugs should be closed during cleaning. Acids, solvents or any other cleaning chemical should never be used.

Capacity and Rating

The capacity of a battery is measured in ampere-hours. This is the equal to the current multiplied by the time (in hours) the battery will last. The ampere-hour varies inversely with the discharging current, so a 50 ampere-hour battery will supply 50 A for 1 hour or 10 A for 5 hours.

Batteries are rated according to their rate of discharge and ampere-hour capacity. Most batteries are rated with a discharge during a 20-hour period. What this means is that the battery will be discharged in 20 hours, providing 20 A per hour. This indicates a capacity of 400 ampere-hours. Unfortunately, most aircraft batteries are not that efficient. The rating for aircraft batteries is at a 1-hour rate of discharge.

Even though batteries are rated for 20 hours, if the load demands more than 20 ampere-hour, the battery will not last the full 20 hours.

Charging Batteries

There are two methods of charging a battery: the constant-voltage method and the constant-current method.

Constant-Voltage Method

In this method of charging, a regulated constant voltage forces current through the battery. At the beginning of the charging process, the current starts out high but tapers off. By the time the charging process has finished, the current is 1 A. The benefit of this charging process is that it requires less time and supervision. This is also the method of keeping the battery charged while installed.

Constant-Current Method

Like the name says, the current during this charging method stays constant. The time that it takes to charge the battery is longer, and the charging process must be monitored. Toward the end of the charging process, it becomes essential to make sure that the battery does not overcharge. The benefit of this method is that multiple batteries can be charged at once as long as they are connected in series.

Section 2

Generators

Generators are widely used in the field of aviation for a source of power. In this section the generator and the units used to control it are discussed. Construction and the maintenance techniques that are commonly performed in the field are also covered. Finally, the type of equipment used to regulate a generator is discussed.

Generator Theory

Whenever a conductor is moved along a magnetic field, the conductor cuts the magnetic flux lines and produces a voltage in the conductor. (Flux lines are the lines of force that extend from a magnet.) This is the principle of generator theory. The amount voltage can depend on four things:

- The strength of the magnetic field
- The angle at which the flux lines are being cut
- The speed at which the conductor is being moved
- The length of the conductor inside the magnetic field

Another aspect to think about is the polarity of the voltage. To determine this, the direction of the flux lines and the direction of movement must be known. Once this is known use a method called the *left-hand rule for generators* (Figure 4-2-1). This is done by

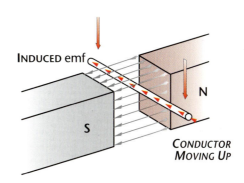

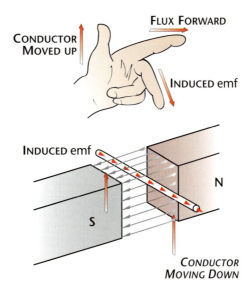

Figure 4-2-1. Application of left-hand rule

4-8 | Generation and Storage of Electricity

POSITION 1

Rotating conductors moving parallel to magnetic field, cutting minimum lines of force.

ZERO VOLTAGE

POSITION 2
ONE-QUARTER TURN COMPLETED

Conductors cutting directly across the magnetic field as conductor A passes across the north magnetic pole and B passes across the south pole.

MAXIMUM POSITIVE VOLTAGE

POSITION 3
ONE-HALF TURN COMPLETED

Conductors again moving parallel to magnetic field cutting minimum lines of force.

VOLTAGE DROPS TO ZERO

POSITION 4
THREE-QUARTER TURN COMPLETED

Conductors again moving directly across magnetic field. A passes across South magnetic pole and B across North magnetic pole.

MAXIMUM NEGATIVE VOLTAGE

POSITION 5
FULL TURN COMPLETED

Conductor A has made one complete cycle and is in same position as position 1. The generator has generated one complete cycle of alternating voltage or current.

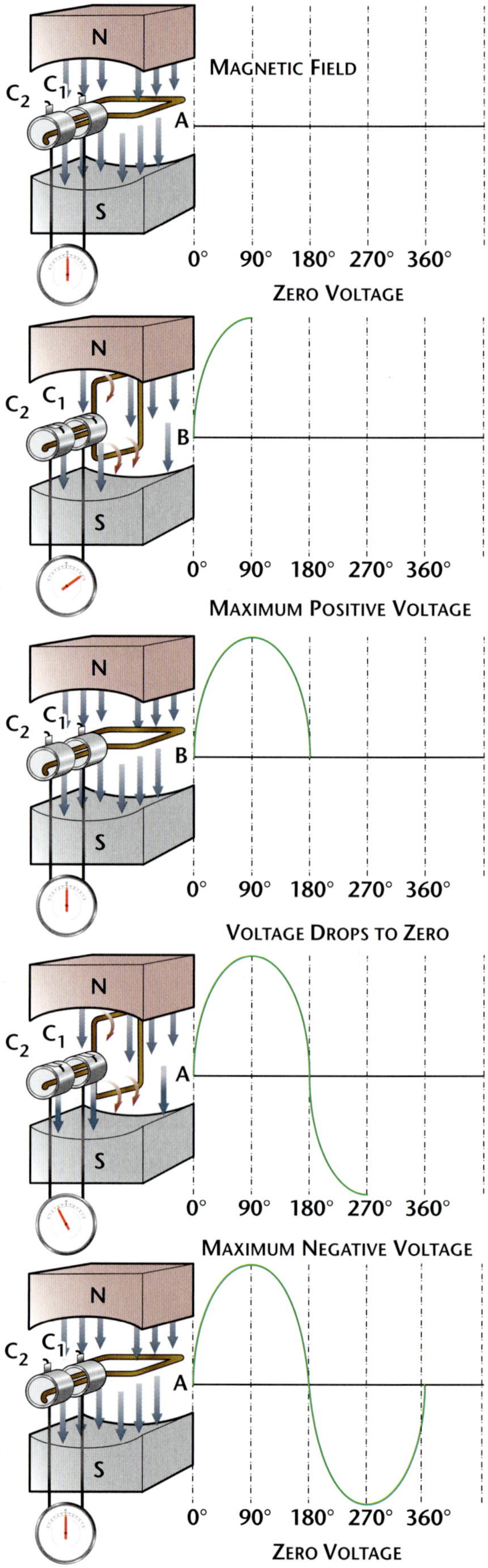

ZERO VOLTAGE

Figure 4-2-2. Generation of a sine wave

extending your thumb, forefinger, and middle finger of your left hand at right angles from each other. The thumb represents the direction that the conductor is moving, the forefinger points in the direction of the flux lines, and the middle finger represents the direction of current flow.

AC Generator

The simplest type of generator is the AC generator. For this reason they are studied first and then the DC generator is covered.

The most basic type of generator consists of a wire loop that is rotated between two magnets, commonly called the field coil. As the wire is rotated, a voltage is produced. Since the wire is rotating there must be a way to remove the voltage. This is accomplished using brushes and slip rings. As mentioned earlier, one of the dependent factors for voltage is the length of the conductor. So instead of just having one loop of wire inside of the magnetic field, there could be many different loops of wire. This group of wires is called the *armature*. At the end of the armature are the slip rings, and riding on top are the brushes. The brushes are usually made of carbon.

At 0° (when the loop is completely perpendicular), also referred to the neutral plane, the conductor is not cutting any flux lines as seen in Figure 4-2-2. As the conductor starts to move, more and more flux lines are being cut until it reaches 90°. At 90° the conductor is cutting the maximum amount of flux lines and is producing its maximum voltage. As the conductor moves down back down toward the 180° mark, the voltage decreases back to 0. The conductor continues to the 270° position, where again it is cutting the maximum number of flux lines and producing the most voltage possible. The big difference between the 90° and 270° mark is at 90°, the generator is producing a positive voltage, and at 270° it is producing a negative voltage. Once past the 270° mark, the conductor moves back to the 0° position, where it starts the whole process over again. AC generators are covered in more detail in the next section.

DC Generator

The DC generator (Figure 4-2-3) is very similar to the AC generator on the principle of how it works, but it differs in that there is no longer a slip ring. Instead of a slip ring a device called a *commutator* is used (Figure 4-2-4). The main difference between the slip ring and commutator is their construction. In a slip ring is a solid piece of metal that the brushes ride along. In a commutator there are pieces of metal segmented

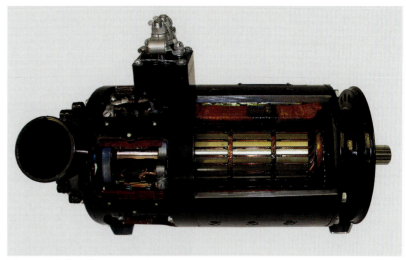

Figure 4-2-3. DC generator cutaway

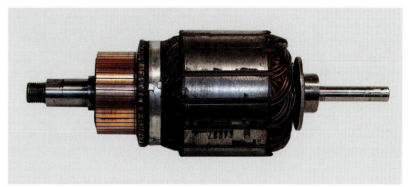

Figure 4-2-4. DC generator commutator

from each other by an insulator called *mica*. One thing to always make sure of is that the mica is not too long. The mica should be cut below the metal surface at a distance equal to its width.

The commutator's function is to mechanically reverse the armature loop connections to an external circuit whenever the polarity of the voltage changes. This process produces a pulsating DC voltage. This pulsating voltage is unidirectional and will vary twice during each revolution, between zero and the maximum. This variation is referred to as a ripple.

The pulsating DC is undesirable for most aircraft applications. To counter this condition more loops are added to the armature and more segments to the commutator. With this, the output generates less of a ripple and an almost smooth DC voltage is the outcome. The same results can be seen from adding another set of magnets surrounding the armature.

Since there is still a slight ripple in the output voltage of the generator, most aircraft have a capacitor wired to the generator before it reaches the voltage regulator. This capacitor will smooth out the DC voltage even more and produce a usable voltage.

4-10 | Generation and Storage of Electricity

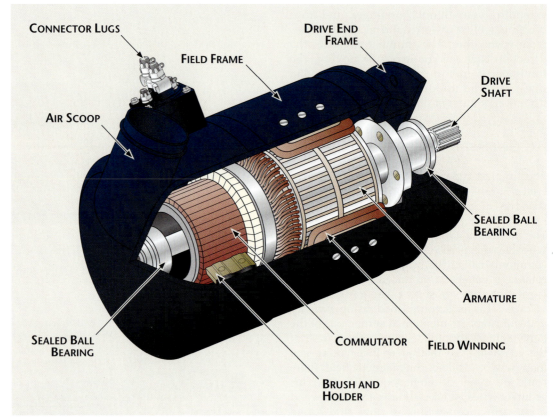

Figure 4-2-5. Construction of a DC generator

Generator Construction

The discussion to this point has been about the major parts that make up a generator. How these parts look and are assembled to create a generator is covered next. (Figure 4-2-5).

The magnets, or *field winding*, are attached on the outside case of the generator. Each field winding is housed inside of what is called a *pole* or *pole shoe*. Rotating inside of the generator is the *armature*. Remember that the armature cuts the flux lines from the field windings. Attached to the armature is the commutator, made up of many segments separated by mica. Riding on top of the commutator are the brushes. The brushes, made of carbon, remove the induced voltage from the commutator and send it to a *pig tail*, which sends the voltage to a lug nut on the outside of the generator. Attached to the brushes are springs to hold them in place and to help prevent arcing.

Common Generator Faults

To understand how the generator works and to better troubleshoot a possible problem, the technician must understand of what kind of

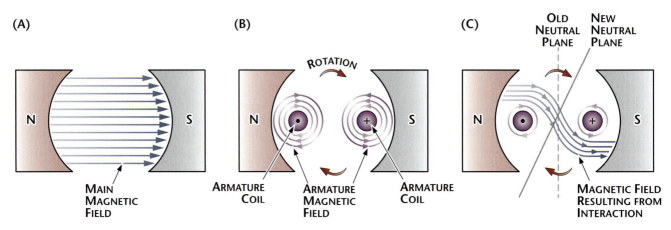

Figure 4-2-6. Armature reaction

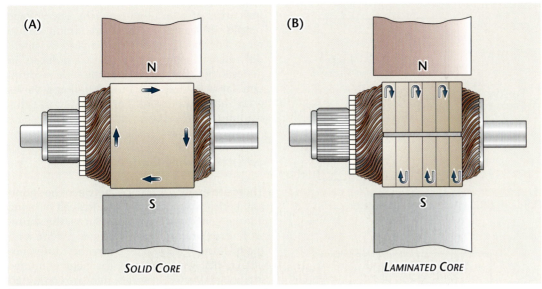

Figure 4-2-7. Eddy currents in DC generator armature cores

faults can happen inside of the generator. The following is a list of the common faults and their fixes.

NOTE: *Most problems that happen inside of the generator cannot be fixed by a field technician. Generators for the most part are a remove-and-replace item.*

Armature reaction. All current carrying conductors produce a magnetic field. The same is true for the armature. The armature affects the flux pattern and distorts the main field, causing a shift in the neutral plane. This is called *armature reaction* (Figure 4-2-6). In the long run, this can cause arcing between the commutator and the brushes. To correct this, change the position of the brushes or add *interpoles*. These interpoles will produce a magnetic field that varies directly with the armature current, eliminating the effects of armature reaction.

Copper losses. This form of loss is the result of heat in the armature windings. The amount of heat generated in the armature depends on the amount of current flowing through it (use I^2R to figure the amount of heat produced), and the amount of resistance of the armature itself. To keep this at a minimum, manufacturers use a larger diameter of wire in the armature windings.

Hysteresis losses. This also is a heat loss like the copper loss, but it deals with the magnetic properties of the armature. Particles in the core of the armature tend to line up with the magnetic field. Since the armature is in constant rotation during use, the particles are in a constant state of rotation. This will cause a molecular friction that will in turn produce heat. The heat then can be transferred into the windings, causing the resistance of those windings to increase. The counteractive measure used to prevent this is the use of heat-treated silicon steel laminations.

Armature losses. This type of loss is actually the combination copper loss, eddy current loss and hysteresis loss.

Motor reaction. Since the generator delivers current to a load, the armature will create a magnetic force. This magnetic force will oppose the rotation of the armature..

Eddy currents. This is unwanted induced current that is found in the armature (Figure 4-2-7). To prevent this, the windings inside the armature are laminated, increasing the resistance. Although there will be some eddy current still induced into the windings, the current is so small that it is considered negligible.

Commutator-to-brush arcing. As time goes on the carbon brushes wear down. Depending on how the brushes wear, arcing can occur. If at some point the brushes do not set smoothly on the commutator, a gap will occur between the two. This gap will cause the electricity to arc from the commutator to the brush. The way to determine if this is happening is by looking on the commutator for scorch marks. To fix this problem, use a piece of No. 000 sandpaper and run the brushes along it and the commutator. This will reform the brushes into the curvature of the commutator and remove the scorch marks from the commutator.

Failures can also happen inside of the armature windings. To check for these errors, use a *growler*. A growler is a standard device to check the armature for grounds and shorts. To do this test, place the armature on the growler. Now slowly rotate the armature while holding a hacksaw blade over it. If the hacksaw

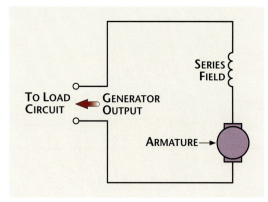

Figure 4-2-8. Series-wound generator

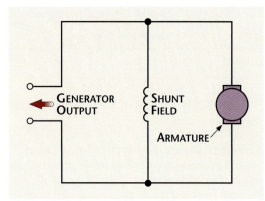

Figure 4-2-9. Shunt-wound generator

blade starts to vibrate over a certain segment of the armature, this could be an indication of a shorted armature coil.

Although some generators use electromagnets, a lot of them use permanent magnets. After a certain amount of time these magnets will start to lose their magnetic characteristics. If this happens, there will be a drop in voltage produced by the generator. To compensate for this, perform a process called *flashing the field*. To do this, reverse the power leads so that the battery is charging the magnets. This process will only take a few seconds and the magnets will be fully restored.

Types of Generators

There are three types of generators used in the field: series wound, shunt wound and compound wound.

Series-Wound Generators

The basic description of a series-wound generator is one in which the field windings and armature are wired in series with each other (Figure 4-2-8). In this type of generator the field coils have a low resistance and have very few turns of a large-gauge wire. The voltage output increases as the load circuit draws more current. If the load demand is small, only a small amount of voltage is induced. In general, the characteristic of the series-wound generator is that the output voltage varies with the load current. For everyday use this is undesirable.

Shunt-Wound Generators

There are many differences between the shunt- and series-wound generators. Instead of using a large-gauge wire with few turns, the shunt-wound generator uses a small-gauge wire with many turns (Figure 4-2-9). Another difference is that the armature and the field windings are not connected in series; they are connected in parallel. Because of this, the output voltage will remain more relatively constant than with the series-wound generator. In use, the shunt-wound generator output voltage will vary inversely with the load current. That means that the voltage will decrease as load current increases.

Compound-Wound Generators

This type of generator is a combination of the series-wound and shunt-wound generators (Figure 4-2-10). In the compound-wound generator, when load current increases, the armature voltage decreases, just like in the shunt-wound generator. This will then cause the voltage applied to the shunt field winding to decrease. This will then cause a decrease in the magnetic field. On the series side of the circuit, the same increase in field current will cause an increase in the magnetic field. The increase and decrease in the field will cause the field to remain equal and produce a constant voltage output even under the varying loads.

Starter Generators

On some smaller turbine engines, a starter generator (Figure 4-2-11) is installed. The starter generator is a combination of a generator and a motor. When the turbine engine is being started, the starter generator turns the engine to facilitate the ignition process. This unit has the advantage of being one unit in a position where two were normally used. This saves weight.

When the starter generator is energized, a gear is engaged to run the turbine engine. Once the turbine is able to sustain itself and reaches a given speed, the generator will no longer drive the turbine. At this point the turbine is

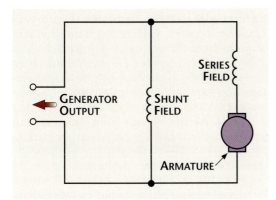

Figure 4-2-10. Compound-wound generator

now running the starter generator. With the starter generator being run by the turbine, it will now act as a generator and supply power to the system.

One thing that must be understood in this system is that only one source of energy can be used at a time. For energizing the starter generator to run the turbine, energy must be supplied from the onboard battery or a ground power unit (GPU). When connecting the GPU, the internal circuitry will automatically disconnect the battery from the system.

Voltage Regulation

The term *regulation* of a generator refers to the voltage change that takes place when the load changes. It usually refers to a change from a no-load condition to a full-load condition or vice versa. Voltage regulation is always calculated as a percentage. To figure out the percentage, use the following equation:

Percent of Regulation = $(E_{nL} - E_{fL}) \div E_{fL} \times 100$

where E_{nL} is the voltage at no-load condition, and E_{fL} is the voltage at full load.

If the output of a generator at full-load is 200 V, and at no-load is 250 V, the percentage of voltage regulation is calculated as:

Percent of Regulation = $(250 - 200) \div 200 \times 100$

Percent of Regulation = $50 \div 200 \times 100$

Percent of Regulation = 0.25×100

Percent of Regulation = 25%

Voltage Control

Controlling the voltage from a generator can be done manually or automatically. For the most part, voltage control is a function of changing the resistance of the field, thereby controlling

Figure 4-2-11. Combination starter-generator for turbine aircraft

the amount of voltage being produced by the generator.

One thing to keep in mind is that voltage control is not the same thing as voltage regulation, even though it is commonly thought to be the same thing. Voltage regulation happens inside of the generator when a load changes, while voltage control happens outside the generator by an external adjustment.

Manual Voltage Control

External to the generator there may be a hand-operated rheostat. A *rheostat* is a resistor that can have its resistance changed. The rheostat will be connected in series with the field circuit. By adjusting it, the amount of voltage that is going into the field coil is controlled.

Automatic Voltage Control

There are a variety of different types of automatic voltage control devices, commonly called voltage regulators. The purpose of these devices is to engage when the load current variation exceeds the built-in ability of the generator to regulate itself.

There are three main types of automatic voltage control devices for DC generators.

Figure 4-2-12. Carbon pile voltage regulator

Figure 4-2-13. Carbon pile

Carbon pile voltage regulator (Figure 4-2-12). This type of voltage regulator consists of a stack of carbon discs (Figure 4-2-13), a spring and a solenoid. The illustration seen in Figure 4-2-14 may be helpful in understanding how a carbon pile voltage regulator works. The carbon discs are wired to the field coil. As the voltage from the generator increases, the solenoid spaces out the carbon discs. This causes an increase in resistance to the field coil and lowers the output voltage. In the opposite circumstance, when a decrease in voltage occurs, the solenoid pulls the discs in and causes the resistance to the field coil to lessen; the output voltage then rises. The overall result is a steady output of voltage to the systems.

Vibrating type voltage regulator. This type of regulator is similar to the carbon pile type. It consists of a solenoid and rheostat. As voltage increases the solenoid opens a switch, allowing the voltage to go through the rheostat and increasing the resistance to the field. When the voltage is low the solenoid will pull the switch closed and short the rheostat. This will cause the terminal voltage to the field to increase. Vibrating type voltage regulators are not great for high-voltage generators since they have a tendency to get hot. For higher voltage, use a carbon pile voltage regulator.

Three-unit regulator (Figure 4-2-15). This type of regulator is preferred in most small aircraft. It includes a voltage regulator, a current limiter and a reverse current cut-out relay.

- Voltage regulator—The function of the voltage regulator in this device is similar

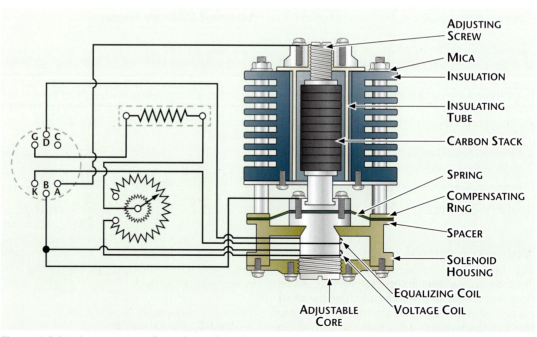

Figure 4-2-14. Construction of a carbon pile voltage regulator

to the vibrating type voltage regulator. Inside the voltage regulator section there are two inductors wrapped around a core, a resistor and a switch held by a spring. The first inductor provides magnetism for the core; the other is used as a way to short the circuit to the resistor when voltage is high. When voltage is low, the switch is held down in its normal position, closed. This allows the terminal voltage to rise.

- Current limiter—The purpose of a current limiter is to limit the output current from the generator, and ultimately to protect the generator. This section has the same parts as the voltage regulator except it only has one inductor wrapped around a core. If the current increases more than the allowed limit, the switch is pulled up by the magnet. This causes the voltage leaving the voltage regulator to go through another resistor. The result is a lower voltage to the field coil and a lower current.

- Reverse current cut-out relay—This is the last section in the three-unit regulator. Unlike in the sections, where the field is strengthened or weakened by the resulting actions, this unit's sole purpose is to prevent damage to the generator. Part of the function of a generator is to charge the battery. If at any point the voltage produced by the generator is lower than the voltage of the battery, the voltage will reverse directions. This will cause the generator to start to act like a motor. If this condition is detected by the reverse current cut-out relay, it will open the circuit and prevent the voltage from entering the regulator.

Figure 4-2-15. Three-unit voltage regulator

Inverters

The inverter is an essential component when using a DC generator. A lot of systems, especially in large aircraft, operate on AC. The inverter's job is to change DC voltage into AC voltage. There are two types of inverters used—the rotary inverter (Figure 4-2-16) and the static inverter (Figure 4-2-17). These two types of inverter do the same thing, but in completely different manners.

Rotary Inverter

This type of inverter is very simple in design; it is a DC motor driving an AC generator. The intricate design of this device has the shaft for both devices as one. To provide cooling for the inverter, fan blades are installed on the shaft. Attached to the top of the inverter is the control box for the voltage going into the motor. The

Figure 4-2-16. Rotary inverter

Figure 4-2-17. Static inverter

input to the motor is usually around 26 VDC, while the output can be 115 V single phase, 115 V three phase, or 200 V three phase, all of which is 400 Hz.

Maintenance of the inverter is very similar to that for a generator or motor. If there is a problem with the control box, the control box must be sent to a qualified repair facility. If there is ever a question in performing maintenance, consult the maintenance manual.

Static Inverter

Instead of using mechanical means to convert DC voltage into AC voltage, a static inverter uses solid-state components to produce 115 V at a 400-Hz frequency. The components inside comprise diodes, crystals, capacitors, transistors and transformers. The circuitry inside a static inverter is similar to a radio transmitter circuit, which is discussed later. The crystal is used in an oscillator circuit to provide the desired frequency, while the transformer can be used to transform the current into the proper wave shape and the proper voltage.

There is not any maintenance that can be done to the static inverter. The most that can be done is bench testing. If it is found that the inverter requires repair, it must be sent to a qualified repair station.

Between the two types of inverters, the static inverter is the most desirable type for use in aircraft since it has no moving parts and is lighter then a rotary inverter.

Generator Control Unit

This component in the power supply system acts more as a check and balance system. It can contain the voltage regulators, current limiters and other devices to protect the system and alert the crew of error conditions. The generator control unit (GCU) helps control the voltage by constantly monitoring the output of the generator and comparing it with an internal reference signal. If this comparison detects anything, the GCU sends an adjustment current to the field of the generator.

In normal conditions, the GCU ensures that the generators on each engine only have to provide an equal amount of energy. Basically if there are two generators, each generator will provide 50 percent of the energy required and neither generator will be overloaded. Even if one generator fails, the generators are not fully loaded down. Each generator on an aircraft is built to be able to supply 100 percent of the aircraft's power needs.

If the GCU detects anything out of the norm, such as an over-voltage or over-current, the GCU will operate relays in the system to separate it from the rest of the circuitry. If something happens to a generator to make it fail, the GCU will disconnect it from the rest of the systems and even out the load among the operable generators.

Section 3
Alternators

Most aircraft use alternators (Figure 4-3-1) or AC generators. (The two terms are considered interchangeable, but the construction does vary.) AC generators and alternators are more often used in aircraft than DC generators because alternators weigh less than their DC counterparts. For the same weight, the alternator produces more power.

Alternator Construction

The construction of the alternator is very different than a generator. There are three major components in a modern alternator: the rotor, stator and slip rings (Figure 4-3-2).

The first component that will be discussed is the *slip rings*. Like the slip rings discussed in the previous section, these slip rings transfer energy from a stationary object to one that is rotating. Unlike the slip rings previously dis-

Figure 4-3-1. Alternator

cussed, the purpose of these slip rings is to provide energy to an electromagnet.

The second component is the *rotor*. This is the electromagnet that receives energy from the slip rings. It is called a rotor because it rotates as the core of the alternators. The electromagnet provides the flux lines that are cut to supply voltage. The increase or decrease of voltage into the electromagnet is the way that the generator output is controlled. Since this is an electromagnet instead of a permanent magnet, like in the DC generator, the magnet does not need to be flashed to restore its magnetism.

Surrounding the rotor is a component called the *stator*. The stator contains windings that cut the lines of flux. The windings of the stator can come in two different fashions—*delta* and *wye* windings (Figure 4-3-3). The delta winding is named so because of its schematic representation looking like the Greek letter delta (Δ). The wye winding is named so because of its schematic representation as well. On a schematic it is drawn like the letter Y.

AC Generator Construction

An AC generator is built almost exactly like a DC generator. It has the field coil that houses the permanent magnet. The armature as the core of the generator is the same. The main difference between the two is that the DC generator has a commutator, while the AC generator uses a slip ring. Remember from the previous section that the commutator facilitated the changing from AC to DC, as well as transferring the voltage from a rotating body to a stationary body. The slip ring is a solid piece of copper that has a set of brushes riding along it.

There are some other parts in an AC generator that differ from the DC generator. One of these parts is the *exciter circuit*. The purpose of the exciter is to supply the electrical energy to the rotor to maintain the alternator field. Simply

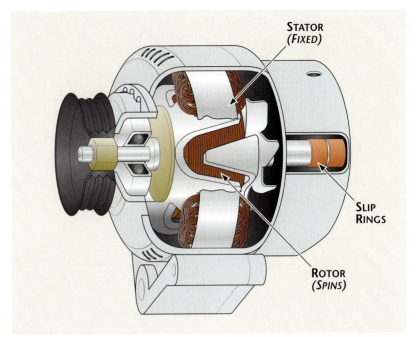

Figure 4-3-2. Alternator construction

put, the exciter is a miniature, shunt-wound DC generator in some cases. The use of a DC generator gives the magnetic field of the rotor a fixed polarity at all times. In other cases the exciter supplies voltage to the rotor from a GCU.

Characteristics of the Alternator

An alternator is rated according to the voltage that it can produce, as well as the maximum current that it can supply. The current supplied depends on heating loss that is sustained by the armature. Heating loss can be detrimental to the conductors. If it heats up to an excessive amount, the insulation can be destroyed. The unit for rating of an alternator is *volt-ampere* for small alternators, and *kilovolt-amperes* for large ones.

When an alternator is built at a factory, it is designed to rotate at a certain speed, produce a given voltage, current limits and other char-

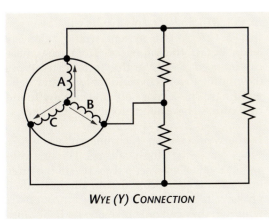
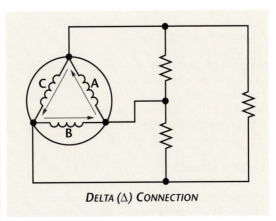

Figure 4-3-3. Delta and wye windings

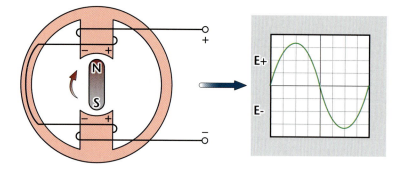

Figure 4-3-4. Single-phase alternator

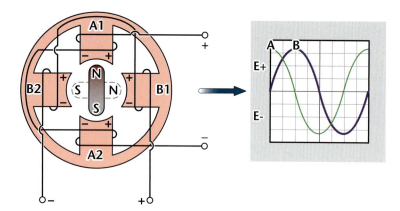

Figure 4-3-5. Two-phase alternator

acteristics. If any questions on the characteristics of the alternator arise, look on the data plate first, then consult any available technical data.

Single-Phase

The term single-phase means that the alternator is producing a single, continuously alternating voltage (Figure 4-3-4). So far, the discussion has been on single-phase alternators. The stator for a single-phase is connected in series. Each individual voltage produced is added up to produce a single AC voltage.

Do not confuse this meaning of the word phase with others. Think of the word *phase* to mean voltage as in a single voltage.

Many applications use single-phase alternators. They are often used when the loads being driven are light. Some power ships, homes and shops. Common hand-held power tools and small appliances use this power to operate.

Two-Phase

As discussed previously, phase means single voltage. The term *two-phase*, then, means two single voltages. Each voltage by itself can be considered a single-phase voltage. Each is generated completely independent of the other.

How Two-Phase Power Is Generated

There are two sets of windings for a two-phase alternator (Figure 4-3-5), both of which are 90° apart from each other. Because of the 90° separation, the two voltages will be 90° out of phase with each other as well.

To put things a little more simply, the stator consists of two single-phase windings that are separated from each other. Each winding is made of two windings connected in series with each other so that their voltages add together. The rotor is still the same as that in a single-phase alternator.

When the voltage is at a maximum for the first phase, the second phase is at a zero. The reverse is same as well: If the second phase is at a maximum, the first is at zero.

There is an advantage to having two separate voltages. In this aspect, one alternator is producing the same amount of power that two alternators do. This is all done with a minimal weight difference. The only disadvantages are that the size of the stator doubles, and the stator becomes more complex.

The two-phase alternator is seldom used. But understanding the two-phase alternators helps us to understand the three-phase alternators that are more commonly used in commercial and corporate aviation.

Three-Phase

Just as the name implies, these alternators supply three single phases of voltage. Unlike the two-phase version that has the two phases 90° from each other, the three-phase alternator (Figure 4-3-6) has each phase 120° apart.

In the windings, it could be easily assumed that a three-phase system would need six leads. In fact, the same leads from each phase can be used. Earlier in this section two types of windings were covered, the wye and delta windings. These types of windings are found in all three-phase alternators.

In the wye winding, each line voltage is 1.73 times one of the phase voltages. The line voltage, or total voltage, across any two of the three line leads is the vector sum of the individual phase voltage. When current flows through the winding, they can only take one path. Because of this, the line current will equal the phase current.

In the delta winding the stators are connected so that the phases are connected end-to-end. The delta winding is an exact opposite when it comes to the voltage and current produced. What this means is that the line and phase voltage are equal to each other, and the line current is equal to 1.73 times the phase current.

Three-Phase Connections

As discussed previously, the stator coils of the alternator are joined in a wye or delta connection. Only three wires come out of the alternator. Because of this, the alternator allows connection to three-phase motors or power distribution transformers.

The three-phase transformer could be made up of three single-phase transformers connected in a delta formation, a wye formation, or a combination of the two. If the primary windings and the secondary windings are both connected in a wye formation, the transformer is referred to as a wye-wye. When the primary and secondary windings are connected in a delta fashion, it is called a delta-delta.

There is no angular relationship between the windings of the individual transformers, but the windings and connections form a delta circuit. For example, the three primary windings are wired in a closed loop; this goes for the secondary as well. Each junction is fed with the phase voltage received by a three-phase alternator. The way that they are connected, whether it be delta or wye, is dependent on the load and voltage requirements, as well as the design of the system in use.

Most of the large commercial and corporate aircraft operate on three-phase 115 VAC. Systems that operate motors will be three-phase, but down the line the three phases are split into three separate single-phase voltages for power distribution to a variety of different systems.

Frequency

All AC generators and alternators, in addition to putting out a voltage and current, also produce a frequency. The frequency that the alternator produces is dependent on a couple things:

1. The number of poles on the rotor. With an increase in the number of poles on

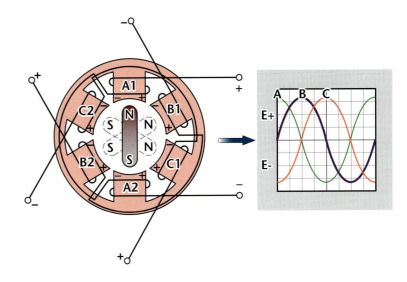

Figure 4-3-6. Three-phase alternator

the rotor, the frequency will be higher. When the rotor has completed one rotation with one set of poles, one cycle has been induced into the windings. If there are more poles, the speed of rotation can be reduced.

2. The speed at which the alternator is spinning. The faster that the rotor spins, the higher the frequency will be. Likewise, the slower the rotor spins, the lower the frequency will be.

This principle can be illustrated by using the following equation:

$$F = NP \div 120$$

where:

F = Frequency
P = Number of poles
N = Speed of rotation
120 = A constant for conversion from minutes to seconds

By using this equation, calculate the frequency at different engine speeds. For example, a four-pole alternator with an engine speed of 4,000 r.p.m. will provide what frequency?

$$F = (4 \times 4,000) \div 120$$
$$F = 16,000 \div 120$$
$$F = 133.33 \text{ Hz or cycles per second}$$

A frequency of 400 Hz is used for aircraft. The reason for the higher frequency is that the electronics on board are small. Compare the transformer used for household electronics to one in an aircraft. The use of the smaller electronics allows for smaller, lighter equipment.

4-20 | Generation and Storage of Electricity

Figure 4-3-7. Rectifier

Voltage Regulation

Voltage regulation for alternators is exactly like that for DC generators. It still deals with the three main points of load, no load and percent of regulation. Use the same equation to determine the percent of regulation.

AC Voltage Control

In alternators, the AC voltage is induced into the stator windings. The amount of voltage depends on three factors:

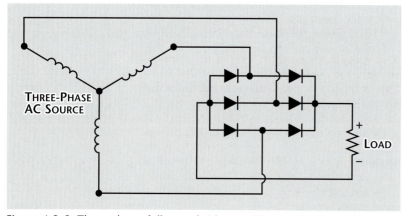

Figure 4-3-8. Three phase, full-wave bridge rectifier circuit schematic

1. The speed (r.p.m.) at which the rotor is spinning. Because the frequency output has to remain stable, the speed cannot be adjusted because the speed of the alternator determines the cycles per second.

2. The number of conductors in series per winding. The number of windings is fixed during the manufacturing of the alternator. A technician cannot change it.

3. The strength of the magnetic field. This is the one aspect that a technician can control. This is done by changing the amount of voltage going to the field coil, just like in a generator.

In the generator section, a few different types of voltage regulators were covered—the carbon pile, the three unit and the vibrating reed. In alternators, the three-unit voltage regulator or another type called the transistorized voltage regulator are used.

Transistorized Voltage Regulator

This type of voltage regulator is made of solid-state components, usually a transistor and a *zener diode*. The zener diode supplies a reference voltage to the transistor. The transistor receives the actual voltage being produced as well as the reference voltage. If the two match, the transistor does not change anything, but if there is a difference between the two, the transistor varies its internal voltage to match the reference. The output of the transistor is then sent to the field circuit of the alternator to increase or decrease the output voltage.

Rectifiers

One of the key advantages of AC voltage is its capability to be changed into DC voltage. The

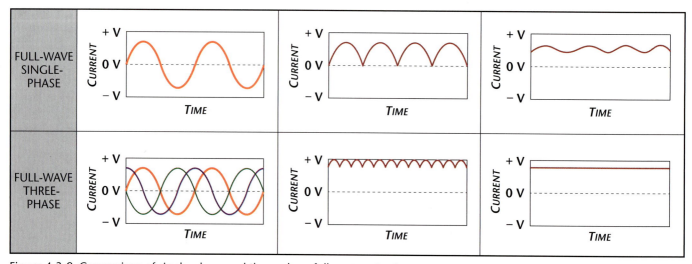

Figure 4-3-9. Comparison of single-phase and three-phase full-wave outputs

rectifier (Figure 4-3-7) is a device that does just that. The rectifier can be an outside circuit, mostly seen on large aircraft that use AC voltage, or it can be built into the alternator, like in small aircraft.

Most rectifiers consist of four to six diodes. A diode acts as a one-way check valve, letting voltage go in only one direction. Since AC voltage flows in two directions, the positive peaks are passed and the negative peaks are eliminated. After the diodes, the voltage goes through a capacitor to help even out the voltage and supply a solid DC voltage.

The six-diode rectifier is called a three-phase rectifier. This type of rectifier is used in three-phase systems like the one discussed earlier in this section. Each pair of diodes rectifies one phase of the incoming sine waves. As seen in Figure 4-3-8, each of the three windings are connected to one of the windings that are 120° apart from each other. The output of the three-phase rectifier can be seen as a smoother DC output as compared to a single-phase rectifier even after a filtering process (Figure 4-3-9).

Frequency Control

Frequency control is just as important as voltage control. As discussed before, frequency is directly proportional to the speed of the engine. Unfortunately, the aircraft engine does not run at a constant r.p.m. To overcome this situation, large aircraft that depend on frequency control use one of two different components: a constant-speed drive (CSD) or an integrated drive generator (IDG).

Constant-Speed Drive (CSD)

The CSD (Figure 4-3-10) device helps maintain a constant speed for the generator. It consists of a gear box called an *axial gear differential*. The input of the CSD is the turbine engine to which it is attached. Through the axial gear differential and hydraulics, the CSD will speed up or slow down depending on what is needed to maintain a 400-Hz output.

Integrated Drive Generator (IDG)

On modern aircraft, the CSD is a thing of the past. It has been replaced by the IDG (Figure 4-3-11). The IDG has a few advantages over the CSD. First, it weighs a lot less then the CSD. The second advantage is that it is more compact then the CSD. The IDG has made it possible to reduce the size of the alternator and keep it producing the amount of voltage it needs by incorporating the alternator and the CSD into one unit. The

Figure 4-3-10. Constant-speed drive cutaway

main downfall of the IDG is that if one aspect of it breaks, the speed regulation side or the alternator side, the whole IDG has to be replaced.

CSD and IDG Maintenance

The technician must maintain the oil level for a CSD or IDG. On the side of the unit, there is a sight glass that shows the level of its oil reservoir. The oil inside is used for lubrication of the gears as well as to help keep the unit cool. One other key piece of information for any technician to know about both CSDs and IDGs is that if there is a failure, they can be mechanically disconnected from the system through a switch in the flight deck. The drawback to this is that they cannot be reconnected in flight. Once the pilot lands, the technician can reconnect it while the engine is not running.

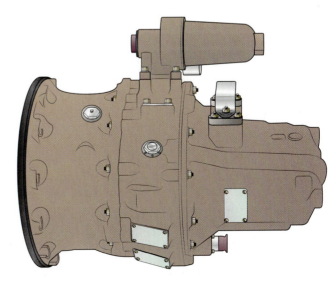

Figure 4-3-11. Integrated drive generator

5
Introduction to Solid-State Components

Section 1

Introduction to Solid-State Devices

Semiconductors have electrical properties somewhere between those of insulators and conductors. The use of semiconductor materials in electronic components is not new; some devices are as old as the electron tube. Two of the most widely known semiconductors in use today are the *junction diode* and *transistor*.

These semiconductors fall under a more general heading called solid-state devices. A *solid state device* is nothing more than an electronic device that operates by virtue of the movement of electrons within a solid piece of semiconductor material.

Since the invention of the transistor, solid-state devices have been developed and improved at an unbelievable rate. Great strides have been made in the manufacturing techniques, and there is no foreseeable limit to the future of these devices. Solid-state devices made from semiconductor materials offer compactness, efficiency, ruggedness and versatility. Consequently, these devices have invaded virtually every field of science and industry.

In addition to the junction diode and transistor, a whole new family of related devices has been developed: the *zener diode, light-emitting diode, field effect transistor*, and many more. One development that has dominated solid-state technology, and probably has had a greater impact on the electronics industry than the electron tube or transistor, is the **integrated circuit**. The *integrated circuit* is a minute piece of semiconductor material that can produce complete electronic circuit functions.

Learning Objective

DESCRIBE
- the function of a transistor
- the function of a diode
- the function of integrated circuits

EXPLAIN
- the makeup of a semiconductor
- the role of diode in a rectifier
- the proper biasing for a transistor
- how a transistor functions
- the different classes of amplifiers
- the different configurations for transistors

APPLY
- identify the proper polarity for a diode
- identify the proper polarity for a transistor
- troubleshoot a diode or transistor

Left. Integrated circuits have almost eliminated the use of individual electronic components as the building blocks of electronic circuits.

Introduction to Solid-State Components

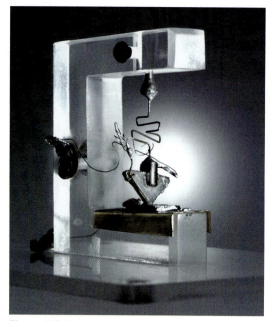

Figure 5-1-1. Point-contact transistor

As the applications of solid-state devices mount, the need for knowledge of these devices becomes increasingly important. Technicians today will have to understand solid-state devices if they are to become proficient in the repair and maintenance of electronic equipment. Therefore, the objective of this chapter is to provide a broad coverage of solid-state devices and, as a broad application, power supplies. The discussion begins with some background information on the development of the semiconductor. After this, the text proceeds to the semiconductor diode, the transistor, special devices and, finally, solid-state power supplies.

Semiconductor Development

Although the semiconductor was late in reaching its present development, its story began long before the electron tube. Historically, as far back as 1883 when Michael Faraday discovered that silver sulfide, a semiconductor, has a negative temperature coefficient. The term negative temperature coefficient is just another way of saying its resistance to electrical current flow decreases as temperature increases. The opposite is true of the conductor. It has a positive temperature coefficient. Because of this particular characteristic, semiconductors are used extensively in power-measuring equipment.

Only two years later, another valuable characteristic was reported by Munk A. Rosenshold. He found that certain materials have rectifying properties. Strange as it may seem, his finding was given such little notice that it had to be rediscovered 39 years later by F. Braun.

Toward the close of the 19th century, experimenters began to notice the peculiar characteristics of the chemical element selenium. They discovered that in addition to its rectifying properties (the ability to convert AC into DC), selenium was also light sensitive—its resistance decreased with an increase in light intensity.

This discovery eventually led to the invention of the photophone by Alexander Graham Bell. The photophone, which converted variations of light into sound, was a predecessor of the radio receiver; however, it wasn't until the actual birth of radio that selenium was used to any extent. Today, selenium is an important and widely used semiconductor.

Many other materials were tried and tested for use in communications. Silicon was found to be the most stable of the materials tested, while galena, a crystalline form of lead sulfide, was found the most sensitive for use in early radio receivers. By 1915, Carl Beredicks discovered that germanium, another metallic element, also had rectifying capabilities. Later, it became widely used in electronics for low-power, low-frequency applications.

Although the semiconductor was known long before the electron tube was invented, the semiconductor devices of that time could not match the performance of the tube. Radio needed a device that could not only handle power and amplify but rectify and detect a signal as well. Since tubes could do all these things, and semiconductor devices of that day could not, the semiconductor soon lost out.

It wasn't until the beginning of World War II that interest was renewed in the semiconductor. There was a dire need for a device that could work within the ultra-high frequencies of radar. Electron tubes had inter-

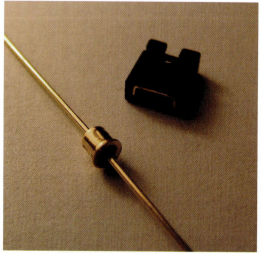

Figure 5-1-2. Tunnel diode

electrode capacitances that were too high to do the job. The point-contact semiconductor diode, on the other hand, had a very low internal capacitance. Consequently, it could be designed to work within the ultra-high frequencies used in radar, whereas the electron tube could not.

As radar took on greater importance and communication electronic equipment became more sophisticated, the demands for better solid-state devices mounted. The limitations of the electron tube made necessary a quest for something new and different. An amplifying device was needed that was smaller, lighter, more efficient and capable of handling extremely high frequencies. This was asking a lot, but if progress was to be made, these requirements had to be met. A serious study of semiconductor materials began in the early 1940s and has continued since.

In June 1948, a significant breakthrough took place in semiconductor development. This was the discovery of the *point-contact transistor* (Figure 5-1-1). Here at last was a semiconductor that could amplify. This discovery brought the semiconductor back into competition with the electron tube. A year later, junction diodes and transistors were developed. The junction transistor was found superior to the point-contact type in many respects. By comparison, the junction transistor was more reliable, generated less noise, and had higher power handling ability than its point-contact brother. The junction transistor became a rival of the electron tube in many uses previously uncontested.

Semiconductor diodes were not to be slighted. The initial work of Dr. Carl Zener led to the development of the zener diode, which is frequently used today to regulate power supply voltages at precise levels. Considerably more interest in the solid-state diode was generated when Dr. Leo Esaki, a Japanese scientist, fabricated a diode that could amplify. The device, named the *tunnel diode* (Figure 5-1-2), has amazing gain and fast switching capabilities. Although it is used in conventional amplifying and oscillating circuits, its primary use is in computer logic circuits.

Another breakthrough came in the late 1950s when it was discovered that semiconductor materials could be combined and treated so that they functioned as an entire circuit or sub-assembly rather than as a circuit component. Many names have been given to this solid-circuit concept, such as integrated circuits, microelectronics and microcircuitry.

So the semiconductor is not something new, but it has come a long way in a short time.

Figure 5-1-3. Transistors on a circuit board

Semiconductor Applications

The previous section mentioned just a few of the many different applications of semiconductor devices. The use of these devices has become so widespread that it would be impossible to list all their different applications. Instead, a broad coverage of their specific application is presented.

Semiconductor devices are all around us. They can be found in just about every commercial product, from the family car to the pocket calculator. Semiconductor devices are contained in television sets, portable radios, stereo equipment and much more.

Science and industry also rely heavily on semiconductor devices. Research laboratories use these devices in all sorts of electronic instruments to perform tests, measurements and numerous other experimental tasks. Industrial control systems (such as those used to manufacture automobiles) and automatic telephone exchanges also use semiconductors. Even today, heavy-duty versions of the solid state rectifier diode are being used to convert large amounts of power for electric railroads. Of the many different applications for solid-state devices, space systems, computers and data processing equipment are some of the largest consumers.

Various modern aviation equipment is literally loaded with semiconductor devices. For example, many types of radar, communication and airborne equipment are transistorized. Data display systems, data processing units, computers and aircraft guidance-control assemblies are also good examples of electronic equipment that uses semiconductor devices. Figure 5-1-3 shows an aircraft circuit board containing transistors. All of the specific applications

Figure 5-1-4. Size comparisons of electron tubes and semiconductors

of semiconductor devices would make a long, impressive list. The fact is, semiconductors are being used extensively in commercial products, industry and the military

Semiconductor Competition

Semiconductor devices can and do perform all the conventional functions of rectification, amplification, oscillation, timing, switching and sensing. Simply stated, these devices perform the same basic functions as the electron tube, but they perform more efficiently, economically, and for a longer period of time. Therefore, it should be no surprise to see these devices used in place of electron tubes. With this in mind, it is only natural and logical to compare semiconductor devices with electron tubes.

Physically, semiconductor devices are much smaller than tubes. Figure 5-1-4 shows that the difference is quite evident. This illustration shows some commonly used tube sizes alongside semiconductor devices of similar capabilities. The reduction in size can be as great as 100:1 by weight and 1,000:1 by volume. It is easy to see that size reduction favors the semiconductor device. Therefore, whenever miniaturization is required or is convenient, transistors are favored over tubes. Bear in mind that the extent of practical size reduction is a big factor. Many things must be considered when designing for miniaturization. Miniature electron tubes, for example, may be preferred in certain applications to transistors, thus keeping size reduction to a competitive area.

Power is also a two-sided story. For low-power applications, where efficiency is a significant factor, semiconductors have a decided advantage. This is true mainly because semiconductor devices perform very well with an extremely small amount of power; in addition, they require no filaments or heaters as in the case of the electron tube. For example, a computer operating with more than 4,000 solid-state devices may require no more than 20 W of power. The same number of tubes would require several kilowatts of power.

For high-power applications, it is a different story—tubes have the upper hand. The high-power tube has no equivalent in any semiconductor device. This is because a tube can be designed to operate with more than 1,000 V applied to its plate whereas the maximum allowable voltage for a transistor is limited to about 200 V (and usually 50 V or less). A tube can also handle thousands of watts of power. The maximum power output for transistor generally ranges from 30 milliwatts to slightly over 100 W.

When it comes to ruggedness and life expectancy, the tube is still in competition. Design and functional requirements usually dictate the choice of device. However, semiconductor devices are rugged and long-lived. They can be constructed to withstand extreme vibration and mechanical shock. They have been known to withstand impacts that would completely shatter an ordinary electron tube.

Although some specially designed tubes render extensive service, the life expectancy of transistors is more than three to four times that of ordinary electronic tubes. There is no known failure mechanism (such as an open filament in a tube) to limit the semiconductor's life. However, semiconductor devices do have some limitations. They are usually affected more by temperature, humidity and radiation than tubes are. Today the only place that tubes are found is in recording studios. For the most part, all elctronics have moved to semiconductor components.

Semiconductor Theory

To understand why solid-state devices function as they do, it is necessary to examine closely the composition and nature of semiconductors. This entails theory that is fundamental to the study of solid-state devices.

Rather than beginning with theory, however, it is helpful to first become reacquainted with some of the basic information studied earlier concerning matter and energy.

Atomic Structure

The universe, as understood today, is divided into two parts: matter and energy. Matter, our main concern at this time, is anything that occupies space and has weight. Rocks, water, air, automobiles, clothing and even our own bodies are good examples of matter. From this, it is possible to conclude that matter may be found in any one of three states: solid, liquid or gas. All matter is composed of either an element or combination of elements. As covered previously, an element is a substance that cannot be reduced to a simpler form by chemical means. Examples of elements seen every day are iron, gold, silver, copper and oxygen. At present, there are more than 100 known elements of which all matter is composed.

Further down the size scale is the atom, the smallest particle into which an element can be broken down and still retain all of its original properties. The atoms of one element, however, differ from the atoms of all other elements. Since there are more than 100 known elements, there must be more than 100 different atoms, or a different atom for each element.

Now consider more than one element at a time. A *compound* is a chemical combination of two or more elements. Water, table salt, ethyl alcohol and ammonia are all examples of compounds. The smallest part of a compound, which has all the characteristics of the compound, is the molecule. Each molecule contains some of the atoms of each of the elements forming the compound, as illustrated in the sugar molecule in Figure 5-1-5.

Consider sugar, for example. Sugar in general terms is matter, since it occupies space and has weight. It is also a compound because it consists of two or more elements. Take a lump of sugar and crush it into small particles; each of the particles still retains its original identifying properties of sugar. The only thing that changed was the physical size of the sugar. If this subdividing process is continued by grinding the sugar into a fine powder, the results are the same. Even dissolving sugar in water does not change its identifying properties, in spite of the fact that the particles of sugar are now too small to be seen even with a microscope.

Eventually, a quantity of sugar is left that cannot be further divided without its ceasing to be sugar. This quantity is known as a molecule of sugar. If the molecule is further divided, it is found to consist of three simpler kinds of matter: carbon, hydrogen and oxygen. These simpler forms are called elements. Therefore, since elements consist of atoms, then a molecule of sugar is made up of atoms of carbon, hydrogen and oxygen.

The atom is basically composed of electrons, protons and neutrons. Furthermore, the elec-

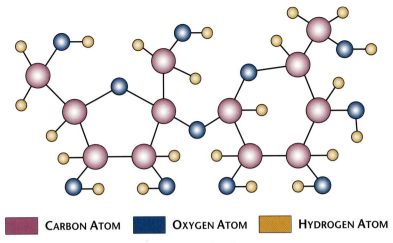

Figure 5-1-5. Composition of a sugar molecule

trons, protons and neutrons of one element are identical to those of any other element. There are different kinds of elements because the number and the arrangement of electrons and protons are different for each element.

The electron carries a small negative charge of electricity. The proton carries a positive charge of electricity equal and opposite to the charge of the electron. Scientists have measured the mass and size of the electron and proton, and they know how much charge each possesses. Both the electron and proton have the same quantity of charge, although the mass of the proton is approximately 1,827 times that of the electron. In all atoms except hydrogen, there exists a neutral particle called a neutron. The neutron has a mass approximately equal to that of a proton, but it has no electrical charge.

According to theory, the electrons, protons and neutrons of the atoms are thought to be arranged in a manner similar to a miniature solar system. Notice the helium atom in Figure 5-1-6. Two protons and two neutrons form the heavy nucleus with a positive charge around

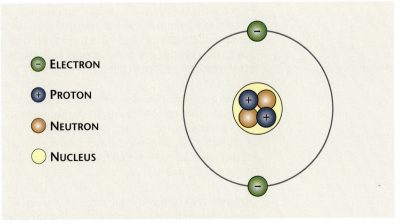

Figure 5-1-6. Composition of a simple helium atom

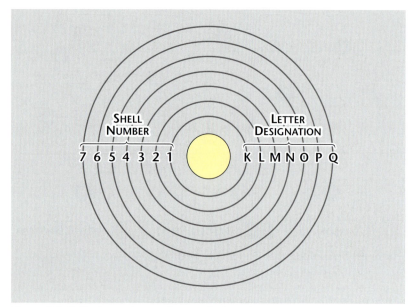

Figure 5-1-7. Shell number and letter designation

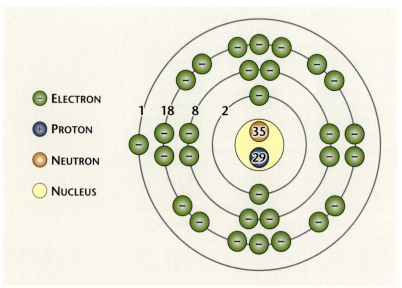

Figure 5-1-8. Copper atom

alone, the electron contains kinetic energy. Because of its position, it also contains potential energy. The total energy contained by an electron (kinetic energy plus potential energy) is the main factor that determines the radius of the electron's orbit. For an electron to remain in this orbit, it must neither gain nor lose energy.

The orbiting electrons do not follow random paths; instead they are confined to definite energy levels. Visualize these levels as shells with each successive shell being spaced a greater distance from the nucleus. The shells, and the number of electrons required to fill them, may be predicted by using Pauli's exclusion principle. Simply stated, this principle specifies that each shell will contain a maximum of $2n^2$ electrons, where n is the shell number starting with the one closest to the nucleus. By this principle, the second shell, for example, would contain $2(2)^2$ or 8 electrons when full.

In addition to being numbered, the shells are also given letter designations starting with the shell closest to the nucleus and progressing outward as shown in Figure 5-1-7. The shells are considered to be full, or complete, when they contain the following quantities of electrons: 2 in the K (first) shell, 8 in the L (second) shell, 18 in the M (third) shell, and so on, in accordance with the exclusion principle. Each of these shells is a major shell and can be divided into sub-shells, of which there are five, labeled s, p, d, f and g.

Like the major shells, the sub-shells are also limited as to the number of electrons they contain. Thus, the s sub-shell is complete when it contains 2 electrons, the p sub-shell when it contains 6, the d sub-shell when it contains 10, the f sub-shell when it contains 14 electrons, and the g sub-shell when it contains 18 electrons.

Inasmuch as the K shell can contain no more than 2 electrons, it must have only one sub-shell, the s sub-shell. The M shell is composed of three sub-shells: s, p and d. If the electrons in the s, p and d sub-shells are added together, their total is found to be 18, the exact number required to fill the M shell.

Notice the electron configuration of copper illustrated in Figure 5-1-8. The copper atom contains 29 electrons, which completely fill the first three shells and sub-shells, leaving one electron in the s sub-shell of the N shell. A list of all the other known elements, with the number of electrons in each atom, is contained in the Periodic Table of Elements.

Valence is an atom's ability to combine with other atoms. The number of electrons in the outermost shell of an atom determines its valence. For this reason, the outer shell of an atom is called *valence shell*, and the electrons contained in this shell are

which two very light electrons revolve. The path each electron takes around the nucleus is called an orbit. The electrons are continuously being acted upon in their orbits by the force of attraction of the nucleus. To maintain an orbit around the nucleus, the electrons travel at a speed that produces a counterforce equal to the attraction force of the nucleus.

Just as energy is required to move a space vehicle away from the earth, energy is also required to move an electron away from the nucleus. Like a space vehicle, the electron is said to be at a higher energy level when it travels a larger orbit.

Scientific experiments have shown that the electron requires a certain amount of energy to stay in orbit. This quantity is called the electron's energy level. By virtue of just its motion

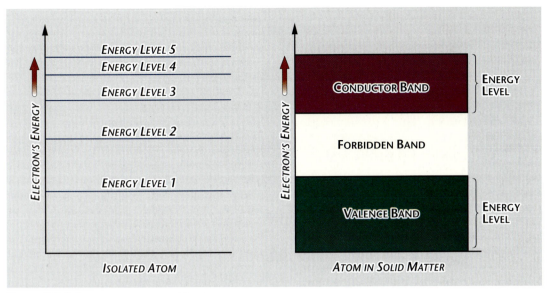

Figure 5-1-9. Energy arrangement in atoms

called *valence electrons*. The valence of an atom determines its ability to gain or lose an electron, which in turn determines the chemical and electrical properties of the atom.

An atom that is lacking only one or two electrons from its outer shell will easily gain electrons to complete its shell, but a large amount of energy is required to free any of its electrons. An atom having a relatively small number of electrons in its outer shell in comparison to the number of electrons required to fill the shell will easily lose these valence electrons. The valence shell always refers to the outermost shell.

Energy Bands

Now that matter and energy have been reviewed, the discussion continues with electron behavior.

As stated earlier, orbiting electrons contain energy and are confined to definite energy levels. The various shells in an atom represent these levels. Therefore, to move an electron from a lower shell to a higher shell, a certain amount of energy is required. This energy can be in the form of electric fields, heat, light and even bombardment by other particles. Failure to provide enough energy to the electron, even if the energy supplied is just short of the required amount, will cause it to remain at its present energy level.

Supplying more energy than is needed will only cause the electron to move to the next higher shell and the remaining energy will be wasted. In simple terms, energy is required in definite units to move electrons from one shell to the next higher shell. These units are called *quanta*.

Electrons can also lose energy. When an electron loses energy, it moves to a lower shell. The lost energy, in some cases, appears as heat.

If a sufficient amount of energy is absorbed by an electron, it is possible for that electron to be completely removed from the influence of the atom. This is called *ionization*. When an atom loses electrons or gains electrons in this process of electron exchange, it is said to be ionized. For ionization to take place, there must be a transfer of energy that results in a change in the internal energy of the atom. An atom having more than its normal amount of electrons acquires a negative charge. It is called a negative ion. The atom that gives up some of its normal electrons is left with fewer negative charges than positive charges and is called a positive ion. Thus, ionization is defined as the process by which an atom loses or gains electrons.

Up to this point, the text has only discussed isolated atoms. When atoms are spaced far enough apart, as in a gas, they have very little influence upon each other, and are very much like lone atoms. But atoms within a solid have a marked effect upon each other. The forces that bind these atoms together greatly modify the behavior of the other electrons. One consequence of this close proximity of atoms is to cause the individual energy levels of an atom to break up and form bands of energy.

Discrete (separate and complete) energy levels still exist within these energy bands, but there are many more energy levels than there were with the isolated atom. In some cases, energy levels will have disappeared. Figure 5-1-9 shows the difference in the energy arrangement between an isolated atom and the atom in a solid. Notice that the isolated atom (such as in gas) has energy levels, whereas the atom in a solid has energy levels grouped into *energy bands*.

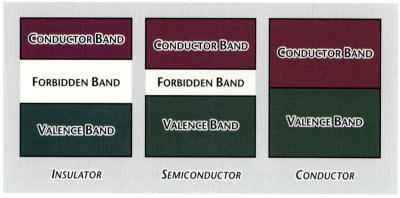

Figure 5-1-10. Energy level diagram

The upper band in the solid lines in Figure 5-1-9 is called the *conduction band* because electrons in this band are easily removed by the application of external electric fields. Materials that have a large number of electrons in the conduction band act as good conductors of electricity.

Below the conduction band is the *forbidden band*, or energy gap. Electrons are never found in this band, but may travel back and forth through it, provided they do not come to rest in the band.

The last band, or *valence band*, is composed of a series of energy levels containing valence electrons. Electrons in this band are more tightly bound to the individual atom than the electrons in the conduction band. However, the electrons in the valence band can still be moved to the conduction band with the application of energy, usually thermal energy.

The concept of energy bands is particularly important in classifying materials as conductors, semiconductors and insulators. An electron can exist in either of two energy bands—the conduction band or the valence band. All that is necessary to move an electron from the valence band to the conduction band, so it can be used for electric current, is enough energy to carry the electron through the forbidden band. The width of the forbidden band or the separation between the conduction and valence bands determines whether a substance is an insulator, semiconductor or conductor. Figure 5-1-10 uses energy level diagrams to show the difference between insulators, semiconductors and conductors.

The energy diagram for the insulator shows the insulator with a very wide energy gap. The wider this gap, the greater the amount of energy required to move the electron from the valence band to the conduction band. Therefore, an insulator requires a large amount of energy to obtain a small amount of current. The insulator "insulates" because of the wide forbidden band or energy gap.

The semiconductor, on the other hand, has a smaller forbidden band and requires less energy to move an electron from the valence band to the conduction band. Therefore, for a certain amount of applied voltage, more current will flow in the semiconductor than in the insulator.

The last energy level diagram in Figure 5-1-10 is that of a conductor. Notice, there is no forbidden band or energy gap, and the valence and conduction bands overlap. With no energy gap, it takes a small amount of energy to move electrons into the conduction band; consequently, conductors pass electrons very easily.

Covalent Bonding

The chemical activity of an atom is determined by the number of electrons in its valence shell. When the valence shell is complete, the atom is stable and shows little tendency to combine with other atoms to form solids. Only atoms that possess eight valence electrons have a complete outer shell. These atoms are referred to as inert or inactive atoms. However, if the valence shell of an atom lacks the number of electrons required to complete the shell, then the activity of the atom increases.

Silicon and germanium, for example, are the most frequently used semiconductors. Both are quite similar in their structure and chemical behavior. Each has four electrons in the valence shell. Consider just silicon. Since it has fewer than the eight electrons needed to complete the outer shell, its atoms will unite with other atoms until eight electrons are shared. This gives each atom a total of eight electrons in its valence shell; four of its own and four that it borrowed from the surrounding atoms.

The sharing of valence electrons between two or more atoms produces a *covalent bond*

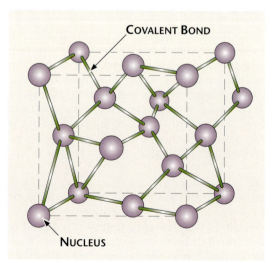

Figure 5-1-11. A typical crystal structure

between the atoms. It is this bond that holds the atoms together in an orderly structure called a crystal. A *crystal* is just another name for a solid whose atoms or molecules are arranged in a three-dimensional geometrical pattern commonly referred to as a lattice. Figure 5-1-11 shows a typical crystal structure. Each sphere in the figure represents the nucleus of an atom, and the arms that join the atoms and support the structure are the covalent bonds.

As a result of this sharing process, the valence electrons are held tightly together. This can best be illustrated by the two-dimensional view of the silicon lattice in Figure 5-1-12. The circles in the figure represent the nuclei of the atoms. The +4 in the circles is the net charge of the nucleus plus the inner shells (minus the valence shell). The short lines indicate valence electrons. Because every atom in this pattern is bonded to four other atoms, the electrons are not free to move within the crystal. As a result of this bonding, pure silicon and germanium are poor conductors of electricity. The reason they are not insulators but semiconductors is that with the proper application of heat or electrical pressure, electrons can be caused to break free of their bonds and move into the conduction band. Once in this band, they wander aimlessly through the crystal.

Conduction Process

As stated earlier, energy can be added to electrons by applying heat. When enough energy is absorbed by the valence electrons, it is possible for them to break some of their covalent bonds. Once the bonds are broken, the electrons move to the conduction band where they are capable of supporting electric current. When a voltage is applied to a crystal containing these conduction-band electrons, the electrons move through the crystal toward the applied voltage. This movement of electrons in a semiconductor is referred to as electron current flow.

There is still another type of current in a pure semiconductor. This current occurs when a covalent bond is broken and a vacancy is left in the atom by the missing valence electron. This vacancy is commonly referred to as a *"hole."* The hole is considered to have a positive charge because its atom is deficient by one electron, which causes the protons to outnumber the electrons. As a result of this hole, a chain reaction begins when a nearby electron breaks its own covalent bond to fill the hole, leaving another hole. Then another electron breaks its bond to fill the previous hole, leaving still another hole. Each time an electron in this process fills a hole, it enters into a covalent bond. Even though an electron has moved from one covalent bond to another, the most important thing to remember is that the hole is also moving.

Therefore, since this process of conduction resembles the movement of holes rather than electrons, it is termed *hole flow* (short for hole current flow or conduction by holes). Hole flow is very similar to electron flow except that the holes move toward a negative potential and in an opposite direction to that of the electron. Since hole flow results from the breaking of covalent bonds, which are at the valence-band level, the electrons associated with this type of conduction contain only valence-band energy and must remain in the valence band. However, the electrons associated with electron flow have conduction-band energy and can, therefore, move throughout the crystal.

A good analogy of hole flow is the movement of a hole through a tube filled with balls (Figure 5-1-13). When ball number 1 is removed from the tube, a hole is left. This hole is then filled by ball number 2, which leaves still another hole. Ball number 3 then moves into the hole left by ball number 2. This causes still another hole to appear where ball 3 was. Notice the holes are moving to the right side of the tube. This action continues until all the balls have moved one space to the left, in which time the hole moved eight spaces to the right and came to rest at the right-hand end of the tube.

In the theory just described, two current carriers were created by the breaking of covalent bonds: the negative electron and the positive hole. These carriers are referred to as *electron-hole pairs*. Since

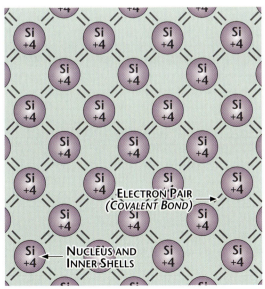

Figure 5-1-12. A two-dimensional view of a silicon cubic lattice

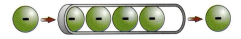

Figure 5-1-13. Electron movement

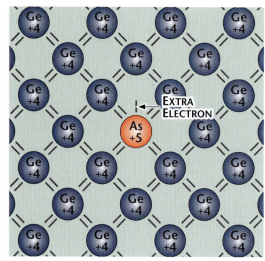

Figure 5-1-14. Germanium crystal doped with arsenic

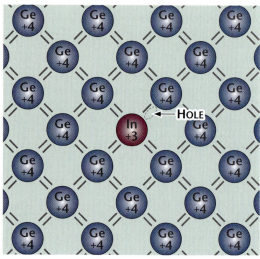

Figure 5-1-15. Germanium crystal doped with indium

the semiconductor in this discussion contains no impurities, the number of holes in the electron-hole pairs is always equal to the number of conduction electrons. Another way of describing this condition where no impurities exist is by saying the semiconductor is *intrinsic*. The term intrinsic is also used to distinguish the pure semiconductor, like the one in this example, from one containing impurities.

Doping Process

The pure semiconductor mentioned earlier is basically neutral. It contains no free electrons in its conduction bands. Even with the application of thermal energy, only a few covalent bonds are broken, yielding a relatively small current flow. A much more efficient method of increasing current flow in semiconductors is by adding very small amounts of selected additives to them, generally no more than a few parts per million. These additives are called impurities and the process of adding them to crystals is referred to as *doping*.

The purpose of semiconductor doping is to increase the number of free charges that can be moved by an external applied voltage. When an impurity increases the number of free electrons, the doped semiconductor is *negative* or N-type, and the impurity that is added is known as an N-type impurity. However, an impurity that reduces the number of free electrons, causing more holes, creates a *positive* or P-type semiconductor, and the impurity that was added to it is known as a P-type impurity. Semiconductors that are doped in this manner, either with N- or P-type impurities, are referred to as *extrinsic* semiconductors.

N-type semiconductor. The N-type impurity loses its extra valence electron easily when added to a semiconductor material, and in so doing, increases the conductivity of the material by contributing a free electron. This type of impurity has five valence electrons and is called a *pentavalent* impurity. Arsenic, antimony, bismuth and phosphorous are pentavalent impurities. Because these materials give or donate one electron to the doped material, they are also called *donor* impurities.

When a pentavalent (donor) impurity, like arsenic, is added to germanium, it will form covalent bonds with the germanium atoms. Figure 5-1-14 illustrates this by showing an arsenic atom (As) in a germanium (Ge) lattice structure. Notice the arsenic atom in the center of the lattice. It has five valence electrons in its outer shell but uses only four of them to form covalent bonds with the germanium atoms, leaving one electron relatively free in the crystal structure. Pure germanium may be converted into an N-type semiconductor by doping it with any donor impurity having five valence electrons in its outer shell. Since this type of semiconductor (N-type) has a surplus of electrons, the electrons are considered *majority* carriers, while the holes, being few in number, are the *minority* carriers.

P-type semiconductor. The second type of impurity, when added to a semiconductor material, tends to compensate for its deficiency of one valence electron by acquiring an electron from its neighbor. Impurities of this type have only three valence electrons and are called *trivalent* impurities. Aluminum, indium, gallium and boron are trivalent impurities. Because these materials accept one electron from the doped material, they are also called *acceptor* impurities.

A trivalent (acceptor) impurity element can also be used to dope germanium. In this case, the impurity is one electron short of the required number of electrons needed to establish covalent bonds with four neighboring atoms. Thus, in a single covalent bond, there will be only one electron instead of two. This arrangement leaves a hole in that covalent bond. Figure 5-1-15 illustrates this theory by showing what happens when germanium is doped with an indium (In) atom. Notice, the indium atom in Figure 5-1-15 is one electron short of the number needed to form covalent bonds with four neighboring atoms and, therefore, creates a hole in the structure.

Gallium and boron, which are also trivalent impurities, exhibit these same characteristics when added to germanium. The holes can only be present in this type semiconductor when a trivalent impurity is used. Note that a hole carrier is not created by the removal of an electron from a neutral atom, but is created when a trivalent impurity enters into covalent bonds with a tetravalent (four valence electrons) crystal structure. The holes in this type of semiconductor (P-type) are considered the *majority* carriers since they are present in the material in the greatest quantity. The electrons, on the other hand, are the *minority* carriers.

Section 2

Semiconductor Diodes

When joining a section of N-type semiconductor material with a similar section of P-type semiconductor material, a device known as a *PN junction* is created. (The area where the N and P regions meet is appropriately called the junction.) The usual characteristics of this device make it extremely useful in electronics as a diode rectifier. The diode rectifier or PN junction diode performs the same function as its counterpart in electron tubes but in a different way.

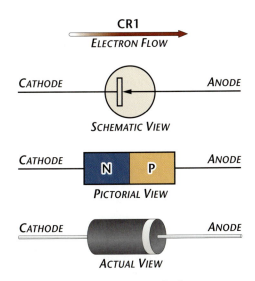

Figure 5-2-1. The PN junction diode

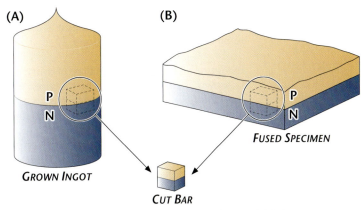

Figure 5-2-2. Grown and fused PN junctions from which bars are cut

The diode is nothing more than a two-element semiconductor device that makes use of the rectifying properties of a PN junction to convert alternating current into direct current by permitting current flow in only one direction. The schematic symbol of a PN junction diode is shown in Figure 5-2-1. The vertical bar represents the cathode (N material) since it is the source of electrons, and the arrow represents the anode (P material) since it is the destination of the electrons.

The label "CR1" is an alphanumerical code used to identify the diode. In this figure, there is only one diode so it is labeled CR1 (crystal rectifier number one). If there were four diodes shown in the diagram, the last diode would be labeled CR4. The heavy dark line shows electron flow. Notice it is against the arrow. For further clarification, a pictorial diagram of a PN junction and an actual semiconductor (one of many types) are also illustrated.

Construction

Merely pressing together a section of P material and a section of N material, however, is not sufficient to produce a rectifying junction. The semiconductor should be in one piece to form a proper PN junction, but divided into a P-type impurity region and an N-type impurity region. This can be done in various ways. One way is to mix P-type and N-type impurities into a single crystal during the manufacturing process. By so doing, a P region is grown over part of a semiconductor's length and an N region is grown over the other part.

This is called a *grown* junction and is illustrated in Figure 5-2-2A. Another way to produce a PN junction is to melt one type of impurity into a semiconductor of the opposite type impurity. For example, a pellet of acceptor impurity is placed on a wafer of N-type germanium and heated. Under controlled temperature conditions, the acceptor impurity fuses into the wafer to form a P-region within it, as shown in

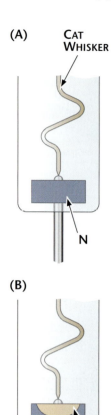

Figure 5-2-3. The point-contact type of diode construction

Figure 5-2-2B. This type of junction is known as an *alloy* or *fused-alloy* junction, and is one of the most commonly used junctions.

In Figure 5-2-3, a *point-contact* type of construction is shown. It consists of a fine metal wire, called a cat whisker, which makes contact with a small area on the surface of an N-type semiconductor, as shown in Figure 5-2-3A. The PN union is formed in this process by momentarily applying a high-surge current to the wire and the N-type semiconductor. The heat generated by this current converts the material nearest the point of contact to a P-type material (Figure 5-2-3B).

Still another process is to heat a section of semiconductor material to near melting and then diffuse impurity atoms into a surface layer. Regardless of the process, the objective is to have a perfect bond everywhere along the union (interface) between P and N materials. Proper contact along the union is important because, as shown later, the union is the rectifying agent in the diode.

PN Junction Operation

Building on this knowledge of P- and N-type materials, how these materials are joined together to form a diode, and the function of the diode, the discussion continues with the operation of the PN junction. The current flow in the materials that make up the junction and what happens initially within the junction when these two materials are joined together must be considered to understand how the PN junction works.

Current Flow in the N-Type Material

Conduction in the N-type semiconductor, or crystal, is similar to conduction in a copper wire. That is, with voltage applied across the material, electrons will move through the crystal just as current would flow in a copper wire. This is shown in Figure 5-2-4. The positive potential of the battery attracts the free electrons in the crystal. These electrons leave the crystal and flow into the positive terminal of the battery. As an electron leaves the crystal, an electron from the negative terminal of the battery enters the crystal, completing the current path. Therefore, the majority current carriers in the N-type material (electrons) are repelled by the negative side of the battery and move through the crystal toward the positive side of the battery.

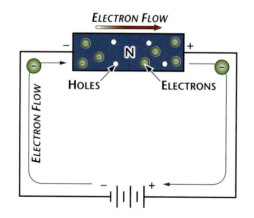

Figure 5-2-4. Current flow in N-type material

Current Flow in the P-Type Material

Current flow through the P-type material is illustrated in Figure 5-2-5. Conduction in the P material is by positive holes instead of by negative electrons. A hole moves from the positive terminal of the P material to the negative terminal. Electrons from the external circuit enter the negative terminal of the material and fill holes in the vicinity of this terminal. At the positive terminal, electrons are removed from the covalent bonds, creating new holes. This process continues as the steady stream of holes (hole current) moves toward the negative terminal.

Notice in both N-type and P-type materials, current flow in the external circuit consists of electrons moving out of the negative terminal of the battery and into the positive terminal of the battery. Hole flow, on the other hand, only exists within the material itself.

Junction Barrier

Although the N-type material has an excess of free electrons, it is still electrically neutral. This is because the donor atoms in the N material were left with positive charges after free electrons became available by covalent bonding (the protons outnumbered the electrons). Therefore, for every free electron in the N material, there is a corresponding positively charged atom to balance it. The end result is that the N material has an overall charge f zero.

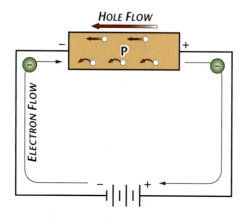

Figure 5-2-5. Current flow in P-type material

By the same reasoning, the P-type material is also electrically neutral because the excess of holes in this material is exactly balanced by the number of electrons. Keep in mind that the holes and electrons are still free to move in the material because they are only loosely bound to their parent atoms.

It would seem that if the N and P materials were joined together by one of the processes mentioned earlier, all the holes and electrons would pair up. But this does not happen. Instead the electrons in the N material diffuse (move or spread out) across the junction into the P material and fill some of the holes. At the same time, the holes in the P material diffuse across the junction into the N material and are filled by N-material electrons. This process, called *junction recombination*, reduces the number of free electrons and holes in the vicinity of the junction. Because there is a depletion, or lack of free electrons and holes in this area, it is known as the *depletion region*.

The loss of an electron from the N material created a positive ion in the N material, while the loss of a hole from the P material created a negative ion in that material. These ions are fixed in place in the crystal lattice structure and cannot move. Thus, they make up a layer of fixed charges on the two sides of the junction as shown in Figure 5-2-6 On the N side of the junction, there is a layer of positively charged ions; on the P side of the junction, there is a layer of negatively charged ions.

An electrostatic field, represented by a small battery in Figure 5-2-6, is established across the junction between the oppositely charged ions. The diffusion of electrons and holes across the junction will continue until the magnitude of the electrostatic field is increased to the point where the electrons and holes no longer have enough energy to overcome it, and are repelled by the negative and positive ions respectively. At this point equilibrium is established and, for all practical purposes, the movement of carriers across the junction ceases. For this reason, the electrostatic field created by the positive and negative ions in the depletion region is called a *barrier*.

The action just described occurs almost instantly when the junction is formed. Only the carriers in the immediate vicinity of the junction are affected. The carriers throughout the remainder of the N and P material are relatively undisturbed and remain in a balanced condition.

Forward bias. An external voltage applied to a PN junction is called *bias*. If, for example, a battery is used to supply bias to a PN junction and is connected so that its voltage opposes the junction field, it will reduce the junction barrier and, therefore, aid current flow through the junction. This type of bias is known as *forward*

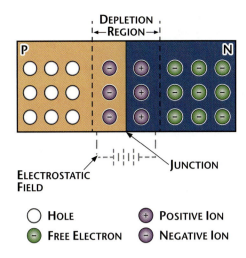

Figure 5-2-6. PN junction barrier formation

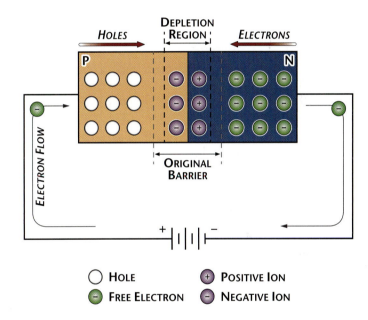

Figure 5-2-7. Forward-biased PN junction

bias, and it causes the junction to offer only minimal resistance to the flow of current.

Forward bias is illustrated in Figure 5-2-7. Notice the positive terminal of the bias battery is connected to the P-type material and the negative terminal of the battery is connected to the N-type material. The positive potential repels holes toward the junction, where they neutralize some of the negative ions. At the same time the negative potential repels electrons toward the junction, where they neutralize some of the positive ions. Since ions on both sides of the barrier are being neutralized, the width of the barrier decreases. Thus, the effect of the battery voltage in the forward-bias direction is to reduce the barrier potential across the junction and to allow majority carriers to cross the junction.

Current flow in the forward-biased PN junction is relatively simple. An electron leaves the negative

5-14 | Introduction to Solid-State Components

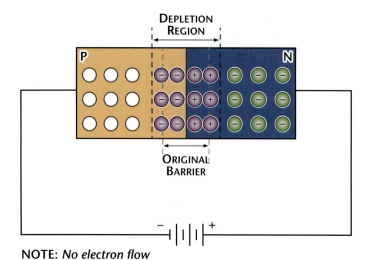

NOTE: *No electron flow*

Figure 5-2-8. Reverse-biased PN junction

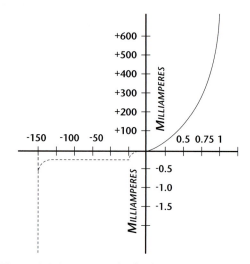

Figure 5-2-9. Junction diode characteristic curve

terminal of the battery and moves to the terminal of the N material. It enters the N material, where it is the majority carrier and moves to the edge of the junction barrier. Because of forward bias, the barrier offers less opposition to the electron and it will pass through the depletion region into the P material. The electron loses energy in overcoming the opposition of the junction barrier, and upon entering the P material, combines with a hole. The hole was produced when an electron was extracted from the P material by the positive potential of the battery. The created hole moves through the P material toward the junction where it combines with an electron.

It is important to remember that in the forward biased condition, conduction is by majority current carriers (holes in the P material and electrons in the N material). Increasing the battery voltage will increase the number of majority carriers arriving at the junction and will therefore increase the current flow. If the battery voltage is increased to the point where the barrier is greatly reduced, a heavy current will flow and the junction may be damaged from the resulting heat.

Reverse bias. If the battery mentioned earlier is connected across the junction so that its voltage aids the junction, it will increase the junction barrier and thereby offer a high resistance to the current flow through the junction. This type of bias is known as *reverse bias*.

To reverse bias a junction diode, the negative battery terminal is connected to the P-type material, and the positive battery terminal to the N-type material, as shown in Figure 5-2-8. The negative potential attracts the holes away from the edge of the junction barrier on the P side, while the positive potential attracts the electrons away from the edge of the barrier on the N side. This action increases the barrier width because there are more negative ions on the P side of the junction and more positive ions on the N side of the junction.

Notice Figure 5-2-8 that the width of the barrier has increased. This increase in the number of ions prevents current flow across the junction by majority carriers. However, the current flow across the barrier is not quite zero because of the minority carriers crossing the junction.

When the crystal is subjected to an external source of energy (light, heat, etc.), electron-hole pairs are generated. The electron-hole pairs produce minority current carriers. There are minority current carriers in both regions: holes in the N material and electrons in the P material. With reverse bias, the electrons in the P material are repelled toward the junction by the negative terminal of the battery. As the electron moves across the junction, it will neutralize a positive ion in the N material. Similarly, the holes in the N material will be repelled by the positive terminal of the battery toward the junction. As the hole crosses the junction, it will neutralize a negative ion in the P material. This movement of minority carriers is called *minority current flow*, because the holes and electrons involved come from the electron-hole pairs that are generated in the crystal lattice structure, and not from the addition of impurity atoms.

Therefore, when a PN junction is reverse biased, there will be no current flow because of majority carriers but a very small amount of current because of minority carriers crossing the junction. However, at normal operating temperatures, this small current may be neglected.

In summary, the most important point to remember about the PN junction diode is its capability to offer very little resistance to current flow in the forward-bias direction but maximum resistance to current flow when reverse biased. A good way of illustrating this point is by plotting a graph of the applied voltage versus the measured current. Figure 5-2-9 shows a plot of this voltage-current relationship (characteristic curve) for a typical PN junction diode.

To determine the resistance from the curve in this figure use Ohm's law:

R = E ÷ I

For example, at point A the forward-bias voltage is 1 V and the forward-bias current is 5 mA. This represents 200 Ω of resistance (1 V/5mA = 200 Ω). However, at point B the voltage is 3 V and the current is 50 mA. This results in 60 Ω of resistance for the diode. Notice that when the forward-bias voltage was tripled (1 V to 3 V), the current increased 10 times (5 mA to 50 mA). At the same time the forward-bias voltage increased, the resistance decreased from 200 Ω to 60 Ω. In other words, when forward bias increases, the junction barrier gets smaller and its resistance to current flow decreases.

On the other hand, the diode conducts very little when reverse biased. Notice at point C the reverse-bias voltage is 80 V and the current is only 100 microamperes (μA). This results in 800 kilohms (800,000 Ω) of resistance, which is considerably larger than the resistance of the junction with forward bias. Because of these unusual features, the PN junction diode is often used to convert AC into DC (rectification).

PN Junction Application

Until now, only one application for the diode has been mentioned—rectification—but there are many more that have not yet been discussed. Variations in doping agents, semiconductor materials and manufacturing techniques have made it possible to produce diodes that can be used in many different applications. Examples of these types of diodes are signal diodes, rectifying diodes, zener diodes (voltage protection diodes for power supplies), varactors (amplifying and switching diodes), and many more. Only applications for two of the most commonly used diodes, the signal diode and rectifier diode, will be presented in this chapter

Half-Wave Rectifier

One of the most important uses of a diode is rectification. The normal PN junction diode is well-suited for this purpose as it conducts very heavily when forward biased and only slightly when reverse biased. If the diode is placed in series with a source of AC power, the diode will be forward and reverse biased every cycle. Since in this situation current flows more easily in one direction than the other, rectification

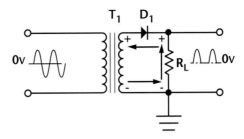

Figure 5-2-10. Half-wave rectifier output

is accomplished. The simplest rectifier circuit is a half-wave rectifier (Figure 5-2-10 and Figure 5-2-11), which consists of a diode, an AC power source and a load resistor.

The transformer (T1) in the figure provides the AC input to the circuit; the diode (CR1) provides the rectification; and the load resistor (RL) serves two purposes: it limits the amount of current flow in the circuit to a safe level, and it also develops the output signal because of the current flow through it.

Before describing how this circuit operates, the definition of the word *load* as it applies to power supplies must be understood. Load is defined as any device that draws current. A device that draws little current is considered a light load, whereas a device that draws a large amount of current is a heavy load. Remember that when speaking of load, that means the device that draws current from the power source. This device may be a simple resistor, or one or more complicated electronic circuits.

During the positive half-cycle of the input signal (solid line) in Figure 5-2-10, the top of the transformer is positive with respect to ground. The dots on the transformer indicate points of the same polarity. With this condition the diode is forward biased, the depletion region is narrow, the resistance of the diode is low, and current flows through the circuit in the direction of the solid lines. When this current flows through the load resistor, it develops a negative-to-positive voltage drop across it, which appears as a positive voltage at the output terminal.

When the AC input goes in a negative direction (Figure 5-2-10), the top of the transformer becomes negative and the diode becomes reverse biased. With reverse bias applied to the diode, the depletion region increases, the resistance of the diode is high, and minimum current flows through the diode. For all practical purposes, there is no output developed across the load resistor during the negative alternation of the input signal, as indicated by the broken lines in the figure.

Although only one cycle of input is shown, it should be realized that the action described

5-16 | Introduction to Solid-State Components

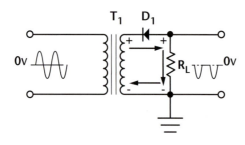

Figure 5-2-11. Half-wave rectifier output reversed diode

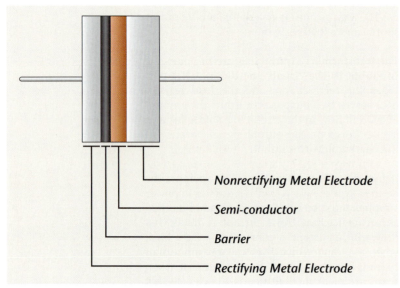

Figure 5-2-12. Metallic rectifier

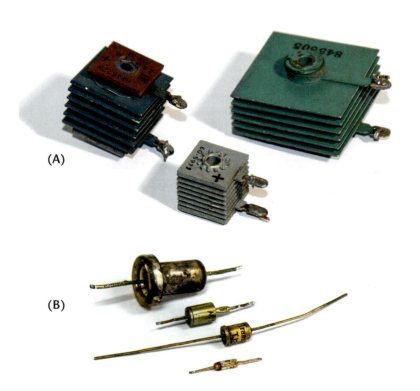

Figure 5-2-13. Various types of; (A) Metallic rectifiers (B) Crystal rectifiers

above continually repeats itself as long as there is an input. Therefore, since only the positive half-cycles appear at the output this circuit converts the AC input into a positive, pulsating DC voltage. The frequency of the output voltage is equal to the frequency of the applied AC signal since there is one pulse out for each cycle of the AC input. For example, if the input frequency is 60 Hz (60 cycles per second), the output frequency is 60 pulses per second (pps).

However, if the diode is reversed, as shown in Figure 5-2-11, a negative output voltage would be obtained. This is because the current would flow from the top of RL toward the bottom, making the output at the top of RL negative with respect to the bottom or ground. Because current flows in this circuit only during half of the input cycle, it is called a half-wave rectifier.

The semiconductor diode shown in Figure 5-2-11 can be replaced by a metallic rectifier and still achieve the same results. The metallic rectifier, sometimes referred to as a dry-disc rectifier, is a metal-to-semiconductor, large-area contact device. Its construction is distinctive; a semiconductor is sandwiched between two metal plates, or electrodes, as shown in Figure 5-2-12. Note in the figure that a barrier, with a resistance many times greater than that of the semiconductor material, is constructed on one of the metal electrodes. The contact having the barrier is a rectifying contact; the other contact is nonrectifying.

Metallic rectifiers act just like the diodes previously discussed in that they permit current to flow more readily in one direction than the other. However, the metallic rectifier is fairly large compared to the crystal diode, as can be seen in Figure 5-2-13. The reason for this is that metallic rectifier units are stacked (to prevent inverse voltage breakdown), have large-area plates (to handle high currents), and usually have cooling fins (to prevent overheating).

There are many known metal-semiconductor combinations that can be used for contact rectification. Copper oxide and selenium devices are by far the most popular. These are frequently used over other types of metallic rectifiers because they have a large forward current per unit of contact area, low forward voltage drop, good stability and a lower aging rate. In practical application, the selenium rectifier is used where a relatively large amount of power is required. On the other hand, copper oxide rectifiers are generally used in small-current applications such as AC meter movements or for delivering direct current to circuits requiring not more than 10 A.

Since metallic rectifiers are affected by temperature, atmospheric conditions and aging (in the case of copper oxide and selenium), they are being replaced by the improved silicon crystal rectifier. The silicon rectifier replaces the bulky selenium rectifier as to current and voltage rating, and can operate at higher ambient temperatures.

Diode Switch

In addition to their use as simple rectifiers, diodes are also used in circuits that mix signals together (mixers), detect the presence of a signal (detector), and act as a switch to open or close a circuit. Diodes used in these applications are commonly referred to as *signal diodes*. The simplest application of a signal diode is the basic diode switch shown in Figure 5-2-14.

When the input to this circuit is at zero potential, the diode is forward biased because of the zero potential on the cathode and the positive voltage on the anode. In this condition, the diode conducts and acts as a straight piece of wire because of its very low forward resistance. In effect, the input is directly coupled to the output resulting in zero volts across the output terminals. Therefore, the diode, acts as a closed switch when its anode is positive with respect to its cathode.

If a positive input voltage (equal to or greater than the positive voltage supplied to the anode) is applied to the diode's cathode, the diode will be reverse biased. In this situation, the diode is cut off and acts as an open switch between the input and output terminals. Consequently, with no current flow in the circuit, the positive voltage on the diode's anode will be felt at the output terminal. Therefore, the diode acts as an open switch when it is reverse biased.

Diode Characteristics

Semiconductor diodes (Figure 5-2-15) have properties that enable them to perform many different electronic functions. To do their jobs, engineers and technicians must be supplied with data on these different types of diodes. The information presented for this purpose is called *diode characteristics*.

These characteristics are supplied by manufacturers either in their manuals or on specification or data sheets. Because of the scores of

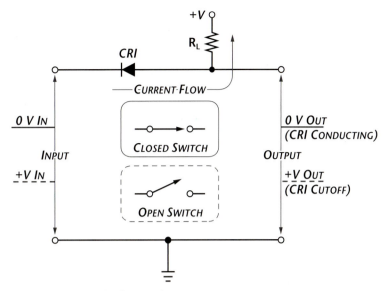

Figure 5-2-14. Basic diode switch

manufacturers and numerous diode types, it is not practical to call a specification sheet for a single component "typical." Aside from the difference between manufacturers, a single manufacturer may supply specification sheets that differ both in format and content. Despite these differences, certain performance and design information is normally required.

A standard specification sheet usually has a brief description of the diode. Included in this description is the type of diode, the major area of application and special features. Of particular interest is the application for which the diode is suited. The manufacturer also provides a drawing of the diode that gives dimension, weight and, if appropriate, identification marks. In addition to this data, the following information is also provided: a static operating table (giving spot values of parameters under fixed conditions); sometimes a characteristic curve similar to the one in Figure 5-2-9 (showing how parameters vary over the full operating range); and diode ratings (which are the limiting values of operating conditions outside which could cause diode damage).

Manufacturers specify these various diode operating parameters and characteristics with letter symbols in accordance with fixed

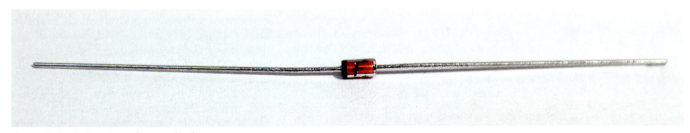

Figure 5-2-15. Semiconductor diode

definitions. Below are lists, by letter symbol, of the major electrical characteristics for the rectifier and signal diodes.

Rectifier Diodes

- DC Blocking Voltage [V_R]—The maximum reverse DC voltage that will not cause breakdown
- Average Forward Voltage Drop [$V_{F(AV)}$]—The average forward voltage drop across the rectifier given at a specified forward current and temperature
- Average Rectifier Forward Current [$I_{F(AV)}$]—The average rectified forward current at a specified temperature, usually at 60 Hz with a resistive load
- Average Reverse Current [$I_{R(AV)}$]—The average reverse current at a specified temperature, usually at 60 Hz
- Peak Surge Current [I_{SURGE}]—The peak current specified for a given number of cycles or portion of a cycle

Signal Diodes

- Peak Reverse Voltage [PRV]—The maximum reverse voltage that can be applied before reaching the breakdown point. (PRV also applies to the rectifier diode.)
- Reverse Current [I_R]—The small value of direct current that flows when a semiconductor diode has reverse bias
- Maximum Forward Voltage Drop at Indicated Forward Current [$V_F@I_F$]—The maximum forward voltage drop across the diode at the indicated forward current
- Reverse Recovery Time [t_{rr}]—The maximum time taken for the forward-bias diode to recover its reverse bias

The ratings of a diode (as stated earlier) are the limiting values of operating conditions, which if exceeded could cause damage to a diode by either voltage breakdown or overheating. The PN junction diodes are generally rated for maximum average forward current, peak recurrent forward current, maximum surge current and peak reverse voltage.

- Maximum average forward current is usually given at a special temperature, usually 77°F (25°C), and refers to the maximum amount of average current that can be permitted to flow in the forward direction. If this rating is exceeded, structure breakdown can occur.
- Peak recurrent forward current is the maximum peak current that can be permitted to flow in the forward direction in the form of recurring pulses.
- Maximum surge current is the maximum current permitted to flow in the forward direction in the form of nonrecurring pulses. Current should not equal this value for more than a few milliseconds.
- Peak reverse voltage (PRV) is one of the most important ratings. PRV indicates the maximum reverse-bias voltage that may be applied to a diode without causing junction breakdown.

All of the above ratings are subject to change with temperature variations. If, for example, the operating temperature is above that stated for the ratings, the ratings must be decreased.

Semiconductor Diodes

Another check often performed by avionics technicians is on rectifier diodes. Diodes are checked with an ohmmeter by testing the resistance of the diode and then by reversing the ohmmeter leads to test resistance in the reverse direction. The diode should have low resistance when forward-biased (positive meter lead on the anode) and high resistance when reverse-biased. If the diode has low resistance in both directions, it is shorted; if it exhibits high resistance in both directions, it is open. In either instance, it must be replaced. It may be necessary, in many situations, to disconnect one of the diode's leads from its associated circuit before making this test.

Section 3
Introduction to Transistors

The discovery of the first transistor in 1948 by a team of physicists at Bell Telephone Laboratories sparked an interest in solid-state research that spread rapidly. The transistor, which began as a simple laboratory oddity, was rapidly developed into a semiconductor device of major importance. The transistor demonstrated for the first time in history that amplification in solids was possible.

Before the transistor, amplification was achieved only with electron tubes. Transistors now perform numerous electronic tasks with new and improved designs being continually put on the market. In many cases, transistors are more desirable than tubes because they are small, rugged, require no filament power, and operate at low voltages with comparatively high efficiency. The development of a family of transistors has even made possible the miniaturization of electronic circuits. Figure 5-3-1 shows a sample of the many different types of transistors encountered when working with electronic equipment.

Transistors have infiltrated virtually every area of science and industry, from the family car to satellites. Even the aviation industry depends heavily on transistors. The ever increasing uses for transistors have created an urgent need for sound and basic information regarding their operation.

The study of the PN junction diode in section 2 supplied the basic knowledge needed to grasp the principles of transistor operation. In this section the basic types of transistors, their construction and their theory of operation are covered. Then the discussion moves on to how and why transistors amplify. Once this basic information is understood, transistor terminology, capabilities, limitations and identification will be discussed. Finally, this section examines transistor maintenance, integrated circuits, circuit boards and modular circuitry.

Transistor Fundamentals

The first solid-state device discussed was the two-element semiconductor diode. The next device on our list is more advanced. It not only has one more element than the diode but it can amplify as well. Semiconductor devices that have three or more elements are called transistors. The term *transistor* was derived by combining "trans" from the word transistor, and "istor" from the word resistor. This term was adopted because it best describes the operation of the transistor—the transfer of an input signal current from a low-resistance circuit to a high-resistance circuit. Basically, the transistor is a solid-state device that amplifies by controlling the flow of current carriers through its semiconductor materials.

There are many different types of transistors, but their basic theory of operation is all the same. As a matter of fact, the theory that will be used to explain the operation of a transistor is the same theory used earlier with the PN junction diode except that now two such junctions are required to form the three elements of a transistor. The three elements of the two-junction transistor are the emitter, which gives off, or emits, current carriers (electrons or holes); the base, which controls the flow of current carriers; and the collector, which collects the current carriers.

Classification

Transistors are classified as either NPN or PNP according to the arrangement of their N and P materials. Their basic construction and chemi-

Figure 5-3-1. An assortment of different types of transistors

cal treatment is implied by their names. That is, an NPN transistor is formed by introducing a thin region of P-type material between two regions of N-type material. On the other hand, a PNP transistor is formed by introducing a thin region of N-type material between two regions of P-type material. Transistors constructed in this latter manner have two PN junctions, as shown in Figure 5-3-2. One PN junction is between the emitter and the base; the other PN junction is between the collector and the base. The two junctions share one section of semiconductor material so that the transistor actually consists of three elements.

Since the majority and minority current carriers are different for N and P materials, it stands to reason that the internal operation of NPN and PNP transistors will also be different. The theory of operation of NPN and PNP transistors will be discussed separately in the next few paragraphs. Additional information about the PN junction will be given as the theory of transistor operation is developed.

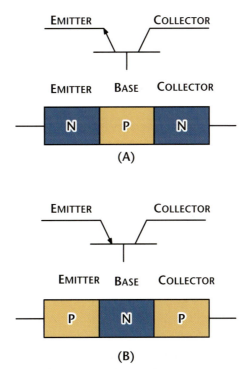

Figure 5-3-2. NPN and PNP transistors

TYPE		CONSTRUCTION
(A)	Point Contact	Emitter / Collector / Base
(B)	Grown Junction or Rate Grown Junction	Emitter / Collector / N or P / N or P / N or P / Base
(C)	Alloy or Fused Junction	Collector / Base / Emitter
(D)	Diffused Junction	Collector / Base / Emitter

Figure 5-3-3. Transistor construction

To prepare for the forthcoming information, the two basic types of transistors along with their circuit symbols are shown in Figure 5-3-2. It should be noted that the two symbols are different. The horizontal line represents the base; the angular line with the arrow on it represents the emitter; and the other angular line represents the collector. The direction of the arrow on the emitter distinguishes the NPN from the PNP transistor. If the arrow points in, (Points "iN") the transistor is a PNP. On the other hand, if the arrow points out, the transistor is an NPN (Not Pointing "iN").

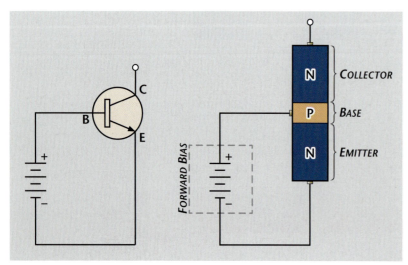

Figure 5-3-4. NPN transistor operation

Another item that should be kept in mind is that the arrow always points in the direction of hole flow, or from the P to N sections, no matter whether the P section is the emitter or base. On the other hand, electron flow is always toward or against the arrow, just like in the junction diode.

Construction

The very first transistors were known as point-contact transistors. Their construction is similar to the construction of the point-contact diode. The difference, of course, is that the point-contact transistor has two P or N regions instead of one. Each of the two regions constitutes an electrode (element) of the transistor. One is named the emitter and the other is named the collector, as shown in Figure 5-3-3A.

Point-contact transistors are now practically obsolete. They have been replaced by junction transistors, which are superior in nearly all respects. The junction transistor generates less noise, handles more power, provides higher current and voltage gains, and can be mass-produced more cheaply than the point-contact transistor. Junction transistors are manufactured in much the same manner as the PN junction diode discussed earlier. However, when the PNP or NPN material is grown (Figure 5-3-3B) the impurity mixing process must be reversed twice to obtain the two junctions required in a transistor. Likewise, when the alloy-junction (Figure 5-3-3C) or the diffused-junction (Figure 5-3-3D) process is used, two junctions must also be created within the crystal.

Although there are many ways to manufacture transistors, one of the most important parts of any manufacturing process is quality control. Without good quality control, many transistors would prove unreliable because the construction and processing of a transistor govern its thermal ratings, stability and electrical characteristics. Even though there are many variations in the transistor manufacturing processes, certain structural techniques that yield good reliability and long life are common to all processes:

- Wire leads are connected to each semiconductor electrode.
- The crystal is specially mounted to protect it against mechanical damage.
- The unit is sealed to prevent harmful contamination of the crystal.

Transistor Theory

Recall from the earlier discussion that a forward-biased PN junction is comparable to a low-resistance circuit element because it passes a high current for a given voltage. In turn, a reverse-biased PN junction is comparable to a high-resistance circuit element. By using the Ohm's law formula for power ($P = I^2R$) and assuming current is held constant, it can be concluded that the power developed across a high resistance is greater than that developed across a low resistance. Thus, if a crystal were to contain two PN junctions (one forward-biased and the other reverse-biased), a low-power signal could be injected into the forward-biased junction and produce a high-power signal at the reverse-biased junction. In this manner, a power gain would be obtained across the crystal.

NPN Transistor Operation

Just as in the PN junction diode, the N material comprising the two end sections of the NPN transistor contains a number of free electrons, while the center P section contains an excess of holes. The action at each junction between these sections is the same as that previously described for the diode; that is, depletion regions develop and the junction barrier appears.

To use the transistor as an amplifier, each of these junctions must be modified by some external bias voltage. For the transistor to function in this capacity, the first PN junction (emitter-base junction) is biased in the forward, or low-resistance, direction. The second PN junction (base-collector junction) is biased in the reverse, or high-resistance, direction. A simple way to remember how to properly bias a transistor is to observe the NPN or PNP elements that make up the transistor. The letters of these elements indicate what polarity voltage to use for correct bias. For instance, notice the NPN transistor in Figure 5-3-4:

1. The emitter, which is the first letter in the NPN sequence, is connected to the negative side of the battery while the base, which is the second letter (P), is connected to the positive side.

2. However, since the second PN junction is required to be reverse biased for proper transistor operation, the collector must be connected to an opposite polarity voltage (positive) than that indicated by its letter designation. The voltage on the collector must also be more positive than the base, as shown in Figure 5-3-5. This is now a properly biased NPN transistor. An example of a properly biased transistor in a circuit is pictured in Figure 5-3-6.

In summary, the base of the NPN transistor must be positive with respect to the emitter,

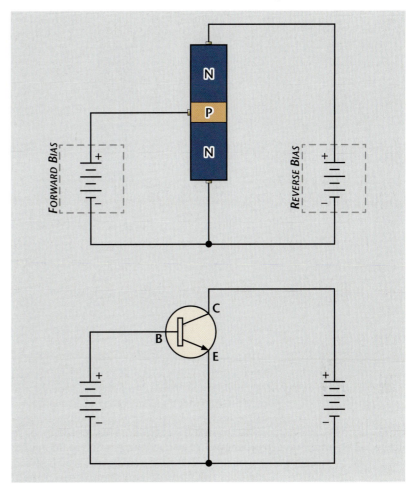

Figure 5-3-5. Properly biased transistor

Figure 5-3-6. Properly biased transistors installed on a PC board

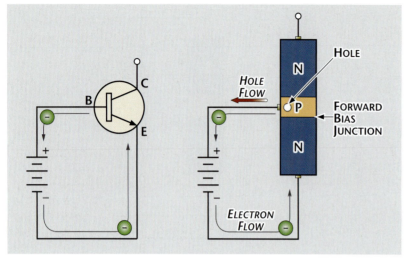

Figure 5-3-7. The forward-biased junction in an NPN transistor

the P material (base). For each electron that fills a hole in the P material, another electron will leave the P material (creating a new hole) and enter the positive terminal of the battery.

NPN reverse-biased junction. The second PN junction (base-to-collector), or reverse-biased junction as it is called in Figure 5-3-8, blocks the majority current carriers from crossing the junction. However, there is a very small current, mentioned earlier, that does pass through this junction. This current is called minority current, or reverse current, and was produced by the electron-hole pairs. The minority carriers for the reverse-biased PN junction are the electrons in the P material and the holes in the N material. These minority carriers conduct the current for the reverse-biased junction when electrons from the P material enter the N material, and the holes from the N material enter the P material. However, the minority current electrons play the most important part in the operation of the NPN transistor.

and the collector must be more positive than the base.

NPN forward-biased junction. An important point to bring out at this time, which was not mentioned during the explanation of the diode, is the fact that the N material on one side of the forward-biased junction is more heavily doped than the P material. This results in more current being carried across the junction by the majority carrier electrons from the N material than the majority carrier holes from the P material. Therefore, conduction through the forward-biased junction, as shown in Figure 5-3-7, is mainly by majority carrier electrons from the N material (emitter).

With the emitter-to-base junction in the figure biased in the forward direction, electrons leave the negative terminal of the battery and enter the N material (emitter). Since electrons are majority current carriers in the N material, they pass easily through the emitter, cross over the junction, and combine with holes in

Why is the second PN junction (base-to-collector) not forward biased like the first PN junction (emitter-to-base) is a common question at this point. If both junctions were forward biased, the electrons would have a tendency to flow from each end section of the NPN transistor (emitter and collector) to the center P section (base). In essence, there would be two junction diodes possessing a common base, thus eliminating any amplification and defeating the purpose of the transistor.

A word of caution is in order at this time. If the second PN junction is mistakenly biased in the forward direction, the excessive current could develop enough heat to destroy the junctions, making the transistor useless. Therefore, be sure the bias voltage polarities are correct before making any electrical connections.

NPN junction interaction. It is now time to see what happens when the two junctions of the NPN transistor are placed in operation at the same time. For a better understanding of just how the two junctions work together, refer to Figure 5-3-9 during the discussion.

The bias batteries in this figure have been labeled V_{CC} for the collector voltage supply, and V_{BB} for the base voltage supply. Also notice the base supply battery is quite small, as indicated by the number of cells in the battery, usually 1 V or less. However, the collector supply is generally much higher than the base supply, normally around 6 V. As shown later, this difference in supply voltages is necessary to have current flow from the emitter to the collector.

As stated earlier, the current flow in the external circuit is always due to the movement of

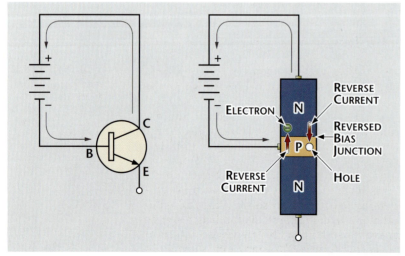

Figure 5-3-8. The reverse-biased junction in an NPN transistor

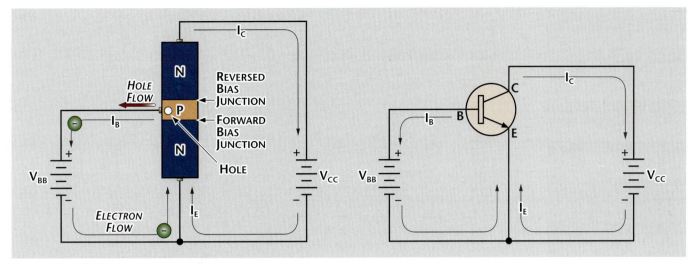

Figure 5-3-9. NPN transistor operation

free electrons. Therefore, electrons flow from the negative terminals of the supply batteries to the N-type emitter. This combined movement of electrons is known as *emitter current* (I_E). Since electrons are the majority carriers in the N material, they will move through the N material emitter to the emitter-base junction. With this junction forward biased, electrons continue on into the base region. Once the electrons are in the base, which is a P-type material, they become minority carriers. Some of the electrons that move into the base recombine with available holes. For each electron that recombines, another electron moves out through the base lead as base current I_B (creating a new hole for eventual combination) and returns to the base supply battery V_{BB}.

The electrons that recombine are lost as far as the collector is concerned. Therefore, to make the transistor more efficient, the base region is made very thin and lightly doped. This reduces the opportunity for an electron to recombine with a hole and be lost. Thus, most of the electrons that move into the base region come under the influence of the large collector reverse bias. This bias acts as forward bias for the minority carriers (electrons) in the base and, as such, accelerates them through the base-collector junction and into the collector region. Since the collector is made of an N-type material, the electrons that reach the collector again become majority current carriers. Once in the collector, the electrons move easily through the N material and return to the positive terminal of the collector supply battery V_{CC} as collector current (I_C).

To further improve on the efficiency of the transistor, the collector is made physically larger than the base for two reasons: to increase the chance of collecting carriers that diffuse to the side as well as directly across the base region, and to enable the collector to handle more heat without damage.

In summary, total current flow in the NPN transistor is through the emitter lead. Therefore, in terms of percentage, I_E is 100 percent. On the other hand, since the base is very thin and lightly doped, a smaller percentage of the total current (emitter current) will flow in the base circuit than in the collector circuit. Usually no more than 2 to 5 percent of the total current is base current (I_B) while the remaining 95 to 98 percent is collector current (I_C). A very basic relationship exists between these two currents:

$$I_E = I_B + I_C$$

In simple terms this means that the emitter current is separated into base and collector current. Since the amount of current leaving the emitter is solely a function of the emitter-base bias, and because the collector receives most of this current, a small change in emitter-base bias will have a far greater effect on the magnitude of collector current than it will have on base current. In conclusion, the relatively small emitter-base bias controls the relatively large emitter-to-collector current.

PNP Transistor Operation

The PNP transistor works essentially the same as the NPN transistor. However, since the emitter, base and collector in the PNP transistor are made of materials that are different from those used in the NPN transistor, different current carriers flow in the PNP unit. The majority current carriers in the PNP transistor are holes. This is in contrast to the NPN transistor, where the majority current carriers are electrons. To support this different type of current (hole flow), the bias batteries are reversed for the PNP transistor. A typical bias setup for the PNP transistor is shown in Figure 5-3-10.

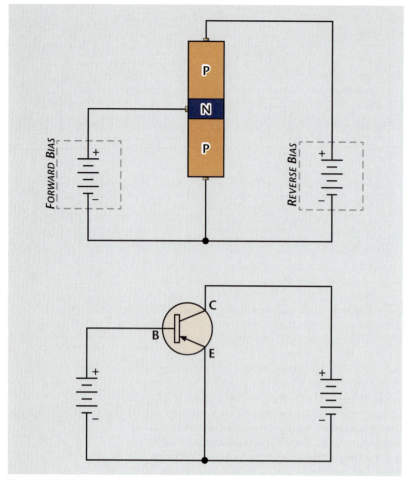

Figure 5-3-10. A properly biased PNP transistor

tor. Thus, the base of the PNP transistor must be negative with respect to the emitter, and the collector must be more negative than the base.

Remember, just as in the case of the NPN transistor, this difference in supply voltage is necessary to have current flow (hole flow in the case of the PNP transistor) from the emitter to the collector. Although hole flow is the predominant type of current flow in the PNP transistor, hole flow only takes place within the transistor itself, while electrons flow in the external circuit. However, it is the internal hole flow that leads to electron flow in the external wires connected to the transistor.

PNP forward-biased junction. Now let us consider what happens when the emitter-base junction in Figure 5-3-11 is forward biased. With the bias setup shown, the positive terminal of the battery repels the emitter holes toward the base, while the negative terminal drives the base electrons toward the emitter. When an emitter hole and a base electron meet, they combine. For each electron that combines with a hole, another electron leaves the negative terminal of the battery, and enters the base. At the same time, an electron leaves the emitter, creating a new hole, and enters the positive terminal of the battery. This movement of electrons into the base and out of the emitter constitutes base current flow (I_B), and the path these electrons take is referred to as the emitter-base circuit.

PNP reverse-biased junction. In the reverse-biased junction (Figure 5-3-12), the negative voltage on the collector and the positive voltage on the base block the majority current carriers from crossing the junction. However, this same negative collector voltage acts as forward bias for the minority current holes in the base, which cross the junction and enter the collector. The minority current electrons in the collector also sense forward bias—the positive base voltage—and move into the base.

The holes in the collector are filled by electrons that flow from the negative terminal of the battery. At the same time the electrons leave the negative terminal of the battery, other electrons in the base break their covalent bonds and enter the positive terminal of the battery. Although there is only minority current flow in the reverse-biased junction, it is still very small because of the limited number of minority current carriers.

PNP junction interaction. The interaction between the forward- and reverse-biased junctions in a PNP transistor is very similar to that in an NPN transistor, except that in the PNP transistor, the majority current carriers are holes. In the PNP transistor shown in Figure 5-3-13, the positive voltage on the emitter repels the holes toward the base. Once in the

Notice that the procedure used earlier to properly bias the NPN transistor also applies here to the PNP transistor. The first letter in the PNP sequence indicates the polarity of the voltage required for the emitter (positive), and the second letter indicates the polarity of the base voltage (negative). Since the base-collector junction is always reverse biased, then the opposite polarity voltage (negative) must be used for the collec-

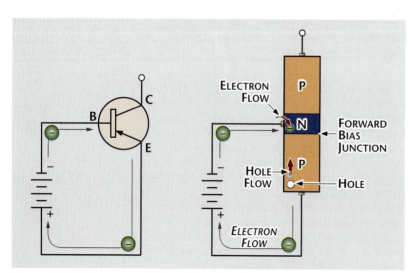

Figure 5-3-11. The forward-biased junction in a PNP transistor

base, the holes combine with base electrons. But again, remember that the base region is made very thin to prevent the recombination of holes with electrons. Therefore, well over 90 percent of the holes that enter the base become attracted to the large negative collector voltage and pass right through the base. However, for each electron and hole that combine in the base region, another electron leaves the negative terminal of the base battery (V_{BB}) and enters the base as base current (I_B).

At the same time an electron leaves the negative terminal of the battery, another electron leaves the emitter as I_E (creating a new hole) and enters the positive terminal of V_{BB}. Meanwhile, in the collector circuit, electrons from the collector battery (V_{CC}) enter the collector as I_C and combine with the excess holes from the base. For each hole that is neutralized in the collector by an electron, another electron leaves the emitter and starts its way back to the positive terminal of V_{CC}.

Although current flow in the external circuit of the PNP transistor is opposite in direction to that of the NPN transistor, the majority carriers always flow from the emitter to the collector. This flow of majority carriers also results in the formation of two individual current loops within each transistor. One loop is the base-current path, and the other is the collector-current path. The combination of the current in both of these loops ($I_B + I_C$) results in total transistor current (I_E).

The most important thing to remember about the two different types of transistors is that the emitter-base voltage of the PNP transistor has the same controlling effect on collector current as that of the NPN transistor. In simple terms, increasing the forward-bias voltage of a transistor reduces the emitter-base junction barrier. This action allows more carriers to reach the collector, causing an increase in current flow

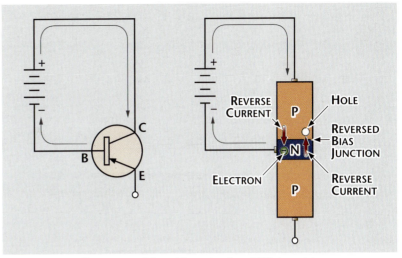

Figure 5-3-12. The reverse-biased junction in a PNP transistor

from the emitter to the collector and through the external circuit. Conversely, a decrease in the forward-bias voltage reduces collector current.

The Basic Transistor Amplifier

In the preceding pages the internal workings of the transistor were explained and new terms introduced, such as emitter, base and collector. This provides the background for the study of the basic transistor amplifier.

To understand the overall operation of the transistor amplifier, only the current in and out of the transistor and through the various components in the circuit need be considered. Therefore, from this point on, only the schematic symbol for the transistor will be used in the illustrations, and rather than thinking about majority and minority carriers, start thinking in terms of emitter, base and collector current.

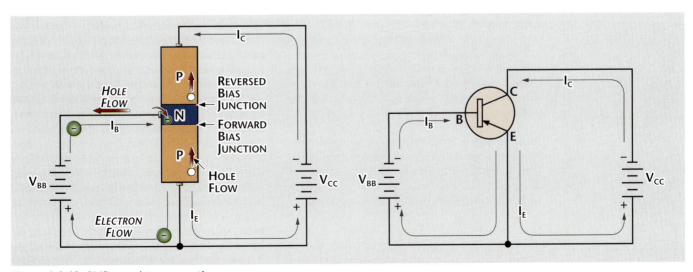

Figure 5-3-13. PNP transistor operation

5-26 | Introduction to Solid-State Components

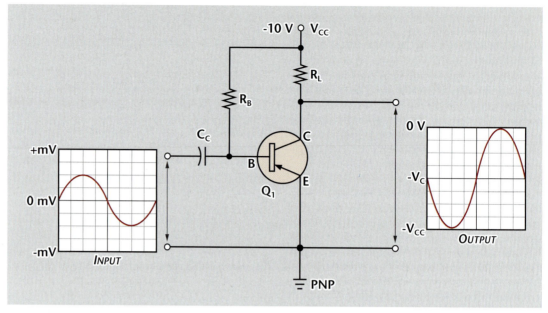

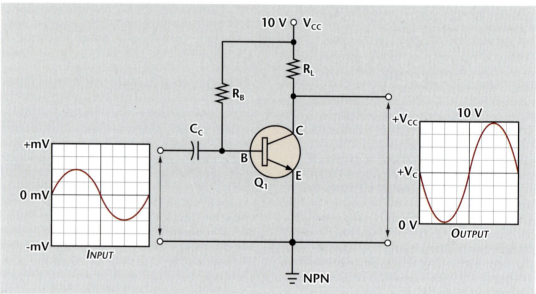

Figure 5-3-14. The basic transistor amplifier

Before examining the basic transistor amplifier, there are two terms one should be familiar with: amplification and amplifier. *Amplification* is the process of increasing the strength of a signal. (A signal is just a general term used to refer to any particular current, voltage or power in a circuit.) An *amplifier* is the device that provides amplification without appreciably altering the original signal.

Transistors are frequently used as amplifiers. Some transistor circuits are current amplifiers, with a small load resistance; other circuits are designed for voltage amplification and have a high load resistance; others amplify power.

Now look at the NPN version of the basic transistor amplifier in Figure 5-3-14 and see how it works. A practical example of a basic transistor amplifier is pictured in Figure 5-3-15.

So far in this discussion, a separate battery has been used to provide the necessary forward-bias voltage. Although a separate battery has been used in the past for convenience, it is not practical to use a battery for emitter-base bias. For instance, it would take a battery slightly greater than 0.2 V to properly forward bias a germanium transistor, while a similar silicon transistor would require a voltage slightly more than 0.6 V. However, common batteries do not have such voltage values. Also, since bias voltages are quite critical and must be held within a few tenths of a volt, it is easier to work with bias currents flowing through resistors of high ohmic values than with batteries.

By inserting one or more resistors in a circuit, different methods of biasing may be achieved and the emitter-base battery eliminated. In addition to eliminating the battery, some of these biasing

Figure 5-3-15. The basic transistor amplifier shown in place on a PC board

methods compensate for slight variations in transistor characteristics and changes in transistor conduction resulting from temperature irregularities. Notice in Figure 5-3-14 that the emitter-base battery has been eliminated and the bias resistor R_B has been inserted between the collector and the base. Resistor R_B provides the necessary forward bias for the emitter-base junction.

Current flows in the emitter-base bias circuit from ground to the emitter, out the base lead, and through R_B to V_{CC}. Since the current in the base circuit is very small (a few hundred microamperes) and the forward resistance of the transistor is low, only a few tenths of a volt of positive bias will be felt on the base of the transistor. However, this is enough voltage on the base, along with ground on the emitter and the large positive voltage on the collector, to properly bias the transistor.

With Q_1 properly biased, direct current flows continuously, with or without an input signal, throughout the entire circuit. The direct current flowing through the circuit develops more than just base bias; it also develops the collector voltage (V_C) as it flows through Q_1 and R_L. Notice the collector voltage on the output graph. Since it is present in the circuit without an input signal, the output signal starts at the V_C level and either increases or decreases. These DC voltages and currents that exist in the circuit before the application of a signal are known as *quiescent* voltages and currents.

Resistor R_L, the collector load resistor, is placed in the circuit to keep the full effect of the collector supply voltage off the collector. This permits the collector voltage (V_C) to change with an input signal, which in turn allows the transistor to amplify voltage. Without R_L in the circuit, the voltage on the collector would always be equal to V_{CC}.

The coupling capacitor (C_C) is another addition to the transistor circuit. It is used to pass the AC input signal and block the DC voltage from the preceding circuit. This prevents DC in the circuitry on the left of the coupling capacitor from affecting the bias on Q_1. The coupling capacitor also blocks the bias of Q_1 from reaching the input signal source.

The input to the amplifier is a sine wave that varies a few millivolts above and below zero. It is introduced into the circuit by the coupling capacitor and is applied between the base and emitter. As the input signal goes positive, the voltage across the emitter-base junction becomes more positive. This in effect increases forward bias, which causes base current to increase at the same rate as that of the input sine wave.

Emitter and collector currents also increase but much more than the base current. With an increase in collector current, more voltage is developed across R_L. Since the voltage across R_L and the voltage across Q_1 (collector

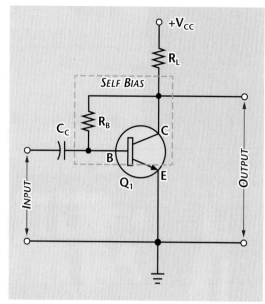

Figure 5-3-16. A basic transistor amplifier with self-bias

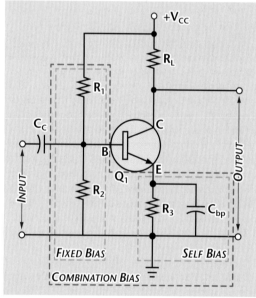

Figure 5-3-17. A basic transistor amplifier with combination bias

to emitter) must add up to V_{CC}, an increase in voltage across R_L results in an equal decrease in voltage across Q_1. Therefore, the output voltage from the amplifier, taken at the collector of Q_1 with respect to the emitter, is a negative alternation of voltage that is larger than the input, but has the same sine wave characteristics.

During the negative alternation of the input, the input signal opposes the forward bias. This action decreases base current, which results in a decrease in both emitter and collector currents. The decrease in current through R_L decreases its voltage drop and causes the voltage across the transistor to rise along with the output voltage. Therefore, the output for the negative alternation of the input is a positive alternation of voltage that is larger than the input but has the same sine wave characteristics.

By examining both input and output signals for one complete alternation of the input, one can see that the output of the amplifier is an exact reproduction of the input except for the reversal in polarity and the increased amplitude (a few millivolts as compared to a few volts).

The PNP version of this amplifier is shown in the upper part of Figure 5-3-14. The primary difference between the NPN and PNP amplifier is the polarity of the source voltage. With a negative V_{CC}, the PNP base voltage is slightly negative with respect to ground, which provides the necessary forward bias between the emitter and base.

When the PNP input signal goes positive, it opposes the forward bias of the transistor. This action cancels some of the negative voltage across the emitter-base junction, which reduces the current through the transistor. Therefore, the voltage across the load resistor decreases, and the voltage across the transistor increases. Since V_{CC} is negative, the voltage on the collector (V_C) goes in a negative direction (as shown on the output graph) toward $-V_{CC}$ (for example, from -5 V to -7 V). Thus, the output is a negative alternation of voltage that varies at the same rate as the sine wave input, but is opposite in polarity and has a much larger amplitude.

During the negative alternation of the input signal, the transistor current increases because the input voltage aids the forward bias. Therefore, the voltage across R_L increases, and consequently, the voltage across the transistor decreases or goes in a positive direction (for example, from -5 V to -3 V). This action results in a positive output voltage, which has the same characteristics as the input except that it has been amplified and the polarity is reversed.

In summary, the input signals in the preceding circuits were amplified because the small change in base current caused a large change in collector current. And, by placing resistor R_L in series with the collector, voltage amplification was achieved.

Types of Bias

One of the basic problems with transistor amplifiers is establishing and maintaining the proper values of quiescent current and voltage in the circuit. This is accomplished by selecting the proper circuit-biasing conditions and ensuring these conditions are maintained despite variations in ambient temperature, which cause changes in amplification and even *distortion* (an unwanted change in a signal). Thus a need arises for a method to properly bias the transistor amplifier and at the same time stabilize its DC operating point (i.e., the no-signal values of collector voltage and collector current). As mentioned earlier, various biasing methods can be used to accomplish both of these functions. Although there are numerous biasing methods, only three basic types will be considered.

Base-Current Bias (Fixed Bias)

The first biasing method, called *base-current* bias or sometimes *fixed bias*, was used in Figure 5-3-14. To review, it consisted basically of a resistor (R_B) connected between the collector supply voltage and the base. Unfortunately, this simple arrangement is thermally unstable. If the temperature of the transistor rises for any reason, due to a rise in ambient temperature or due to current flow through it, collector current will increase. This increase in current also causes the DC operating point to move away from its desired level. This reaction to temperature is undesirable because it affects amplifier gain (the number of times of amplification) and could result in distortion, as will be shown later in this discussion.

Self-Bias

A better method of biasing is obtained by inserting the bias resistor directly between the base and collector, as shown in Figure 5-3-16. By tying the collector to the base in this manner, feedback voltage can be fed from the collector to the base to develop forward bias. This arrangement is called *self-bias*. Now, if an increase in temperature causes an increase in collector current, the collector voltage (V_C) will fall because of the increase of voltage produced across the load resistor (R_L). This drop in V_C will be fed back to the base and will result in a decrease in the base current. The decrease in base current will oppose the original increase in collector current and tend to stabilize it. The exact opposite effect is produced when the collector current decreases.

Self-bias has two small drawbacks:

- It is only partially effective and, therefore, is only used where moderate changes in ambient temperature are expected.
- It reduces amplification since the signal on the collector also affects the base voltage.

This is because the collector and base signals for this particular amplifier configuration are 180° out of phase (opposite in polarity) and the part of the collector signal that is fed back to the base cancels some of the input signal. This process of returning a part of the output back to its input is known as *degeneration* or *negative feedback*. Sometimes degeneration is desired to prevent amplitude distortion (an output signal that fails to follow the input exactly) and self-bias may be used for this purpose.

Combination Bias

A combination of fixed and self-bias can be used to improve stability and at the same time overcome some of the disadvantages of the other two biasing methods. One of the most widely used combination-bias systems is the voltage-divider type shown in Figure 5-3-17. Fixed bias is provided in this circuit by the voltage-divider network consisting of R_1, R_2, and the collector supply voltage (V_{CC}). The DC current flowing through the voltage-divider network biases the base positive with respect to the emitter. Resistor R_3, which is connected in series with the emitter, provides the emitter with self-bias. Should I_E increase, the voltage drop across R_3 would also increase, reducing V_C. This reaction to an increase in I_E by R_3 is another form of degeneration, which results in less output from the amplifier. However, to provide long-term or DC thermal stability, and at the same time allow minimal AC signal degeneration, the bypass capacitor (C_{bp}) is placed across R_3. If C_{bp} is large enough, rapid signal variations will not change its charge materially and no degeneration of the signal will occur.

In summary, the fixed-bias resistors, R_1 and R_2, tend to keep the base bias constant while the emitter bias changes with emitter conduction. This action greatly improves thermal stability and at the same time maintains the correct operating point for the transistor.

Amplifier Classes of Operation

In the previous discussions, it was assumed that for every portion of the input signal there was an output from the amplifier. This is not always the case with amplifiers. It may be desirable to have the transistor conducting for only a portion of the input signal. The portion of the input for which there is an output determines the class of operation of the amplifier. There are four classes of amplifier operations: A, AB, B and C.

Class A Amplifier Operation

Class A amplifiers are biased so that variations in input signal polarities occur within the limits of *cutoff* and *saturation*. In a PNP transistor, for example, if the base becomes positive with respect to the emitter, holes will be repelled at the PN junction and no current can flow in the collector circuit. This condition is known

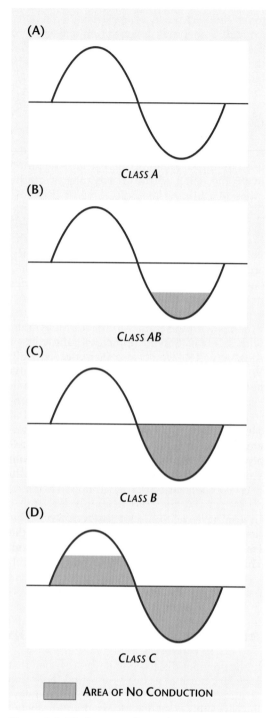

Figure 5-3-18. A comparison of output signals for the different amplifier classes of operation

as cutoff. Saturation occurs when the base becomes so negative with respect to the emitter that changes in the signal are not reflected in collector-current flow.

Biasing an amplifier in this manner places the DC operating point between cutoff and saturation and allows collector current to flow during the complete cycle (360°) of the input signal, thus providing an output that is a replica of the input. Figure 5-3-14 is an example of a class A amplifier. Although the output from this amplifier is 180° out of phase with the input, the output current still flows for the complete duration of the input.

The Class A–operated amplifier is used as an audio- and radio-frequency amplifier in radio, radar and sound systems, just to mention a few examples. For a comparison of output signals for the different amplifier classes of operation, refer to Figure 5-3-18 during the following discussion.

Class AB Amplifier Operation

Amplifiers designed for Class AB operation are biased so that collector current is zero (cutoff) for a portion of one alternation of the input signal. This is accomplished by making the forward-bias voltage less than the peak value of the input signal. By doing this, the base-emitter junction will be reverse biased during one alternation for the amount of time that the input signal voltage opposes and exceeds the value of forward-bias voltage. Therefore, collector current will flow for more than 180° but less than 360° of the input signal, as shown in Figure 5-3-18B. As compared to the Class A amplifier, the DC operating point for the class AB amplifier is closer to cutoff.

The Class AB–operated amplifier is commonly used as a push-pull amplifier to overcome a side effect of Class B operation called crossover distortion.

Class B Amplifier Operation

Amplifiers biased so that collector current is cut off during one-half of the input signal are called Class B. The DC operating point for this class of amplifier is set up so that base current is zero with no input signal. When a signal is applied, one half-cycle will forward bias the base-emitter junction and I_C will flow. The other half-cycle will reverse bias the base-emitter junction and I_C will be cut off. Thus, for Class B operation, collector current will flow for approximately 180° (half) of the input signal, as shown in Figure 5-3-18C.

The Class B–operated amplifier is used extensively for audio amplifiers that require high-power outputs. It is also used as the driver- and power-amplifier stages of transmitters.

Class C Amplifier Operation

In Class C operation, collector current flows for less than one-half cycle of the input signal, as shown in Figure 5-3-18D. The Class C operation is achieved by reverse biasing the emitter-base junction, which sets the DC operating point below cutoff and allows only the portion of the

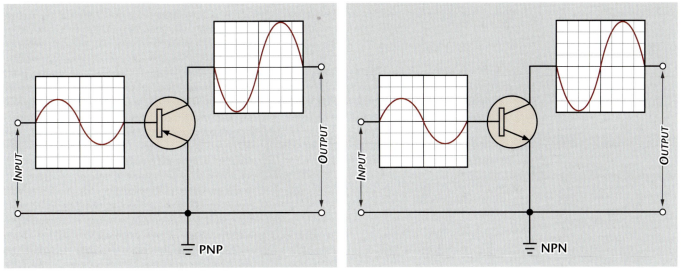

Figure 5-3-19. Transistor connected in common emitter configuration

input signal that overcomes the reverse bias to cause collector current flow.

The Class C–operated amplifier is used as a radio-frequency amplifier in transmitters.

Amplifier Operation Terms

There are two primary items that determine the class of operation of an amplifier.

- The amount of bias
- The amplitude of the input signal

With a given input signal and bias level, the operation of an amplifier can be changed from Class A to Class B just by removing forward bias. Also, a class A amplifier can be changed to Class AB by increasing the input signal amplitude. However, if the input signal amplitude is increased to the point that the transistor goes into saturation and cutoff, it is then called an *overdriven* amplifier.

Be familiar with two terms used in conjunction with amplifiers: fidelity and efficiency. *Fidelity* is the faithful reproduction of a signal. In other words, if the output of an amplifier is just like the input except in amplitude, the amplifier has a high degree of fidelity. The opposite of fidelity is a term mentioned earlier: *distortion*. Therefore, a circuit that has high fidelity has low distortion. In conclusion, a Class A amplifier has a high degree of fidelity. A class AB amplifier has less fidelity, and Class B and Class C amplifiers have low or "poor" fidelity.

The *efficiency* of an amplifier refers to the ratio of output-signal power to the total input power. An amplifier has two input power sources: one from the signal and one from the power supply. Since every device takes power to operate, an amplifier that operates for 360° of the input signal uses more power than if operated for 180° of the input signal. By using more power, an amplifier has less power available for the output signal; thus the efficiency of the amplifier is low.

This is the case with the Class A amplifier. It operates for 360° of the input signal and requires a relatively large input from the power supply. Even with no input signal, the Class A amplifier still uses power from the power supply. Therefore, the output from the Class A amplifier is relatively small compared to the total input power. This results in low efficiency, which is acceptable in Class A amplifiers because they are used where efficiency is not as important as fidelity.

Class AB amplifiers are biased so that collector current is cut off for a portion of one alternation of the input, which results in less total input power than the Class A amplifier. This leads to better efficiency.

Class B amplifiers are biased with little or no collector current at the DC operating point. With no input signal, there is little wasted power. Therefore, the efficiency of Class B amplifiers is higher still.

The efficiency of Class C is the highest of the four classes of amplifier operations.

Transistor Configurations

A transistor may be connected in any one of three basic configurations: common emitter (CE) (Figure 5-3-19), common base (CB) (Figure 5-3-20), and common collector (CC) (Figure 5-3-21). The term *common* is used to denote the element that is common to both input and output circuits. Because the common element is often grounded, these configurations are frequently referred to as grounded emitter, grounded base and grounded collector.

Each configuration has particular characteristics that make it suitable for specific applications. An easy way to identify a specific transistor configuration is to follow these three steps:

1. Identify the element (emitter, base or collector) to which the input signal is applied.
2. Identify the element (emitter, base or collector) from which the output signal is taken.
3. The remaining element is the common element and gives the configuration its name.

Therefore, by applying these three steps to the circuit in Figure 5-3-14, one can conclude that this circuit is more than just a basic transistor amplifier. It is a common-emitter amplifier.

Common Emitter

The common-emitter configuration (CE) shown in Figure 5-3-19 is the arrangement most frequently used in practical amplifier circuits, since it provides good voltage, current and power gain. The CE also has a somewhat low input resistance (500 to 1,500 Ω), because the input is applied to the forward-biased junction, and a moderately high output resistance (30 to 50 kΩ or more), because the output is taken off the reverse-biased junction. Since the input signal is applied to the base-emitter circuit and the output is taken from the collector-emitter circuit, the emitter is the element common to both input and output.

Since what is now known to be a common-emitter amplifier has already been covered (Figure 5-3-14), let's take a few minutes and review its operation, using the PNP common-emitter configuration shown in Figure 5-3-19.

When a transistor is connected in a CE configuration, the input signal is injected between the base and emitter, which is a low-resistance, low-current circuit. As the input signal swings positive, it also causes the base to swing positive with respect to the emitter. This action decreases forward bias, which reduces collector current (I_C) and increases collector voltage (making V_C more negative).

During the negative alternation of the input signal, the base is driven more negative with respect to the emitter. This increases forward bias and allows more current carriers to be released from the emitter, which results in an increase in collector current and a decrease in collector voltage (making V_C less negative or swing in a positive direction). The collector current that flows through the high-resistance reverse-biased junction also flows through a high-resistance load (not shown), resulting in a high level of amplification.

Since the input signal to the common emitter goes positive when the output goes negative, the two signals (input and output) are 180° out of phase. The common-emitter circuit is the only configuration that provides a phase reversal.

The CE is the most popular of the three transistor configurations because it has the best combination of current and voltage gain. The term gain is used to describe the amplification capabilities of the amplifier. It is basically a ratio of output versus input. Each transistor configuration gives a different value of gain even though the same transistor is used. The transistor configuration used is a matter of design consideration. However, a technician is interested in understanding gain in order to determine whether the transistor is working properly in the circuit.

The current gain in the CE circuit is called *beta* (β). Beta is the relationship of collector current (output current) to base current (input current). To calculate beta, use the following formula:

$$\beta = \Delta I_C \div \Delta I_B$$

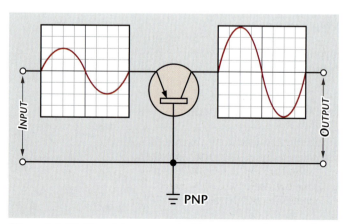 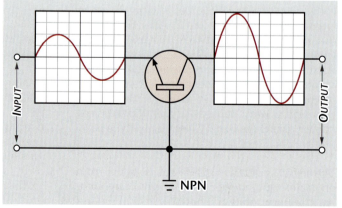

Figure 5-3-20. Transistor connected in common base configuration

(Δ is the Greek letter delta; it is used to indicate a change.)

For example, if the input current (I_B) in a CE changes from 75 μA to 100 μA and the output current (I_C) changes from 1.5 mA to 2.6 mA, the current gain (β) will be 44.

$$\beta = \Delta I_C \div \Delta I_B$$
$$\beta = (11 \times 10^{-3}) \div (25 \times 10^{-6})$$
$$\beta = 44$$

This simply means that a change in base current produces a change in collector current that is 44 times as large.

The term h_{fe} may be used in place of β. These are equivalent and may be used interchangeably. This is because h_{fe} means:

- h = hybrid (meaning mixture)
- f = forward current transfer ratio
- e = common-emitter configuration

The resistance gain of the common emitter can be found in a method similar to the one used for finding beta:

$$R = R_{out} \div R_{in}$$

Once the resistance gain is known, the voltage gain is easy to calculate since it is equal to the current gain (β) multiplied by the resistance gain ($E=\beta R$). And, the power gain is equal to the voltage gain multiplied by the current gain β ($P=E\beta$).

Common Base

The common-base configuration (CB) shown in Figure 5-3-20, is mainly used for impedance matching, since it has low input resistance (30 to 160 Ω) and high output resistance (250 to 550 kΩ). However, two factors limit its usefulness in some circuit applications:

- Its low input resistance
- Its current gain of less than 1

Since the CB configuration will give voltage amplification, there are some additional applications, which require both a low-input resistance and voltage amplification, that could use a circuit configuration of this type—some microphone amplifiers, for example.

In the CB configuration, the input signal is applied to the emitter, the output is taken from the collector, and the base is the element common to both input and output. Since the input is applied to the emitter, it causes the emitter-base junction to react in the same manner as it did in the common-emitter circuit. For example, an input that aids the bias will increase transistor current, and one that opposes the bias will decrease transistor current.

Unlike the common-emitter circuit, the input and output signals in the common-base circuit are in phase. To illustrate this point, assume the input to the PNP version of the CB circuit in Figure 5-3-20 is positive. The signal adds to the forward bias, since it is applied to the emitter, causing the collector current to increase. This increase in I_C results in a greater voltage drop across the load resistor R_L (not shown), thus lowering the collector voltage V_C. The collector voltage, in becoming less negative, is swinging in a positive direction, and is therefore in phase with the incoming positive signal.

The current gain in the common-base circuit is calculated in a method similar to that of the common emitter except that the input current is I_E rather than I_B and the term *alpha* (α) is used in place of beta for gain. Alpha is the relationship of collector current (output current) to emitter current (input current). Alpha is calculated using the formula:

$$\alpha = \Delta I_C \div \Delta I_E$$

For example, if the input current (I_E) in a common base changes from 1 mA to 3 mA and the output current (I_C) changes from 1 mA to 2.8 mA, the current gain (α) will be 0.90 or:

$$\alpha = \Delta I_C \div \Delta I_E$$
$$\alpha = (18 \times 10^{-3}) \div (2 \times 10^{-3})$$
$$\alpha = 0.90$$

This is a current gain of less than 1.

Since part of the emitter current flows into the base and does not appear as collector current, collector current will always be less than the emitter current that causes it. (Remember, $I_E = I_B + I_C$.) Therefore, alpha is *always less than* one for a common-base configuration.

Another term for α is h_{fb}. These terms are equivalent and may be used interchangeably. The meaning for the term h_{fb} is derived in the same manner as the term h_{fe} mentioned earlier, except that the last letter *e* has been replaced with *b* to stand for common base configuration.

Many transistor manuals and data sheets only list transistor current gain characteristics in terms of β or h_{fe}. To find alpha (α) when given beta (β), use the following formula to convert β to α for use with the CB configuration:

$$\alpha = \beta \div (\beta + 1)$$

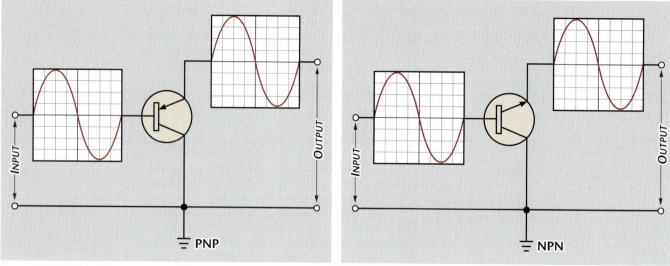

Figure 5-3-21. Transistor connected in common collector configuration

To calculate the other gains (voltage and power) in the CB configuration when the current gain (α) is known, follow the procedures described earlier under the common-emitter section.

Common Collector

The common collector configuration (CC) shown in Figure 5-3-21, is used mostly for impedance matching. It is also used as a current driver because of its substantial current gain. It is particularly useful in switching circuitry since it has the ability to pass signals in either direction (bilateral operation). An example of a transistor connected in common collector configuration is pictured in Figure 5-3-22.

Figure 5-3-22. Transistor connected in common collector configuration

In the CC circuit, the input signal is applied to the base, the output is taken from the emitter, and the collector is the element common to both input and output. The common collector is equivalent to our old friend the electron-tube cathode follower. Both have high input and low output resistance. The input resistance for the common collector ranges from 2 to 500 kΩ, and the output resistance varies from 50 to 1,500 Ω.

The current gain is higher than that in the common emitter, but it has a lower power gain than either the common base or common emitter. Like the common base, the output signal from the common collector is in phase with the input signal. The common collector is also referred to as an emitter-follower because the output developed on the emitter follows the input signal applied to the base.

Transistor action in the CC is similar to the operation explained for the common base, except that the current gain is not based on the emitter-to-collector current ratio, alpha (α). Instead, it is based on the emitter-to-base current ratio called *gamma* (γ), because the output is taken off the emitter. Since a small change in base current controls a large change in emitter current, it is still possible to obtain high current gain in the CC. However, since the emitter current gain is offset by the low output resistance, the voltage gain is always less than 1 (unity), exactly as in the electron-tube cathode follower.

The CC current gain, gamma (γ), is defined as:

$$\gamma = \Delta I_E \div \Delta I_B$$

and is related to collector-to-base current gain, beta (β), of the common-emitter circuit by the formula:

$$\gamma = \beta + 1$$

Since a given transistor may be connected in any of three basic configurations, there is a definite relationship, as pointed out earlier, between alpha (α), beta (β), and gamma (γ). These relationships are listed again:

α = β ÷ (β + 1)
β = α ÷ (1 - α)
γ = β + 1

Take, for example, a transistor that is listed on a manufacturer's data sheet as having an alpha of 0.90. The goal is to use it in a CE configuration. This means beta must be determined. The calculations are:

β = α ÷ (1 - α)
β = 0.90 ÷ (1 - 0.90)
β = 0.90 ÷ 0.10
β = 9

Therefore, a change in base current in this transistor will produce a change in collector current that will be nine times as large.

To use this same transistor in a CC, find gamma (γ) by using the following process:

γ = β + 1
γ = 9 + 1
γ = 10

To summarize the properties of the three transistor configurations, a comparison chart is provided in Table 5-3-1.

Now that the basic transistor amplifier has been analyzed in terms of bias, class of operation and circuit configuration, apply what has been covered to Figure 5-3-14.

This illustration is not just the basic transistor amplifier shown earlier in Figure 5-3-14 but a Class A amplifier configured as a common emitter using fixed bias. From this, one should be able to conclude the following:

- Because of its fixed bias, the amplifier is thermally unstable.
- Because of its class A operation, the amplifier has low efficiency but good fidelity.
- Because it is configured as a common emitter, the amplifier has good voltage, current and power gain.

In conclusion, the type of bias, class of operation and circuit configuration are all clues to the function and possible application of the amplifier.

Transistor Specifications

Transistors are available in a large variety of shapes and sizes, each with its own unique characteristics. The characteristics for each of these transistors are usually presented on specification sheets or may be included in transistor manuals. Although many properties of a transistor could be specified on these sheets, manufacturers list only some of them. The specifications listed vary with different manufacturers, the type of transistor and the application of the transistor. The specifications usually cover the following items.

Transistor description. A general description of the transistor that includes:

- The kind of transistor. This covers the material used, such as germanium or silicon; the type of transistor (NPN or PNP); and the construction of the transistor (alloy-junction, grown or diffused junction, etc.).
- Some of the common applications for the transistor, such as audio amplifier, oscillator, RF amplifier, etc.
- General sales features, such as size and packaging data

AMPLIFIER TYPE	COMMON BASE	COMMON EMITTER	COMMON COLLECTOR
Input/Output Phase Relationship	0°	180°	0°
Voltage Gain	High	Medium	Low
Current Gain	Low(α)	Medium(β)	High(γ)
Power Gain	Low	High	Medium
Input Resistance	Low	Medium	High
Output Resistance	High	Medium	Low

Table 5-3-1. Transistor configuration comparison chart

5-36 | Introduction to Solid-State Components

Step 1

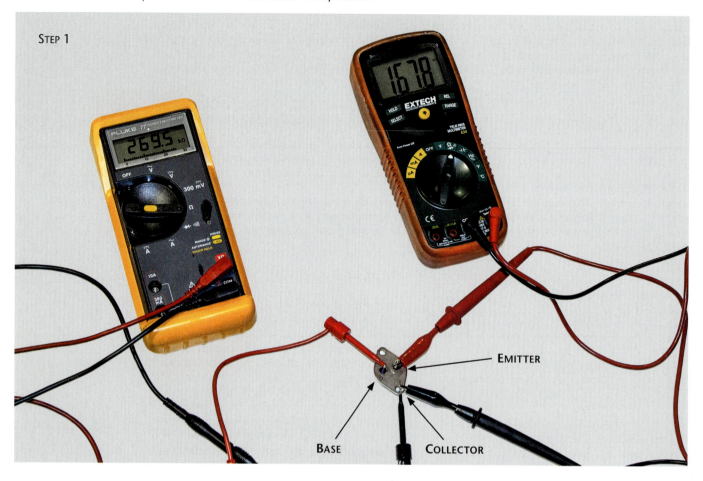

Step 2

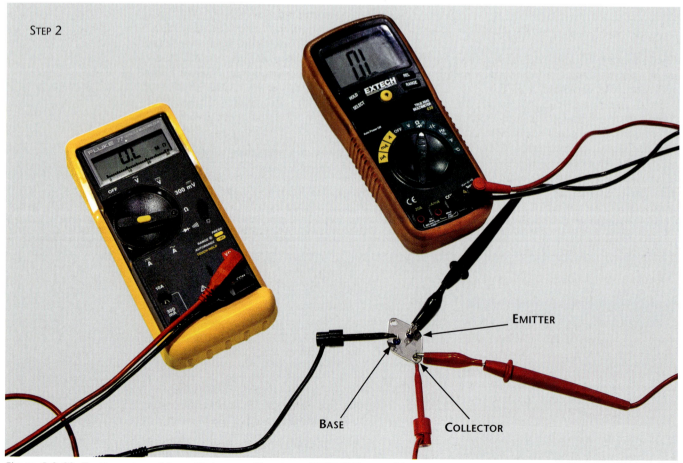

Figure 5-3-23. Testing a transistor with two multimeters; (STEP 1) Forward biasing and, (STEP 2) Reverse biasing

Absolute Maximum Ratings. The "Absolute Maximum Ratings" of the transistor are the direct voltage and current values that if exceeded in operation may result in transistor failure. Maximum ratings usually include collector-to-base voltage, emitter-to-base voltage, collector current, emitter current and collector power dissipation.

The typical operating values of the transistor. These values are presented only as a guide. The values vary widely, are dependent upon operating voltages, and also upon which element is common in the circuit. The values listed may include collector-emitter voltage, collector current, input resistance, load resistance, current-transfer ratio (another name for alpha or beta), and collector cutoff current, which is leakage current from collector to base when no emitter current is applied. Transistor characteristic curves may also be included in this section. A transistor characteristic curve is a graph plotting the relationship between currents and voltages in a circuit. More than one curve on a graph is called a "family of curves."

Additional information for engineering design purposes. So far, many letter symbols, abbreviations and terms have been introduced, some frequently used and others only rarely used.

Transistor Maintenance

Transistors are very rugged and are expected to be relatively trouble free. Encapsulation and conformal coating techniques now in use promise extremely long life expectancies. In theory, a transistor should last indefinitely. However, if transistors are subjected to current overloads, the junctions will be damaged or even destroyed. In addition, the application of excessively high operating voltages can damage or destroy the junctions through arc-over or excessive reverse currents. One of the greatest dangers to the transistor is heat, which will cause excessive current flow and eventual destruction of the transistor.

To determine whether a transistor is good or bad, check it with an ohmmeter or a transistor tester (Figure 5-3-23). In many cases, a transistor that is known to be good can be substituted for one that is questionable and thus determine the condition of a suspected transistor. This method of testing is highly accurate and sometimes the quickest, but it should be used only after making certain that there are no circuit defects that might damage the replacement transistor.

If more than one defective transistor is present in the equipment where the trouble has been localized, this testing method becomes cumbersome, as several transistors may have to be replaced before the trouble is corrected. To determine which stages failed and which transistors are not defective, all the removed transistors must be tested. This test can be made by using a standard ohmmeter, a transistor tester, or by observing whether the equipment operates correctly as each of the removed transistors is reinserted into the equipment. A word of caution: Indiscriminate substitution of transistors in critical circuits should be avoided.

When transistors are soldered into equipment, substitution is not practicable; it is generally desirable to test these transistors in their circuits.

Precautions

Transistors, although generally more rugged mechanically than electron tubes, are susceptible to damage by electrical overload, heat, humidity and radiation. Damage of this nature often occurs during transistor servicing by applying the incorrect polarity voltage to the collector circuit or excessive voltage to the input circuit.

Careless soldering techniques that overheat the transistor have also been known to cause considerable damage. One of the most frequent causes of damage to a transistor is the electrostatic discharge from the human body when the device is handled. To avoid such damage before starting repairs, the technician should discharge the static electricity from his or her body to the chassis containing the transistor. Simply touching the chassis will transfer the electricity from the body to the chassis.

To prevent transistor damage and avoid electrical shock, observe the following precautions when working with transistorized equipment:

- Test equipment and soldering irons should be checked to make certain there is no leakage current from the power source. If leakage current is detected, isolation transformers should be used.

- Always connect a ground between test equipment and circuit before attempting to inject or monitor a signal.

- Ensure test voltages do not exceed maximum allowable voltage for circuit components and transistors. Also, never connect test equipment outputs directly to a transistor circuit.

- Ohmmeter ranges that require a current of more than 1 mA in the test circuit should not be used for testing transistors.

- The heat applied to a transistor, when soldered connections are required, should be

5-38 | Introduction to Solid-State Components

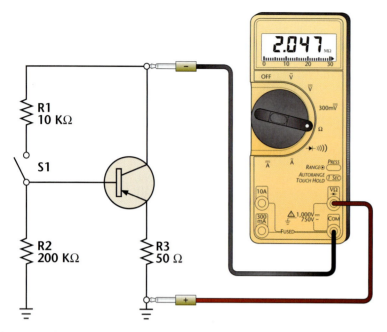

Figure 5-3-24. Testing a transistor's gain with an ohmmeter

kept to a minimum by using a low-wattage soldering iron and heat shunts, such as long-nose pliers, on the transistor leads.

- When it becomes necessary to replace transistors, never pry transistors to loosen them from printed circuit boards.
- All circuits should be checked for defects before replacing a transistor.
- The power must be removed from the equipment before replacing a transistor.
- Using conventional test probes on equipment with closely spaced parts often causes accidental shorts between adjacent terminals. These shorts rarely cause damage to an electron tube but may ruin a transistor. To prevent these shorts, the probes can be covered with insulation, except for a very short length of the tips.

Transistor Testing

There are several ways of testing transistors. They can be tested while in the circuit, by the substitution method, or with a transistor tester or ohmmeter.

Transistor testers are nothing more than the solid-state equivalent of electron-tube testers (although they do not operate on the same principle). With most transistor testers, it is possible to test the transistor in or out of the circuit.

There are four basic tests required for transistors in practical troubleshooting: gain, leakage, breakdown and switching time. For mainte-nance and repair, however, a check of two or three parameters is usually sufficient to determine whether a transistor needs to be replaced.

Since it is impractical to cover all the different types of transistor testers and since each tester comes with its own operator's manual, it is time to move on to a tool used more frequently for testing transistors: the ohmmeter.

Two tests that can be done with an ohmmeter are gain and junction resistance. Tests of a transistor's junction resistance will reveal leakage, shorts and opens.

Transistor gain test. A basic transistor gain test can be made using an ohmmeter and a simple test circuit. The test circuit can be made with just a couple of resistors and a switch, as shown in Figure 5-3-24. The principle behind the test lies in the fact that little or no current will flow in a transistor between emitter and collector until the emitter-base junction is forward biased. The only precaution that should be observed is with the ohmmeter. Any internal battery may be used in the meter provided that it does not exceed the maximum collector-emitter breakdown voltage.

With the switch in Figure 5-3-24 in the open position as shown, no voltage is applied to the PNP transistor's base, and the emitter-base junction is not forward biased. Therefore, the ohmmeter should read a high resistance, as indicated on the meter. When the switch is closed, the emitter-base circuit is forward biased by the voltage across R_1 and R_2. Current now flows in the emitter-collector circuit, which causes a lower resistance reading on the ohmmeter. A 10-to-1 resistance ratio in this test between meter readings indicates a normal gain for an audio-frequency transistor.

To test an NPN transistor using this circuit, simply reverse the ohmmeter leads and carry out the procedure described above.

Transistor junction resistance test. An ohmmeter can be used to test a transistor for leakage (an undesirable flow of current) by measuring the base-emitter, base-collector and collector-emitter forward and reverse resistances.

For simplicity, consider the transistor under test in Figure 5-3-25 as two diodes connected back to back. Therefore, each diode will have a low forward resistance and a high reverse resistance. By measuring these resistances with an ohmmeter as shown in the figure, it is possible to determine whether the transistor is leaking current through its junctions. When making these measurements, avoid using the R_1 scale on the meter or a meter with a high internal battery voltage. Either of these conditions can damage a low-power transistor.

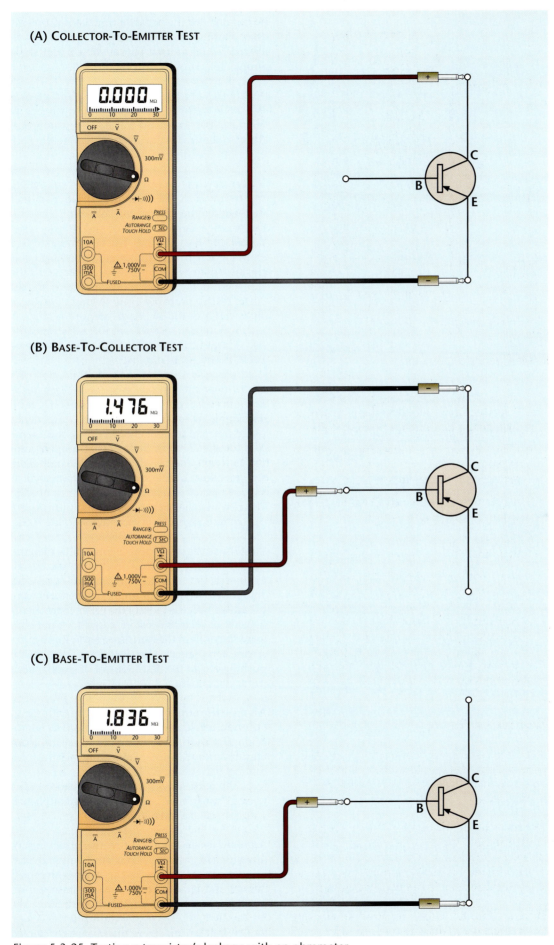

Figure 5-3-25. Testing a transistor's leakage with an ohmmeter

Now consider the possible transistor problems that could exist if the indicated readings in Figure 5-3-25 are not obtained. A list of these problems is provided in Table 5-3-2.

Notice that the transistor used in Figure 5-3-25 is a PNP transistor. If the technician needs to test an NPN transistor for leakage, the procedure is identical to that used for testing the PNP except the readings obtained are reversed.

When testing transistors (PNP or NPN), remember that the actual resistance values depend on the ohmmeter scale and the battery voltage. Typical forward and reverse resistances are insignificant. The best indicator for showing whether a transistor is good or bad is the ratio of forward-to-reverse resistance. If the transistor being tested shows a ratio of at least 30 to 1, it is probably good. Many transistors show ratios of 100 to 1 or greater.

Microelectronics

Up to now the various semiconductors, resistors and capacitors in our discussions have been considered as separately packaged components, called discrete components. In this section some of the more complex devices that contain complete circuits packaged as a single component are introduced. These devices are referred to as *integrated circuits* and the broad term used to describe the use of these devices to miniaturize electronic equipment is *microelectronics*.

With the advent of the transistor and the demand by the military for smaller equipment, design engineers set out to miniaturize electronic equipment. In the beginning, their efforts were frustrated because most of the other components in a circuit such as resistors, capacitors and coils were larger than the transistor. Soon these other circuit components were miniaturized, thereby pushing ahead the development of smaller electronic equipment.

Along with miniature resistors, capacitors and other circuit elements, the production of components that were actually smaller than the space required for the interconnecting wiring and cabling became possible. The next step in the research process was to eliminate these bulky wiring components. This was accomplished with the printed circuit board.

A *printed circuit board* is a flat insulating surface upon which printed wiring and miniaturized components are connected in a predetermined design, and attached to a common base. Figure 5-3-26 shows a typical printed circuit board.

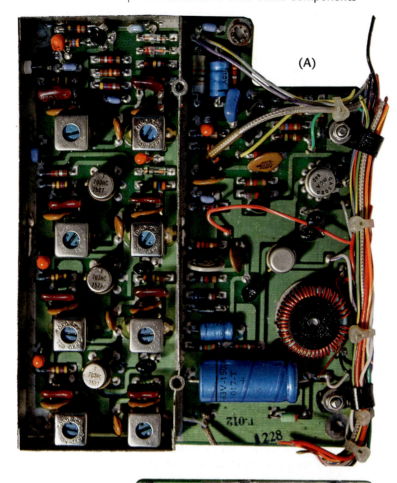

Figure 5-3-26. A typical printed circuit board (PCB); (A) Front side (B) Reverse side

Notice that various components are connected to the board and the printed wiring is on the

Figure 5-3-27. Integrated circuit

Table 5-3-2. Possible transistor problems from ohmmeter readings

RESISTANCE READINGS		PROBLEMS
Forward	Reverse	The Transistor Is:
Low (not shorted)	Low (not shorted)	Leaking
Low (shorted)	Low (shorted)	Shorted
High	High	Open*
*Except collector-to-emitter test.		

reverse side. With this technique, all interconnecting wiring in a piece of equipment, except for the highest power leads and cabling, is reduced to lines of conducting material (copper, silver, gold, etc.) deposited directly on the surface of an insulating "circuit board." Since printed circuit boards are readily adapted as plug-in units, the elimination of terminal boards, fittings and tie points, not to mention wires, results in a substantial reduction in the overall size of electronic equipment.

After printed circuit boards were perfected, efforts to miniaturize electronic equipment shifted to assembly techniques, which led to *modular circuitry*. In this technique, printed circuit boards are stacked and connected to form a module. This increases the packaging density of circuit components and results in a considerable reduction in the size of electronic equipment. Since the module can be designed to perform any electronic function, it is also a very versatile unit.

However, the drawback to this approach was that the modules required a considerable number of connections that took up too much space and increased costs. In addition, tests showed the reliability was adversely affected by the increase in the number of connections.

A new technique was required to improve reliability and further increase packaging density. The solution was integrated circuits (Figure 5-3-27).

An *integrated circuit* is a device that integrates (combines) both the active components (transistors, diodes, etc.) and passive components (resistors, capacitors, etc.) of a complete electronic circuit in a single chip (a tiny slice or wafer of semiconductor crystal or insulator). Integrated circuits have almost eliminated the use of individual electronic components as the building blocks of electronic circuits. Instead, tiny chips have been developed whose functions are not that of a single part, but of dozens of transistors, resistors, capacitors, and other electronic elements, all interconnected to perform the task of a complex circuit.

Often these comprise a number of complete conventional circuit stages, such as a multistage amplifier in one extremely small component. These chips are frequently mounted on a printed circuit board which plugs into an electronic unit (Figure 5-3-28).

Figure 5-3-28. Integrated circuits mounted on a printed circuit board

Integrated circuits have several advantages over conventional wired circuits of discrete components. These advantages include:

- Drastic reduction in size and weight
- Large increase in reliability
- Lower cost
- Possible improvement in circuit performance

However, integrated circuits are composed of parts so closely associated with one another that repair becomes almost impossible. In case of trouble, the entire circuit is replaced as a single component.

Basically, there are two general classifications of integrated circuits: monolithic and hybrid.

In the *monolithic* integrated circuit, all elements associated with the circuit are fabricated inseparably within a continuous piece of material (called the substrate), usually silicon. The monolithic integrated circuit is made very much like a single transistor. While one part of the crystal is being doped to form a transistor, other parts of the crystal are being acted upon to form the associated resistors and capacitors. Thus, all the elements of the complete circuit are created in the crystal by the same processes and in the same time required to make a single transistor. This produces a considerable cost savings over the same circuit made with discrete components by lowering assembly costs.

Hybrid integrated circuits are constructed somewhat differently. The passive components (resistors, capacitors) are deposited onto a substrate made of glass, ceramic, or other insulating material. Then the active components (diodes, transistors) are attached to the substrate and connected to the passive circuit components on the substrate using very fine (0.001 in.) wire. The term *hybrid* refers to the fact that different processes are used to form the passive and active components of the device.

Hybrid circuits are of two general types: thin film and thick film. "Thin" and "thick" film refer to the relative thickness of the deposited material used to form the resistors and other passive components. Thick-film devices are capable of dissipating more power, but are somewhat more bulky.

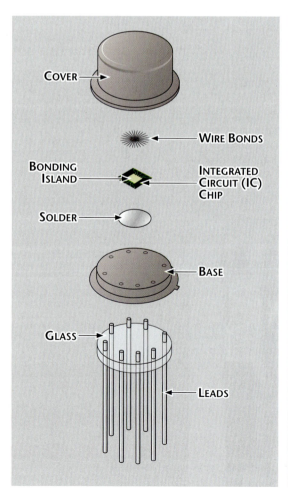
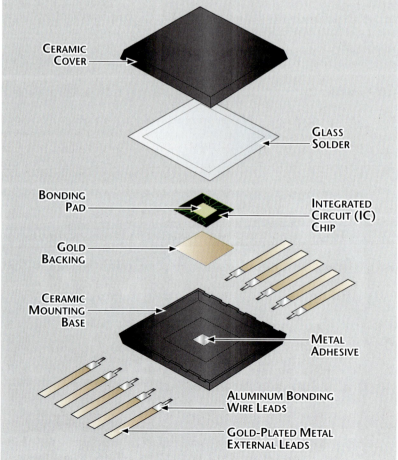

Figure 5-3-29. A typical integrated circuit packaging sequence

Figure 5-3-30. Common integrated circuit packaging styles

Integrated circuits are being used in an ever increasing variety of applications. Small size, low weight and high reliability make them ideally suited for use in airborne equipment, missile systems, computers, spacecraft and portable equipment. They are often easily recognized because of the unusual packages that contain the integrated circuit. A typical packaging sequence is shown in Figure 5-3-29. These tiny packages protect and help dissipate heat generated in the device. One of these packages may contain one or several stages, often having several hundred components. Some of the most common package styles are shown in Figure 5-3-30.

Section 4
Electrostatic Discharge Sensitive Components

Microelectronic devices, such as integrated circuits and microprocessors, incorporate semiconductor material measuring only a few millionths-of-an-inch thick. These subminiature structures are extremely vulnerable to damage from static electricity. Devices made of complementary metal oxide semiconductor (CMOS) components are especially vulnerable to static discharge.

Components that are electrostatic discharge sensitive are commonly referred to as ESDS parts. Since these components are popular on all types of avionics equipment, the avionics technician must be aware of the potential dangers from static electricity. Thousands of warranty repairs and unnecessary failures are created in avionics shops annually. Awareness and proper precautions for ESDS components can increase productivity, customer satisfaction and improve air safety.

Electrostatic Discharge

Electrostatic discharge is the discharge, or movement of electrons, created when any material containing a static charge comes in contact with a material containing a different or neutral charge. A static charge is present when a material possesses an excess or deficiency of electrons. A neutral charge is present when a material possesses an equal number of electrons and protons. Any time two components of different static charge get close enough together, a static discharge will occur. Typically, a distance of 10 mm or less is required to produce a discharge of static electricity generated through normal maintenance activities.

Production of a Static Charge

Friction between two different materials produces the majority of static electricity. As two dissimilar materials rub together, there is often a transfer of electrons from one surface to another. The amount of electron transfer is a function of the type of materials making contact, the amount of friction between the two, and the relative humidity of the surrounding air.

Most everyone has experienced the production of a static charge while walking across a nylon carpet with plastic sole shoes. In this situation approximately 35,000 V can be generated if the relative humidity is 20 percent or less. Normally, the static charge is not noticed until contact is made with another object, such as a doorknob. At that time the static electricity is discharged to the doorknob creating a noticeable shock. This type of discharge will damage ESDS parts.

The minimum perception level to feel a static electrical discharge is typically 3,000 V. For a discharge to be heard requires approximately 5,000 V; and the discharge cannot be seen if less than 10,000 V. The current during discharge is

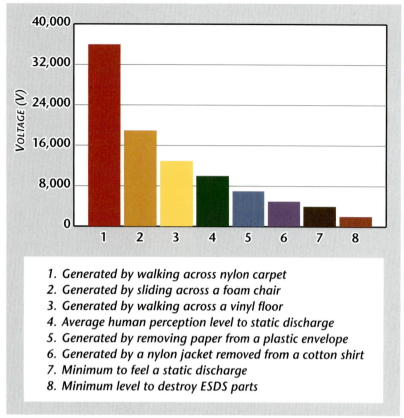

Figure 5-4-1. Graph showing various static voltage levels

1. Generated by walking across nylon carpet
2. Generated by sliding across a foam chair
3. Generated by walking across a vinyl floor
4. Average human perception level to static discharge
5. Generated by removing paper from a plastic envelope
6. Generated by a nylon jacket removed from a cotton shirt
7. Minimum to feel a static discharge
8. Minimum level to destroy ESDS parts

Figure 5-4-2. Common labels used to identify ESDS parts

Identifying ESDS Components

In order to protect components from static discharge one must first identify ESDS parts and then take the necessary precautions. The most common labels are shown in Figure 5-4-2. One or more of these labels should be placed on all ESDS parts. The label should be easily visible to anyone who might come in contact with the component. The identification labels must be used on components installed in the aircraft, as well as components found in shipping, storage or in a repair facility.

ESDS parts come in all shapes and sizes. Components on any modern aircraft are likely electrostatic sensitive and should be handled using proper precautions. Each equipment rack containing a sensitive component must be labeled with the appropriate decal. Other vulnerable components include computer cards, circuit boards and certain integrated circuits. These components are most vulnerable during removal and installation, as well as shipping, handling and bench repair.

Protecting Components

The basic premise for the protection of all ESDS parts is to prevent a static charge from entering that component. This is accomplished by:

- Electrically neutralizing anyone or anything coming in contact with or near the part, or
- Electrically insulating the sensitive part from potential static discharge

A charged body does not need to contact the ESDS component to damage it. If a sensitive component is close enough, less than approximately one-half inch to the static charge, the part can be damaged.

Neutralization is typically accomplished by connecting all personnel and equipment to an electrical ground source. Prior to working with an ESDS part the technician must connect a grounding strap to bare skin and ensure its security. A wrist strap connected to ground through a flexible wire is typically used for this purpose (Figure 5-4-3). All test equipment, including bench tops, must also be grounded. If equipment installed in the aircraft is labeled ESDS, always connect a wrist strap to the aircraft's ground prior to touching any component. A grounding socket is often provided in the aircraft's electrical equipment bay for this purpose.

CAUTION: *Always use an approved wrist strap. Commercially available straps contain a resistor in series with the ground circuit to*

extremely low and produces only minor discomfort to humans, however, a static discharge of as little as 100 V can damage certain electronic components. Figure 5-4-1 shows voltage potential from common materials. Almost any situation can create enough static charge to damage sensitive components.

protect the user from electrocution if contact is accidentally made with a hot wire.

To electrically insulate a component, place all sensitive parts in the appropriate conductive container. These containers are often specially designed boxes for specific line replaceable units or conductive bags used for smaller items such as cards or integrated circuits. Once an item has been placed in its protective container, be sure it is labeled with an ESDS decal.

Technicians should be aware that there are two types of protective bags currently available:

1. The pink antistatic polyethylene bag is used to protect components from generating a static charge caused by movement while stored inside the bag
2. The dark gray antistatic bag will protect the component from static fields outside the bag, static discharge current and static fields generated inside the bag (Figure 5-4-4). The gray-colored bag offers the most protection and should be used under most circumstances.

Other means to protect components include the use of antistatic caps that should be placed over all connections of sensitive LRUs, and metal clips or conductive foam used to short together the leads of individual components or cards. Whenever using any protective device be sure to inspect it for defects or unacceptable wear.

At the workstation, the ESDS components should not be set directly onto the tabletop. The workstation should be equipped with either a conductive or static dissipative mat. The conductive mat may be used whenever a component is serviced in a power off condition. If the component is operated while placed on the conductive-type mat, the mat itself may bridge the connections between any components and cause component failure. In the case where components are operated while in contact with the mat surface, a static dissipating mat must be used. Be sure to check that all workstations are equipped with the correct type of protection.

Nonconductors at the workstation are also a source of problems when working around ESDS parts. If plastic tools or pens, for example, come into contact with a sensitive component damage may occur. Nonconductive plastic does not dissipate its charge easily. A grounded technician holding that tool is not enough. If nonconductors are used at workstations, the best solution is to install an ionization air blower. An ionization air blower will safely delete any static charge formed on nonconductors. It is also helpful to maintain a relatively high humidity level in all work areas.

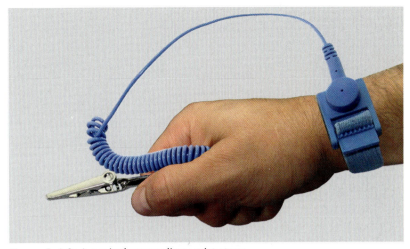

Figure 5-4-3. A typical grounding wrist strap

Figure 5-4-4. A circuit card in an antistatic bag

High humidity helps to dissipate static charges before they become a problem.

Types of Static Damage

Damage from static discharge can take two forms. They are commonly referred to as hard and soft failures. A *hard failure* caused by static discharge will create an immediate system defect. A *soft failure* caused by static discharge may only injure the component and cause erratic operations and/or eventual failure. A component that experienced a soft failure is often said to be wounded. A wounded part may pass all bench and/or preflight tests and still fail during flight. Wounded parts account for approximately 90 percent of all static damage. Often wounded parts cycle from aircraft to shop several times before the fault can be detected and repaired.

Modern avionics equipment contains a variety of ESDS parts. Every technician must be aware of the problems involved with static electricity and take the necessary precautions. The defects to a sensitive component caused by a static discharge will not be visible to the naked eye; however, the results could be catastrophic. When in doubt, assume the component is ESDS and take the necessary precautions.

6

Advanced Solid-State Components

Introduction to Special Devices

Considering the sensitive nature and the various interacting properties of semiconductors, it is not surprising that solid-state devices can be designed for many different purposes. In fact, devices with special features are so numerous and new designs are so frequently introduced that it would be beyond the scope of this chapter to describe all of the devices in use today. These devices have been grouped into three categories: diodes, optoelectronic devices and transistors.

Learning Objective

DESCRIBE
- the different energy bands
- depletion region
- the avalanche effect
- the purpose of zener diodes and where you can find them
- the purpose of a tunnel diode

EXPLAIN
- function of a varactor
- function of an SCR
- function of a TRIAC
- function of a UJT
- function of a FET
- function of a JFET
- function of a MOSFET

Section 1

Special Diodes

Diodes are two-terminal semiconductors of various types that are used in seemingly endless applications. The operation of normal PN junction diodes has already been discussed, but there are a number of diodes with special properties with which the technician should be familiar. A discussion of all of the developments in the diode field would be impossible so some of the more commonly used special diodes have been selected for explanation. These include zener diodes, tunnel diodes, varactors, silicon controlled rectifiers (SCR) and TRIACs.

Zener Diodes

When a PN junction diode is reverse biased, the majority carriers (holes in the P-type material and electrons in the N-type material) move away from the junction. The barrier or depletion

Left. LED recognition lights, used in many modern aircraft, are examples of electronic devices that source, detect and control light.

Photo courtesy of Lufthansa

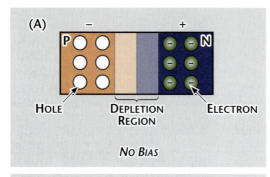
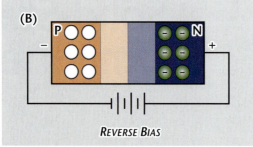
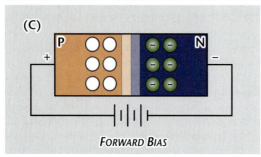

Figure 6-1-1. Effects of bias on the depletion region of a PN junction diode

region becomes wider, as illustrated in Figure 6-1-1, and majority carrier current flow becomes very difficult across the high resistance of the wide depletion region. The presence of minority carriers causes a small leakage current that remains nearly constant for all reverse voltages up to a certain value. Once this value has been exceeded, there is a sudden increase in the reverse current. The voltage at which the sudden increase in current occurs is called the *breakdown voltage*. At breakdown, the reverse current increases very rapidly with a slight increase in the reverse voltage. Any diode can be reverse biased to the point of breakdown, but not every diode can safely dissipate the power associated with breakdown. A zener diode is a PN junction designed to operate in the reverse-bias breakdown region.

There are two distinct theories used to explain the behavior of PN junctions during breakdown: one is the Zener effect and the other is the avalanche effect. The Zener effect was first proposed by Dr. Carl Zener in 1934. According to Dr. Zener's theory, electrical breakdown in solid dielectrics occurs by a process called quantum-mechanical tunneling. The Zener effect accounts for the breakdown below 5 V, whereas above 5 V the breakdown is caused by the avalanche effect. Although the avalanche effect is now accepted as an explanation of diode breakdown, the term zener diode is used to cover both types.

The true Zener effect in semiconductors can be described in terms of energy bands; however, only the two upper energy bands are of interest. The two upper bands, illustrated in Figure 6-1-2A, are called the conduction band and the valence band.

The *conduction band* is a band in which the energy level of the electrons is high enough that the electrons will move easily under the influence of an external field. Since current flow is the movement of electrons, the readily mobile electrons in the conduction band are capable of maintaining a current flow when an external field in the form of a voltage is applied. Therefore, solid materials that have many electrons in the conduction band are called conductors.

The *valence band* is a band in which the energy level is the same as the valence electrons of the atoms. Since the electrons in these levels are attached to the atoms, the electrons are not free to move around as are the conduction-band electrons. With the proper amount of energy added, however, the electrons in the valence band may be elevated to the conduction band energy level. To do this, the electrons must cross a gap between the valence band energy level and the conduction band energy level. This gap is known as the forbidden energy band or forbidden gap. The energy difference across this gap determines whether a solid material will act as a conductor, a semiconductor or an insulator.

A conductor is a material in which the forbidden gap is so narrow that it can be considered nonexistent. A semiconductor is a solid that contains a forbidden gap, as shown in Figure 6-1-2A. Normally, a semiconductor has no electrons at the conduction band energy level. Room temperature heat, however, provides enough energy to overcome the binding force of a few valence electrons and to elevate them to the conduction band energy level. The addition of impurities to the semiconductor material increases both the number of free electrons in the conduction band and the number of electrons in the valence band that can be elevated to the conduction band.

Insulators are materials in which the forbidden gap is so large that practically no electrons can be given enough energy to cross the gap. Therefore, unless extremely large amounts of heat energy are available, these materials will not conduct electricity.

Figure 6-1-2B shows an energy diagram of a reverse-biased zener diode. The energy bands of the P and N materials are naturally at differ-

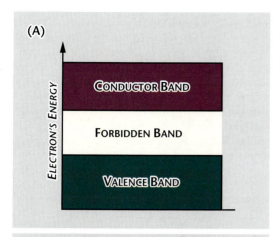

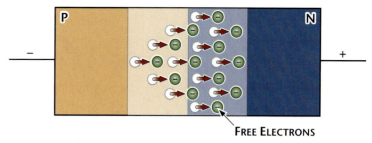

Figure 6-1-3. Avalanche multiplication

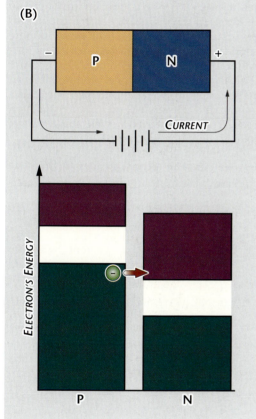

Figure 6-1-2. Energy diagrams for Zener diode

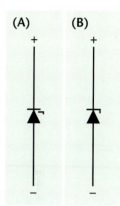

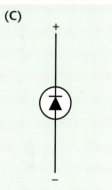

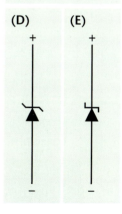

Figure 6-1-4. Five examples of Zener diode schematic symbols shown in (A) through (E)

of breakdown diode has a depletion region that is deliberately made narrower than the depletion region in the normal PN junction diode, but thicker than that in the zener diode. The thicker depletion region is achieved by decreasing the doping level from the level used in zener diodes. The breakdown is at a higher voltage because of the higher resistivity of the material. Controlling the doping level of the material during the manufacturing process can produce breakdown voltages ranging from about 2 to 200 V.

The mechanism of avalanche breakdown is different from that of the Zener effect. In the depletion region of a PN junction, thermal energy is responsible for the formation of electron-hole pairs. The leakage current is caused by the movement of minority electrons, which is accelerated in the electric field across the barrier region. As the reverse voltage across the depletion region is increased, the reverse voltage eventually reaches a critical value. Once the critical or breakdown voltage has been reached, sufficient energy is gained by the thermally released minority electrons to enable the electrons to rupture covalent bonds as they collide with lattice atoms. The released electrons are also accelerated by the electric field, resulting in the release of further electrons, and so on, in a chain or avalanche effect. This process is illustrated in Figure 6-1-3.

For reverse voltage slightly higher than breakdown, the avalanche effect releases an almost unlimited number of carriers so that the diode essentially becomes a short circuit. The current flow in this region is limited only by an external series current-limiting resistor. Operating a diode in the breakdown region does not damage it, as long as the maximum power dissipation rating of the diode is not exceeded. Removing the reverse voltage permits all carriers to return to their normal energy values and velocities.

Some of the symbols used to represent zener diodes are illustrated in Figure 6-1-4. Note that the polarity markings indicate that electron flow is with the arrow symbol instead of against it as in a normal PN junction diode. This is because breakdown diodes are operated in the reverse-bias mode, which means the current flow is by minority current carriers.

ent levels, but reverse bias causes the valence band of the P material to overlap the energy level of the conduction band in the N material. Under this condition, the valence electrons of the P material can cross the extremely thin junction region at the overlap point without acquiring any additional energy. This action is called *tunneling*. When the breakdown point of the PN junction is reached, large numbers of minority carriers "tunnel" across the junction to form the current that occurs at breakdown. The tunneling phenomenon only takes place in heavily doped diodes such as zener diodes.

The second theory of reverse breakdown effect in diodes is known as *avalanche breakdown* and occurs at reverse voltages beyond 5 V. This type

Advanced Solid-State Components

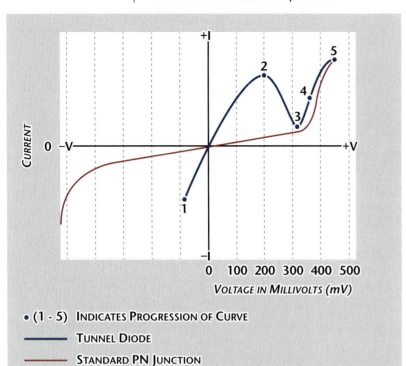

Figure 6-1-5. Characteristic curve of a tunnel diode compared to that of a standard PN junction

Tunnel Diodes

In 1958, Leo Esaki, a Japanese scientist, discovered that if a semiconductor junction diode is heavily doped with impurities, it will have a region of negative resistance. The normal junction diode uses semiconductor materials that are lightly doped with one impurity atom per 10 million semiconductor atoms. This low doping level results in a relatively wide depletion region. Conduction occurs in the normal junction diode only if the voltage applied to it is large enough to overcome the potential barrier of the junction.

In the tunnel diode, the semiconductor materials used in forming a junction are doped to the extent of 1,000 impurity atoms per 10 million semiconductor atoms. This heavy doping produces an extremely narrow depletion zone similar to that in the zener diode. Also because of the heavy doping, a tunnel diode exhibits an unusual current-voltage characteristic curve as compared with that of an ordinary junction diode. The characteristic curve for a tunnel diode is shown in Figure 6-1-5

The three most important aspects of this characteristic curve are:

- Forward current increase to a peak (I_P) with a small applied forward bias
- Decreasing forward current with an increasing forward bias to a minimum valley current (I_V)
- Normal increasing forward current with further increases in the bias voltage

The portion of the characteristic curve between I_P and I_V is the region of negative resistance.

Zener diodes of various sorts are used for many purposes, but their most widespread use is as voltage regulators. Once the breakdown voltage of a zener diode is reached, the voltage across the diode remains almost constant regardless of the supply voltage. Therefore they hold the voltage across the load at a constant level. This characteristic makes zener diodes ideal voltage regulators, and they are found in almost all solid-state circuits in this capacity.

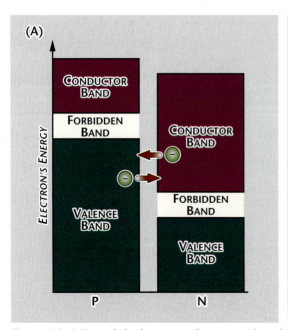

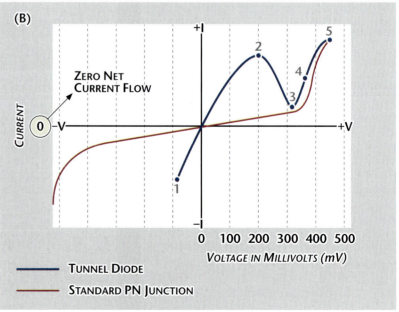

Figure 6-1-6. Tunnel diode energy diagram with no bias

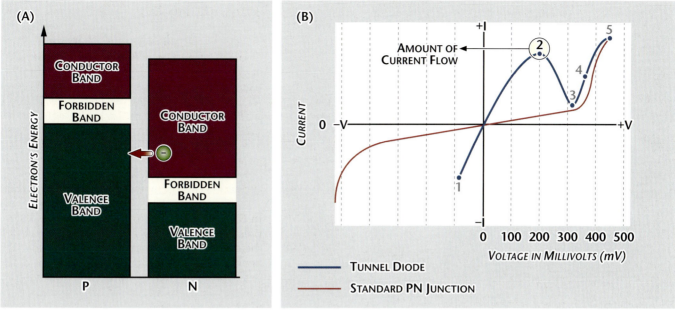

Figure 6-1-7. Tunnel diode energy diagram with 50 millivolts bias

An explanation of why a tunnel diode has a region of negative resistance is best understood by using energy levels as in the previous explanation of the Zener effect.

Simply stated, the theory known as quantum-mechanical tunneling is an electron crossing a PN junction without having sufficient energy to do so otherwise. Because of the heavy doping the width of the depletion region is only one-millionth of an inch. It is easy to think of the process simply as an arc-over between the N and the P sides across the depletion region.

Figure 6-1-6 shows the equilibrium energy level diagram of a tunnel diode with no bias applied.

Note in Figure 6-1-6A that the valence band of the P-type material overlaps the conduction band of the N-type material. The majority electrons and holes are at the same energy level in the equilibrium state. If there is any movement of current carriers across the depletion region due to thermal energy, the net current flow will be zero because equal numbers of current carriers flow in opposite directions. The zero net current flow is marked by a "0" on the current-voltage curve illustrated in Figure 6-1-6B.

Figure 6-1-7A shows the energy diagram of a tunnel diode with a small forward bias (50 mV) applied. The bias causes unequal energy levels between some of the majority carriers at

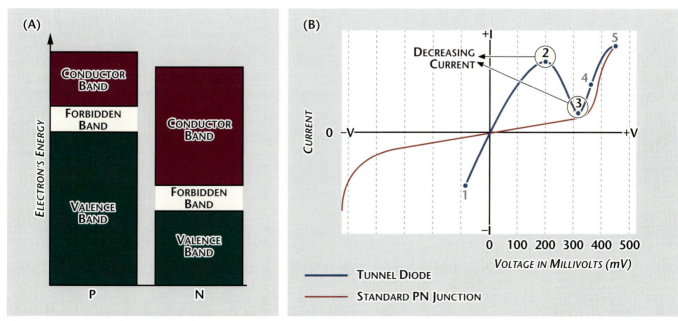

Figure 6-1-8. Tunnel diode energy diagram with 450 millivolts bias

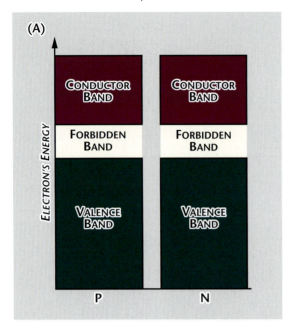
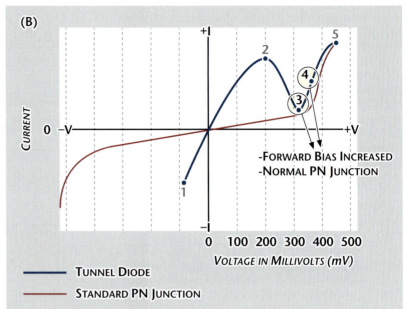

Figure 6-1-9. Tunnel diode energy diagram with 600 millivolts bias

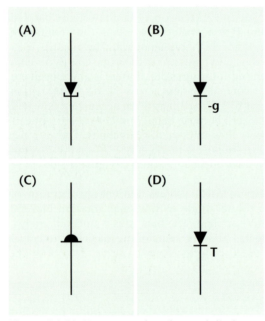

Figure 6-1-10. Four examples of tunnel diode schematic symbols seen in (A) through (D)

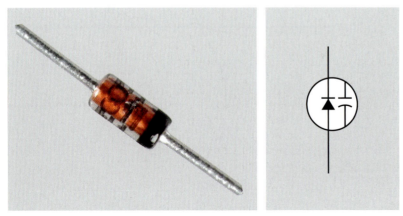

Figure 6-1-11. Varactor diode and schematic symbol

the energy band overlap point, but not enough of a potential difference to cause the carriers to cross the forbidden gap in the normal manner. Since the valence band of the P material and the conduction band of the N material still overlap, current carriers tunnel across at the overlap and cause a substantial current flow. The amount of current flow is marked by point 2 on the curve in Figure 6-1-7B. Note in Figure 6-1-7A that the amount of overlap between the valence band and the conduction band decreased when forward bias was applied.

Figure 6-1-8A is the energy diagram of a tunnel diode in which the forward bias has been increased to 450 mV. As shown, the valence band and the conduction band no longer overlap at this point, and tunneling can no longer occur. The portion of the curve in Figure 6-1-8B from point 2 to point 3 shows the decreasing current that occurs as the bias is increased and the area of overlap becomes smaller. As the overlap between the two energy bands becomes smaller, fewer and fewer electrons can tunnel across the junction. The portion of the curve between point 2 and point 3, in which current decreases as the voltage increases, is the negative resistance region of the tunnel diode.

Figure 6-1-9A is the energy diagram of a tunnel diode in which the forward bias has been increased even further. The energy bands no longer overlap and the diode operates in the same manner as a normal PN junction, as shown by the portion of the curve in Figure 6-1-9B from point 3 to point 4.

The negative resistance region is the most important and most widely used characteristic of the tunnel diode. A tunnel diode biased to operate in the negative resistance region can be used as either an oscillator or an amplifier in a wide range of frequencies and applications. Very high frequency applications using the tunnel diode are possible because the tunneling action occurs so rapidly that there is no transit time effect and therefore no signal distortion. Tunnel diodes are also used extensively in high-speed switching circuits because of the speed of the tunneling action.

Several schematic symbols are used to indicate a tunnel diode. These symbols are illustrated in Figure 6-1-10.

Varactors

The varactor, or varicap, as the schematic drawing in Figure 6-1-11 suggests, is a diode that behaves like a variable capacitor, with the PN junction functioning like the dielectric and plates of a common capacitor. Understanding how the varactor operates is an important prerequisite to understanding field-effect transistors, which will be covered later in this chapter.

Figure 6-1-12 shows a PN junction. Surrounding the junction of the P and N materials is a narrow region void of both positively and negatively charged current carriers. This area is called the depletion region.

The size of the depletion region in a varactor diode is directly related to the bias. Forward biasing makes the region smaller by repelling the current carriers toward the PN junction. If the applied voltage is large enough (about 0.5 V for silicon material), the negative particles will cross the junction and join with the positive particles, as shown in Figure 6-1-13. This forward biasing causes the depletion region to decrease, producing a low resistance at the PN junction and a large current flow across it.

This is the condition for a forward-biased diode. On the other hand, if reverse-bias voltage is applied to the PN junction, the size of its depletion region increases as the charged particles on both sides move away from the junction. This condition, shown in Figure 6-1-14, produces a high resistance between the terminals and allows little current flow (only in the microampere range). This is the operating condition for the varactor diode, which is nothing more than a special PN junction.

As Figure 6-1-14 shows, the insulation gap formed by the reverse biasing of the varactor is comparable to the layer of dielectric material between the plates of a common capaci-

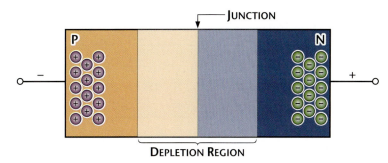

Figure 6-1-12. PN junction

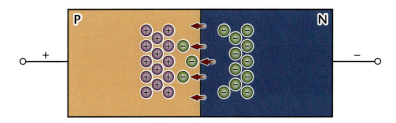

Figure 6-1-13. Forward-biased PN junction

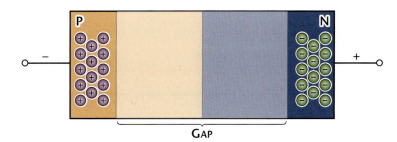

Figure 6-1-14. Reverse-biased PN junction

tor. Furthermore, the formula used to calculate capacitance can be applied to both the varactor and the capacitor.

$C = AK \div d$

Where

A = plate area

K = a constant value

d = distance between plates

In this case, the size of the insulation gap, or depletion region, of the varactor is substituted for the distance between the plates of the capacitor. By varying the reverse-bias voltage applied to the varactor, the width of the gap may be varied. An increase in reverse bias increases the width of the gap (d), which reduces the capacitance (C) of the PN junction. Therefore, the capacitance of the varactor is inversely proportional to the applied reverse bias.

The ratio of varactor capacitance to reverse-bias voltage change may be as high as 10 to 1.

6-8 | Advanced Solid-State Components

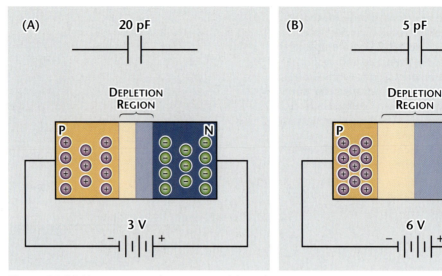

Figure 6-1-15. Varactor capacitance versus bias voltage

Figure 6-1-15 shows one example of the voltage-to-capacitance ratio. Figure 6-1-15A shows that a reverse bias of 3 V produces a capacitance of 20 picofarads (pF) in the varactor. If the reverse bias is increased to 6 V, as shown in Figure 6-1-15B, the depletion region widens and capacitance drops to 5 pF. Each 1-V increase in bias voltage causes a 5-pF decrease in the capacitance of the varactor; the ratio of change is therefore 5 to 1. Of course any decrease in applied bias voltage would cause a proportionate increase in capacitance, as the depletion region narrows. Notice that the value of the capacitance is small in the picofarad range.

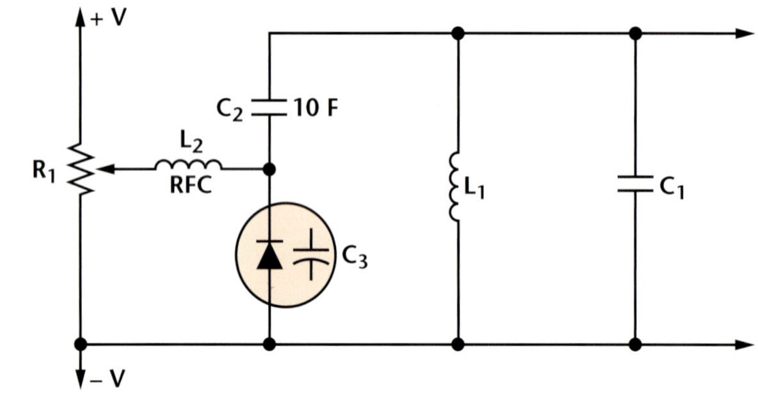

In general, varactors are used to replace the old-style variable capacitor tuning. They are used in tuning circuits of more sophisticated communication equipment and in other circuits where variable capacitance is required. One advantage of the varactor is that it allows a DC voltage to be used to tune a circuit for simple remote control or automatic tuning functions. One such application of the varactor is as a variable tuning capacitor in a receiver or transmitter tank circuit like that shown in Figure 6-1-16.

Figure 6-1-16. Varactor tuned resonant circuit

Figure 6-1-16 shows a DC voltage felt at the wiper of potentiometer R_1, which can be adjusted between +V and –V. The DC voltage, passed through the low resistance of radio frequency choke L_2, acts to reverse bias varactor diode C_3. The capacitance of C_3 is in series with C_2, and the equivalent capacitance of C_2 and C_3 is in parallel with tank circuit L_1-C_1. Therefore, any variation in the DC voltage at R_1 will vary both the capacitance of C_3 and the resonant frequency of the tank circuit. The radio-frequency choke provides high inductive reactance at the tank frequency to prevent tank loading by R_1. C_2 acts to block DC from the tank as well as to fix the tuning range of C_3.

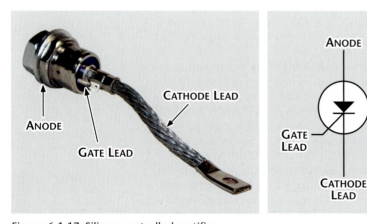

Figure 6-1-17. Silicon controlled rectifier

An ohmmeter can be used to check a varactor diode in a circuit. A 10-to-1 ratio between reverse-bias resistance and a forward-bias resistance is considered normal.

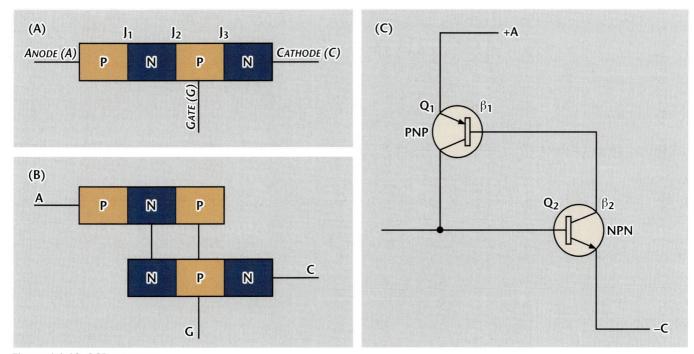

Figure 6-1-18. SCR structure

Silicon Controlled Rectifiers (SCR)

The silicon controlled rectifier, usually referred to as an SCR, is one of the family of semiconductors that includes transistors and diodes. A picture of an SCR and its schematic representation is shown in Figure 6-1-17. Not all SCRs use the casing shown, but this is typical of most of the high-power units.

Although it is not the same as either a diode or a transistor, the SCR combines features of both. Circuits using transistors or rectifier diodes may be greatly improved in some instances through the use of SCRs.

The basic purpose of the SCR is to function as a switch that can turn on or off small or large amounts of power. It performs this function with no moving parts that wear out and no points that require replacing. There can be a tremendous power gain in the SCR; in some units a very small triggering current is able to switch several hundred amperes without exceeding its rated abilities. The SCR can often replace much slower and larger mechanical switches. It even has many advantages over its more complex and larger electron tube equivalent, the thyratron.

The SCR is an extremely fast switch. It is difficult to cycle a mechanical switch several hundred times a minute; however, some SCRs can be switched 25,000 times a second. It takes just microseconds (millionths of a second) to turn these units on or off. Varying the time that a switch is on as compared to the time that it is off regulates the amount of power flowing through the switch. Since most devices can operate on pulses of power (alternating current is a special form of alternating positive and negative pulse), the SCR can be used readily in control applications. Motor-speed controllers, inverters, remote switching units, controlled rectifiers, circuit overload protectors, latching relays and computer logic circuits all use the SCR.

The SCR is made up of four layers of semiconductor material arranged PNPN. The construction is shown in Figure 6-1-18A.

In function, the SCR has much in common with a diode, but the theory of operation of the SCR is best explained in terms of transistors. Consider the SCR as a transistor pair, one PNP and the other NPN, connected as shown in Figure 6-1-18B and Figure 6-1-18C. The anode is attached to the upper P layer; the cathode, C, is part of the lower N layer; and the gate terminal, G, goes to the P layer of the NPN triode.

In operation the collector of Q_2 drives the base of Q_1, while the collector of Q_1 feeds back to the base of Q_2. Beta-1 is the current gain of Q_1, and beta-2 is the current gain of Q_2. The gain of this positive feedback loop is their product, beta-1 times beta-2. When the product is less than one, the circuit is stable; if the product is greater than unity, the circuit is regenerative. A small negative current applied to terminal G will bias the NPN transistor into cutoff, and the loop gain is less than unity. Under these conditions, the only current that can exist between

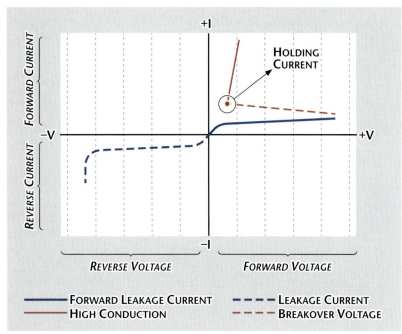

Figure 6-1-19. Characteristic curve for an SCR

output terminals A and C is the very small cut-off collector current of the two transistors. For this reason the impedance between A and C is very high.

When a positive current is applied to terminal G, transistor Q_2 is biased into conduction, causing its collector current to rise. Since the current gain of Q_2 increases with increased collector current, a point (called the *breakover point*) is reached where the loop gain equals unity and the circuit becomes regenerative. At this point, collector current of the two transistors rapidly increases to a value limited only by the external circuit. Both transistors are driven into saturation, and the impedance between A and C is very low. The positive current applied to terminal G, which served to trigger the self-regenerative action, is no longer required since the collector of PNP transistor Q_1 now supplies more than enough current to drive Q_2. The circuit will remain on until it is turned off by a reduction in the collector current to a value below that necessary to maintain conduction.

The characteristic curve for the SCR is shown in Figure 6-1-19. With no gate current, the leakage current remains very small as the forward voltage from cathode to anode is increased until the breakdown point is reached. Here the center junction breaks down, the SCR begins to conduct heavily, and the drop across the SCR becomes very low.

The effect of a gate signal on the firing of an SCR is shown in Figure 6-1-20. Breakdown of the center junction can be achieved at speeds approaching a microsecond by applying an appropriate signal to the gate lead, while holding the anode voltage constant. After breakdown, the voltage across the device is so low that the current through it from cathode to anode is essentially determined by the load it is feeding.

The important thing to remember is that a small current from gate to cathode can fire or trigger the SCR, changing it from practically an open circuit to a short circuit. The only way to change it back again (that is, to commutate it) is to reduce the load current to a value less than the minimum forward-bias current. Gate current is required only until the anode current has built up to a point sufficient to sustain conduction (about 5 microseconds in resistive-load circuits). After conduction from cathode to anode begins, removing the gate current has no effect.

The basic operation of the SCR can be compared to that of the thyratron. The thyratron is an electron tube, normally gas filled, that uses a filament or a heater. The SCR and the thyratron function in a very similar manner. Figure 6-1-21 shows the schematic of each with the corresponding elements labeled. In both types of devices, control by the input signal is lost after they are triggered. The control grid (thyratron) and the gate (SCR) have no further effect on the magnitude of the load current after conduction begins. The load current can be interrupted by one or more of three methods:

- The load circuit must be opened by a switch

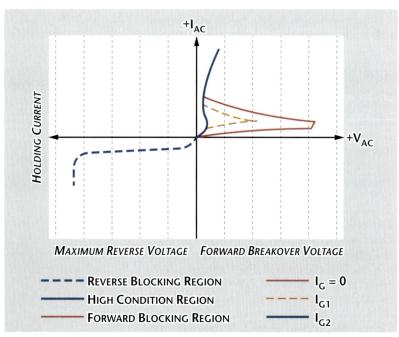

Figure 6-1-20. SCR characteristic curve with various gate signals

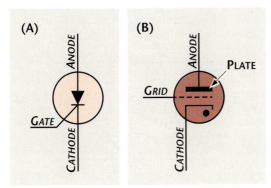

Figure 6-1-21. Comparison of (A) an SCR and, (B) a Thyratron

- The plate (anode) voltage must be reduced below the ionizing potential of the gas (thyratron)
- The forward-bias current must be reduced below a minimum value required to sustain conduction (SCR)

The input resistance of the SCR is relatively low (approximately 100 Ω) and requires a current for triggering; the input resistance of the thyratron is exceptionally high and requires a voltage input to the grid for triggering action.

The applications of the SCR as a rectifier are so many that they give this semiconductor device its name. When alternating current is applied to a rectifier, only the positive or negative halves of the sine wave flow through. All of each positive or negative half-cycle appears in the output. When an SCR is used, however, the controlled rectifier may be turned on at any time during the half-cycle, thus controlling the amount of DC power available from zero to maximum, as shown in Figure 6-1-22. Since the output is actually DC pulses, suitable filtering can be added if continuous direct current is needed. Thus any DC-operated device can have controlled amounts of power applied to it. Notice that the SCR must be turned on at the desired time for each cycle.

When an AC power source is used, the SCR is turned off automatically, since current and voltage drop to zero every half-cycle. By using one SCR on positive alternations and one on negative, full-wave rectification can be accomplished, and control is obtained over the entire sine wave. The SCR serves in this application just as its name implies—as a controlled rectifier of AC voltage.

TRIACs

The TRIAC (from "triode for alternating current") is a three-terminal device similar in construction and operation to the SCR. The TRIAC

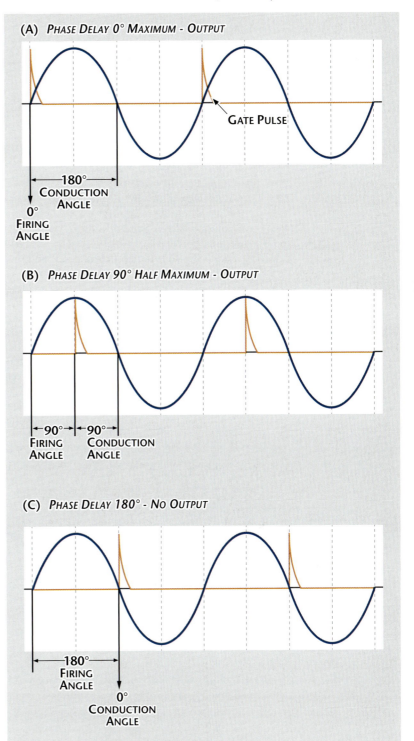

Figure 6-1-22. SCR gate control signals

controls and conducts current flow during both alternations of an AC cycle, instead of only one. The schematic symbols for the SCR and the TRIAC are compared in Figure 6-1-23. Both the SCR and the TRIAC have a gate lead. However, in the TRIAC the lead on the same side as the gate is "main terminal 1," and the lead opposite the gate is "main terminal 2."

This method of lead labeling is necessary because the TRIAC is essentially two SCRs back

6-12 | Advanced Solid-State Components

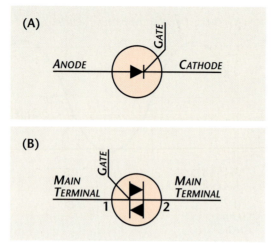

Figure 6-1-23. Comparison of; (A) SCR and, (B) TRIAC symbols

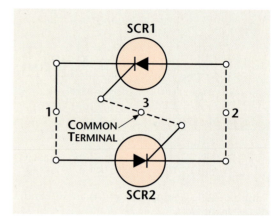

Figure 6-1-24. Back to back SCR equivalent circuit

to back, with a common gate and common terminals. Each terminal is, in effect, the anode of one SCR and the cathode of another and either terminal can receive an input. In fact, the functions of a TRIAC can be duplicated by connecting two actual SCRs as shown in Figure 6-1-24. The result is a three-terminal device identical to the TRIAC. The common anode-cathode connections form main terminals 1 and 2, and the common gate forms terminal 3.

The difference in current control between the SCR and the TRIAC can be seen by comparing their operation in the basic circuit shown in Figure 6-1-25.

In the circuit shown in Figure 6-1-25A, the SCR is connected in the familiar half-wave arrangement. Current will flow through the load resistor (R_L) for one alternation of each input cycle. Diode CR_1 is necessary to ensure a positive trigger voltage.

In the circuit shown in Figure 6-1-25B, with the TRIAC inserted in the place of the SCR, current flows through the load resistor during both alternations of the input cycle. Because either alternation will trigger the gate of the TRIAC, CR_1 is not required in the circuit. Current flowing through the load will reverse direction for half of each input cycle. To clarify this difference, a comparison of the waveforms seen at the input, gate and output points of the two devices is shown in Figure 6-1-26.

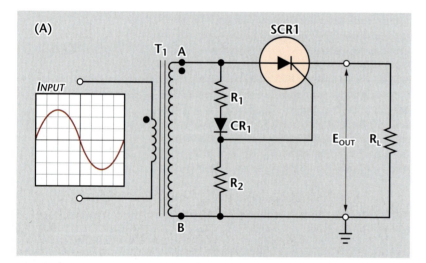

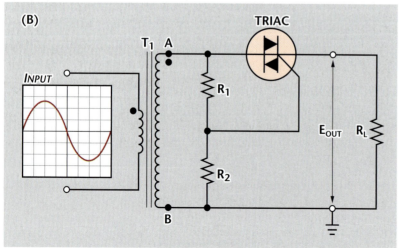

Figure 6-1-25. Comparison of SCR and TRIAC circuits

Optoelectronic Devices

Optoelectronic devices either produce light or use light in their operation. The first of these, the light-emitting diode (LED), was developed to replace the fragile, short-life incandescent light bulbs used to indicate on/off conditions on panels. A *light-emitting diode* is a diode which, when forward biased, produces visible light. The light may be red, green, or amber, depending upon the material used to make the diode.

Figure 6-1-27 shows an LED and its schematic symbol. The LED is designated by a standard diode symbol with two arrows pointing away from the cathode. The arrows indicate light leaving the diode. The circuit symbols for all opto-

Advanced Solid-State Components | 6-13

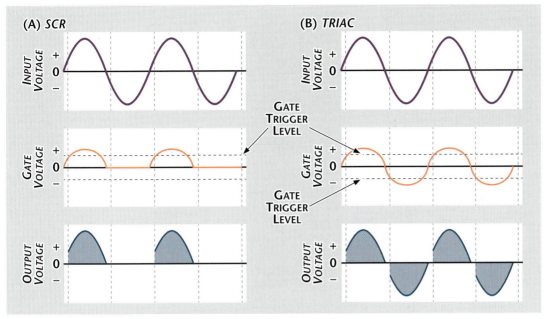

Figure 6-1-26. Comparison of; (A) SCR and, (B) TRIAC waveforms

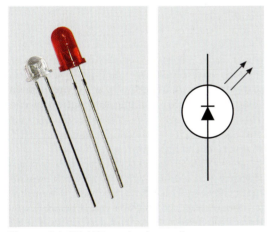

Figure 6-1-27. LED and schematic

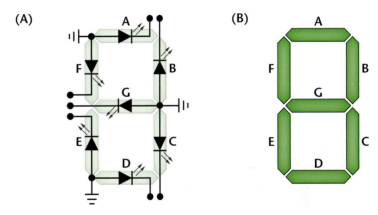

Figure 6-1-28. Seven-segment LED display

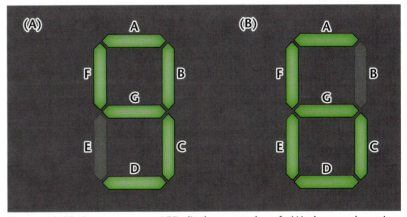

Figure 6-1-29. Seven-segment LED display examples of; (A) the number nine (B) the number six

electronic devices have arrows pointing either toward them (if they use light) or away from them (if they produce light). The LED operating voltage is small, about 1.6 V forward bias and generally about 10 mA. The life expectancy of the LED is very long—more than 100,000 hours of operation.

LEDs are used widely as "power on" indicators of current and as displays for pocket calculators, digital voltmeters, frequency counters, etc. For use in calculators and similar devices, LEDs are typically placed together in seven-segment displays, as shown in Figure 6-1-28. The seven LED segments, or bars (labeled A through G in the figure), can be lit in different combinations to form any number from 0 through 9. The schematic, Figure 6-1-28A, shows a common-anode display.

All anodes in a display are internally connected. When a negative voltage is applied to the proper cathodes, a number is formed. For example, if negative voltage is applied to all cathodes except that of LED "E," the number 9 is produced, as shown Figure 6-1-29A. If the negative voltage is changed and applied to all cathodes except LED "B," the number 9 changes to 6, as shown in Figure 6-1-29B.

Figure 6-1-30. Seven-segment display on a digital voltmeter

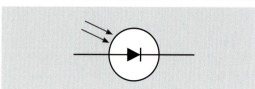

Figure 6-1-31. Photodiode and schematic

Seven-segment displays are also available in common-cathode form, in which all cathodes are at the same potential. When replacing LED displays, the technician must ensure the replacement display is the same type as the faulty display. Since both types look alike, always check the manufacturer's number.

LED seven-segment displays range from the very small, often not much larger than standard typewritten numbers, to about an inch. Several displays may be combined in a package to show a series of numbers, such as the digital voltmeter shown in Figure 6-1-30.

Another special optoelectronic device in common use today is the *photodiode*. Unlike the LED, which produces light, the photodiode uses light to accomplish special circuit functions. Basically, the photodiode is a light-controlled variable resistor. In total darkness, it has a relatively high resistance and therefore conducts little current. However, when the PN junction is exposed to an external light source, internal resistance decreases and current flow increases. The photodiode is operated with reverse bias and conducts current in direct proportion to the intensity of the light source.

Figure 6-1-31 shows a photodiode with its schematic symbol. The arrows pointing toward the symbol indicate that light is required for operation of the device. A light source is aimed at the photodiode through a transparent "window" placed over the semiconductor chip. Switching the light source on or off changes the conduction level of the photodiode. Varying the light intensity controls the amount of conduction. Because photodiodes respond quickly to changes in light intensity, they are extremely useful in digital applications such as computer card readers, paper tape readers, and photographic light meters. They are also used in some types of optical scanning equipment.

A second optoelectronic device that conducts current when exposed to light is the *phototransistor*. A phototransistor, however, is much more sensitive to light and produces more output current for a given light intensity than does a photodiode. Figure 6-1-32 shows one type of phototransistor, which is made by placing a photodiode in the base circuit of an NPN transistor. Light falling on the photodiode changes the base current of the transistor, causing the collector current to be amplified. Phototransistors may also be of the PNP type, with the photodiode placed in the base-collector circuit.

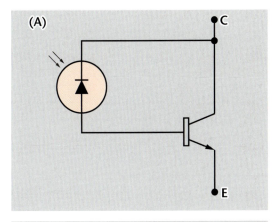

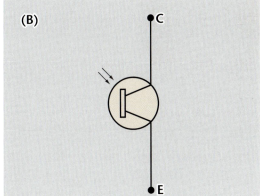

Figure 6-1-32. Phototransistor schematic

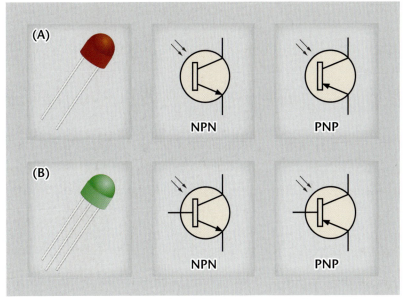

Figure 6-1-33. (A) Two-terminal and, (B) three-terminal phototransistors

Figure 6-1-33 illustrates the schematic symbols for the various types of phototransistors.

Phototransistors may be of the two-terminal type, in which the light intensity on the photodiode alone determines the amount of conduction. They may also be of the three-terminal type, which has an added base lead that allows an electrical bias to be applied to the base. The bias allows an optimum transistor conduction level, and thus compensates for ambient light intensity.

When it is necessary to block the voltage between one electronic circuit and another, and transfer the signal at the same time, an *amplifier coupling capacitor* is often used, as shown in Figure 6-1-34. Although this method of coupling does block DC between the circuits, voltage isolation is not complete. A newer method, making use of optoelectronic devices to achieve electrical isolation, is the *optical coupler*, shown in Figure 6-1-35.

The coupler is composed of an LED and a photodiode contained in a light-conducting medium. As the polarity signs in Figure 6-1-35 show, the LED is forward biased, while the photodiode is reverse biased. When the input signal causes current through the LED to increase, the light produced by the LED increases. This increased light intensity causes current flow through the photodiode to increase. In this way, changes in input current produce proportional changes in the output, even though the two circuits are electrically isolated.

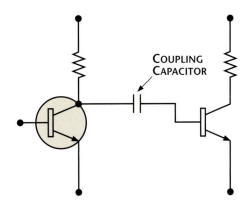

Figure 6-1-34. DC blocking with a coupling capacitor

The optical coupler is suitable for frequencies in the low megahertz range. The photodiode type shown above can handle only small currents; however, other types of couplers, combining phototransistors with the SCR, can be used where more output is required. Optical couplers are replacing transformers in low-voltage and low-current applications. Sensitive digital circuits can use the coupler to control large current and voltages with low-voltage logic levels.

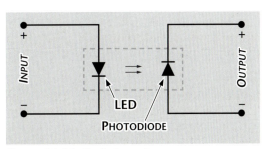

Figure 6-1-35. Optical coupler

6-16 | Advanced Solid-State Components

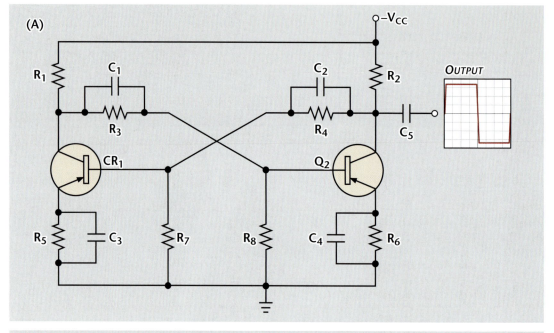

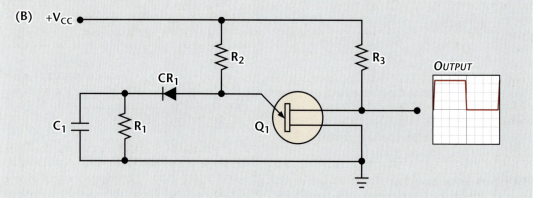

Figure 6-2-1. Comparison of conventional transistors and UJT circuits

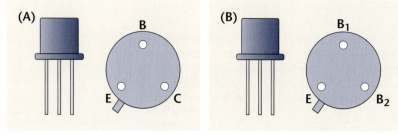

Figure 6-2-2. (A) Transistor and, (B) UJT

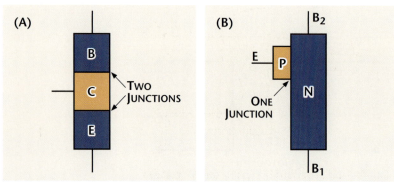

Figure 6-2-3. Transistor and UJT structure

Section 2

Advanced Transistors

Transistors are semiconductor devices with three or more terminals. The operation of normal transistors has already been discussed, but there are several transistors with special properties that should be explained. As with diodes, a discussion of all the developments in the transistor field would be impossible.

Unijunction Transistors (UJT)

The *unijunction transistor* (UJT), originally called a double-based diode, is a three-terminal, solid-state device that has several advantages over conventional transistors. It is very stable over a wide range of temperatures and allows a reduction of components when used in place of conventional transistors. A comparison is shown in Figure 6-2-1. Figure 6-2-

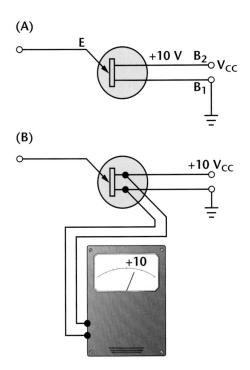

Figure 6-2-4. UJT biasing

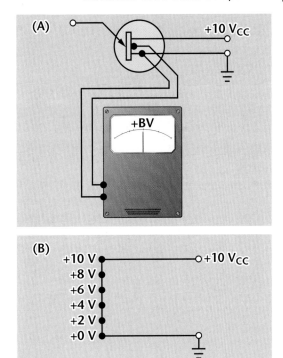

Figure 6-2-5. UJMT voltage gradient

1A shows a circuit using conventional transistors, and Figure 6-2-1B is the same circuit using the UJT. As shown, the UJT circuit has fewer components, and this reduces the cost, size and probability of failure.

In its physical appearance, the UJT is identical to the common transistor. As shown in Figure 6-2-2, both have three leads and the same basic shape; the tab on the case indicates the emitter on both devices. The UJT, however, has a second base instead of a collector.

As indicated in the block diagram shown in Figure 6-2-3A and Figure 6-2-3B, the lead differences are even more pronounced. Unlike the transistor, the UJT has only one PN junction. The area between base 1 and base 2 acts as a resistor when the UJT is properly biased. A conventional transistor needs a certain bias level between the emitter, base and collector for proper conduction. The same principle is true for the UJT; it needs a certain bias level between the emitter and base 1 and also between base 1 and base 2 for proper conduction.

The normal bias arrangement for the UJT is illustrated in Figure 6-2-4A. A positive 10 V is placed on base 2 and a ground on base 1. The area between base 1 and base 2 acts as a resistor. If a reading were taken between base 1 and base 2, the meter would indicate the full 10 V, as shown in Figure 6-2-4B. Theoretically, if one meter lead were connected to base 1 and the other lead to some point between base 1 and base 2, the meter would read some voltage less than 10 V. This concept is illustrated in Figure

6-2-5A. Figure 6-2-5B is an illustration of the voltage levels at different points between the two bases. The sequential rise in voltage is called a voltage gradient.

The emitter of the UJT can be viewed as the wiper arm of a variable resistor. If the voltage level on the emitter is more positive than the voltage gradient level at the emitter-base material contact point, the UJT is forward biased. The UJT will conduct heavily (almost a short circuit) from base 1 to the emitter. The emitter is fixed in position by the manufacturer. The level of the voltage gradient therefore depends upon the amount of bias voltage, as shown in Figure 6-2-6.

If the voltage level on the emitter is less positive than the voltage gradient opposite the emitter, the UJT is reverse biased. No current will flow from base 1 to the emitter. However, a small current, called reverse current, will flow from the

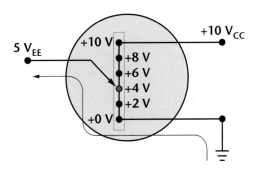

Figure 6-2-6. Forward bias point on UJT voltage gradient

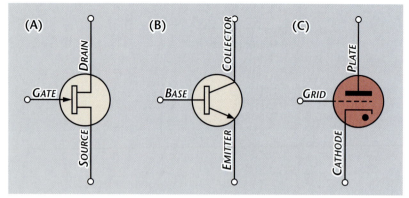

Figure 6-2-7. Comparison of; (A) JFET (B) Transistor (C) Vacuum tube symbols

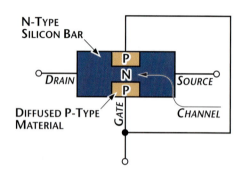

Figure 6-2-8. JFET structure

emitter to base 2. The reverse current is caused by the impurities used in the construction of the UJT and is in the form of minority carriers.

More than 40 distinct types of UJTs are presently in use. One of the most common applications is in switching circuits. They are also used extensively in oscillators and wave-shaping circuits.

Field-Effect Transistors (FET)

Although it has brought about a revolution in the design of electronic equipment, the bipolar (PNP/NPN) transistor still has one very undesirable characteristic. The low input impedance associated with its base-emitter junction causes problems in matching impedances between interstage amplifiers.

For years, scientists searched for a solution that would combine the high input impedance of the vacuum tube with the many other advantages of the transistor. The result of this research is the *field-effect transistor* (FET). In contrast to the bipolar transistor, which uses bias current between base and emitter to control conductivity, the FET uses voltage to control an electrostatic field within the transistor. Because the FET is voltage-controlled, much like a vacuum tube, it is sometimes called the "solid-state vacuum tube."

Junction Gate Field-Effect Transistor

The elements of one type of FET, the junction type (JFET), are compared with the bipolar transistor and the vacuum tube in Figure 6-2-7. As the figure shows, the JFET is a three-element device comparable to the other two. The "gate" element of the JFET corresponds very closely in operation to the base of the transistor and the grid of the vacuum tube. The "source" and "drain" elements of the JFET correspond to the emitter and collector of the transistor and to the cathode and plate of the vacuum tube.

The construction of a JFET is shown in Figure 6-2-8. A solid bar, made either of N-type or P-type material, forms the main body of the device. Diffused into each side of this bar are two deposits of material of the opposite type, which form the "gate." The portion of the bar between the deposits of gate material is of a smaller cross section than the rest of the bar and forms a channel connecting the source and the drain. Figure 6-2-8 shows a bar of N-type material and a gate of P-type material. Because the material in the channel is N-type, the device is called an N-channel JFET.

In a P-channel JFET, the channel is made of P-type material and the gate of N-type material. In Figure 6-2-9, schematic symbols for the two types of JFET are compared with those of the NPN and PNP bipolar transistors. Like the bipolar transistor types, the two types of JFET differ only in the configuration of bias voltages required and in the direction of the arrow within the symbol. Just as it does in transistor symbols, the arrow in a JFET symbol always points towards the N-type material. Thus the symbol of the N-channel JFET

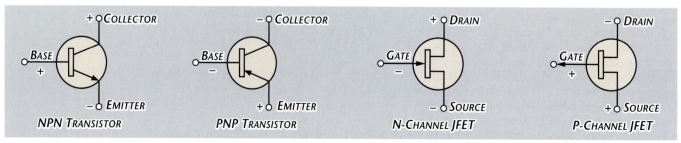

Figure 6-2-9. Symbols and bias voltages for transistors and JFET

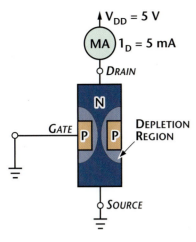

Figure 6-2-10. JFET operation with zero gate bias

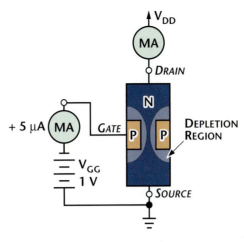

Figure 6-2-12. JFET input impedance

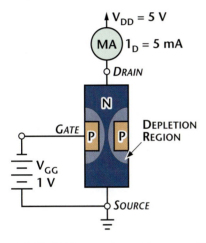

Figure 6-2-11. JFET operation with reverse bias

shows the arrow pointing toward the drain/source channel, whereas the P-channel symbol shows the arrow pointing away from the drain/source channel toward the gate.

The key to FET operation is the effective cross-sectional area of the channel, which can be controlled by variations in the voltage applied to the gate. This is demonstrated in the figures that follow.

Figure 6-2-10 shows how the JFET operates in a zero gate-bias condition. Five volts are applied across the JFET so that current flows through the bar from source to drain, as indicated by the arrow. The gate terminal is tied to ground. This is a zero gate-bias condition. In this condition, a typical bar represents a resistance of about 500 Ω. A milliammeter, connected in series with the drain lead and DC power, indicates the amount of current flow. With a drain supply (V_{DD}) of 5 V, the milliammeter gives a drain current (I_D) reading of 10 mA. The voltage and current subscript letters (V_{DD}, I_D) used for an FET correspond to the elements of the FET just as they do for the elements of transistors.

In Figure 6-2-11, a small reverse-bias voltage is applied to the gate of the JFET. A gate-source voltage (V_{GG}) of –1 V applied to the P-type gate material causes the junction between the P- and N-type material to become reverse biased. Just as it did in the varactor diode, a reverse-bias condition causes a depletion region to form around the PN junction of the JFET. Because this region has a reduced number of current carriers, the effect of reverse biasing is to reduce the effective cross-sectional area of the channel. This reduction in area increases the source-to-drain resistance of the device and decreases current flow.

The application of a large enough negative voltage to the gate causes the depletion region to become so large that conduction of current through the bar stops altogether. The voltage required to reduce drain current (I_D) to zero is called "pinch-off" voltage and is comparable to "cut-off" voltage in a vacuum tube. In Figure 6-2-11, the –1 V applied, although not large enough to completely stop conduction, has caused the drain current to decrease markedly (from 10 mA under zero gate-bias conditions to 5 mA). Calculation shows that the 1-volt gate bias has also increased the resistance of the JFET (from 500 Ω to 1 kΩ). In other words, a 1-volt change in gate voltage has doubled the resistance of the device and cut current flow in half.

These measurements, however, show only that a JFET operates in a manner similar to a bipolar transistor, even though the two are constructed differently. As stated before, the main advantage of an FET is that its input impedance is significantly higher than that of a bipolar transistor. The higher input impedance of the JFET under reverse gate-bias conditions can be seen by connecting a microammeter in series with the gate-source voltage (V_{GG}), as shown in Figure 6-2-12.

With a V_{GG} of 1 V, the microammeter reads 0.5 µA. Applying Ohm's law (1 V/0.5 µA) illustrates that this very small amount of current flow

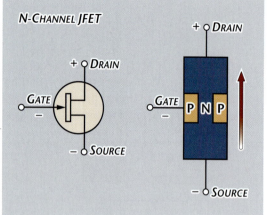
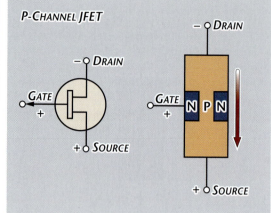

Figure 6-2-13. JFET symbols and bias voltages

results in a very high input impedance (about 2 MΩ). By contrast, a bipolar transistor in similar circumstances would require higher current flow (e.g., 0.1 to -1 mA), resulting in a much lower input impedance (about 1,000 Ω or less). The higher input impedance of the JFET is possible because of the way reverse-bias gate voltage affects the cross-sectional area of the channel.

The preceding example of JFET operation uses an N-channel JFET. However, a P-channel JFET operates on identical principles. The differences between the two types are shown in Figure 6-2-13.

Because the materials used to make the bar and the gate are reversed, source voltage potentials must also be reversed. The P-channel JFET therefore requires a positive gate voltage to be reverse biased, and current flows through it from drain to source.

Figure 6-2-14 shows a basic common-source amplifier circuit containing an N-channel JFET. An example of a basic common-source amplifier is seen in Figure 6-2-15. The characteristics of this circuit include high input impedance and a high voltage gain. The function of the circuit components in Figure 6-2-14 is very similar to those in a triode vacuum tube common-cathode amplifier circuit. C_1 and C_3 are the input and output coupling capacitors.

R_1 is the gate return resistor and functions much like the grid return resistor in a vacuum tube circuit. It prevents unwanted charge buildup on the gate by providing a discharge path for C_1. R_2 and C_2 provide source self-bias for the JFET, which operates like cathode self-bias. R_3 is the drain load resistor, which acts like the plate or collector load resistor.

The phase shift of 180° between input and output signals is the same as that of common cathode vacuum tube circuits and common-emitter transistor circuits. The reason for the phase shift can be seen easily by observing the operation of the N-channel JFET. On the positive alternation of the input signal, the amount of reverse bias on the P-type gate material is reduced, thus increasing the effective cross-sectional area of the channel and decreasing source-to-drain resistance.

Figure 6-2-15. Basic common source amplifier

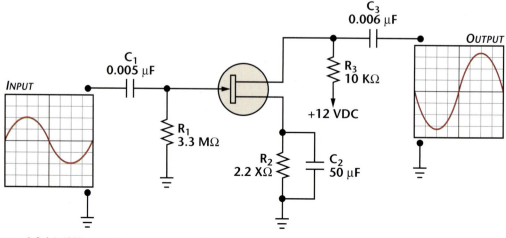

Figure 6-2-14. JFET common-source amplifier

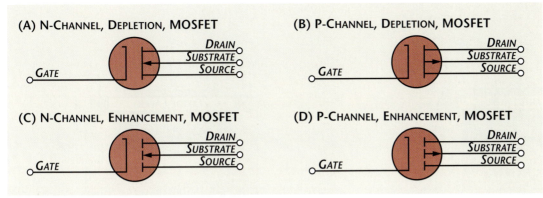

Figure 6-2-16. MOSFET symbols

When resistance decreases, current flow through the JFET increases. This increase causes the voltage drop across R_3 to increase, which in turn causes the drain voltage to decrease. On the negative alternation of the cycle, the amount of reverse bias on the gate of the JFET is increased and the action of the circuit is reversed. The result is an output signal, which is an amplified 180°-out-of-phase version of the input signal.

Metal Oxide Semiconductor Field-Effect Transistor

A second type of field-effect transistor introduced in recent years that has some advantages over the JFET. This device is the *metal oxide semiconductor field-effect transistor* (MOSFET). The MOSFET has an even higher input impedance than the JFET (10 to 100 million MΩ). Therefore, the MOSFET is even less of a load on preceding circuits. The extremely high input impedance, combined with a high gain factor, makes the MOSFET a highly efficient input device for RF/IF amplifiers and mixers and for many types of test equipment.

The MOSFET is normally constructed so that it operates in one of two basic modes: the depletion mode or the enhancement mode. The depletion-mode MOSFET has a heavily doped channel and uses reverse bias on the gate to cause a depletion of current carriers in the channel. The JFET also operates in this manner. The enhancement-mode MOSFET has a lightly doped channel and uses forward bias to enhance the current carriers in the channel. A MOSFET can be constructed that will operate in either mode depending upon what type of bias is applied, thus allowing a greater range of input signals.

In addition to the two basic modes of operation, the MOSFET, like the JFET, is of either the P-channel type or the N-channel type. Each type has four elements: gate, source, drain and substrate. The schematic symbols for the four basic

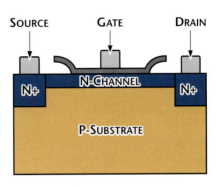

Figure 6-2-17. MOSFET structure

variations of the MOSFET are shown in Figure 6-2-16.

The construction of an N-channel MOSFET is shown in Figure 6-2-17. Heavily doped N-type regions (indicated by the N+) are diffused into a P-type substrate or base. A channel of regular N-type material is diffused between the heavily doped N-type regions. A metal oxide insulating layer is then formed over the channel, and a metal gate layer is deposited over the insulating layer. There is no electrical connection between the gate and the rest of the device. This construction method results in the extremely high input impedance of the MOSFET. Another common name for the device, derived from the construction method, is the *insulated gate field-effect transistor* (IGFET).

The operation of the MOSFET, or IGFET, is basically the same as the operation of the JFET. The current flow between the source and drain can be controlled by using either of two methods or by using a combination of the two methods. In one method the drain voltage controls the current when the gate potential is at zero volts. A voltage is applied to the gate in the second method. An electric field is formed by the gate voltage that affects the current flow in the channel by either depleting or enhancing the number of current carriers available. As previously stated, a reverse bias applied to

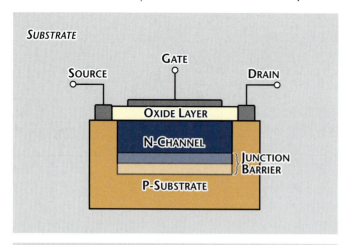
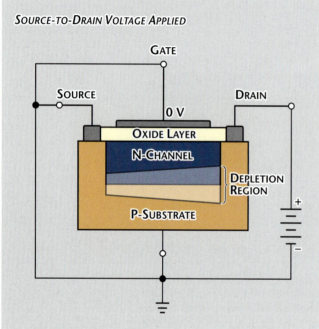
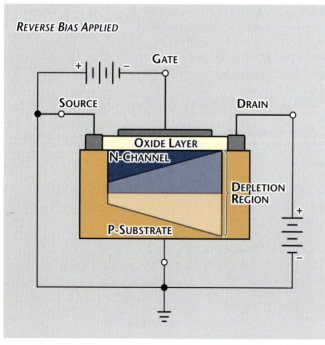

Figure 6-2-18. Effects of bias on N-channel depletion MOSFET

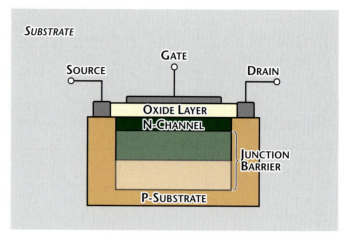
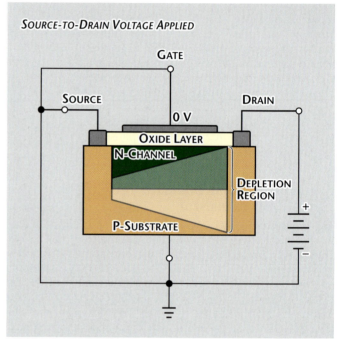
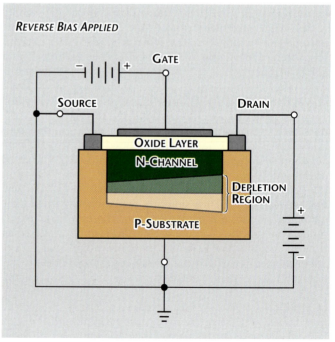

Figure 6-2-19. Effects of bias on N-channel enhancement MOSFET

the gate depletes the carriers, and a forward bias enhances the carriers. The polarity of the voltages required to forward or reverse bias a MOSFET depends upon whether it is of the P-channel type or the N-channel type. The effects of reverse-bias voltage on a MOSFET designed to operate in the depletion mode are illustrated in Figure 6-2-18. The amount of reverse bias applied has a direct effect on the width of the current channel and, thus, the amount of drain current (I_D).

Figure 6-2-19 illustrates the effect of forward bias on an enhancement-mode N-channel MOSFET. In this case, a positive voltage applied to the gate increases the width of the current channel and the amount of drain current (I_D).

Another type of MOSFET is the induced-channel MOSFET. Unlike the MOSFETs discussed so far, the induced-channel type has no actual channel between the source and the drain. The induced-channel MOSFET is constructed by making the channel of the same type of material as the substrate, or the opposite of the source and the drain material. As shown in Figure 6-2-20, the source and the drain are of P-type material, and the channel and the substrate are of N-type material.

The induced-channel MOSFET is caused to conduct from source to drain by the electric field that is created when a voltage is applied to the gate. For example, assume that a negative voltage is applied to the MOSFET in Figure 6-2-20. The effect of the negative voltage modifies the conditions in the substrate material. As the gate builds a negative charge, free electrons are repelled, forming a depletion region. Once a certain level of depletion has occurred (determined by the composition of the substrate material), any additional gate bias attracts positive holes to the surface of the substrate.

When enough holes have accumulated at the surface channel area, the channel changes from an N-type material to a P-type material, since it now has more positive carriers than negative carriers. At this point the channel is considered to be too inverted, and the two P-type regions at the source and the drain are now connected by a P-type inversion layer or channel. As with the MOSFET, the gate signal determines the amount of current flow through the channel as long as the source and drain voltages remain constant. When the gate voltage is at zero, essentially no current flows since a gate voltage is required to form a channel.

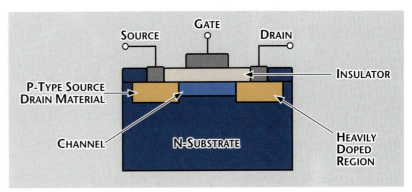

Figure 6-2-20. Induced channel MOSFET construction

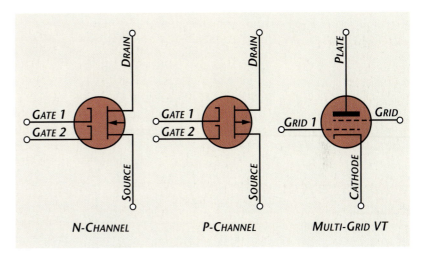

Figure 6-2-21. Dual-gate MOSFET

The MOSFETs discussed up to this point have been single-gate MOSFETs. Another type of MOSFET, the dual-gate type, is shown in Figure 6-2-21. As the figure shows, the gates in a dual-gate MOSFET can be compared to the grids in a multi-grid vacuum tube. Because the substrate has been connected directly to the source terminal, the dual-gate MOSFET still has only four leads: one each for source and drain, and two for the gates. Either gate can control conduction independently, making this type of MOSFET a truly versatile device.

One problem with both single- and dual-gate MOSFETs is that the oxide layer between gate and channel can be destroyed very easily by ordinary static electricity. Replacement MOSFETs come packaged with their leads shorted together by a special wire loop or spring to avoid accidental damage. The rule to remember with these shorting springs is that they must not be removed until after the MOSFET has been soldered or plugged into a circuit. One such spring is shown in Figure 6-2-22.

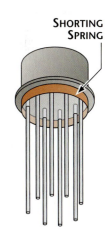

Figure 6-2-22. MOSFET shorting spring

7

Frequency Generation

How alternators produce a frequency for use in AC systems was discussed in chapter three. There are other types of circuitry that will produce a frequency, as well. Most of these systems are used in radar or radios. In this chapter simple oscillator circuitry, amplifiers, filters and wave shaping devices will be discussed.

Learning Objective

DESCRIBE
- types of oscillators
- filter circuits
- counting circuits

EXPLAIN
- how amplifiers are classified
- how limiters work
- integration and differentiation

APPLY
- read circuit diagrams and graph the outputs
- shape a circuit

Section 1

Amplifiers

Amplifiers are devices that provide amplification. That doesn't explain much, but it does describe an amplifier if it's known what amplification is and what it is used for. This section covers what amplifiers are, what amplification is and how it takes place.

Amplification

Just as an amplifier is a device that provides amplification, amplification is the process of providing an increase in *amplitude*. Amplitude is a term that describes the size of a signal. In terms of AC, amplitude usually refers to the amount of voltage or current. A 5-V peak-to-peak AC signal would be larger in amplitude than a 4-V peak-to-peak AC signal. *Signal* is a general term used to refer to any alternating or direct current of interest in a circuit (e.g., input signal and output signal). A signal can be large or small; AC or DC; a sine wave or nonsinusoidal; or even electric or nonelectrical such as sound or light.

Perhaps the concept of the relationship of amplifier-amplification-amplitude will be

Left. Frequency producing circuits, like this aviation radio circuit, are used extensively in modern aircraft.

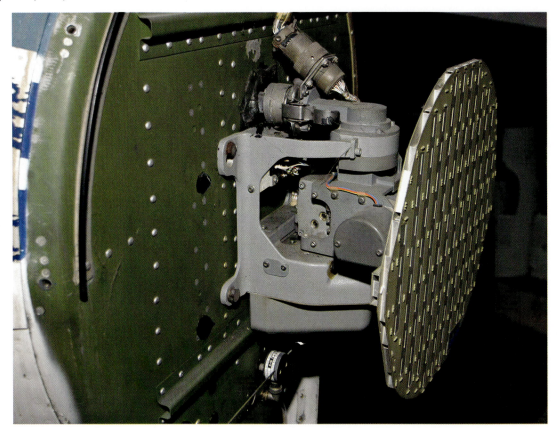
Figure 7-1-1. Radar antennas require power amplifiers for proper function

clarified by looking at a parallel situation. A magnifying glass is a magnifier. As such, it provides magnification, which is an increase in the magnitude (size) of an object. This relationship of magnifier-magnification-magnitude is the same as the relationship of amplifier-amplification-amplitude. The analogy is true in one other aspect as well. The magnifier does not change the object that is being magnified; only the image is larger, not the object itself. With the amplifier, the output signal differs in amplitude from the input signal, but the input signal still exists unchanged. So, the object (input signal) and the magnifier (amplifier) control the image (output signal).

An *amplifier* can be defined as a device that enables an input signal to control an output signal. The output signal will have some (or all) of the characteristics of the input signal but will generally be larger than the input signal in terms of voltage, current or power.

How Amplification Is Used

Most electronic devices use amplifiers to provide various amounts of signal amplification. Since most signals are originally too small to control or drive the desired device, some amplification is needed. For example, the audio signal taken from a digital recording is too small to drive a speaker, so amplification is needed. The signal will be amplified several times between the laser of the compact disc player and the speaker.

Each time the signal is amplified it is said to go through a stage of amplification. Almost every electronic device contains at least one stage of amplification, so amplifiers are present in many devices that technicians work on regularly.

Classification of Amplifiers

Most electronic devices use at least one amplifier, but there are many types of amplifiers. This chapter will not try to describe all the different types of amplifiers. Instead, the general principles of amplifiers and some typical amplifier circuits are covered.

Most amplifiers can be classified in two ways. The first classification is by their function. This means they are basically voltage amplifiers or power amplifiers. The second classification is by their frequency response. In other words, what frequencies are they designed to amplify?

If an amplifier is described by these two classifications (function and frequency response) the technician will have a good working description of the amplifier. The exact circuitry may not be known, but what the amplifier does and the frequencies that it is designed to handle will be understood.

Voltage Amplifiers and Power Amplifiers

All amplifiers are current-control devices. The input signal to an amplifier controls the current output of the amplifier. The connections of the amplifying device (electron tube, transistor, magnetic amplifier, etc.) and the circuitry of the amplifier determine the classification. Amplifiers are classified as voltage or power amplifiers.

Voltage amplifier. This is an amplifier in which the output signal voltage is larger than the input signal voltage. In other words, a voltage amplifier amplifies the voltage of the input signal.

Power amplifier. This an amplifier in which the output signal power is greater than the input signal power. In other words, a power amplifier amplifies the power of the input signal. Most power amplifiers are used as the final amplifier (stage of amplification) and control (or drive) the output device. The output device could be a speaker, an indicating device, or an an antenna (Figure 7-1-1). Whatever the device, the power to make it work comes from the final stage of amplification, which is a power amplifier.

The classification of an amplifier as a voltage or power amplifier is made by comparing the characteristics of the input and output signals. If the output signal is larger in voltage amplitude than the input signal, the amplifier is a voltage amplifier. If there is no voltage gain, but the output power is greater than the input power, the amplifier is a power amplifier.

Transistor Amplifiers

A transistor amplifier (Figure 7-1-2) is a current-control device. The current in the base of the transistor (which is dependent on the emitter-base bias) controls the current in the collector. A vacuum-tube amplifier is also a current-control device. The grid bias controls the plate current.

Some will say that a vacuum tube (Figure 7-1-3) is a voltage-operated device (since the grid does not need to draw current) while the transistor is a current-operated device. While there is truth to this statement, both the vacuum tube and the transistor are still current-control devices. The whole secret to understanding amplifiers is to remember that fact. Current control is the name of the game. Once current is controlled the designer can use it to create a voltage gain or a power gain.

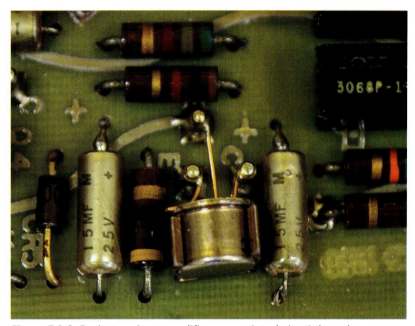

Figure 7-1-2. Basic transistor amplifier on a printed circuit board

Classes of Amplifiers

The class of operation of an amplifier is determined by the amount of time (in relation to the input signal) that current flows in the output circuit. This is a function of the operating point of the amplifying device. The operating point of the amplifying device is determined by the bias applied to the device. There are four classes of operation for an amplifier: A, AB, B and C. Each class of operation has certain uses and characteristics. No one class of operation is "better" than any other class. The selection of the "best" class of operation is determined by the use of the amplifying circuit. The best class of operation for a CD player is not the best class for a radio transmitter.

Figure 7-1-3. Transistor operation is similar to vacuum tube operation

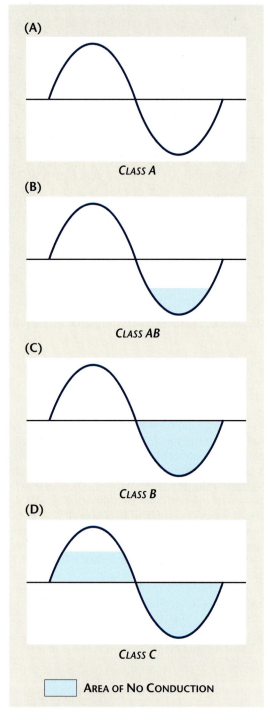

Figure 7-1-4. A comparison of output signals for the different amplifier classes of operation

Class A amplifiers. A simple transistor amplifier that is operating Class A is one that amplifies 100 percent of the input signal (Figure 7-1-4A). Since the output signal is a 100-percent (or 360°) copy of the input signal, current in the output circuit must flow for 100 percent of the input signal time. This is the definition of a Class A amplifier: amplifier current flows for 100 percent of the input signal.

The Class A amplifier has good fidelity and low efficiency. *Fidelity* means that the output signal is just like the input signal in all respects except amplitude. It has the same shape and frequency. In some cases, there may be a phase difference between the input and output signal (usually 180°), but the signals are still considered to be "good copies." If the output signal is not like the input signal in shape or frequency, the signal is said to be distorted. Distortion is any undesired change in a signal from input to output.

The *efficiency* of an amplifier refers to the amount of power delivered to the output compared to the power supplied to the circuit. Since every device takes power to operate, if the amplifier operates for 360° of input signal, it uses more power than if it only operates for 180° of input signal. If the amplifier uses more power, less power is available for the output signal and efficiency is lower. Since Class A amplifiers operate (i.e., have current flow) for 360° of input signal, they are low in efficiency. This low efficiency is acceptable in Class A amplifiers because they are used where efficiency is not as important as fidelity.

Class AB amplifiers. If the amplifying device is biased in such a way that current flows in the device for 51 to 99 percent of the input signal, the amplifier is operating Class AB (Figure 7-1-4B).

The output signal no longer has the same shape as the input signal. The portion of the output signal that appears to be cut off is caused by the lack of current through the transistor. When the emitter becomes positive enough, the transistor cannot conduct because the base-to-emitter junction is no longer forward biased. Any further increase in input signal will not cause an increase in output signal voltage.

Class AB amplifiers (Figure 7-1-5) have better efficiency and poorer fidelity than Class A amplifiers. They are used when the output signal need not be a complete reproduction of the input signal, but both positive and negative portions of the input signal must be available at the output.

Class AB amplifiers are usually defined as amplifiers operating between Class A and Class B because Class A amplifiers operate on 100 percent of the input signal and Class B amplifiers (discussed next) operate on 50 percent of the input signal. Any amplifier operating between these two limits is operating Class AB.

Class B amplifiers. As stated above, a Class B amplifier operates for 50 percent of the input signal (Figure 7-1-4C). The base-emitter bias in a Class B amplifier will not allow the transistor to conduct whenever the input signal becomes positive. Therefore, only the negative portion of the input signal is reproduced in the output signal. Why use a Class B amplifier instead of a simple rectifier if only half the input signal is desired in the output? The answer is that a rectifier does not amplify. The output signal of a rectifier cannot be higher in amplitude than the input signal. The Class B amplifier not only reproduces half the input signal, but amplifies it as well.

Class B amplifiers are twice as efficient as Class A amplifiers since the amplifying device only conducts (and uses power) for half of the input signal. Class B amplifiers are used in cases where exactly 50 percent of the input signal must be amplified. If less than 50 percent of the input signal is needed, a Class C amplifier is used.

Class C amplifiers. In a simple Class C amplifier only a small portion of the input signal is actually amplified (Figure 7-1-4D). Since the transistor does not conduct except during a small portion of the input signal, this is the most efficient amplifier. It also has the worst fidelity. The output signal bears very little resemblance to the input signal.

Class C amplifiers are used where the output signal need only be present during part of one-half of the input signal. Any amplifier that operates on less than 50 percent of the input signal is operated Class C.

Impedance and Amplifiers

As previously discussed, efficiency and impedance are important in amplifiers. The reasons for this may not be clear. It has been shown that every amplifier is a current-control device. Now there are two other principles to keep in mind. First, there is no such thing as "something for nothing" in electronics. That means every time something is done to a signal, it costs something. It might mean a loss in fidelity to get high power. Some other compromise might also be made when a circuit is designed.

Regardless of the compromise, every stage will require and use power. This brings up the second principle: Do things as efficiently as possible. The improvement and design of electronic circuits is an attempt to do things as cheaply as possible, in terms of power, when all the other requirements (fidelity, power output, frequency range, etc.) have been met.

This brings the third principle: efficiency. The most efficient device is the one that does the job with the least loss of power. One of the largest losses of power is caused by impedance differences between the output of one circuit and the input of the next circuit. Perhaps the best

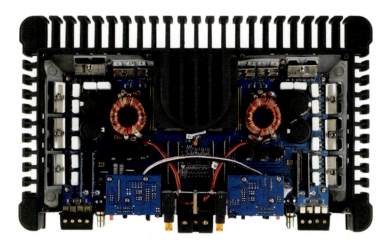

Figure 7-1-5. Most modern audio amplifier designs employ Class AB topology. Quality is similar to that of Class A, while efficiency is comparable to Class B.

way to think of an impedance difference (mismatch) between circuits is to think of different-sized water pipes. If a one-inch water pipe is connected to a two-inch water pipe without an adapter, significant quantities of water will be lost. An adapter is required for proper operation. An impedance-matching device is like that adapter. It allows the connection of two devices with different impedances without the loss of power.

Two important points to remember about impedance matching are as follows.

- Maximum power transfer requires matched impedance.
- To get maximum voltage at the input of a circuit requires an intentional impedance mismatch with the circuit that is providing the input signal.

Amplifier Feedback

Occasionally a public address system will emit a squeal or high-pitched noise from the speaker. Someone will turn down the volume and the noise will stop. That noise is an indication that the amplifier (at least one stage of amplification) has begun oscillating. For now, the important thing is to realize that the oscillation is caused by a small part of the signal from the amplifier output being sent back to the input of the amplifier. This signal

7-6 | Frequency Generation

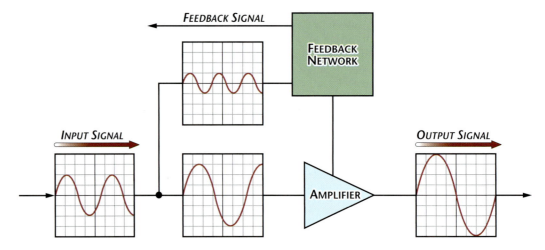

Figure 7-1-6. Positive feedback in an amplifier

is amplified and again sent back to the input where it is amplified again. This process continues and the result is a loud noise out of the speaker. The cycle in which part of the output signal of an amplifier is sent back to the input of the amplifier is called *feedback*.

There are two types of feedback in amplifiers: positive feedback, also called regenerative feedback; and negative feedback, also called degenerative feedback. The difference between these two types is whether the feedback signal is in phase or out of phase with the input signal.

Sometimes feedback that is not desired occurs in an amplifier. This happens at high frequencies and limits the high-frequency response of an amplifier. Unwanted feedback also occurs as the result of some circuit components used in the biasing or coupling network. The usual solution to unwanted feedback is a feedback network of the opposite type. For example, a positive feedback network would counteract unwanted, negative feedback.

Feedback is also used to get the ideal input signal. Normally, the maximum output signal is desired from an amplifier. The amount of the output signal from an amplifier is dependent on the amount of the input signal. However, if the input signal is too large, the amplifying device will be saturated or cut off during part of the input signal. This causes the output signal to be distorted and reduces the fidelity of the amplifier. Amplifiers must provide the proper balance of gain and fidelity.

Positive feedback (Figure 7-1-6). Positive feedback is accomplished by adding part of the output signal in phase to the input signal. In

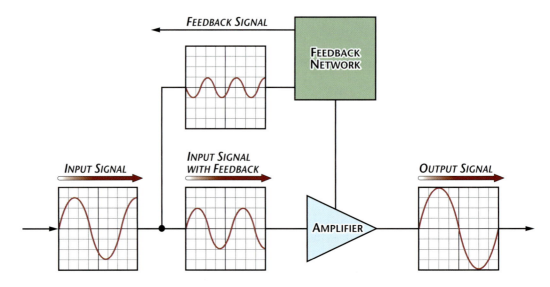

Figure 7-1-7. Negative feedback in an amplifier

a common-base transistor amplifier, it is fairly simple to provide positive feedback. Since the input and output signals are in phase, the technician need only couple part of the output signal back to the input.

Negative feedback (Figure 7-1-7). Negative feedback is accomplished by adding part of the output signal out of phase to the input signal. It has been demonstrated that an emitter resistor in a common-emitter transistor amplifier will develop a negative feedback signal. Other methods of providing negative feedback are similar to those methods used to provide positive feedback. The phase relationship of the feedback signal and the input signal is the only difference.

Section 2

Oscillators

An oscillator (Figure 7-2-1) is a device that converts a DC input into an output with a wave, sometimes similar to that of an AC voltage. The oscillator can be classified into two broad categories in accordance with their output wave: sinusoidal and nonsinusoidal.

Sinusoidal Oscillators

The output of this type of oscillator is an AC sine wave (Figure 7-2-2). The sine wave will have constant amplitude with no variation from its assigned frequency. To get to this ideal state, there are certain factors that must be depended on:

- Class of amplifier operation
- Amplifier characteristics
- Frequency stability
- Amplitude stability

Oscillators can produce many different frequencies, ranging from low audio frequencies to ultra-high radio and microwave frequencies. To produce these different ranges there are three types of oscillators:

- RC oscillator—By the use of a resistor and capacitor, an RC oscillator is able to produce low audio frequencies. The combination of the resistor and capacitor form a frequency determining network.

- LC oscillator—This type of oscillator uses inductors and capacitors to form what is

Figure 7-2-1. Crystal oscillator on circuit board

called a tank circuit. This type of configuration is widely used in radios because of its capability to be used in the higher frequencies. Unfortunately they are not ideal to use for lower frequencies because of cost and size.

- Crystal-controlled oscillator—A very versatile type of oscillator with excellent frequency stability. The crystal-controlled type is often used from middle-range frequencies to the radio frequency range.

All three types of oscillators will be talked about in length later in this section.

Nonsinusoidal Oscillators

These types of oscillators will produce complex wave forms at their output. A complex wave

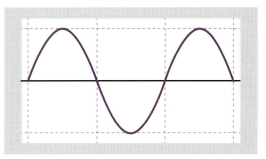

Figure 7-2-2. AC sine wave

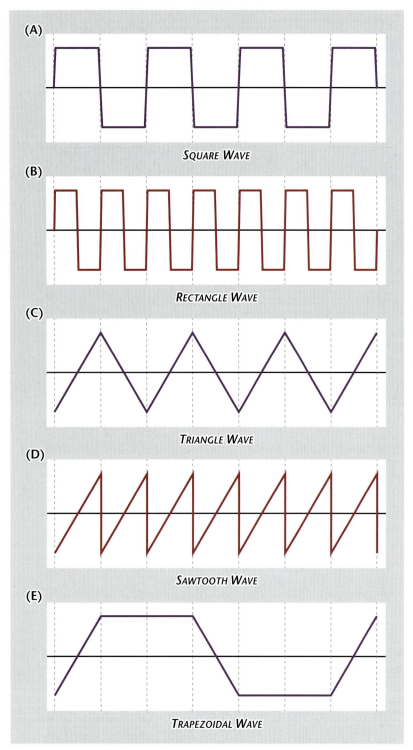

Figure 7-2-3. Nonsinusoidal waves

form comes in a variety of different forms as seen in Figure 7-2-3:

- Square waves
- Rectangular waves
- Triangle waves
- Sawtooth waves
- Trapezoidal waves

These are all known as complex wave forms because their outputs are generally characterized by a sudden change, or relaxation.

The oscillators used to create these wave forms are commonly referred to as *relaxation oscillators*. The signals of these oscillators are governed by the charge and discharge time of a capacitor in series with a resistor. The oscillator may also include an inductor to help with the output frequency.

Like sinusoidal oscillators, the RC and LC networks are used for determining the frequency of oscillation. Within the category of nonsinusoidal oscillators are multivibrators, blocking oscillators, sawtooth generators and trapezoidal generators.

Basic Oscillators

An oscillator can be thought of as an amplifier that provides itself with an input signal. It could be said that an oscillator is a non-rotating device for producing an AC current. The primary purpose of the oscillator is to generate a given wave form at a constant peak amplitude and specific frequency to maintain the wave form within its limits.

Oscillators must provide amplification. The amplification of the power signal occurs from the input to the output. In an oscillator, some of the output is fed back to sustain the input. Enough power must be fed back to the input circuitry for the oscillator to drive itself, like a signal generator.

To cause the oscillator to become self-driven, the feedback signal must also be regenerative, or positive. These regenerative signals must have a high enough power to compensate for any losses and maintain oscillation.

Since the oscillator will produce a predetermined frequency, a frequency determining device must be installed into the circuitry. This device will act as a filter, only letting the desired frequency pass. Without this device, the output frequency would be random rather than constant.

Every piece of equipment that uses oscillators has two basic requirements:

- Amplitude stability—This refers to the capability of the oscillator to maintain a constant amplitude output wave form.
- Frequency stability—This refers to the ability of the oscillator to maintain its operating frequency.

A constant frequency and amplitude can be achieved by taking care to prevent variations in

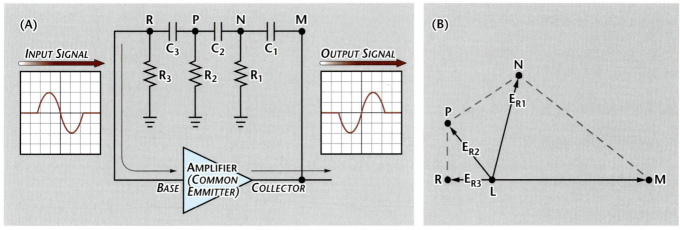

Figure 7-2-4. RC oscillator; (A) Amplifier with an RC feedback network, (B) Vector analysis

load, bias and component characteristics. Load variations can affect amplitude and frequency stability. For this reason, it is always important to keep the load as constant as possible.

Remember how bias variations can affect the operating point of the transistor. These variations can also affect the amplitude capabilities of the oscillator. To help overcome this effect, a regulated power supply and bias stabilizing circuit is required to keep a constant output

Changes in temperature and humidity can change the value of the internal components of the oscillator. This change will affect the output of the oscillator. For this reason, built-in fans and vents must be kept clean to help regulate the atmosphere in the oscillator.

The output power of the oscillator is another factor that must be considered. Generally, high power is obtained at some sacrifice to the stability of the oscillator. When requirements are met, the low-power stable output from the oscillator can be then sent to a higher-powered buffer amplifier. This amplifier will provide isolation between the oscillator and the load.

Sine-Wave Oscillators

RC networks, LC tanks and crystals may appear in the sine-wave oscillator circuit. An amplifier can be made into a sine-wave oscillator if there is a regenerative feedback through an RC network. The next few subsections discuss the three oscillator circuits in more detail.

RC Network

A basic block diagram of an RC network with a regenerative feedback is shown in Figure 7-2-4. To analyze the operation of the circuit, assume that the amplifier is in a common-emitter configuration. The signal from point M will be 180° out of phase with the input to the base of the amplifier. For the circuit to produce regenerative feedback, the RC network must provide a 180° phase shift of the collector signal. When power is applied to the circuit, a noise voltage (noise contains many different frequencies) will appear on the collector. This noise signal is represented by vector LM in Figure 7-2-4B.

As the signal couples through C_1 and across R_1 (Figure 7-2-4A), a phase shift occurs. The voltage across R_1 (E_{R1}), represented by vector LN, has been shifted in phase (about 60°) and reduced in amplitude. The signal at point N (Figure 7-2-4A) is then coupled to the next RC section (R_2 and C_2). Using the same size resistor and capacitor as before will cause another 60° phase shift to take place. The signal at point P is the voltage across R_2, represented by vector LP. Now the signal at point P has been shifted about 120° and its amplitude is reduced still further.

The same actions occur for the last section (R_3 and C_3). This signal experiences another 60° phase shift and has further amplitude reduction. The signal at point R (E_{R3}) has been shifted 180° and is represented by vector LR. Notice that point R is the input to the base of the common-emitter amplifier. Also, vector LR shows that the signal on the base is regenerative (aiding the circuit operation). This meets the regenerative feedback requirement. An exact 60° phase shift per stage is not required, but the sum of the three phase shifts must equal 180°.

For a given RC network, only one frequency of the initial noise signal will be shifted exactly 180°. In other words, the network is frequency selective. Therefore, the RC network is the frequency determining device since the lengths of the vectors and their phase relationships depend on frequency. The frequency

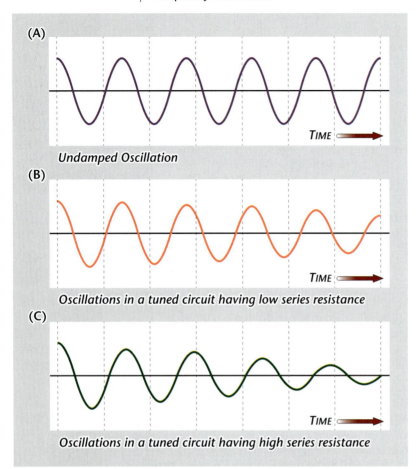

Figure 7-2-5. Effects of damping

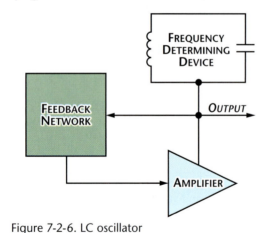

Figure 7-2-6. LC oscillator

Figure 7-2-7. A quartz crystal enclosed in a sealed package. The frequency is marked on the unit.

of oscillations is governed by the values of resistance and capacitance in these sections. Variable resistors and capacitors may be used to provide tuning in the feedback network to allow for minor variations in phase shift. For an RC phase-shift oscillator, the amplifier is biased for Class A operation to minimize distortion of the wave or signal.

LC Network

Some sine-wave oscillators use resonant circuits consisting of inductance and capacitance. In an LC tank circuit, a capacitor and inductor are connected to each other in series. Off to the side of the capacitor will be the input voltage. Once the capacitor is charged from the input voltage, the capacitor will discharge and send the voltage to the inductor. The inductor will then store the voltage in an electromagnetic field, which expands until it reaches the peak of the voltage. Once the peak is reached, the magnetic field will collapse on itself. During this process, the polarity of the voltage has reversed and the reversed voltage is then sent back to the capacitor, where the process is repeated all over again.

If there were absolutely no internal resistances in a tank circuit, oscillations would continue indefinitely as shown in Figure 7-2-5A. Each resonant circuit does, however, contain some resistance that dissipates power. This power loss causes the amplitude to decrease, as shown in Figure 7-2-5B and Figure 7-2-5C. The reduction of amplitude in an oscillator circuit is referred to as *damping*. Damping is caused by both tank and load resistances. The larger the tank resistance, the greater the amount of damping. Loading the tank causes the same effect as increasing the internal resistance of the tank. The effect of this damping can be overcome by applying regenerative feedback.

Figure 7-2-6 shows a block diagram of a typical LC oscillator. Notice that the oscillator contains the three basic requirements for sustained oscillations: amplification, a frequency-determining device and regenerative feedback.

The amplifier supplies energy to begin what is known as the *flywheel effect*. The flywheel effect is the maintenance of oscillations in a circuit in the intervals between pulses of excitation energy. The LC network provides initial oscillations. A portion of the output of the LC network is then returned to the input of the amplifier through the regenerative feedback network to sustain the oscillations. When a tank circuit is used to develop oscillations in an oscillator, the output frequency of the oscillator is primarily the resonant frequency

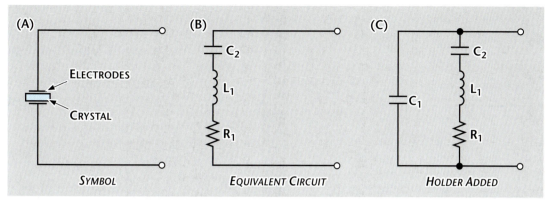

Figure 7-2-8. Crystal symbol and equivalent circuits

Figure 7-2-10. Tickler coil

of the tank circuit and can be found by the formula:

$$F_r = 1 \div 2\pi \sqrt{LC}$$

Crystals

Another frequency-determining device is the crystal (Figure 7-2-7). The crystal may be used with a tank circuit, or it may perform alone. Crystals exhibit a characteristic known as the *piezoelectric effect*. The piezoelectric effect is the property of a crystal by which mechanical forces produce electrical charges and, conversely, electrical charges produce mechanical forces. This effect is a form of oscillation similar to the flywheel effect in a tank circuit. The piezoelectric effect can be seen in a number of crystal substances. The most important of these are the minerals quartz and Rochelle salt (potassium sodium tartrate). Although quartz does not exhibit the piezoelectric effect to the degree that Rochelle salt does, quartz is used for frequency control in oscillators because of its greater mechanical strength. Another mineral, tourmaline, is physically strong like quartz; but used less frequently because it is more expensive.

The crystals used in oscillator circuits are thin sheets, or wafers, cut from natural or synthetic quartz and ground to a specific thickness to obtain the desired resonant frequency. The crystals are mounted in holders, which support them physically and provide electrodes by which voltage is applied. The holder must allow the crystals freedom for vibration. There are many different types of holders.

The frequency for which a crystal is ground is referred to as the *natural resonant frequency* of the crystal. Voltage applied to the crystal produces mechanical vibrations, which, in turn, produce an output voltage at the natural resonant frequency of the crystal. A vibrating crystal can be represented by an equivalent electrical circuit composed of capacitance, inductance and resistance.

Figure 7-2-8A, illustrates the symbol of a crystal; Figure 7-2-8B shows an equivalent circuit for the crystal. Figure 7-2-8C shows an equivalent circuit for the crystal and the holder; C_1 represents the capacitance between the metal plates of the holder.

Types of Feedback

The feedback signal is coupled from the circuit by two methods. The first method is to take some of the energy from the inductor. This can be done by any one of the three ways (Figure 7-2-9A, Figure 7-2-9B, Figure 7-2-9C,). When an oscillator uses a tickler coil (Figure 7-2-10) it is referred to as an *Armstrong oscillator*. When an oscillator uses a tapped coil or a split coil it is referred to as a *Hartley oscillator*.

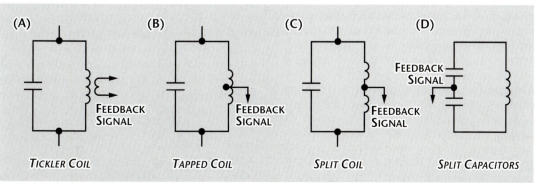

Figure 7-2-9. Feedback signals

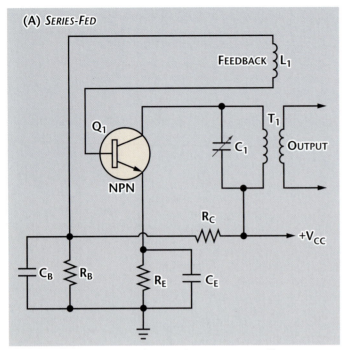
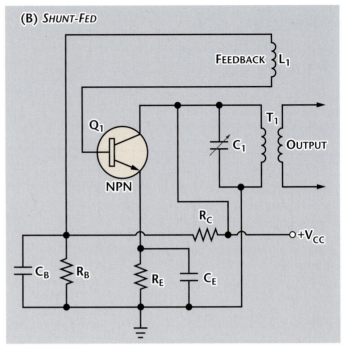

Figure 7-2-11. Series and shunt-fed Armstrong oscillators

The second method of coupling the feedback signal is to use two capacitors in the tank circuit and tap the feedback signal between them (Figure 7-2-9D). An oscillator using this method is referred to as a *Colpitts oscillator*. Each of these particular oscillators is named after the person who originally designed them.

Transistor Configuration

As discussed earlier, there are three configurations to transistors: common emitter, common collector and common base. Certain considerations in the application of the circuit, such as the operating frequency and output power required, usually determine which of the three configurations is to be used.

Common emitter. The common-emitter configuration has high power gain and is used in low-frequency applications. For the energy that is fed back from the output to be in phase with the energy at the input, the feedback network of a common-emitter oscillator must provide a phase shift of approximately 180°. An advantage of the common-emitter configuration is that the medium resistance range of the input and output simplifies the job of impedance matching.

Common collector. Since there is no phase reversal between the input and output circuits of a common-collector configuration, the feedback network does not need to provide a phase shift. However, since the voltage gain is less than unity and the power gain is low, the common-collector configuration is very seldom used in oscillator circuits.

Common base. The power gain and voltage gain of the common-base configuration are high enough to give satisfactory operation in an oscillator circuit. The wide range between the input resistance and the output resistance make impedance matching slightly harder to achieve in the common-base circuit than in the common-emitter circuit. An advantage of the common-base configuration is that it exhibits better high-frequency response than does the common-emitter configuration.

Oscillator Circuits

Oscillators may be classified by name, such as Armstrong, Hartley, Colpitts, or by the man-

Figure 7-2-12. Oscillator circuit

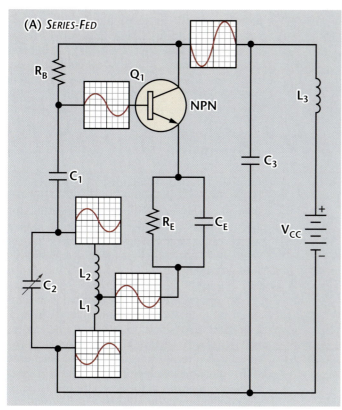
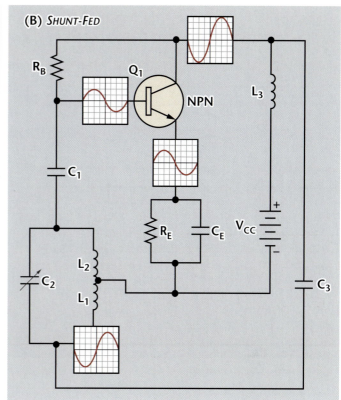

Figure 7-2-13. Series and shunt-fed Hartley oscillators

ner in which DC power is applied. An oscillator in which DC power is supplied to the transistor through the tank circuit, or a portion of the tank circuit, is said to be *series fed* (Figure 7-2-11A). An oscillator that receives its DC power for the transistor through a path separate and parallel to the tank circuit is said to be *parallel fed* or *shunt fed* (Figure 7-2-11B). All the oscillators in this chapter can be constructed either way, series or shunt fed. The construction depends on the characteristics of the oscillator circuit the designer is interested in. An example of an oscillator circuit is pictured in Figure 7-2-12.

A series-fed, tuned-collector Armstrong oscillator is illustrated in Figure 7-2-11A. The DC path is from the negative side (ground) of V_{CC} through RE, Q_1, T_1, and back to the positive side of V_{CC}. The figure clearly illustrates that both the AC and DC components flow through the tank circuit.

By modifying the circuit slightly, it becomes a shunt-fed, tuned-collector Armstrong oscillator as shown in Figure 7-2-11B. The DC component flows from ground through RE to Q_1 to positive V_{CC}. The DC is blocked from the tank circuit by capacitor C_2. Only the AC component flows in the tank circuit.

Armstrong Oscillator

The Armstrong oscillator is used to produce a sine-wave output of constant amplitude and of fairly constant frequency within the RF range. It is generally used as a local oscillator in receivers; as a source in signal generators; and as a radio-frequency oscillator in the medium- and high-frequency range. The identifying characteristics of the Armstrong oscillator are:

- It uses an LC tuned circuit to establish the frequency of oscillation.
- Feedback is accomplished by mutual inductive coupling between the tickler coil and the LC tuned circuit.
- It uses a Class C amplifier with self-bias.
- Its frequency is fairly stable, and the output amplitude is relatively constant.

Hartley Oscillator

The Hartley oscillator is an improvement over the Armstrong oscillator. Although its frequency stability is not the best possible of all the oscillators, the Hartley oscillator can generate a wide range of frequencies and is very easy to tune. The Hartley will operate Class C with self-bias for ordinary operation. It will operate Class A when the output waveform must be of a constant voltage level or of a linear wave shape.

There are two versions of this oscillator: the series fed (Figure 7-2-13A) and the shunt fed

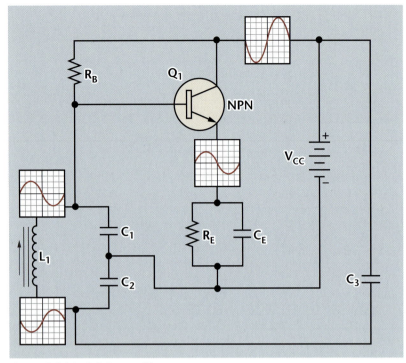

Figure 7-2-14. Colpitts oscillator

because of junction capacitance. In comparison, the Colpitts oscillator (Figure 7-2-14) has fairly good frequency stability, is easy to tune, and can be used for a wide range of frequencies. The large value of split capacitance is in parallel with the junctions and minimizes the effect on frequency stability.

Harmonics

From the study of oscillators, it was shown that the oscillator will oscillate at the resonant frequency of the tank circuit. Although the tank circuit is resonant at a particular frequency, many other frequencies are present in the oscillator. These other frequencies are referred to as harmonics.

A *harmonic* is defined as a sinusoidal wave having a frequency that is a multiple of the fundamental frequency. In other words, a sine wave that is twice that of the fundamental frequency is referred to as the second harmonic. It is important to remember that the current in circuits operating at the resonant frequency is relatively large in amplitude.

(Figure 7-2-13B). The main difference between the Armstrong and the Hartley oscillators lies in the design of the feedback (tickler) coil. A separate coil is not used. Instead, in the Hartley oscillator, the coil in the tank circuit is a split inductor. Current flow through one section induces a voltage in the other section to develop a feedback signal.

Colpitts Oscillator

Both the Armstrong and the Hartley oscillators have a tendency to be unstable in frequency

The harmonic frequency amplitudes are relatively small. For example, the second harmonic of a fundamental frequency has only 20 percent of the amplitude of the resonant frequency. A third harmonic has perhaps 10 percent of the amplitude of the fundamental frequency.

One useful purpose of harmonics is frequency multiplication. It can be used in circuits to multiply the fundamental frequency to a higher frequency. The need for frequency-multiplier circuits results from the fact that the frequency stability of most oscillators decreases as frequency increases. Relatively good stability can be achieved at the lower frequencies. Thus, to achieve optimum stability, an oscillator is operated at a low frequency, and one or more stages of multiplication are used to raise the signal to the desired operating frequency.

Frequency Multiplication

Frequency multipliers are special Class C amplifiers that are biased at 3 to 10 times the normal cutoff bias. They are used to generate a frequency that is a multiple (harmonic) of a lower frequency. Such circuits are called frequency multipliers or harmonic generators.

One type of frequency multiplier is known as a frequency doubler (Figure 7-2-15) or second harmonic generator. The multiplier input could be 1 MHz and the output is 2 MHz, or twice the input frequency. In other words, the sec-

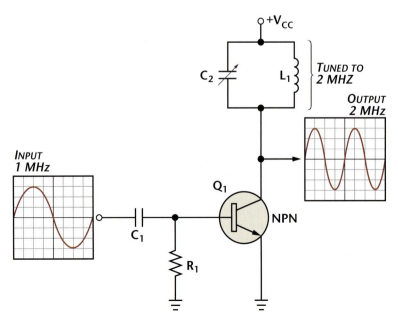

Figure 7-2-15. Frequency doubler

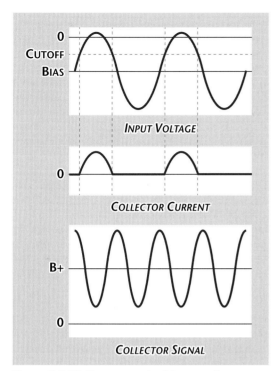

Figure 7-2-16. Frequency doubler waveforms

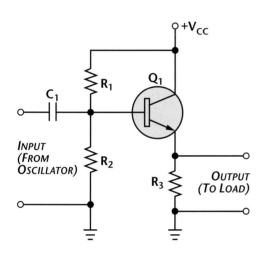

Figure 7-2-17. Buffer amplifier

ond harmonic of 1 MHz is 2 MHz. The third harmonic (frequency tripler) would be 3 MHz, or three times the input signal. The fourth harmonic (quadruplet) would be 4 MHz, or four times the 1-MHz input signal. The fourth harmonic generator (frequency quadruplet) is normally as high in multiplication as is practical, because at harmonics higher than the fourth, the output signal becomes very weak.

Frequency multipliers are operated by the pulses of collector current produced by a Class C amplifier. Although the collector current flows in pulses, the AC voltage is sinusoidal because of the action of the tank circuit. When the output tank circuit is tuned to the required harmonic, the tank circuit acts as a filter, accepting the desired frequency and rejecting all others.

Figure 7-2-16 illustrates the waveforms in a typical doubler circuit. The illustration shows that the pulses of collector current are the same frequency as the input signal. These pulses of collector current energize the tank circuit and cause it to oscillate at twice the base-signal frequency. Between the pulses of collector current, the tank circuit continues to oscillate. Therefore, the tank circuit receives a current pulse for every other cycle of its output.

Buffer Amplifier

Coupling the resonant frequency from the oscillator by different coupling methods also affects the oscillator frequency and amplitude. A *buffer amplifier* decreases the loading effect on the oscillator by reducing the interaction (matching impedance) between the load and the oscillator.

Figure 7-2-17 is the schematic diagram of a buffer amplifier. This circuit is a common-collector amplifier. A common-collector amplifier has a high input impedance and a low output impedance. Since the output of an oscillator is connected to the high impedance of the common-collector amplifier, the buffer has little effect on the operation of the oscillator. The output of the common-collector buffer is then connected to an external load; therefore, the changes in the output load cannot reflect back to the oscillator circuit. Thus, the buffer amplifier reduces interaction between the load and the oscillator.

Section 3

Filters

While the output of a rectifier is a pulsating DC, most electronic circuits require a substantially pure DC for proper operation. This type of output is provided by single- or multi-section filter circuits placed between the output of the rectifier and the load.

There are four basic types of filter circuits:

- Simple capacitor filter
- LC choke-input filter
- RC capacitor-input filter (pi-type)
- LC capacitor-input filter (pi-type)

7-16 | Frequency Generation

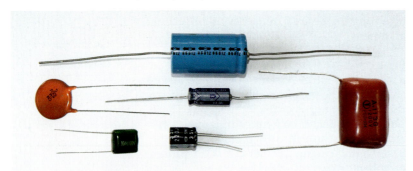

Figure 7-3-1. Capacitors

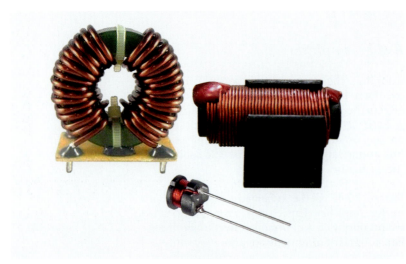

Figure 7-3-2. Inductors

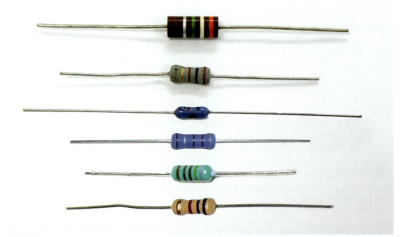

Figure 7-3-3. Resistors

Filtering is accomplished by the use of capacitors (Figure 7-3-1), inductors (Figure 7-3-2) and resistors (Figure 7-3-3) in various combinations. Inductors are used as series impedances to oppose the flow of alternating (pulsating DC) current. Capacitors are used as shunt elements to bypass the alternating components of the signal around the load (to ground). Resistors are used in place of inductors in low-current applications.

Let's briefly review the properties of a capacitor. First, a capacitor opposes any change in voltage. The opposition to a change in current is called capacitive reactance (X_C) and is measured in ohms. The capacitive reactance is determined by the frequency (f) of the applied voltage and the capacitance (C) of the capacitor.

$$X_C = 1 \div 2\pi fC$$
or
$$0.159 \div fC$$

The formula shows that if frequency or capacitance is increased, the X_C decreases. Since filter capacitors are placed in parallel with the load, a low X_C will provide better filtering than a high X_C. For this to be accomplished, a better shunting effect of the AC around the load is provided, as shown in Figure 7-3-4.

To obtain a steady DC output, the capacitor must charge almost instantaneously to the value of applied voltage. Once charged, the capacitor must retain the charge as long as possible. The capacitor must have a short charge time constant (Figure 7-3-4A). This can be accomplished by keeping the internal resistance of the power supply as small as possible (fast charge time) and the resistance of the load as large as possible (for a slow discharge time), as illustrated in Figure 7-3-4B.

From the earlier studies in basic electricity, remember that one time constant is defined as the time it takes a capacitor to charge to

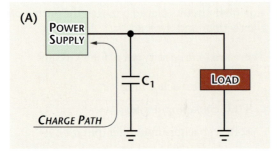 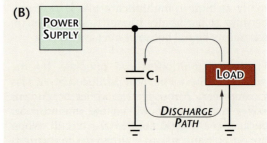

Figure 7-3-4. Fast charge and slow discharge capacitor filters

63.2 percent of the applied voltage or to discharge to 36.8 percent of its total charge. This action can be expressed by the following equation:

t = RC

Where R represents the resistance of the charge or discharge path and C represents the capacitance of the capacitor.

Remember that a capacitor is considered fully charged after five RC time constants (Figure 7-3-5). A steady DC output voltage is obtained when the capacitor charges rapidly and discharges as slowly as possible.

In filter circuits the capacitor is the common element to both the charge and the discharge paths. Therefore, to obtain the longest possible discharge time, the capacitor should be as large as possible. Another way to look at it: The capacitor acts as a short circuit around the load (as far as the AC component is concerned), and since the larger the value of the capacitor (C), the smaller the opposition (X_C) or reactance to AC.

$X_C = 1 \div 2\pi fC$

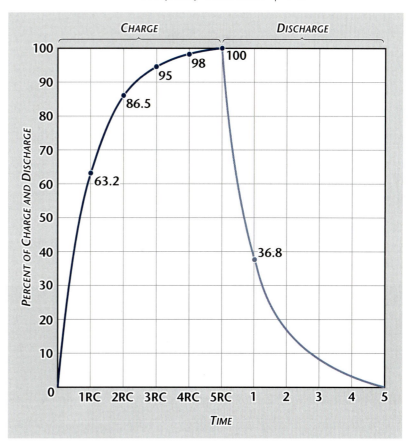

Figure 7-3-5. RC time constant

Now examine inductors and their application in filter circuits. Remember that an inductor opposes any change in current, and that a change in current through an inductor produces a changing electromagnetic field. The changing field, in turn, cuts the windings of the wire in the inductor and thereby produces a counter electromotive force (cemf). It is the cemf that opposes the change in circuit current. Opposition to a change in current at a given frequency is called inductive reactance (X_L) and is measured in ohms. The inductive reactance (X_L) of an inductor is determined by the applied frequency and the inductance of the inductor.

$X_L = 2\pi fL$

If frequency or inductance is increased, the X_L increases. Since inductors are placed in series with the load (Figure 7-3-6), the larger the X_L, the larger the AC voltage developed across the load.

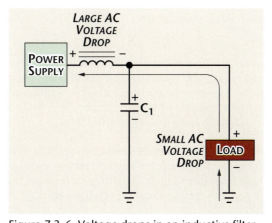

Figure 7-3-6. Voltage drops in an inductive filter

Now refer to Figure 7-3-7. When the current starts to flow through the coil, an expanding magnetic field builds up around the inductor. This magnetic field around the coil develops the cemf that opposes the change in current. When the rectifier current decreases, as shown

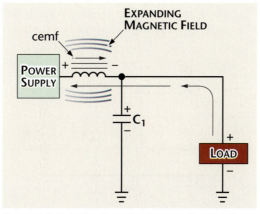

Figure 7-3-7. Inductive filter (expanding field).

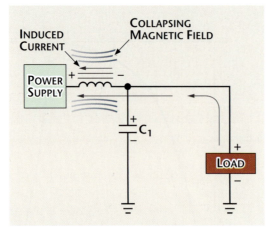

Figure 7-3-8. Inductive filter (collapsing field)

Figure 7-3-9. Most aircraft fuel pump motors use an internal capacitor filter.

in Figure 7-3-8, the magnetic field collapses and again cuts the turns (windings) of wire, thus inducing current into the coil. This additional current merges with the rectifier current and attempts to keep it at its original level.

Building on the understanding of how the components in a filter circuit react to current flow from the rectifier, the different types of filter circuits in use today will be discussed.

Capacitor Filters

The simple capacitor filter (Figure 7-3-9) is the most basic type of power supply filter. Its application is very limited. It is sometimes used on extremely high-voltage, low-current power supplies for cathode-ray and similar electron tubes, which require very little load current from the supply. The capacitor filter is also used where the power supply ripple frequency is not critical; this frequency can be relatively high. The capacitor (C_1) shown in Figure 7-3-10 is a simple filter connected across the output of the rectifier in parallel with the load.

When this filter is used, the RC charge time of the filter capacitor (C_1) must be short and the RC discharge time must be long to eliminate ripple action. In other words, the capacitor must charge up fast, preferably with no discharge at all. Better filtering also results when the input frequency is high; therefore, the full-wave rectifier output is easier to filter than that of the half-wave rectifier because of its higher frequency.

To have a better understanding of the effect that filtering has on E_{avg}, a comparison of a rectifier circuit with a filter and one without a filter is illustrated in Figure 7-3-11A and Figure 7-3-11B. The output waveforms in the diagram represent the unfiltered and filtered outputs of the half-wave rectifier circuit. Current pulses flow through the load resistance (R_L) each time a diode conducts. The dashed line indicates the average value of output voltage. For the half-wave rectifier, E_{avg} is less than half (or approximately 0.318) of the peak output voltage. This value is still much less than that of the applied voltage. With no capacitor connected across the output of the rectifier circuit, the waveform in Figure 7-3-11A has a large pulsating component (ripple) compared with the average or DC component. When a capacitor is connected across the output (Figure 7-3-11B), the average value of output voltage (E_{avg}) is increased due to the filtering action of capacitor C_1.

The value of the capacitor is fairly large (several microfarads), and thus it presents a relatively low reactance to the pulsating current and it stores a substantial charge.

The rate of charge for the capacitor is limited only by the resistance of the conducting diode, which is relatively low. Therefore, the RC charge time of the circuit is relatively short. As a result, when the pulsating voltage is first applied to the circuit, the capacitor charges rapidly and almost reaches the peak value of the rectified voltage within the first few cycles. The capacitor attempts to charge to the peak value of the rectified voltage anytime a diode is conducting, and tends to retain its charge when the rectifier output falls to zero. (The capacitor cannot discharge immediately.) The capacitor slowly discharges through the load

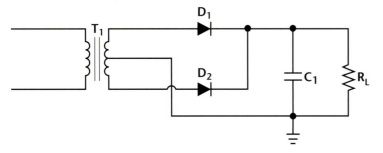

Figure 7-3-10. Full-wave rectifier with a capacitor filter

resistance (R_L) during the time the rectifier is nonconducting.

The rate of discharge of the capacitor is determined by the value of capacitance and the value of the load resistance. If the capacitance and load-resistance values are large, the RC discharge time for the circuit is relatively long.

A comparison of the waveforms shown in Figure 7-3-11 illustrates that the addition of C_1 to the circuit results in an increase in the average of the output voltage (E_{avg}) and a reduction in the amplitude of the ripple component (E_r) which is normally present across the load resistance.

Now, consider a complete cycle of operation using a half-wave rectifier, a capacitive filter (C_1), and a load resistor (R_L). As shown in Figure 7-3-12A, the capacitive filter (C_1) is assumed to be large enough to ensure a small reactance to the pulsating rectified current. The resistance of R_L is assumed to be much greater than the reactance of C_1 at the input frequency. When the circuit is energized, the diode conducts on the positive half-cycle and current flows through the circuit, allowing C_1 to charge. C_1 will charge to approximately the peak value of the input voltage. (The charge is less than the peak value because of the voltage drop across the diode [D_1].)

In Figure 7-3-12A, the charge on C_1 is indicated by the heavy solid line on the waveform. As illustrated in Figure 7-3-12B, the diode cannot conduct on the negative half-cycle because the anode of D_1 is negative with respect to the cathode. During this interval, C_1 discharges through the load resistor (R_L). The discharge of C_1 produces the downward slope as indicated by the solid line on the waveform in Figure 7-3-12B. In contrast to the abrupt fall of the applied AC voltage from peak value to zero, the voltage across C_1 (and thus across R_L) during the discharge period gradually decreases until the time of the next half-cycle of rectifier operation. Keep in mind that for good filtering, the filter capacitor should charge up as fast as possible and discharge as little as possible.

Since practical values of C_1 and R_L ensure a more or less gradual decrease of the discharge voltage, a substantial charge remains on the capacitor at the time of the next half-cycle of operation. As a result, no current can flow through the diode until the rising AC input voltage at the anode of the diode exceeds the voltage on the charge remaining on C_1. The charge on C_1 is the cathode potential of the diode. When the potential on the anode exceeds the potential on the cathode (the

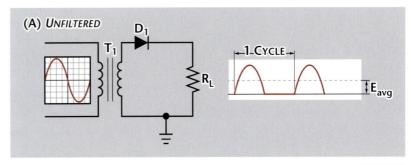

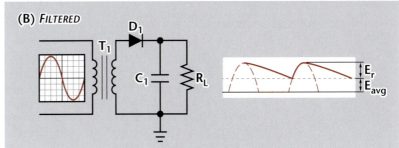

Figure 7-3-11. Unfiltered and filtered half-wave rectifier

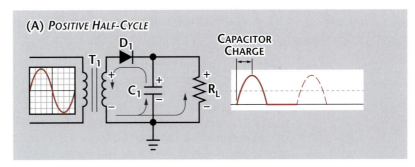

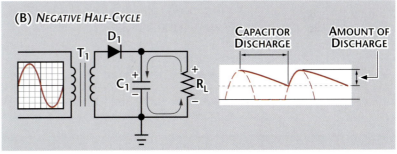

Figure 7-3-12. Capacitor filter circuit: positive and negative half-cycle

charge on C_1), the diode again conducts, and C_1 begins to charge to approximately the peak value of the applied voltage.

After the capacitor has charged to its peak value, the diode cuts off and the capacitor starts to discharge. Since the fall of the AC input voltage on the anode is considerably more rapid than the decrease on the capacitor voltage, the cathode quickly becomes more positive than the anode, and the diode ceases to conduct.

Operation of the simple capacitor filter using a full-wave rectifier is basically the same as that discussed for the half-wave rectifier. Referring

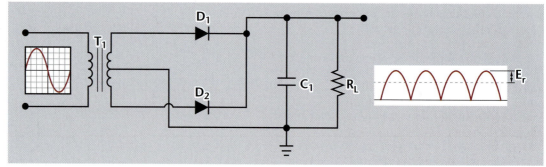

Figure 7-3-13. Full-wave rectifier with capacitor filter

to Figure 7-3-13, notice that because one of the diodes is always conducting on either alternation, the filter capacitor charges and discharges during each half-cycle. Note that each diode conducts only for that portion of time when the peak secondary voltage is greater than the charge across the capacitor.

Another thing to keep in mind is that the ripple component (E_r) of the output voltage is an AC voltage and the average output voltage (E_{avg}) is the DC component of the output. Since the filter capacitor offers a relatively low impedance to AC, the majority of the AC component flows through the filter capacitor. The AC component is therefore bypassed (shunted) around the load resistance, and the entire DC component (or E_{avg}) flows through the load resistance. This statement can be clarified by using the formula for X_C in a half-wave and full-wave rectifier. First, establish some values for the circuit.

HALF-WAVE RECTIFIER

Frequency at rectifier output: 60 Hz
Value of filter capacitor: 30 μF
Load resistance: 10kΩ

$X_C = 1 \div 2\pi fC$
$X_C = .159 \div fC$
$X_C = .159 \div (60 \times .000030)$
$X_C = .159 \div .0018$
$X_C = 88.3\Omega$

FULL-WAVE RECTIFIER

Frequency at rectifier output: 120 Hz
Value of filter capacitor: 30 μF
Load resistance: 10kΩ

$X_C = 1 \div 2\pi fC$
$X_C = .159 \div fC$
$X_C = .159 \div (120 \times .000030)$
$X_C = .159 \div .0036$
$X_C = 44.16\Omega$

As seen from the calculations, by doubling the frequency of the rectifier, the impedance of the capacitor is reduced by one-half. This allows the AC component to pass through the capacitor more easily. As a result, a full-wave rectifier output is much easier to filter than that of a half-wave rectifier. Remember, the smaller the X_C of the filter capacitor with respect to the load resistance, the better the filtering action. The largest possible capacitor will provide the best filtering.

$X_C = 1 \div 2\pi fC$

Remember, also, that the load resistance is an important consideration. If load resistance is made small, the load current increases, and the average value of output voltage (E_{avg}) decreases. The RC discharge time constant is a direct function of the value of the load resistance; therefore, the rate of capacitor voltage discharge is a direct function of the current through the load. The greater the load current, the more rapid the discharge of the capacitor, and the lower the average value of output voltage. For this reason, the simple capacitive filter is seldom used with rectifier circuits that must supply a relatively large load current. Using the simple capacitive filter in conjunction with a full-wave or bridge rectifier provides

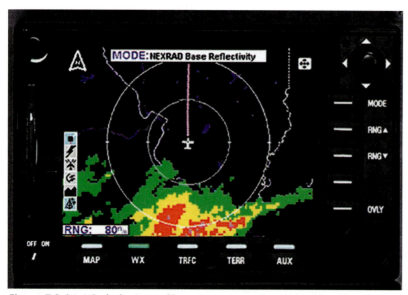

Figure 7-3-14. LC choke-input filters are commonly used in aircraft radar.

improved filtering because the increased ripple frequency decreases the capacitive reactance of the filter capacitor.

LC Choke-Input Filters

The LC choke-input filter is used primarily in power supplies where voltage regulation is important and where the output current is relatively high and subject to varying load conditions. This filter is used in high-power applications such as those found in radars (Figure 7-3-14) and communication transmitters.

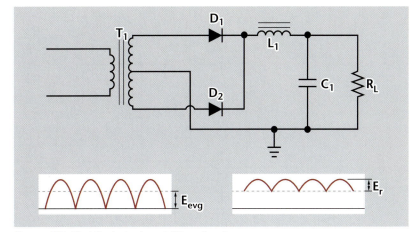

Figure 7-3-15. LC choke-input filter circuit

Notice in Figure 7-3-15 that this filter consists of an input inductor (L_1), or filter choke, and an output filter capacitor (C_1). Inductor L_1 is placed at the input to the filter and is in series with the output of the rectifier circuit. Since the action of an inductor is to oppose any change in current flow, the inductor tends to keep a constant current flowing to the load throughout the complete cycle of the applied voltage. As a result, the output voltage never reaches the peak value of the applied voltage. Instead, the output voltage approximates the average value of the rectified input to the filter, as shown in the Figure 7-3-15. The reactance of the inductor (X_L) reduces the amplitude of ripple voltage without reducing the DC output voltage by an appreciable amount. (The DC resistance of the inductor is just a few ohms.)

The shunt capacitor (C_1) charges and discharges at the ripple frequency rate, but the amplitude of the ripple voltage (E_r) is relatively small because the inductor (L_1) tends to keep a constant current flowing from the rectifier circuit to the load. In addition, the reactance of the shunt capacitor (X_C) presents a low impedance to the ripple component existing at the output of the filter, and thus shunts the ripple component around the load. The capacitor attempts to hold the output voltage relatively constant at the average value of the voltage.

The value of the filter capacitor (C_1) must be relatively large to present a low opposition (X_C) to the pulsating current and to store a substantial charge. The rate of the charge for the capacitor is limited by the low impedance of the AC source (the transformer), by the small resistance of the diode, and by the cemf developed by the coil. Therefore, the RC charge time constant is short compared to its discharge time. (This comparison in RC charge and discharge paths is illustrated Figure 7-3-16A and Figure 7-3-16B) Consequently, when the pulsating voltage is first applied to the LC choke-input filter, the inductor (L_1) produces a cemf that opposes the constantly increasing input voltage.

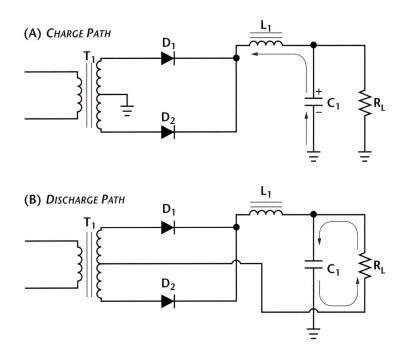

Figure 7-3-16. LC choke-input filter; (A) Charge and, (B) Discharge path

The net result is to effectively prevent the rapid charging of the filter capacitor (C_1). Thus, instead of reaching the peak value of the input voltage, C_1 only charges to the average value of the input voltage. After the input voltage reaches its peak and decreases sufficiently, the capacitor (C_1) attempts to discharge through the load resistance (R_L). C_1 will only partially discharge, as indicated in Figure 7-3-16B, because of its relatively long discharge time constant. The larger the value of the filter capacitor, the better the filtering action. However, physical size is a practical limitation to the maximum value of the capacitor.

The inductor (also referred to as the filter choke or coil) serves to maintain the current flow to the filter output (R_L) at a nearly constant level during the charge and discharge

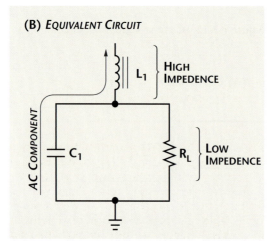

Figure 7-3-17. (A) LC choke-input filter and, (B) Equivalent circuit

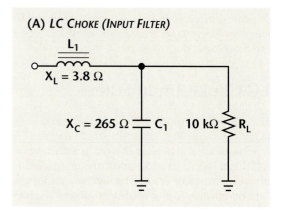

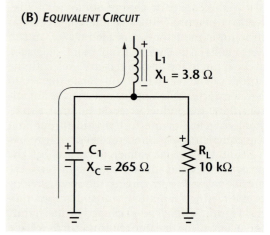

Figure 7-3-20. AC component in an; (A) LC choke-input filter and, (B) Equivalent circuit

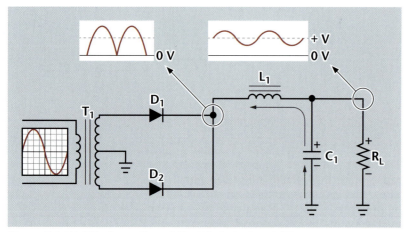

Figure 7-3-18. Filtering action of the LC choke-input filter

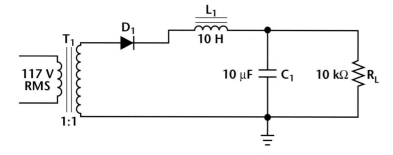

Figure 7-3-19. Half-wave rectifier with an LC choke-input filter

periods of the filter capacitor. The inductor (L_1) and the capacitor (C_1) form a voltage divider for the AC component (ripple) of the applied input voltage. This is shown in Figure 7-3-17A and Figure 7-3-17B.

As far as the ripple component is concerned, the inductor offers a high impedance (Z) and the capacitor offers a low impedance (Figure 7-3-17B). As a result, the ripple component (E_r) appearing across the load resistance is greatly attenuated (reduced). The inductance of the filter choke opposes changes in the value of the current flowing through it; therefore, the average value of the voltage produced across the capacitor contains a much smaller value of ripple component (E_r) than the value of ripple produced across the choke.

Now look at Figure 7-3-18, which illustrates a complete cycle of operation for a full-wave rectifier circuit used to supply the input voltage to the filter. The rectifier voltage is developed across the capacitor (C_1). The ripple voltage at the output of the filter is the alternating component of the input voltage reduced in amplitude by the filter section. Each time the anode of a diode goes positive with respect to the cathode, the diode conducts and C_1 charges.

Conduction occurs twice during each cycle for a full-wave rectifier. For a 60-Hz supply, this produces a 120-Hz ripple voltage. Although the diodes alternate (one conducts while the other is nonconducting), the filter input voltage is not steady. As the anode voltage of the conducting diode increases on the positive half of the cycle, capacitor C_1 charges—the charge being limited by the impedance of the secondary transformer winding, the diode's forward (cathode-to-anode) resistance, and the cemf developed by the choke. During the nonconducting interval (when the anode voltage drops below the capacitor charge voltage), C_1 discharges through the load resistor (R_L). The components in the discharge path have a long time constant; thus, C_1 discharges more slowly than it charges.

The choke (L_1) is usually a large value, from 1 to 20 henries, and offers a large inductive reactance to the 120-Hz ripple component produced by the rectifier. Therefore, the effect that L_1 has on the charging of the capacitor (C_1) must be considered. Since L_1 is connected in series with the parallel branch consisting of C_1 and R_L, a division of the ripple (AC) voltage and the output (DC) voltage occurs. The greater the impedance of the choke, the less the ripple voltage that appears across C_1 and the output. The DC output voltage is fixed mainly by the DC resistance of the choke.

Remember how the LC choke-input filter functions, and study the following examples that discuss it with actual component values applied. For simplicity, the input frequency at the primary of the transformer will be 117 V at 60 Hz. Both half-wave and full-wave rectifier circuits will be used to provide the input to the filter.

Starting with the half-wave configuration shown in Figure 7-3-19, the basic parameters are: with 117 V AC root mean square (rms) applied to the T_1 primary, 165 V AC peak is available at the secondary [(117 V) x (1.414) = 165 V]. Recall that the ripple frequency of this half-wave rectifier is 60 Hz. Therefore, the capacitive reactance of C_1 is:

$X_C = 1 \div 2\pi fC$
$X_C = 1 \div (2)(3.14)(60)(10)(10^{-6})$
$X_C = (1)(10^6) \div 3{,}768$
$X_C = 265\Omega$

This means that the capacitor (C_1) offers 265Ω of opposition to the ripple current. Note, however, that the capacitor offers an infinite impedance to direct current. The inductive reactance of L_1 is:

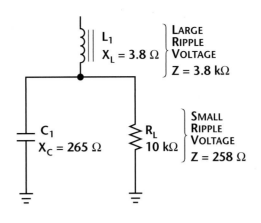

Figure 7-3-21. Equivalent circuit of an LC choke-input filter

$X_L = 2\pi fL$
$X_L = (2)(3.14)(60)(10)$
$X_L = 3.8\Omega$

The above calculation shows that L_1 offers a relatively high opposition (3.8Ω) to the ripple in comparison to the opposition offered by C_1 (265Ω). Thus, more ripple voltage will be dropped across L_1 than across C_1. In addition, the impedance of C_1 (265Ω) is relatively low with respect to the resistance of the load (10Ω). Therefore, more ripple current flows through C_1 than the load. In other words, C_1 shunts most of the AC component around the load.

Taking this a step further, redraw the filter circuit to show the voltage divider action (Figure 7-3-20A). Remember, the 165 V peak 60 Hz provided by the rectifier consists of both an AC and a DC component. This first discussion will be about the AC component. The figure shows that the capacitor (C_1) offers the least opposition (265Ω) to the AC component. Therefore, the greater amount of AC will flow through C_1. (The heavy line in Figure 7-3-20B indicates the AC current flow through the capacitor.) Thus the capacitor bypasses, or shunts, most of the AC around the load.

By combining the X_C of C_1 and the resistance of R_L into an equivalent circuit (Figure 7-3-20B), an equivalent impedance of 265Ω is created.

As a formula;

$RT = (R_1)(R_2) \div (R_1 + R_2)$

This is now a voltage divider, as illustrated in Figure 7-3-21. Because of the impedance ratios, a large amount of ripple voltage is dropped across L_1, and a substantially smaller amount is dropped across C_1 and R_L. The ripple voltage

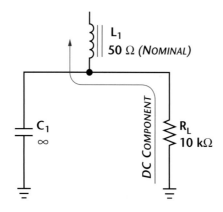

Figure 7-3-22. DC component in an LC choke-input

can be further increased across L_1 by increasing the inductance ($X_L = 2\pi fL$).

The DC component of the applied voltage will now be discussed. Remember, a capacitor offers an infinite impedance to the flow of direct current. The DC component, therefore, must flow through R_L and L_1. As far as the DC is concerned, the capacitor does not exist. The coil and the load are therefore in series with each other. The DC resistance of a filter choke is very low (50Ω average). Consequently, most of the DC component is developed across the load and a very small amount of the DC voltage is dropped across the coil, as shown in Figure 7-3-22.

As shown, both the AC and the DC components flow through L_1. Because it is frequency sensitive, the coil provides a large resistance to AC and a small resistance to DC. In other words, the coil opposes any change in current. This property makes the coil a highly desirable filter component. Note that the filtering action of the LC choke-input filter is improved when the filter is used in conjunction with a full-wave rectifier, as shown in Figure 7-3-23. This is due to the decrease in the X_C of the filter capacitor and the increase in the X_L of the choke. Remember, ripple frequency of a full-wave rectifier is twice that of a half-wave rectifier. For 60-Hz input, the ripple will be 120 Hz. The X_C of C_1 and the X_L of L_1 are calculated as follows:

$X_C = 1 \div 2\pi fC$
$X_C = 1 \div (2)(3.14)(120)(10)(10^{-6})$
$X_C = (1)(10^6) \div 7,536$
$X_C = 132.5\Omega$

$X_L = 2\pi fL$
$X_L = (2)(3.14)(120)(10)$
$X_L = 7.5\Omega$

When the X_C of a filter capacitor is decreased, it provides less opposition to the flow of AC. The greater the AC flow through the capacitor, the lower the flow through the load. Conversely, the larger the X_L of the choke, the greater the amount of AC ripple developed across the choke; consequently, less ripple is developed across the load and better filtering is obtained.

Failure Analysis of an LC Choke-Input Filter

The filter capacitors are subject to open circuits, short circuits and excessive leakage. The series inductor is subject to open windings and, occasionally, shorted turns or a short circuit to the core.

The filter capacitor in the LC choke-input filter circuit is not subject to extreme voltage surges because of the protection offered by the inductor. However, the capacitor can become open, leaky or shorted.

Shorted turns in the choke may reduce the value of inductance below the critical value. This will result in excessive peak rectifier current, accompanied by an abnormally high output voltage, excessive ripple amplitude and poor voltage regulation.

A choke winding that is open, or a choke winding that is shorted to the core, will result in a no-output condition. A choke winding that is shorted to the core may cause overheating of the rectifier elements and blown fuses.

With the supply voltage removed from the input to the filter circuit, one terminal of the capacitor can be disconnected from the circuit. The capacitor should be checked with a capacitance analyzer to determine its capacitance and leakage resistance. When the capacitor is electrolytic, the correct polarity must be used at all times. A decrease in capacitance or losses within the capacitor can decrease the efficiency of the filter and can produce excessive ripple amplitude.

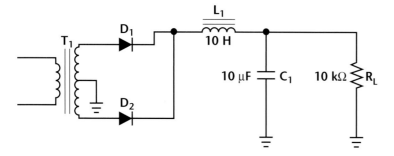

Figure 7-3-23. Full-wave rectifier with an LC choke-input filter

RC Capacitor-Input Filters

The RC capacitor-input filter is limited to applications in which the load current is small. This type of filter is used in power supplies where the load current is constant and voltage regulation is not necessary. For example, RC filters are used in high-voltage power supplies for cathode-ray tubes and in decoupling networks for multistage amplifiers (Figure 7-3-24).

Figure 7-3-25 shows an RC capacitor-input filter and associated waveforms. Both half-wave and full-wave rectifiers are used to provide the inputs. The waveform shown in Figure 7-3-25A represents the unfiltered output from a typical rectifier circuit. Note that the dashed lines in Figure 7-3-25A indicate the average value of output voltage (E_{avg}) for the half-wave rectifier. E_{avg} is less than half (approximately 0.318) the amplitude of the voltage peaks. The average value of output voltage (E_{avg}) for the full-wave rectifier is greater than half (approximately 0.637), but is still much less than, the peak amplitude of the rectifier output waveform. With no filter circuit connected across the output of the rectifier circuit, the waveform has a large value of pulsating component (ripple) as compared to the average (or DC) component.

Figure 7-3-24. RC capacitor input filters are used in applications with limited current loads.

The RC filter in Figure 7-3-25 consists of an input filter capacitor (C_1), a series resistor (R_1), and an output filter capacitor (C_2). (This filter is sometimes referred to as an RC pi-section filter because its schematic symbol resembles the Greek letter π.)

The single-capacitor filter is suitable for many noncritical, low-current applications. However, when the load resistance is very low or when

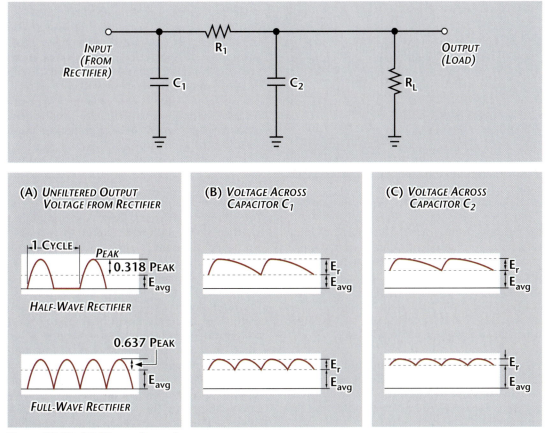

Figure 7-3-25. RC filter and waveforms

FRONT

BACK

Figure 7-3-26. LC capacitor-input filters are found in the amplifier section of most aircraft radio receivers.

Figure 7-3-27. LC capacitor-input filter

the percent of ripple must be held to an absolute minimum, the capacitor value required must be extremely large. While electrolytic capacitors are available in sizes up to 10,000 µF or greater, the large sizes are quite expensive. A more practical approach is to use a more sophisticated filter that can do the same job but that has lower capacitor values, such as the RC filter.

Figure 7-3-25A, Figure 7-3-25B and Figure 7-3-25C show the output waveforms of a half-wave and a full-wave rectifier. Each waveform is shown with an RC filter connected across the output. The following explanation of how a filter works shows that an RC filter of this type does a much better job than the single-capacitor filter.

C_1 performs exactly the same function as it did in the single-capacitor filter. It is used to reduce the percentage of ripple to a relatively low value. Thus, the voltage across C_1 might consist of an average DC value of +100 V with a ripple voltage of 10 V peak-to-peak. This voltage is passed on to the R_1-C_2 network, which reduces the ripple even further.

C_2 offers an infinite impedance (resistance) to the DC component of the output voltage. Thus, the DC voltage is passed to the load, but reduced in value by the amount of the voltage drop across R_1. However, R_1 is generally small compared to the load resistance. Therefore, the drop in the DC voltage by R_1 is not a drawback.

Component values are designed so that the resistance of R_1 is much greater than the reactance (X_C) of C_2 at the ripple frequency. C_2 offers a very low impedance to the AC ripple frequency. Thus, the AC ripple senses a voltage divider consisting of R_1 and C_2 between the output of the rectifier and ground. Therefore, most of the ripple voltage is dropped across R_1. Only a trace of the ripple voltage can be seen across C_2 and the load. In extreme cases where the ripple must be held to an absolute minimum, a second stage of RC filtering can be added. In practice, the second stage is rarely required. The RC filter is extremely popular because smaller capacitors can be used with good results.

The RC filter has some disadvantages. First, the voltage drop across R_1 takes voltage away from the load. Second, power is wasted in R_1 and is dissipated in the form of unwanted heat. Finally, if the load resistance changes, the voltage across the load will change. Even so, the advantages of the RC filter overshadow these disadvantages in many cases.

Failure Analysis of the RC Filter

The shunt capacitors (C_1 and C_2) are subject to an open circuit, a short circuit or excessive leakage. The series filter resistor (R_1) is subject to changes in value and occasionally opens. Any of these troubles can be easily detected.

The input capacitor (C_1) has the greatest pulsating voltage applied to it and is the most susceptible to voltage surges. As a result, the input capacitor is frequently subject to voltage breakdown and shorting. The remaining shunt capacitor (C_2) in the filter circuit is not subject to voltage surges because of the protection offered by the series filter resistor (R_1). However, a shunt capacitor can become open, leaky or shorted.

A shorted capacitor or an open filter resistor results in a no-output indication. An open filter resistor results in an abnormally high DC voltage at the input to the filter and no voltage at the output of the filter. Leaky capacitors or filter resistors that have lost their effectiveness, or filter resistors that have decreased in value, result in an excessive ripple amplitude in the output of the supply.

LC Capacitor-Input Filters

The LC capacitor-input filter is one of the most commonly used filters. This type of filter is used primarily in radio receivers (Figure 7-3-26), small audio amplifier power supplies, and in any type of power supply where the output current is low and the load current is relatively constant. An example of an LC capacitor-input filter used in a circuit is pictured in Figure 7-3-27.

Figure 7-3-28 shows an LC capacitor-input filter and associated waveforms. Both half-wave and full-wave rectifier circuits are used to provide the input. The waveforms shown in Figure 7-3-28A represent the unfiltered output from a typical rectifier circuit. Note that the average value of output voltage (E_{avg}), indicated by the dashed lines, for the half-wave rectifier is less than half the amplitude of the voltage peaks. The average value of output voltage (E_{avg}) for the full-wave rectifier is greater than half, but is still much less than the peak amplitude of the rectifier-output waveform. With no filter connected across the output of the rectifier circuit (which results in unfiltered output voltage), the waveform has a large value of pulsating component (ripple) as compared to the average (or DC) component.

C_1 reduces the ripple to a relatively low level (Figure 7-3-28B). L_1 and C_2 form the LC filter, which reduces the ripple even further. L_1 is a large-value iron-core induct (choke). L_1 has a high value of inductance and therefore, a high value of X_L, which offers a high reactance to the ripple frequency. At the same time, C_2 offers a very low reactance to AC ripple. L_1 and C_2 form an AC voltage divider, and because the reactance of L_1 is much higher than that of C_2, most of the ripple voltage is dropped across L_1. Only a slight trace of ripple appears across C_2 and the load (Figure 7-3-28C).

While the L_1-C_2 network greatly reduces AC ripple, it has little effect on DC. Recall that an inductor offers no reactance to DC. The only opposition to current flow is the resistance of the wire in the choke. Generally, this resistance is very low and the DC voltage drop across the coil is minimal. Thus, the LC filter overcomes the disadvantages of the RC filter.

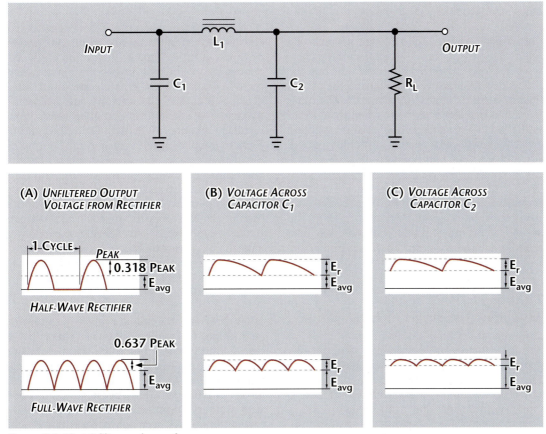

Figure 7-3-28. LC filter and waveforms

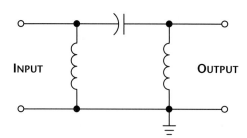

Figure 7-3-29. Schematic of a high-pass filter

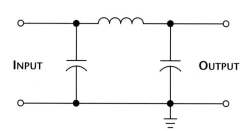

Figure 7-3-31. Schematic of a low-pass filter

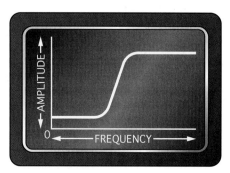

Figure 7-3-30. An example of a high-pass filter reading on an oscilloscope

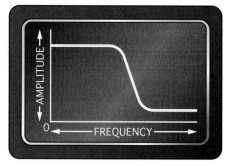

Figure 7-3-32. A low-pass filter reading example as it would appear on an oscilloscope

Aside from the voltage divider effect, the inductor improves filtering in another way. Recall that an inductor resists changes in the magnitude of the current flowing through it. Consequently, when the inductor is placed in series with the load, the inductor maintains steady current. In turn, this helps the voltage across the load remain constant when size of components is a factor.

The LC filter provides good filtering action over a wide range of currents. The capacitor filters best when the load is drawing little current. Thus, the capacitor discharges very slowly and the output voltage remains almost constant. On the other hand, the inductor filters best when the current is highest. The complementary nature of these two components ensures that good filtering will occur over a wide range of currents.

The LC filter has two disadvantages. First, it is more expensive than the RC filter because an iron-core choke costs more than a resistor. The second disadvantage is size. The iron-core choke is bulky and heavy, a fact that may render the LC filter unsuitable for many applications.

Failure Analysis of an LC Capacitor-Input Filter

Shunt capacitors are subject to open circuits, short circuits and excessive leakage; series inductors are subject to open windings and, occasionally, shorted turns or a short circuit to the core.

The input capacitor (C_1) has the greatest pulsating voltage applied to it, is the most susceptible to voltage surges, and has a generally higher average voltage applied. As a result, the input capacitor is frequently subject to voltage breakdown and shorting. The output capacitor (C_2) is not as susceptible to voltage surges because of the series protection offered by the series inductor (L_1), but the capacitor can become open, leaky or shorted.

A shorted capacitor, an open filter choke (L_1) or a choke winding that is shorted to the core, results in a no-output indication. A shorted capacitor, depending on the magnitude of the short, may cause a shorted rectifier, transformer or filter choke, and may result in a blown fuse in the primary of the transformer. An open filter choke results in an abnormally high DC voltage at the input to the filter and no voltage at the output of the filter. A leaky or open capacitor in the filter circuit results in a low DC output voltage. This condition is generally accompanied by an excessive ripple amplitude. Shorted turns in the winding of a filter choke reduce the effective inductance of the choke and decrease its filtering efficiency. As a result, the ripple amplitude increases.

Frequency Sensitive Filters

Filters are available that are sensitive to certain frequencies or frequency ranges. This type of filter is often used in receivers. Their operating principle is mainly based upon resonant frequencies. The types of filters are the high-pass, low-pass, band-pass, and the band-reject. These four are very common in the world of receivers, but there are more out there. This text will mainly be covering the four listed above.

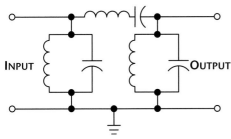

Figure 7-3-33. Schematic of a band-pass filter

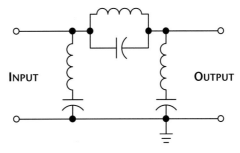

Figure 7-3-35. Schematic of a band-reject filter

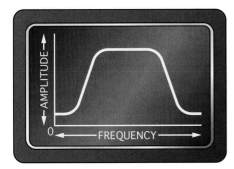

Figure 7-3-34. An example reading of a band-pass filter on an oscilloscope

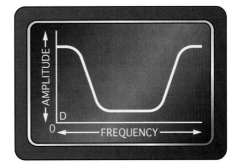

Figure 7-3-36. A sample reading of a band-reject filter on an oscilloscope

In general a high-pass filter will pass high frequencies and cancel out low-pass frequencies. The low-pass filter will pass low frequencies and cancel out high frequencies. The band-pass filter passes frequencies in a specific range of the frequency band and will block out higher and lower frequencies, while its opposite, the band-reject filter, will pass all other frequencies and block out the resonant frequency.

High-Pass Filters

Figure 7-3-29 shows the schematic of the high-pass filter. Notice the arrangement of the capacitor and inductor. In this circuit the capacitor is in series, while the inductor is in parallel. The reason for this arrangement is because as the frequency increases, the resistance (capacitive reactance) decreases. This allows high frequencies to pass through the capacitor. The lower frequencies go through the inductor because as frequencies get lower the resistance on the inductor (inductive reactance) decreases. Therefore the high frequencies will be passed on through the circuit and the low frequencies will be separated and canceled out. If the filter were read by an oscilloscope, the reading would look like Figure 7-3-30.

Low-Pass Filters

A schematic of a low-pass filter is shown in Figure 7-3-31 The arrangement of the capacitor is in parallel and the inductor is in series, unlike in the high-pass filter. In a low-pass filter, high frequencies are passed by the capacitor while low frequencies are passed by the inductor. Figure 7-3-32 shows the reading of a low-pass filter on the oscilloscope.

Band-Pass Filters

In a band-pass filter there are two sets of inductors and capacitors. The first set is in series, while the second is in parallel, as seen in Figure 7-3-33 In the series LC circuit the impedance is high except at the resonant frequency; therefore, the current will flow at the resonant frequency. On the parallel portion of the circuit, the impedance is high at the resonant frequency. So, in the series portion of the circuit, the resonant frequency is passed and all others are blocked, while the parallel section blocks the resonant frequency and passes all the others. The bandwidth of the frequency is also very important. The bandwidth determines the number of circuit elements and the resistance of the circuit. If a wide bandwidth is desired, use a higher resistance. Figure 7-3-34 shows the reading of a band-pass filter on an oscilloscope.

Band-Reject Filter

In a band-reject filter, the parallel element and series element have flipped compared to the band-pass filter. See the schematic of a band-reject filter in Figure 7-3-35. In this arrangement the resonant frequency is bypassed into the parallel portion and all other frequencies are passed through the series portion. A reading of a band-reject filter on an oscilloscope is shown in Figure 7-3-36. A

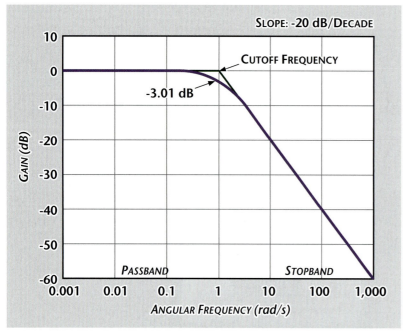

Figure 7-3-37. Cutoff frequency is the point where the amount of frequency blocking is accelerated

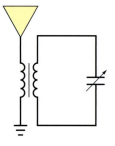

Figure 7-3-38. Simple tuning circuit schematic

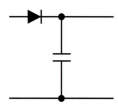

Figure 7-3-39. Simple demodulator circuit schematic

band-reject filter may also be referred to as a band-stop filter.

Cutoff Frequency

The cutoff frequency is another key element in frequency sensitive filters. This is a boundary in a system's frequency response where energy flow begins to be reduced rather than passing through. A typical characterization is where the frequency level, rather above or below, fails to operate. An example of the cutoff is show in Figure 7-3-37.

Tuning circuits

Tuning circuits are very similar to filters; in fact many filters can be used as tuners. Frequently tuners are made up of a variable capacitor and a fixed inductor, although it is possible to have a variable inductor with a fixed capacitor. Tuners typically are very selective in what frequency they let pass. All other frequencies that are not the tuned frequency will be canceled out.

The operation of a tuner is as follows. The desired frequency is picked up by the antenna and sent to the antenna's primary coil and then to ground. The primary creates a magnetic field that will be picked up by a secondary coil. The secondary is connected in parallel with the tuning capacitor. Because of this configuration, only the resonant frequency is allowed to pass through, which happens to be the tuned in frequency. This is a very simple type of tuner.

There are many types of tuners in use, but for the most part they all do the same thing. They pass on the frequency that was selected by the radio. In many case that frequency also happens to be the resonant frequency of the tuner section. A simple tuning circuit is shown in Figure 7-3-38.

Demodulator

The demodulator, also referred to as a detector circuit, is a component that typically comes after the tuner. When a radio wave is received by a radio, the radio wave is a combination of a carrier wave and the actual intelligence that is meant to be received. The purpose of the carrier wave is to give information enough power to travel long distances. The demodulator's purpose is to separate the carrier wave from the intelligence.

A simple demodulator can be made up of a diode and a capacitor as seen in Figure 7-3-39. When the wave enters the diode the radio signal will be rectified. The capacitor will act as a filter, removing the rest of the carrier wave to let the intelligence pass on to the next stage.

There are many different types of demodulation circuits, but they all do the same thing: rectify and filter the incoming carrier wave. Figure 7-3-40 illustrates the step-by-step process the carrier wave goes through.

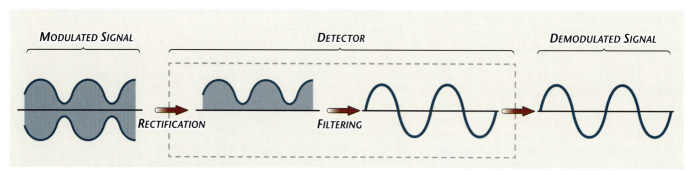

Figure 7-3-40. Step-by-step function of a demodulation circuit

Section 4
Waves and Wave Shaping

Limiters

A technician will often be confronted with many different types of limiting circuits. A *limiter* is a device that limits some part of a waveform from exceeding a specified value. Limiting circuits are used primarily for wave shaping and circuit-protection applications. An example of a limiter is pictured in Figure 7-4-1.

A limiter is little more than the half-wave. By using a diode, a resistor and sometimes a DC bias voltage, the technician can build a limiter that will eliminate the positive or negative alternations of an input waveform. Such a circuit can also limit a portion of the alternations to a specific voltage level. This section introduces five types of limiters:

- Series-positive
- Series-negative
- Parallel-positive
- Parallel-negative
- Dual-diode limiters

The diode in these circuits is the voltage-limiting component. Its polarity and location, with respect to ground, are the factors that determine circuit action. In series limiters, the diode is in series with the output. In parallel limiters, the diode is in parallel with the output.

Series Limiters

Remember that a diode will conduct when the anode voltage is positive with respect to the cathode voltage. The diode will not conduct when the anode is negative in respect to the cathode. Keeping these two simple facts in mind while studying limiters will help with an understanding of their operation.

In a *series limiter*, a diode is connected in series with the output, as shown in Figure 7-4-2A. The input signal is applied across the diode and resistor and the output is taken across the resistor. The series-limiter circuit can limit either the positive or negative alternation, depending on the polarity of the diode connection with respect to ground. The circuit shown in Figure 7-4-2B is a series-positive limiter. Reversing D_1 would change the circuit to a series-negative limiter.

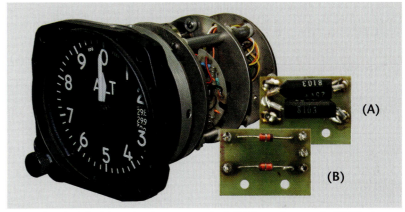

Figure 7-4-1. A limiting circuit composed of; (A)Capacitors and, (B) Diodes can be found in this aircraft simulator altimeter.

Series-Positive Limiter

Look at the series-positive limiter and its outputs in Figure 7-4-2. Diode D_1 is in series with the output and the output is taken across resistor R_1. The input must be negative with respect to the anode of the diode to make the diode conduct. When the positive alternation of the input signal (T0 to T1) is applied to the circuit, the cathode is positive with respect to the anode. The diode is reverse biased and will not conduct. Since no current can flow, no output is

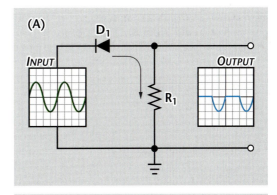

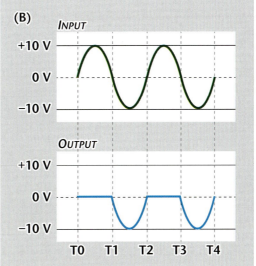

Figure 7-4-2. Series-positive limiter

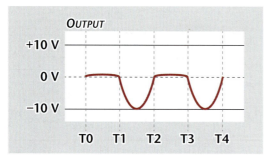

Figure 7-4-3. Output of a series-positive limiter with a reverse biased diode

developed across the resistor during the positive alternation of the input signal.

During the negative half cycle of the input signal (T1 to T2), the cathode is negative with respect to the anode. This causes D_1 to be forward biased. Current flows through R_1 and an output is developed. The output during each negative alternation of the input is approximately the same as the input (–10 V) because most of the voltage is developed across the resistor.

Ideally, the output wave shape should be exactly the same as the input wave shape with only the limited portion removed. When the diode is reverse biased, the circuit has a small amount of reverse current flow, as shown just above the 0 V reference line in Figure 7-4-3. During the limiting portion of the input signal, the diode resistance should be high compared to the resistor. During the time the diode is conducting, the resistance of the diode should be small as compared to that of the resistor. In other words, the diode should have a very high front-to-back ratio (forward resistance compared to reverse resistance). This relationship can be better understood by studying the effects that a front-to-back resistance ratio has on circuit output.

The following formula can be used to determine the output amplitude of the signal:

$E_{out} = R \div (R + R_{ac}) \times E_{in}$

Where:

E_{out} = amplitude voltage
R = value of R_1
R_{ac} = value of AC resistance of the diode (under forward and reverse biased conditions)
E_{in} = input of signal amplitude

Use the formula to compare the front-to-back ratio of the diode in the forward- and reverse-biased conditions.

R_1 = 1,000 ohms
R_{ac} = 1Ω (forward-biased condition)
R_{ac} = 100,000Ω (reverse-biased condition)
E_{in} = 10 V

FORWARD BIAS

$E_{out} = R \div (R + R_{ac}) \times E_{in}$
$E_{out} = 1,000 \div (1,000 + 1) \times 10 \text{ V}$
$E_{out} = (1,000 \div 1,001) \times 10 \text{ V}$
$E_{out} = .999 \times 10 \text{ V}$
$E_{out} = 0.09 \text{ V}$

REVERSE BIAS

$E_{out} = R \div (R + R_{ac}) \times E_{in}$
$E_{out} = 1,000 \div (1,000 + 100,000) \times 10 \text{ V}$
$E_{out} = (1,000 \div 101,000) \times 10 \text{ V}$
$E_{out} = .009 \times 10 \text{ V}$
$E_{out} = .09 \text{ V}$

This formula comparison of the forward- and reverse-bias resistance conditions shows that a small amount of reverse current flows during the limited portion of the input waveform. This small amount of reverse current develops as the small positive voltage (0.09 V) shown in Figure 7-4-3 (T0 to T1 and T2 to T3). The actual amount of voltage developed will depend on the type of diode used. For the remainder of

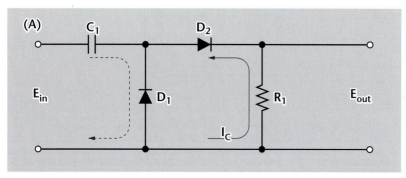

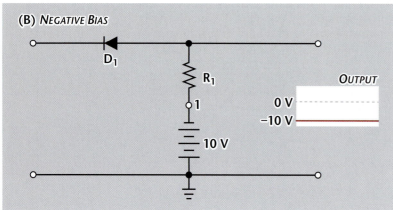

Figure 7-4-4. Positive and negative bias

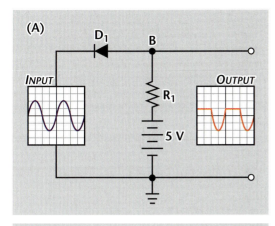

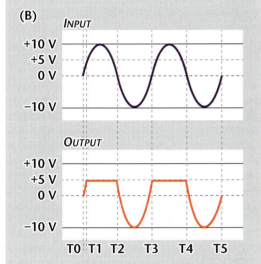

Figure 7-4-5. Series-positive limiter with positive bias

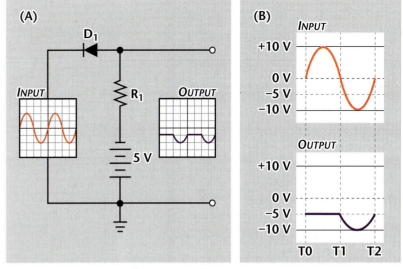

Figure 7-4-6. Series-positive limiter with negative bias

this chapter, to simplify the discussion, only idealized waveforms are used and this small voltage will be disregarded.

Series-Positive Limiter with Bias

In the series-positive limiter shown in Figure 7-4-2A, the reference point at the bottom of resistor R_1 is ground, or 0 V. Placing a DC potential at point 1 in Figure 7-4-4A and Figure 7-4-4B, changes the reference point. The reference point changes by the amount of DC potential that is supplied by the battery. The battery can either aid or oppose the flow of current in the series-limiter circuit. Positive bias (aiding) is shown in Figure 7-4-4A and negative bias (opposing) is shown in Figure 7-4-4B.

When the DC aids forward bias, as in Figure 7-4-4A, the diode conducts even with no signal applied. An input signal sufficiently positive to overcome the DC bias potential is required to reverse bias and cut off the diode.

Look at a series-positive limiter with positive bias as shown in Figure 7-4-5. The diode will conduct until the input signal exceeds +5 V at T1 on the positive alternation of the input signal. When the positive alternation exceeds +5 V, the diode becomes reverse biased and limits the positive alternation of the output signal to +5 V. This is because there is no current flow through resistor R_1 and battery voltage is felt at point B. The diode will remain reverse biased until the positive alternation of the input signal decreases to just under +5 V at T2. At this time, the diode again becomes forward biased and conducts. The diode remains forward biased from T2 to T3. During this period the negative alternation of the input is passed through the diode without being limited. From T3 to T4 the diode is again reverse biased and the output is again limited.

Now look at what takes place when reverse bias is aided, as shown in Figure 7-4-6A. The diode is negatively biased with -5 V from the battery. In Figure 7-4-6B, compare the output to the input signal applied. From T0 to T1 the diode is reverse biased and limiting takes place. The output is at -5 V (battery voltage) during this period. As the negative alternation increases toward -10 V (T1), the cathode of the diode becomes more negative than the anode and is forward biased. From T1 to T2 the input signal is passed to the output. The diode remains forward biased until the negative alternation has decreased to -5 V at T2. At T2 the cathode of the diode becomes more positive than the anode, and the diode is again reverse biased and remains so until T3.

Series-Negative Limiter

In Figure 7-4-7A, the series-negative limiter limits the negative portion of the waveform, as shown in Figure 7-4-7B. Consider the input signal and

7-34 | Frequency Generation

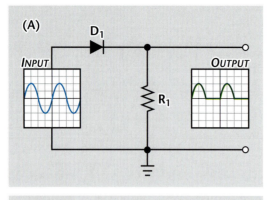

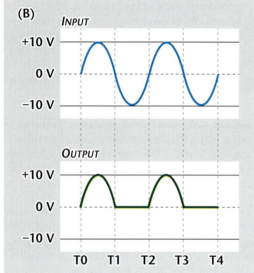

Figure 7-4-7. Series-negative limiter

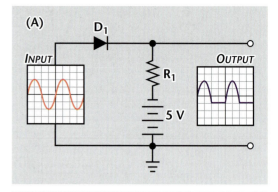

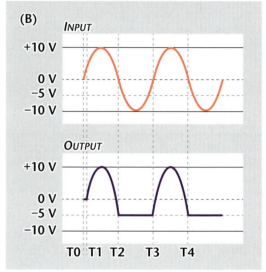

Figure 7-4-8. Series-negative limiter with negative bias

determine how the output is produced. During T0 to T1 (Figure 7-4-7B), the anode is more positive than the cathode and the diode conducts. Current flows up through the resistor and the diode, and a positive voltage is developed at the output. The voltage across the resistor is essentially the same as the voltage applied to the circuit.

During T1 to T2 the anode is negative with respect to the cathode and the diode does not conduct. This portion of the output is limited because no current flows through the resistor. The only difference between series-positive and series-negative limiters is that the diode is reversed in the negative limiters.

Series-Negative Limiter with Bias

Figure 7-4-8A shows a series-negative limiter with negative bias. The diode is forward biased and conducts with no input signal. In Figure 7-4-8B it continues to conduct as the input signal swings first positive and then negative (but only to -5 V) from T0 through T1. At T1 the input becomes negative with respect to the -5 V battery bias. The diode becomes reverse biased and is cut off until T2, when the anode again becomes positive with respect to the battery voltage (-5 V) on the cathode. No voltage is developed in the output by R_1 (no current flow) and the output is held at -5 V from T1 to T2. With negative bias applied to a series-negative limiter, only a portion of the negative signal is limited.

Now look at a series-negative limiter with positive bias, as shown in Figure 7-4-9. This begins by removing all of the negative alternation and part of the positive alternation of the input signal. A full explanation of the series-positive limiter, series-positive limiter with bias, series-negative limiter and series-negative limiter with negative bias has been presented. This is the basis for easily understanding what is happening in the circuit in the figure.

The series-negative limiter with positive bias is different in only one aspect from the series-positive limiter with bias (Figure 7-4-6). The difference is that the diode is reversed and the output is of the opposite polarity.

Parallel Limiters

A parallel-limiter circuit uses the same diode theory and voltage divider action as series limiters. A resistor and diode are connected in

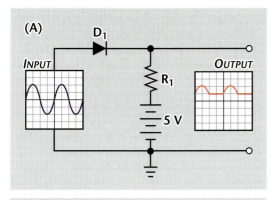

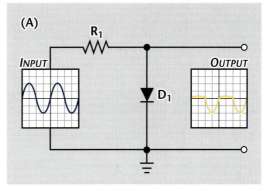

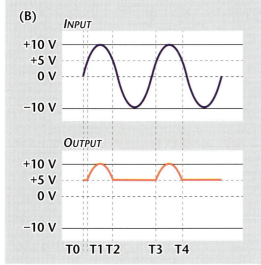

Figure 7-4-9. Series-negative limiter with positive bias

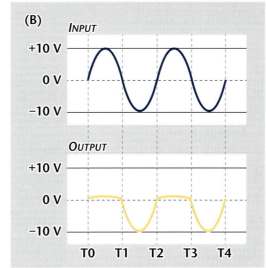

Figure 7-4-10. Parallel-positive limiter

series with the input signal and the output signal is developed across the diode. The output is in parallel with the diode, hence the circuit name, parallel limiter. The parallel limiter can limit either the positive or negative alternation of the input signal.

Recall that in the series limiter the output was developed while the diode was conducting. In the parallel limiter the output will develop when the diode is cut off. Rather than memorize the outputs of these circuits the technician should study their actions and be able to figure them out.

Parallel-Positive Limiter

The schematic diagram shown in Figure 7-4-10A is a parallel-positive limiter. The diode is in parallel with the output and only the positive half cycle of the input is limited. When the positive alternation of the input signal is applied to the circuit (T0 to T1), the diode is forward biased and conducts. This action can be seen in Figure 7-4-10B. As current flows up through the diode and the resistor, a voltage is dropped across each. Since R_1 is much larger than the forward resistance of D_1, most of the input signal is developed across R_1. This leaves only a very small voltage across the diode (output). The positive alternation of the input signal has been limited.

From T1 to T2 the diode is reverse biased and acts as an extremely high resistance. The negative alternation of the input signal appears across the diode at approximately the same amplitude as the input. The negative alternation of the input is not limited.

As with the series limiter, the parallel limiter should provide maximum output voltage for the unlimited part of the signal. The reverse-bias resistance of the diode must be very large compared to the series resistor. To determine the output amplitude, use the following formula:

$$E_{out} = R \div (R + R_{ac}) \times E_{in}$$

Where:

E_{out} = amplitude voltage
R = value of R_1
R_{ac} = value of AC resistance of the diode
  (under forward- and reverse-biased conditions)
E_{in} = input of a signal amplitude

7-36 | Frequency Generation

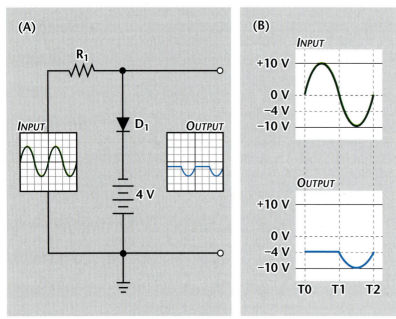

Figure 7-4-11. Parallel limiter with negative bias

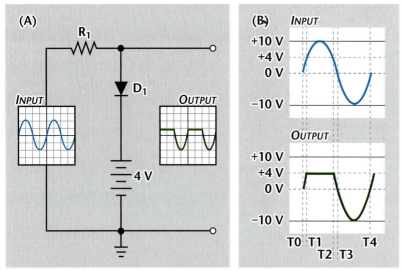

Figure 7-4-12. Parallel-positive limiter with positive bias

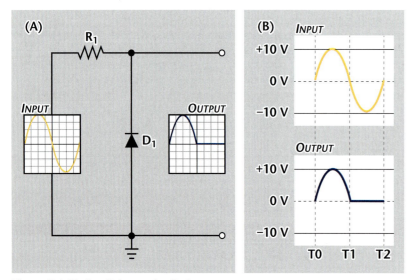

Figure 7-4-13. Parallel-negative limiter

Parallel-Positive Limiter with Bias

Figure 7-4-11A shows the schematic diagram of a parallel-positive limiter with negative bias. The diode is forward biased and conducts without an input signal. D_1 is essentially a short circuit. The voltage at the output terminals is -4 V.

As the positive alternation of the input signal is applied to the circuit, the diode remains forward biased and limits the entire positive alternation, as shown in Figure 7-4-11B. As the signal goes in a negative direction (just before T1), the diode remains forward biased (limiting is still present) until the input signal exceeds -4 V (T1). D_1 becomes reverse biased as the anode becomes more negative than the cathode. While the input signal is more negative than the -4 V of the bias battery (T1 to T2), the diode is reverse biased and remains cut off. The output follows the input signal from T1 to T2. At all other times during that cycle, the diode is forward biased and limiting occurs. This circuit is called a parallel-positive limiter with negative bias because the positive output is limited and the bias in the circuit is negative with reference to ground. Limiting takes place at all points more positive than -4 V.

The circuit shown in Figure 7-4-12A is a parallel-positive limiter with positive bias. The positive terminal of the battery is connected to the cathode of the diode. This causes the diode to be reverse biased at all times except when the input signal is more positive than the bias voltage (T1 to T2), as shown in Figure 7-4-12B.

As the positive alternation of the input signal is applied (T0), the output voltage follows the input signal. From T1 to T2 the input signal is more positive than +4 V. The diode is forward biased and conducts. At this time the output voltage equals the bias voltage and limiting takes place. From T2 to T4 of the input signal, the diode is reverse biased and does not conduct. The output signal follows the input signal and no limiting takes place.

This circuit is called a parallel-positive limiter with positive bias because limiting takes place in the positive alternation and positive bias is used on the diode.

Parallel-Negative Limiter

A parallel-negative limiter is shown in Figure 7-4-13A. Notice the similarity of the parallel-negative limiter and the parallel-positive limiter shown in Figure 7-4-10A. From T0 to T1 of the input signal, the diode is reverse biased and does not conduct, as shown in Figure 7-4-13B. The output signal follows the input signal and the positive alternation is not limited.

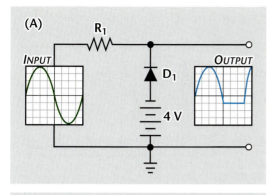

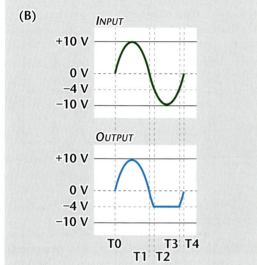

Figure 7-4-14. Parallel-negative limiter with negative bias

During the negative alternation of the input signal (T1 to T2), the diode is forward biased and conducts. The relatively low forward bias of D_1 develops a very small voltage and, therefore, limits the output to nearly 0 V. A voltage is developed across the resistor as current flows through the resistor and diode.

Parallel-Negative Limiter with Bias

The circuit shown in Figure 7-4-14A is a parallel-negative limiter with negative bias. With no input, the battery maintains D_1 in a reverse-bias condition. D_1 cannot conduct until its cathode is more negative than its anode. D_1 acts as an open until the input signal dips below -4 V at T2 in Figure 7-4-14B. At T2 the input signal becomes negative enough to forward bias the diode, D_1 conducts and acts like a short, and the output is limited to the -4 V from the battery from T2 to T3. Between T3 and T4 the diode is again reverse biased. The output signal follows the input signal and no limiting occurs.

Figure 7-4-15A shows a parallel-negative limiter with positive bias. The operation is similar to those circuits already explained. Limiting

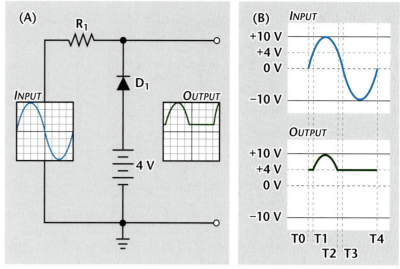

Figure 7-4-15. Parallel-negative limiter with positive bias

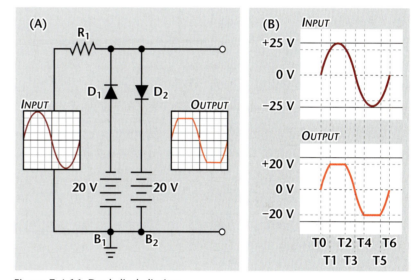

Figure 7-4-16. Dual-diode limiter

occurs when the diode conducts. No limiting occurs when the diode is reverse biased. In this circuit, the bias battery provides forward bias to the diode without an input signal. The output is at +4 V, except where the input goes above +4 V (T1 to T2), as shown in Figure 7-4-15B. The parts of the signal more negative than +4 V are limited.

Dual-Diode Limiters

The last type of limiter to be discussed in this section is the *dual-diode limiter*, shown in Figure 7-4-16A. This limiter combines a parallel-negative limiter with negative bias (D_1 and B_1) and a parallel-positive limiter with positive bias (D_2 and B_2). Parts of both the positive and negative alternations are removed in this circuit. Each battery aids the reverse bias of the diode in its circuit; the circuit has no current flow with no input

7-38 | Frequency Generation

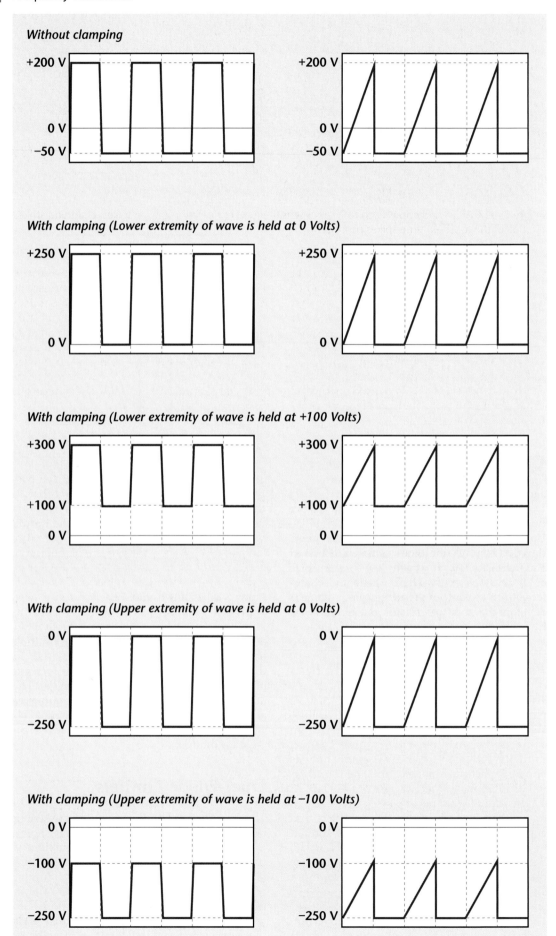

Figure 7-4-18. Clamping waveforms

Figure 7-4-17. A diode clamp is used to protect sensitive electronics from voltage spikes. Lightning strikes are one of the most extreme spikes possible.

signal. When the input signal is below the value of the biasing batteries, both D_1 and D_2 are reverse biased. With D_1 and D_2 reverse biased, the output follows the input. When the input signal becomes more positive than +20 V (Figure 7-4-16B), D_2 conducts and limits the output to +20 V. When the input signal becomes more negative than -20 V, D_1 conducts and limits the output to this value. When neither diode conducts, the output follows the input waveform.

Clampers

Certain applications in electronics require that the upper or lower extremity of a wave be fixed at a specific value. In such applications, a *clamping* (or *clamper*) circuit is used. A clamping circuit clamps or restrains either the upper or lower extremity of a waveform to a fixed DC potential. This circuit is also known as a direct-current restorer or a baseline stabilizer. Such circuits are used in test equipment, radar systems, electronic countermeasure systems and sonar systems. A diode clamp can be used to protect sensitive electronics from voltage spikes induced on connected wires (Figure 7-4-17). Depending upon the equipment, a technician may find negative or positive clampers with or without bias. Figure 7-4-18 illustrates some examples of waveforms created by clampers. However, before discussing clampers, a review of some relevant points about series RC circuits is necessary.

Series RC Circuits

Series RC circuits are widely used for coupling signals from one stage to another. If the time constant of the coupling circuit is comparatively long, the shape of the output waveform will be almost identical to that of the input. However, the output DC reference level may be different from that of the input. Figure 7-4-19A shows a typical RC coupling circuit in which the output reference level has been changed to 0 V. In this circuit, the values of R_1 and C_1 are chosen so that the capacitor will charge (during T0 to T1) to 20

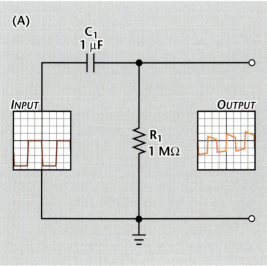
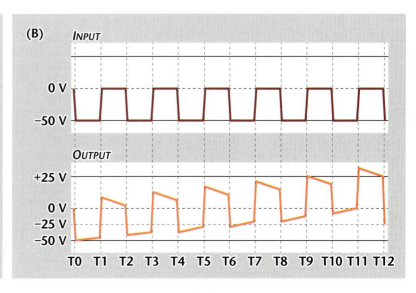

Figure 7-4-19. RC coupling

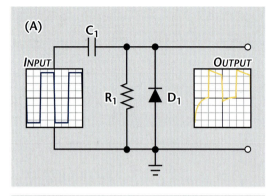

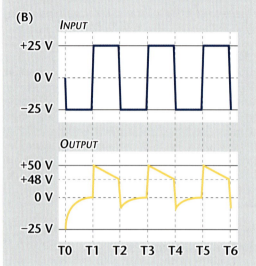

Figure 7-4-20. Positive clamper and waveform

percent of the applied voltage, as shown in Figure 7-4-19B. With this in mind, let's consider the operation of the circuit.

At T0 the input voltage is -50 V and the capacitor begins charging. At the first instant the voltage across C is 0 V and the voltage across R is -50 V. As C charges, its voltage increases. The voltage across R, which is the output voltage, begins to drop as the voltage across C increases. At T1 the capacitor has charged to 20 percent of the -50 V input, or -10 V. Because the input voltage is now 0 V, the capacitor must discharge. It discharges through the low impedance of the signal source and through R, developing +10 V across R at the first instant. C discharges 20 percent of the original 10-V charge from T1 to T2. Thus, C discharges to +8 V and the output voltage also drops to 8 V.

At T2 the input signal becomes -50 V again. This -50 V is in series opposition to the 8-V charge on the capacitor. Thus, the voltage across R totals -42 V (-50 V plus +8 V). Notice that this value of voltage is smaller in amplitude than the amplitude of the output voltage that occurred at T0 (-50 V). Capacitor C now charges from +8 V to +16 V. When continuing to follow the operation of the circuit, the technician will find that the output wave shape would become exactly distributed around the 0-V reference point. At that time, the circuit operation would have reached a stable operating point. Note that the output wave shape has the same amplitude and approximately the same shape as the input wave shape, but now "rides" equally above and below 0 V. Clampers use this RC time so that the input and output waveforms will be almost identical, as shown from T11 to T12.

Positive-Diode Clampers

Figure 7-4-20A illustrates the circuit of a positive-diode clamper. Resistor R_1 provides a discharge path for C_1. This resistance is large in value so that the discharge time of C_1 will be long compared to the input pulse width. The diode provides a fast charge path for C_1. After C_1 becomes charged, it acts as a voltage source. The input wave shape shown in Figure 7-4-20B is a square wave and varies between +25 V and -25 V. Compare each portion of the input wave shape with the corresponding output wave shape. Keep Kirchhoff's law in mind: The sum of the voltage drops around a closed loop is 0 at any instant.

At T0 the -25 V input signal appears across R_1 and D_1 (the capacitor is a short at the first instant). The initial voltage across R_1 and D_1 causes a voltage spike in the output. Because the charge time of C_1 through D_1 is almost instantaneous, the duration of the pulse is so short that it has only a negligible effect on the output. The -25 V across D_1 makes the cathode negative with respect to the anode and the diode conducts heavily. C_1 quickly charges through the small resistance of D_1. As the voltage across C_1 increases, the output voltage decreases at the same rate. The voltage across C_1 reaches -25 V and the output is at 0 V.

At T1 the +25 V already across the capacitor and the +25 V from the input signal are in series and aid each other (*series aiding*). Thus, +50 V appears across R_1 and D_1. At this time, the cathode of D_1 is positive with respect to the anode, and the diode does not conduct. From T1 to T2, C_1 discharges to approximately +23 V (because of the large values of R and C) and the output voltage drops from +50 V to +48 V.

At T2 the input signal changes from +25 V to -25 V. The input is now *series opposing* with the +23 V across C_1. This leaves an output voltage of -2 V (-25 V plus +23 V). The cathode of D_1 is negative with respect to the anode and D_1 conducts. From T2 to T3, C_1 quickly charges through D_1 from +23 V to +25 V; the output voltage changes from -2 V to 0 V.

At T3 the input signal and capacitor voltage are again series aiding. Thus, the output voltage felt across R_1 and D_1 is again +50 V. During T3 and T4, C_1 discharges 2 V through R_1. Notice that circuit operation from T3 to T4 is the same as it was from T1 to T2. The circuit operation for each square-wave cycle repeats the operation that occurred from T2 to T4.

Compare the input wave shape of Figure 7-4-20B with the output wave shape. Note the following important points:

- The peak-to-peak amplitude of the input wave shape has not been changed by the clamper circuit.
- The shape of the output wave shape has not been significantly changed from that of the input by the action of the clamper circuit.
- The output wave shape is now all above 0 V, whereas the input wave shape is both above and below 0 V.

Thus, the lower part of the input wave shape has been clamped to a DC potential of 0 V in the output. This circuit is referred to as a *positive clamper* since all of the output wave shape is above 0 V and the bottom is clamped at 0 V.

The positive clamper circuit is self-adjusting. This means that the bottom of the output waveform remains clamped at 0 V during changes in input signal amplitude. Also, the output wave shape retains the form and peak-to-peak amplitude (50 V in this case) of the input wave shape. When the input amplitude becomes greater, the charge of the capacitor becomes greater and the output amplitude becomes larger. When the input amplitude decreases, the capacitor does not charge as high as before and clamping occurs at a lower output voltage. The capacitor charge, therefore, changes with signal strength.

The size of R_1 and C_1 has a direct effect on the operation of the clamper. Because of the small resistance of the diode, the capacitor charge time is short. If either R_1 or C_1 is made smaller, the capacitor discharges faster (t = RC).

The ability of a smaller value capacitor to quickly discharge to a lower voltage is an *advantage* when the amplitude of the input wave shape is suddenly reduced. However, for normal clamper operation, quick discharge time is a *disadvantage*. This is because one objective of clamping is to keep the output wave shape the same as the input wave shape. If the small capacitor allows a relatively large amount of the voltage to discharge with each cycle, then distortion occurs in the output wave shape. A larger portion of the wave shape then appears on the wrong side of the reference line.

Increasing the value of the resistor increases the discharge time (again, t = RC). This increased value causes the capacitor to discharge more slowly and produces an output wave shape that is

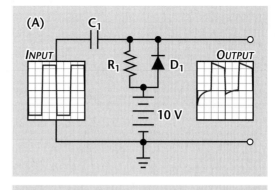

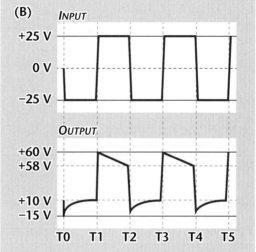

Figure 7-4-21. Positive clamper with positive bias

a better reproduction of the input wave shape. A disadvantage of increasing the resistance value is that the larger resistance increases the discharge time of the capacitor and slows the self-adjustment rate of the circuit, particularly if a sudden decrease in input amplitude should occur. The larger resistance has no effect on self-adjustment with a sudden rise in input amplitude. This is because the capacitor charges through the small resistance of the conducting diode.

Circuits often incorporate a compromise between a short RC time constant (for self-adjustment purposes) and a long RC time constant for less distortion. A point to observe is that the reverse resistance of the diode sometimes replaces the physical resistor in the discharge path of the capacitor.

Positive-Diode Clamper with Bias

Biased clamping circuits operate in exactly the same manner as unbiased clampers, with one exception: the addition of a DC bias voltage in series with the diode and resistor. The size and polarity of this bias voltage determines the output clamping reference.

Figure 7-4-21A illustrates the circuit of a positive clamper with positive bias. It can be identified as a positive clamper because the cathode of the diode is connected to the capacitor. Positive bias can be observed by noting that the negative side of the battery is connected to ground. The purposes and actions of the capacitor, resistor and diode are the same as in the unbiased clamper circuit just discussed.

With no input, D_1 is forward biased and the +10 V battery is the output. C_1 will charge to +10 V and hold this charge until the first pulse is applied. The battery establishes the DC reference level at +10 V. The input wave shape at the top of Figure 7-4-21B is a square wave that alternates between +25 and -25 V. The output wave shape is shown at the bottom half of Figure 7-4-21B.

Here, as with previous circuits, apply Kirchhoff's voltage law to determine circuit operation. With no input signal, the output is just the +10 V supplied by the battery.

At time T0 the -25 V signal applied to the circuit is instantly felt across R_1 and D_1. The -25-V input signal forward biases D_1, and C_1 quickly charges to 35 V. This leaves +10 V across the output terminals for much of the period from T0 to T1. The polarity of the charged capacitor is, from the left to the right, minus to plus.

At T1 the 35 V across the capacitor is series aiding with the +25-V input signal. At this point (T1) the output voltage becomes +60 V; the voltage across R_1 and D_1 is +50 V, and the battery is +10 V. The cathode of D_1 is positive with respect to the anode and the diode does not conduct. From T1 to T2, C_1 discharges only slightly through the large resistance of R_1. Assume that, because of the size of R_1 and C_1, the capacitor discharges just 2 V (from +35 V to +33 V) during this period. Thus, the output voltage drops from +60 V to +58 V.

At T2 the -25-V input signal and the +33 V across C_1 are series opposing. This makes the voltage across the output terminals +8 V. The cathode of the diode is 2 V negative with respect to its anode and D_1 conducts. Again, since the forward-biased diode is essentially a short, C_1 quickly charges from +33 V to +35 V. During most of the time from T2 to T3, then the output voltage is +10 V.

At T3 the +25 V of the input signal is series aiding with the +35 V across C_1. Again the output voltage is +60 V. Observe that at T3 the conditions in the circuit are the same as they were at T1. Therefore, the circuit operation from T3 to T4 is the same as it was from T1 to T2. Circuit operation continues as a duplication of the operations that occurred from T1 to T3.

Compare the input and output wave shapes and note the following:

- The peak-to-peak amplitude of the input wave shape has not been changed in the output (for all practical purposes) by the action of the clamper circuit.

- The shape of the input wave has not been changed.

- The output wave shape is now clamped above +10 V.

Remember that this clamping level is determined by the bias battery.

Positive-Diode Clamper with Negative Bias

Figure 7-4-22A is a positive clamper with negative bias. Observe that with no input signal, the capacitor charges through R_1 to the bias battery voltage; the output voltage equals -10 V. The circuit has negative bias because the positive side of the battery is grounded. The output waveform is shown in Figure 7-4-22B. Study

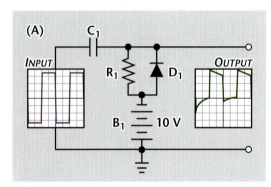
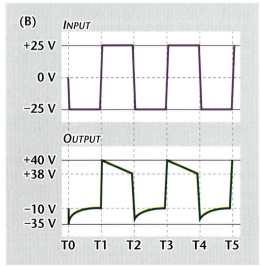

Figure 7-4-22. Positive clamper with negative bias

the figure and waveforms carefully and note the following important points. Once again the peak-to-peak amplitude and shape of the output wave are, for all practical purposes, the same as the input wave. The lower extremity of the output wave is clamped to -10 V, the value of the battery.

Look at the circuit operation. The capacitor is initially charged to -10 V with no input signal, and diode D_1 does not conduct. The -25-V input signal provides forward bias for D_1. The capacitor charges to +15 V and retains most of its charge because its discharge through R_1 is negligible. The +25-V input signal is series aiding the capacitor voltage and develops +40 V between the output terminals. When the input voltage is -25 V, D_1 conducts and the output voltage is -10 V (-25 V plus +15 V). In this way the output reference is clamped at -10 V. Changing the size of the battery changes the clamping reference level to the new voltage.

Negative-Diode Clampers

Figure 7-4-23A illustrates the circuit of a negative-diode clamper. Compare this with the positive-diode clamper in Figure 7-4-20A. Note that the diode is reversed with reference to ground. Like the positive clamper, resistor R_1 provides a discharge path for C_1; the resistance must be a large value for C_1 to have a long discharge time. The low resistance of the diode provides a fast charge path for C_1. Once C_1 becomes charged, it acts as a source of voltage that will help determine the maximum and minimum voltage levels of the output wave shape.

The input wave shape shown in Figure 7-4-23B is a square wave that varies between +25 and -25 V. The output wave shapes are shown in the bottom half of Figure 7-4-23B. The operation of the negative clamper is similar to that of the positive clamper, except for the reversal of polarities.

At T0 the +25 V input signal applied to the circuit appears across R_1 and D_1. This makes the anode of D_1 positive with respect to the cathode and it conducts heavily. Diode resistance is very small, causing C_1 to charge quickly. As the voltage across C_1 increases, the output voltage decreases. The voltage across C_1 reaches 25 V quickly; during most of T0 to T1, the output voltage is 0.

At T1 the voltage across the capacitor and the input voltage are series aiding and result in -50 V appearing at the output. At this time the diode is reverse biased and does not conduct. Because of the size of R and C, the

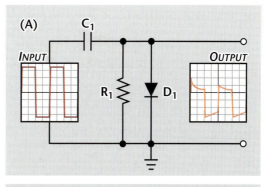

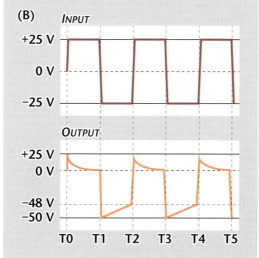

Figure 7-4-23. Positive clamper with negative bias

capacitor discharges only 2 V, to approximately 23 V, from T1 to T2. Using Kirchhoff's voltage law to determine voltage in the circuit, the output voltage decreases from -50 to -48 V.

At T2 the +25-V input signal and the 23 V across C_1 are series opposing. The output voltage is +2 V. The anode of D_1 is positive with respect to the cathode and D_1 will conduct. From T2 to T3, C_1 charges quickly from 23 V to 25 V through D_1. At the same time, the output voltage falls from +2 V to 0 V.

At T3 the input and capacitor voltages are series aiding and the total output voltage is -50 V. From T3 to T4, D_1 is reverse biased and C discharges through R. The circuit operation is now the same as it was from T1 to T2. The circuit operation for the following square-wave cycles duplicates the operation that occurred from T1 to T3.

As was the case with the positive clamper, the amplitude and wave shape of the output are almost identical to that of the input. However, note that the upper extremity of the output wave shape is clamped to 0 V; that is, the output wave shape, for all practical purposes, lies entirely below the 0 V reference level.

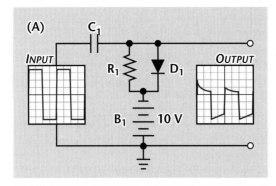
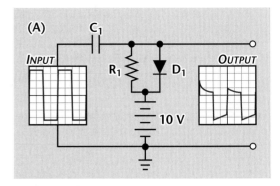

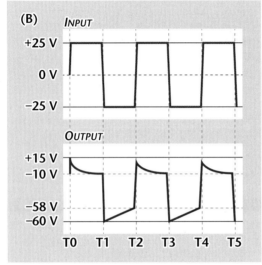

Figure 7-4-24. Negative damper with negative bias

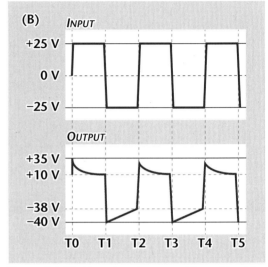

Figure 7-4-25. Negative clamper with positive bias

Negative-Diode Clamper with Negative Bias

Figure 7-4-24A is the circuit of a negative clamper with negative bias. Again, with no input signal the capacitor charges to the battery voltage and the output is negative because the positive side of the battery is ground. The bottom of Figure 7-4-24B shows the output of the circuit. Study the figure carefully, and note the following important points. The peak-to-peak amplitude and shape of the output wave, for all practical purposes, are the same as that of the input wave. The output wave is clamped to -10 V, which is the value of the battery. Since this is a negative clamper, the upper extremity of the waveform touches the -10 V-reference line and the rest of it lies below this voltage level.

Now review the important points of circuit operation. The capacitor is initially charged to -10 V with no input signal. Apply Kirchhoff's law to see that the +25-V input signal and the 10-V battery are series opposing. This series opposing forward biases D_1 and the capacitor charges to -35 V. The output voltage is equal to the sum of the capacitor voltage and the input voltage. Thus, the output voltage is -10 V and the wave shape is clamped to -10 V. With a -25 V input, the charge maintained across C_1 and the input are series aiding and provide a -60 V output. C_1 will discharge just before the next cycle begins and the input becomes positive. The +25-V input signal and the approximately -23 V charge remaining on C_1 will forward bias D_1 and the output will be clamped to the battery voltage. C_1 will quickly charge to the input signal level. Thus, the output voltage varies between -10 V and -60 V and the wave shape is clamped to -10 V.

Negative Clamper With Positive Bias

Figure 7-4-25A illustrates the circuit of a negative clamper with positive bias. With no input signal the capacitor charges to the battery voltage and the output is positive because the negative side of the battery is grounded. The output is illustrated in the bottom half of Figure 7-4-25B. Study the figure carefully and note the following important points. The peak-to-peak amplitude and shape of the output waveform, for all practical purposes, are the same as that of the input. The output wave is clamped to +10 V, the value of the battery. Since this is a negative clamper (cathode to ground), the top of the output wave touches the +10 V reference line.

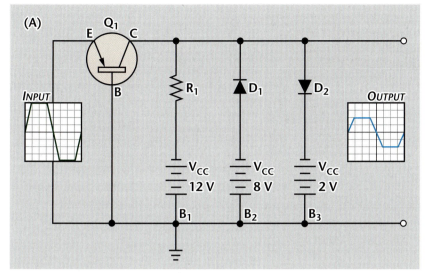 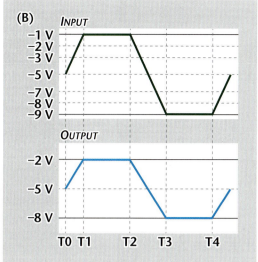

Figure 7-4-26. Common-base configuration clamper

To review, study the following summary of the circuit operation. With no input signal the capacitor charges to 10 V. The +25-V input signal forward biases D_1. With the 10 V battery and the input in series, the capacitor charges to -15 V. The capacitor remains charged, for all practical purposes, since its discharge through R_1 is almost negligible. The output voltage is equal to the sum of the capacitor voltage and the input voltage. The +25-V input signal added to the -15 V capacitor charge provides a +10 V output. With a -25-V input at T1, D_1 is reverse biased and the charge across C_1 adds to the input voltage to provide a -40-V output. From T1 to T2, the capacitor loses only a small portion of its charge. At T2 the input signal is +25 V and the input returns to +10 V. The wave shape is negatively clamped to +10 V by the battery.

This shows then that positive clamping sets the wave shape above (i.e., the negative peak is on) the reference level, and negative clamping places the wave shape below (i.e., the positive peak is on) the reference level.

Common-Base Transistor Clamper

The common-base transistor clamper is similar to a dual-diode limiter, except for the addition of a transistor. In the previous clampers, the output signal was clamped to a reference. In the common-base transistor clamper, it is necessary to clamp the amplitude of the input to no more than nor no less than certain values in the output. Also, phase inversion in the output is not desirable. Figure 7-4-26A shows such a circuit. The transistor does not amplify the input and the output is not inverted. However, the two diode circuits serve to clamp the output between -2 and -8 V, no matter the varying input positive and negative extremes.

Look at Figure 7-4-26B. The input signal is a square-wave pulse-type signal that varies in amplitude. Without an input signal, Q_1 conducts and provides current through R_1. This develops the output (collector-to-ground) potential, which is assumed to be approximately -5 V (V_{CC} - E_{R1}) for this discussion.

From T0 to T1 the output follows the input because of the increasing emitter-base forward bias. However, at T1 the collector voltage reaches -2 V and D_2 is forward biased. D_2 conducts and limits the output to -2 V (the value of B_3). D_2 conducts until T2, when the input decreases below -2 V. At this time, D_2 cuts off and the output again follows the input because of the decreasing forward bias on Q_1. At T3 the input reaches -8 V and forward biases D_1. D_1 conducts and any further increase (beyond -8 V) of the input has no effect on the output. When the input returns to a value more positive than -8 V, D_1 cuts off and the output again follows the input. This circuit action is the same for all inputs. The output remains the same as the input except that both positive and negative extremes are clamped at -2 V and -8 V, respectively.

Shaping Circuits

Timing circuits and circuits that require a particular shape or "spike" of voltage, may use shaping circuits. Shaping circuits can be used to cause wave shapes (e.g., square waves, sawtooth waves, trapezoidal waves) to change their shape. Shaping circuits may be either series RC or series RL circuits. The time constant is controlled in respect to the duration of the applied waveform. Notice that the wave shapes mentioned did not include the sine wave. These RC or RL shaping circuits do not change the shape of a pure sine wave.

Composition of Nonsinusoidal Waves

Pure sine waves are basic wave shapes from which other wave shapes can be constructed. Any waveform that is not a pure sine wave consists of two or more sine waves. Adding the correct frequencies at the proper phase and amplitude will form square waves, sawtooth waves and other nonsinusoidal waveforms.

The series RC and RL circuits electrically perform the mathematical operations of integration and differentiation. Therefore, the circuits used to perform these operations are called integrators and differentiators. These names are applied to these circuits even though they do not always completely perform the operations of mathematical integration and differentiation.

A waveform other than a sine wave is called a *complex wave*. A complex wave consists of a fundamental frequency plus one or more harmonic frequencies. The shape of a nonsinusoidal waveform is dependent upon the type of harmonics present as part of the waveform, their relative amplitudes and their relative phase relationships. In general, the steeper the sides of a waveform—that is, the more rapid its rise and fall—the more harmonics it contains.

The sine wave that has the lowest frequency in the complex periodic wave is referred to as the *fundamental frequency*. The type and number of harmonics included in the waveform are dependent upon the shape of the waveform. Harmonics have two classifications: *even numbered* and *odd numbered*.

Harmonics are always a whole number of times higher than the fundamental frequency and are designated by an integer. For example, the frequency twice as high as the fundamental frequency is the second harmonic (or the first even harmonic).

Figure 7-4-27A compares a square wave with sine waves. Sine wave K is the same frequency as the square wave (its fundamental frequency). If another sine wave (L) of smaller amplitude but three times the frequency (referred to as the third harmonic) is added to sine wave K, curve M is produced. The addition of these two waveforms is accomplished by adding the instantaneous values of both sine waves algebraically. Curve M is called the *resultant*. Notice that curve M begins to assume the shape of a square wave. Curve M is shown again in Figure 7-4-27B.

As shown in Figure 7-4-27B, when the fifth harmonic (curve N, with its decreased amplitude) is added, the sides of the new resultant (curve P) are steeper than before. In Figure 7-4-27C, the addition of the seventh harmonic (curve Q), which is of even smaller amplitude, makes the sides of the composite waveform (R) still steeper. The addition of more odd harmonics will bring the composite waveform nearer the shape of the perfect square wave. A perfect square wave is, therefore, composed of an infinite number of odd harmonics. In the composition of square waves, all the odd harmonics cross the reference line in phase with the fundamental.

A sawtooth wave, shown in Figure 7-4-28, is made up of both even and odd harmonics. Notice that each higher harmonic is added in phase as it crosses the 0 reference in Figure 7-4-28A, Figure 7-4-28B, Figure 7-4-28C and Figure 7-4-28D. The resultant, shown in Figure 7-4-28D, closely resembles a sawtooth waveform.

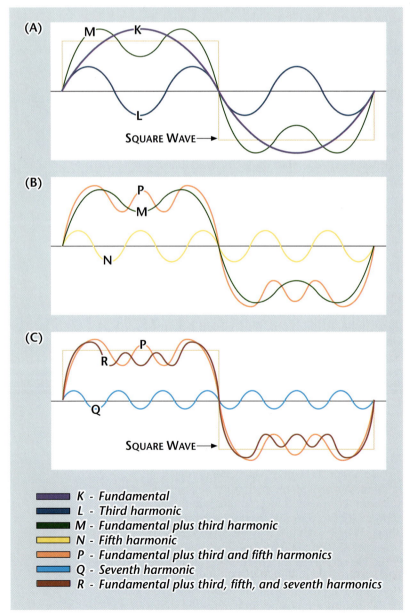

Figure 7-4-27. Harmonic composition of a square wave

Frequency Generation | 7-47

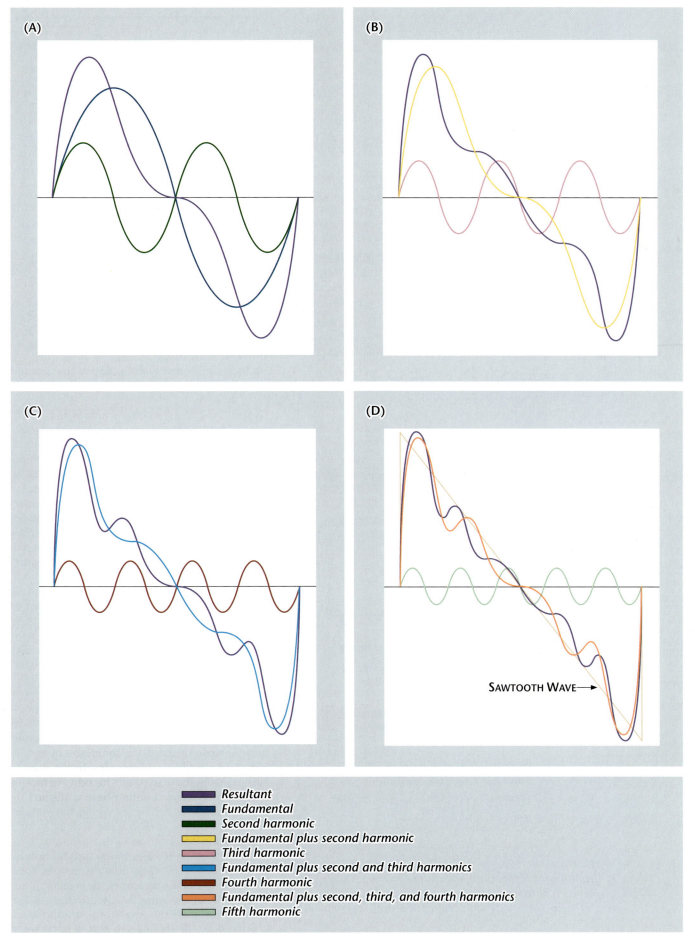

Figure 7-4-28. Composition of a sawtooth wave

7-48 | Frequency Generation

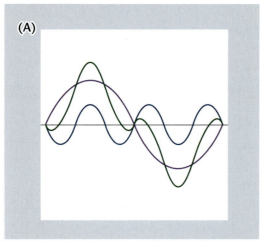

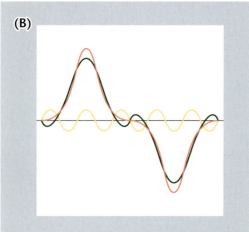

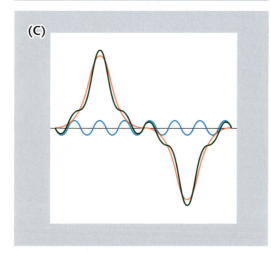

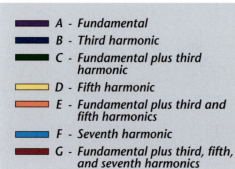

- A - Fundamental
- B - Third harmonic
- C - Fundamental plus third harmonic
- D - Fifth harmonic
- E - Fundamental plus third and fifth harmonics
- F - Seventh harmonic
- G - Fundamental plus third, fifth, and seventh harmonics

Figure 7-4-29. Composition of a peaked wave

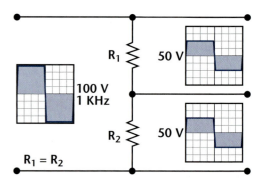

Figure 7-4-30. Square wave applied to a resistive circuit

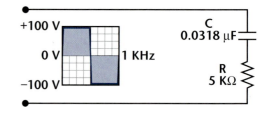

Figure 7-4-31. Square wave applied to an RC circuit

Figure 7-4-29 shows the composition of a peaked wave. Notice how the addition of each odd harmonic makes the peak of the resultant higher and the sides steeper. The phase relationship between the harmonics of the peaked wave is different from the phase relationship of the harmonics in the composition of the square wave. In the composition of the square wave, all the odd harmonics cross the reference line in phase with the fundamental. In the peaked wave, harmonics such as the third, seventh, and so forth, cross the reference line 180° out of phase with the fundamental; the fifth, ninth, and so forth, cross the reference line in phase with the fundamental.

Nonsinusoidal voltages applied to an RC circuit. The harmonic content of a square wave must be complete to produce a pure square wave. If the harmonics of the square wave are not of the proper phase and amplitude relationships, the square wave will not be pure. The term *pure*, as applied to square waves, means that the waveform must be perfectly square.

Figure 7-4-30 shows a pure square wave that is applied to a series-resistive circuit. If the values of the two resistors are equal, the voltage developed across each resistor will be equal; that is, from one pure square-wave input, two pure square waves of a lower amplitude will be produced. The value of the resistors does not affect the phase or amplitude relationships of the harmonics contained within the square waves. This is true because the same opposition is offered by the resistors to all the harmonics presented. However, if the same square wave

Figure 7-4-32. RC integrator and waveshaping networks are critical to the function of radar systems.

is applied to a series RC circuit, as shown in Figure 7-4-31, the circuit action is not the same.

RC Integrator

The *RC integrator* is used as a waveshaping network in communications, radar and computers (Figure 7-4-32). The harmonic content of the square wave is made up of odd multiples of the fundamental frequency. Therefore, *significant harmonics* (those that have an effect on the circuit) as high as 50 or 60 times the fundamental frequency will be present in the wave. The capacitor will offer a reactance (X_C) of a different magnitude to each of the harmonics

$$X_C = \frac{1}{2\pi fc}$$

This means that the voltage drop across the capacitor for each harmonic frequency present is not the same. To low frequencies, the capacitor offers a large opposition, providing a large voltage drop across the capacitor. To high frequencies, the reactance of the capacitor is extremely small, causing a small voltage drop across the capacitor. This is no different than was the case for low- and high-pass filters. If the voltage component of the harmonic is not developed across the reactance of the capacitor, it will be developed across the resistor, as stated by Kirchhoff's voltage law.

The harmonic amplitude and phase relationship across the capacitor is not the same as that of the original frequency input; therefore, a perfect square wave will not be produced across the capacitor. Remember that the reactance offered to each harmonic frequency will cause a change in both the amplitude and phase of each of the individual harmonic frequencies with respect to the current reference. The amount of phase and amplitude change taking place across the capacitor depends on the X_C of the capacitor. The value of the resistance offered by the resistor must also be considered here; it is part of the ratio of the voltage development across the network.

The circuit in Figure 7-4-33 will help show the relationships of R and X_C more clearly. The square wave applied to the circuit is 100 V peak at a frequency of 1 kHz. The odd harmonics will be 3 kHz, 5 kHz, 7 kHz, etc. Table 7-4-1 shows the

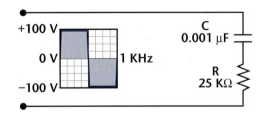

Figure 7-4-33. Partial integration circuit

HARMONIC	X_C	R
Fundamental	159kΩ	25kΩ
3rd	53kΩ	25kΩ
5th	31.8kΩ	25kΩ
7th	22.7kΩ	25kΩ
9th	17.7kΩ	25kΩ
11th	14.5kΩ	25kΩ

Table 7-4-1. Resistive and reactive values

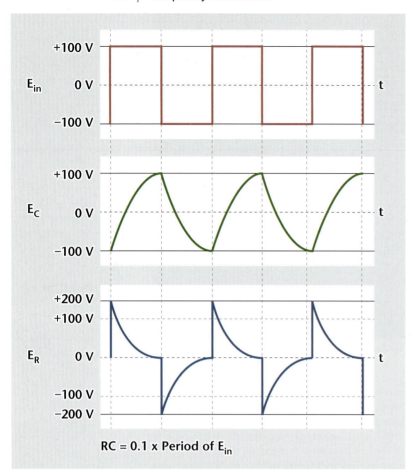

Figure 7-4-34. Partial waveform integration

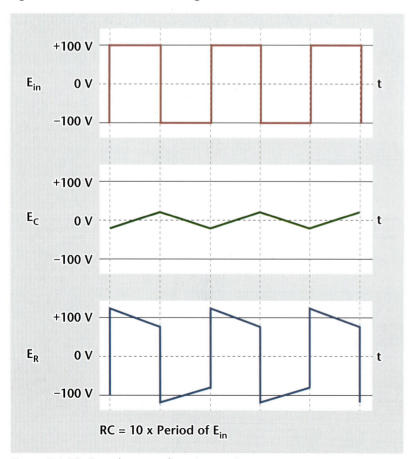

Figure 7-4-35. Complete waveform integration

values of X_C and R offered to several harmonics and indicates the approximate value of the cutoff frequency (X_C = R). The table clearly shows that the cutoff frequency lies between the fifth and seventh harmonics. Between these two values, the capacitive reactance will equal the resistance.

Therefore, for all harmonic frequencies above the fifth, the majority of the output voltage will not be developed across the output capacitor. Rather, most of the output will be developed across R. The absence of the higher order harmonics will cause the leading edge of the waveform developed across the capacitor to be rounded. An example of this effect is shown in Figure 7-4-34. If the value of the capacitance is increased, the reactances to each harmonic frequency will be further decreased. This means that even fewer harmonics will be developed across the capacitor.

The harmonics not effectively developed across the capacitor must be developed across the resistor to satisfy Kirchhoff's voltage law. Note the pattern of the voltage waveforms across the resistor and capacitor. If the waveforms across both the resistor and the capacitor were added graphically, the resultant would be an exact duplication of the input square wave.

When the capacitance is increased sufficiently, full integration of the input signal takes place in the output across the capacitor. An example of complete integration is shown in Figure 7-4-35 (waveform E_C). This effect can be caused by significantly decreasing the value of capacitive reactance. The same effect would take place by increasing the value of the resistance. Integration takes place in an RC circuit when the output is taken across the capacitor.

The amount of integration is dependent upon the values of R and C. The amount of integration may also be dependent upon the time constant of the circuit. The time constant of the circuit should be at least 10 times greater than the time duration of the input pulse for integration to occur. The value of 10 is only an approximation. When the time constant of the circuit is 10 or more times the value of the duration of the input pulse, the circuit is said to possess a *long time constant*. When the time constant is long, the capacitor does not have the ability to charge instantly to the value of the applied voltage. Therefore, the result is the long, sloping integrated waveform.

RL Integrator

The RL circuit may also be used as an integrating circuit. An integrated waveform may be obtained from the series RL circuit by taking the output across the resistor. The characteristics of the inductor are such that at the first instant of time in which voltage is applied, current flow through the inductor is minimum and the voltage developed across it is maximum. Therefore, the value of the voltage drop across the series resistor at that first instant must be 0 V because there is no current flow through it. As time passes, current begins to flow through the circuit and voltage develops across the resistor. Since the circuit has a long time constant, the voltage across the resistor does *not* respond to the rapid changes in voltage of the input square wave. Therefore, the conditions for integration in an RL circuit are a long time constant with the output taken across the resistor. These conditions are shown in Figure 7-4-36.

Integrator Waveform Analysis

If either an RC or RL circuit has a time constant 10 times greater than the duration of the input pulse, the circuits are capable of integration. Compute and graph the actual waveform that would result from a long time constant (10 times the pulse duration), a short time constant (1/10 of the pulse duration), and a medium time constant (that time constant between the long and the short). To accurately plot values for the capacitor output voltage, use the Universal Time Constant Chart shown in Figure 7-4-37.

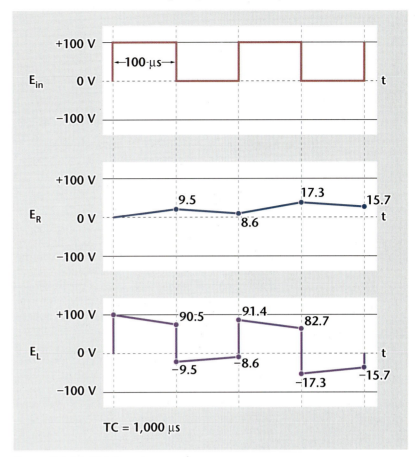

Figure 7-4-36. RL integrator waveform

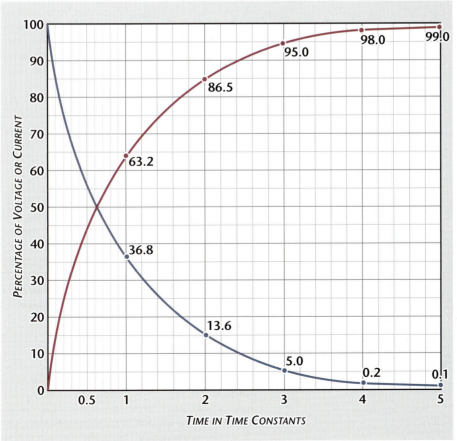

Figure 7-4-37. Universal Time Constant Chart

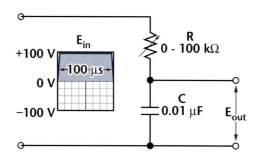

Figure 7-4-38. RC integrator circuit

As previously discussed, the capacitor charge follows the shape of the curve shown in Figure 7-4-37. This curve may be used to determine the amount of voltage across either component in the series RC circuit. As long as the time constant or a fractional part of the time constant is known, the voltage across either component may be determined.

Short time-constant integrator. In Figure 7-4-38, a 100-microsecond (μs) pulse at an amplitude of 100 V is applied to the circuit. The circuit is composed of the 0.01-μF capacitor and the variable resistor, R. The square wave applied is a pure square wave. The resistance of the variable resistor is set at a value of 1,000Ω. The time constant of the circuit is given by the equation:

$$TC = RC$$

Substituting values:

$$T = 1,000 \times 0.01 \; \mu F$$
$$T = (1 \times 10^3) \times (1 \times ^{-8})$$
$$T = 1 \times 10^{-5} \text{ vor 10 microseconds}$$

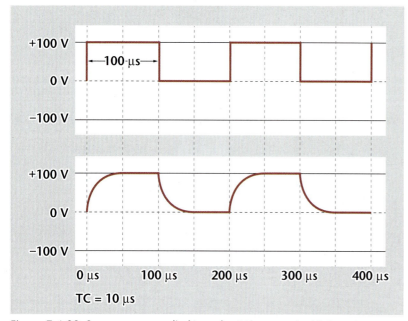

Figure 7-4-39. Square wave applied to a short time-constant integrator

Since the time constant of the circuit is 10 μs and the pulse duration is 100 μs, the time constant is short (1/10 of the pulse duration). The capacitor is charged exponentially through the resistor. In five time constants, the capacitor will be, for all practical purposes, completely charged. At the first time constant, the capacitor is charged to 63.2 V; at the second, 86.5 V; at the third, 95 V; at the fourth, 98 V; and finally at the end of the fifth time constant (50 μs), the capacitor is fully charged. This is shown in Figure 7-4-39.

Notice that the leading edge of the square wave taken across the capacitor is rounded. If the time constant were made extremely short, the rounded edge would become square.

Medium time-constant integrator. The time constant in Figure 7-4-39 can be changed by increasing the value of the variable resistor (Figure 7-4-38) to 10,000Ω. The time constant will then be equal to 100 μs.

This time constant is known as a medium time constant. Its value lies between the extreme ranges of the short and long time constants. In this case, its value happens to be exactly equal to the duration of the input pulse, 100 μs. The output waveform, after several time constants, is shown in Figure 7-4-40. The long, sloping rise and fall of voltage is caused by the inability of the capacitor to charge and discharge rapidly through the 10,000-Ω series resistance.

At the first instant of time, 100 V is applied to the medium time-constant circuit. In this circuit, 1 TC is exactly equal to the duration of the input pulse. After 1 TC the capacitor has charged to 63.2 percent of the input voltage (100 V). Therefore, at the end of 1 TC (100 μs), the voltage across the capacitor is equal to 63.2 V. However, as soon as 100 μs has elapsed and the initial charge on the capacitor has risen to 63.2 V, the input voltage suddenly drops to 0. It remains there for 100 μs.

The capacitor will now discharge for 100 μs. Since the discharge time is 100 μs (1 TC), the capacitor will discharge 63.2 percent of its total 63.2-V charge, a value of 23.3 V. During the next 100 μs, the input voltage will increase from 0 V to 100 V instantaneously. The capacitor will again charge for 100 μs (1 TC). The voltage available for this charge is the difference between the voltage applied and the charge on the capacitor (100 V - 23.3 V), or 76.7 V. Since the capacitor will only be able to charge for 1 TC, it will charge to 63.2 percent of the 76.7 V, or 48.4 V. The total charge on the capacitor at the end of 300 μs will be 23.3 V + 48.4 V, or 71.7 V.

Notice that the capacitor voltage at the end of 300 μs is greater than the capacitor voltage at the end of 100 μs. The voltage at the end of 100 μs is 63.2 V, and the capacitor voltage at the end of 300 μs is 71.7 V, an increase of 8.5 V.

The output waveform in this graph (E_C) is the waveform that will be produced after many cycles of input signal to the integrator. The capacitor will charge and discharge in a step-by-step manner until it finally charges and discharges above and below the 50 V level. The 50 V level is controlled by the maximum amplitude of the symmetrical input pulse, the average value of which is 50 V.

Long time-constant integrator. If the resistance in the circuit in Figure 7-4-38 is increased to 100,000Ω, the time constant of the circuit will be 1,000 μs. This time constant is 10 times the pulse duration of the input pulse. It is, therefore, a long time-constant circuit.

The shape of the output waveform across the capacitor is shown in Figure 7-4-41. The shape of the output waveform is characterized by a long, sloping rise and fall of capacitor voltage.

At the first instant of time, 100 V is applied to the long time-constant circuit. The value of charge on the capacitor at the end of the first 100 μs of the input signal can be found by using the Universal Time Constant Chart (Figure 7-4-37). Assume that a line is projected up from the point on the baseline corresponding to 0.1 TC. The line will intersect the curve at a point that is the percentage of voltage across the capacitor at the end of the first 100 μs. Since the applied voltage is 100 V, the charge on the capacitor at the end of the first 100 μs will be approximately 9.5 V. At the end of the first 100 μs, the input signal will fall suddenly to 0 and the capacitor will begin to discharge. It will be able to discharge for 100 μs.

Therefore, the capacitor will discharge 9.5 percent of its accumulated 9.5 V (.095 × 9.5 V = 0.90 V). The discharge of the 0.90 V will result in a remaining charge on the capacitor of 8.6 V. At the end of 200 μs, the input signal will again suddenly rise to a value of 100 V. The capacitor will be able to charge to 9.5 percent of the difference (100 V - 8.6 V = 91.4 V). This may also be figured as a value of 8.7 V plus the initial 8.6 V. This results in a total charge on the capacitor (at the end of the first 300 μs) of 8.7 V + 8.6 V = 17.3 V.

Notice that the capacitor voltage at the end of the first 300 μs is greater than the capacitor voltage at the end of the first 100 μs. The voltage at the end of the first 100 μs is 9.5 V; the capacitor voltage at the end of the first 300 μs is 17.3 V, an increase of 7.8 V.

The capacitor charges and discharges in this step-by-step manner until, finally, the capacitor charges and discharges above and below

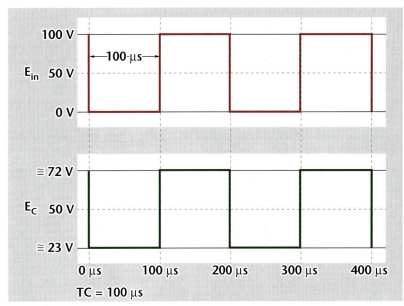

Figure 7-4-40. Medium time-constant integrator

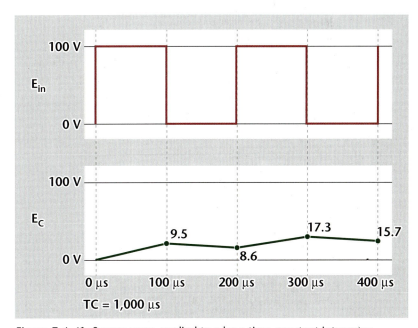

Figure 7-4-41. Square wave applied to a long time-constant integrator

the 50 V level. The 50 V level is controlled by the maximum amplitude of the square-wave input pulse, the average value of which is 50 V.

Differentiators

Differentiation is the direct opposite of integration. In the RC integrator, the output is taken from the capacitor. In the differentiator, the output is taken across the resistor. Likewise, this means that when the RL circuit is used as a differentiator, the differentiated output is taken across the inductor.

An application of Kirchhoff's law shows the relationship between the waveforms across

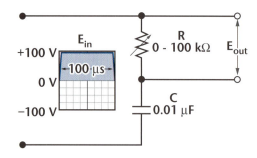

Figure 7-4-42. RC circuit as a differentiator

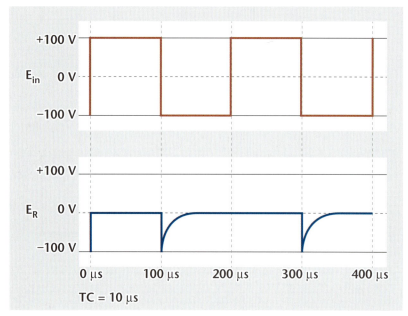

Figure 7-4-43. Square wave applied to a short time-constant differentiator

the resistor and capacitor in a series network. Since the sum of the voltage drops in a closed loop must equal the total applied voltage, the graphical sum of the voltage waveforms in a closed loop must equal the applied waveform. Figure 7-4-42 shows a differentiator circuit with the output taken across a variable resistor.

Short time-constant differentiator. With the variable resistor set at 1,000Ω and the capacitor value of 0.01 μF, the time constant of the circuit is 10 μs. Since the input waveform has a duration of 100 μs, the circuit is a short time-constant circuit.

At the first instant of time in the short time-constant circuit, the voltage across the capacitor is 0 V. Current flows through the resistor and causes a maximum voltage to be developed across it. This is shown at the first instant of time in the graph of Figure 7-4-43.

As the capacitor begins accumulating a charge, the voltage developed across the resistor will begin to decrease. At the end of the first time constant, the voltage developed across the resistor will have decreased by a value equal to 63.2 percent of the applied voltage. Since 100 V is applied, the voltage across the resistor after 1 TC will be 36.8 V. After the second time constant, the voltage across the resistor will be down to 13.5 V. At the end of the third time constant, E_R will be 5 V, and at the end of the fourth time constant, 2 V. At the end of the fifth time constant, the voltage across the resistor will be very close to 0 V. Since the time constant is equal to 10 μs, it will take a total of 50 μs to completely charge the capacitor and stop current flow in the circuit.

As shown in Figure 7-4-43, the slope of the charge curve will be very sharp. The voltage across the resistor will remain at 0 V until the end of 100 μs. At that time, the applied voltage suddenly drops to 0, and the capacitor will now discharge through the resistor. At this time, the discharge current will be at its maximum, causing a large discharge voltage to develop across the resistor. This is shown as the negative spike in Figure 7-4-43.

Since the current flow from the capacitor, which now acts like a source, is decreasing exponentially, the voltage across the resistor will also decrease. The resistor voltage will decrease exponentially to 0 V in 5 time constants. All of this discharge action will take a total of 50 μs. The discharge curve is also shown in Figure 7-4-43. At the end of 200 μs, the action begins again. The output waveform taken across the resistor in this short time-constant circuit is an example of differentiation. With the square wave applied, positive and negative spikes are produced in the output. These spikes approximate the rate of change of the input square wave.

Medium time-constant differentiator. The output across the resistor in an RC circuit of a medium time constant is shown in Figure 7-4-44. The value of the variable resistor has been increased to a value of 10,000Ω. This means that the time constant of the circuit is equal to the duration of the input pulse or 100 μs. For clarity, the voltage waveforms developed across both the resistor and the capacitor are shown. As before, the sum of the voltages across the resistor and capacitor must be equal to the applied voltage of 100 V.

At the first instant of time, a pulse of 100 V in amplitude with a duration of 100 μs is applied. Since the capacitor cannot respond quickly to the change in voltage, all of the applied voltage is felt across the resistor. Figure 7-4-44 shows the voltage across the resistor (E_R) to be 100 V and the voltage across the capacitor (E_C) to be 0 V. As time progresses, the capacitor charges. As the capacitor voltage increases, the resistor voltage decreases. Since the time that the capacitor is permitted to charge is 100 µs (equal to 1 TC in this circuit), the capacitor will charge to 63.2 percent of the applied voltage at the end of 1 TC, or 63.2 V. Because Kirchhoff's law must be followed at all times, the voltage across the resistor must be equal to the difference between the applied voltage and the charge on the capacitor (100 V - 63.2 V), or 36.8 V.

At the end of the first 100 µs, the input voltage suddenly drops to 0 V. The charge on the capacitor (-63.2 V) becomes the source and the entire voltage is developed across the resistor for the first instant.

The capacitor discharges during the next 100 µs. The voltage across the resistor decreases at the same rate as the capacitor voltage and total voltage is maintained at 0 V. This exponential decrease in resistor voltage is shown during the second 100 µs in Figure 7-4-42. The capacitor will discharge 63.2 percent of its charge to a value of 23.3 V at the end of the second 100 µs. The resistor voltage will rise in the positive direction to a value of -23.3 V to maintain the total voltage at 0 V.

At the end of 200 µs, the input voltage again rises suddenly to 100-V. Since the capacitor cannot respond to the 100-V increase instantaneously, the 100-V change takes place across the resistor. The voltage across the resistor suddenly rises from -23.3 V to +76.7 V. The capacitor will now begin to charge for 100 µs. The voltage will decrease across the resistor. This charge and discharge action will continue for many cycles. Finally, the voltage across the capacitor will rise and fall by equal amounts both above and below about a 50-V level. The resistor voltage will also rise and fall by equal amounts to about a 0-V level.

Long time-constant differentiator. If the time constant for the circuit in Figure 7-4-42 is increased to make it a long time-constant circuit, the differentiator output will appear more like the input. The time constant for the circuit can be changed by increasing the value of either capacitance or resistance. In this circuit, the time constant will be increased by increasing the value of resistance from 10,000Ω to 100,000Ω. Increasing the value of resistance will result in a time constant of 1,000 µs. This time constant is 10 times the duration of the input pulse. The output of this long time-constant circuit is shown in Figure 7-4-45.

At the first instant of time, a pulse of 100-V amplitude with a duration of 100 µs is applied.

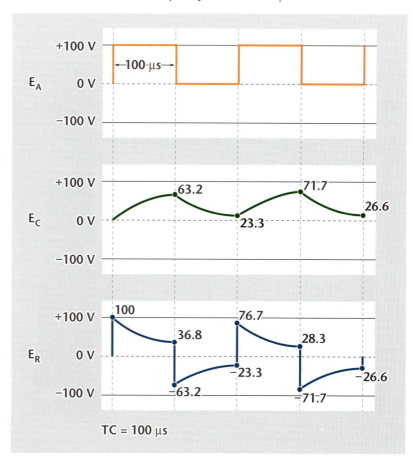

Figure 7-4-44. Voltage outputs in a medium time-constant differentiator

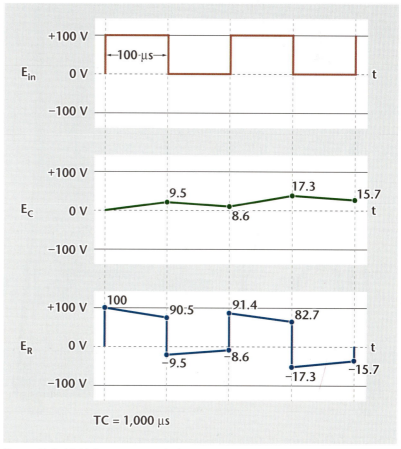

Figure 7-4-45. Voltage outputs in long time-constant differentiator

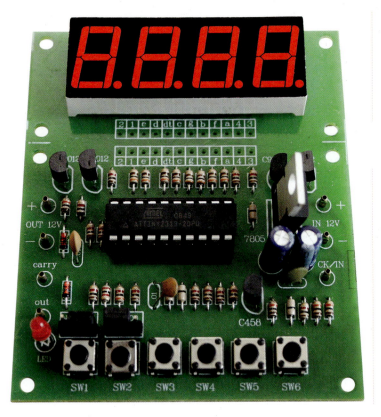

Figure 7-4-46. Four-digit counter

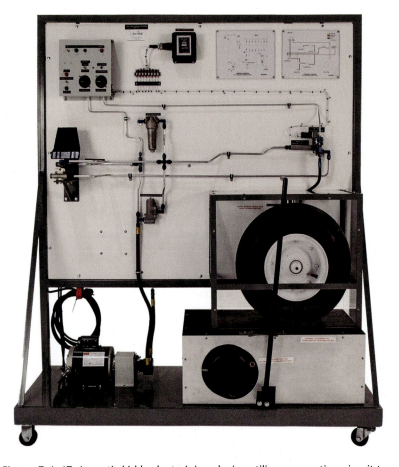

Figure 7-4-47. An anti-skid brake training device utilizes a counting circuit to register wheel speed.

Since the capacitor cannot respond instantaneously to a change in voltage, all of the applied voltage is felt across the resistor. As time progresses, the capacitor will charge and the voltage across the resistor will be reduced. Since the time that the capacitor is permitted to charge is 100 μs, the capacitor will charge for only 1/10 of 1 TC, or to 9.5 percent of the applied voltage. The voltage across the resistor must be equal to the difference between the applied voltage and the charge on the capacitor (100 V - 9.5 V), or 90.5 V.

At the end of the first 100 μs of input, the applied voltage suddenly drops to 0 V, a change of 100 V. Since the capacitor is not able to respond to so rapid a voltage change, it becomes the source of 9.5 V. This causes a -9.5 V to be felt across the resistor in the first instant of time. The sum of the voltage across the two components is now 0 V.

During the next 100 μs, the capacitor discharges. The total circuit voltage is maintained at 0 by the voltage across the resistor decreasing at exactly the same rate as the capacitor discharge. This exponential decrease in resistor voltage is shown during the second 100 μs of operation. The capacitor will now discharge 9.5 percent of its charge to a value of 8.6 V. At the end of the second 100 μs, the resistor voltage will rise in a positive direction to a value of -8.6 V to maintain the total circuit voltage at 0 V.

At the end of 200 μs, the input voltage again suddenly rises to 100 V. Since the capacitor cannot respond to the 100-V change instantaneously, the 100-V change takes place across the resistor. This step-by-step action will continue until the circuit stabilizes. After many cycles have passed, the capacitor voltage varies by equal amounts above and below the 50 V level. The resistor voltage varies by equal amounts both above and below a 0-V level.

The RC networks that have been discussed in this chapter may also be used as coupling networks. When an RC circuit is used as a coupling circuit, the output is taken from across the resistor. Normally, a long time-constant circuit is used. This will cause an integrated wave shape across the capacitor if the applied signal is nonsinusoidal. However, in a coupling circuit, the signal across the resistor should closely resemble the input signal, and will if the time constant is sufficiently long. Refer to the diagram in Figure 7-4-45 and notice that the voltage across the resistor closely resembles the input signal. Consider what would happen if a pure sine wave were applied to a long time-constant RC circuit (where R is much greater than X_C). A large percentage of the applied voltage would be developed across the resistor and only a small amount across the capacitor.

Counters

A counting circuit (Figure 7-4-46) receives uniform pulses representing units to be counted. It provides a voltage that is proportional to the frequency of the units.

With slight modification, the counting circuit can be used with a blocking oscillator to produce trigger pulses that are a submultiple of the frequency of the pulses applied. In this case the circuit acts as a frequency divider.

The pulses applied to the counting circuit must be of the same duration if accurate frequency division is to be made. Counting circuits are generally preceded by shaping circuits and limiting circuits (both discussed in this chapter) to ensure uniformity of amplitude and pulse width. Under those conditions, the pulse repetition frequency is the only variable, and frequency variations may be measured.

Positive Counters

The *positive-diode counter circuit* is used in timing or counting circuits in which the number of input pulses are represented by the output voltage. The output may indicate frequency, count the r.p.m. of a shaft, or register a number of operations (Figure 7-4-47). The counter establishes a direct relationship between the input frequency and the average DC output voltage. As the input frequency increases, the output voltage also increases; conversely, as the input frequency decreases, the output voltage decreases. In effect, the positive counter counts the number of positive input pulses by producing an average DC output voltage proportional to the repetition frequency of the input signal. For accurate counting, the pulse repetition frequency must be the only variable parameter in the input signal. Therefore, careful shaping and limiting of the input signal is essential to ensure that the pulses are of uniform width and that the amplitude is constant. When properly filtered and smoothed, the DC output voltage of the counter may be used to operate a direct reading indicator.

Solid-state and electron-tube counters operate in manners similar to each other. The basic solid-state (diode) counter circuit is shown in Figure 7-4-48A. Capacitor C_1 is the input coupling capacitor. Resistor R_1 is the

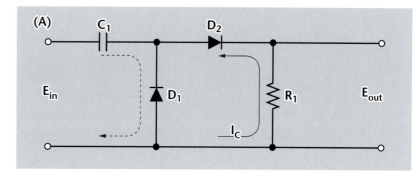

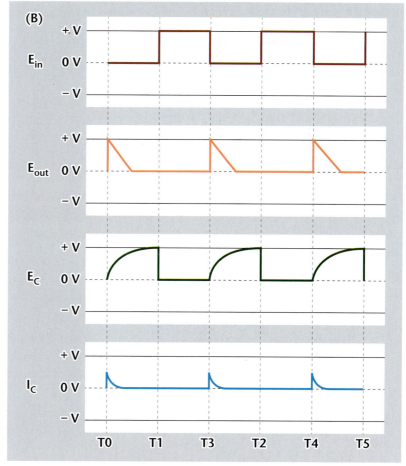

Figure 7-4-48. Positive-diode counter and waveform

load resistor across which the output voltage is developed. For the purpose of circuit discussion, assume that the input pulses (Figure 7-4-48B) are of constant amplitude and time duration and that only the pulse repetition frequency changes. At time T0, the positive-going input pulse is applied to C_1 and causes the anode of D_2 to become positive. D_2 conducts and current I_C flows through R_1 and D_2 to charge C_1. Current I_C develops an output voltage across R_1, shown as E_{out}.

The initial heavy flow of current produces a large voltage across R_1 that tapers off exponentially as C_1 charges. The charge on C_1 is determined by the time constant of R_1 and the conducting resistance of the diode times the capacitance of C_1. For ease of explanation,

7-58 | Frequency Generation

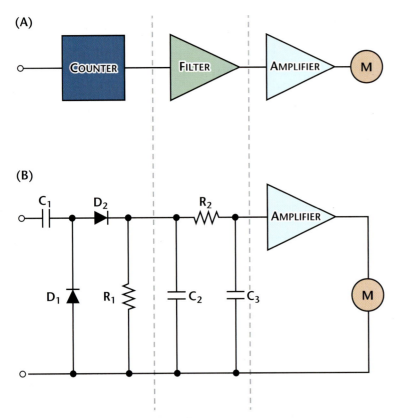

Figure 7-4-49. A basic frequency counter includes a filter and an amplifier.

assume that C_1 is charged to the peak value before T1.

At T1 the input signal reverses polarity and becomes negative-going. Although the charge on capacitor C_1 cannot change instantly, the applied negative voltage is equal to or greater than the charge on C_1. This causes the anode of D_2 to become negative and conduction ceases. When D_2 stops conducting Eout is at 0. C_1 quickly discharges through D_1 since its cathode is now negative with respect to ground. Between T1 and T2 the input pulse is again at the 0-V level and D_2 remains in a nonconducting state. Since the very short time constant provided by the conduction resistance of D_1 and C_1 is so much less than the long time constant offered by D_2 and R_1 during the conduction period, C_1 is always completely discharged between pulses. Thus, for each input pulse, a precise level of charge is deposited on C_1. For each charge of C_1 an identical output pulse is produced by the flow of Ic through R_1. Since this current flow always occurs in the direction indicated by the solid arrow, the DC output voltage is positive.

At T2 the input signal again becomes positive and the cycle repeats. The time between pulses is the interval represented by the period between T_1 and T_2 or between T_3 and T_4. If the input pulse frequency is reduced, these intervals become longer. On the other hand, if the frequency is increased, these intervals become shorter. With shorter periods, more pulses occur in a given length of time and a higher average DC output voltage is produced; with longer periods, fewer pulses occur and a lower average DC output voltage is produced. Thus, the DC output is directly proportional to the repetition frequency of the input pulses. If the current and voltage are sufficiently large, a direct-reading meter can be used to indicate the count. If they are not large enough to actuate a meter directly, a DC amplifier may be added. In the latter case, a pi-type filter network is inserted at the output of R_1 to absorb the instantaneous pulse

Figure 7-4-50. Navigation indicators, like these, are output devices that uses a counter circuit to measure the relationship of output voltage to input frequency.

variations and produce a smooth direct current for amplification.

It was noted in the preceding discussion that the voltage across the output varies in direct proportion to the input pulse repetition rate. Hence, if the repetition rate of the incoming pulses increases, the voltage across R_1 also increases. For the circuit to function as a frequency counter, some method must be employed to use this frequency-to-voltage relationship to operate an indicator. The block diagram in Figure 7-4-49A represents one simple circuit that may be used to perform this function. In this circuit, the basic counter is fed into a low-pass filter and an amplifier with a meter that is calibrated in units of frequency.

A typical schematic diagram is shown in Figure 7-4-49B. The positive pulses from the counter are filtered by C_2, R_2 and C_3. The positive DC voltage from the filter is applied to the input of amplifier A. This voltage increases with frequency; as a consequence, the current through the device increases. Since emitter or cathode current flows through M1, an increase in amplifier current causes an increase in meter deflection. The meter may be calibrated in units of time, frequency, revolutions per minute or any function based upon the relationship of output voltage to input frequency (Figure 7-4-50).

Negative Counters

Reversing the connections of diodes D_1 and D_2 in the positive-counter circuit (Figure 7-4-48A) causes the circuit to respond to negative pulses and become a *negative-counter circuit*. Diode D_2 conducts during the time the negative pulse is applied and current flows in the opposite direction through R_1, as indicated by the arrow. At the end of the negative pulse, D_1 conducts and discharges C_1. The current through R_1 increases with an increase in pulse frequency as before. However, if the voltage developed across R_1 is applied to the same control circuit, as shown in Figure 7-4-49A, the increase in current will be in a negative direction and the amplifier will conduct less. Thus, the effect is opposite to that of the positive counter.

Step-by-Step (Step) Counters

The *step-by-step (step) counter* is used as a voltage multiplier when a stepped voltage must be provided to any device that requires such an input. The step counter provides an output that increases in one-step increments for each cycle of the input. At some predetermined level, the output voltage reaches a point that causes a circuit, such as a blocking oscillator, to be triggered.

A schematic diagram of a positive step counter is shown in Figure 7-4-51A. For step counting, the load resistor of the positive-counter circuit is replaced by capacitor C_2. This capacitor is relatively large in comparison to C_1. Each time D_2 conducts, the charge on C_2 increases as shown in Figure 7-4-51B. The steps are not the same height each time. They decrease exponentially with time as the voltage across C_2 approaches the input voltage.

As long as C_2 has no discharge path, the voltage across its terminals increases with each successive step until it is equal in amplitude to the applied pulse. The voltage across C_2 could be applied to a blocking-oscillator circuit to cause the oscillator to pulse after a certain amount of voltage is applied to it.

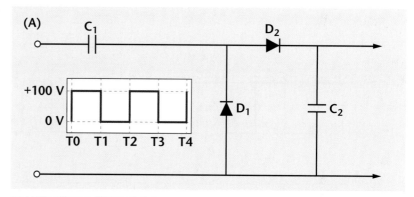

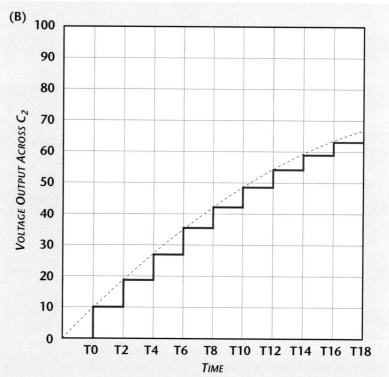

Figure 7-4-51. Basic step counter and waveforms

7-60 | Frequency Generation

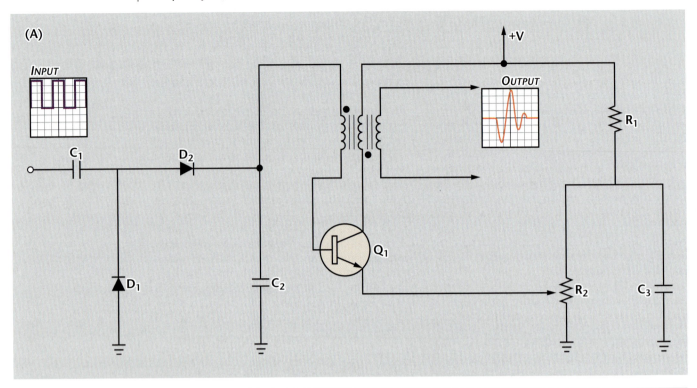

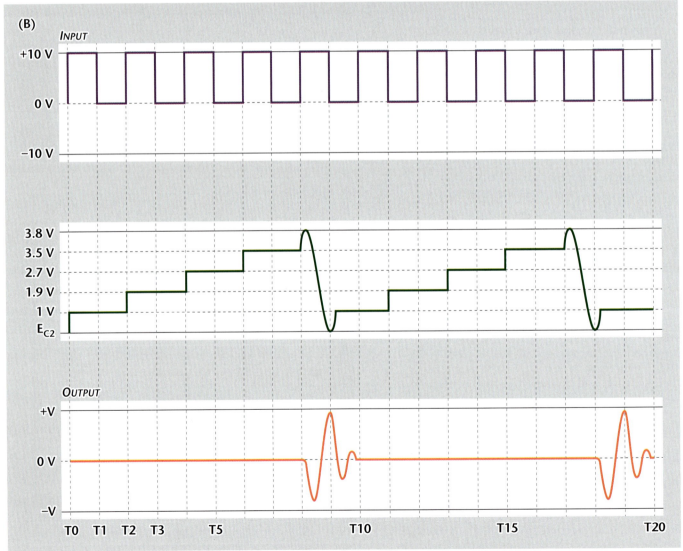

Figure 7-4-52. Step counter as frequency divider and waveforms

The circuit in Figure 7-4-52 may be used as a frequency divider. When used in this manner, Q_1 is used as a single-swing blocking oscillator that is triggered when the voltage across C_2 becomes great enough to forward bias Q_1. At other times, the transistor is cut off by the bias voltage developed in the section of R_2 that is between the ground and the slide.

The action of the counter can best be understood by referring back to Figure 7-4-51. Assume C_2 is 10 times larger than C_1 and the peak voltage is 10 V. C_1 will assume 9/10 of the positive input voltage at T0, while C_2 will assume only 1/10, or 1 V, in this example. At T1 the input will drop in a negative direction and D_2 will be cut off. The cathode of D_1 will become more negative than its anode and conduct, discharging C_1. The charge on C_2 will remain at 1 V because it has no discharge path. At T2 the second pulse will be applied. The 1-V charge on C_2 will oppose the 10 V of the second pulse, and the applied voltage for the capacitors to charge will be 9 V. C_2 will again charge 10 percent, or 0.9 V. This is in addition to the initial charge of 1 V. At the end of the second pulse, the voltage on C_2 will be 1.9 V. At T3 the third pulse will be 10 V, but 1.9 V will oppose it. Therefore, the applied voltage will be 10 V - 1.9 V, or 8.1 V. C_2 will charge to 10 percent of 8.1 V, or 0.81 V. The voltage on C_2 will become 1 V + 0.9 V + 0.81 V, or 2.71 V. Successive input pulses will raise C_2 by 10 percent of the remaining voltage toward 10 V until the blocking oscillator works. If the oscillator bias is set so that Q_1 begins conduction at 3.8 V, this will continue until 3.8 V is exceeded. Since the fourth step is 3.5 V and the fifth is 4.1 V, the 3.8 V level is crossed at the fifth step. If the oscillator goes through one cycle of operation every fifth step and C_2 is discharged at this point, this circuit would be a 5-to-1 divider.

The circuit can be made to divide by 3, 4, or some other value by setting the bias at a different level. For example, if the bias is set at 2.9 V, conduction will occur at the fourth step, making it a 4-to-1 divider.

The counting stability of the step counter is dependent upon the exponential charging rate of capacitor C_2. As C_2 increases to higher steps, the voltage increments are less and less. If the ratio becomes too great, the higher steps become almost indiscernible. For this reason, accuracy decreases as the ratio increases. . When it is necessary to count by a large number, 24 for example, a 6-to-1 counter and a 4-to-1 counter are connected in cascade (series). A more stable method of counting 24 would be to use 2-to-1, 3-to-1, and 4-to-1 counters connected in cascade. Most step counters operate on a ratio of 5-to-1 or less.

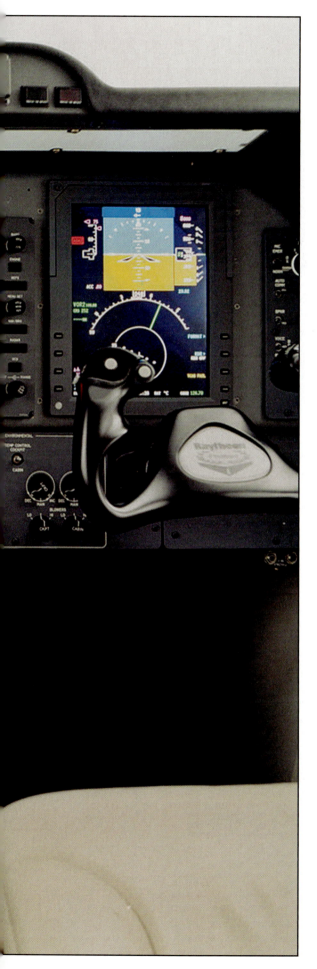

8

Digital Theory

Section 1

Numbering Systems

Computers where originally used wherever repeated calculations or the processing of huge amounts of data was needed. Today, computers have become inexpensive enough that they are used in almost all consumer electronics. More advanced computer systems are used in many commercial and industrial applications. Modern commercial aircraft have computer controls integrated into systems throughout the aircraft.

A significant advantage of computers is the speed, accuracy and work hour savings they can provide. Early computers were used to take over routine jobs and release personnel for more important work—work that could not be handled by a computer. As computer technology has advanced, there are more places where computers are integrated into work processes. Today personnel frequently use computerized equipment to speed up or automate processes that were previously completely manual.

Computerized systems have become so prevalent in our world that we often don't even recognize that we are using a computer. Things as simple as kitchen appliances often have computer circuits to control functions and features. A typical automobile would not operate if its computer systems failed.

The aviation world uses computers for many beneficial purposes. A major use is enabling more efficient navigation, which creates fuel savings. Modern engine designs also integrate computers into their controls allowing more energy efficient operation, also creating sig-

> **Learning Objective**
>
> **DESCRIBE**
> - characteristics of number systems
> - logic functions
> - counters
>
> **EXPLAIN**
> - binary, octal, and hexadecimal number systems
> - AND, OR, NOT, and other logic gates
>
> **APPLY**
> - perform calculations using various number systems
> - convert bases
> - use truth tables

Left. A thorough understanding of digital theory is key to working with modern computerized aircraft systems.

Figure 8-1-1. Computers are used in many new production aircraft cockpit control systems.

nificant fuel savings. Elsewhere, computers are integrated into control systems (Figure 8-1-1), creating lighter, yet more accurate systems. This permits higher payloads and reduces maintenance and troubleshooting time.

People and computers do not normally speak the same language. Methods of translating information into forms that are understandable and usable to both are necessary. Humans generally speak in words and numbers expressed in the decimal number system, while computers only understand coded electronic pulses that represent digital information.

Types of Number Systems

The commonly used number system is the decimal system. Some schools also teach the Roman numeral system as part of their history studies, even though this system is only rarely used today.

The Decimal Number System

This chapter studies modern number systems. All numbering systems have certain things in common. These common terms will be defined using the decimal system as a base of reference.

Each of the number systems covered are built around the following components: the unit, the number and the base (radix).

Unit and Number

The terms *unit* and *number*, when used with the decimal system, are almost self-explanatory. By definition the unit is a single object—an apple, a dollar, a day. A number is a symbol representing a unit or a quantity. The numerals 0, 1, 2, and 3 through 9 are the symbols used in the decimal system. These symbols are called Arabic numerals or figures. Other symbols may be used for different number systems. For example, the symbols used with the Roman numeral system are normally used in writing as letters—V is the symbol for 5, X for 10, M for 1,000, and so forth. Arabic numerals and letters are used in the number system discussions in this chapter.

Base (Radix)

The *base*, or *radix*, of a number system tells a user the number of unique symbols used in that system. The base of any system is always expressed in decimal numbers. The base, or radix, of the decimal system is 10. This means that 10 symbols —0, 1, 2, 3, 4, 5, 6, 7, 8 and 9— are used in the system. A number system using three symbols—0, 1 and 2—would be base-3; four symbols would be base-4; and so forth. Remember to count the zero or the symbol used for zero when determining the number of symbols used in a number system.

The base of a number system is indicated by a subscript (decimal number) following the value of the number. The following are examples of numerical values in different bases with the subscript to indicate the base: 7592_{10}; 214_5; 123_4; and 656_7.

The highest value symbol used in a number system is always one less than the base of the system. In base-10 the largest value symbol possible is 9; in base-5, it is 4; in base-3, it is 2.

Positional Notation and Zero

Two principles must be observed when counting or writing quantities or numerical values: the positional notation and the zero principles.

Positional notation is a system where the value of a number is defined not only by the symbol but by the symbol's position. Let's examine the decimal (base-10) value of 427.5. From experience, the user knows that this value is four hundred twenty-seven and one-half.

If 427.5 is the quantity to be expressed, then each number must be in the exact position. If the positions of the 2 and the 7 are exchanged, then change the value changes.

Each position in the positional notation system represents a power of the base, or radix. A *power* is the number of times a base is multiplied by itself. The power is written above and to the right of the base and is called an *exponent*. Examine the following base-10 line graph:

Radix Point ⟶
10^3 10^2 10^1 10^0 . 10^{-1} 10^{-2} 10^{-3}

10^3 = 10 x 100, or 1000
10^2 = 10 x 10, or 100
10^1 = 10 x 1, or 10
10^0 = 1 (any number raised to the power of 0 equals 1)
10^{-1} = 1 ÷ 10, or .1
10^{-2} = 1 ÷ 100, or .01
10^{-3} = 1 ÷ 1000, or .001

Now let's look at the value of the base-10 number 427.5 with the positional notation line graph:

Radix Point ⟶
10^2 10^1 10^0 . 10^{-1}
 4   2   7 . 5

10^2 = 4 x 100, or 400
10^1 = 2 x 10, or 20
10^0 = 7 x 1, or 7
10^{-1} = 5 x .1, or .5

This shows that the power of the base is multiplied by the number in that position to determine the value for that position. The following graph illustrates the progression of powers of 10:

Radix Point ⟶
10^4 10^3 10^2 10^1 10^0 . 10^{-1} 10^{-2} 10^{-3}

All numbers to the left of the decimal point are whole numbers, and all numbers to the right of the decimal point are fractional numbers. A *whole number* is a symbol that represents one or more complete objects, such as one apple or $5. A *fractional number* is a symbol that represents a portion of an object, such as half of an apple (0.5 apples) or a quarter of a dollar ($0.25). A *mixed number* represents one or more complete objects and some portion of an object, such as one-and-a-half apples (1.5 apples). When using any base other than the decimal system, the division between whole numbers and fractional numbers is referred to as the *radix point*. The decimal point is actually the radix point of the decimal system, but the term radix point is normally not used with the base-10 number system.

Just as important as positional notation is the use of the zero. The placement of the zero in a number can have quite an effect on the value being represented. Sometimes a position in a number does not have a value between 1 and 9. Consider how this would affect a paycheck. If the technician were expecting a check for $605.47, then they wouldn't want it to be $65.47. Leaving out the zero in this case means a difference of $540.00. In the number 605.47, the zero indicates that there are no tens. By placing this value on a bar graph, it can be observed that there are no multiples of 10^1.

10^2 10^1 10^0 . 10^{-1} 10^{-2}
 6   0   5 . 4   7
Radix Point ⟶

Most Significant Digit and Least Significant Digit (MSD and LSD)

Other important factors of number systems that should be recognized are the *most significant digit* (MSD) and the *least significant digit* (LSD). The MSD in a number is the digit that has the *greatest* effect on that number. The LSD in a number is the digit that has the *least* effect on that number. Look at the following examples:

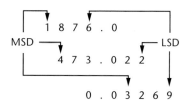

+	0	1	2	3	4	5	6	7	8	9
0	0	1	2	3	4	5	6	7	8	9
1	1	2	3	4	5	6	7	8	9	10
2	2	3	4	5	6	7	8	9	10	11
3	3	4	5	6	7	8	9	10	11	12
4	4	5	6	7	8	9	10	11	12	13
5	5	6	7	8	9	10	11	12	13	14
6	6	7	8	9	10	11	12	13	14	15
7	7	8	9	10	11	12	13	14	15	16
8	8	9	10	11	12	13	14	15	16	17
9	9	10	11	12	13	14	15	16	17	18

Table 8-1-1. Decimal addition table

This shows that a change in the MSD will increase or decrease the value of the number the greatest amount. Changes in the LSD will have the smallest effect on the value. The nonzero digit of a number that is the farthest left is the MSD, and the nonzero digit farthest right is the LSD.

Carry and Borrow Principles

Soon after learning how to count, students were taught how to add and subtract. At that time, most students learned some concepts that are used almost every day. Those concepts will be reviewed using the decimal system. They will also be applied to the other number systems that will be studied.

Addition. Addition is a form of counting in which one quantity is added to another. The following definitions identify the basic terms of addition:

- *Addend*—A number to be added to a preceding number
- *Augend*—The quantity to which an addend is added
- *Sum*—The result of an addition. (The sum of 5 and 7 is 12.)
- *Carry*—A carry is produced when the sum of two or more digits in a vertical column equals or exceeds the base of the number system in use.

How is the carry handled? That is, how to handle the two-digit number generated when a carry is produced? The lower-order digit becomes the sum of the column being added; the higher-order digit (the carry) is added to the next higher-order column.

The rules for addition are basically the same regardless of the number system being used. Each number system, because it has a different number of digits, will have a unique digit addition table. These addition tables will be described during the discussion of the adding process for each number system.

A decimal addition table is shown in Table 8-1-1. The numbers in row X and column Y may represent either the addend or the augend. If the numbers in X represent the augend, then the numbers in Y must represent the addend and vice versa. The sum of X + Y is located at the point in array Z where the selected X row and Y column intersect.

To add 5 and 7 using the table, first locate one number in the X row and the other in the Y column. The point in field Z where the row and column intersect is the sum. In this case, the sum is 12.

Subtraction. Subtraction is to take away, as a part from the whole or one number from another. The following definitions identify the basic terms needed to understand subtraction operations:

- *Minuend*—The number from which another number is to be subtracted
- *Subtrahend*—The quantity to be subtracted
- *Remainder* or *difference*—That which is left after subtraction
- *Borrow*—To transfer a digit (equal to the base number) from the next higher-order column for the purpose of subtraction

Since the process of subtraction is the opposite of addition, the addition Table 8-1-1 may be used to illustrate subtraction facts for any number system that may be discussed.

In addition,

$X + Y = Z$

In subtraction, the reverse is true; that is,

$Z - Y = X$

or

$Z - X = Y$

Thus, in subtraction the minuend is always found in array Z and the subtrahend in either row X or column Y. If the subtrahend is in row X, then the remainder will be in column Y. Conversely, if the subtrahend is in column Y, then the difference will be in row X. For example, to subtract 8 from 15, find 8 in either the X row or Y column. Find where this row or column intersects with a value of 15 for Z; then move to the remaining row or column to find the difference.

The Binary Number System

The simplest possible number system is the *binary*, or base-2, system. The information just covered about the decimal system can be used to relate the same terms to the binary system.

Unit and Number

The base, or radix, is the number of symbols used in the number system. Since this is the base-2 system, only two symbols, 0 and 1, are used. The base is indicated by a subscript, as shown in the following example:

1_2

When working with the decimal system, the subscript is not normally used. When working with number systems other than the decimal system, it is important that to use and understand the subscript in order to be sure of the system being referred to. Consider the following two numbers:

11 11

With no subscript the technician would assume both values were the same. If subscripts are added to indicate their base system, as shown below, then their values are quite different:

11_{10} 11_2

The base-10 number 11_{10} is eleven, but the base-2 number 11_2 is only equal to three in base-10. There will be occasions when more than one number system will be discussed at the same time, so using the proper subscript is very important.

	DECIMAL	BINARY	
10^0	0	0	2^0
	1	1	
	2	10	2^1
	3	11	
	4	100	2^2
	5	101	
	6	110	
	7	111	
	8	1000	2^3
	9	1001	
10^1	10	1010	
	11	1011	
	12	1100	
	13	1101	
	14	1110	
	15	1111	
	16	10000	2^4
	17	10001	
	18	10010	
	19	10011	
	20	10100	

Table 8-1-2. Decimal and binary comparison

Positional Notation

As in the decimal number system, the principle of positional notation applies to the binary number system. Recall that the decimal system uses powers of 10 to determine the value of a position. The binary system uses powers of 2 to determine the value of a position. An example showing the positions and the powers of the base is shown below:

2^4 2^3 2^2 2^1 2^0 . 2^{-1} 2^{-2} 2^{-3}

$2^4 = 2 \times 2 \times 2 \times 2$, or 16_{10}

$2^3 = 2 \times 2 \times 2$, or 8_{10}

$2^2 = 2 \times 2$, or 4_{10}

$2^1 = 2 \times 1$, or 2_{10}

$2^0 = 1_{10}$

$2^{-1} = 1 \div 2$, or $.5_{10}$

$2^{-2} = 1 \div 4$, or $.25_{10}$

$2^{-3} = 1 \div 8$, or $.125_{10}$

All numbers or values to the left of the radix point are whole numbers, and all numbers to the right of the radix point are fractional numbers.

Table 8-1-2 provides a comparison of decimal and binary numbers. Notice that each time

8-6 | Digital Theory

Figure 8-1-2. A simple binary counting device

Figure 8-1-3. Diode

1_2 may be indicated when a device is active (on), and 0_2 may be indicated when a device is nonactive (off).

Look at Figure 8-1-2. It illustrates a very simple binary counting device. Notice that 1_2 is indicated by a lighted lamp and 0_2 is indicated by an unlighted lamp. The reverse will work equally well. The unlighted state of the lamp can be used to represent a binary 1 condition, and the lighted state can represent the binary 0 condition. Both methods are used in digital computer applications. Many other devices are used to represent binary conditions. They include switches, relays, diodes (Figure 8-1-3), transistors (Figure 8-1-4) and integrated circuits (Figure 8-1-5).

MSD and LSD

When determining the MSD and LSD for binary numbers, use the same guidelines used with the decimal system. When reading from left to right, the first nonzero digit encountered is the MSD, and the last nonzero digit is the LSD. If the number is a whole number, then the first digit to the left of the radix point is the LSD.

Here, as in the decimal system, the MSD is the digit that will have the most effect on the number; the LSD is the digit that will have the least effect on the number.

The two numerals of the binary system (1 and 0) can easily be represented by many electrical or electronic devices. For example, the total number of binary symbol positions increases, the binary number indicates the next higher power of 2. This example illustrates that more symbol positions are needed in the binary system to represent the equivalent value in the decimal system.

Addition of Binary Numbers

Addition of binary numbers is basically the same as addition of decimal numbers. Each system has an augend, an addend, a sum and carries. Since only two symbols, 0 and 1, are used with the binary system, only four combinations of addition are possible.

0 + 0
1 + 0
0 + 1
1 + 1

The sum of each of the first three combinations is obvious:

$0 + 0 = 0_2$
$0 + 1 = 1_2$
$1 + 0 = 1_2$

The fourth combination presents a different situation. The sum of 1 and 1 in any other number system is 2, but the numeral 2 does not exist in the binary system. Therefore, the

Figure 8-1-4. Common transistor package styles

sum of 1_2 and 1_2 is 10_2 (spoken as, "One zero, base-two"), which is equal to 2_{10}. Study the following examples using the four combinations mentioned:

$$\begin{array}{r} 101_2 \\ +\ 010_2 \\ \hline 111_2 \end{array}$$

$$\begin{array}{r} 1\\ 101_2 \\ +\ 101_2 \\ \hline 010_2 \end{array}$$

When a carry is produced, it is noted in the column of the next higher-order value or in the column immediately to the left of the one that produced the carry.

EXAMPLE: Add 1011_2 and 1101_2.

SOLUTION: Write out the problem as shown:

$$\begin{array}{r} 1011_2 \\ +\ 1101_2 \end{array}$$

As previously noted, the sum of 1 and 1 is 2, which cannot be expressed as a single digit in the binary system. Therefore, the sum of 1 and 1 produces a carry:

$$\begin{array}{r} 1\\ 1011_2 \\ +\ 1101_2 \\ \hline 0_2 \end{array}$$

The following steps, with the carry indicated, show the completion of the addition:

$$\begin{array}{r} 1+\\ 1011_2 \\ +\ 1101_2 \\ \hline 00_2 \end{array}$$

When the carry is added, it is marked through to prevent adding it twice.

$$\begin{array}{r} 1+\!\!+\\ 1011_2 \\ +\ 1101_2 \\ \hline 000_2 \end{array}$$

$$\begin{array}{r} 1\!+\!\!+\!\!+\\ 1011_2 \\ +\ 1101_2 \\ \hline 11000_2 \end{array}$$

In the final step the remaining carry is brought down to the sum.

Figure 8-1-5. Common integrated circuit package styles

Subtraction of Binary Numbers

Now that addition of binary numbers has been explained, subtraction will be easy. The following are the four rules that must be observed when subtracting:

Rule 1: $0_2 - 0_2 = 0_2$
Rule 2: $1_2 - 0_2 = 1_2$
Rule 3: $0_2 - 1_2 = -1_2$
Rule 4: $10_2 - 1_2 = 1_2$ with a borrow

The following example ($10110_2 - 1100_2$) demonstrates the four rules of binary subtraction:

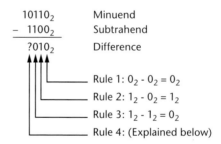

Rule 1: $0_2 - 0_2 = 0_2$
Rule 2: $1_2 - 0_2 = 1_2$
Rule 3: $1_2 - 1_2 = 0_2$
Rule 4: (Explained below)

Rule 4 presents a different situation because 1 cannot be subtracted from 0. Because 1 cannot be subtracted from 0 and have a positive difference, borrow the 1 from the next higher-order column of the minuend. The borrow may be indicated as shown below:

$$\begin{array}{rl} 10 & \text{Borrow} \\ 0 & \text{After borrow} \\ \cancel{1}0110_2 & \text{Minuend} \\ -\ 1100_2 & \text{Subtrahend} \\ \hline 1010_2 & \text{Difference} \end{array}$$

Rule 4: $10_2 - 1_2 = 1_2$

Complementary Subtraction

When working with computers, it soon becomes apparent that most digital systems cannot subtract—they can only add. This requires a method of adding that gives the results of subtraction. Does that sound confusing? Really, it is quite simple. A *complement* is used for subtractions. A complement is something used to complete something else.

In most number systems there are two types of complements. The first is the amount necessary to complete a number up to the highest number in the number system having the same number of digits. In the decimal system, this would be the difference between a given number and a number with the same number of digits composed of all 9s. This is called the *9's complement* or the radix-1 or (r's)-1 complement. As an example, the nines complement of 254 is 999 - 254, or 745.

The second type of complement is the difference between a number and the next higher power of the number base. As an example, the next higher power of 10 above 254 is 1,000. The difference between 1,000 and 254 is 746. This is called the 10's complement in the decimal number system. It is also called the radix or *r's complement*.

Complements can be used to subtract. Let's look at the magic of this process. There are three important points that need to be mentioned before starting:

1. Never complement the minuend in a problem.

2. Always disregard any carry beyond the number of positions of the largest of the original numbers.

3. Add the r's complement of the original subtrahend to the original minuend. This will have the same effect as subtracting the original number.

Let's look at a base-10 example in which 38 is subtracted from 59:

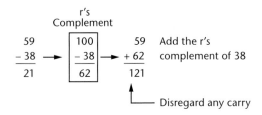

Now let's look at the number system that most computers use, the binary system. Just as the decimal system had the 9's ([r's]-1) and 10's (r's) complements, the binary system also has two complement methods. They are the 1's ([r's]-1) complement and the 2's (r's) complement. The binary system (r's)-1 complement is the difference between the binary number and a number composed of all 1s with the same number of digits. The r's complement is the difference between the binary number and the next higher power of 2.

Let's look at a quick and easy way to form the (r's)-1 complement. To do this, change each 1 in the original number to 0 and each 0 in the original number to 1 as has been done in the example below.

1011011_2

0100100_2 is the (r's)-1 complement

There are two methods of achieving the r's complement. In the first method perform the (r's)-1 complement and then add 1. This is much easier than subtracting the original number from the next higher power of 2. If subtraction had been used, it would have been necessary to borrow.

Saying it another way, to reach the r's complement of any binary number, change all 1s to 0s and all 0s to 1s, and then add 1.

As an example let's determine the r's complement of 10101101_2:

The second method of obtaining the r's complement will be demonstrated on the binary number 0010110100_2.

STEP 1

Starting with the LSD and working toward the MSD, write the digits as they are up to and including the first 1.

First 1

0010110100_2

100_2

STEP 2

Now find the (r's)-1 complement for the remaining digits:

First 1

1101001100_2

r-1's complement of remaining digits

Now let's find the r's complement of the same number, using both methods:

METHOD 1

$$1001100_2$$
$$0110011_2 \quad \text{r-1's complement}$$
$$+ \quad\quad 1_2 \quad \text{Add 1}$$
$$0110100_2 \quad \text{r's complement answer}$$

METHOD 2

$$1001100_2$$
$$0110100_2 \quad \text{r-1's complement}$$

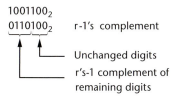

Unchanged digits
r's-1 complement of remaining digits

Now let's do some subtracting by using the r's complement method. This practice set will go through the subtraction of 3_{10} from 9_{10} (0011_2 from 1001_2).

STEP 1

Leave the minuend alone: 1001_2 remains 1001_2.

STEP 2

Using either method, r's complement the subtrahend: 1101_2 is the r's complement of the subtrahend.

STEP 3

Add the r's complement found in step 2 to the minuend of the original problem:

$$\quad\quad 1001_2 \quad \text{Original minuend}$$
$$+ \quad 1101_2 \quad \text{r's complement of subtrahend}$$
$$10110_2 \quad \text{Difference of original problem}$$

STEP 4

Remember to discard any carry beyond the size of the original number (i.e., the minuend). The original problem had four digits, so discard the carry that expanded the difference to five digits. This disregarded carry is significant to the computer. It indicates that the difference is positive. Because there is a carry, the difference can be read directly without any further computations. Let's check the answer:

$$\quad\quad 1001_2 = 9_{10}$$
$$- \quad\quad 0011_2 = -3_{10}$$
$$1\,0110_2 = 6_{10}$$

When there is *not* a carry, it indicates the difference is a negative number. In that case, the difference must be r's complemented to produce the correct answer.

Looking at an example that will explain this:

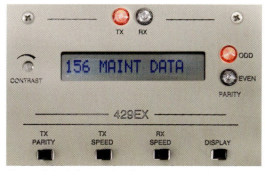

Figure 8-1-6. Example of an octal number

Subtract 9_{10} from 5_{10} (1001_2 from 0101_2):

$$5_{10} \quad\quad 0101_2 \quad \text{Minuend}$$
$$-9_{10} \quad -1001_2 \quad \text{Subtrahend}$$
$$-4_{10}$$

STEP 1

Leave the minuend alone: 0101_2 remains 0101_2.

STEP 2

r's complement the subtrahend: 0111_2 is the r's complement of the subtrahend.

STEP 3

Add the r's complement found in step 2 to the minuend of the original problem:

$$\quad\quad 0101_2 \quad \text{Original minuend}$$
$$+ \quad 0111_2 \quad \text{Two's complement}$$
$$1100_2 \quad \text{Difference of original problem}$$

STEP 4

This example does *not* have a carry; and this tells us, and any computer, that the difference is negative. With no carry, we must find r's complement of the difference from step 3. This then arrives at the answer to the original problem. Let's do this r's complement step and then check the answer:

0100_2 is the r's complement of the difference in step 3.

Remember, there was no carry in step 3. That showed us the answer was going to be negative. Make sure to indicate that the difference is negative.

The Octal Number System

The octal, or base-8, number system is a common system used with computers. An example of a octal number is seen on the display in Figure 8-1-6. Because of its relationship with

	BINARY	OCTAL	
2^0	0	0	8^0
	1	1	
2^1	10	2	
	11	3	
2^2	100	4	
	101	5	
	110	6	
	111	7	
2^3	1000	10	8^1
	1001	11	
	1010	12	
	1011	13	
	1100	14	
	1101	15	
	1110	16	
	1111	17	
2^4	10000	20	
	10001	21	
	10010	22	
	10011	23	
	10100	24	
	10101	25	
	10110	26	
	10111	27	
	11000	30	

Table 8-1-3. Binary and octal comparison

the binary system, it is useful in programming some types of computers.

Look closely at the comparison of binary and octal number systems in Table 8-1-3. The following examples of the conversion of 225_8 to binary and back again further illustrate this comparison.

Unit and Number

The terms learned in the decimal and binary sections are also used with the octal system. The unit remains a single object, and the number is still a symbol used to represent one or more units.

Base (Radix)

As with the other systems, the radix, or base, is the number of symbols used in the system. The octal system uses eight symbols—0 through 7. The base, or radix, is indicated by the subscript 8.

Positional Notation

The octal number system is a positional notation number system. Just as the decimal system uses powers of 10 and the binary system uses powers of 2, the octal system uses powers of 8 to determine the value of a number's position. The following bar graph shows the positions and the power of the base:

$$8^3 \quad 8^2 \quad 8^1 \quad 8^0 \; . \; 8^{-1} \quad 8^{-2} \quad 8^{-3}$$

Remember, that the power, or exponent, indicates the number of times the base is multiplied by itself. The value of this multiplication is expressed in base-10 as shown below:

$8^3 = 8 \times 8 \times 8$, or 512_{10}
$8^2 = 8 \times 8$, or 64_{10}
$8^1 = 8_{10}$
$8^0 = 1_{10}$
$8^{-1} = 1 \div 8$, or $.125_{10}$
$8^{-2} = 1 \div (8 \times 8)$, or $1 \div 64$, or $.015625_{10}$
$8^{-3} = 1 \div (8 \times 8 \times 8)$, or $1 \div 512$, or $.0019531_{10}$

All numbers to the left of the radix point are whole numbers, and those to the right are fractional numbers.

MSD and LSD

When determining the most and least significant digits in an octal number, use the same rules that were used with the other number systems. The digit farthest to the left is the MSD, and the one farthest right is the LSD.

If the number is a whole number, the MSD is the nonzero digit farthest to the left of the radix point and the LSD is the digit immediately to the left of the radix point. Conversely, if the number is a fraction only, the nonzero digit closest to the radix point is the MSD and the LSD is the nonzero digit farthest to the right of the radix point.

Addition of Octal Numbers

The addition of octal numbers is not difficult provided the user remembers that anytime the sum of two digits exceeds 7, a carry is produced. Compare the two examples shown below:

$$\begin{array}{r} 4_8 \\ + \; 2_8 \\ \hline 6_8 \end{array} \qquad \begin{array}{r} 4_8 \\ + \; 4_8 \\ \hline 10_8 \end{array}$$

The octal addition table in Table 8-1-4 will be of benefit to the user until becoming more accustomed to adding octal numbers.

To use the table, follow the directions used in this example: add 6_8 and 5_8. Locate the 6 in the X column of Table 8-1-4. Next locate the 5 in the Y column. The point in area Z where these two columns intersect is the sum. Therefore,

$$\begin{array}{r} 6_8 \\ +\ 5_8 \\ \hline 13_8 \end{array}$$

+	0	1	2	3	4	5	6	7
0	0	1	2	3	4	5	6	7
1	1	2	3	4	5	6	7	10
2	2	3	4	5	6	7	10	11
3	3	4	5	6	7	10	11	12
4	4	5	6	7	10	11	12	13
5	5	6	7	10	11	12	13	14
6	6	7	10	11	12	13	14	15
7	7	10	11	12	13	14	15	16

Table 8-1-4. Octal addition table

When using the concepts of addition that were already learned, the technician is now ready to add octal numbers.

As was mentioned earlier, each time the sum of a column of numbers exceeds 7, a carry is produced. More than one carry may be produced if there are three or more numbers to be added, as in this example:

$$\begin{array}{r} 7_8 \\ 7_8 \\ +\ 7_8 \end{array}$$

The sum of the augend and the first addend is 6_8 with a carry. The sum of 6_8 and the second addend is 5_8 with a carry. Write down the 5_8 and add the two carries and bring them down to the sum, as shown below:

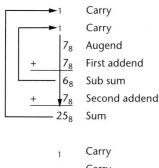

Subtraction of Octal Numbers

The subtraction of octal numbers follows the same rules as the subtraction of numbers in any other number system. The only variation is in the quantity of the borrow. In the decimal system, it was necessary to borrow a group of 10_{10}. In the binary system, it was necessary to borrow a group of 2_{10}. In the octal system a group of 8_{10} is borrowed.

Consider the subtraction of 1 from 10 in decimal, binary and octal number systems:

Decimal	Binary	Octal
10_{10}	10_2	10_8
$-\ 1_{10}$	$-\ 1_2$	$-\ 1_8$
9_{10}	1_2	7_8

In each example, 1 cannot be subtracted from 0 and have a positive difference. A borrow must be used from the next column of numbers. Let's examine the above problems and show the borrow as a *decimal* quantity for clarity:

$$\begin{array}{ccc} 10 & 2 & 8 \quad \text{Borrow} \\ \cancel{1}0_{10} & \cancel{1}0_2 & \cancel{1}0_8 \\ -\ 1_{10} & -\ 1_2 & -\ 1_8 \\ \hline 9_{10} & 1_2 & 7_8 \end{array}$$

When using the borrow, the column that is borrowed from is reduced by 1, and the amount of the borrow is added to the column of the minuend being subtracted. The following examples show this procedure:

$$\begin{array}{rl} 10 & \text{Borrow (Base 10)} \\ 2 & \text{After borrow} \\ \cancel{3}4_{10} & \text{Minuend} \\ -\ 9_{10} & \text{Subtrahend} \\ \hline 25_{10} & \text{Difference} \end{array}$$

$$\begin{array}{rl} 10 & \text{Borrow (Base 10)} \\ 3 & \text{After borrow} \\ \cancel{4}6_8 & \text{Minuend} \\ -\ 7_8 & \text{Subtrahend} \\ \hline 37_8 & \text{Difference} \end{array}$$

In the octal example, 7_8 cannot be subtracted from 6_8, so there must be a borrow from the 4. Reduce the 4 by 1 and add 10_8 (the borrow) to the 6_8 in the minuend. Subtract 7_8 from 16_8, and get a difference of 7_8. Write this number in the difference line and bring down the 3.

Figure 8-1-7. Example of a hexadecimal number

Table 8-1-4 may need to be referred to, the octal addition table, until developing a good familiarization with octal numbers. To use the table for subtraction, locate the subtrahend in column Y. Now find where this line intersects with the minuend in area Z. The remainder, or difference, will be in row X directly above this point.

The Hexadecimal (Hex) Number System

The hex number system is a more complex system in use with computers. The name is derived from the fact the system uses 16 symbols. It is beneficial in computer programming because of its relationship to the binary system. An example of a hexadecimal number is seen on the display in Figure 8-1-7. Since 16 in the decimal system is the fourth power of 2 (or 2^4), each single hex digit can be represented by up to four binary digits. Table 8-1-5 shows the relationship between the two systems.

Unit and Number

As in each of the previous number systems, a unit stands for a single object. A number in the hex system is the symbol used to represent a unit or quantity. The Arabic numerals 0 through 9 are used along with the first six letters of the Latin alphabet. Letters are often used in math problems to represent unknown quantities, but in the hex system A, B, C, D, E and F each have a definite value as shown below:

$A_{16} = 10_{10}$
$B_{16} = 11_{10}$
$C_{16} = 12_{10}$
$D_{16} = 13_{10}$
$E_{16} = 14_{10}$
$F_{16} = 15_{10}$

Base (Radix)

The base, or radix, of this system is 16, which represents the number of symbols used in the

	BINARY	HEXADECIMAL	
2^0	0	0	16^0
	1	1	
2^1	10	2	
	11	3	
2^2	100	4	
	101	5	
	110	6	
	111	7	
2^3	1000	8	
	1001	9	
	1010	A	
	1011	B	
	1100	C	
	1101	D	
	1110	E	
	1111	F	
2^4	10000	10	16^1
	10001	11	
	10010	12	
	10011	13	
	10100	14	
	10101	15	
	10110	16	
	10111	17	
	11000	18	
	11001	19	
	11010	1A	
	11011	1B	
	11100	1C	

Table 8-1-5. Binary and hexadecimal comparison

system. A quantity expressed in hex will be annotated by the subscript 16, as shown below:

$A3EF_{16}$

Positional Notation

Like the binary, octal and decimal systems, the hex system is a positional notation system. Powers of 16 are used for the positional values of a number. The following bar graph shows the positions:

$16^3\ 16^2\ 16^1\ 16^0\ .\ 16^{-1}\ 16^{-2}\ 16^{-3}$

Multiplying the base times itself the number of times indicated by the exponent will show the equivalent decimal value:

+	0	1	2	3	4	5	6	7	8	9	A	B	C	D	E	F
0	0	1	2	3	4	5	6	7	8	9	A	B	C	D	E	F
1	1	2	3	4	5	6	7	8	9	A	B	C	D	E	F	10
2	2	3	4	5	6	7	8	9	A	B	C	D	E	F	10	11
3	3	4	5	6	7	8	9	A	B	C	D	E	F	10	11	12
4	4	5	6	7	8	9	A	B	C	D	E	F	10	11	12	13
5	5	6	7	8	9	A	B	C	D	E	F	10	11	12	13	14
6	6	7	8	9	A	B	C	D	E	F	10	11	12	13	14	15
7	7	8	9	A	B	C	D	E	F	10	11	12	13	14	15	16
8	8	9	A	B	C	D	E	F	10	11	12	13	14	15	16	17
9	9	A	B	C	D	E	F	10	11	12	13	14	15	16	17	18
A	A	B	C	D	E	F	10	11	12	13	14	15	16	17	18	19
B	B	C	D	E	F	10	11	12	13	14	15	16	17	18	19	1A
C	C	D	E	F	10	11	12	13	14	15	16	17	18	19	1A	1B
D	D	E	F	10	11	12	13	14	15	16	17	18	19	1A	1B	1C
E	E	F	10	11	12	13	14	15	16	17	18	19	1A	1B	1C	1D
F	F	10	11	12	13	14	15	16	17	18	19	1A	1B	1C	1D	1E

Table 8-1-6. Hexadecimal addition table

$16^3 = 16 \times 16 \times 16$, or 4096_{10}

$16^2 = 16 \times 16$, or 256_{10}

$16^1 = 16_{10}$

$16^0 = 1_{10}$

$16^{-1} = 1 \div 16$, or $.0625_{10}$

$16^{-2} = 1 \div (16 \times 16)$, or $.0039062_{10}$

$16^{-3} = 1 \div (16 \times 16 \times 16)$, or $.0002441_{10}$

A look at the positional values show that fewer hex symbol positions are usually required to express a number than are required in decimal. The following example shows this comparison:

$625_{16} = 1573_{10}$

MSD and LSD

The most significant and least significant digits will be determined in the same manner as the other number systems. The following examples show the MSD and LSD of whole, fractional and mixed hex numbers:

7 9 E 4 . $_{16}$
↑ ↑ ↑
MSD LSD — Radix Point

. 1 8 2 A_{16}
↑ ↑ ↑
Radix Point — MSD LSD

3 B C . E 4 2 F_{16}
↑ ↑ ↑
MSD Radix Point LSD

Addition of Hex Numbers

The addition of hex numbers may seem intimidating at first glance, but it is no different than addition in any other number system. The same rules apply. Certain combinations of symbols produce a carry while others do not. Some numerals combine to produce a sum represented by a letter. After a little practice the technician can be as confident adding hex numbers as when adding decimal numbers.

Study the hex addition table in Table 8-1-6. Using the table, add 7 and 7. Locate the number 7 in both columns X and Y. The point in area Z where these two columns intersect is the sum; in this case, 7 + 7 = E. As long as the sum of two numbers is 15_{10} or less, only one symbol is used for the sum. A carry will be produced when the sum of two numbers is 16_{10} or greater, as in the following examples:

$\begin{array}{r} 8_{16} \\ + \ 8_{16} \\ \hline 10_{16} \end{array}$ $\begin{array}{r} A_{16} \\ + \ D_{16} \\ \hline 17_{16} \end{array}$ $\begin{array}{r} D_{16} \\ + \ 9_{16} \\ \hline 16_{16} \end{array}$

Use the addition table and follow the solution of the following problems:

$\begin{array}{rl} 456_{16} & \text{Augend} \\ + \ 784_{16} & \text{Addend} \\ \hline BDA_{16} & \text{Sum} \end{array}$

In this example each column is straight addition with no carry.

Now add the addend (784_{16}) and the sum (BDA_{16}) of the previous problem.

```
  1 1          Carry
  784₁₆        Augend
+ BDA₁₆        Addend
  135E₁₆       Sum
```

Here the sum of 4 and A is E. Adding 8 and D is 15_{16}; write down 5 and carry a 1. Add the first carry to the 7 in the next column and add the sum, 8, to B. The result is 13_{16}; write down 3 and carry a 1. Since only the last carry is left to add, bring it down to complete the problem.

Now observe the procedures for a more complex addition problem. In some cases, it may be easier to add the Arabic numerals in each column first:

```
  1 1 1        Carry
  C14₁₆        Augend
  19E₁₆        Addend
  571₁₆        Addend
+ BB3₁₆        Addend
  1ED6₁₆       Sum
```

The sum of 4, E, 1 and 3 in the first column is 16_{16}. Write down the 6 and the carry. In the second column, 1, 1, 9 and 7 equals 12_{16}. Write the carry over the next column. Add B and 2—the sum is D. Write this in the sum line. Now add the final column, 1, 1, 5 and C. The sum is 13_{16}. Write down the carry; then add 3 and B—the sum is E. Write down the E and bring down the final carry to complete the problem.

Subtraction of Hex Numbers

The subtraction of hex numbers looks more difficult than it really is. In the preceding sections all the rules for subtraction were covered. Now it is time to apply those rules to a new number system. The symbols may be different and the amount of the borrow is different, but the rules remain the same.

Use the hex addition table (Table 8-1-6) to follow the solution of the following problems:

```
  ABC₁₆        Minuend
-  642₁₆       Subtrahend
```

Working from left to right, first locate the subtrahend (2) in column Y. Follow this line across area Z until reaching C. The difference is located in column X directly above the C—in this case, A. Use this same procedure to reach the solution:

```
  ABC₁₆        Minuend
-  642₁₆       Subtrahend
   47A₁₆       Difference
```

Now examine the following solutions:

```
  7E5E₁₆       Minuend
-  471₁₆       Subtrahend
  3744₁₆       Difference
```

```
  1E9C₄₁₆      Minuend
-  F4A1₁₆      Subtrahend
   F523₁₆      Difference
```

In the previous example, when F was subtracted from 1E, a borrow was used. Since F cannot be subtracted from E and have a positive difference, a borrow of 10_{16} was taken from the next higher-value column. The borrow was added to E, and the higher-value column was reduced by 1.

```
      10₁₆         Borrow
       2           Minuend reduced by 1
   4 A̶ 3̶ 7₁₆       Minuend
 - 2 C 4 B₁₆       Subtrahend
           C₁₆     Difference
```

In this first step, B cannot be subtracted from 7, so take a borrow of 10_{16} from the next higher-value column. Add the borrow to the 7 in the minuend; then subtract ($17_{16} - B_{16} = C_{16}$). Reduce the number from which the borrow was taken (3) by 1.

To subtract 4_{16} from 2_{16} also requires a borrow, as shown here:

```
     10₁₆ 10₁₆    Borrow
       9   2      Minuend reduced by 1
   4 A̶ 3̶ 7₁₆      Minuend
 - 2 C 4 B₁₆      Subtrahend
         E C₁₆    Difference
```

Borrow 10_{16} from the A and reduce the minuend by 1. Add the borrow to the 2 and subtract 4_{16} from 12_{16}. The difference is E.

When solved the problem looks like this:

```
     10 10 10     Borrow (Base 16)
      3  9  2     Minuend reduced by 1
   4 A̶ 3̶ 7₁₆      Minuend
 - 2 C 4 B₁₆      Subtrahend
   1 D E C₁₆      Difference
```

Remember that the borrow is 10_{16}—not 10_{10}.

There may be times when it is necessary to borrow from a column that has a 0 in the minuend. In that case, borrow from the next highest-value column, which will provide a value in the 0 column that can be borrowed from.

```
     F      Borrow reduced by 1
    10 10   Borrow (Base 16)
     1      Minuend reduced by 1
     2 0 7₁₆   Minuend
  −    A₁₆     Subtrahend
     1 F D₁₆   Difference
```

To subtract A from 7, use a borrow. To borrow, first borrow from the 2. The 0 becomes 10_{16}, which can give up a borrow. Reduce the 10_{16} by 1 to provide a borrow for the 7. Reducing 10_{16} by 1 equals F. Subtracting A_{16} from 17_{16} gives D_{16}. Bring down the 1 and F for a difference of $1FD_{16}$.

Conversion Of Bases

As mentioned in the introduction to this chapter, digital computers operate on electrical pulses. These pulses, or their absence, is easily represented by binary numbers. A pulse can represent a binary 1, and the lack of a pulse can represent a binary 0, or vice versa.

The sections that discussed octal and hex numbers both mentioned that their number systems were beneficial to programmers. This section shows how octal and hex numbers are easily converted to binary numbers and vice versa.

When working with computers, there will be many times when it will be necessary to convert decimal numbers to binary, octal and hex numbers. It will also be necessary to be able to convert binary, octal and hex numbers to decimal numbers. Converting each number system to each of the others will be explained. This background will enable the technician to convert from any base to any other base when needed.

Decimal Conversion

Some computer systems have the capability to convert decimal numbers to binary numbers. They do this by using additional circuitry. Many of these systems require that the decimal numbers be converted to another form before entry.

Decimal to Binary

Conversion of a decimal number to any other base is accomplished by dividing the decimal number by the radix of the system that is being converted to. The following definitions identify the basic terms used in division:

- *Dividend*—The number to be divided
- *Divisor*—The number by which a dividend is divided
- *Quotient*—The number resulting from the division of one number by another
- *Remainder*—The final undivided part after division that is less than or of a lower degree than the divisor

To convert a base-10 whole number to its binary equivalent, first set up the problem for division:

$$2\overline{)5_{10}}$$

STEP 1

Divide the base-10 number by the radix (2) of the binary system and extract the remainder. (This becomes the binary number's LSD.)

```
        2      Quotient
    2⌡ 5₁₀
        4
        ─
        1      Remainder ⟶ 1
```

STEP 2

Continue the division by dividing the quotient from step 1 by the radix.

```
        1      Quotient from step 1
    2⌡ 2
        2
        ─
        0      Remainder ⟶ 0
```

STEP 3

Continue dividing quotients by the radix until the quotient becomes smaller that the divisor; then do one more division. The remainder is the MSD.

```
        0      Quotient from step 2
    2⌡ 1
        0
        ─
        1      Remainder ⟶ 1
```

The remainder in step 1 is the LSD. Now rewrite the solution, and see that 5_{10} equals 101_2. Now follow the conversion of 23_{10} to binary:

STEP 1

Set up the problem for division.

$$2\overline{)23_{10}}$$

STEP 2

Divide the number and extract the remainder.

8-16 | Digital Theory

```
    11
2 ⟌ 23
    2
   ─
   03
    2
   ─
    1    Remainder ⟶ 1(LSD)
```

```
    5
2 ⟌ 11
   10
   ─
    1    Remainder ⟶ 1
```

```
    2
2 ⟌ 5
    4
   ─
    1    Remainder ⟶ 1
```

```
    1
2 ⟌ 2
    2
   ─
    0    Remainder ⟶ 0
```

```
    0
2 ⟌ 1
    0
   ─
    1    Remainder ⟶ 1 (MSD)
```

STEP 3

Rewrite the solution from MSD to LSD.

10111_2

No matter how large the decimal number may be, use the same procedure. Try the problem below. It has a larger dividend:

```
    52
2 ⟌ 105
   10
   ─
   05
    4
   ─
    1    ⟶ 1(LSD)
```

```
    26
2 ⟌ 52
    4
   ─
   12
   12
   ─
    0    ⟶ 0
```

```
    13
2 ⟌ 26
    2
   ─
   06
    6
   ─
    0    ⟶ 0
```

```
    6
2 ⟌ 13
   12
   ─
    1    ⟶ 1
```

```
    3
2 ⟌ 6
    6
   ─
    0    ⟶ 0
```

```
    1
2 ⟌ 3
    2
   ─
    1    ⟶ 1
```

```
    0
2 ⟌ 1
    0
   ─
    1    ⟶ 1 (MSD)
```

$105_{10} = 1101001_2$

Fractional decimal numbers can be converted by multiplying the fraction by the radix and extracting the portion of the product to the *left* of the radix point. Continue to multiply the fractional portion of the previous product until the desired degree of accuracy is attained.

Let's go through this process and convert 0.25_{10} to its binary equivalent.

```
              .25₁₀
          ×      2
         ─────────
MSD ⟵ 0 ⟵ 0.50
          ×      2
         ─────────
LSD ⟵ 1 ⟵ 1.00
```

The *first* figure to the left of the radix point is the MSD, and the last figure of the computation is the LSD. Rewrite the solution from MSD to LSD preceded by the radix point as shown.

0.01_2

Now try converting 0.625_{10} to binary.

```
              .625
          ×      2
         ─────────
MSD ⟵ 1 ⟵ 1.250
          ×      2
         ─────────
       0 ⟵ 0.500
          ×      2
         ─────────
LSD ⟵ 1 ⟵ 1.000
          ×      2
         ─────────
           0.000
```

$.625_{10} = .101_2$

As was mentioned, continue the operations until reaching the desired accuracy. For example, convert 0.425_{10} to five places in the binary system.

```
                .425
              x   2
MSD ← 0 ← 0.850
              x   2
      1 ← 1.700
              x   2
      1 ← 1.400
              x   2
      0 ← 0.800
              x   2
      1 ← 1.600
              x   2
      1 ← 1.200
              x   2
LSD ← 0 ← 0.400
```

Although the multiplication was carried out for seven places, in practice only use what is required. Write out the solution as shown.

0.01101_2

To convert a mixed number such as 37.625_{10} to binary, split the number into its whole and fractional components and solve each one separately. In this problem, carry the fractional part to four places. When the conversion of each is completed, recombine it with the radix point as shown below:

$37_{10} = 100101_2$
$.625_{10} = .1010_2$
$37.625_{10} = 100101.1010_2$

Decimal to Octal

The conversion of a decimal number to its base-8 equivalent is done by the repeated division method. Simply divide the base-10 number by 8 and extract the remainders. The first remainder will be the LSD, and the last remainder will be the MSD.

Look at the following example. To convert 15_{10} to octal, set up the problem for division.

$8\ \overline{)15_{10}}$

Since 8 goes into 15 one time with a remainder of 7, 7 is the LSD. Next divide 8 into the quotient (1). The result is a 0 quotient with a remainder of 1. The 1 is the MSD:

```
        1
  2 | 15₁₀
        8
        7   → 7(LSD)
```

```
         0
  8 | 1
       0
       1   → 1(MSD)
```

Now write out the number from MSD to LSD as shown.

17_8

The same process is used regardless of the size of the decimal number. Naturally, more divisions are needed for larger numbers, as in the following example.

Convert 264_{10} to octal.

```
         33
  8 | 264₁₀
       24
       24
       24
        0   → 0 (LSD)

         4
  8 | 33
       32
        1   → 1

         0
  8 | 4
       0
       4   → 4 (MSD)
```

By rewriting the solution, find that the octal equivalent of 264_{10} is as follows:

410_8

To convert a decimal fraction to octal, multiply the fraction by 8. Extract everything that appears to the left of the radix point. The first number extracted will be the MSD and will follow the radix point. The last number extracted will be the LSD.

Convert 0.05_{10} to octal:

```
                 .05
              x    8
MSD ← 0 ← 0.40
              x    8
      3 ← 3.20
              x    8
      1 ← 1.60
              x    8
      4 ← 4.80
              x    8
LSD ← 6 ← 6.40
```

Write the solution from MSD to LSD.

0.03146_8

Digital Theory

The conversion can be carried out to as many places as needed, but usually four or five places are enough.

To convert a mixed decimal number to its octal equivalent, split the number into whole and fractional portions and solve as shown below.

Convert 105.589_{10} to octal.

$$\begin{array}{r} 13 \\ 8\overline{)105} \\ 8 \\ \overline{25} \\ 24 \\ \overline{1} \end{array} \rightarrow 1 \text{ (LSD)}$$

$$\begin{array}{r} 1 \\ 8\overline{)13} \\ 8 \\ \overline{5} \end{array} \rightarrow 5$$

$$\begin{array}{r} 0 \\ 8\overline{)1} \\ 0 \\ \overline{1} \end{array} \rightarrow 1 \text{ (MSD)}$$

$$\begin{array}{r} 0.589 \\ \times \quad 8 \\ \hline \text{MSD} \leftarrow 4 \leftarrow 4.712 \\ \times \quad 8 \\ \hline 5 \leftarrow 5.696 \\ \times \quad 8 \\ \hline 5 \leftarrow 5.568 \\ \times \quad 8 \\ \hline \text{LSD} \leftarrow 4 \leftarrow 4.544 \end{array}$$

Combine the portions into a mixed number.

151.4554_8

Decimal to Hex

To convert a decimal number to hex, follow the repeated division procedures used above, but divide by 16. Let's look at an example.

Convert 63_{10} to hex.

$$\begin{array}{r} 3 \\ 16\overline{)63_{10}} \\ 48 \\ \overline{15_{10}} \end{array} \rightarrow F_{16} \rightarrow \text{(LSD)}$$

$$\begin{array}{r} 0 \\ 16\overline{)3} \\ 0 \\ \overline{3} \end{array} \rightarrow 3_{16} \rightarrow \text{(MSD)}$$

Therefore, the hex equivalent of 63_{10} is $3F_{16}$.

Remember that the remainder is in base-10 and must be converted to hex if it exceeds 9. Let's work through another example:

Convert 174_{10} to hex.

$$\begin{array}{r} 10 \\ 16\overline{)174} \\ 16 \\ \overline{14} \\ 0 \\ \overline{14_{10}} \end{array} \rightarrow E_{16} \rightarrow \text{(LSD)}$$

$$\begin{array}{r} 0 \\ 16\overline{)10} \\ 0 \\ \overline{10_{10}} \end{array} \rightarrow A_{16} \rightarrow \text{(MSD)}$$

Write the solution from MSD to LSD.

AE_{16}

There will probably be very few times when it is necessary to convert a decimal fraction to a hex fraction. If the occasion should arise, the conversion is done in the same manner as binary or octal. Use the following example as a pattern:

Convert 0.695_{10} to hex.

$$\begin{array}{r} .695 \\ \times \quad 16 \\ \hline 4.170 \\ 6.950 \\ \hline \text{MSD} \leftarrow B_{16} \leftarrow 11.120 \\ \times \quad 16 \\ \hline .720 \\ 1.200 \\ \hline 1_{16} \leftarrow 1.920 \\ \times \quad 16 \\ \hline 5.520 \\ 9.200 \\ \hline E_{16} \leftarrow 14.720 \\ \times \quad 16 \\ \hline 4.320 \\ 7.200 \\ \hline \text{LSD} \leftarrow B_{16} \leftarrow 11.520 \end{array}$$

The solution: $0.B1EB_{16}$

Should the need arise to convert a decimal mixed number to hex, convert the whole number and the fraction separately. Then recombine for the solution.

Binary Conversion

Earlier in this chapter, it was mentioned that the octal and hex number systems are useful to computer programmers. It is much easier to provide data to a computer in one or the other of these systems. Likewise, it is important to be able to convert data from the computer into one or the other number systems for ease of understanding the data.

Binary to Octal

Look at the following numbers:

10111001001101_2

27115_8

Obviously, the octal number is much easier to say. Although the two numbers look completely different, they are equal.

Since 8 is equal to 2^3, then one octal digit can represent three binary digits, as shown below:

$0_8 = 000_2$
$1_8 = 001_2$
$2_8 = 010_2$
$3_8 = 011_2$
$4_8 = 100_2$
$5_8 = 101_2$
$6_8 = 110_2$
$7_8 = 111_2$

With the use of this principle, the conversion of a binary number is quite simple. As an example, follow the conversion of the binary number at the beginning of this section.

Write out the binary number to be converted. Starting at the radix point and moving left, break the binary number into groups of three as shown. This grouping of binary numbers into three-bit groups is called *binary-coded octal* (BCO). Add 0s to the left of the MSD as needed to fill a group of three.

010 111 001 001 101 . $_2$
↑
└── Radix Point

Next, write down the octal equivalent of each group.

010	111	001	001	101.$_2$
2	7	1	1	5.$_8$

To convert a binary fraction to its octal equivalent, starting at the radix point and moving right, group the digits to form groups of three.

. 100 001 110 011$_2$
↑
└── Radix Point

Add 0s to the right of the LSD as needed to form a group of three. Now write the octal digit for each group of three, as shown below:

.100	001	110	011.$_2$
.4	1	6	3.$_8$

To convert a mixed binary number, starting at the radix point, form groups of three both right and left.

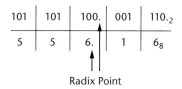

101	101	100.	001	110.$_2$
5	5	6.	1	6$_8$

↑
Radix Point

Binary to Hex

The table below shows the relationship between binary and hex numbers. Four binary digits may be used to represent one hex digit. This is because 16 is equal to 2^4.

HEX		Binary
0	=	0000
1	=	0001
2	=	0010
3	=	0011
4	=	0100
5	=	0101
6	=	0110
7	=	0111
8	=	1000
9	=	1001
A	=	1010
B	=	1011
C	=	1100
D	=	1101
E	=	1110
F	=	1111

Using this relationship, binary numbers can easily be converted to hex. Starting at the radix point and moving either right or left, break the number into groups of four. The grouping of binary into four-bit groups is called *binary-coded hexadecimal* (BCH).

Convert 111010011_2 to hex.

┌── Radix Point
0001	1101	0011.$_2$
1	D	3.$_{16}$
↑
└── Radix Point

Add 0s to the left of the MSD of the whole portion of the number and to the right of the LSD of the fractional part to form a group of four.

Convert 0.111_2 to hex:

.110	$_2$
.E	$_{16}$

In this case, if a 0 had not been added, the conversion would have been 0.7_{16}, which is incorrect.

Octal Conversion

The conversion of one number system to another, as explained earlier, is done to simplify computer programming or interpreting of data.

Octal to Binary

For some computers to accept octal data, the octal digits must be converted to binary. This process is the reverse of binary to octal conversion. To convert a given octal number to binary, write out the octal number in the following format. This example will convert 567_8.

5	6	7_8

Next, below each octal digit write the corresponding three-digit binary-coded octal equivalent:

5	6	7_8
101	110	111_2

Solution: 567_8 equals 101 110 111_2, or

101110111_2

With experience, it may not be necessary to use the block format. An octal fraction is converted in the same manner, as shown below:

.1	2	3
.001	010	011_2

Solution: 0.123_8 equals 0.001010011_2

Apply these principles to convert mixed numbers as well.

Convert 32.25_8 to binary.

3	2 .	2	5_8
011	010 .	010	101_2

Solution: 32.25_8 equals 011010.010101_2

Octal to Hex

Occasionally it is necessary to convert octal numbers to hex. Should the need arise, conversion is a two-step procedure. Convert the octal number to binary; then convert the binary number to hex. The steps to convert 53.7_8 to hex are shown below:

5	3 .	7_8
101	011 .	111_2

Regroup the binary digits into groups of four and add zeros where needed to complete groups. Then convert the binary to hex.

0010	1011 .	1110_2
2	B .	E_{16}

Solution: 53.7_8 equals $2B.E_{16}$

Hex Conversion

The procedures for converting hex numbers to binary and octal are the reverse of the binary and octal conversions to hex.

Hex to Binary

To convert a hex number to binary, set up the number in the block format used in earlier conversions. Below each hex digit, write the four-digit binary equivalent. Observe the following example:

Convert ABC_{16} to binary.

A	B	C_{16}
1010	1011	1100_2

Solution: $ABC_{16} = 101010111100_2$

Hex to Octal

Just like the conversion of octal to hex, conversion of hex to octal is a two-step procedure. First, convert the hex number to binary; and second, convert the binary number to octal. Let's use the same example that was used above in the hex-to-binary conversion and convert it to octal:

A	B	C_{16}
1010	1011	1100_2

101	010	111	100₂
5	2	7	4₈

Conversion to Decimal

Computer data will have little meaning without an understanding of the various number systems. It is often necessary to convert binary, octal or hex numbers to decimal numbers. The need for understanding is better illustrated by showing a paycheck printed in binary. A check in the amount of $10,010,101.00$_2$ looks impressive, but in reality, it only amounts to 149.00_{10}$.

Binary to Decimal

The computer that calculates a technician's pay probably operates with binary numbers, so a conversion takes place in the computer before the amount is printed on the check. Some computers, however, don't automatically convert from binary to decimal. There are times when the conversion must be done mathematically.

To convert a base-2 number to base-10, the decimal equivalent of each power of 2 must be known. The decimal value of a power of 2 is obtained by multiplying 2 by itself the number of times indicated by the exponent for whole numbers; for example, $2_4 = 2 \times 2 \times 2 \times 2$, or 16_{10}.

For fractional numbers, the decimal value is equal to 1 divided by 2 multiplied by itself the number of times indicated by the exponent. Look at this example:

$2^{-3} = 1 \div (2 \times 2 \times 2)$ or $.125_{10}$

The table below shows a portion of the positions and decimal values of the binary system:

```
Radix Point ─────────────┐
2⁵  2⁴  2³  2²  2¹  2⁰  . 2⁻¹  2⁻²  2⁻³
32  16  8   4   2   1  .  .5   .25  .125
Radix Point ─────────────┘
```

Remember, earlier in this chapter it was discussed that any number to the 0 power is equal to 1_{10}. Another method of determining the decimal value of a position is to multiply the preceding value by 2 for whole numbers and to divide the preceding value by 2 for fractional numbers, as shown:

```
Radix Point ──────────────┐
2⁵  2⁴  2³  2²  2¹  2⁰  . 2⁻¹  2⁻²  2⁻³  2⁻⁴
32  16  8   4   2   1  .  .5   .25  .125 .0625
Multiply by 2  ←────────→  Divide by 2
```

Let's convert a binary number to decimal by using the positional notation method. First, write out the number to be converted; then, write in the decimal equivalent for each position with a 1 indicated. Add these values to determine the decimal equivalent of the binary number. Look at this example:

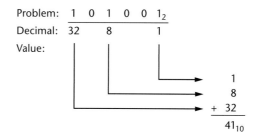

As easy method is to write the decimal equivalent for each position as done in the following example. Add only the values indicated by a 1.

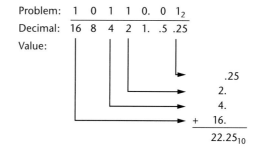

Make sure that the decimal values for each position are properly aligned before adding.

Octal to Decimal

Conversion of octal numbers to decimal is best done by the positional notation method. This process is the one used to convert binary numbers to decimal.

First, determine the decimal equivalent for each position by multiplying 8 by itself the number of times indicated by the exponent. Set up a bar graph of the positions and values as shown below:

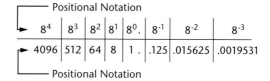

To convert an octal number to decimal, write out the number to be converted, placing each digit under the proper position.

EXAMPLE:

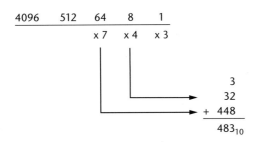

Next, multiply the decimal equivalent by the corresponding digit of the octal number; then, add this column of figures for the final solution:

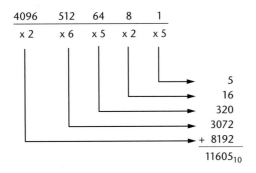

SOLUTION: 743_8 is equal to 483_{10}.

Now follow the conversion of 26525_8 to decimal.

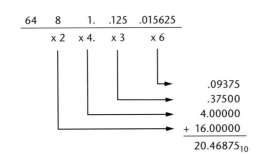

SOLUTION: $11,605_{10}$ is the decimal equivalent of $26,525_8$.

To convert a fraction or a mixed number, simply use the same procedure.

EXAMPLE: Change 0.5_8 to decimal.

```
   .125
  x 5₈
   ─────
   .625₁₀
```

EXAMPLE: Convert 24.36_8 to decimal.

```
 64    8    1.   .125   .015625
x 2   x 4.  x 3   x 6
                        .09375
                       .37500
                      4.00000
                    + 16.00000
                     ──────────
                      20.46875₁₀
```

SOLUTION: 24.36_8 equals 20.46875_{10}.

If your prefer or find it easier, you may want to convert the octal number to binary and then to decimal.

Hex to Decimal

It is difficult to comprehend the magnitude of a base-16 number until it is presented in base-10; for instance, $E0_{16}$ is equal to 224_{10}. Remember that usually fewer digits are necessary to represent a decimal value in base-16.

When converting from base-16 to decimal, use the positional notation system for the powers of 16 (a bar graph). Another option is to convert the base-16 number to binary and then convert to base-10.

Note in the bar graph below that each power of 16 results in a tremendous increase in the decimal equivalent. Only one negative power (16^{-1}) is shown for demonstration purposes.

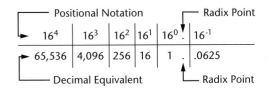

Just as with octal conversion, write out the hex number, placing each digit under the appropriate decimal value for that position. Multiply the decimal value by the base-16 digit and add the values. (Convert A through F to their decimal equivalent before multiplying.) Let's take a look at an example.

Convert $2C_{16}$ to decimal.

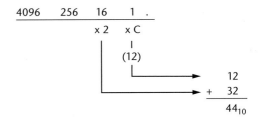

The decimal equivalent of $2C_{16}$ is 44_{10}.

Use the same procedure used with binary and octal to convert base-16 fractions to decimal.

When converting the hex number to binary and then to decimal, the solution will look like this:

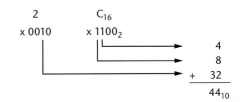

Binary-Coded Decimal

In today's technology, a great deal is heard about microprocessors. A microprocessor is an integrated circuit designed for two purposes: data processing and control.

Computers and microprocessors both operate on a series of electrical pulses called words. A *word* can be represented by a binary number such as 10110011_2. The word length is described by the number of digits or *bits* in the series. A series of 4 digits would be called a 4-bit word and so forth. The most common are 4-, 8- and 16-bit words. Quite often, these words must use binary-coded decimal inputs.

Binary-coded decimal, or BCD, is a method of using binary digits to represent the decimal digits 0 through 9. A decimal digit can be represented by four binary digits, as shown below:

BCD		Decimal
0000	=	0
0001	=	1
0010	=	2
0011	=	3
0100	=	4
0101	=	5
0110	=	6
0111	=	7
1000	=	8
1001	=	9

Note in the table above that the BCD coding is the binary equivalent of the decimal digit.

Since many devices use BCD, knowing how to handle this system is important. The technician should realize that BCD and binary are not the same. For example, 49_{10} in binary is 110001_2, but 49_{10} in BCD is 01001001_{BCD}. Each decimal digit is converted to its binary equivalent.

BCD Conversion

As shown in the above table, the conversion of decimal to BCD or BCD to decimal is similar to the conversion of hexadecimal to binary and vice versa.

For example, let's go through the conversion of 264_{10} to BCD. Start by using the block format that was used in earlier conversions. First, write out the decimal number to be converted; then, below each digit write the BCD equivalent of that digit:

2	6	4_{10}
0010	0110	0100_{BCD}

The BCD equivalent of 264_{10} is 001001100100_{BCD}. To convert from BCD to decimal, simply reverse the process as shown:

1001	1000	0011_{BCD}
9	8	3_{10}

BCD Addition

The procedures followed in adding BCD are the same as those used in binary. There is, however, the possibility that addition of BCD values will result in invalid totals. The following example shows this.

Add 9 and 6 in BCD.

$$\begin{array}{r} 1001_{BCD} = 9_{10} \\ +\ 1001_{BCD} = 6_{10} \\ \hline \text{Invalid BCD} \longrightarrow 1111 \quad 15_{10} \end{array}$$

The sum 11112 is the binary equivalent of 15_{10}; however, 1111 is not a valid BCD number. 1001 cannot be exceeded in BCD, so a correction factor must be made. To do this, you add 6_{10} (0110_{BCD}) to the sum of the two numbers. The "add 6" correction factor is added to any BCD group larger than 1001_2. Remember, there is no 1010_2, 1011_2, 1100_2, 1101_2, 1110_2, or 1111_2 in BCD:

$$\begin{array}{rl} 1111 & \longleftarrow \text{Invalid BCD} \\ +\ 0110_{BCD} & \text{Add } 6_{10} \\ \hline 0001\quad 0101 & \longleftarrow \text{New BCD} \end{array}$$

The sum plus the add-6 correction factor can then be converted back to decimal to check the answer. Put any carries that were developed in the add-6 process into a new 4-bit word.

0001	0101_{BCD}
1	5_{10}

Now observe the addition of 60_{10} and 55_{10} in BCD.

$$\begin{array}{l} 60_{10} = 0110\ 0000_{BCD} \\ 55_{10} = 0101\ 0101_{BCD} \\ \hline \phantom{55_{10} =\ }1011\ 0101 \longleftarrow \text{Invalid BCD} \end{array}$$

In this case, the higher order group is invalid, but the lower order group is valid. Therefore, the correction factor is added only to the higher order group.

$$\begin{array}{l} 1011\ 0101 \\ +\ 0110\ 0000 \quad \text{Add } 6_{10} \\ \hline 0001\ 0001\ 0101_{BCD} \end{array}$$

Figure 8-2-1. All computers, regardless of brand, platform or age, use TRUE and FALSE logic conditions to make programming decisions.

Convert this total to decimal to check the answer.

$$\frac{0001 \quad 0001 \quad 0101_{BCD}}{1 \quad\quad 1 \quad\quad 5_{10}}$$

Remember that the correction factor is added only to groups that exceed 9_{10} (1001_{BCD}).

Section 2

Logic Functions

To review the previous section, two digits of the binary number system can be represented by the state or condition of electrical or electronic devices. A binary 1 can be represented by a switch that is closed, a lamp that is lit or a transistor that is conducting. Conversely, a binary 0 would be represented by the same devices in the opposite state: the switch open, the lamp off or the transistor in cutoff.

This chapter covers the four basic logic gates that make up the foundation for digital equipment. The types of logic that are used in equipment to accomplish the desired results is also examined.

This chapter includes an introduction to Boolean algebra, the logic mathematics system used with digital equipment. Certain Boolean expressions are used in explanation of the basic logic gates.

Computer Logic

Logic is defined as the science of reasoning. In other words, it is the development of a reasonable or logical conclusion based on known information.

General Logic

Consider the following example: If it is true that all airports have runway(s) and that Washington-Dulles International is an airport, then a logical conclusion is that the Washington-Dulles International has runway(s).

To reach a logical conclusion, first assume the qualifying statement is a condition of truth. For each statement there is also a corresponding false condition. The statement "Washington-Dulles International is an airport" is true; therefore, the statement "Washington-Dulles International is not an airport" is false. There are no in-between conditions.

Computers operate on the principle of logic and use the TRUE and FALSE logic conditions of a logical statement to make a programmed decision (Figure 8-2-1).

The conditions of a statement can be represented by symbols (variables); for instance,

EXAMPLE 1: ASSUME TODAY IS PAYDAY					
STATEMENT	SYMBOL	CONDITION	LOGIC STATE	LOGIC LEVEL
ORIGINAL: TODAY IS PAYDAY	P	True	1	High
COMPLEMENT: TODAY IS NOT PAYDAY	$\overline{P}$	False	0	Low
EXAMPLE 2: ASSUME TODAY IS NOT PAYDAY				
ORIGINAL: TODAY IS NOT PAYDAY	P	False	0	Low
COMPLEMENT: TODAY IS NOT PAYDAY	$\overline{P}$	True	1	High

Table 8-2-1. Relationship of digital logic concepts and terms

the statement "Today is payday" might be represented by the symbol P. If today actually is payday, then P is TRUE. If today is not payday, then P is FALSE. As shown, a statement has two conditions. In computers, these two conditions are represented by electronic circuits operating in two *logic states*. These logic states are 0 (zero) and 1 (one). Respectively, 0 and 1 represent the FALSE and TRUE conditions of a statement.

When the TRUE and FALSE conditions are converted to electrical signals, they are referred to as *logic levels* called HIGH and LOW. The 1 state might be represented by the presence of an electrical signal (HIGH), while the 0 state might be represented by the absence of an electrical signal (LOW).

If the statement "Today is payday" is FALSE, then the statement, "Today is NOT payday" must be TRUE. This is called the *complement* of the original statement. In the case of computer math, complement is defined as the opposite or negative form of the original statement or variable. If today were payday, then the statement "Today is not payday" would be FALSE. The complement is shown by placing a bar, or *vinculum*, over the statement symbol (in this case, $\bar{P}$). This variable is spoken as, "Not P." Table 8-2-1 shows this concept and the relationship with logic states and logic levels.

In some cases, more than one variable is used in a single expression. For example, the expression $AB\bar{C}D$ is spoken as, "A and B and not C and D."

Positive And Negative Logic

To this point, the discussion has dealt with one type of logic polarity, positive. Let's further define logic polarity and expand to cover in more detail the differences between positive and negative logic.

Logic polarity is the type of voltage used to represent the logic 1 state of a statement. The two logic states can be represented by electrical signals. Any two distinct voltages may be used. For instance, a positive voltage can represent the 1 state, and a negative voltage can represent the 0 state. The opposite is also true.

Logic circuits are generally divided into two broad classes according to their polarity—positive logic and negative logic. The voltage levels used and a statement indicating the use of positive or negative logic will usually be specified on logic diagrams supplied by manufacturers.

In practice, many variations of logic polarity are used; for example, from a high positive to a low positive voltage, or from positive to ground; or from a high-negative to a low negative voltage, or from negative to ground. A brief discussion of the two general classes of logic polarity is presented in the following paragraphs.

EXAMPLE 1	ACTIVE SIGNAL	True, 1, High	+10 Volts
	COMPLEMENT	False, 0, Low	0 Volts
EXAMPLE 2	ACTIVE SIGNAL	True, 1, High	0 Volts
	COMPLEMENT	False, 0, Low	-10 Volts

Table 8-2-2. Examples of positive logic

EXAMPLE 1	ACTIVE SIGNAL	True, 1, Low	+5 Volts
	COMPLEMENT	False, 0, High	+10 Volts
EXAMPLE 2	ACTIVE SIGNAL	True, 1, Low	-10 Volts
	COMPLEMENT	False, 0, High	-5 Volts

Table 8-2-3. Examples of negative logic

Positive Logic

Positive logic is defined as follows: If the signal that activates the circuit (the 1 state) has a voltage level that is more positive than the 0 state, then the logic polarity is considered to be positive. Table 8-2-2 shows the manner in which positive logic may be used.

As shown in the table, in positive logic the 1 state is at a more positive voltage level than the 0 state.

Negative Logic

As might be suspected, negative logic is the opposite of positive logic and is defined as follows: If the signal that activates the circuit (the 1 state) has a voltage level that is more negative than the 0 state, then the logic polarity is considered to be negative. Table 8-2-3 shows the manner in which negative logic may be used.

NOTE: *The logic level LOW now represents the 1 state. This is because the 1-state voltage is more negative than the 0-state voltage.*

In the examples shown for negative logic, the voltage for the logic 1 state is more negative with respect to the logic 0 state voltage. This holds true in example 1 where both voltages are positive. In this case, it may be easier to think of the TRUE condition as being less positive than the FALSE condition. Either way, the end result is negative logic.

8-26 | Digital Theory

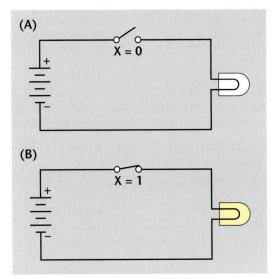

Figure 8-2-2. Logic switch; (A) Logic 0 state (B) Logic 1 state

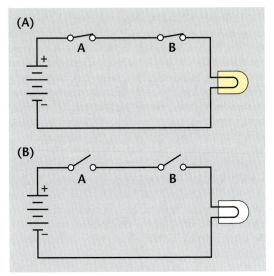

Figure 8-2-4. AND gate equivalent circuit; (A) Logic 1 state (B) Logic 0 state

The use of positive or negative logic for digital equipment is a choice to be made by design engineers. The difficulty for the technician in this area is limited to understanding the type of logic being used and keeping it in mind when troubleshooting.

NOTE: *Unless otherwise noted, the remainder of this book will deal only with positive logic.*

Logic Inputs And Outputs

In the study of logic circuits, a variety of symbols (variables) are used to represent the inputs and outputs. The purpose of these symbols is to let inform the user as to what inputs are required for the desired output.

If the symbol A is shown as an input to a logic device, then the logic level that represents A must be HIGH to activate the logic device. That is, it must satisfy the input requirements of the logic device before the logic device will issue the TRUE output.

Look at Figure 8-2-2A. The symbol X represents the input. As long as the switch is open, the lamp is not lit. The open switch represents the logic 0 state of variable X.

Closing the switch Figure 8-2-2B, represents the logic 1 state of X. Closing the switch completes the circuit, causing the lamp to light. The 1 state of X satisfied the input requirement and the circuit therefore produced the desired output (logic HIGH); current was applied to the lamp causing it to light.

When considering the lamp as the output of a logic device, the same conditions exist. The TRUE (1 state) output of the logic device is to have the lamp lit. If the lamp is not lit, then the output of the logic device is FALSE (0 state).

When studying logic circuits, it is important to remember the state (1 or 0) of the inputs and outputs.

So far in this chapter, the two conditions of logical statements have been discussed, the logic states representing these two conditions, logic levels and associated electrical signals and positive and negative logic. It is now time to proceed with individual logic device operations. These make up the majority of computer circuitry.

As each of the logic devices are presented, a chart called a *truth table* will be used to illustrate all possible input and corresponding output combinations. Truth tables are particularly helpful in understanding a logic device and for showing the differences between devices.

The logic operations that are covered in this section are the AND, OR, NOT, NAND, NOR and XOR. The devices that accomplish these operations are called *logic gates*, or more informally, *gates*. These gates are the foundation for all digital equipment. They are the "decision-making" circuits of computers and other types of digital equipment. The term "making deci-

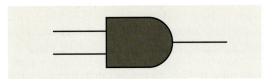

Figure 8-2-3. AND gate

sions" means that certain conditions must exist to produce the desired output.

In studying each gate, various mathematical symbols known as *Boolean algebra* expressions are introduced. These expressions are nothing more than descriptions of the input requirements necessary to activate the circuit and the resultant circuit output.

The AND Gate

The *AND gate* is a logic circuit that requires all inputs to be TRUE at the same time in order for the output to be TRUE.

Logic Symbol

The standard symbol for the AND gate is shown in Figure 8-2-3. Variations of this standard symbol may be encountered. These variations become necessary to illustrate that an AND gate may have more than one input.

If two variables, A and B, are applied to the inputs of the AND gate, then both A and B have to be TRUE at the same time to produce a TRUE output. The symbol *f* designates the output function. The *Boolean expression* for this operation is f = A•B or f = AB. The expression is spoken as, "f = A AND B." The dot, or lack of, indicates the AND function.

AND Gate Operation

The operation of the AND gate can be demonstrated with a simple circuit that has two switches in series, as shown in Figure 8-2-4. Both switches have to be closed at the same time to light the lamp (Figure 8-2-4A). Any other combination of switch positions (Figure 8-2-4B) results in an open circuit and the lamp will not light (logic 0).

Now look at Figure 8-2-5. Signal A is applied to one input of the AND gate and signal B to the other. At time T0, both inputs are LOW (logic 0) and f is LOW. At T1, A goes HIGH (logic 1); B remains LOW; and as a result, f remains LOW. At T2, A goes LOW and B goes HIGH; f, however, is still LOW because the proper input conditions have not been satisfied (A and B both HIGH at the same time). At T4, both A and B are HIGH. As a result, f is HIGH. The input requirements have been satisfied, so the output is HIGH (logic 1).

Truth Table

Now look at Figure 8-2-6. A truth table and a table of combinations are shown. The latter is a deviation of the truth table. It uses the HIGH and LOW logic levels to depict the gate's inputs and resultant output combinations rather than the 1 and 0 logic states. By comparing the inputs and outputs of the two tables, see how one can easily be converted to the other (remember, 1 = HIGH and 0 = LOW). The table of combinations is shown here only to familiarize the technician with its existence; it will not be seen again in this book. As mentioned earlier, the truth table is a chart that shows all possible combinations of inputs and the resulting outputs. Compare the AND gate truth table (Figure 8-2-6) with the input signals shown in Figure 8-2-5.

The first combination (A = 0, B = 0) corresponds to T0 in Figure 8-2-5; the second to T1; the third to T2; and the last to T4. When constructing a truth table, first include all possible combinations of the inputs, including the all-0s combination.

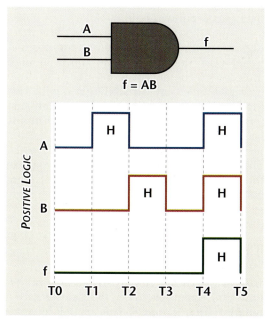

Figure 8-2-5. AND gate input and output signals

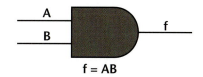

TRUTH TABLE			TABLE OF COMBINATIONS		
A	B	f	A	B	f
0	0	0	L	L	L
0	1	0	L	H	L
1	0	0	H	L	L
1	1	1	H	H	H

Figure 8-2-6. AND gate logic symbol, truth table, and table of combinations

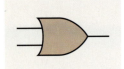

Figure 8-2-7. OR gate

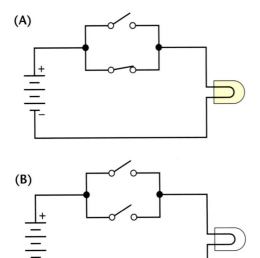

Figure 8-2-8. OR gate equivalent circuit; (A) Logic 1 state (B) Logic 0 state

A truth table representing an AND gate with three inputs (X, Y and Z) is shown in the following equation. Remember that the two-input AND gate has four possible combinations, with only one of those combinations providing a HIGH output. An AND gate with three inputs has eight possible combinations, again with only one combination providing a HIGH output. Make sure to include all possible combinations. To check if all combinations are included, raise 2 to the power equal to the number of input variables. This will give the total number of possible combinations. For example:

EXAMPLE 1:
AB = 2^2 = 4 combinations

EXAMPLE 2:
XYZ = 2^3 = 8 combinations

X Y Z f
0 0 0 0
0 0 1 0
0 1 0 0
0 1 1 0
1 0 0 0
1 0 1 0
1 1 0 0
1 1 1 1
f = XYZ

As with all AND gates, all the inputs must be HIGH at the same time to produce a HIGH output. Don't be confused if the complement of a variable is used as an input. When a complement is indicated as an input to an AND gate, it must also be HIGH to satisfy the input requirements of the gate. The Boolean expres-

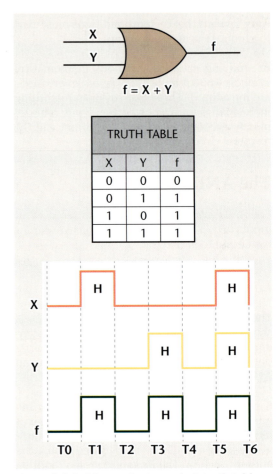

Figure 8-2-9. OR gate logic symbol, truth table, and input and output signals

sion for the output is formulated based on the TRUE inputs that give a TRUE output. Here is a summary that might help better explain the AND gate:

In order to produce a 1 output, all the inputs must be 1. If any or all of the inputs is or are 0, then the output will be 0.

Remember, the inputs, whether the original variable or the complement, must be high in order for the output to be high. The three examples given are all AND gates with two inputs. Keep in mind the Boolean expression for the output is the result of all the inputs being HIGH.

The technician will soon be able to recognize the truth table for the other types of logic gates without having to look at the logic symbol.

The OR Gate

The *OR gate* differs from the AND gate in that only ONE input has to be HIGH to produce a HIGH output. In an OR gate, *any* HIGH input will yield a HIGH output.

OR Gate Logic Symbol

Figure 8-2-7 shows the standard symbol for the OR gate. The number of inputs will vary according to the needs of the designer.

The OR gate may also be represented by a simple circuit as shown in Figure 8-2-8. In the OR gate, two switches are placed in parallel. If either or both of the switches are closed (Figure 8-2-8A), the lamp will light. The only time the lamp will not be lit is when both switches are open (Figure 8-2-8B).

Let's assume two variables, X and Y, are applied to the inputs of an OR gate. For the circuit to produce a HIGH output, either variable X, variable Y or both must be HIGH. The Boolean expression for this operation is $f = X + Y$ and is spoken as, "f equals X OR Y." The plus sign indicates the OR function and should not be confused with addition.

OR Gate Operation

Look at Figure 8-2-9. At time T0, both X and Y are LOW and f is LOW. At T1, X goes HIGH producing a HIGH output. At T2 when both inputs go LOW, f goes LOW. When Y goes HIGH at T3, f also goes HIGH and remains HIGH until both inputs are again LOW. At T5, both X and Y go HIGH, causing f to go HIGH.

Truth Table

The discussion of Figure 8-2-9 showed that there are four combinations of inputs X and Y. The truth table in Figure 8-2-9 lists each of these combinations of inputs and the respective outputs for the OR gate.

When writing or stating the Boolean expression for an OR gate with more than two inputs, simply place the OR sign (+) between each input and read or state the sign as OR. For example, the Boolean expression for an OR gate with the inputs of A, B, C and D would be:

$f = A+B+C+D$

This expression is spoken as, "f equals A OR B OR C OR D."

The complements can be substituted for the original statements as done with the AND gate or use negative logic; but for an output from an OR gate, at least one of the inputs must be TRUE.

The Inverter (NOT)

The *inverter*, often referred to as a *NOT gate*, is a logic device that has an output opposite of the input. It is sometimes called a *negator*. It may be used alone or in combination with other logic devices to fulfill equipment requirements.

When an inverter is used alone, it is represented by the symbol shown in Figure 8-2-10A. It will more often be seen in conjunction with the symbol for an amplifier (Figure 8-2-10B). Symbols for inverters used in combination with other devices will be shown later in the chapter.

Let's go back to the statement, "Today is payday." This example stated that P represents the TRUE state. If P is applied to the input of the inverter as shown in Figure 8-2-11, then the output will be the opposite of the input. The output, in this case, is $\bar{P}$. At T0 through T2, P is LOW. Consequently, the output ($\bar{P}$) is HIGH. At T2, P goes HIGH and as a result $\bar{P}$ goes LOW. $\bar{P}$ remains LOW as long as P is HIGH and vice versa. The Boolean expression for the output of this gate is $f = \bar{P}$.

Recall that $\bar{P}$ is the complement of P.

The truth table for an inverter is shown in Figure 8-2-11.

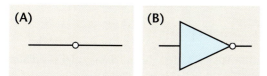

Figure 8-2-10. Inverter; (A) Symbol for inverter used alone (B) Symbol for an amplifier/inverter

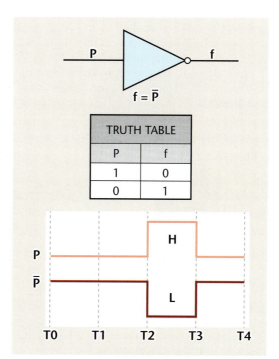

Figure 8-2-11. Inverter logic symbol, truth table, and input and resultant output

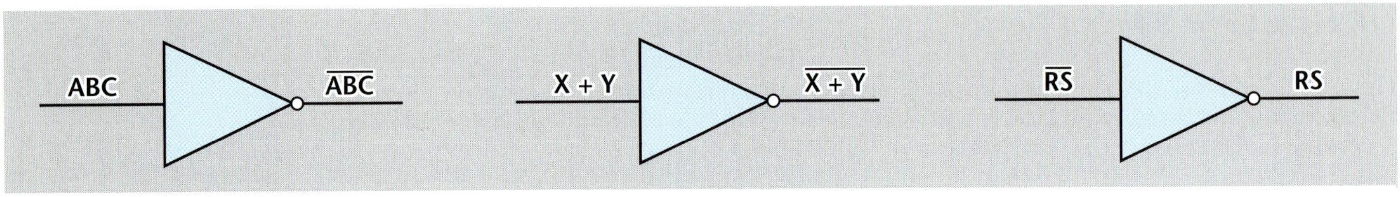

Figure 8-2-12. Various inputs to inverters and the resulting outputs

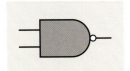

Figure 8-2-13. NAND gate

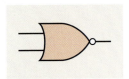

Figure 8-2-16. NOR gate

The output of an inverter will be the complement of the input. Figure 8-2-12 show various inputs to inverters and the resulting outputs.

The NAND Gate

The *NAND* gate is another logic device commonly found in digital equipment. This gate is simply an AND gate with an inverter (NOT gate) at the output.

NAND Gate Logic Symbol

The logic symbol for the NAND gate is shown in Figure 8-2-13.

The NAND gate can have two or more inputs. The output will be LOW only when all the inputs are HIGH. Conversely, the output will be HIGH when any or all of the inputs are LOW.

The NAND gate performs two functions, AND and NOT. Separating the NAND symbol to show these two functions would reveal the equivalent circuits depicted in Figure 8-2-14. This should help develop a better understanding of how the NAND gate functions.

Inputs X and Y are applied to the AND gate. If either X or Y or both are LOW (Figure 8-2-14A), then the output of the AND gate is LOW. A LOW (logic 0) on the input of the inverter results in a HIGH (logic 1) output. When both X and Y are HIGH (Figure 8-2-14B), the output of the AND gate is HIGH; thus the output of the inverter is LOW. The Boolean expression for the output of a NAND gate with these inputs is $f = \overline{X \cdot Y}$. The expression is spoken as, "X AND Y quantity not." The output of any NAND gate is the negation of the input. For example, if the inputs are X and $\overline{Y}$, the output will be $\overline{XY}$.

NAND Gate Operation

Now, let's observe the logic level inputs and corresponding outputs as shown in Figure 8-2-15. At time T0, X and Y are both LOW. The output is HIGH; the opposite of an AND gate with the same inputs. At T1, X goes HIGH and Y remains LOW. As a result, the output remains HIGH. At T2, X goes LOW and Y goes HIGH. Again, the output remains HIGH. When both X and Y are HIGH at T4, the output goes LOW. The output will remain LOW only as long as both X and Y are HIGH.

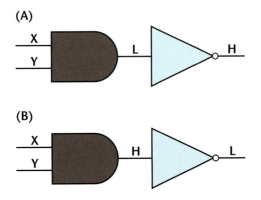

Figure 8-2-14. NAND gate equivalent circuit;
(A) Either X or Y or both are LOW
(B) Both X and Y are HIGH

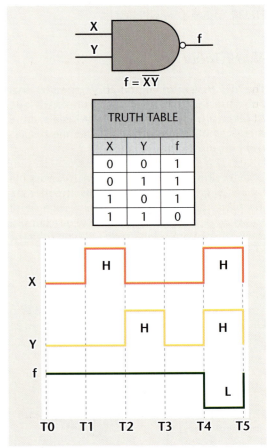

Figure 8-2-15. NAND gate logic symbol, truth table, and input and output signals

Truth Table

The truth table for a NAND gate with X and Y as inputs is shown in Figure 8-2-15.

The NOR Gate

As might be expected, the *NOR gate* is an OR gate with an inverter on the output.

NOR Gate Logic Symbol

The standard logic symbol for this gate is shown in Figure 8-2-16. More than just the two inputs may be shown.

The NOR gate will have a HIGH output only when all the inputs are LOW.

When broken down, the two functions performed by the NOR gate can be represented by the equivalent circuit depicted in Figure 8-2-17. When both inputs to the OR gate are LOW, the output is LOW. A LOW applied to an inverter gives a HIGH output. If either or both of the inputs to the OR gate are HIGH, the output will be HIGH. When this HIGH output is applied to the inverter, the resulting output is LOW. The Boolean expression for the output of this NOR gate is $f = \overline{K + L}$. The expression is spoken as, "K OR L quantity not."

NOR Gate Operation

The logic level inputs and corresponding outputs for a NOR gate are shown in Figure 8-2-18. At time T0, both K and L are LOW; as a result, f is HIGH. At T1, K goes HIGH, L remains LOW, and f goes LOW. At T2, K goes LOW, L goes HIGH, and the output remains LOW. The output goes HIGH again at T3 when both inputs are LOW. At T4, when both inputs are HIGH, the output goes LOW and remains LOW until T5, when both inputs go LOW. Remember the output is just opposite of what it would be for an OR gate.

Truth Table

The truth table for a NOR gate with K and L as inputs is shown in Figure 8-2-18.

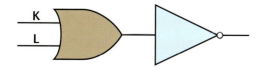

Figure 8-2-17. NOR gate equivalent circuit

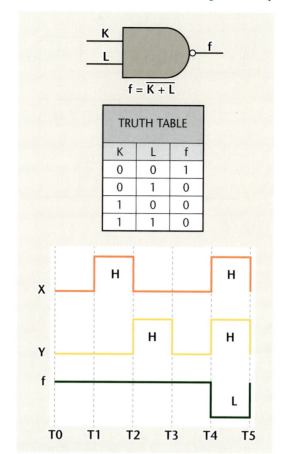

Figure 8-2-18. NOR gate ogic symbol, truth table, and input and output signals

The Exclusive OR Gate (XOR)

The *exclusive OR* (XOR) gate is a modified OR gate that produces a HIGH output when one and only one of the inputs is HIGH. The abbreviation XOR is often used to identify this gate. When both inputs are HIGH or when both inputs are LOW, the output is LOW.

The standard symbol for an exclusive OR gate is shown in Figure 8-2-19 along with the

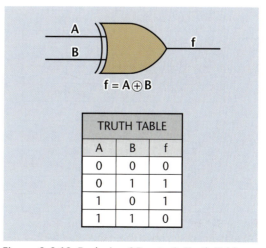

Figure 8-2-19. Exclusive OR gate & Truth Table

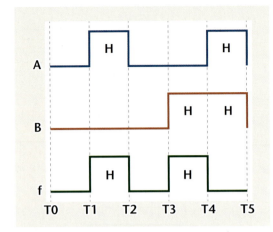

Figure 8-2-20. Exclusive OR gate timing diagram

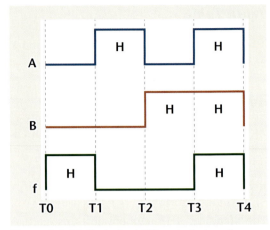

Figure 8-2-22. Exclusive NOR gate timing diagram

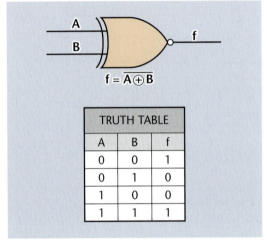

Figure 8-2-21. Exclusive NOR gate and truth table

associated truth table. The expression for the exclusive OR gate is f = A⊕B.

If observing the input and output signals of an XOR gate, the results would be similar to those shown in Figure 8-2-20. At T0, both inputs are LOW and the output is LOW. At T1, A goes to HIGH and remains HIGH until T2. During this time the output is HIGH. At T3, B goes HIGH and remains HIGH through T5. At T4, A again goes HIGH and remains HIGH through T5. Between T3 and T4, the output is HIGH. At T4, when both A and B are HIGH, the output goes LOW.

The Exclusive NOR Gate (XNOR)

The *exclusive NOR (XNOR) gate* is nothing more than an XOR gate with an inverted output. It produces a HIGH output when the inputs are either all HIGH or all LOW. The standard symbol and the truth table are shown in Figure 8-2-21. The expression for the XNOR gate is $f = \overline{A \oplus B}$.

A timing diagram for the XNOR gate is shown in Figure 8-2-22. From T0 to T1, when both inputs are LOW, the output is HIGH. The output goes LOW when the inputs are opposite; one HIGH and the other LOW. At T3, both inputs go HIGH, causing the output to go HIGH.

Flip-Flops

Flip-flops (FF) are devices used in the digital field for a variety of purposes. When properly connected, flip-flops may be used to store data temporarily, to multiply or divide, to count operations, or to receive and transfer information.

Flip-flops are bistable multivibrators. The types used in digital equipment are identified by the inputs. They may have from two to five inputs depending on the type. They are all common in one respect. They have two, and only two, distinct output states. The outputs are normally labeled Q and $\overline{Q}$ and should always be complementary. When Q = 1, then $\overline{Q}$ = 0 and vice versa.

Four types of FFs that are common to digital equipment are discussed. They are the R-S, D, T and J-K FFs.

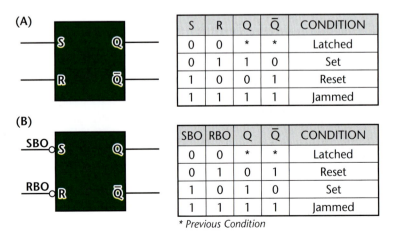

Figure 8-2-23. R-S flip-flop; (A) Standard symbol (B) R-S flip-flop with inverted inputs

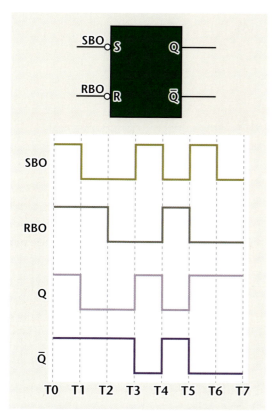

Figure 8-2-24. R-S flip-flop with inverted inputs timing diagram

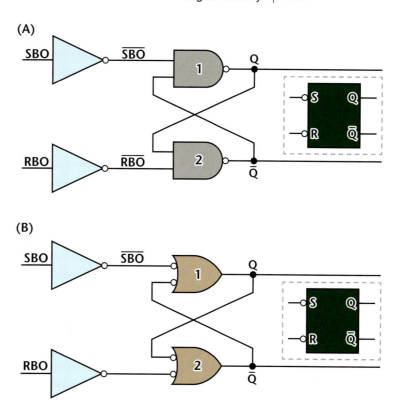

Figure 8-2-25. R-S flip-flop construction; (A) Using cross-coupled NAND gates (B) Using cross OR gates

R-S Flip-Flop

The *R-S FF* is used to temporarily hold or store information until it is needed. A single R-S FF will store one binary digit, either a 1 or a 0. Storing a four-digit binary number would require four R-S FFs.

The standard symbol for the R-S FF is shown in Figure 8-2-23A. The name is derived from the inputs—R for reset and S for set. It is often referred to as an *R-S latch*. The outputs Q and $\overline{Q}$ are complements, as mentioned earlier.

The R-S FF has two output conditions. When the Q output is HIGH and $\overline{Q}$ is LOW, the FF is set. When Q is LOW and $\overline{Q}$ is HIGH, the FF is reset. When the R and S inputs are both LOW, the outputs will both be HIGH. When this condition exists, the FF is considered to be *jammed* and the outputs cannot be used. The jammed condition is corrected when either S or R goes HIGH.

To set the flip-flop requires a HIGH on the S input and a LOW on the R input. To reset, the opposite is required; S input LOW and R input HIGH. When both R and S are HIGH, the FF will hold or "latch" the condition that existed before both inputs went HIGH.

Because the S input of this FF requires a logic LOW to set, a more easily understood symbol is shown in Figure 8-2-23B. Refer to this figure while reading the following paragraph.

In the description of R-S FF operation, let's assume that the signals applied to the S and R inputs are the LSDs of two different binary numbers. Let's also assume that these two binary numbers represent the speed and range of a target ship. The LSDs will be called SB0 (speed bit 0) and RB0 (range bit 0) and will be applied to the S and R inputs respectively (Figure 8-2-23B and Figure 8-2-24). At T0, both SB0 and RB0 are HIGH; as a result, both Q and $\overline{Q}$ are HIGH. This is the jammed state, which, as mentioned earlier, cannot be used in logic circuitry. At T1, SB0 goes LOW and RB0 remains HIGH; Q goes LOW and $\overline{Q}$ remains HIGH; the FF is reset. At T2 RB0 goes LOW and SB0 remains LOW; the FF is latched in the reset condition. At T3, SB0 goes HIGH and RB0 remains LOW; the FF sets. At T4 SB0 goes LOW and RB0 goes HIGH; the FF resets. When SB0 and RB0 input conditions reverse at T5, the FF sets. The circuit is put in the latch condition at T6, when SB0 goes LOW. Notice that the output changes states only when the inputs are in opposite states.

Figure 8-2-25 shows two methods of constructing an R-S FF. These diagrams can be used to prove the truth table for the R-S FF.

Look at Figure 8-2-25A. Let's assume SB0 is HIGH and RB0 is LOW. Remember from ear-

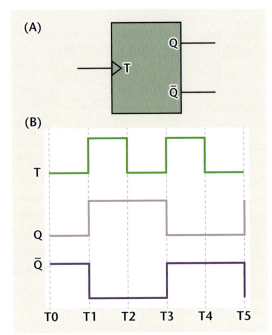

Figure 8-2-26. Toggle (T) flip-flop; (A) Standard symbol (B) Timing diagram

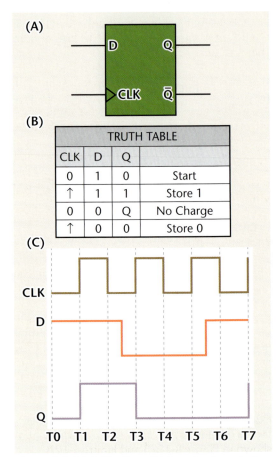

Figure 8-2-27. D flip flop; (A) Standard symbol (B) Truth table (C) Timing diagram

lier that the output of an inverter is the complement of the input. In this case, since SB0 is HIGH, $\overline{SB0}$ will be LOW. The LOW input to NAND gate 1 causes the Q output to go HIGH. This HIGH Q output is also fed to the input of NAND gate 2. The other input to NAND gate 2, $\overline{RB0}$, is HIGH. With both inputs to gate 2 HIGH, the output goes LOW. The LOW $\overline{Q}$ output is also fed to NAND gate 1 to be used as the latch signal. If SB0 goes LOW while this condition exists, there will be no change to the outputs because the FF would be in the latched condition, with both SB0 and RB0 LOW.

When RB0 is HIGH and SB0 is LOW, $\overline{RB0}$ being LOW drives the output, $\overline{Q}$, to a HIGH condition. The HIGH $\overline{Q}$ and HIGH $\overline{SB0}$ inputs to gate 1 cause the output, Q, to go LOW. This LOW is also fed to NAND gate 2 to be used as the latch signal. Since SB0 is LOW, the FF will again go into the latched mode if RB0 goes LOW.

The cross-coupled OR gates in Figure 8-2-25B perform the same functions as the NAND gate configuration of view A. A HIGH input at SB0 produces a HIGH Q output, and a LOW at RB0 produces a LOW $\overline{Q}$ output. The cross-coupled signals ($\overline{Q}$ to gate 1 and Q to gate 2) are used as the latch signals just as in view A. Other changes of the inputs can be traced using knowledge of basic logic gates.

Toggle Flip-Flop

The *toggle*, or *T, FF* is a bistable device that changes state on command from a common input terminal.

The standard symbol for a T FF is illustrated in Figure 8-2-26A. The T input may be preceded by an inverter. An inverter indicates an FF will toggle on a HIGH-to-LOW transition of the input pulse. The absence of an inverter indicates the FF will toggle on a LOW-to-HIGH transition of the pulse.

The timing diagram in Figure 8-2-26B shows the toggle input and the resulting outputs. Begin by assuming an initial condition (T0) of Q being LOW and $\overline{Q}$ being HIGH. At T1, the toggle changes from a LOW to a HIGH and the device changes state; Q goes HIGH and $\overline{Q}$ goes LOW. The outputs remain the same at T2 since the device is switched only by a LOW-to-HIGH

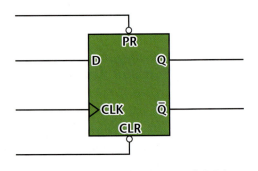

Figure 8-2-28. D flip-flop with PR and CLR inputs

transition. At T3, when the toggle goes HIGH, Q goes LOW and $\overline{Q}$ goes HIGH; they remain that way until T5.

Between T1 and T5, two complete cycles of T occur. During the same period, only one cycle is observed for Q or $\overline{Q}$. Since the output cycle is one-half the input cycle, this device can be used to divide the input by 2.

The most commonly used T FFs are J-K FFs wired to perform a toggle function. This use will be demonstrated later in this section.

D Flip-Flop

The *D FF* is a two-input FF. The inputs are the data (D) input and a clock (CLK) input. The clock is a timing pulse generated by the equipment to control operations. The D FF is used to store data at a predetermined time and hold it until it is needed. This circuit is sometimes called a *delay FF*. In other words, the data input is delayed up to one clock pulse before it is seen in the output.

The simplest form of a D FF is shown in Figure 8-2-27A. Now, follow the explanation of the circuit using the truth table and the timing diagram shown in Figure 8-2-27B and Figure 8-2-27C.

Depending on the circuit design, the clock can be a square wave, a constant frequency or asymmetrical pulses. In this example the clock (CLK) input will be a constant input at a given frequency. This frequency is determined by the control unit of the equipment. The data (D) input will be present when there is a need to store information. Notice in the truth table that output Q reflects the D input only when the clock transitions from 0 to 1 (LOW to HIGH).

Let's assume that at T0, CLK is 0, D is 1, and Q is 0. Input D remains at 1 for approximately $2\text{-}1/2$ clock pulses. At T1, when the clock goes to 1, Q also goes to 1 and remains at 1 even though D goes to 0 between T2 and T3. At T3, the positive-going pulse of the clock causes Q to go to 0, reflecting the condition of D. The positive-going clock pulse at T5 causes no change in the output because D is still LOW. Between T5 and T6, D goes HIGH, but Q remains LOW until T7 when the clock goes HIGH.

The key to understanding the output of the D FF is to remember that the data input is seen in the output only after the clock has gone HIGH.

D FF symbols may be seen with two additional inputs—clear (CLR) and preset (PR). These inputs are used to set the start condition of the FF—CLR sets Q to 0; PR sets Q to 1. Figure 8-2-28 shows the standard symbol with the CLR and PR inputs. Since these inputs are preceded by inverters (part of the FF), a LOW-going signal is necessary to activate the FF. These signals (CLR and PR) override the existing condition of the output.

An inverter may also be seen at the clock input. In this case, the output will change when the clock pulse goes negative.

J-K Flip-Flop

The *J-K FF* is the most widely used FF because of its versatility. When properly used it may perform the function of an R-S, T or D FF. The standard symbol for the J-K FF is shown in Figure 8-2-29A.

The J-K FF is a five-input device. The J and K inputs are for data. The CLK input is for the clock; and the PS and CLR inputs are the preset and clear inputs, respectively. The outputs Q and $\overline{Q}$ are the normal complementary outputs.

Observe the truth table and timing diagram in Figure 8-2-29B and Figure 8-2-29C, as the circuit is explained.

Line 1 of the truth table corresponds to T0 in the timing diagram. The PS and CLR inputs are both LOW. The CLK, J and K inputs are irrelevant. At this point the FF is jammed, and both Q and $\overline{Q}$ are HIGH. As with the R-S FF, this state cannot be used.

At T1, PS remains LOW while CLR goes HIGH. The Q output remains HIGH and $\overline{Q}$ goes LOW. The FF is in the preset condition (line 2 of the truth table).

At T2, PS goes HIGH, CLR goes LOW, Q goes LOW and $\overline{Q}$ goes HIGH. At this point the FF is cleared (line 3 of the truth table). The condition of the CLK, J and K inputs have no effect on the PS and CLR actions since these inputs override the other inputs. Starting at T3, PS and CLR will be held at HIGHs so as not to override the other actions of the FF. Using the PS and CLR inputs only, the circuit functions as an R-S FF.

Between T2 and T3, the CLK input is applied to the device. Since the CLK input has an inverter, all actions will take place on the negative-going transition of the clock pulse.

Line 4 of the truth table shows both PS and CLR HIGH, a negative-going CLK, and J and K at 0, or LOW. This corresponds to T3 on the timing diagram. In this condition, the FF holds the previous condition of the output. In this case the FF is reset. If the circuit were set when these inputs occurred, it would remain set.

At time T5, there is a negative-going clock pulse and a HIGH on the J input. This causes

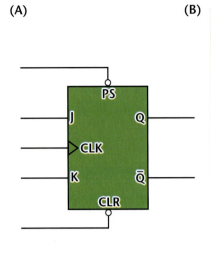
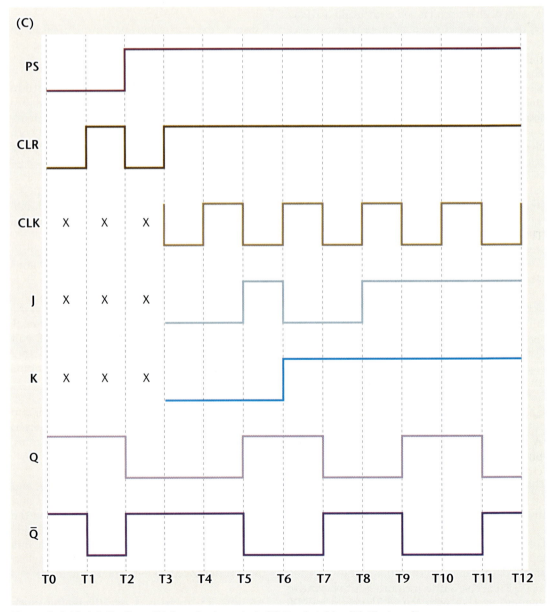

Figure 8-2-29. J-K flip-flop; (A) Standard symbol (B) Truth table (C) Timing diagram

the circuit to set, Q to go HIGH, and $\overline{Q}$ to go LOW. See line 5 of the truth table.

At T6, J goes LOW, K goes HIGH, and the clock is in a positive-going transition. There is no change in the output because all actions take place on the negative clock transition.

At T7, when J is LOW, K is HIGH, and the clock is going negative, the FF resets, Q goes LOW, and $\overline{Q}$ goes HIGH (line 6).

With both J and K HIGH and a negative-going clock (as at T9 and line 7), the FF toggles or changes state with each clock pulse. It will continue to toggle as long as J and K both remain HIGH.

Line 8 of the truth table indicates that as long as the clock is in any condition other than a negative going transition, there will be no change in the output regardless of the state of J or K.

As mentioned at the beginning of this section, J-K FFs may be used as R-S, T or D FFs. Figure 8-2-30 shows how a J-K can be made to perform the other functions. In Figure 8-2-30A, using just the PS and CLR inputs of the J-K will cause it to react like an R-S FF. In Figure 8-2-30B, data is applied to the J input. This same data is applied to the K input through an inverter to ensure that the K input is in the opposite state. In this configuration, the J-K performs the same function as a D FF. Figure 8-2-30C shows both the J and K inputs held at 1, or HIGH. The FF will change state or toggle with each negative-going transition of the clock, just as a T FF will.

This shows the versatility of the J-K FF.

Adders

Adders are combinations of logic gates that combine binary values to obtain a sum. They are classified according to their ability to accept and combine the digits. In this section quarter adders, half adders and full adders are discussed.

Quarter Adder

A *quarter adder* is a circuit that can add two binary digits but will not produce a carry. This circuit will produce the following results:

0 + 0 = 0
0 + 1 = 1
1 + 0 = 1
1 + 1 = 0 (no carry)

Notice that the output produced is the same as the truth table of an XOR gate. Therefore, an XOR gate can be used as a quarter adder.

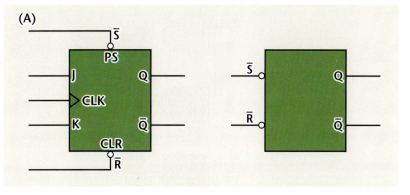

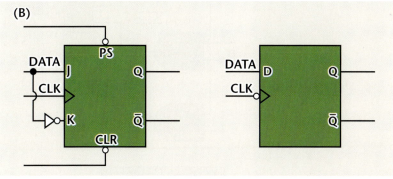

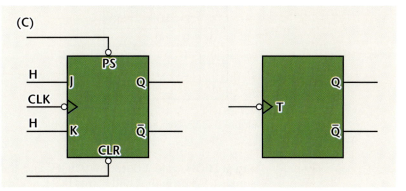

Figure 8-2-30. J-K versatility; (A) Using just the PS and CLR inputs (B) Data applied to the J input (C) Both J and K inputs held HIGH

The combination of gates in Figure 8-2-31 will also produce the desired results. When A and B are both LOW (0), the output of each AND gate is LOW (0); therefore, the output of the OR gate is LOW (0).

When A is HIGH and B is LOW, then $\overline{B}$ is HIGH and AND gate 1 produces a HIGH output, resulting in a sum of 1 at gate 3. With A LOW

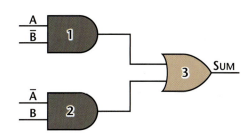

Figure 8-2-31. Quarter adder

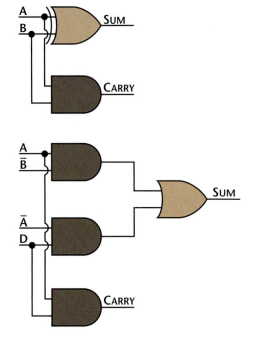

Figure 8-2-32. Half adders and truth table

Figure 8-2-32 shows two ways of constructing a half adder. An AND gate is added in parallel to the quarter adder to generate the carry. The Sum column of the truth table represents the output of the quarter adder, and the Carry column represents the output of the AND gate.

As previously discussed, the output of the quarter adder is HIGH when either input, but not both, is HIGH. It is only when both inputs are HIGH that the AND gate is activated that a carry is produced. The largest sum that can be obtained from a half adder is 10_2 ($1_2 + 1_2$).

Full Adder

The *full adder* becomes necessary when a carry input must be added to the two binary digits to obtain the correct sum. A half adder has no input for carries from previous circuits.

One method of constructing a full adder is to use two half adders and an OR gate as shown in Figure 8-2-33. The inputs A and B are applied to gates 1 and 2. These make up one half adder. The sum output of this half adder and the carry from a previous circuit become the inputs to the second half adder. The carry from each half adder is applied to gate 5 to produce the carry-out for the circuit.

Now let's add a series of numbers and see how the circuit operates.

First, let's add 1_2 and 0. When either A or B is HIGH, gate 1 has an output. This output is applied to gates 3 and 4. Since the carry-in is 0, only gate 3 will produce an output. The sum of 1_2 and 0 is 1_2.

Now let's add 1_2 and 1_2. If A and B are both HIGH, the output of gate 1 is LOW. When the carry-in is 0 (LOW), the output of gate 3 is LOW. Gate 2 produces an output that is applied to gate 5, which produces the carry-out. The

and B HIGH, gate 2 output is HIGH, and the sum is 1. When both A and B are HIGH, neither AND gate has an output, and the output of gate 3 is LOW (0); no carry is produced.

Half Adder

A *half adder* is designed to combine two binary digits and produce a carry.

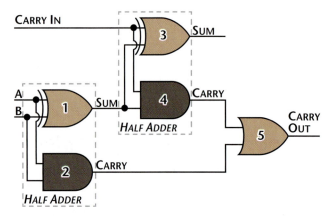

Figure 8-2-33. Full adder & truth table

A	B	CARRY IN	SUM OUT	CARRY OUT
0	0	0	0	0
0	1	0	1	0
1	0	0	1	0
1	1	0	0	1
0	0	1	1	0
0	1	1	0	1
1	0	1	0	1
1	1	1	1	1

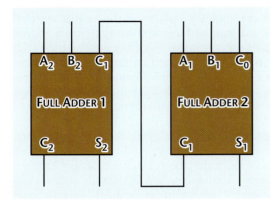

Figure 8-2-34. Parallel binary adder

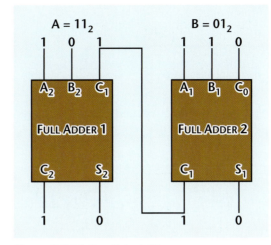

Figure 8-2-35. Parallel addition

sum of 1_2 and 1_2 is 10_2, just as it was for the half adder.

When A and B are both LOW and the carry-in is 1, only gate 3 has an output and produces a sum of 1_2 with no carry-out.

Now, let's add A or B and a carry-in. For example, let's assume that A is HIGH and B is LOW. With these conditions, gate 1 will have an output. This output and the carry-in applied to gates 3 and 4 will produce a sum out of 0 and a carry of 1. This carry from gate 4 will cause gate 5 to produce a carry-out. The sum of A and a carry ($1_2 + 1_2$) is 10_2.

When A, B, and the carry-in are all HIGH, a sum of 1 and a carry-out are produced. First, consider A and B. When both are HIGH, the output of gate 1 is LOW, and the output of gate 2 is HIGH, giving us a carry-out at gate 5. The carry-in produces a 1 output at gate 3, giving us a sum of 1. The output of the full adder is 11_2. The sum of 1_2, 1_2 and 1_2 is 11_2.

Parallel Adders

The adders discussed in the previous section have been limited to adding single-digit binary numbers and carries. The largest sum that can be obtained using a full adder is 11_2.

Parallel adders let us add multiple-digit numbers. By placing full adders in parallel, it is possible to add two- or four-digit numbers or any other size desired.

Figure 8-2-34 uses *standard symbols* to show a parallel adder capable of adding two two-digit binary numbers. The previous discussions have depicted circuits with individual logic gates shown. Standard symbols (blocks) allow us to analyze circuits with inputs and outputs only. One standard symbol may actually contain many and various types of gates and circuits. The addend would be input on the A inputs (A2 = MSD, A1 = LSD), and the augend input on the B inputs (B2 = MSD, B1 = LSD). For this explanation, assume there is no input to C_0 (carry from a previous circuit).

Now add some two-digit numbers. To add 10_2 (addend) and 01_2 (augend), assume there are numbers at the appropriate inputs. The addend inputs will be 1 on A_2 and 0 on A_1. The augend inputs will be 0 on B_2 and 1 on B_1. Working from right to left, as done in normal addition, calculate the outputs of each full adder.

With A_1 at 0 and B_1 at 1, the output of adder 1 will be a sum (S_1) of 1 with no carry (C_1). Since A_2 is 1 and B_2 is 0, there is a sum (S_2) of 1 with no carry (C_2) from adder 1. To determine the sum, read the outputs (C_2, S_2 and S_1) from left to right. In this case, $C_2 = 0$, $S_2 = 1$ and $S_1 = 1$. The sum, then, of 10_2 and 01_2 is 011_2 or 11_2.

As previously discussed, the highest binary number with two digits is 11_2. Using the parallel adder, let's add 11_2 and 11_2.

First, apply the addend and augend to the A and B inputs. Calculate the output of each full adder beginning with full adder 1. With A_1 and B_1 at 1, S_1 is 0 and C_1 is 1. Since all three inputs (A2, B2 and C1) to full adder 2 are 1, the output will be 1 at S_2 and 1 at C_2. The output of the circuit, as read left to right, is 110_2, the sum of 11_2 and 11_2.

Parallel adders may be expanded by combining more full adders to accommodate the number of digits in the numbers to be added. There must be one full adder for each digit.

To add 11_2 and 01_2, assume one number is applied to A_1 and A_2, and the other to B_1 and B_2, as shown in Figure 8-2-35. Adder 1 produces a sum (S_1) of 0 and a carry (C_1) of 1. Adder 2 gives us a sum (S_2) of 0 and a carry (C_2) of 1. By reading the outputs (C_2, S_2 and S_1), notice that the sum of 11_2 and 01_2 is 100_2.

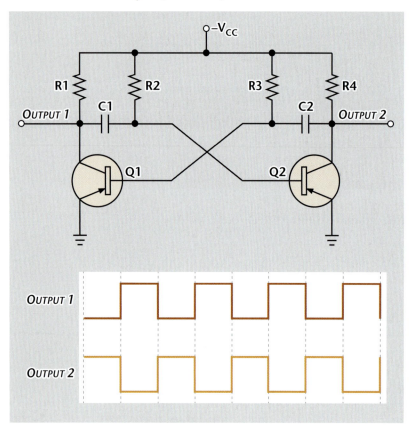

Figure 8-2-36. Free-running multivibrator

Clocks And Counters

Clocks and counters are found in all types of digital equipment. Although they provide different functions, they are all constructed of circuits with which the technician is familiar. By changing the way the circuits are interconnected, timing circuits, multipliers and dividers, and storage units can be built.

Clocks

The simplest form of a clock is the astable or free-running multivibrator. A schematic diagram of a typical free-running multivibrator is shown, along with its output waveforms, in Figure 8-2-36. This multivibrator circuit is called free running because it alternates between two output voltages during the time it is active. Outputs 1 and 2 will be equal and opposite since Q_1 and Q_2 conduct alternately. The frequency of the outputs may be altered within certain limits by varying the values of R_2C_1 and R_3C_2.

Figure 8-2-37. Monostable multivibrator block diagram

The frequency stability of the astable multivibrator can be increased by applying a trigger pulse to the circuit. The frequency of the trigger must be higher than the free-running frequency of the multivibrator. The output frequency will match the trigger frequency and produce a more stable output.

Another method of producing a stable clock pulse is to use a triggered monostable or one-shot multivibrator. A block diagram of a monostable multivibrator with input and output signals is shown in Figure 8-2-37. The duration of the output pulse is dependent on the charge time of an RC network in the multivibrator. Each trigger input results in a complete cycle in the output, as shown in Figure 8-2-37. Trigger pulses are supplied by an oscillator.

The circuits described previously are very simple clocks. However, as the complexity of the system increases, so do the timing requirements. Complex systems have multiphase clocks to control a variety of operations. Multiphase clocks allow functions involving more than one operation to be completed during a single clock cycle. They also permit an operation to extend over more than one clock cycle.

A block diagram of a two-phase clock system is shown in Figure 8-2-38A. The astable multivibrator provides the basic timing for the circuit, while the one-shot multivibrators are used to shape the pulses. Outputs Q and $\overline{Q}$ are input to one-shot multivibrators 1 and 2, respectively. The resulting outputs are in phase with the inputs, but the duration of the pulse is greatly reduced, as shown in Figure 8-2-38B.

Clocks are designed to provide the most efficient operation of the equipment. During the design phase, the frequency, pulse width, and the number of phases required is determined; and the clock circuit is built to meet those requirements.

Most modern high-speed equipment uses crystal-controlled oscillators as the basis for their timing networks. Crystals are stable even at extremely high frequencies.

Counters

A *counter* is simply a device that counts. Counters may be used to count operations, quantities or periods of time. They may also be used for dividing frequencies, for addressing information in storage, or for temporary storage.

Counters are a series of FFs wired together to perform the type of counting desired. They will count up or down by ones, twos or more.

The total number of counts or stable states a counter can indicate is called *modulus*. For instance, the modulus of a four-stage counter would be 16_{10}, since it is capable of indicating from 0000_2 to 1111_2. The term *modulo* is used to describe the count capability of counters; that is, modulo-16 for a four-stage binary counter, modulo-11 for a decade counter, modulo-8 for a three-stage binary counter, and so forth.

Ripple Counters

Ripple counters are so named because the count is like a chain reaction that ripples through the counter because of the time involved. This effect will become more evident with the explanation of the following circuit.

Figure 8-2-39A shows a basic four-stage, or modulo-16, ripple counter. The inputs and outputs are shown in Figure 8-2-39B. The four J-K FFs are connected to perform a toggle function, which divides the input by 2. The HIGHs on the J and K inputs enable the FFs to toggle. The inverters on the clock inputs indicate that the FFs change state on the negative-going pulse.

Assume that A, B, C and D are lamps and that all the FFs are reset. The lamps will all be out,

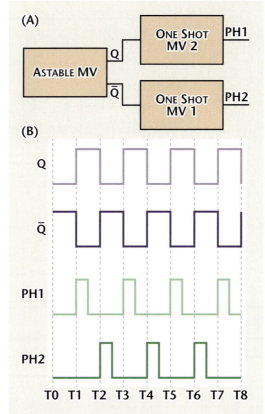

Figure 8-2-38. Two-phase clock; (A) Block diagram (B) Timing diagram

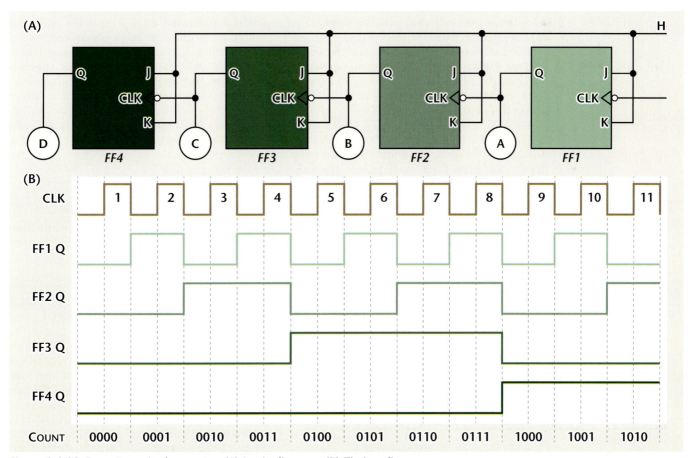

Figure 8-2-39. Four-stage ripple counter; (A) Logic diagram (B) Timing diagram

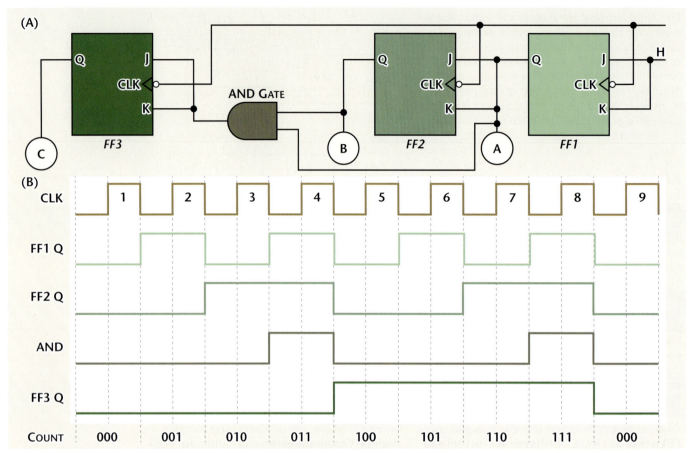

Figure 8-2-40. Three-stage synchronous counter; (A) Logic diagram (B) Timing diagram

and the count indicated will be 00000_2. The negative-going pulse of clock pulse 1 causes FF1 to set. This lights lamp A, and the count becomes 0001_2. The negative-going pulse of clock pulse 2 toggles FF1, causing it to reset. This negative-going input to FF2 causes it to set and causes B to light. The count after two clock pulses is 0010_2, or 2_{10}. Clock pulse 3 causes FF1 to set and lights lamp A. The setting of FF1 does not affect FF2, and lamp B stays lit. After three clock pulses, the indicated count is 0011_2 (3_{10}).

Clock pulse 4 causes FF1 to reset, which causes FF2 to reset, which causes FF3 to set, giving us a count of 0100_2 (4_{10}). This step shows the ripple effect.

This setting and resetting of the FFs will continue until all the FFs are set and all the lamps are lit. At that time the count will be 1111_2 (15_{10}). Clock pulse 16 will cause FF1 to reset and lamp A to go out. This will cause FF2 through FF4 to reset, in order, and will extinguish lamps B, C and D. The counter would then start at 0001_2 on clock pulse 17. To display a count of 10000_2 (16_{10}), another FF would need to be added.

The ripple counter is also called an *asynchronous* counter. Asynchronous means that the events (setting and resetting of FFs) occur one after the other rather than all at once. Because the ripple count is asynchronous, it can produce erroneous indications when the clock speed is high. A high-speed clock can cause the lower-stage FFs to change state before the upper stages have reacted to the previous clock pulse. The errors are produced by the FFs' inability to keep up with the clock.

Synchronous Counter

High-frequency operations require that all the FFs of a counter be triggered at the same time to prevent errors. A *synchronous* counter is used for this type of operation.

The synchronous counter is similar to a ripple counter with two exceptions: The clock pulses are applied to each FF, and additional gates are added to ensure that the FFs toggle in the proper sequence.

A logic diagram of a three-state (modulo-8) synchronous counter is shown in Figure 8-2-40A. The clock input is wired to each of the FFs to prevent possible errors in the count. A HIGH is wired to the J and K inputs of FF1 to make the FF toggle. The output of FF1 is wired to the J and K inputs of FF2, one input of the AND gate, and indicator A. The output of FF2 is wired to the other input of the AND gate and indicator B. The AND output is connected to the J and K inputs of FF3. The C indicator is the only output of FF3.

During the explanation of this circuit, follow the logic diagram in Figure 8-2-40A and the pulse sequences in Figure 8-2-40B.

Assume the following initial conditions: The outputs of all FFs, the clock and the AND gate are 0; and the J and K inputs to FF1 are HIGH. The negative-going portion of the clock pulse will be used throughout the explanation.

Clock pulse 1 causes FF1 to set. This HIGH lights lamp A, indicating a count of 001_2. The HIGH is also applied to the J and K inputs of FF2 and one input of the AND gate. Notice that FF2 and FF3 are unaffected by the first clock pulse because the J and K inputs were LOW when the clock pulse was applied.

As clock pulse 2 goes LOW, FF1 resets, turning off lamp A. In turn, FF2 will set, lighting lamp B and showing a count of 010_2. The HIGH from FF2 is also felt by the AND gate. The AND gate is not activated at this time because the signal from FF1 is now a LOW. A LOW is present on the J and K inputs of FF3, so it is not toggled by the clock.

Clock pulse 3 toggles FF1 again and lights lamp A. Since the J and K inputs to FF2 were LOW when pulse 3 occurred, FF2 does not toggle but remains set. Lamps A and B are lit, indicating a count of 011_2 (3_{10}). With both FF1 and FF2 set, HIGHs are sent to both inputs of the AND gate, resulting in HIGHs to J and K of FF3. No change occurred in the output of FF3 on clock pulse 3 because the J and K inputs were LOW at the time.

Just before clock pulse 4 occurs, the following conditions exist: FF1 and FF2 are set, and the AND gate is outputting a HIGH to the J and K inputs of FF3. With these conditions, all of the FFs will toggle with the next clock pulse.

At clock pulse 4, FF1 and FF2 are reset, and FF3 sets. The output of the AND gate goes to 0, and there is a count of 100_2 (4_{10}).

It appears that the clock pulse and the AND output both go to 0 at the same time, but the clock pulse arrives at FF3 before the AND gate goes LOW because of the transit time of the signal through FF1, FF2 and the AND gate.

Between pulses 4 and 8, FF3 remains set because the J and K inputs are LOW. FF1 and FF2 toggle in the same sequence as they did on clock pulses 1, 2 and 3.

Clock pulse 7 results in all of the FFs being set and the AND gate output being HIGH. Clock pulse 8 causes all the FFs to reset and all the lamps to turn off, indicating a count of 000_2. The next clock pulse (9) will restart the count sequence.

Decade Counter

A *decade counter* is a binary counter that is designed to count to 10_{10}, or 1010_2. An ordinary four-stage counter can be easily modified to a decade counter by adding a NAND gate, as shown in Figure 8-2-41. Notice that FF2 and FF4 provide the inputs to the NAND gate. The NAND gate outputs are connected to the CLR input of each of the FFs.

The counter operates as a normal counter until it reaches a count of 1010_2. At that time, both inputs to the NAND gate are HIGH, and the output goes LOW. This LOW applied to the CLR input of the FFs causes them to reset to 0. Remember from the discussion of J-K FFs that CLR and PS or PR override the existing condition of the FF. Once the FFs are reset, the count

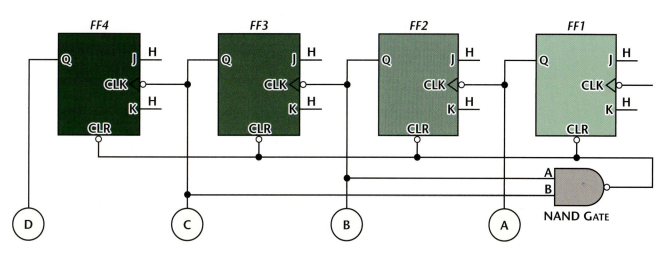

Figure 8-2-41. Decade counter

Binary Count	NAND Gate Input		NAND Gate Output
*******	A	B	*******
0000	0	0	1
0001	0	0	1
0010	1	0	1
0011	1	0	1
0100	0	0	1
0101	0	0	1
0110	1	0	1
0111	1	0	1
1000	0	1	1
1001	0	1	1
1010	1	1	0

Table 8-2-4. NAND Gate input, output and binary count

may begin again. Table 8-2-4 shows the binary count and the inputs and outputs of the NAND gate for each count of the decade counter:

Changing the inputs to the NAND gate can cause the maximum count to be changed. For instance, if FF4 and FF3 were wired to the NAND gate, the counter would count to 1100_2 (12_{10}) and then reset.

Ring Counter

A *ring counter* is defined as a loop of bistable devices (FFs) interconnected in such a manner that only one of the devices may be in a specified state at a time. If the specified condition is HIGH, then only one device may be HIGH at a time. As the clock, or input, signal is received, the specified state will shift to the next device at a rate of one shift per clock, or input, pulse.

Figure 8-2-42 shows a typical four-stage ring counter. This particular counter is composed of

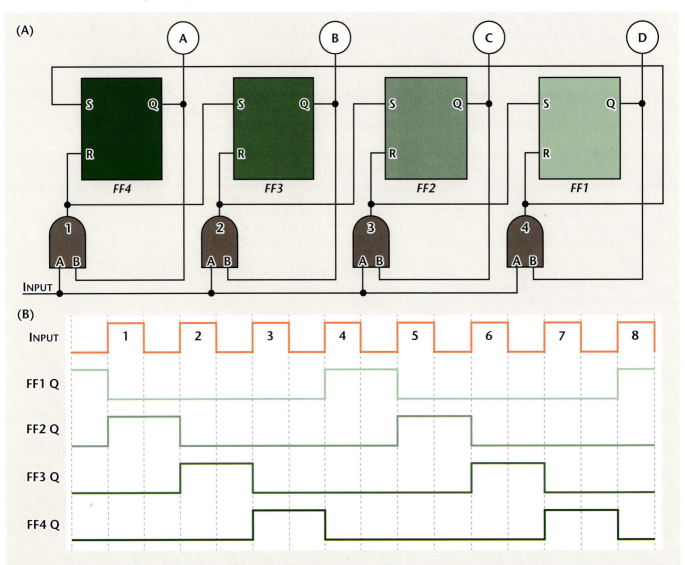

Figure 8-2-42. Ring counter; (A) Logic diagram (B) Timing diagram

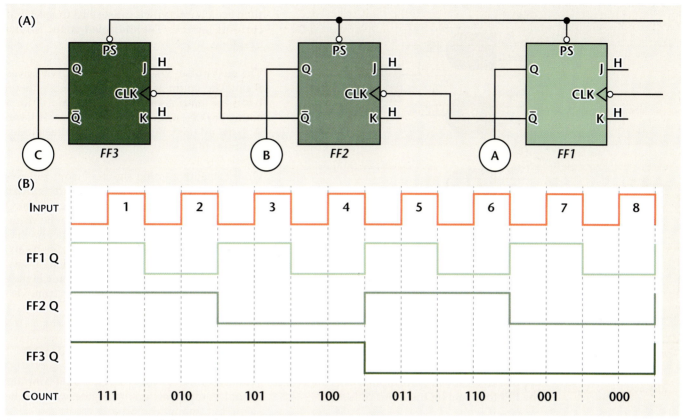

Figure 8-2-43. Down counter; (A) Logic diagram (B) Timing diagram

R-S FFs, but J-K FFs may also be used. Notice that the output of each AND gate is input to the R, or reset side, of the nearest FF and to the S, or set side, of the next FF. The Q output of each FF is applied to the B input of the AND gate that is connected to its own R input.

The circuit input may be normal CLK pulses or pulses from elsewhere in the equipment that would indicate some operation has been completed.

Now, let's look at the circuit operation and observe the signal flow as shown in Figure 8-2-42B.

For an initial condition, let's assume that the output of FF1 is HIGH and that the input and FF2, FF3 and FF4 are LOW. Under these conditions, lamp A will be lit, and lamps B, C and D will be extinguished. The HIGH from FF1 is also applied to the B input of AND gate 1.

The first input pulse is applied to the A input of each of the AND gates. The B inputs to AND gates 2, 3 and 4 are LOW since the outputs of FF2, FF3 and FF4 are LOW. AND gate 1 now has HIGHs on both inputs and produces a HIGH output. This HIGH simultaneously resets FF1 and sets FF2. Lamp A then goes out, and lamp B goes on. There is now a HIGH on AND gate 2 at the B input. There is also a LOW on AND gate 1 at input B.

Input pulse 2 will produce a HIGH output from AND gate 2 since AND gate 2 is the only one with HIGHs on both inputs. The HIGH from AND gate 2 causes FF2 to reset and FF3 to set. Indicator B goes out and C goes on.

Pulse 3 will cause AND gate 3 to go HIGH. This results in FF3 being reset and FF4 being set. Pulse 4 causes FF4 to reset and FF1 to set, bringing the counter full circle to the initial conditions. As long as the counter is operational, it will continue to light the lamps in sequence: 1, 2, 3, 4; 1, 2, 3, 4; etc.

As stated at the beginning of this section, only one FF may be in the specified condition at a given time. The specified condition shifts one position with each input pulse.

Down Counters

Up to this point the counters discussed have been up counters (with the exception of the ring counter). An up counter starts at 0 and counts to a given number. This section will discuss *down counters*, which start at a given number and count down to 0.

Up counters are sometimes called *increment counters*. Increment means to increase. Down counters are called *decrement counters*. Decrement means to decrease.

A three-stage, ripple down counter is shown in Figure 8-2-43A. Notice that the PS input of

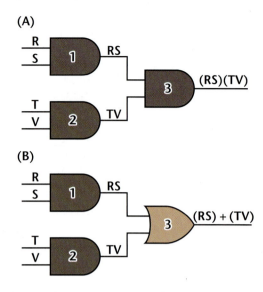

Figure 8-2-44. Logic gate combinations;
(A) Simple combination of AND gates (B) Simple combination of AND gates and OR gate

the J-K FFs is used in this circuit. HIGHs are applied to all the J and K inputs. This enables the FFs to toggle on the input pulses.

A negative-going pulse is applied to all PS terminals to start the countdown. This causes all the FFs to set and also lights indicators A, B and C. The beginning count is 111_2 (7_{10}). At the same time, LOWs are applied to the CLK inputs of FF2 and FF3, but they do not toggle because the PS overrides any change. All actions in the counter will take place on the negative-going portion of the input pulse. Let's go through the pulse sequences in Figure 8-2-43B.

Clock pulse 1 causes FF1 to toggle and output Q to go LOW. Lamp A is turned off. Notice that $\overline{Q}$ goes HIGH, but no change occurs in FF2 or FF3. Lamps B and C are now on, A is off, and the indicated count is 110_2 (6_{10}).

Clock pulse 2 toggles FF1 again and lights lamp A. When Q goes HIGH, $\overline{Q}$ goes LOW. This negative-going signal causes FF2 to toggle and reset. Lamp B is turned off, and a HIGH is felt at the CLK input of FF3. The indicated count is 101_2 (5_{10}); lamps A and C are on, and B is off.

At clock pulse 3, FF1 toggles and resets. Lamp A is turned off. A positive-going signal is applied to the CLK input of FF2. Lamp B remains off and C remains on. The count at this point is 100_2 (4_{10}).

Clock pulse 4 toggles FF1 and causes it to set, lighting lamp A. Now FF1, output $\overline{Q}$, goes LOW, causing FF2 to toggle. This causes FF2 to set and lights lamp B. Output of FF2, $\overline{Q}$, then goes LOW, which causes FF3 to reset and turn off lamp C. The indicated count is now 011_2 (3_{10}).

The next pulse, 5, turns off lamp A but leaves B on. The count is now 010_2. Clock pulse 6 turns on lamp A and turns off lamp B, for a count of 001_2. Clock pulse 7 turns off lamp A. Now all the lamps are off, and the counter indicates 000.

On the negative-going signal of clock pulse 8, all FFs are set, and all the lamps are lighted. The CLK pulse toggles FF1, making output Q go HIGH. As output $\overline{Q}$ goes LOW, the negative-going signal causes FF2 to toggle. As FF2, output Q, goes HIGH, output $\overline{Q}$ goes LOW, causing FF3 to toggle and set. As each FF sets, its indicator lamp lights. The counter is now ready to again start counting down from 111_2 with the next CLK pulse.

Logic Gates in Combination

When looking at logic circuit diagrams for digital equipment, a single gate will not be seen, but many combinations of gates. At first it may seem confusing and complex. If the technician interprets one gate at a time, it is possible to work through any network. In this section, several combinations of gates are analyzed and followed by a number of practice problems.

Figure 8-2-44A shows a simple combination of AND gates. The outputs of gates 1 and 2 are the inputs to gate 3. As previously discussed, both inputs to an AND gate must be HIGH at the same time in order to produce a HIGH output.

The output Boolean expression of gate 1 is RS, and the output expression of gate 2 is TV. These two output expressions become the inputs to gate 3. Remember, the output Boolean expression is the result of the inputs—in this case (R•S)•(T•V). The output can also be written (RS)(TV). Both are spoken as, "Quantity R AND S AND quantity T AND V."

In Figure 8-2-44B gate 3 is changed to an OR gate. The outputs of gates 1 and 2 remain the same but the output of gate 3 changes as might be expected. The output of gate 3 is now (R•S)+(T•V), spoken as, "Quantity R AND S OR quantity T AND V."

In Figure 8-2-45A, the outputs of two OR gates are applied as the input to third OR gate. The output for gate 1 is R+S, and the output for gate 2 is T+V. With these inputs, the output expression of gate 3 is (R+S)+(T+V).

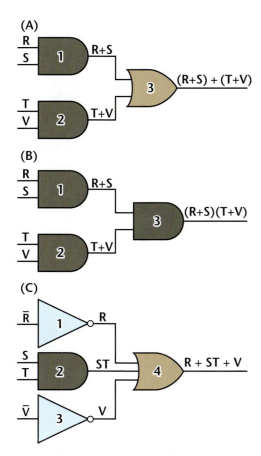

Figure 8-2-45. Logic gate combinations;
(A) Simple combination of OR gates
(B) Simple combination of OR gates and AND gate
(C) Output expression without the parentheses

In Figure 8-2-45B, gate 3 has been changed to an AND gate. The outputs of gates 1 and 2 do not change, but the output expression of gate 3 does. In this case, the gate 3 output expression is (R+S)•(T+V), or, "Quantity R OR S AND quantity T OR V." The parentheses are used to separate the input terms and to indicate the AND function. Without the parentheses the output expression would read R+ST+V, which is representative of the circuit in Figure 8-2-45C. As shown, this is not the same circuit as the one depicted in Figure 8-2-45B. It is very important that the Boolean expressions be written and spoken correctly.

The truth table for the output expression of gate 3 (Figure 8-2-45B) will help in understanding the output. When studying this truth table, notice that the only time f is HIGH (logic 1) is when either or both R and S AND either or both T and V are HIGH (logic 1).

```
R S T V f
0 0 0 0 0
0 0 0 1 0
0 0 1 0 0
0 0 1 1 0
0 1 0 0 0
0 1 0 1 1
0 1 1 0 1
0 1 1 1 1
1 0 0 0 0
1 0 0 1 1
1 0 1 0 1
1 0 1 1 1
1 1 0 0 0
1 1 0 1 1
1 1 1 0 1
1 1 1 1 1
f = (R+S)•(T+V)
```

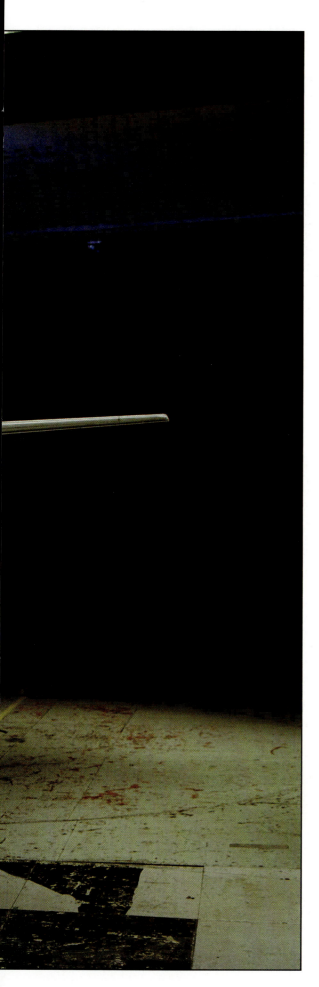

9

Fundamentals of Flight

Section 1

Theory of Flight

Even though modern computer-based design programs have taken the place of many years of struggle by design teams, a human brain still has to be in control. The design principles that control heavier-than-air flight exist in the mind; the computer just makes assumptions based on human input.

In order to properly maintain any aircraft, the technician must make assumptions based on human input. In the process, understanding the relationship of the various control surfaces to each other, as well as the complete airplane, is essential. As you read this chapter, remember that, in aviation, nothing exists and operates alone.

Aerodynamics. Aerodynamics is the science of the action of air on an object. It is further defined as that branch of dynamics that deals with the motion (current) of air and with the forces acting upon an object in the current of air. In effect, aerodynamics is concerned with three distinct parts: the atmosphere, the relative wind and the aircraft.

The atmosphere. Obviously, an aircraft operates in the air; therefore, the properties of air that affect aircraft control and performance must be understood to actually know what an airplane is doing when it flies.

Since air is a combination of gases, it adheres to the laws of gases. Air is considered a fluid because it answers the definition of a fluid; namely, a substance that may be made to flow or change its shape by the application of moderate pressure. Air has weight, therefore

Learning Objective

DESCRIBE
- atmospheric conditions
- fundamental laws of motion
- airfoils
- subsonic and supersonic airflow

EXPLAIN
- Bernoulli's principle
- the forces that act on an aircraft
- aircraft control surfaces

APPLY
- calculate lift
- predict the effects of aircraft controls

Left. Full-span model in wind tunnel.
Photo courtesy of NASA Langley Research Center

Figure 9-1-1. Measurement of atmospheric pressure using a column of mercury

something lighter than air, such as a balloon filled with helium, will rise in the air.

Pressure. If a 1-inch² column of air extending from sea level to the top of the atmosphere could be weighed, it would be found to weigh about 14.69 lbs. Thus, atmospheric pressure at sea level is 14.69 p.s.i. (pounds per square inch). However, p.s.i. is rather a crude unit for the measurement of a light substance such as air. Therefore, atmospheric pressure is usually measured in terms of inches of mercury.

The apparatus for measuring atmospheric pressure is shown in Figure 9-1-1. A glass tube, 36 inches long, open at one end and closed at the other, is filled with mercury. The open end is sealed temporarily and then submerged into a small container partly filled with mercury, after which the end is unsealed. This allows the mercury in the tube to descend, leaving a vacuum at the top of the tube. Some of the mercury flows into the container, while a portion of it remains in the tube. The weight of the atmosphere pressing on the mercury in the open container exactly balances the weight of the mercury in the tube, which has no atmospheric pressure pushing down on it due to the vacuum in the top of the tube. As the pressure of the surrounding air decreases or increases, the mercury column lowers or rises correspondingly. At sea level, the height of the mercury in the tube measures approximately 29.92 inches and varies slightly with atmospheric conditions.

Another unit of measure for barometric pressure is *millibars* which is defined as 1000 dyne/cm². The most common usage is in weather maps, which use millibars to show levels of barometric pressure. At sea level, the pressure is 1,013.25 millibars (mb).

An important consideration is that atmospheric pressure varies with altitude. The higher an object rises above sea level, the shorter the column of air above it. This means the lower the pressure. On a normal day, the pressure drop can be calculated and charted for each altitude. At the same time, temperature changes with a change in altitude. This temperature change with a change in altitude is called a *lapse rate*. When all things are equal, it changes at a predictable rate. This is called the *adiabatic lapse rate*.

There are some other specific changes, brought about by various atmospheric conditions that have a definite relation to flying. The effect of temperature, combined with altitude, affects the density of the air and affects aircraft performance.

Temperature. Temperature is a dominant factor affecting the physical properties of fluids. It is of particular concern when calculating changes in the state of gases.

There are three temperature scales used extensively. They are:

- Celsius
- Fahrenheit
- Kelvin, or absolute

The Celsius scale is constructed by using the freezing and boiling points of water under standard conditions, as fixed points of 0° and 100°, respectively, with 100 equal divisions between.

The Fahrenheit scale uses 32°F as the freezing point of water and 212°F as the boiling point, with 180 equal divisions between.

The absolute, or Kelvin, scale is constructed with its zero point established as -273°C, or -459°F, below the freezing point of water. The relationships of all the fixed points of the scales are shown in Figure 9-1-2.

Absolute zero, one of the fundamental constants of physics, is commonly used in the study of gases. It is usually expressed in terms of the Celsius scale. If the heat energy of a given gas sample could be progressively reduced, some temperature would be reached at which the motion of the molecules would cease entirely. If accurately determined, this temperature could then be taken as a natural reference, or as a true *absolute zero* value.

Experiments with hydrogen indicated that if a gas were cooled to -273.16°C (used as -273°C for most calculations), all molecular motion would cease, and no additional heat could be extracted from the substance.

When temperatures are measured with respect to the absolute zero reference, they are expressed as 0 in the absolute, or Kelvin, scale. Thus, absolute zero may be expressed as 0°K, as –273°C, or as –459.4°F (used as –460°F for most calculations).

When working with temperatures, always make sure which system of measurement is being used and know how to convert from one to another. The conversion formulas are shown in Figure 9-1-2.

For purposes of calculations, the Rankine scale, illustrated in Figure 9-1-2, is commonly used to convert Fahrenheit to absolute.

For Fahrenheit readings above zero, 460° is added. Thus, 72°F equals 460° plus 72°, or 532°F absolute. If the Fahrenheit reading is below zero, it is subtracted from 460°. Thus, -40°F equals 460° minus 40°, or 420° absolute.

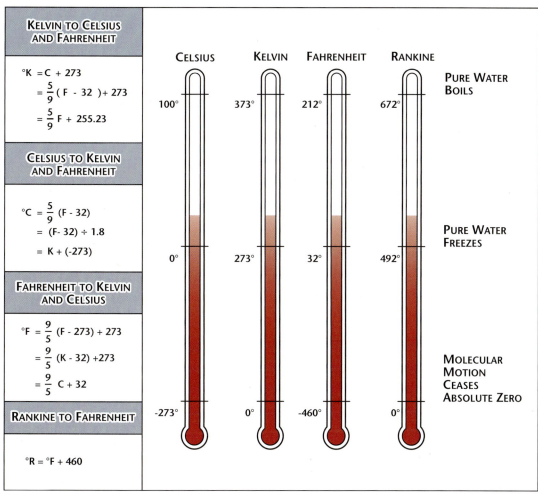

Figure 9-1-2. Common temperatures compared in the temperature measurement systems normally encountered. The Rankine scale is used to convert Fahrenheit to absolute

The Rankine scale does not indicate absolute temperature readings in accordance with the Kelvin scale, but these conversions may be used for the calculations of changes in the state of gases.

The Kelvin and Celsius scales are used more extensively in scientific work; therefore, some technical manuals may use these scales in giving directions and operating instructions. The Fahrenheit scale is commonly used in the United States, and most people are familiar with it. Therefore, the Fahrenheit scale is used in most areas of this text.

Density. Density is a term that means weight per unit volume. Since air is a mixture of gases, it can be compressed. If the air in one container is under one-half as much pressure as the air in another identical container, the air under the greater pressure weighs twice as much as that in the container under lower pressure. The air under greater pressure is twice as dense as that in the other container. Additionally, for equal weights of air, that which is under the greater pressure will only occupy half the volume.

The density of gases is governed by the following rules:

- Density varies in direct proportion with the pressure.
- Density varies inversely with the temperature.

Thus, air at high altitudes is less dense than air at low altitudes, and a mass of hot air is less dense than a mass of cool air.

Changes in density affect the aerodynamic performance of aircraft. With the same horsepower, an aircraft can fly faster at a high altitude, where the density is low, than at a low altitude, where the density is great. This is because air offers less resistance to the aircraft when it contains a smaller number of air particles per unit volume.

Humidity. Humidity is the amount of *water vapor* in the air. The maximum amount of water vapor that air can hold varies with the temperature. The higher the temperature of the air, the more water vapor air can absorb.

By itself, water vapor weighs approximately five-eighths as much as an equal amount of perfectly dry air. Therefore, when air contains water vapor, it is not as heavy as air containing no moisture at all. An airplane will not perform as well in high humidity conditions, because they produce a higher density altitude.

Absolute humidity. Absolute humidity is the actual amount of the water vapor in a mixture of air and water. It is sometimes expressed in grams per cubic meter (g/m^3), sometimes in pounds per cubic feet (lb/ft^3). The amount of water vapor that can be present in the air is dependent upon the temperature and pressure. The higher the temperature, the more water vapor the air is capable of holding, assuming constant pressure. When air has all the water vapor it can hold at the prevailing temperature and pressure, it is considered saturated.

Relative humidity. Relative humidity is the ratio of the amount of water vapor actually present in the atmosphere to the amount that would be present if the air were saturated at the prevailing temperature and pressure. This ratio is usually multiplied by 100 and expressed as a percentage. Suppose, for example, that a weather report says that the temperature is 75°F (24°C) and the relative humidity is 56 percent. This indicates that the air holds 56 percent of the water vapor required to saturate it at 75°F. (24°C) If the temperature drops and the absolute humidity remains constant, the relative humidity will increase. This is because less water vapor is required to saturate the air at the lower temperature.

Standard Day

While all the above may be interesting, it also has a very important purpose. It is the basis for defining a *standard day*. A standard day is a derived set of parameters that are used for many things, including designing airplanes and measuring their performance. It is also used in weather forecasting.

A standard day is defined as being 29.92 inches of mercury (1,013.25 mb), 14.7 p.s.i. at mean sea level altitude with a temperature of 59°F (15°C).

Law of Conservation of Energy

Energy is required for all forms of work. It is possible for man to convert one form of energy to another, but we cannot destroy it. However, it normally appears that a portion of the energy is lost during transformation. What actually happens is that some of the energy used transfers to different types of energy, and that is our primary concern.

For instance, an electric motor is a means of changing electrical energy to mechanical energy. A loss of 6 percent is common. This energy cannot be accounted for in friction or power. However, it has become heat. The same processes must be considered in flight. In flight, we change chemical energy into heat energy through combustion. This, in turn, is converted into mechanical energy, which powers the aircraft. During each of these processes, some of this energy becomes a byproduct of the transformation. Because of this, we must do whatever is possible to obtain the best flight characteristics for the energy consumed.

Velocity and acceleration. The terms *speed* and *velocity* are often used interchangeably, but they do not mean the same thing. Speed is the rate of motion, and velocity is the rate of motion in a particular direction in relation to time.

An aircraft starts from New York City and flies 10 hours at an average speed of 260 m.p.h. At the end of this time, the aircraft may be over the Atlantic Ocean, the Pacific Ocean, the Gulf of Mexico or, if its flight were in a circular path, it may even be back over New York. If this same aircraft flew at a velocity of 260 m.p.h. in a southwestward direction, it would arrive in Los Angeles in about 10 hours. Only the rate of motion is indicated in the first example, denoting the speed of the aircraft. In the last example, the particular direction is included with the rate of motion, thus denoting the velocity of the aircraft.

Acceleration is defined as the rate of change of velocity. An aircraft increasing in velocity is an example of positive acceleration, while an aircraft reducing its velocity is an example of *negative acceleration*. Positive acceleration is commonly referred to simply as acceleration and negative acceleration as deceleration.

Motion. Motion is the act or process of changing place or position. An object may be in motion with respect to one object and motionless with respect to another. For example, a person sitting quietly in an aircraft flying at 200 knots is at rest, or motionless, with respect to the aircraft. However, the person is in motion with respect to the air or the Earth, the same as is the aircraft.

Air has no force or power, except pressure, unless it is in motion. When it is moving, however, its force becomes apparent. A moving object in motionless air has a force exerted on it as a result of its own motion. It makes no difference in the effect then, whether an object is moving with respect to the air or the air is moving with respect to the object. The result is the same.

The flow of air around an object caused by the movement of either the air or the object, or both, is called the *relative wind*.

Newton's laws of motion. The fundamental laws governing the action of air around an airfoil are Newton's laws of motion.

Newton's First Law of Motion is normally referred to as the law of inertia. It simply means that a body at rest will not move unless force is applied to it. If it is moving at uniform speed in a straight line, additional force must be applied to increase or decrease that speed.

Since air has mass, it is a *body* in the meaning of the law. When an aircraft is on the ground with its engines stopped, inertia keeps the aircraft at rest. An aircraft is moved from its state of rest by the thrust force created by the propeller, by the expanding exhaust gases, or both. When it is flying at uniform speed in a straight line, inertia tends to keep the aircraft moving. Some external force is required to change the aircraft from its path of flight.

Newton's Second Law of Motion, that of force, also applies to objects. This law states, *"if a body moving with uniform speed is acted upon by an external force, the change of motion will be proportional to the amount of the force, and motion will take place in the direction in which the force acts."* This law may be stated mathematically as follows:

Force = mass × acceleration or F = ma

Newton's Third Law of Motion is the law of action and reaction. This law states that *"for every action* (force) *there is an equal and opposite reaction"* or (force). This law is well illustrated by someone rowing a boat. As the oars push the water aft, it propels the boat forward, since the water resists the action of the oars. When the force of lift on an aircraft's wing equals the force of gravity, the aircraft maintains level flight.

The three laws of motion are closely related and apply to the theory of flight. In many cases, all three laws may be operating on an aircraft at the same time.

Bernoulli's Principle and Subsonic Flow

Bernoulli's principle states that when a fluid (air) flowing through a tube reaches a constriction, or narrowing of the tube, the speed of the fluid flowing through that constriction is increased and its pressure is decreased. This is the principle of a *venturi* and is what makes a carburetor work. The *cambered* (curved) surface of an airfoil (wing)

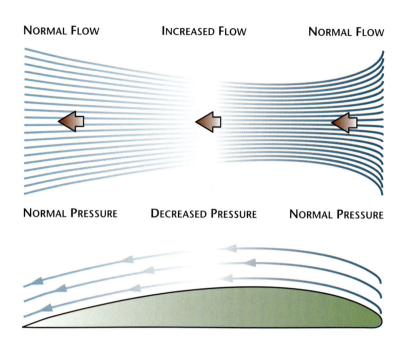

Figure 9-1-3. Bernoulli's principle is best explained by examining the actions of a venturi.

affects the airflow exactly as constriction in a tube affects airflow; in essence, half of a venturi. This is illustrated in Figure 9-1-3.

The top portion of Figure 9-1-3 illustrates the effect of air passing through a constriction in a tube. In the bottom illustration on Figure 9-1-3, the air is flowing past a cambered surface, such as an airfoil, and the effect is similar to that of air passing through a restriction.

As the air flows over the upper surface of an airfoil, its speed, or velocity, increases and its pressure decreases. An area of low pressure is thus formed. There is an area of greater pressure on the lower surface of the airfoil, and this greater pressure tends to move the wing upward. This difference in pressure between the upper and lower surfaces of the wing is called *lift*. Three-fourths of the total lift of an airfoil is the result of the decrease in pressure over the upper surface. The impact of air on the under surface produces the other one-fourth of the lift generated by the airfoil. At the trailing edge of the airfoil, the upper air, traveling faster, will strike the slower air passing under the airfoil and force it downward at an angle, producing a *downwash*. The downwash produced will extend the full width of the wing and add significantly to the total lift.

An aircraft in flight is acted upon by four forces:

- *Gravity* (or weight) — the force that pulls the aircraft toward the earth
- *Lift* — the force that pushes the aircraft upward

- *Thrust* — the force that moves the aircraft forward
- *Drag* — the force that exerts a braking action

Figure 9-2-2. Fineness ratio of chord to thickness

Section 2

Airfoils

An *airfoil* is a surface designed to obtain a desirable reaction from the air through which it moves. Thus, we can say that any part of the aircraft that converts air resistance into a force useful for flight is an airfoil. The blades of a propeller are so designed that when they rotate, their shape and position cause a higher pressure to be built up behind them than in front of them so that they will pull the aircraft forward. The profile of a conventional wing, shown in Figure 9-2-1, is an excellent example of an airfoil. Notice that the top surface of the wing profile has greater curvature than the lower surface.

The difference in curvature of the upper and lower surfaces of the wing builds up the lift force. When a fluid, in this case air, flows over an object, the air molecules, because they are not tightly bound to each other are free to move around the object. Because of this ability there is a velocity associated with the air and this velocity has dissimilar values at various locations near the object.

Bernoulli's equation relates the pressure in a fluid to the local velocity; as the velocity increases the pressure decreases by an inverse proportion. By adding all the pressure variations and multiplying by the area of the object, the aerodynamic force on the body is determined. Lift is the component of the aerodynamic force which is perpendicular to the original air flow direction, while the drag is parallel to the flow direction. When the velocity variations are added up it can be seen that the velocity of the fluid also determine the aerodynamic force. The sum of all these variations results in a turning of the airflow. When Newton's third law, of action and reaction, is applied to this turning, a reaction force behind the object is the result. This turning of the airflow is sometimes called the downwash. So it can be seen that lift is a combination of Bernoulli's theory and Newton's laws of motion.

The theoretical amount of lift of the airfoil at a velocity of 100 m.p.h. can be determined by sampling the pressure above and below the airfoil at the point of greatest air velocity. As shown in Figure 9-2-1, this pressure is 14.54 p.s.i. above the airfoil. Subtracting this pressure from the pressure below the airfoil, 14.67 p.s.i., gives a difference in pressure of 0.13 p.s.i. Multiplying 0.13 by 144 (number of square inches in a square foot) shows that each square foot of this wing will lift 18.72 lbs. The equation for figuring lift — when P_1 is the air pressure at the point of greatest velocity above the airfoil, P_2 is the air pressure under the airfoil, D is the difference between the two pressures, and L is the lift per square foot — is as follows:

$$P_2 - P_1 = D$$

$$D / 144 = L$$

Thus, a small pressure differential across an airfoil section can produce a large lifting force. Within limits, lift can be increased by increasing the angle of attack, the wing area, the free stream velocity, the density of the air or by changing the shape of the airfoil.

Shape of the Airfoil

The shape of the airfoil determines the amount of turbulence, or *skin friction*, that it will produce. The shape of a wing consequently affects its efficiency.

Airfoil section properties differ from wing or aircraft properties because of the effect of the wing *planform*. A wing may have various airfoil sections from root to tip, with taper, twist and sweepback. The resulting aerodynamic properties of the wing are determined by the action of each section along the span.

Turbulence and skin friction are controlled mainly by the *fineness ratio*, which is defined as

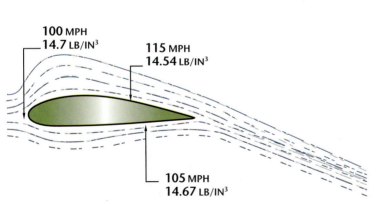

Figure 9-2-1. Airflow over a wing section, showing the various velocities, pressures and the downwash angle

the ratio of the chord of the airfoil to the maximum thickness. See Figure 9-2-2.

If the wing has a high fineness ratio, it is a very thin wing and produces a large amount of skin friction. A thick wing has a low fineness ratio, producing a large amount of turbulence. The best wing is a compromise between these two extremes to hold both turbulence and skin friction to a minimum.

Efficiency of a wing is measured in terms of the *lift-over-drag (L/D) ratio*. This ratio varies with the angle of attack but reaches a definite maximum value for a particular angle of attack. At this angle, the wing has reached its maximum efficiency. The shape of the airfoil is the factor that determines the angle of attack at which the wing is most efficient; it also determines the degree of efficiency.

Research has shown that the most efficient airfoils for general use have the maximum thickness occurring about one-third of the way back from the leading edge of the wing.

Some modern airliners use a wing with the maximum thickness further back. This provides a better lift to drag ratio at higher speeds, improving fuel efficiency at cruising speeds.

High-lift wings, as well as high-lift devices for wings, have been developed by shaping the airfoils to produce the desired effect. The amount of lift produced by an airfoil will increase with an increase in wing *camber*.

Camber refers to the curvature of an airfoil above and below the *chord line* surface. Upper camber refers to the upper surface, lower camber to the lower surface and *mean camber* to the *mean line* of the section. Camber is positive when departure from the chord line is outward and negative when it is inward. See Figure 9-2-3. Thus, high-lift wings have a large positive camber on the upper surface and a slight negative camber on the lower surface. Wing flaps cause an ordinary wing to approximate this same condition by increasing the upper camber and by creating a negative lower camber.

Aspect ratio. It is also known that the longer the wingspan compared to the chord, the greater the lift obtained. This comparison is called *aspect ratio*. The higher the aspect ratio, the greater the lift. Despite benefits from an increase in aspect ratio, there are limitations where the structural and drag considerations outweigh the gain from a high aspect ratio. See Figure 9-2-4.

Modern aircraft have airfoils that strike a medium between extremes, with the shape varying according to the aircraft for which it is designed.

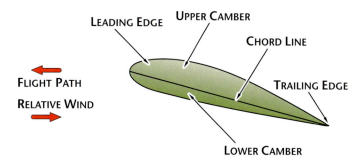

Figure 9-2-3. Wing terminology

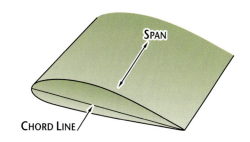

Figure 9-2-4. Aspect ratio; span to chord

Angle of incidence. The acute angle that the wing chord makes with the longitudinal axis of the aircraft is called the *angle of incidence* (Figure 9-2-5), or the angle of wing setting. The angle of incidence in most cases is a fixed, built-in angle. When the leading edge of the wing is higher than the trailing edge, the angle of incidence is said to be positive. The angle of incidence is negative when the leading edge is lower than the trailing edge of the wing.

Do not confuse the angle of incidence with the angle of attack, which is the angle between the chord line of the wing and the relative wind. A good way to keep the two separated in your mind is to remember that the angle of incidence is established by the attachment of the wing to the airframe.

Angle of attack. Before beginning the discussion on *angle of attack* (Figure 9-2-6) and its effect on airfoils, we first need to consider the terms chord and center of pressure.

The *chord* of an airfoil or wing section is an imaginary straight line passing through the section from the leading edge to the trailing edge, as shown in Figure 9-2-6. The chord line provides one side of an angle that ultimately forms the *angle of attack*. The other side of the angle is formed by a line indicating the direction of the *relative wind*. The relative wind is opposite to the direction in which the wing is moving. Thus, angle of attack is defined as the angle between the chord line of the wing and the direction of the relative wind.

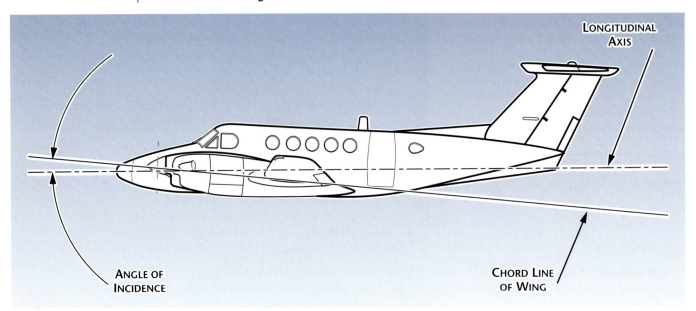

Figure 9-2-5. The angle of incidence is the angle between the centerline of the airplane and the bottom of the wing. For rigging purposes, the angle of incidence is adjustable through a very small range on some aircraft.

On each minute part of an airfoil or wing surface, a small force is present. This force is different in magnitude and direction from any forces acting on other areas forward or rearward from this point. It is possible to add all of these small forces mathematically, and the sum is called the *resultant force,* or *lift*. This resultant force has magnitude, direction and location, and can be represented as a *vector*, as shown in Figure 9-2-6. The point of intersection of the resultant force line with the chord line of the airfoil is called the *center of pressure*. The center of pressure moves along the airfoil chord as the angle of attack changes. Throughout most of the flight range, the center of pressure moves forward with the increasing angle of attack and rearward as the angle decreases. The effect of increasing the angle of attack on the center of pressure is shown in Figure 9-2-7.

The angle of attack changes as the aircraft's attitude changes. Since the angle of attack has a great deal to do with determining lift, it is of primary consideration when designing airfoils. In a properly designed airfoil, the lift increases as the angle of attack is increased.

When the angle of attack is increased gradually toward a positive angle of attack, the lift component increases rapidly up to a certain point and then suddenly drops off. During this action, the *drag component* increases slowly at first, and then rapidly, as lift begins to drop off.

When the angle of attack increases to the angle of maximum lift, the *burble point* is reached. This is known as the *critical angle*. When the critical angle is reached, the air ceases to flow smoothly over the top surface of the airfoil and begins to burble, or eddy. This means that air breaks away from the upper camber line of the wing. What was formerly an area of decreased pressure is now filled by this burbling air. When this occurs, the amount of lift drops, downwash is reduced, and drag becomes excessive. The force of gravity exerts itself and the nose of the aircraft drops. Thus, we see that the burble point is the *stalling angle*.

The distribution of the pressure forces over the airfoil varies with the angle of attack. The application of the *resultant force*, the center of pressure, varies correspondingly. As this angle increases, the center of pressure moves forward. As the angle decreases, the center of pressure moves back. The instability of the center of pressure is characteristic of most airfoils.

Boundary layer and stall. The ideal situation would be for the air to flow over the airfoil smoothly in layers. This does not occur for two reasons: the air is *viscous* and the airfoil is not perfectly smooth.

Because air is viscous, it has a tendency to stick to the airfoil surface. Because the airfoil is not

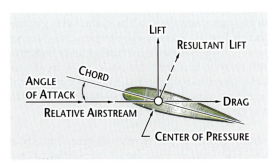

Figure 9-2-6. Angle of attack is the angle between the relative wind and the chordline of the airfoil.

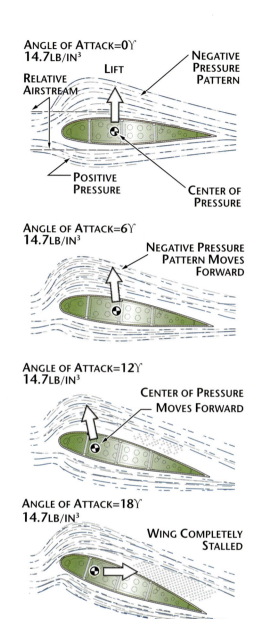

Figure 9-2-7. Angle of attack is extremely important to the safe operation of the aircraft.

perfectly smooth, turbulence is created where the surface is rough. These two factors result in what is referred to as the *boundary layer*.

In the design of a wing, it is desirable to keep this boundary layer as thin as possible. As the boundary layer becomes thicker, more turbulence is created. This turbulence will lead to stall. Under normal circumstances, the boundary layer becomes thicker when the angle of attack is increased. The airflow will eventually break away, and stall will occur. This is why the surface of the airfoil should remain as smooth as possible.

Downwash. For many years, lift was explained using just the Bernoulli principle. Indeed, many textbooks still rely solely upon it. What was ignored was the effect of the down-

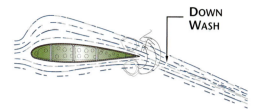

Figure 9-2-8. The downwash is an example of Newton's third law.

wash coming off the trailing edge of the surface. Created by the airflow around an airfoil, the downwash is a classic example of Newton's third law. Many aerodynamicists now believe that the actual lift is created by the downwash, and the airflow around an airfoil is for the purpose of creating the downwash. See Figure 9-2-8 for an example of downwash angle.

Obviously, designers must adhere closely to the Bernoulli principle, because any disruption of airflow will cause a change in both the lift of the airfoil and the reaction of the downwash. Careful observation of a modern high-performance airplane, like a jet fighter, will show that all efforts have been made to preserve both principles.

Section 3

Thrust and Drag

An aircraft in flight is the center of a continuous battle of forces. Actually, this conflict is not as violent as it sounds, but it is the key to all maneuvers performed in the air. There is nothing mysterious about these forces; they are definite and known. The directions in which they act can be calculated, and the aircraft itself is designed to take advantage of each of them. In all types of flying, flight calculations are based on the magnitude and direction of four forces: weight, lift, drag and thrust (Figure 9-3-1).

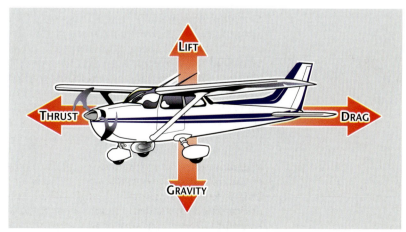

Figure 9-3-1. The four forces of flight in action

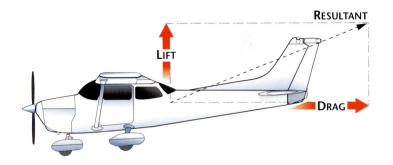

Figure 9-3-2. The resultant of lift and drag

Weight is the force of gravity acting downward upon everything that goes into the aircraft, such as the aircraft itself, the crew, the fuel and the cargo.

Lift acts vertically and by so doing counteracts the effects of weight.

Drag is a backward deterrent force and is caused by the disruption of the airflow by the wings, fuselage and protruding objects.

Thrust produced by the powerplant is the forward force that overcomes the force of drag.

Notice that these four forces are only in perfect balance when the aircraft is in straight and level unaccelerated flight.

The force of lift and drag are the direct result of the relationship between the relative wind and the aircraft. *The force of lift always acts perpendicular to the relative wind, and the force of drag always acts parallel to the relative wind and in the same direction.* These forces are actually the components that produced a resultant lift force on the wing, as shown in Figure 9-3-2.

Weight has a definite relationship with lift, as has thrust with drag. This relationship is quite simple, but very important in understanding the aerodynamics of flying. Remember that lift is the upward force on the wing acting perpendicular to the relative wind. Lift is required to counteract the aircraft's weight, caused by the force of gravity acting on the mass of the aircraft. This weight force acts downward through a point called the *center of gravity*; the point at which all the weight of the aircraft is considered to be concentrated. When the lift force is in equilibrium with the weight force, the aircraft neither gains nor loses altitude.

If lift becomes less than weight, the aircraft loses altitude. When the lift is greater than weight, the aircraft gains altitude.

Drag must be overcome in order for the aircraft to move, and movement is essential to obtain lift. To overcome the drag and move the aircraft forward, another force is essential. This force is thrust. Thrust is derived from jet propulsion or from a propeller-and-engine combination. Jet propulsion theory is based on Newton's third law of motion, which states *"for every action there is an equal and opposite reaction."* For example, in firing a gun, the action is the bullet going forward, while the reaction is the gun recoiling backward. The turbine engine causes a mass of air to be moved backward at high velocity, resulting in a forward reaction that moves the aircraft.

In a propeller/engine combination, the propeller is actually two or more revolving airfoils mounted on a horizontal shaft. The motion of the blades through the air produces lift and downwash similar to a wing, but acts in a horizontal direction, pulling the aircraft forward.

We have seen that increasing the lift means that the aircraft moves upward, whereas decreasing the lift so it is less than the weight causes the aircraft to lose altitude. A similar rule applies to the two forces of thrust and drag. If the r.p.m. of the engine is reduced, the thrust is lessened, and the aircraft slows down. As long as the thrust is less than the drag, the aircraft travels more and more slowly until its speed is insufficient to support it in the air.

Likewise, if the r.p.m. of the engine is increased, thrust becomes greater than drag, and the speed of the aircraft increases. As long as the thrust continues to be greater than the drag, the aircraft continues to accelerate. When drag equals thrust, the aircraft flies at a steady speed.

To make things a bit more complicated, an airplane has a design cruising speed. Design cruising speed is where a specific power setting produces a speed where all forces are equal and the airplane flies at a steady speed and altitude. Trimmed for level flight and left to its own devices, this is where the airplane wants to fly.

Increased thrust means more speed, which equals greater airflow over the wings, which in turn equals more lift. With lift becoming greater, the aircraft will increase in altitude. It will continue to increase in altitude until the excess engine power is used up and all the forces reach a balance again. With the forces in balance, the airplane will now resume its design cruising speed at the new altitude. The opposite is true for a reduction in power. The speed will decrease and drag will now be greater than lift. The nose of the airplane will drop and the airplane will descend. Descent will result in an increase in speed. Once the increase in speed produces enough lift to balance the forces again, the design cruise speed will resume.

The pilot can change the results somewhat by manipulating the controls. When the airplane starts to descend, he can raise the nose somewhat to counteract the decent. The result will be a slower speed at the same altitude. The reverse is also true. To increase speed, the pilot adds power, the airplane tries to climb, and the pilot must lower the nose to maintain the same altitude at a higher speed.

Unlike an automobile, where more power means more speed, airplanes behave differently. In an airplane, *power controls altitude and pitch controls speed*. Step on the gas and you go up; let off the gas and you go down. Pull the nose up and you go slower; push the nose down and you go faster.

The relative motion of the air over an object that produces lift also produces drag. Drag is the resistance of the air to objects moving through it. If an aircraft is flying in level flight, the lift force acts vertically to support it while the drag force acts horizontally to hold it back. The total amount of drag on an aircraft is made up of many drag forces, but for our purposes, we will only consider three:

- Parasite drag
- Profile drag
- Induced drag

Parasite drag is made up of a combination of many different drag forces. Any exposed object on an aircraft offers some resistance to the air, and the more objects in the airstream, the more parasite drag. While parasite drag can be minimized by reducing the number of exposed parts and streamlining their shape, *skin friction* is the type of parasite drag most difficult to reduce. No surface is perfectly smooth. Even machined surfaces when inspected under magnification have a ragged, uneven appearance. These ragged surfaces deflect the air near the surface causing resistance to smooth airflow. Skin friction can be reduced by using glossy, smooth finishes and eliminating protruding rivet heads, roughness and other irregularities.

Profile drag may be considered the parasite drag of the airfoil itself. The various components of parasite drag are all of the same nature as profile drag.

The action of the airfoil that gives us lift also causes *induced drag*. Remember that the pressure above the wing is less than atmospheric, and the pressure below the wing is equal to or greater than atmospheric pressure. Since fluids always move from high pressure toward low pressure, there is a spanwise movement of air from the bottom of the wing outward from the fuselage and upward around the wing tip. This flow of air results in *spillage* up and over the wing tip. The spilled air is then pulled downward into the low-pressure air flowing above the wing. This sets up a whirlpool of disturbed

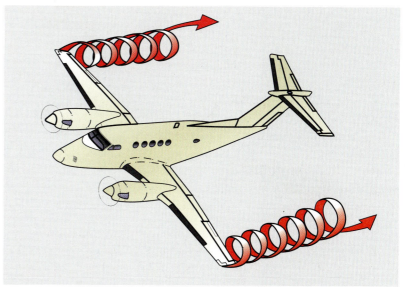

Figure 9-3-3. Wing tip vortices grow larger the further away from the airplane they progress.

air called a *vortex* (Figure 9-3-3). When viewed from the rear of the airplane, a tip vortex spirals clockwise off the left tip and counterclockwise off the right tip. The spiraling air contains a large amount of energy and can be a danger to other airplanes flying too close behind.

The air on the upper surface has a tendency to move in toward the fuselage and off the trailing edge. This air current forms a similar vortex at the inner portion of the trailing edge of the wing. Inner vortex control is the prime reason for wing fillets and fairings. Control of the inner vortex reduces drag and reduces interference with the tail surfaces. These vortices increase drag because of the turbulence produced and constitute-induced drag. Additionally, a wing tip vortex has a major effect on the downwash pattern. Any disruption caused to the downwash also constitutes a reduction in lift, or an increase in induced drag.

Section 4
Aircraft Stability

Center of gravity. Gravity is the pulling force that draws all things toward the center of the earth. The center of gravity may be considered as a point at which all the weight of the aircraft is concentrated. If the aircraft were supported at its exact center of gravity, it would balance in any position. Center of gravity is of major importance in an aircraft, for its position has a great bearing upon *stability*.

The center of gravity is determined by the general design of the aircraft. The designer esti-

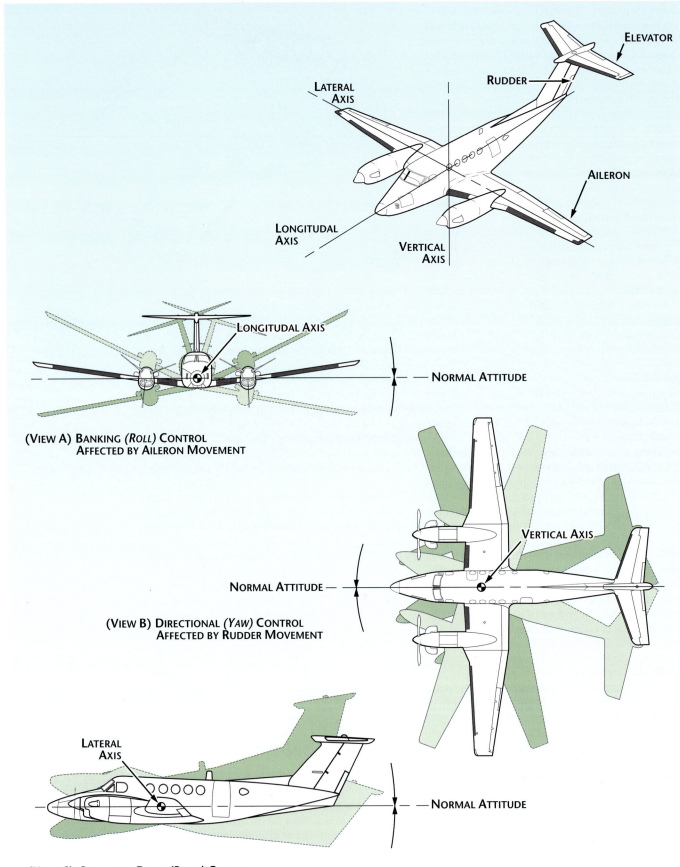

Figure 9-4-1. Motion of an aircraft around its axes

mates how far the *center of pressure* will travel. He then fixes the center of gravity in front of the center of pressure for the corresponding design cruise speed in order to provide an adequate *restoring moment* for flight equilibrium.

Axes of an aircraft. Whenever an aircraft changes its attitude in flight, it must turn from one or more of three *axes*. Figure 9-4-1 shows the three axes, which are imaginary lines passing through the center of the aircraft. The axes of an aircraft can be considered as imaginary axles around which the aircraft turns like a wheel. At the center, where all three axes intersect, each is perpendicular to the other two. The *axis* that extends lengthwise through the fuselage from the nose to the tail is called the *longitudinal axis*. The axis that extends crosswise, from wing tip to wing tip, is the *lateral axis*. The axis that passes through the center, from top to bottom, is called the *vertical axis*.

Motion around the longitudinal axis resembles the roll of a ship from side to side. In fact, the names used in describing the motion about an aircraft's three axes were originally nautical terms. They have been adapted to aeronautical terminology because of the similarity of motion between an aircraft and a ship.

The motion around the longitudinal axis is called *roll*; motion around the lateral (crosswing) axis is called *pitch*. Finally, an aircraft moves around its vertical axis in a motion termed *yaw*. This is a horizontal movement of the nose of the aircraft.

Roll, pitch and yaw, the motions an aircraft makes around its longitudinal, lateral and vertical axes, are controlled by three control surfaces. Roll is produced by the *ailerons*, which are located at the trailing edges of the wings. Pitch is affected by the *elevators*, the rear portion of the horizontal tail assembly. Yaw is controlled by the *rudder*, the rear portion of the vertical tail assembly.

Stability and control. An aircraft must have sufficient stability to maintain a uniform flight path and recover from the various upsetting forces. Also, to achieve the best performance, the aircraft must have the proper response to the movement of the controls.

Three terms that appear in any discussion of stability and control are:

- Stability
- Maneuverability
- Controllability

Stability is the characteristic of an aircraft that causes it to fly (hands off) in a straight and level flight path. *Maneuverability* is the ability of an aircraft to be directed along a desired flight path and

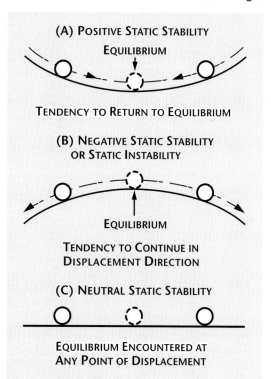

Figure 9-4-2. The three types of stability; (A) Positive, (B) Negative and (C) Static

to withstand the stresses imposed. *Controllability* is the quality of the response of an aircraft to the pilot's commands while maneuvering the aircraft.

Stability. An aircraft is in a state of equilibrium when the sum of all the forces acting upon the aircraft and all the moments are equal to zero. (A *moment* is equal to the weight, multiplied by the distance from the pivot point, or center of gravity.) An aircraft in equilibrium experiences no accelerations, and the aircraft continues in a steady flight. A gust of wind or a deflection of the controls disturbs the equilibrium, and the aircraft experiences acceleration due to the unbalance of moment or force.

The three types of *static stability* are defined by the character of the movements following some disturbance from equilibrium. *Positive static stability* exists when the disturbed object tends to return to equilibrium. *Negative static stability* or *static instability* exists when the disturbed object tends to continue in the direction of disturbance. *Neutral static stability* exists when the disturbed object has neither the tendency to return nor continue in the displacement direction, but remains in equilibrium in the direction of disturbance. These three types of stability are illustrated in Figure 9-4-2.

Dynamic stability. While static stability deals with the tendency of a displaced body to return to equilibrium, *dynamic stability* deals with the resulting motion with time. If an object is disturbed from equilibrium, the time history of the

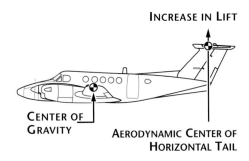

Figure 9-4-3. The majority of horizontal tail surfaces are designed to produce lift.

resulting motion defines the dynamic stability of the object. In general, an object demonstrates positive dynamic stability if the amplitude of motion decreases with time. If the amplitude of motion increases with time, the object is said to possess dynamic instability.

Any aircraft must demonstrate the required degrees of static and dynamic stability. If an aircraft were designed with static instability and a rapid rate of dynamic instability, the aircraft would be very difficult, if not impossible, to fly. Usually, positive dynamic stability is required in an aircraft design to prevent objectionable continued oscillations.

Longitudinal stability. When an aircraft has a tendency to keep a constant angle of attack with reference to the relative wind, that is, when it does not put its nose down and dive or lift its nose and stall, it is said to have *longitudinal stability*. Longitudinal stability refers to motion in pitch. The *horizontal stabilizer* is the primary surface that controls longitudinal stability. The action of the stabilizer depends upon the speed and angle of attack of the aircraft. Figure 9-4-3 illustrates the contribution of tail lift to stability. If the aircraft changes its angle of attack, a change in lift takes place at the aerodynamic center (center of pressure) of the horizontal stabilizer.

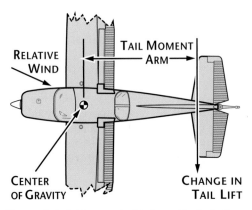

Figure 9-4-4. The vertical tail, particularly the fin portion, is a major contributor to directional stability.

Under certain conditions of speed, load and angle of attack, the flow of air over the horizontal stabilizer creates a force that pushes the tail up or down. When conditions are such that the airflow creates equal forces up and down, the forces are said to be in equilibrium. This condition is usually found in level flight in calm air.

Directional stability. Stability around the vertical axis is referred to as *directional stability*. The aircraft should be designed so that when it is in straight and level flight it remains on its course heading, even though the pilot takes his hands and feet off the controls. If an aircraft recovers automatically from a skid, it has been well designed and possesses good directional balance. The *vertical stabilizer* is the primary surface controlling directional stability.

As shown in Figure 9-4-4, when an aircraft is in a sideslip, or yawing, the vertical tail experiences a change in angle of attack with a resulting change in lift (not to be confused with the lift created by the wing). The change in lift, or side force, on the vertical tail creates a yawing moment about the center of gravity that tends to return the aircraft to its original flight path.

Sweepback wings aid in directional stability. If the aircraft yaws from its direction of flight, the wing which is farther ahead presents more leading edge surface to the apparent wind, offering more drag than the wing which is aft and presents less surface to the apparent wind. The effect of this drag is to hold back the wing that is farther ahead and to let the other wing catch up.

In subsonic flight, directional stability is also aided by using a large *dorsal fin* and a long fuselage.

The high Mach numbers of supersonic flight reduce the contribution of the vertical tail to directional stability. To produce the required directional stability at high Mach numbers, a very large vertical tail area may be necessary. *Ventral (belly) fins* may be added as an additional contribution to directional stability.

Lateral stability. We have seen that pitching is motion around the aircraft's lateral axis, and yawing is motion around its vertical axis. Motion around its longitudinal (fore and aft) axis is a lateral, or rolling, motion. The tendency to return to the original attitude from such motion is called *lateral stability*.

The lateral stability of an airplane involves consideration of rolling moments due to *sideslip*. A sideslip tends to produce both a rolling and a yawing motion. If an airplane has a favorable rolling moment, a sideslip will tend to return the airplane to a level flight attitude.

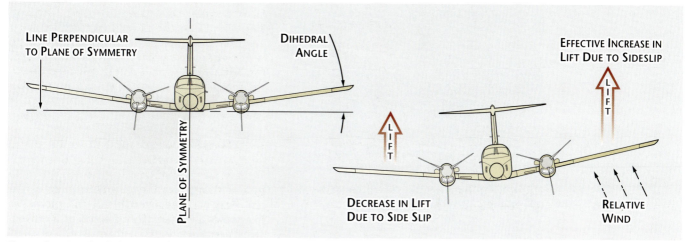

Figure 9-4-5. Dihedral is a major contributor to lateral stability. It helps an airplane hold its course without constant control.

The principal surface contributing to the lateral stability of an airplane is the wing. The effect of the *geometric dihedral* of a wing is a powerful contribution to lateral stability. As shown in Figure 9-4-5, a wing with dihedral develops stable rolling moments with sideslip. With the relative wind from the side, the wing into the wind is subject to an increase in angle of attack and develops an increase in lift. The wing away from the wind is subject to a decrease in angle of attack and develops less lift. The changes in lift effect a rolling moment tending to raise the windward wing.

When a wing is swept back, the effective dihedral increases rapidly with a change in the lift coefficient of the wing. *Sweepback* is the angle between a line perpendicular to the fuselage centerline and the quarter chord of each wing airfoil section. Sweepback in combination with dihedral causes the dihedral effect to be excessive. As shown in Figure 9-4-6, the swept-wing aircraft in a sideslip has the wing that is into the wind operating with an effective decrease in sweepback, while the wing out of the wind is operating with an effective increase in sweepback. The wing into the wind develops more lift, and the wing out of the wind develops less. This tends to restore the aircraft to a level flight attitude.

Dutch roll. The amount of effective dihedral necessary to produce satisfactory flying qualities varies greatly with the type and purpose of the aircraft. Generally, the effective dihedral is kept low, since high roll due to sideslip can create problems. Excessive dihedral effect can lead to *Dutch roll*, a yaw and roll combination that makes rudder coordination more difficult in rolling maneuvers, or place extreme demands for lateral control of power during crosswind takeoff and landing. Transport and larger executive aircraft provide an automatic control system for the rudder, called a *yaw damper*, to reduce this tendency. Dutch roll can be a very unpleasant experience for passengers. See Figure 9-4-7. Yaw damper systems are designed to correct for Dutch roll.

Section 5
Aircraft Control

Control is the action taken to make the aircraft follow any desired flight path. When an aircraft is said to be controllable, it means that the craft responds easily and promptly to movement of the controls. Different control surfaces are used to control the aircraft about each of the three axes. Moving the control surfaces on an aircraft changes the airflow over the aircraft's surface. This, in turn, creates changes in the balance of forces acting to keep the aircraft flying straight and level.

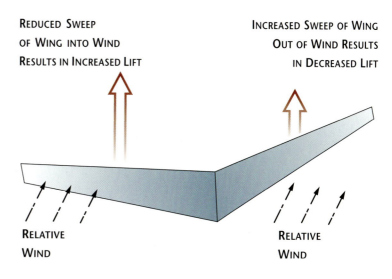

Figure 9-4-6. Sweepback is also important to lateral stability. It helps maintain a heading.

Figure 9-4-7. Dutch roll is a lateral oscillation with both rolling and yawing components at the same time.

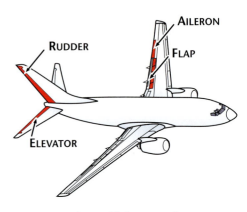

Figure 9-5-1. Primary flight controls on a conventional airplane

Flight control surfaces. The flight control surfaces are hinged or movable airfoils designed to change the attitude of the aircraft during flight.

The primary group includes the ailerons, elevators and rudder (Figure 9-5-1). These surfaces are used for moving the aircraft around its three axes. The concepts of these three control systems and their interaction were developed by the Wright brothers. It is the prime reason they were successful in establishing powered flight and controllability.

Ailerons and elevators are operated from the cockpit by a wheel-and-yoke assembly. Rudders are operated by foot pedals.

Control around the longitudinal axis. The motion of the aircraft around the longitudinal axis is called *rolling* or *banking*. The ailerons (Figure 9-5-2) are used to control this movement. The ailerons form a part of the wing and are located in the trailing edge of the wing toward the tips. Ailerons are the movable surfaces of an otherwise fixed-surface wing. The aileron is in neutral position when it is streamlined with the trailing edge of the wing.

Ailerons respond to side pressure applied to the control wheel. Pressure applied to move the wheel toward the right raises the right aileron and lowers the left aileron, causing the aircraft to bank to the right. Ailerons are linked together by control cables so that when one aileron is down, the opposite aileron is up. The function of the lowered aileron is to increase the lift by increasing the wing camber, thereby raising the wing. The up aileron, on the opposite end of the wing, decreases lift on that end of the wing and subsequently lowers that wing. This causes the aircraft to roll around its longitudinal axis.

As a result of the increased lift on the wing with the lowered aileron, drag on that side is also increased. This drag attempts to pull the nose in the direction of the drag. Since the ailerons are

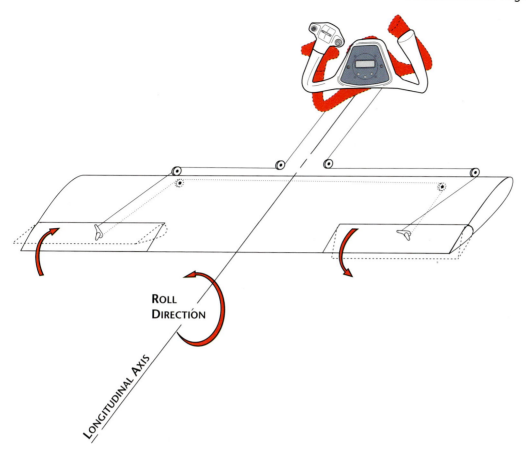

Figure 9-5-2. The aileron is the control surface that controls rolling, or banking around the longitudinal axis.

used with the rudder when making turns, the increased drag tries to turn the aircraft in the direction opposite to that desired. To avoid this undesirable effect called adverse yaw, aircraft are designed with *differential travel* of the ailerons.

Differential aileron travel provides more aileron up travel than down travel for a given movement of the control wheel in the cockpit.

In modern transport aircraft, the action of the ailerons is supplemented by the use of *spoilers*.

The spoilers are plates hinged to the upper surface of the wing. They are usually deflected upward by hydraulic actuators in response to control-wheel movement in the cockpit. The purpose of the spoilers is to disturb the smooth airflow across the top of the airfoil, thereby creating an increased amount of drag and a decreased amount of lift on that airfoil.

Spoilers are used primarily for lateral control. When banking the airplane, the spoilers function with the ailerons. The spoilers on the up aileron side raise with that aileron to further decrease the lift on that wing. The spoiler on the opposite side remains in the faired position.

During lateral control at high speed, use of the ailerons would cause a large amount of bending pressure to be applied to the wing and excessive loads on the ailerons themselves. Therefore, the ailerons are automatically disconnected from the system at high speed. Lateral control is then by action of the spoilers only.

When the spoilers are used as a *speed brake*, they are all deflected upward simultaneously. A separate control is provided for operating the spoilers as speed brakes.

Control around the lateral axis. When the nose of an aircraft is raised or lowered, it is rotated around its lateral axis. Elevators are the movable control surfaces that cause this rotation (Figure 9-5-3). They are normally hinged to the trailing edge of the horizontal stabilizer.

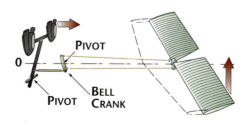

Figure 9-5-3. An up or down motion of the elevators causes the nose of the aircraft to move up or down in relation to the lateral axis.

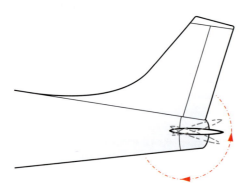

Figure 9-5-4. A stabilator acts as a horizontal stabilizer-and-elevator in one. Pivoting as a unit, the stabilator portion ahead of the pivot point serves as an aerodynamic balance.

The elevators can be moved either up or down and are used to make the aircraft pitch nose up or nose down.

If the elevator is rotated up, it decreases the lift force on the tail, causing the tail to lower and the nose to rise. If the elevator is rotated downward, it increases the lift force on the tail, causing it to rise and the nose to lower. Lowering the aircraft's nose increases forward speed, and raising the nose decreases forward speed.

Some aircraft use a movable horizontal surface called a *stabilator* (Figure 9-5-4). The stabilator serves the same purpose as the horizontal stabilizer and elevator combined. When the cockpit control is moved, the complete stabilator is moved to raise or lower the leading edge, thus changing the angle of attack and the amount of lift on the tail surfaces.

Control around the vertical axis. Turning the nose of the aircraft causes the aircraft to rotate around its vertical axis. Rotation of the aircraft around the vertical axis is called *yawing*. This motion is controlled by using the rudder, as illustrated in Figure 9-4-1B.

The rudder is a movable control surface attached to the trailing edge of the vertical stabilizer. The main function of the rudder is to turn the nose of the aircraft in flight. A turn is maintained by the side pressure of the air moving past the vertical surfaces. To turn the aircraft to the right, the rudder is moved to the right. The rudder protrudes into the airstream, causing a force to act upon it. This is the force necessary to give a turning movement around the center of gravity, which turns the aircraft to the right. If the rudder is moved to the left, it induces a counterclockwise rotation and the aircraft similarly turns to the left. Rudder-only turns produce a skidding turn that is not very effective. To be effective, a turn must be a coordinated effort involving the rudder, ailerons and the elevator.

To make a coordinated turn, first the pilot applies a little rudder to get the nose swinging, then establishes a bank with the ailerons. The nose will start swinging in the desired direction, but the airplane still needs some help to make a good turn. Because of the lift lost by banking, the nose will start to drop a bit, which is corrected by a little up-elevator pressure. At the same time, the rudder pressure is relaxed, and the airplane starts making a coordinated turn. Rudder is then used to keep the nose of the airplane on the horizon so the turn can be made without losing altitude. To roll out of the turn requires the exact opposite control movements, in reverse order.

Making smooth coordinated turns takes a bit of practice. Some airplanes even have a control interconnect between the rudder and the ailerons in an attempt to help the pilot make coordinated turns. When an aircraft begins to slip or skid, rudder pressure is applied to keep the aircraft balanced, or headed in the desired direction.

Slip, or *side-slipping*, refers to any motion of the aircraft to the side and downward toward the inside of a turn. *Skid*, or *skidding*, refers to any movement upward and outward away from the center of a turn.

Vee tails. Aircraft *empennages*, or tail sections, have been designed which combine the vertical and horizontal stabilizers. Such empennages have the stabilizers set at an angle, as shown

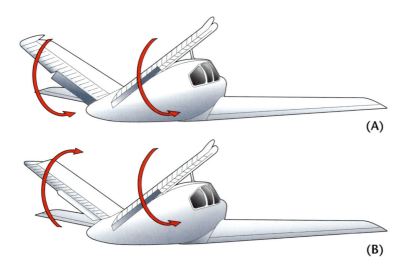

Figure 9-5-5. The vee tail configuration was first popularized by the Beechcraft Bonanza. In this configuration, the controls are called ruddervators. They combine the elevator and rudder inputs.

Figure 9-5-6. This Beechcraft Bonanza is one example of a vee-tailed aircraft.

in Figure 9-5-5. This arrangement is referred to as a butterfly or *vee tail*. The Bonanza in Figure 9-5-6 is an illustration of a modern vee-tailed aircraft.

The control surfaces are hinged to the stabilizers at the trailing edges. The stabilizing portion of this arrangement is called a stabilator, and the control portion is called the *ruddervator*. The ruddervators can be operated both up or both down at the same time.

When used in synchronization in this manner, — as in Figure 9-5-5A — the result is the same as with any other type of elevator. This action is controlled by the control column.

The ruddervators can be made to move opposite each other by pushing the left or right rudder pedal. If the right rudder pedal is pushed, the right ruddervator moves down and the left ruddervator moves up. As seen in illustration B of Figure 9-5-5, this produces turning moments to move the nose of the aircraft to the right.

The newer vee-tailed military aircraft are frequently fly-by-wire control systems, therefore controlled by computer. The older civil aircraft use a mechanical mixer box to combine different inputs. Without the mixer, a pilot couldn't apply elevator and rudder at the same time.

Section 6

Transport Aircraft Control Surfaces

On most light aircraft, the longitudinal control is accomplished by the *elevator system*. This system uses a fixed horizontal stabilizer with a moveable elevator hinged to the rear of the stabilizer. In most instances, the elevator is equipped with a moveable trim tab so that minor corrections in the pitch of the aircraft can be made. This enables the pilot to fly without having to hold fore or aft pressure on the control column; in essence, *hands off*.

A typical light aircraft elevator control system is shown in Figure 9-5-3. This system is strictly a mechanical system, using cables and bellcranks to transfer motion. An airplane featuring a *canard* system would work in the same manner, only the canard would be in the front and travel in the opposite direction.

Two control columns are present in such a system. The fore and aft movement of the column moves the elevator. The two columns move in unison to move a bellcrank in the lower section of the floor. This bellcrank has a cable attached to the top and bottom of the arm. These, in turn, lead to a second bellcrank in the empennage of the aircraft.

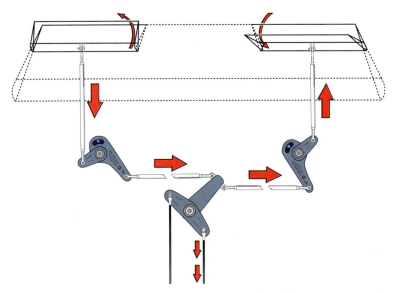

Figure 9-6-1. Aileron systems are connected in a closed loop system. Each wing bellcrank is connected to its opposite side by linkage.

plished with the use of a *cable, bellcranks* and *push-pull tubes*.

The movement of the control wheel is a rotating movement for the ailerons. This is accomplished by a chain-and-sprocket arrangement behind the instrument panel. The chain is attached to a cable that rotates a bellcrank. This bellcrank changes the rotary motion to linear motion. Cables go out each side from the bellcrank to the aileron bellcranks. Running between the two bellcranks is an additional cable that is often referred to as the *balance cable*. This completes the closed loop and ensures that one aileron movement is transferred to the other aileron. Attached to the wing bellcrank is a push-pull tube that connects to a fitting near the leading edge of the aileron.

The rudder system is quite simple, as shown in Figure 9-6-2. This system operates the rudder pedals by pushing with the foot. A *torque tube* attached at the base of the pedals transfers the pedal motion to pull on the cables, which in turn are attached to horns on the base of the rudder. As the pedals are depressed left or right, the rudder is deflected in the same direction.

The rudder pedals are often connected to the nose gear for steering on light aircraft, which may be a either rigid connection or spring connection. Even in advanced aircraft that use hydraulic or electrical control actuators instead of control cables, the same basic process applies.

The second bellcrank attaches to a push-pull tube and horn that attaches to the elevator. When the elevator down-cable is pulled, the bottom of the bellcrank moves forward. This causes the push-pull tube to pull the elevator down. This operation is reversed when the up-cable is pulled.

Lateral and directional controls. As we already discussed, the ailerons control bank and the rudder controls direction. In order to turn the aircraft, a coordinated turn requires both aileron and rudder. Figure 9-6-1 is a view of a typical light aircraft aileron system.

The aileron system connects the control column to the two ailerons. This, again, is accom-

Tabs. Even though an aircraft has inherent stability, it does not always tend to fly straight and level. The weight of the load and its distribution affect stability. Various speeds also

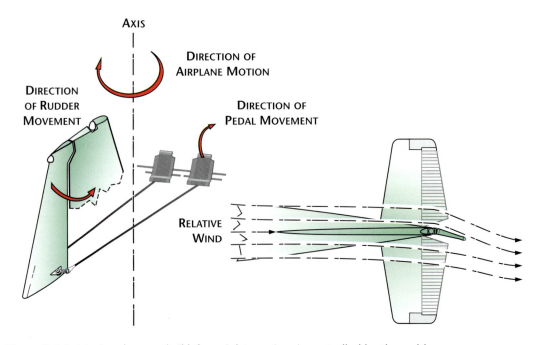

Figure 9-6-2. Moving the nose/tail left or right, yawing, is controlled by the rudder.

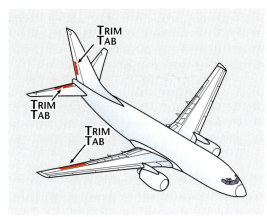

Figure 9-6-3. Trim tabs

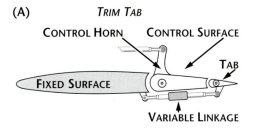

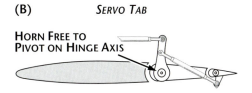

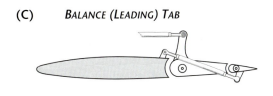

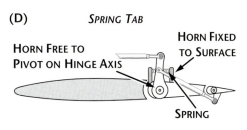

Figure 9-6-4. Trim and control tabs can come in a bewildering array of types and operating principles. Almost all use air pressure exerted by the slipstream to help move the surface.

affect its flight characteristics. If the fuel in one wing tank is used before that in the other wing tank, the aircraft tends to roll toward the full tank. All of these variations require constant exertion of pressure on the controls for correction. While climbing or descending, it is necessary to apply pressure on the controls to keep the aircraft in the desired attitude.

To offset the forces that tend to unbalance an aircraft in flight, ailerons, elevators and rudders are provided with auxiliary controls known as *trim tabs*. These are small, hinged control surfaces (Figure 9-6-3) on the trailing edge of the primary control surfaces. Tabs can be moved up or down by means of a control or moved electrically from the cockpit. These tabs can be used to balance the forces on the controls so that the aircraft flies hands-off straight and level, or may be set so that the aircraft maintains either a climbing or descending attitude. See Figure 9-6-4A.

Servo tabs. *Servo tabs* (Figure 9-6-4B) are very similar in operation and appearance to the trim tabs just discussed. Servo tabs, sometimes referred to as flight tabs, are used primarily on the large main control surfaces. They aid in moving the control surface and holding it in the desired position. Only the servo tab moves in response to movement of the cockpit control. (The servo tab horn is free to pivot to the main control surface hinge axis.) The force of the airflow on the servo tab then moves the primary control surface. With the use of a servo tab, less force is needed to move the main control surface.

Balance tabs. A *balance tab*, also called a leading tab, is shown in Figure 9-6-4C. The linkage is designed in such a way that when the main control surface is moved, the tab moves in the opposite direction. Thus, aerodynamic forces acting on the tab assists in moving the main control surface.

Spring tabs. *Spring tabs* (Figure 9-6-4D) are similar in appearance to trim tabs, but serve an entirely different purpose. Spring tabs are used for the same purpose as hydraulic actuators: that is, to aid in moving a primary control surface. There are various spring arrangements used in the linkage of the spring tab.

On some aircraft, a spring tab is hinged to the trailing edge of each aileron and is actuated by a spring-loaded push-pull rod assembly that is also linked to the aileron control linkage. The linkage is connected in such a way that movement of the aileron in one direction causes the spring tab to be deflected in the opposite direction. This provides a balanced condition, thus reducing the amount of force required to move the ailerons.

Anti–servo tabs. The anti–servo tab is used on stabilators to help dampen out a tendency for the surface to move abruptly in the direction of deflection. The abrupt movement occurs when the nose of the stabilator is moved out of the airstream by the pilot and is forced to continue in the direction of the movement by the action of the air pushing against the front of the con-

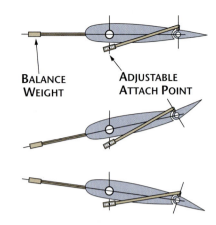

Figure 9-6-5. Anti-servo tab on an all-movable tail surface.

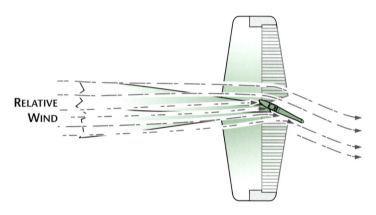

Figure 9-6-6. In many aerodynamic balances, additional weight is used to also create a static balance. If repairs or refinishing disturbs the static balance, the surface will have to be rebalanced.

trol surface. The anti-servo tab moves up when the nose of the control moves down and acts to dampen out the tendency of the stabilator to continue in the direction of the deflection. The anti-servo tab can also be used as a trim tab with a control in the cockpit and a drum and jackscrew mechanism. See Figure 9-6-5.

Ground-adjustable tabs. Ground-adjustable trim tabs are adjusted on the ground before taking off. Their purpose is to compensate for minor differences between different airplanes and allow the airplane to be trimmed for hands-off at a specific speed (usually cruising). This will allow a full range of movement of the regular trim tabs to be available to the pilot to compensate for varying loads and conditions.

Control surface balance. To lessen the force required to operate the control surfaces, they are usually balanced statically and aerodynamically. *Aerodynamic balance* is usually achieved by extending a portion of the control surface ahead of the hinge line. This utilizes the airflow around the aircraft to aid in moving the surface. This method, applied to a rudder, is shown in Figure 9-6-6.

Static balance is accomplished by adding weight to the section forward of the hinge line until it weighs the same as the section aft of it. Some designs use a small aerodynamic balance to provide a longer arm, lessening the amount of weight needed to achieve balance. When repairing a control surface, use care to prevent upsetting or disturbing the static balance. An unbalanced surface has a tendency to flutter as air passes over it. Flutter increases the pressure on the surface attach points and control system. It is possible for a fluttering surface to depart the airplane, resulting in an accident. Should a repair or refinishing operation cause an imbalance to a surface, check the maintenance manual for the correct rebalancing procedure for the specific surface. NEVER allow a statically balanced control surface to be installed in an out of balance condition.

An *adjustable stabilizer* is used on some aircraft rather than using a tab for the elevator. This device generally uses the *jackscrew* and a hinge point, as shown in Figure 9-6-7, which can be raised or lowered by an electric motor running a jackscrew. Normally, a switch is used on the control column for its operation. On some aircraft, this is controlled by a manually operated trim wheel.

High-lift devices. High-lift devices are used in combination with airfoils in order to reduce the takeoff or landing speed by changing the lift characteristics of an airfoil during the landing or takeoff phases. When these devices are no longer needed, they are retracted to a position within the wing to regain the normal characteristics of the airfoil.

The most common high-lift device is known as a *flap*. It is a hinged surface on the trailing edge of the wing. It is controlled from the cockpit and, when not in use, fits smoothly into the lower surface of the wing. The use of flaps increases the camber of a wing, and therefore, the lift of the wing, making it possible for aircraft speed to be decreased without stalling. This also permits a steeper gliding angle to be obtained in the landing approach without increasing speed.

Flaps. Flaps are primarily used during takeoff and landing. As the two uses are opposite, each has their own settings. On a large airplane, if not enough flap is used for takeoff, the airplane will be short on lift. If the flaps are set in the landing range, there will be too much drag. A wrong flap setting will not allow the airplane to perform correctly.

The types of flaps in use on aircraft include:
- Plain
- Split
- Fowler
- Slotted

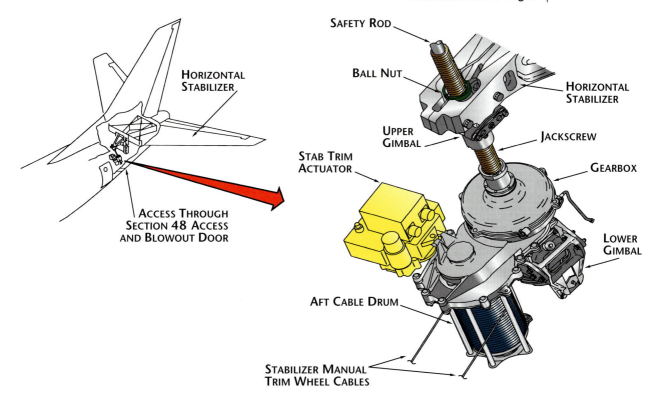

Figure 9-6-7. Many transport category airplanes use a jackscrew system to raise or lower the stabilizer. Most are hydraulic, operated by either cable or electrical inputs.

The *plain flap* (Figure 9-6-8A) is simply hinged to the wing and forms a part of the wing surface when raised.

The *split flap* (Figure 9-6-8B) gets its name from the hinge at the bottom part of the wing near the trailing edge, permitting it to be lowered from the fixed top surface.

The *Fowler flap* (Figure 9-6-8C) fits into the lower part of the wing, flush with the surface. In operation, it slides backward on tracks and tilts downward at the same time. In addition to increasing wing camber, Fowler flaps also increase the wing area, thus providing added lift without unduly increasing drag.

The *slotted flap* (Figure 9-6-8D) is like the Fowler flap in operation, but in appearance it is similar to a plain flap. This flap is equipped with either tracks and rollers or hinges of a special design. During operation, the flap moves downward and rearward away from the position of the wing. The *slot*, thus opened, allows a flow of air over the upper surface of the flap. The effect is to streamline the airflow and to improve the efficiency of the flap. Often, more than one panel is used with the slotted flap.

Boundary layer control devices. The layer of air over the surface that is slower-moving in relation to the rest of the slipstream is called the *boundary layer*. The initial airflow on a smooth surface (Figure 9-6-8) gives evidence of a very-

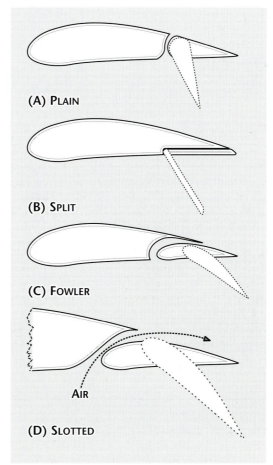

Figure 9-6-8. Principal flap systems with common usage. The transport category "split flap" is a modified Fowler flap.

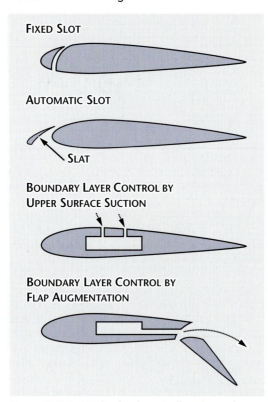

Figure 9-6-9. Methods of controlling boundary layer air

thin boundary layer, with the flow occurring in smooth laminations of air sliding smoothly over one another. Therefore, the term for this type of flow is the *laminar boundary layer*.

As the flow continues back from the leading edge, friction forces in the boundary layer continue to dissipate the energy of the airstream, slowing it down. The laminar boundary layer increases in thickness with increased distance from the wing's leading edge. Some distance from the leading edge, the laminar flow begins an oscillatory disturbance that is unstable. A waviness occurs in the laminar boundary layer that ultimately grows larger and more severe and destroys the smooth laminar flow. Thus, a transition takes place in which the laminar boundary layer decays into a turbulent boundary layer. The same sort of transition can be noticed in the smoke from a burning cigarette. At first, the smoke ribbon is smooth and laminar, then develops a definite waviness and decays into a random turbulent smoke pattern.

Boundary layer control devices are additional means of increasing the maximum lift coefficient of a section. The thin layer of air adjacent to the surface of an airfoil shows reduced local velocities from the effect of skin friction. At high angles of attack, the boundary layer on the upper surface tends to *stagnate*, or come to a stop. When this happens, the airflow separates from the surface and stall occurs.

Boundary layer control for high-lift applications features various devices to maintain high velocity in the boundary layer and delay separation of the airflow. Control of the boundary layer's kinetic energy can be accomplished using slats and the application of suction to draw off the stagnant air and replace it with high-velocity air from outside the boundary layer.

One of the simplest of these devices is the *slot*. The device is simply an opening aft of the forward edge of the wing. When the angle of attack is increased, the air passing through the slot prevents the boundary layer from thickening by increasing the airflow. This will retard the point where stall will occur. On some high-performance Short Takeoff and Landing (STOL) airplanes, the slots are forward of the ailerons. This allows positive airflow over the ailerons, providing control during a stall.

Slats. (Figure 9-6-9) are movable control surfaces attached to the leading edge of the wing. When the slat is closed, it forms the leading edge of the wing. When in the open position (extended forward), a slot is created between the slat and the wing leading edge. Thus, high-energy air is introduced into the boundary layer over the top of the wing. This is a form of *boundary layer control*. At low airspeeds this improves

Figure 9-6-10. Leading-edge flaps on large transport airplanes can be quite complicated. By clever linkage design, this leading-edge flap can unfold and extend, as in this view of a Kruger flap on a Boeing 747.

handling characteristics, allowing the aircraft to be controlled laterally at airspeeds below the otherwise normal landing speed.

Controlling boundary layer air by surface suction allows the wing to operate at higher angles of attack. The effect on lift characteristics is similar to that of a slot, because the slot is essentially a boundary layer control device, ducting high-energy air to the upper surface. This type of boundary layer control is normally reserved for military airplane designs.

Boundary layer control can also be accomplished by directing high-pressure engine bleed air through a narrow orifice located just forward of the wing flap leading edge. This directs a *laminar flow* (air in layers) over the wing and flaps when opened sufficiently to expose the orifice. The high-temperature, high-velocity laminar air passing over the wing and flaps delays *flow separation* (when the airstream over an airfoil no longer follows the contour of the airfoil), hence reducing turbulence and drag (Figure 9-6-9). This results in a lower stall speed and allows slower landing speeds. The first application of *blown flaps* was on the Grumman F9F jet fighter in the 1950s.

Some leading-edge flaps actually change the camber of the leading edge of the wing. These are normally made of composite material and are driven hydraulically or electrically. In most cases, both systems are used, with one as primary and the other as a back-up. An excellent example is the *Kruger flap* (Figure 9-6-10).

Aerodynamic twist. Most aircraft produced today have an aerodynamic twist designed into the wing structure (Figure 9-6-11). Normally, the outer section of the wing is twisted down, or has a lower angle of attack, than the wing root. When the wing stalls, the root section will reach the critical angle of attack first and will thus stall first. With the root stalling first, the pilot should have time to push the

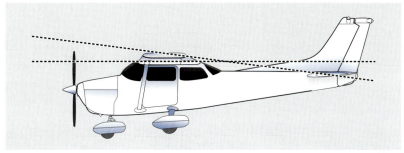

Figure 9-6-11. Aerodynamic twist in a wing is easy to observe. Stand opposite the tip. Move your eye up or down until the trailing edge lines up at both the tip and root.

nose down, increase speed and have some degree of aileron control still available.

Many older aircraft have wing designs that do not allow the root of the wing to stall before the outer portion of the wing. This feature is undesirable, since the ailerons should aid in control when the stall occurs. Ideally, a small triangular strip, called a *stall strip*, is added to the root portion of the wing. This creates enough disturbance to stall the root before the tip at high angles of attack. The result is a much more gentle stall with some aileron control. If the stall strips were removed, a complete wing stalling would result. In that scenario, the only control surface with some positive reaction is the rudder. Trying to use any other surface would result in a spin (Figure 9-6-12).

Winglets. One major method of controlling wingtip vortices is the design of the wingtip itself. The current trend toward the installation of *winglets* on the tips of wings is an example of attempting to control the vortex by design.

Because air is viscous, it has a tendency to slide off the wingtip at right angles to the chord of the wing. The higher pressure air then flows, or curls, into the low-pressure area formed on top of the wing. A whirlwind effect is created.

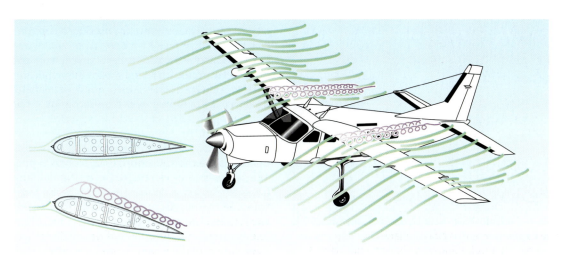

Figure 9-6-12. Stall strips are an important part of aerodynamics and should not be removed.

Figure 9-6-13. Winglets add considerable weight and structural complexity but do provide excellent drag reduction.

Figure 9-6-14. The Cozy series of homebuilt airplanes is currently one of the most popular examples of a canard design.

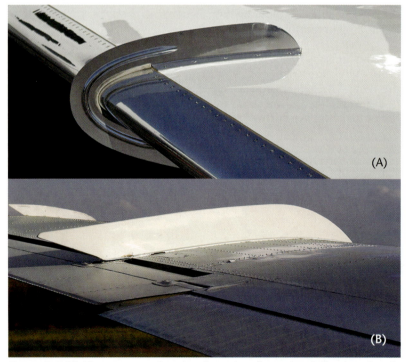

Figure 9-6-15. The purpose of a wing fence is to keep the air flowing chordwise across the wing. Some span little more than the leading edge of the wing (A), while others reach all the way back to the trailing edge (B).

The "whirlwind" continues to grow in size and plays out behind the wing tip as the airplane flies on. This causes a great deal of turbulence and reduces the effectiveness of the wing by destroying downwash. Additionally, the turbulence can remain organized for some time, producing a danger to following aircraft.

In its simplest form, a winglet is a vertical extension of the wing. It keeps the air from sliding off the wing and combining with the air on top. The actual tip of the winglet can now be a symmetrical airfoil. This reduces and relocates the wing tip vortex, thus reducing loss of downwash caused by the disturbance. Additionally, a winglet increases the aspect ratio of the wing. Increasing the aspect ratio always produces an increase in lift (Figure 9-6-13 for an example of a winglet).

Winglets are not a cure-all for induced drag. As with all other factors aircraft designers consider, there are trade-offs. Winglets require more structural strength, and many wings would need complete redesign to accommodate them. There is also a trade-off between the gain they produce and the cost and complexity they add to the manufacture of the airplane.

Just as lift increases with an increase in angle of attack, induced drag also increases as the angle of attack becomes greater. This occurs because, as the angle of attack is increased, there is a greater pressure difference between the top and bottom of the wing. This causes more violent vortices to be set up, resulting in more turbulence and more induced drag.

Canard. A *canard* is a fixed or moveable surface mounted on the forward fuselage, much as a horizontal stabilizer is placed on the rear of the fuselage. The canard is a very old idea. The Wright brothers placed their elevator on the front of their aircraft. A fixed canard adds to the lift of the forward portion of the fuselage. This allows the wing to be placed further aft on the fuselage. A fixed canard also reduces the size requirement of the horizontal stabilizer. In some designs, a canard actually eliminates the need for a horizontal stabilizer; in effect, it becomes a horizontal stabilizer located in front. The best current example of a fixed canard is on jet fighter aircraft, while the Varieze homebuilt series is an example of a canard used in place of tail surfaces (Figure 9-6-14).

To understand the operation of a moveable canard requires some further explanation. On a conventional tail assembly, the horizontal stabilizer provides a down force, or reverse lift, on the aft of the fuselage. At design cruise speed, this down force balances the fuselage nose's down force from weight ahead of the center of gravity. A reduction of power causes the horizontal stabilizer to lose some lift, or down pressure, and the nose drops in response. As speed increases from the nose-down attitude, the lift will increase faster on the horizontal stabilizer than on the wings, pushing the tail down and raising the nose, with the aircraft resuming level flight.

A canard works in reverse. The canard provides lift, or upward pressure, on the forward fuselage. At design cruise speed, this upward pressure balances the lift of the wings, and the airplane flies straight and level. When power is reduced, lift is lost more quickly on the canard than on the wings and the nose drops. As speed builds, the canard builds lift faster than the wings, raising the nose to level flight. It is possible to design an airplane with a canard planform that, for practical purposes, will not stall.

Wing fences. Wing fences have been used for many years with the advent of the swept-back wing. The purpose of the fence is to direct the airflow over the chord of the wing rather than at the angle of the sweepback, and to stop the movement of air towards the wingtip (Figure 9-6-15).

Section 7

Control Systems

Control systems in modern transports can quickly become complicated. Transport aircraft use several control surfaces in conjunction with each other in most flight configurations.

The input commands for each flight control are generally managed by an electronic device that will provide the commands to the various systems simultaneously. Most of these controls are hydraulically assisted, generally from two or more hydraulic systems. This redundancy in the flight controls is a safety measure to ensure the operation of the system in an emergency.

Some aircraft have electrical backup control mechanisms on some of the hydraulic controls, while others may have a mechanical backup system.

An aircraft may have control surfaces that are moved electrically with electrical backup systems — called *fly-by-wire* systems. Because of all the various systems and variations in use, it is easiest to follow one particular system through its operation, rather than portions of several unrelated systems. Our example aircraft, in Figure 9-7-1, has control surfaces of this type.

The primary control surfaces are the ailerons, elevator and the rudder. These surfaces are operated by control cables running from the flight deck to the hydraulic-control actuators. For reliability, they utilize the two hydraulic systems of the aircraft.

The secondary controls include the spoilers, speed brakes, stabilizer, slats and flaps.

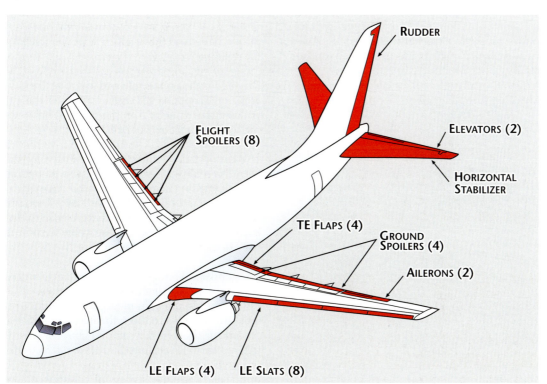

Figure 9-7-1. Primary control surfaces on a transport aircraft are the same rudder, elevator and ailerons as used on any other conventional airplane.

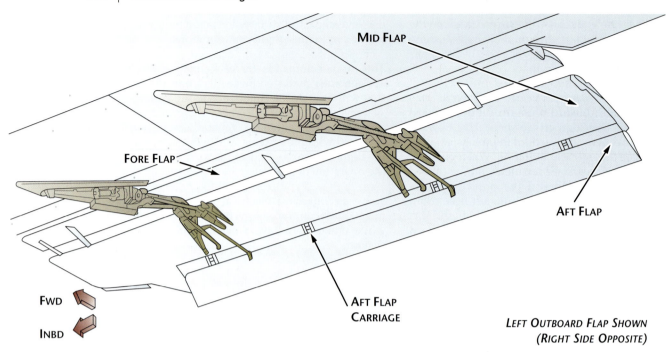

Figure 9-7-2. Inboard trailing edge flaps extended

The spoilers consist of six units on the top of each wing. The four center panels are used for roll control, while all six panels are used for flight and ground-speed brakes. The autospeed brakes are for landing and are refused activation by the computer system for takeoff. The spoilers are hydraulically powered and electronically controlled.

The stabilizer is moved up and down by the use of cable linkages controlling the hydraulic power output to a mechanical jackscrew. Again, two hydraulic systems are used to ensure reliability.

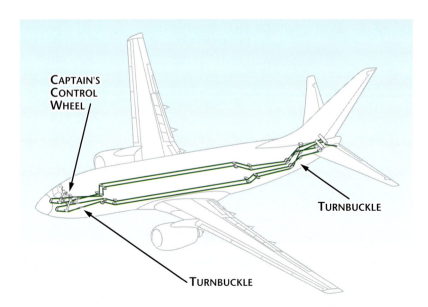

Figure 9-7-3. Stabilizer cable-operated trim system

The system of slats consists of eight units, four on each wing. These have three programmed positions: cruise, landing and takeoff. They are hydraulically powered, with torque tube drives and electric power backup.

This aircraft utilizes an outboard and inboard flap on each wing. The outboard flap is a single-slotted flap. The inboard flap is single-slotted for takeoff and double-slotted for landing. These are lowered by a hydraulically powered torque tube and have electric power backup for reliability.

During landings, the inboard ailerons are lowered, or drooped, 10°. This improves the lift and reduces drag by filling in the gap between the inboard and outboard flaps.

The droop is controlled mechanically by the flap-drive angle gearbox. The droop begins as the trailing edge flaps extend beyond 5° down. The droop is completed at 10° down. This cycle is reversed when the trailing edge flaps are retracted. The wing cable system is not affected by the aileron droop.

The outboard aileron becomes inoperative when 235 knots of airspeed is reached, with roll control being provided by the spoiler system. This greatly reduces the bending stresses placed on the wing structure. This is accomplished through an automatic lockout system.

The spoiler system assists in aileron control by raising the flight spoilers on one wing to destroy lift. In addition to this function, the spoiler may be deployed as speed brakes, both in the air and on the ground.

The operation of the speed brakes on the ground may be accomplished by the speed brake lever or automatically by an electrical actuator after the aircraft is on the ground.

Flaps and slats are used for high-lift systems. The flap system is made up of two double-slotted flaps (shown in Figure 9-7-2) on the inboard and two single-slotted flaps on the outboard wing. There are a total of twelve slats. These have a small seal flap between the inboard slat and the engine strut. The flap and slats are operated by a single lever.

The horizontal stabilizer is movable and used to trim the aircraft. To accomplish this, the stabilizer is pivoted at the rear attachments. It is raised and lowered by a hydraulically powered ball screw actuator assembly.

Control switches on each cockpit control wheel horn provide manual electric trim. The flight control computers provide autopilot trim. Manual control of the stabilizer is accomplished with a manual lever cable system. Figure 9-7-3 is an illustration of a stabilizer trim system.

The elevator system consists of an inboard and outboard elevator on each side. The inboard and outboard elevators are connected by links that move the elevators as a single unit. The two systems normally operate as one. However, if a problem developed in one of the systems, the other would be sufficient to operate the plane.

Other features of the (dual-path) elevator control system include *artificial feel, autopilot input* and a *stick nudger*. The stick nudger is used to reproduce the feel of a conventional control system when it approaches a stall.

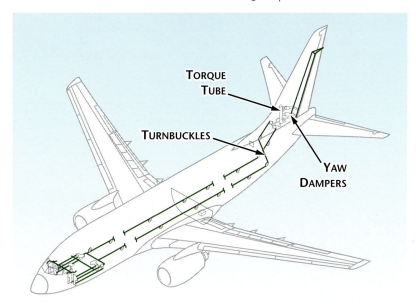

Figure 9-7-4. Although they appear conventional, large aircraft include additional control inputs, including automatic yaw dampers.

The rudder system consists of two pedal systems that mechanically drive a pair of quadrants. The quadrants are tied together, enabling either set of pedals to control the rudder.

The directional autopilot servos receive control inputs from the flight control computer and provide directional control in *auto-land mode* on final approach and runway rollout.

The feel centering unit provides a feel force to the pedal input and a centering force to return the pedals to neutral when the input is removed.

The *yaw damper* provides control input to the rudder actuators (Figure 9-7-4). Two yaw-damper servos receive inputs from control modules and provide turn coordination and protection against uncommanded yaw inputs.

10
Corrosion Control

Section 1

Corrosion Prevention and Control

Corrosion is the single greatest threat to the integrity of airframe structures. It is a natural chemical or electrochemical process that occurs on metals and metal alloys. Corrosion weakens the metals it attacks and, if left untreated, will cause metal parts to fail.

A number of factors promote the spread of corrosion. These include air pollution, the type of metal used in components, or the type of stress the metal is subjected to. However, unless a metal part suffers direct chemical attack by acid or a mercury spill, *corrosion will only occur in the presence of water and oxygen.*

Chemical corrosion. This occurs when a strong acid or base chemically dissolves metal. An example would be a piece of copper or zinc immersed in acid. The acid attacks and dissolves the metal until nothing is left. Aircraft are exposed to a number of corrosive chemicals. For example, aircraft batteries are a source of both strong acids and bases. In addition, acids can be produced in aircraft structures when certain conditions are present. It is common to find growths of microorganisms in aircraft fuel tanks. Certain bacteria have metabolisms that cause them to secrete corrosive fluids. These fluids form acids that attack metal structures.

Electrochemical corrosion. *Electrochemical corrosion* occurs in the presence of different metals that have different susceptibilities to corrosion. The mechanism involved is similar to the way a primary cell works. As you recall from your study of electricity, a primary cell consists of an

Learning Objective

DESCRIBE
- factors that promote corrosion
- corrosion-prone areas of an aircraft

EXPLAIN
- methods of preventing or controlling corrosion

APPLY
- recognize types of corrosion
- inspect an aircraft for corrosion

Left. An extreme example of the effects of corrosion, this P-63 was shot down during World War II and spent several decades decaying in a jungle before being retrieved.

CONTACTING METALS	ALUMINUM ALLOY	CADMIUM PLATE	ZINC PLATE	CARBON AND ALLOY STEELS	LEAD	TIN COATING	COPPER AND ALLOYS	NICKEL AND ALLOYS	TITANIUM ALLOYS	CHROMIUM PLATE	CORROSION RESISTING STEEL	MAGNESIUM ALLOYS
Aluminum Alloy												
Cadmium Plate												
Zinc Plate												
Carbon and Alloy Steels												
Lead												
Tin Coating												
Copper and Alloys												
Titanium and Alloys												
Chromium Plate												
Corrosion Resisting Steel												
Magnesium Alloys												
SHADED AREAS INDICATE DISSIMILIAR METAL CONTACT												

Table 10-1-1. Differences in electrode potential among various structural materials

anode, or donor of electrons, a cathode, or receiver of electrons and a conductive electrolyte. When a conductor completes the circuit between the anode and cathode, a chemical reaction occurs in the cell that produces electricity. As this process takes place the anode is slowly worn away by the chemical reaction. The same process occurs in electrochemical corrosion.

A metal's *electrode potential* refers to the metal's ability to give up or receive electrons. Electrode potential is a function of a material's atomic structure; those with a high electric potential are strong electron donors while those with a low potential are poor electron donors. Refer to Table 10-1-1. Because of its atomic structure, gold is not a good electron donor. Since it is not very susceptible to corrosion, gold is frequently used as a coating on electrical system contacts. On the other end of the scale is magnesium, which is a strong electron donor. This property makes magnesium extremely susceptible to corrosion. However, its strength and light weight make it indispensable for certain aircraft applications.

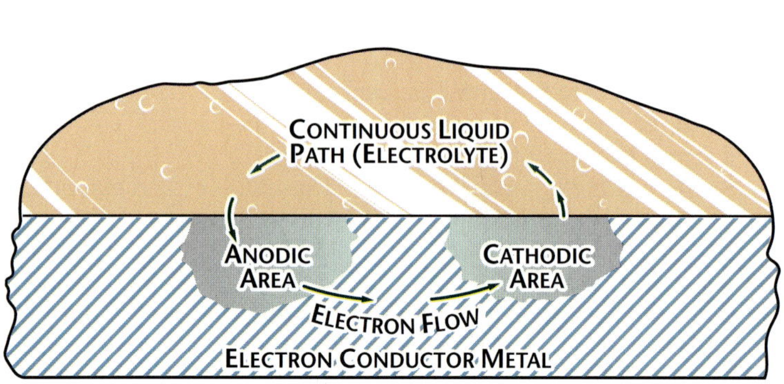

Electrochemical corrosion takes place when two different metals come in contact, either directly or through a conductive electrolyte. The farther apart they are in their electrode potentials, the greater the degree of corrosion.

Moisture and oxygen are always present in the atmosphere. When metal is exposed to moisture, electrochemical corrosion has a place to start. One part of the metal surface will serve as a cathode, receiving electrons. Another part of the metal acts as an anode, giving up electrons. Corrosion will always take place at the anode, as shown in Figure 10-1-1.

A number of factors affect the spread of corrosion. If an aircraft is frequently operated near the ocean, the salt in the atmosphere increases the electrolyte action of the water and the corrosive process is more rapid. The same is true for air pollution. Sulfur and nitrogen compounds in the air dissolve in water and form acid compounds. These

Figure 10-1-1. Water acts as an electrolyte when corrosion occurs on a metal structure

compounds attack structural components directly and provide a good electrolyte for electrochemical corrosion.

Types of Corrosion

Corrosion attacks aircraft structures in a variety of ways, depending on a component's composition and location.

Pitting corrosion. Pitting corrosion starts on the surface and extends down into the material. It is most common in aluminum and magnesium parts and is first noticeable as a white or gray powdery deposit on the surface. When the powdery deposit is cleaned away, tiny pits or holes can be seen in the surface. Pitting corrosion can spread vertically and horizontally from the area of initial surface attack, severely weakening the corroded part. The corrosion can spread rapidly. An example of pitting corrosion can be seen in Figure 10-1-2.

Figure 10-1-2. Example of pitting corrosion

Concentration cell corrosion. Crevice corrosion occurs at joints between metal parts. The joint can be a butt splice, a seam, or an assembly. When the protective finish or sealant between the metals deteriorates, water and air are allowed in. This creates a microenvironment where a corrosive process begins and spreads. In metal ion concentration cells, entrapped water forms a solution with ions from the metal structure. A high concentration of metal ions develops where the water solution is stagnant, while a low concentration of metal ions forms next to the crevice. An electrical potential difference exists between the two points. Metal in contact with the low concentration of ions is anodic and corrodes.

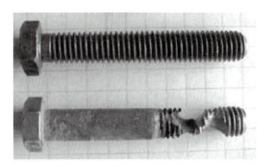

Figure 10-1-3. Normal bolt (Top) compared with corroded bolt (Bottom)

Oxygen concentration. Oxygen concentration cells occur when the solution in contact with the metal surface contains dissolved oxygen. An oxygen cell can develop at any point where the oxygen in the air is not allowed to diffuse into the solution, thereby creating a difference in oxygen concentration between the two points. The area of low oxygen concentration is anodic, and corrosion starts there.

Look at Figure 10-1-3 and contrast the normal bolt on top with the corroded lower bolt. Water exposure allowed an oxygen concentration to start that dissolved the threaded portion.

Filiform corrosion. Filiform corrosion (Figure 10-1-4) is a type of oxygen concentration cell corrosion that occurs on metal surfaces having an organic coating. You can recognize it by its characteristic worm-like or thread-like trace of corrosion products beneath the paint film. Filiform corrosion occurs when the relative humidity is between

Figure 10-1-4. Filiform corrosion is a form of oxygen concentration cell corrosion that occurs under painted surfaces.

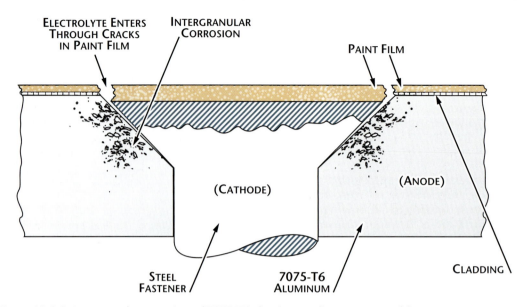

Figure 10-1-5. Intergranular corrosion of 7075-T6 aluminum adjacent to a steel fastener

Figure 10-1-6. An example of exfoliation corrosion

78 and 90 percent, and it most likely to occur under polyurethane finishes. If filiform corrosion is not removed, it can lead to another form, intergranular corrosion.

Intergranular corrosion. Intergranular corrosion is an attack on the grain boundaries of a metal. A magnified cross-section of an alloy will show the granular structure of the metal. This granular structure consists of thousands of individual grains, each of which has a clearly defined boundary that differs chemically from the metal within the grain. The grain boundary and the grain center can react with each other as anode and cathode when in contact with an electrolyte, resulting in rapid corrosion along the grain boundary. Intergranular corrosion is most likely to occur in high-strength aluminum alloys that have been improperly heat-treated. Figure 10-1-5 illustrates a typical area to look for this type of corrosion.

Exfoliation corrosion. Exfoliation corrosion (Figure 10-1-6) is an advanced form of intergranular corrosion characterized by the lifting up of a metal surface's grains by the force of expanding corrosion products occurring at the grain boundaries just below the surface. It is visible evidence of intergranular corrosion and is most often seen on extruded sections.

Galvanic corrosion. Galvanic corrosion, one of the most common types of corrosion, (Figure 10-1-7) occurs when two dissimilar metals make contact in the presence of an electrolyte. It also occurs when certain metals come in contact with carbon fiber reinforced plastic. Galvanic corrosion typically appears as a white or gray powdery substance on fittings, joints, or other structural interfaces.

Stress corrosion. Stress corrosion takes place when a metal part is subjected to a tensile load in a corrosive environment. Internal stress can be trapped in a component during manufacturing when the stress relief operation is omitted or performed improperly. It can be introduced after manufacturing by riveting, welding, press-fitting parts, or improper bolt tightening. For example, when a fastener is overtorqued, stress is introduced into the part. Figure 10-1-8 is an example of stress corrosion.

Fatigue corrosion. Fatigue corrosion involves the cyclic stress of a part in a corrosive environment. Metal parts can withstand cyclic stress indefinitely as long as the stress is below the part's design endurance limit. However, once this limit is exceeded, the part will eventually crack and fail from metal fatigue. When

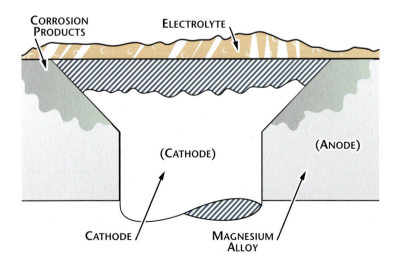

Figure 10-1-7. Galvanic corrosion of magnesium adjacent to steel structure

the stress limit is exceeded in the presence of a corrosive environment, component failure will occur much more rapidly, and can occur at stress levels well below those for which the part was designed.

Fatigue corrosion failure occurs in two stages. In the first stage, the combination of stress and corrosion weakens the metal structure and begins the formation of pitting and cracks. The damage will now continue even if the corrosive agent is removed. In the second stage, the cracks grow until the part fails in use, usually at a very low level of stress.

Fretting corrosion. Fretting corrosion happens when there is movement between two highly loaded surfaces that are not supposed to move against each other. Once this has begun, the rubbing action removes the protective coatings on both pieces of metal. With continued rubbing, metal particles sheared from the two surfaces combine with oxygen to form metal oxides. As these oxides accumulate, they cause further damage by abrasive action. The most common example of fretting corrosion is the "smoking rivet" found on engine cowlings and wing skins.

Corrosion Inspection

The importance of early corrosion detection cannot be overstated. If you find and repair corrosion at an early stage of its development there is less damage to the aircraft, the repair is less expensive to complete, downtime is reduced and safety is not compromised. The longer corrosion is allowed to go untreated, however, the bigger the problem it creates.

Dye penetrant, eddy current, ultrasonic and radiographic inspections are very effective in detecting corrosion damage. These methods are discussed in the section on nondestructive testing.

Visual inspection can be performed using a flashlight, magnifying glass and inspection mirror. On painted surfaces, the appearance and integrity of the paint is your best indicator of the condition of the metal beneath. Corrosion can change the color of the paint or cause the paint to have a scaly or blistered surface. Look for blisters or paint that is chipping and flaking off the surface. Watch for damage to the paint or to adjacent sealant. Figure 10-1-9 shows what can happen when cracks or pinholes in these areas expose the metal underneath to water and oxygen, the first step in the corrosive process.

On bare metal surfaces corrosion will appear as a dulled or darkened area with a pitted surface. You may also observe white, gray or reddish dust or particles.

Corrosive Agents

Corrosive agents are substances that cause a corrosive chemical reaction on metals. The most common corrosive agents are acids, alkalis (bases) and salts. The atmosphere and water, the two most common media for these agents, can sometimes act as corrosive agents themselves.

Acid. An acid is a chemical compound that gives up hydrogen ions when dissolved in water. Depending on the acid's strength, it can corrode most alloys used in aircraft structures. The most destructive are sulfuric acid, halogen acids (hydrochloric, hydrofluoric and hydrobromic) and organic acids found in human and animal waste.

Figure 10-1-8. A typical example of stress corrosion

Figure 10-1-9. This casting developed extensive corrosion when the built-up sealant cracked and allowed water to contact the metal. The part appeared sound until corrosion extended beyond the sealant.

Figure 10-1-10. Extensive magnesium corrosion due to salt water

Figure 10-1-12. Exposure to water and food items makes galley areas especially prone to corrosion

Alkalis. Alkalis, or bases, are chemical compounds that give up hydroxyl ions when dissolved in water. Aluminum is vulnerable to corrosive attack from lime, washing soda, or lye, and potassium hydroxide, an electrolyte used in nickel-cadmium batteries. Aluminum and magnesium alloys are generally more resistant to alkali attack than to acid attack.

Salts. Salts are chemical compounds formed by the chemical reaction that occurs when acids are mixed with alkalis. Sodium chloride, or table salt, is a good example. Solutions containing salts are good electrolytes that actively promote corrosive attack on aluminum and magnesium alloys. Many stainless steel alloys are resistant to attack by salt solutions. Aircraft operated in saltwater environments are especially vulnerable to salt-induced corrosion.

Mercury. Mercury is a heavy metallic element that is liquid at room temperatures and is highly corrosive to aluminum alloys, stainless steel and brass. Through a process known as *amalgamation*, mercury chemically combines with these metals and produces severe corrosion. It can come in contact with aircraft structure through breaks in paint or other protective coatings, and when this happens the chemical attack is extremely rapid. Contamination results in pitting and intergranular attack, leaving the metal embrittled and weakened. Mercury and mercury compounds are frequently shipped on aircraft, and if spills occur, cleanup must be fast and thorough.

Water. Water acts as a corrosive agent on aircraft structures. The degree of corrosivity depends on the type and quantity of dissolved minerals, organic impurities and gases in the water.

The most corrosive natural waters are those that contain salts. Figure 10-1-10 is an example of how destructive salt water can be. Water in the open ocean is extremely corrosive, but waters in harbors are often more so because they are usually contaminated by industrial waste. The corrosiveness of fresh water varies depending on the kinds of dissolved impurities it contains. Certain industrial pollutants can make fresh water extremely corrosive.

Oxygen. The atmosphere contains oxygen, which when mixed with moisture in the air, acts as a corrosive agent. As with water, the pres-

Figure 10-1-11. Exposure to high heat and corrosive exhaust gases make engine exhaust areas susceptible to corrosion

ence of industrial pollutants greatly enhances the corrosiveness of the atmosphere around cities and industrial centers.

Organic growth. Organic growth includes bacteria and fungi that live in aircraft structures such as fuel tanks, water systems and galleys. They promote corrosion in several ways. Some microorganisms produce corrosive agents as waste products, which attack metal structures directly. Bacterial growths can entrap water around the floor structures of galleys, hastening the spread of corrosion.

Corrosion-Prone Areas

Some areas of an aircraft structure receive little exposure to corrosive conditions and thus experience less corrosion damage. Other areas, however, are constantly exposed to corrosives and need much more frequent inspection.

On both turbine and reciprocating engines, the high heat and corrosive compounds of engine exhaust can cause problems for exhaust components and structures in the exhaust gas path. Pay particular attention to gaps, seams, hinges and fairings in the exhaust gas path where deposits may be trapped and not reached by normal cleaning methods (Figure 10-1-11). This includes remote areas such as empennage structures.

Aircraft galley (Figure 10-1-12) and lavatory areas are some of the most corrosion-prone areas you will encounter.

Deck areas behind lavatories, sinks and ranges where spilled food and waste products may collect, if not kept clean, are potential trouble spots. Even if some contaminants are not corrosive in themselves, they will attract and retain moisture and in turn cause corrosive attack. Carefully inspect bilge areas located under galleys and lavatories, clean these areas frequently, and keep paint touched up.

Aircraft battery electrolytes contain acid or strong alkali. As a result, battery compartments and battery vent openings are frequently attacked by corrosion (Figure 10-1-13). Despite improvements in protective paint finishes and in methods of sealing and venting, battery compartments continue to be corrosion problem areas. Fumes from overheated electrolyte are difficult to contain and will spread to adjacent cavities and cause a rapid, corrosive attack on all unprotected metal surfaces.

Battery vent openings on the aircraft skin should be included in the battery compartment inspection and maintenance procedure. Regular cleaning and neutralization of acid deposits will minimize corrosion from this cause.

Figure 10-1-13. Damage due to acid fumes in battery area

Landing gears and wheel wells probably receive more punishment than any other area on the aircraft because of mud, water, salt, gravel and other flying debris that is picked up from ramps, taxiways and runways and thrown by the tires. Because of the many complicated shapes, assemblies and fittings found in the wheel well and landing gear areas, complete area paint film coverage is difficult to attain. A partially applied preservative tends to mask corrosion rather than prevent it. Due to heat generated by braking action, preservatives cannot be used on some main landing gear wheels. During inspection of this area, pay particular attention to the following trouble spots.

- Magnesium wheels, especially around bolt heads, lugs and wheel-web areas, for the presence of entrapped water or its effects.

- Exposed rigid tubing, especially at B-nuts and ferrules, under clamps and tubing identification tapes.

- Exposed position indicator switches and other electrical equipment.

- Crevices between stiffeners, ribs and lower skin surfaces, which are typical water and debris traps.

External aircraft surfaces are readily visible and accessible for inspection and maintenance. Even here, certain types of configurations or combinations of materials become troublesome under certain operating conditions and require special attention. Steel screws in aluminum is one example of this (Figure 10-1-14).

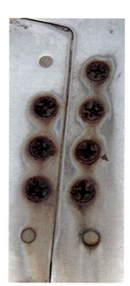

Figure 10-1-14. The steel screws in this wing show signs of dissimilar metal corrosion.

Figure 10-1-15. This piano hinge secures the air conditioning bay door to the fuselage on a Boeing 737. The hinge is aluminum, the pin is steel. It is common to find these hinges corroded.

Relatively little corrosion trouble is experienced with magnesium skins if the original surface finish and insulation are adequately maintained. Trimming, drilling, or riveting destroys some of the original surface treatment, which is never completely restored by touchup procedures. Any inspection for corrosion should include all magnesium skin surfaces with special attention to edges, areas around fasteners and cracked, chipped, or missing paint.

Corrosion of metal skin joined by spot welding is the result of the entrance and entrapment of corrosive agents between the layers of metal. This type of corrosion is evidenced by corrosion products appearing at the crevices through which the corrosive agents enter. More advanced corrosive attack causes skin buckling and eventual spot-weld fracture. Skin buckling in its early stages may be detected by sighting along spot-welded seams or by using a straightedge. The only technique for preventing this condition is to keep potential moisture entry points, including seams and holes created by broken spot welds, filled with a sealant or a suitable preservative compound.

Inaccessible Areas

Because fuel tanks are usually located inside wing and fuselage structures, it is often difficult to gain access to inspect fittings and other hardware on the outside of the tank for corrosion. In addition, as was previously mentioned in this chapter, fuel tanks are targets for bacterial growth, particularly in tanks used for turbine fuels. While inspection inside the tank may be difficult or impossible, bacterial growth can be controlled with the use of growth-inhibiting additives added to the fuel when refueling.

Piano hinges are prime spots for corrosion due to the dissimilar metal contact between the steel pin and aluminum hinge. As you can see from Figure 10-1-15, they are also natural traps for dirt, salt, or moisture. Inspection of hinges should include lubrication and actuation through several cycles to ensure complete lubricant penetration.

Wing flap and spoiler recesses (Figure 10-1-16) accumulate grease, dirt and water. These areas frequently go unnoticed because flaps and spoilers are normally retracted. For this reason, these recesses are potential corrosion problem areas.

Figure 10-1-16. Flap recesses at wing trailing edge

Because of their purpose and location, *engine-mount structures* are subjected to extremes of heat, vibration and torque from the engine and its accessories. To withstand the stresses placed on mount structures, most reciprocating engine mounts are manufactured from welded tubular steel. Therefore, engine-mount structures are inspected for corrosion, and corrosion treated, in much the same manner as other tubular steel airframe components, such as push/pull tubes, airframe structural tubing, tubular landing gear, etc. Particular attention must be paid to areas where moisture or other contaminants could possibly get inside the tubing, such as threaded, riveted, or welded areas. Where economically feasible, corroded tubing should be cleaned, the structural integrity of the material tested (through the use of magnaflux, radiography, or other suitable test procedure) and treated to prevent a recurrence of the same or similar corrosion. Where the cost is prohibitive, the alternative is replacement of the part. In some cases parts of the engine-mount structure can be individually replaced. In other cases the entire mount assembly must be replaced.

All *control cables,* whether plain carbon steel or corrosion-resistant steel, should be inspected to determine their condition at each inspection period. Cables should be inspected for corrosion by random cleaning of short sections with solvent-soaked cloths. Control cable access is easier in large airplanes (Figure 10-1-17) than in some smaller airplanes. If external corrosion is evident, tension should be relieved and the cable checked for internal corrosion. Cables with internal corrosion should be replaced. Light external corrosion should be removed with a stainless steel wire brush. When corrosion products have been removed, recoat the cable with preservative.

Many types of fluxes used in brazing, soldering and welding are corrosive and will chemically attack the metals or alloys on which they are used. Therefore, it is important that residual flux be removed from the metal surface immediately after the joining operation. Flux residues are hydroscopic in nature; that is, they are capable of absorbing moisture, and unless carefully removed, tend to cause severe pitting.

Weld decay is a form of intergranular corrosion that attacks welds in stainless steel. It occurs because the process of welding often produces an undesirable heat treatment adjacent to the welded area (Figure 10-1-18), in turn producing separate phases of the metal, one of which may be preferentially attacked under adverse environmental conditions.

Electronic and electrical package compartments cooled by ram air or compressor bleed air are subjected to the same conditions common to engine and accessory cooling vents and

Figure 10-1-17. Most cable runs in large airplanes are accessible once the floorboards are removed

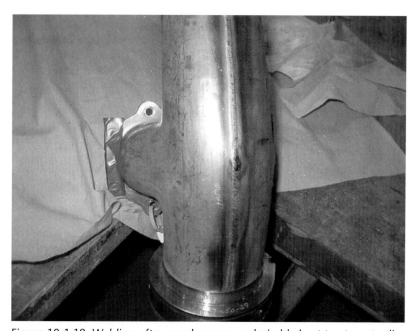

Figure 10-1-18. Welding often produces an undesirable heat treatment adjacent to the welded area

engine frontal areas. While the degree of exposure is less because of a lower volume of air passing through and special design features incorporated to prevent water formation in the enclosed spaces, this is still a trouble area that requires special attention.

Circuit breakers, contact points and switches are extremely sensitive to moisture and corrosive attack and should be inspected for these conditions as thoroughly as design permits. If design features hinder examination of these items while in the installed condition, advantage should be taken of component removals for other reasons with careful inspection for corrosion required before reinstallation.

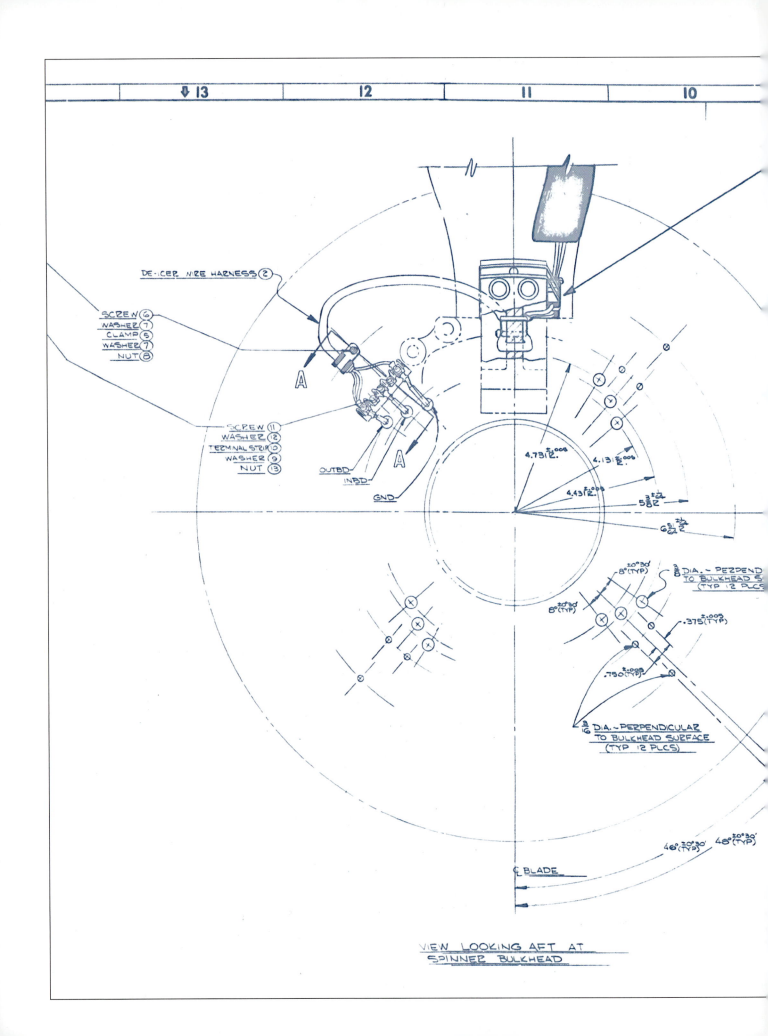

11

Aircraft Manuals and Drawings

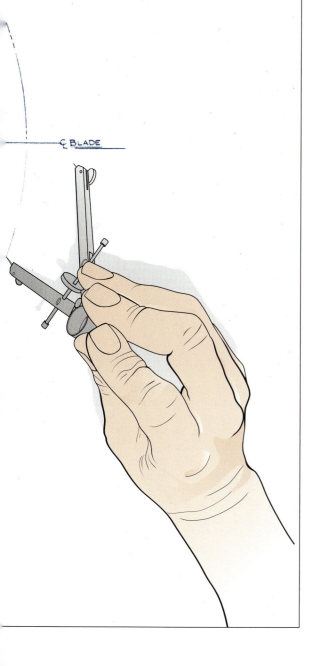

Section 1

Manufacturers' Maintenance Manuals

Maintenance is defined in 14 CFR Part 1.1 as: inspection, overhaul, repair, preservation, and the replacemnt of parts. By federal regulation, each current aircraft manufacturer must provide all the manuals necessary to service, operate, maintain, repair and overhaul each product that they manufacture. Each subcontractor that supplies assemblies to that manufacturer must also have those same types of manuals available. The price of manuals varies significantly. Some small manuals for high-production parts cost just a few dollars. For large, complex airplanes, these same types of manuals can run several hundred dollars each. Hard-to-find manuals for out-of-production airplanes can cost more than a thousand dollars per copy.

While all the FARs in book form might use six or eight feet of shelf space, all the manuals required by a large general aviation shop, in hard copy, might cover forty to fifty feet of shelf space. Within this wall of books would be many of the following:

- Service manuals
- Maintenance manuals
- Parts manuals
- Overhaul manuals
- Standard procedures manual
- Structural repair manuals
- Operations manuals

Learning Objective

DESCRIBE
- manufacturers' maintenance manuals
- methods of illustrating objects

EXPLAIN
- various types of aircraft drawings and their purposes

APPLY
- find the correct documentation for a task
- compare an aircraft part to a drawing

Left. Installation drawing for electric propeller de-ice wiring block

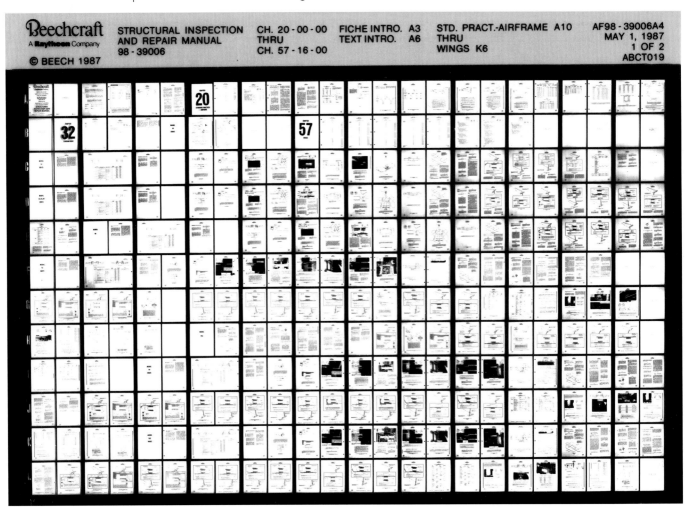

Figure 11-1-1. A full-size representation of a sheet of microfiche

- Inspection manuals (by type of inspection)
- Component service manuals
- Component overhaul manuals
- Component parts manuals
- Electrical system manuals
- Troubleshooting manuals

Now, imagine this list of manuals existing for each different model of each manufacturers airplane. In addition, each engine model will have its own set of manuals, as will each engine accessory.

In the case of transport category airplanes, one model airplane by one manufacturer could produce as much as 20 linear feet of manuals. Boeing 767 component overhaul manuals alone occupy 8 feet of shelving.

This discussion on the sheer volume of material has a point: You don't have to read it all. What you do have to read is the material that covers what it is you are doing today. Once you have read it and understand what it is telling you, you may not have to read it again (though refreshing your memory from time to time is a good idea). What you do have to do is to keep the material available. For the FAA's purposes, that means at the least having it in the same building with you.

Work cards. From all the previous information, it is clear that finding specific information could pose a challenge. It is not possible to start at one end of the bookcase and go through each volume looking for specific directions. That is why airline shops use a work-card system. The card contains not only the job description, but enough information from the proper manual to allow completion of the project. If it doesn't, or if you don't understand the card, then you must look up the material you need. This is where the ATA 100 system is a major benefit. You can find what you need fairly quickly.

Just think it out beforehand so you will be looking for what you need in the place it really is.

The constant revision of maintenance publications and the increasing scope of the printed page requires several full-time personnel who do nothing but try to keep up with the filing and storage of these documents.

Aerofiche. This problem was originally addressed by large aircraft manufacturers who produced maintenance and overhaul data on microfilm. The microfilm was available in rolls and used a special machine to read it. The reader machines had a search feature that made finding information relatively quick. In a shop where all work was done on a single type of airplane, microfilm was hard to beat. However, the system did have some drawbacks: the readers were expensive, and the entire roll of microfilm had to be replaced when any information was updated. Especially troublesome was changing from one type airplane to another. Even at that, microfilm worked and many large airplane shops still use it.

An outgrowth of the microfilm system was Aerofiche. Instead of using roll film, a film card is used. The standard microfiche card uses 24 columns by 12 rows of pictures on a transparent film approximately 4-1/8 inches high by 5-7/8 inches wide (Figure 11-1-1). One microfiche card will accommodate 288 pages of information.

Information retrieval is from a microfiche reader, or reader/printer. The reader has a lens that is 40x, or 40 power, for enlarging the pages and making the information easy to read. Reader/printer models allow for printing single pages and taking them to the job.

Thousands of aircraft industry publications and FAA regulations have been transferred to the microfiche system for use by aircraft repair stations, inspectors and individual technicians.

Some of the features of the microfiche system which are available from the FAA, aircraft manufacturers and private companies are:

- Numerical indexing and dating for control and management
- Bi-weekly updates are standard procedures of most microfiche publishers
- All regulatory data, such as TCDS, supplemental TC information and all ACs
- ADs and manufacturers' service bulletins and letters are collated and indexed by aircraft type
- All Federal Regulations are kept current by subscription
- All powerplant service, repair and overhaul manuals

Many commercial services have a subscription program whereby they send monthly updates. Fiche libraries are kept current simply by replacing the old fiche with the new one.

The FAA regulations state that a shop must have all of the current information in order to do repair and maintenance. Microfiche is an excellent way to keep current without investing large amounts time in the updating process.

Microfiche is available in libraries, which allow a service facility to buy information on an as-needed basis. As needs grow, the facility can simply add the appropriate library.

Computerized Maintenance Manuals. Laptops or computer workstations are now common in the maintenance hanger. These computers access electronic versions of the maintenance and parts manuals for the aircraft. While the programs that are used differ from manufacturer to manufacturer, the information is organized the same way as in printed manuals.

The advantages to using computers are many:

- The most current information is always available
- The technician can printout any page or the diagram needed
- For many aircraft, all the information can be contained on a few compact disks (CDs) or on a hard drive, instead of hundreds of pages of printed material.

NOTE: *Printouts should be disposed of after use to ensure that the most current information will be used in the future.*

Many manufacturers incorporate programs that allow the user to make maintenance entries to the aircraft historical records. These programs can also track the usage of time-critical parts and recommended overhaul times.

Some aftermarket companies have maintenance tracking and scheduling programs that integrate with the various aircraft used by a company. These programs prove vital to cost-effective operations.

Manufacturers allow access to their manuals and databases through the internet. This means that the data is always up-to-date with the latest standards. Information can be input that helps in diagnosing and troubleshooting out of the ordinary problems on an aircraft. Access is usually restricted to paid subscribers.

ATA Specification 100. The *Air Transport Association of America* (ATA) issued the specifications for Manufacturers' Technical Data on

MAINTENANCE MANUAL CHAPTER NUMBERS

AIRCRAFT GENERAL

Time Limits/ Maintenance Checks	5
Dimensions & Charts	6
Lifting & Shoring	7
Leveling & Weighing	8
Towing & Taxiing	9
Parking & Mooring	10
Required Placards	11
Servicing	12
Standard Practices - Airframe	20

AIRPLANE SYSTEMS

Air Conditioning	21
Auto Flight	22
Communication	23
Electrical Power	24
Equipment and Furnishings	25
Fire Protection	26
Flight Controls	27
Fuel	28
Hydraulic Power	29
Ice & Rain Protection	30
Instruments	31
Landing Gear	32
Lights	33
Navigation	34
Oxygen	35
Pneumatic	36
Water/ Waste	38
Airborne Auxiliary Power	49

STRUCTURES

Structures - General	51
Doors	52
Fuselage	53
Nacelles/Pylons	54
Stabilizers	55
Windows	56
Wings	57

POWERPLANT

Standard Practices - Engine	70
Power Plant	71
Engine	72
Engine Fuel & Control	73
Ignition	74
Air	75
Engine Controls	76
Engine Indicating	77
Exhaust	78
Oil	79
Starting	80
Water Injection	82

CHARTS

Charts	91

ATA SPECIFICATION 100 MAINTENANCE INFORMATION SYSTEM

Application of Standard Maintenance Manual Numbering System

The "Chapter-Section" Number: The numbering system used in the Maintenance Manual consists of a three element number separated by dashes:

First and second digits	-	System/Chapter
Third digit	-	Sub-System/ Section
Fourth digit	-	Sub-Sub-System
Fith and sixth digits	-	Unit/Subject

The following example illustrates and describes use of each element of the number:

Typical Chapter - Section - Subject Number

This number designates Chapter 52, the title of which is "Doors." (Designated by ATA 100 Spec.)

52-34-01

This number designates the section breakdown of material in Chapter 52. In this case, 3X represents "Cargo" doors. (Designated by ATA 100 Spec.)

This number designates a specific sub-subsytem within "Cargo" doors. In this case, -34 represents "Cargo" Doors (Designated by ATA 100 Spec.)

This number designates a specific component. In this case, -01 represents the rotary actuator. (Assigned by the manufacturer)

Page Number Blocks

SUBJECT	PAGE BLOCK
Description and Operation	1-100
Trouble Shooting	101-200
Servicing	301-400
Removal/ Installation	401-500
Adjustment/ Test	501-600
Inspection/ Check	601-700
Cleaning/ Painting	701-800
Approved Repairs	801-900

Figure 11-1-2. The ATA 100 numbering system takes a little getting used to. Once fully understood, finding information becomes much simpler.

June 1, 1956. From then until March 2003, the ATA 100 maintenance information numbering system prevailed. In April 2003, the ATA 100 Specification was replaced by another specification, called ATA iSPEC 2200. iSPEC 2200 consists of *ATA Spec 100 Manufacturers' Technical Data* and *ATA Spec 2100 Digital Data Standards for Aircraft Support*. The combined edition is called *ATA Specification iSpec 2200 Information Standards for Aviation Maintenance*.

Because ATA 100 has been used by most major manufacturers for more than 40 years, it will continue to be with us for some time. When manufacturers will start using iSpec 2200 remains to be seen, as does exactly what the new system will look like.

The ATA Specification 100 has the aircraft divided into systems; i.e. electrical, which covers the basic electrical system (ATA 2400). Numbering in each major system provides an arrangement for breaking the system down into several sub-systems. Late model aircraft, both over and under the 12,500 lbs gross weight dividing line, have their parts manuals and maintenance manuals arranged according to the ATA coded system (Figure 11-1-2).

Section 2
Purpose and Function of Aircraft Drawings

The exchange of ideas is essential to everyone, regardless of their vocation or position. Usually, this exchange is carried on by the oral or written word; but under some conditions the use of these alone is impractical. Industry discovered that it could not depend entirely upon written or spoken words for the exchange of ideas because misunderstanding and misinterpretation arose frequently.

Pictures were the earliest form of language used to communicate information and ideas. These pictures were drawn with lines and symbols. Drawing has since evolved along two different lines, artistic and technical. Artistic drawings use lines and forms in the creative expression of cultural things, whereas technical drawings use lines and symbols to express technical ideas and thoughts.

To express in written terms the information required to construct even a simple item would end in disaster. In the design and construction of complex items, drawings are the most accurate way to communicate the information. Each engineering field has made use of drawings. Each field uses standards in the production of drawings, but each has also evolved different symbols.

Drafting is the drawing of an engineering picture of an object. The drawing is a graphic presentation of a real thing. These pictures can be understood by anyone who knows the language of drafting. For this reason drafting is referred to as the *universal language* (see *Lines and Their Meanings*, later in this chapter).

Aircraft drawings originate in the drafting section of the engineering office. These drawings are referred to as engineering drawings. There are many types of engineering drawings. Some of these types of drawings are discussed in the following paragraphs.

Prints are copies of the original engineering drawing, and are the link between the aircraft designers, manufacturers, and the mechanics that repair and maintain the aircraft. A print is a copy of the original working drawing for an aircraft part or group of parts, or for a design of a system or group of systems. It is made by placing a tracing of the drawing over a sheet of chemically treated paper and exposing it to a strong light for a short period of time. When the exposed paper is developed, it turns blue where the light has penetrated the transparent tracing. The inked lines of the tracing, having blocked out the light, show as white lines on a blue background. Other types of sensitized paper have been developed; prints may have a white background with colored lines or a colored background with white lines.

Because copies of prints can shrink, never make a layout directly from the drawing. Use the measurements.

With the introduction of Computer Aided Design (CAD), many engineering drawings today exist only in the computer. Many advanced designs are entirely CAD-drawn from inception to production.

Types of Drawings

Working drawings may be divided into three classes: detail drawings, assembly drawings, and installation drawings. Other types of drawings include sectional drawings, exploded views, block diagrams, logic flow charts, electrical wiring diagrams, schematic diagrams, and pictorial electrical diagrams.

Detail drawing. A detail drawing supplies complete information for the construction of a single part. The drawing shows the size, shape, material, method of manufacture, dimensions, tolerances, and/or specifications for material, finishes, and heat treating. Sectional views, aux-

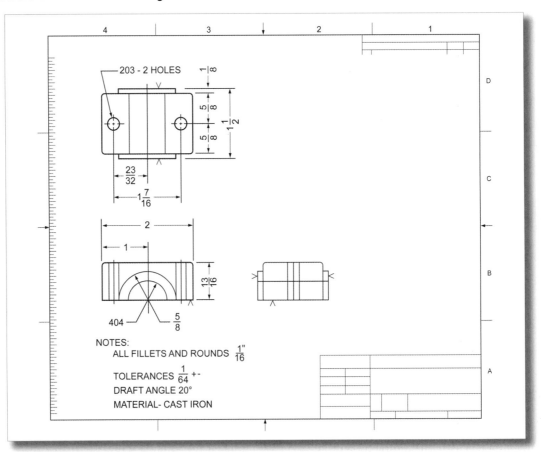

Figure 11-2-1. Single detail drawing

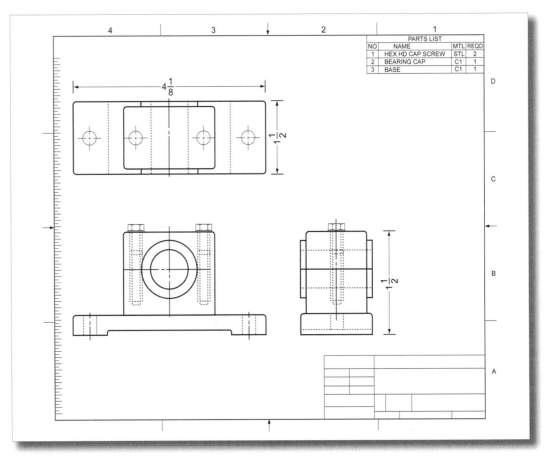

Figure 11-2-2. Assembly drawing

iliary views, or enlarged views may be added for clearer understanding. Detail drawings may be either single-detail or multi-detail drawings. The single-detail drawing, Figure 11-2-1, shows the part and perhaps one detailed view of that part that emphasizes or helps to describe size, shape, or any of the other details previously mentioned. The multi-detail drawing is essentially the same as the single detail drawing except that more than one detailed view may be used to describe or emphasize the previously mentioned details.

Assembly drawing. An assembly drawing depicts the assembled relationships between two or more parts, a combination of parts, or a group of assemblies to form a larger assembly. Assembly drawings vary in the amount and type of information given depending on what the drawing depicts. The function of an assembly drawing is to show an item in its completed shape, to indicate relationships between parts or components, and to show the part number for the parts. Assembly drawings may also show overall dimensions capacities, information for assembly, and operating instructions (Figure 11-2-2).

Installation drawing. An installation drawing shows the general arrangement of the part(s) or its/their position and the information to install the item(s). The information shown on an installation drawing is that needed to complete the installation. Depending on the type of installation, either electrical or mechanical, the information may vary. Generally, the information will give mounting directions, location and dimensions, and attaching hardware.

Sectional drawings. Sectional drawings are usually referred to as sectional views and are used to show internal detail more clearly than is possible in any other type of drawing. There are several types of view drawings available depending on what is to be shown. A cutting plane line is used to indicate what surface and where the surface is cut. The portion that is cut is indicated by the use of section lines. A viewing plane line is used to indicate what surface is being viewed and the direction from which it will be viewed.

A *full section view* indicates the object is cut or viewed as if it were cut in half (Figure 11-2-3). The cutting plane line passes completely through the object. The viewing plane line does not pass through the object.

In a *half section*, the cutting plane extends only halfway across the object, leaving the other half of the object as an exterior view. Half sections are used to advantage with symmetrical objects to show both the interior and exterior.

Exploded views. This type of drawing shows the relationship of parts and can be helpful in assembling components (Figure 11-2-4).

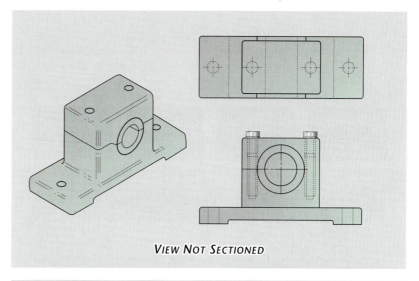
VIEW NOT SECTIONED

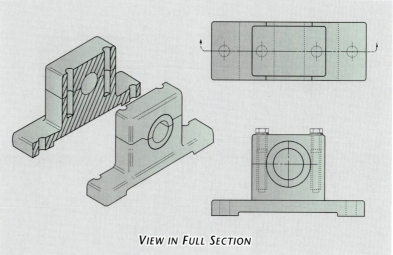
VIEW IN FULL SECTION

Figure 11-2-3. Sectional drawings

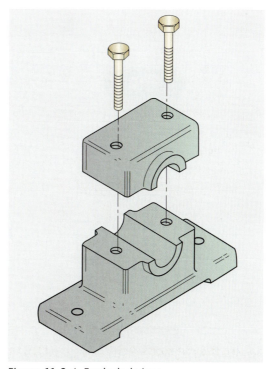

Figure 11-2-4. Exploded view

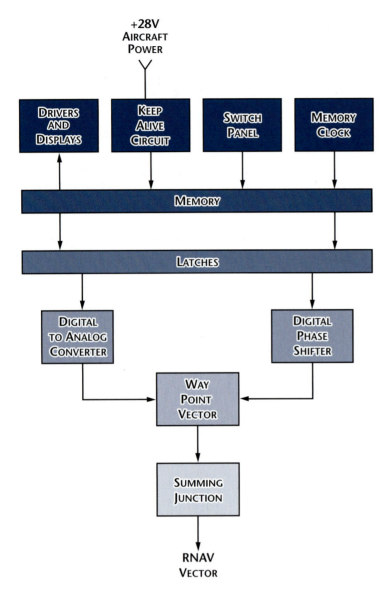

Figure 11-2-5. Block diagram

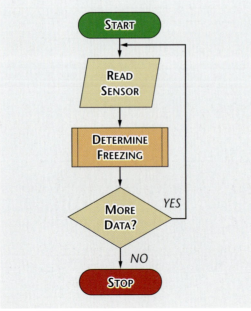

Figure 11-2-6. Logic flow chart

Exploded views are also used to illustrate parts manuals.

Block diagrams. Block diagrams are used to show the relationship and function of each item in the diagram. This type of diagram can be used in electrical, electronic, or mechanical applications. An electrical or electronic block diagram does not show electrical connections (Figure 11-2-5). Block diagrams are so called because each unit is identified by a block or square. Other types of symbols may also be used in block diagrams.

Logic flow charts. The logic flow chart represents the mechanical, electrical, or electronic action without necessarily expressing the construction or engineering information. An understanding of logic symbols is needed to interpret logic flow charts. Figure 11-2-6 shows a logic flow chart.

Electrical wiring diagram. Electrical wiring diagrams are divided into four types: single-line, schematic or elementary, connection or wiring, and interconnect. They will frequently show wire sizes.

A single-line diagram shows the path of an electrical circuit or system and components using graphic symbols as shown in Figure 11-2-7.

The connection or wiring diagram shows the general arrangement of parts and other information needed to trace or make internal or external connections (Figure 11-2-8).

The interconnect diagram shows only external connections between units (Figure 11-2-9).

Schematic diagrams, like installation diagrams, are used extensively in aircraft manuals and in the troubleshooting of aircraft systems.

Pictorial electrical diagrams. A pictorial electrical wiring diagram shows pictorial sketches of the parts and the electrical connections between them. This type of diagram can be used for learning system operation and troubleshooting. It does not show location of equipment (Figure 11-2-10).

Schematic diagrams. An electrical or electronic elementary schematic diagram indicates the electrical connection and function of electrical or electronic circuits. This type of diagram aids in the tracing, function, and troubleshooting of the circuit without regard to size, shape, or location of the components.

A mechanical schematic diagram depicts the relationship of parts, components, or flow of fluids in a system. For ease of reading and tracing the flow, each component is identified by name, and its location within the system can be ascertained by noting the lines that lead into and out of the unit.

CAD drawings. CAD software permits the user to switch between multiple drawings and diagrams within a single computer file. Composite views, which contain elements of multiple types of drawings are also available in some cases.

Methods of Illustrating Objects

The method used to illustrate an object depends on what is to be shown. Each type of drawing

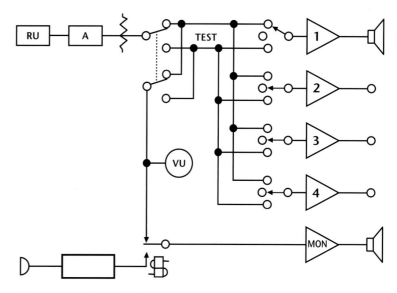

Figure 11-2-7. Single-line diagram

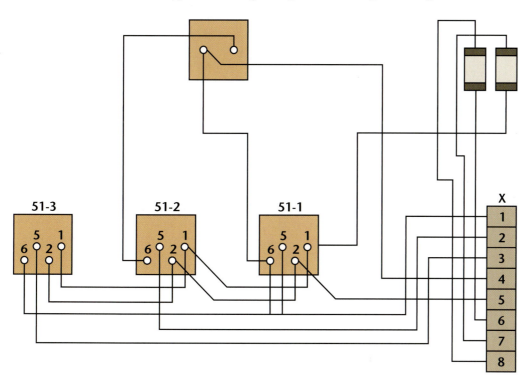

Figure 11-2-8. Connection or wiring diagram

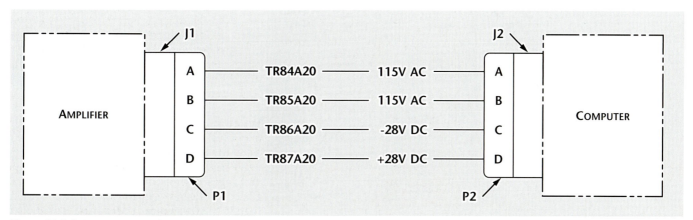

Figure 11-2-9. Interconnect diagram

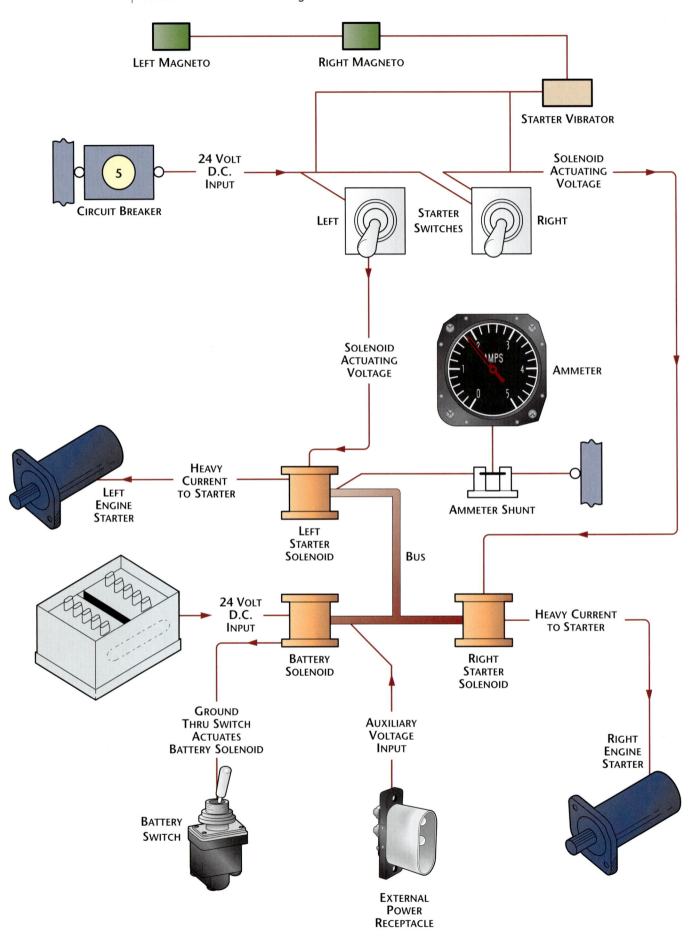

Figure 11-2-10. Pictorial electrical diagram

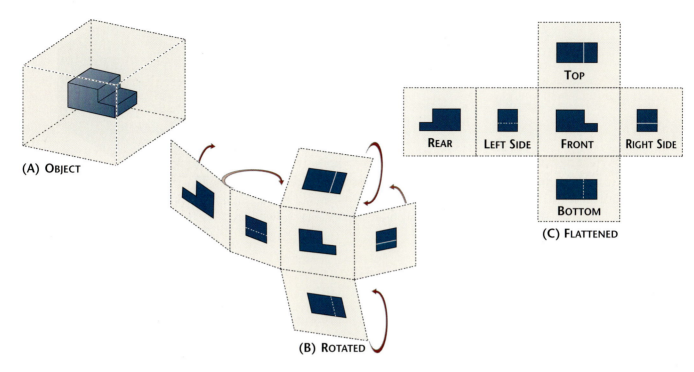

Figure 11-2-11. Orthographic projection

has advantages and disadvantages in presenting the desired information.

Orthographic projection drawings. In order to show the exact size and shape of all the parts of complex objects, a number of views are necessary. This is the system used in orthographic projection.

In orthographic projection, there are six possible views of an object because all objects have six sides front, top, bottom, rear, right side, and left side. Figure 11-2-11A shows an object placed in a transparent box, hinged at the edges. The projections on the sides of the box are the views as seen looking straight at the object through each side. If the outlines of the object are drawn on each surface and the box opened as shown in Figure 11-2-11B, then laid flat as shown in Figure 11-2-11C, the result is a six-view orthographic projection.

It is seldom necessary to show all six views to portray an object clearly; therefore, only those views necessary to illustrate the required characteristics of the object are drawn. One-view, two-view, and three-view drawings are the most common. Regardless of the number of views used, the arrangement is generally as shown in Figure 11-2-11, with the front view being the principal one. If the right-side view is shown, it will be to the right of the front view. If the left-side view is shown, it will be to the left of the front view. The top and bottom views, if included, will be shown in their respective positions relative to the front view. Should a rear view be necessary, it is customary to place it to the left of the left-hand view.

One-view drawings are commonly used for objects of uniform thickness, such as gaskets, shims, and plates. A dimensional note gives the thickness as shown in Figure 11-2-12. One-view drawings are also commonly used for cylindrical, spherical, or square parts, if all the necessary dimensions can be properly shown in one view.

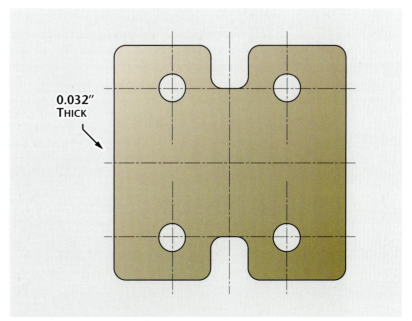

Figure 11-2-12. One-view drawing

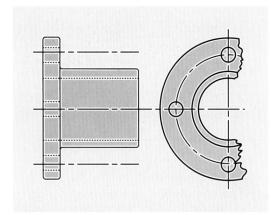

Figure 11-2-13. Symmetrical object with exterior half view

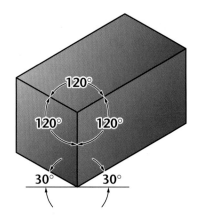

Figure 11-2-14. Isometric drawing

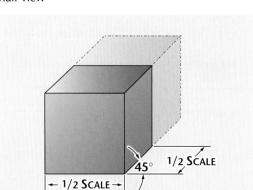

Figure 11-2-15. Cabinet drawing of a cube

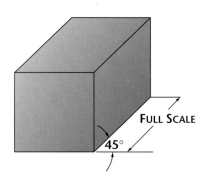

Figure 11-2-16. Cavalier oblique drawing

When space is limited and two views must be shown, symmetrical objects are often represented by half views. (Figure 11-2-13).

Isometric drawings. In an isometric drawing, all the lines that are parallel on the part being drawn are parallel on the drawing. Vertical lines on the part are shown vertical on the drawing, but horizontal lines are drawn at a 30° angle to the horizontal. This type of drawing cannot be used to express complex parts. It may be used to clarify orthographic drawings.

Unlike orthographic projection drawings which present three-dimensional objects on a flat plane with a number of views, isometric drawings present a three-dimensional object on a flat plane approximately the same way the eye views it (Figure 11-2-14). The three dimensions shown on an isometric drawing are height, width, and depth. They are also the three isometric axes and their point of intersection is called the point of origin. The angle between these axes is 120°, as shown in Figure 11-2-14. Isometric drawings show external features only.

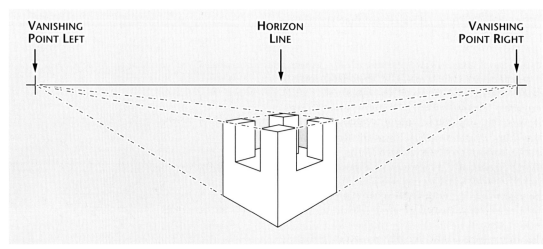

Figure 11-2-17. Perspective drawing

Oblique drawings. The front face of an oblique drawing is shown in true size and shape as if it were an orthographic drawing. The horizontal lines may be drawn at 30°, 45°, or 60° angles to the horizontal. The oblique sides are drawn to any scale to give a realistic depth.

Cabinet drawings. A cabinet drawing is a type of oblique drawing. It gets its name from drawings used for cabinet work. Cabinet drawings are drawn with the oblique side at a 30° or 45° angle to the horizontal and use 1/2 scale of the front view (Figure 11-2-15).

Cavalier drawings. The cavalier drawing uses the same scale of the front view on the oblique side lines. These lines are set at a 45° angle to the horizontal and create a distorted picture of the object's true proportions (Figure 11-2-16).

Perspective drawings. The perspective drawing is the truest representation of an object. This method of drawing allows objects to appear proportionally smaller the further the distance, just as they do when viewed.

A perspective drawing is not used in the manufacture or repair of aircraft. This type of drawing may be used effectively for technical illustrations (Figure 11-2-17).

CAD drawings. Computer Aided Design programs allow the user to select any one of many types of drawings for viewing on the computer screen or printout. They also often allow the user to freely rotate an object and obtain an isometric view or drawing from almost any angle.

Lines and Their Meanings

Every drawing is composed of lines. Lines mark the boundaries, edges, and intersections of surfaces. Lines are used to show dimensions and hidden surfaces, and to indicate centers. Obviously, if the same kind of line is used to show all of these things, a drawing becomes a meaningless collection of lines. For this reason, various kinds of standardized lines are used on aircraft drawings.

Most drawings use three widths or intensities of lines; thin, medium, or thick. These lines vary somewhat on different drawings, but there will always be a noticeable difference between a thin and thick line, with the width of the medium line somewhere between the two.

Visible lines. The visible line is used for all lines on the drawing representing visible lines on the object (Figure 11-2-18A).

Hidden lines. Hidden lines indicate invisible edges or contours. Hidden lines consist of

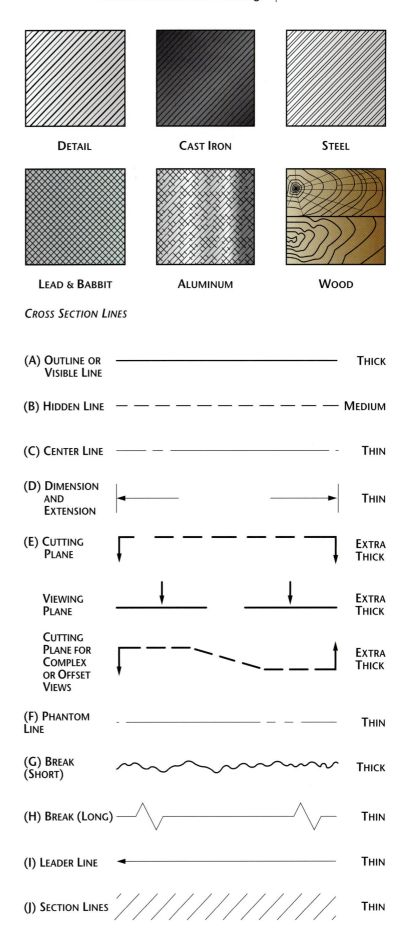

Figure 11-2-18. Lines and their meanings

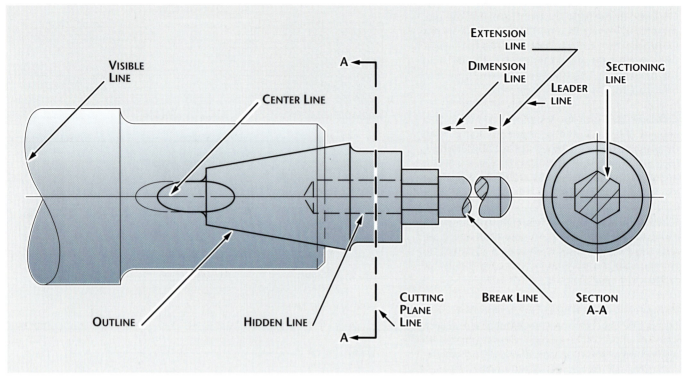

Figure 11-2-19. Correct uses of lines

short, evenly spaced dashes and are frequently referred to as dash lines (Figure 11-2-18B).

Center lines. Center lines are made up of alternate long and short dashes. They indicate the center of an object or part of an object. Where center lines cross, the short dashes intersect symmetrically. In the case of very small circles, the center lines may be shown unbroken (Figure 11-2-18C). Center lines may also be used to indicate the travel of a center and as extension lines.

Dimension lines. A dimension line (Figure 11-2-18D) is a light solid line, broken at the midpoint for insertion of measurement indications, and having opposite pointing arrowheads at each end to show origin and termination of a measurement. Dimension lines are generally parallel to the line for which the dimension is given, and are usually placed outside the outline of the object and between views if more than one view is shown. Dimension lines should not contact the outline of the object.

Extension lines. Extension lines are thin lines used to move the dimension from the surface of the object to a point where the dimension will not interfere with the other lines. Extension lines should not touch the outline of the object, but may cross object lines. They should not begin or end on object lines. See Figure 11-2-19.

Cutting plane lines. Cutting plane lines indicate the plane in which a sectional view of the object is taken. In Figure 11-2-19, plane line A-A indicates the plane in which section A-A is taken (Figure 11-2-18E).

Phantom lines. Phantom lines indicate the alternate position of parts of the object or the relative position of a missing part. Phantom lines are composed of one long and two short evenly spaced dashes (Figure 11-2-18F).

Break lines. Break lines indicate that a portion of the object is not shown on the drawing. Short breaks are made by solid, freehand lines (Figure 11-2-18G). For long breaks, solid ruled lines with zigzags are used (Figure 11-2-18H). Shafts, rods, tubes, and other such parts, which have a portion of their length broken out, have the ends of the break drawn as indicated in Figure 11-2-19.

Leader lines. Leaders are solid lines with one arrowhead and indicate a part or portion to which a note, number, or other reference applies (Figure 11-2-18I).

Sectioning lines. Sectioning lines are generally thin lines, and are sometimes referred to as cross-hatching. Section lines serve two purposes. The lines indicate the surface of an object that has been cut to make it stand out from the rest of the object. Section lines also indicate the type of material from which the object is made. Examples are shown at the top of Figure 11-2-18.

Lettering. Good lettering gives a sketch a professional look. Sloppy lettering will make a good sketch look bad. Good lettering is essential for easy reading; therefore, it is important that you develop skill in lettering. Lettering is drawn, not written, so the standard forms and strokes can be learned through practice. Fancy, ornate lettering does not belong on a technical sketch.

The proportion of one letter to another in lettering, and the order in which the strokes are drawn are as important as the shape of the individual letters. The proportion of the letters gives them style and character, and the order in which the strokes are drawn will affect the ease and rapidity of lettering.

Numbers. The legibility of numbers and fractions on technical sketches is important. If the numbers on the sketch are hard to read, the wrong information may be communicated and time and material could be wasted.

Fractions. Fractions are always drawn with horizontal division lines. This will lessen the chance of misinterpretation with other numbers. Each figure is two-thirds the height of a whole number. To prevent the figures of a fraction from blending with the horizontal line when drawing fractions, leave space above and below the line. Lightly draw in the guide lines and erase them when you complete each set.

Dimensioning

Tolerance. Tolerance is the acceptable variation from the specific dimension given on a print or drawing. A tolerance is usually given in three decimals (0.010). The tolerance may be shown by one of the following ways:

- As a specific tolerance for a specified dimension.
- As a general tolerance note that indicates the tolerance for all dimensions not covered by specific tolerances. (This tolerance is usually found in the title block). Tolerances are shown on prints or drawings in two different ways: either by limit dimensioning or by plus and minus dimensioning.
- In limit dimensioning, Figure 11-2-20, the higher limit is placed above the lower limit. If the tolerance is expressed on a single line, the lower limit is expressed first, followed by the higher limit. A dash will separate the two limits.
- Plus and minus dimensioning indicates the specific size dimension followed by the plus (high limit) and the minus (low limit). The plus limit is shown above the minus limit as shown in Figure 11-2-21.

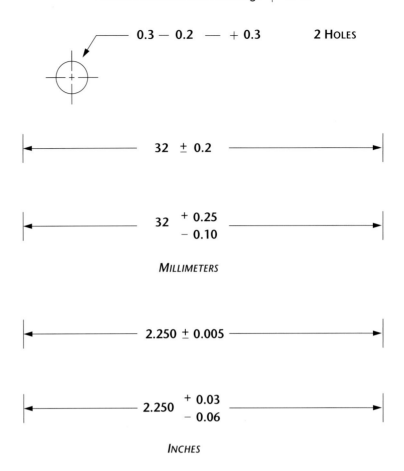

Figure 11-2-20. Bilateral tolerancing

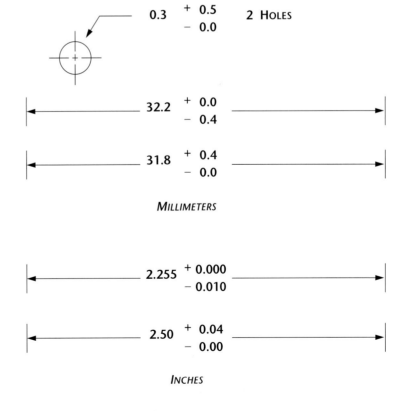

Figure 11-2-21. Unilateral tolerancing

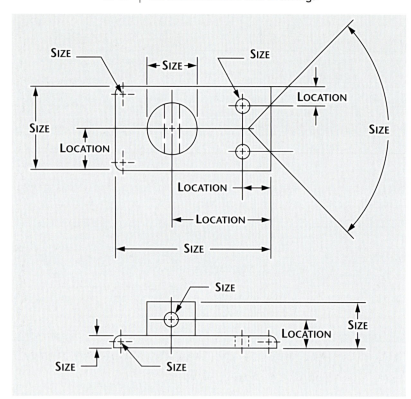

Figure 11-2-22. Size and location of dimension

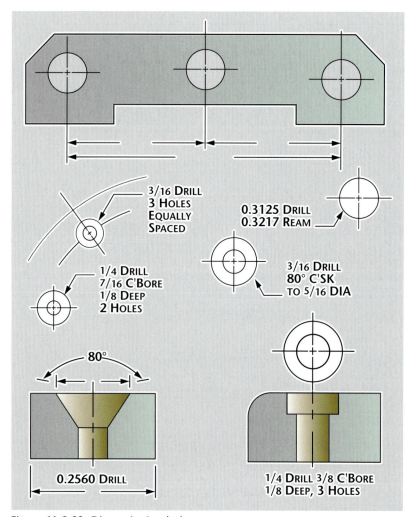

Figure 11-2-23. Dimensioning holes

- Plus and minus tolerancing may be expressed as either bilateral or unilateral tolerances.
- In bilateral tolerancing, the plus and minus limits are generally equal, but designs may dictate unequal values as shown in Figure 11-2-20.
- Unilateral tolerancing is used when only a high or low limit of a tolerance is used, Figure 11-2-21.

Dimension lines. Dimensioning on a drawing or print is indicated by the use of extension lines, leader lines, dimension lines, figures, notes, or symbols. Dimensions on a drawing indicate length, angles, diameters, radius, or locations (Figure 11-2-22).

In dimensioning distances between holes in an object, dimensions are usually given from center to center rather than from outside to outside of the holes. When a number of holes of various sizes are shown, the desired diameters are given on a leader followed by notes indicating the machining operations for each hole. If a part is to have three holes of equal size, equally spaced, this information is given. For precision work, sizes are given in decimals. Diameters and depths are given for counterbored holes. For countersunk holes, the angle of countersinking and the diameters are given. Study the examples shown in Figure 11-2-23.

The dimensions given for fits signify the amount of clearance allowed between moving parts. A positive allowance is indicated for a part that is to slide or revolve upon another part. A negative allowance is one given for a force fit. Whenever possible, the tolerance and allowances for desired fits conform to those set up in the *American Standard for Tolerances, Allowances, and Gages for Metal Fits*. The classes of fits specified in the standard may be indicated on assembly drawings.

Aircraft Production Drawings

From the manufacturing design of an aircraft or part to the assembly, installation, and repair will require several types of engineering drawings. The engineering drawing is a document that pictorially shows the physical shape, function, or other information the designer wants to present.

To show all these requirements, it will normally take a number of different types of engineering drawings. As a rule, the combination of detail, assembly, installation, and diagrammatic drawings will provide the necessary information for a mechanic to complete the job. *Diagrammatic* is the description for usage of various diagrams. It is plural and refers to no specific diagram, but any diagrams that may be required (used). The format for engineering drawings is shown in Figure 11-2-24.

Title blocks. Every print must have some means of identification. This is provided by a title block (Figure 11-2-25). The title block consists of a drawing number and certain other data concerning the drawing and the object it represents. This information is grouped in a prominent place on the print, usually in the lower right-hand corner. Sometimes the title block is in the form of a strip extending almost the entire distance across the bottom of the sheet.

Although title blocks do not follow a standard form insofar as layout is concerned, all of them will present essentially the following information:

- A drawing number to identify the print for filing purposes and to prevent confusing it with any other print.
- The name of the part or assembly
- The scale to which it is drawn
- The date
- The name of the firm
- The name of the draftsperson, the checker and the person approving the drawing

Size. The universal numbering system provides a means of identifying standard drawing sizes. In the universal numbering system, each drawing number consists of six or seven digits. The first digit is always A, B, C, D, E or J (Figure 11-2-26), and indicates the size of the drawing. The remaining digits identify the drawing.

Many firms have modified this basic system to conform to their particular needs. Letters may be used instead of numbers. The letter or number depicting the standard drawing size may be prefixed to the number, separated from it by a dash. Other numbering systems provide a separate box preceding the drawing number for the drawing size identifier. In other modifications of this system, the part number of the depicted assembly is assigned as the drawing number.

Drawing numbers. All prints are identified by a number that appears in a number block in the lower right-hand corner of the title block. It may also be shown in other places, such as near the top border line in the upper right-hand corner or on the reverse side of the print at both ends, so that the number will show when the print is folded or rolled. The purpose of the number is for quick identification of a print.

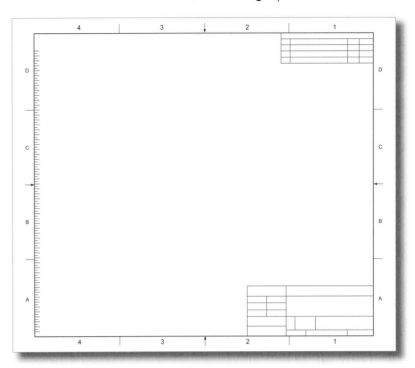

Figure 11-2-24. Engineering drawing format

Figure 11-2-25. Title block

Size	A	B	C	J
Length	11"	17"	22"	Indefinite (Roll)
Width	8½	11"	27"	17, 22, 25, 50, 34, and 36 Inches

Figure 11-2-26. Standard blueprint paper sizes

If a print has more than one sheet and each sheet has the same number, this information is included in the number block, indicating the sheet number and the number of sheets in the series.

Reference numbers that appear in the title block refer a person to the numbers of other prints. When more than one detail is shown on a drawing, dash numbers are used. Both parts would have the same drawing number plus an individual number, such as 40267-1 and 40267-2.

BILL OF MATERIALS			
ITEM	PART NO.	REQUIRED	SOURCE
CONNECTOR	UG-21 D/U	2	STOCK

Figure 11-2-27. A typical bill of materials

In addition to appearing in the title block, dash numbers may appear on the face of the drawing near the parts they identify. Dash numbers are also used to identify right-hand and left-hand parts shown in the drawing. The right-hand part is called for in the title block. Above the title block will be found a notation such as "470204-1LH shown, 470204-2RH opposite". Both parts carry the same number, but the part called for is distinguished by a dash number. Some prints have odd numbers for left-hand parts and even numbers for right-hand parts.

Scale. The scale that is printed on the blueprint indicates the size of the part on the drawing as compared to the size of the actual part.

A scale may be indicated as 1 inch equals 2 inches; 1 inch equals 12 inches; 3/8 inch equals 1 foot, or full size, one-half size, or one-quarter size. The scale *1 inch = 2 inches* indicates that a 1-inch line on the drawing is actually 2 inches on the object. When the scale is shown as *3 inches = 1 inch*, the line on the drawing is 3 inches long and the line on the object is 1 inch long. This type of scale would be used when drawing a very small object.

Never measure a drawing and use that dimension because the drawing may have been enlarged or reduced.

Page. The title block contains a place to number the pages of a drawing. If a drawing has more than one page, it will be indicated by 1 of 3 on the first page, 2 of 3 on the second page, and 3 of 3 on the third page. When drawings are in book form, this number may be used to indicate the page number of the book.

Responsibility. Within the title block is a space for the date and initials or signatures of the designer, draftsperson, checker, and supervisor. Each drawing may not have all of these positions, but each drawing will indicate the responsibility for the drawing.

Standards. There are standards by which all drawings are made. The purpose of these standards is for the uniformity of drawings among the manufacturers. The standards deal with all aspects of the drawing. These standards are set by organizations with an interest in producing uniform meaning of the information presented on the drawings.

Some of the organizations that set standards for drawings are the Department of Defense (DOD), Society of Automotive Engineers (SAE), American Welding Society (AWS), and the American National Standards Institute (ANSI).

Bill of materials. A list of the materials and parts necessary for the fabrication or assembly of a component or system is often included on the drawing. The list usually will be in ruled columns in which are listed the part number, name of the part, material from which the part is to be constructed, the quantity required, and the source of the part or material. A typical bill of materials is shown in Figure 11-2-27. On drawings that do not have a bill of materials, the data may be indicated directly on the drawing.

On assembly drawings, each item is identified by a number in a circle or square. An arrow connecting the number with the item assists in locating it in the bill of materials.

Revision block. Revisions to a drawing are necessitated by changes in dimensions, design, or materials. The changes are usually listed in ruled columns either adjacent to the title block or at one corner of the drawing. All changes to approved drawings must be carefully noted on all existing prints of the drawing.

When drawings contain such corrections, attention is directed to the changes by lettering or numbering them and listing those changes against the symbol in a revision block (Figure 11-2-28). The revision block contains the identification symbol, the date, the nature of the revision, the authority for the change, and the name of the draftsperson who made the change.

To distinguish the corrected drawing from its previous version, many firms are including, as part of the title block, a space for entering the appropriate symbol to designate that the drawing has been changed or revised.

Zone numbers. Zone numbers on drawings are similar to the numbers and letters printed on the borders of a map. They are there to help locate a particular point. To find a point, mentally draw horizontal and vertical lines from the letters and numerals specified; the point where these lines would intersect is the area sought.

Use the same method to locate parts, sections, or views on large drawings, particularly assembly drawings. Parts numbered in the title block can be located on the drawing by finding the numbers in squares along the lower border. Zone numbers read from right to left.

Station numbers. A numbering system is used in the design and manufacture of aircraft in order to identify any given point within the aircraft to within one cubic inch. This system utilizes fuselage stations, waterlines, buttock lines (commonly called butt lines), and wing stations. While each is described in detail in the following paragraphs, each one consists of a set of imaginary lines placed one inch apart, parallel to each other, and measured from a 0, or reference datum line. In addition to using this station numbering system on drawings and in the design and manufacture of aircraft, once produced, the weight and balance of the aircraft is determined by utilizing these imaginary lines.

Fuselage stations. Fuselage stations (FS) are indicated in inches from the datum as set by the engineer. The datum can be at the nose of the aircraft, in front of the aircraft, aft of the nose of the aircraft, or any place the engineer designates. If the datum is aft of the nose of the aircraft, any station towards the nose of the aircraft will be a negative fuselage station. This will be indicated by a minus sign in front of the fuselage station number. For example, FS-15 indicates the station is 15 inches in front of the fuselage datum. When no sign precedes a number, it is positive and indicates that the fuselage station is between the fuselage datum and the tail of the aircraft.

Waterline stations. Waterline stations (WL) indicate, in inches, the vertical distance from the waterline datum to a location on the aircraft. The waterline datum has no set location. This datum may be a point above the ground, the ground itself, or below the ground. If the location of the datum allows any part of the aircraft to fall below the datum, those waterline stations will be negative.

2	CHANGED PART NO. 5	E.O.1	05/02/06	B.K.
1	REVISED DIMENSIONS	J.L.M.	07/01/06	E.K.P.
NO.	REVISION	AUTH.	DATE	SIGN

Figure 11-2-28. Revision block

Buttock line stations. Buttock line (BL) stations are measured in inches from the centerline of the aircraft. This is the only datum that is the same on all aircraft. Buttock line stations are measured to the left and right of the datum looking forward. This is indicated by right buttock line (RBL) and left buttock line (LBL). The right buttock line is given a positive value from 0 (zero) and the left buttock line is given a negative value from 0 (zero).

Some manufacturers use buttock line stations to indicate positions on the wings. Other manufacturers use wing stations.

Wing stations. Wing stations (WS) are measured in inches from the datum, which is the centerline of the aircraft. The wing stations are indicated by left or right. LWS indicates a left-wing station and RWS would indicate a right-wing station. When wing stations and buttock stations are used together, be careful not to confuse the numbers. Wing stations indicate positions on the wing structure only, not positions on the fuselage.

Aircraft Safety

Section 1
Shop Safety

Avionics technicians devote a portion of their aviation career to ground handling aircraft and working with ground-support equipment. The complexity of support equipment and the hazards involved in the ground handling of expensive aircraft require that technicians possess a detailed knowledge of safe procedures to be used in aircraft servicing, taxiing and run-up, and in the use of ground-support equipment. The information provided in this is intended as a general guide for working around all types of aircraft.

Good housekeeping in hangars, in shops and on the flightline is essential to safety and efficient maintenance. The highest standards of orderly work arrangements and cleanliness should be observed during the maintenance of aircraft.

Where continuous work shifts are established, the outgoing shift should remove and properly store personal tools, rollaway boxes, all workstands, maintenance stands, hoses, electrical cords, hoists, crates and boxes that are superfluous to the work to be accomplished.

Signs should be posted to indicate dangerous equipment or hazardous conditions. Signs also provide information on the location of first-aid, fire equipment, exits and other information.

Safety lanes, pedestrian walkways or fire lanes should be painted around the perimeter inside the hangars. This should be done as a safety measure to prevent accidents and to keep pedestrian traffic out of work areas.

Learning Objective

DESCRIBE
- ways to make a shop safer
- types of fires and how to extinguish them

EXPLAIN
- the contents of a Material Safety Data Sheet
- flightline safety precautions

APPLY
- work safely with electricity
- work safely with compressed gasses

Left. A lineman guides a corporate jet into a parking place. Notice the hearing protectors, which are always necessary on the flight line.

Photo courtesy of National Business Aviation Association

GLASS BEADS PART 6700

OSHA regulations require that a Material Safety Data Sheet be available for all users. Material Safety Data Sheets are included with each box of our abrasive. Included with most Skat Blast Cabinets is a small supply of Glass Beads for initial start-up. This is the Material Safety Data Sheet for our Part No. 6700 Glass Beads.

Material Safety Data Sheet

Occupational Safety and Health Administration

PART NO. 6700 — GLASS BEADS — Revised 9-14-98

WARNING: Glass Beads, if spilled on the floor, are as slippery as ice. Sweep up spills promptly.

SECTION I

DISTRIBUTOR NAME:	Distributor---Skat Blast, Inc.
EMERGENCY PHONE NO.	(330) 533-9477
ADDRESS:	7077 State Rt. 446, Canfield, OH 44406
CHEMICAL NAME AND SYNONYMS	Glass (CAS Number 65997-17-3)
TRADE NAME AND SYNONYMS	GLASS BEADS
CHEMICAL FAMILY	GLASS, SODA-LIME TYPE
FORMULA	Sodium Aluminum Silicate base Glass

SECTION II - HAZARDOUS INGREDIENTS

	OSHA-PEL	ACGIH-TLV	
NUISANCE DUST	15mg/m^3	10mg/m^3	ALLOYS AND METALLIC COATINGS
NUISANCE DUST - RESPIRABLE	5mg/m^3	5mg/m^3	N/A

CONTAINS NO FREE SILICA - All components are amorphous and non-crystalline; none are SARA Title III reportable.
NUISANCE DUST - to the best of our knowledge, this material is non-hazardous as per OSHA 29 CFR 1910.1200.

SECTION III - PHYSICAL DATA

BOILING POINT (C)	MELTING POINT (C)	SPECIFIC GRAVITY (@ 60 degrees F)	
N/A	Above 1100°F		2.4-2.6g/cm^3
VAPOR PRESSURE (mm Hg)	N/A	PERCENT SOLID BY WEIGHT	N/A
VAPOR DENSITY (Air = 1)	N/A	EVAPORATION RATE	N/A
SOLUBILITY IN WATER	None	APPEARANCE AND COLOR	White, odorless, tasteless powder.

SECTION IV - FIRE AND EXPLOSION HAZARD DATA

Flash Point (Method Used): None. Flammable Limits: None. Extinguishing Media: Does not burn. Water - avoid creating dust.
Materials to avoid - (Incapability) Concentrated Hydrofluoric Acid, fluosilicic, phosphoric acids, and hot, strong alkaline solutions.

SECTION V - HEALTH HAZARD DATA

ROUTES OF ENTRY	CARCINOGENICITY - This product is not listed as a potential carcinogen
Inhalation, Ingestion	in either the NIP, IARC, or OSHA.

HEALTH HAZARD - Repeated or prolonged inhalation of dust in excess of permissible exposure limits may result in irritation to the respiratory tract.
OVEREXPOSURE - Can aggravate existing respiratory conditions and eye irritation.

EMERGENCY AND FIRST AID PROCEDURE:
Eye Contact: Flush with running water for 15 min. If irritation or redness persists, see a physician. Skin Contact: Wash area well with soap and water. Ingestion: Seek medical help if large quantities of material have been ingested.

SECTION VI - REACTIVITY DATA

STABILITY		CONDITIONS TO AVOID
Stable.	Hazardous Polymerization - Will not occur	Excessive dust, slippery if spilled

HAZARDOUS DECOMPOSITION PRODUCTS
None   Glass Beads will break down into progressively smaller particles during normal use.

SECTION VII - SPILL OR LEAK PROCEDURES

STEPS TO BE TAKEN IN CASE MATERIAL IS RELEASED OR SPILLED. Considered as non-hazardous per EPA 29CFR1910.1200.
Sweep from floor to prevent slipping hazard. Wear NIOSH-approved respirator. If respiratory aggravation, go to a well-ventilated area.

WASTE DISPOSAL METHOD
Collected dust from blast cleaning or shot peening operations always contain contaminates from the surface of the parts being processed; and, therefore, the dust may be classed as a hazardous waste and, as such, must be disposed of according to appropriate Local, State, or Federal regulations. The RCRA status of UNUSED material is non-hazardous, according to the list of CERCLA chemicals.

SECTION VIII - SPECIAL PROTECTION INFORMATION

RESPIRATORY PROTECTION (SPECIFY TYPE)   Use NIOSH/OSHA-approved respiratory equipment. Positive pressure air-supplied type recommended. If beads or dust cause eye irritation, flush eye(s) with water or eye wash.

VENTILATION	LOCAL EXHAUST	Follow OSHA standards; use adequate dust collecting system to remove suspended particulate from equipment and ambient environment.
N/A		

MECHANICAL (GENERAL)	OTHER
As required for nuisance dust.	Provide eyewash station in the area.
PROTECTIVE GLOVES	EYE PROTECTION
As required per job.	Normal for dust---use safety goggles.

OTHER PROTECTIVE EQUIPMENT
If blasting, use appropriate protective clothing, air-supplied hood/respirator & other safety equipment.

SECTION IX - SPECIAL PRECAUTIONS

PRECAUTIONS TO BE TAKEN IN HANDLING AND STORING
Observe maximum floor loading and stacking limitations due to density of product.

OTHER PRECAUTIONS
Keep dry. Store material away from incompatible materials. Avoid generating dust.
The company has no control over this product or its use after it leaves our facility. The company assumes no liability for loss or damage from the proper or improper use of this product. The information presented here has been compiled from sources considered to be reliable and accurate to the best of our knowledge and belief, but is not guaranteed to be so. Revision Date, September 14, 1998.

Rev 3/28/00

Figure 12-1-1. This MSDS represents the information for the basic product

Safety is everyone's business, and communication is key to ensuring everyone's safety. Technicians and supervisors should watch for their own safety and for the safety of others working around them. If someone else is conducting themselves in an unsafe manner, communicate with them, and remind them of their safety and that of others around them.

Material Safety Data Sheets

It is every employer's responsibility to teach employees about the *Hazard Communication Standard*. The Hazard Communication Standard (HCS) is a uniform standard to communicate workplace hazards. It clearly spells out what specific information has to be communicated and how it must be communicated. The Hazard Communication Standard is an *Occupational Safety and Health Administration* (OSHA) requirement to cover handling of workplace chemicals. It addresses both health and safety issues. The standard is a *Right to Know* requirement for potential chemical hazards. It says that everyone handling chemicals needs to know how to protect themselves. This is a federal standard however; there may also be state and local Right to Know laws that must be followed as well.

We are often exposed to chemicals. Improper handling of some of these chemicals is dangerous and could result in illness, injury or incapacitation. The effects may be either external, like burns and rashes, or internal such as nausea or organ damage. Chemicals generally enter the body through the skin, nose, mouth or eyes.

The *Hazard Communication Standard* requires employers to develop, implement and continuously maintain a documented program for the instruction of employees. The written program has to list all the hazardous chemicals used in each specific work area, and explain how to handle them. There has to be information on how to read and understand *Material Safety Data Sheets* (MSDS) and chemical labels. The written methods program must include both how to observe and how to detect a release or presence of hazardous chemicals in the workplace. The last element of the written program is to provide for training of new employees and a means to inform non-employees — either visitors or vendors — about the specific hazardous chemicals handled in each work area.

When any chemical is made or distributed, its potential hazards must be determined. Manufacturers, importers and distributors are required by law to assess the extent of this potential hazard and make this information easily accessible through MSDS. For each chemical used in the workplace, it is the employer's task to make readily available the MSDS and to tell everyone where the MSDS are in your facility. Anyone using a chemical also has to take responsibility for knowing how to read labels, understanding MSDS, handling chemicals with all necessary precautions and knowing what to do if a particular chemical is spilled or comes into contact with someone's skin. An MSDS tells how the chemical would enter the body and gives *emergency first aid procedures*.

The MSDS serves as the vehicle to inform everyone of safety procedures, emergency response opt-ions, chemical components and dangers. The MSDS will generally have the chemical name, its trade name and often even the formula. Addresses and emergency numbers are provided. A sample MSDS is shown in Figure 12-1-1.

Physical data. A material's physical data listing could include: percentage of volatile components, odor, appearance, boiling point, specific gravity, vapor pressure, density, evaporation rate and solubility in water. Also included is information regarding the stability of the chemical, how it reacts and extent of reaction with other chemicals and compounds, along with ways to prevent an unexpected and unwanted chemical reaction.

MSDSs also include information on fire prevention and extinguishing.

Explosion and fire data. This provides information on which fire extinguishers to use and their media, the temperature at which the chemical ignites (flashpoint), any unusual fire hazards and special fire-fighting procedures, any unusual or special dangers, and chemical flammability limits by volume. Any *spill or leak procedure* or process will be identified. All equipment needed in clean-up, and any special precautions, including methods for disposal, will be clearly defined. Also, any *special precautions for handling* will be listed. Safe handling of hazardous chemicals may require protective clothing, gloves, respirators, eye protection and ventilation requirements. Some chemicals require *special storage precautions*, like refrigeration and explosion-proof cabinets.

The *Hazard Communication Standard* also requires that all containers that are used in a work area be labeled with special precautions identified with either words or descriptive symbols. The one exception is a portable container for immediate use by the person transferring the chemical. Everyone must have training in reading the labels and understanding what they mean. The label should identify the chemical, hazard severity, health hazards and any needed protective clothing or equipment. The most common label is illustrated in Figure 12-1-2. In some areas the sign must be placed on the entry doors to indicate what is located inside the building.

Understanding the meaning of labels can prevent serious accidents. Investigate all chemicals that lack labels. Always follow the directions and precautions to ensure safe handling of all chemicals. Don't mix chemicals that you have not positively identified. The end result may be a big, unpleasant surprise. Following instructions and warnings will prevent accidents that could ruin your day.

Hazardous Liquids and Cleaning Solvents

Avionics technicians periodically work with hazardous liquids including acetone, MEK, cleaning products and other solvents. Only nonvolatile solvents should be used to clean electrical or electronic apparatus.

Many cleaning solvents are capable of damaging the human respiratory system, particularly in cases of prolonged exposure. Always follow an employer's policies and procedures. Typical requirements include:

- Do not work alone in a poorly ventilated compartment.
- Do not breathe the vapor of a cleaning solvent.
- Do not spray cleaning solvents on electrical windings or insulation.
- Do not apply solvents to warm or hot equipment. This increases the toxicity hazard.
- Use a blower or other positive pressure ventilating system to provide fresh air to a compartment where cleaning solvent is being used.
- Open all windows, doors and other ventilation sources.
- Keep a fire extinguisher in a readily accessible location.
- Use protective gloves, made of a material other than latex, to prevent direct skin contact with solvents.
- Use goggles when solvent is being sprayed.
- Keep the nozzle close to the object being sprayed to prevent excessive amounts of solvent in the atmosphere.

Common liquids and cleaning materials the avionics technician will work with include:

Safety solvent. Safety solvent is used for general cleaning and grease removal from assembled and disassembled engine components in addition to spot cleaning. It should not be used on painted surfaces. Safety solvent is not suitable for oxygen systems, although it may be used for other cleaning in ultrasonic cleaning devices. It may be applied by wiping, scrubbing, or booth spraying. The term safety solvent is derived from its high flash point.

Methyl ethyl ketone (MEK). MEK is used as a cleaner for bare metal surfaces and areas where sealants are removed. Normally, MEK is applied over small areas using wiping cloths or soft bristle brushes.

> **CAUTION:** *Avoid prolonged breathing and skin contact. MEK should be used only in well ventilated spaces. Extreme care should be used when working around transparent plastics as MEK will damage them upon contact.*

Acetone. Acetone is an organic solvent. It is colorless, volatile and extremely flammable. It is commonly found in paints and polyester resins.

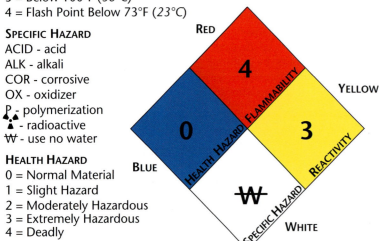

NFPA
- This label is for emergency response and fire fighters.
- Hazard rating is from 0 (no hazard) to 4 (extreme).

FLAMMABILITY (FLASH POINTS)
0 = Will not burn
1 = Above 200°F (93°C)
2 = Between 100 - 200°F (38°-93°C)
3 = Below 100°F (38°C)
4 = Flash Point Below 73°F (23°C)

SPECIFIC HAZARD
ACID - acid
ALK - alkali
COR - corrosive
OX - oxidizer
P - polymerization
☢ - radioactive
W - use no water

HEALTH HAZARD
0 = Normal Material
1 = Slight Hazard
2 = Moderately Hazardous
3 = Extremely Hazardous
4 = Deadly

REACTIVITY
0 = Stable
1 = Unstable if heated
2 = Violent Chemical Change
3 = Shock or heat may detonate
4 = Rapidly capable of detonation or Explosion

Figure 12-1-2. The hazard communication label illustrated is used on all commercial items.

Sodium bicarbonate. Sodium bicarbonate is used as a neutralizing agent on sulfuric acid battery electrolyte deposits.

Sodium bicarbonate may also be used to neutralize urine deposits. It is applied with a sponge using a mixture of 8 ounces of sodium bicarbonate to 1 gallon of fresh water. The area is then flushed with fresh water.

Sodium phosphate. Sodium phosphate is used to neutralize electrolyte spills from nickel cadmium batteries.

Hazardous Materials Disposal

Hazardous materials have specific disposal requirements. Hazardous materials that are no longer needed become hazardous waste. Every employer must follow national, state and local rules for the handling of hazardous waste. In the United States, the Environmental Protection Agency (EPA) has the authority to control hazardous waste, including its generation, transportation, treatment, storage and disposal.

There are very specific rules for handling any materials that can be hazardous or toxic to human health or to the environment. Always follow local and federal laws and any additional employer requirements. Typical requirements include:

- Never pour hazardous materials down the drain. They can enter the water supply, threatening human health. Some materials cause damage to water treatment facilities.

- Never pour hazardous waste down a storm drain. Storm drains often lead directly to a lake, stream, or other body of water. The hazardous waste could contaminate those bodies of water and harm wildlife. They could also be reintroduced into the drinking water supply.

- Store all solvent waste, oily rags and flammable liquids in covered, fire resistant containers. There are specific removal and transportation requirements for these materials. Make sure they are processed by a company licensed and certified in proper disposal. Additionally, always obtain documentation from the company to verify that they have properly handled the material.

Radio Frequency Radiation Hazards

Unlike nuclear radiation, radio frequency (RF) energy does not break down atoms. As a result, radio waves are considered non-ionizing radiation, but they still contain high levels of radio energy that can heat living tissue and cause damage. Radio energy in the microwave spectrum are some of the most harmful to humans. High levels of radiation can cause skin burns, cataracts and internal burns.

A technician exposed to high levels of radio wave radiation for a long period of time may suffer heat exhaustion or heat stroke. If the technician is working in close proximity to a radiating element, such as an antenna, then electrical shock is also possible. Radar systems radiate energy at incredibly high power levels for very short periods of time. As a result, the technician may not feel any sensation as the damage is occurring.

Limits for RF energy are published by The Occupational Safety and Health Administration (OSHA). At frequencies between 10 MHz and 100 GHz, OSHA recommends a maximum permissible exposure limit (PEL) of 10 mW per square centimeter of body surface averaged over a six minute period of time. In addition, weather radar manuals contain information regarding the minimum safe distance a technician must stay from a radiating radar antenna. Weather radar systems can also induce arcs and sparks in metal structures; therefore, they should never be operated in the hangar or around other aircraft or ground vehicles.

Typically, radar is turned off while an aircraft is on the ground. The avionics technician may need to power up the radar to service it, however, in which case, caution must be taken to protect him or herself and others.

EMF Hazards

EMF hazards refer to danger resulting from close proximity to high voltage or electromotive force. On occasion, avionics technicians may work in close proximity to exposed circuits energized with high voltages. When near such circuits, the technician must use extreme care to ensure he or she is not grounded. Do not stand on a wet surface, keep metal tools away from the energized circuit and work with one hand. The other hand should be placed in a pocket to avoid grounding the circuit through the chest cavity. If at all possible, such circuits should be de-energized prior to performing any work.

Compressed Gas Safety

Compressed air, like electricity, is an excellent tool, as long as it is kept under control.

The following DOs and DON'Ts apply when working with or around compressed gases:

- Air hoses should be inspected frequently for breaks and worn spots. Unsafe hose should be replaced immediately.
- All connections should be kept in a no-leak condition.
- In-line oilers, if installed, should be maintained in operating condition.
- The system should have water sumps installed and should be drained at regular intervals.
- Air used for paint spraying should be filtered to remove oil and water.
- Never use compressed air to clean hands or clothing. Pressure can force debris into the flesh, leading to infection.
- Never horseplay with compressed air.
- Air hoses should be straightened, coiled and properly stored when not in use.

Electrical Safety

Physiological safety. Working on or with electrical equipment poses some physiological safety hazards. It is known that when electricity is applied to the human body, it can create severe burns in the areas where it enters and exits the body. In addition, the nervous system is affected, and can be damaged or destroyed.

To safely deal with electricity, the technician must have knowledge of the principles of electricity, and a healthy respect for its capability to do both work and damage.

Wearing or use of proper safety equipment can give a psychological reassurance, while at the same time physically protecting the user. Rubber gloves, safety glasses, rubber or grounded safety mats and other safety equipment can all be used to contribute to the physiological safety of the technician working on or with electrical equipment.

Two factors that affect safety when working with or around electricity are fear and overconfidence. While a certain amount of fear is healthy and a certain level of confidence is necessary, extremes of either can be deadly.

Fear is often born of a lack of knowledge. Those who try to work on electrical equipment with no knowledge of its principles or a lack of confidence in their work, are often fearful of it. Overconfidence leads to risk-taking. The technician who does not respect electricity's capabilities will, sooner or later, become a victim of electricity's awesome power.

Electrical fire safety. Anytime current flows, whether during generation or transmission, a byproduct of that flow is heat. The greater the current flow, the greater the amount of heat created. When this heat becomes too great, protective coatings on wiring and other electrical devices can melt, causing shorting, which leads to more current flow and greater heat. This heat can become so great that metals can melt, liquids vaporize and flammable substances ignite.

The single most important factor in preventing electrical fires is to keep the area around electrical work or electrical equipment clean, uncluttered and free of all unnecessary flammable substances.

Ensure that all power cords, wires and lines are free of kinks and bends, which can damage the wire. When several wires inside a power cord are broken, it causes the current passing through the remaining wires to increase. This generates more heat than the insulation coatings on the wire are designed to withstand, and can lead to a fire.

Lockout/tagout. Lockout/tagout refers to specific practices and procedures to safeguard employees from the unexpected startup of machinery and equipment during service or maintenance activities.

This process requires, in part, that a designated individual turn off and disconnect the machinery or equipment from its energy source before performing service or maintenance.

Lockout devices hold energy-isolation devices in a safe or "off" position. They provide protection by preventing machines or equipment from becoming energized, because they are positive restraints that no one can remove without a key or other unlocking mechanism or through extraordinary means, such as bolt cutters.

Tagout devices, by contrast, are prominent warning devices that an authorized employee fastens to energy-isolating devices to warn employees not to re-energize the machine while he or she services or maintains it.

Tagout devices are easier to remove and, by themselves, provide less protection than do lockout devices.

Employees can be seriously or fatally injured if machinery they service or maintain unexpectedly energizes, starts up or releases stored energy.

OSHA's standard on the Control of Hazardous Energy (Lockout/Tagout), spells out the steps employers must take to prevent accidents associated with hazardous energy. The standard addresses practices and procedures necessary to disable machinery and prevent the release of potentially hazardous energy while maintenance or servicing activities are performed.

Electrical Power Safety

Working on Energized Circuits

When possible, do not work on energized circuits or equipment. Unless authorized by an employer's policies and specifically directed not to do so, always de-energize equipment prior to conducting any maintenance or repair. Follow an employer's safety policies when working on energized equipment. These typically include at least the following:

- Work in adequate lighting. Being able to see the work clearly increases safety.
- Use an approved rubber mat or other approved insulating material to insulate onself from ground sources.
- When possible, use only one hand and ensure that the other hand is not in contact with anything.
- When voltage may exceed 150 V, wear rubber gloves.
- Post an assistant near the main switch or circuit breaker to immediately de-energize the equipment in an emergency.
- Have someone qualified in first aid nearby.
- Do NOT work alone.
- Do NOT work on any electrical apparatus when wearing wet clothing or with wet hands.
- Do NOT wear loose or flapping clothing.
- Wear shoes with thick, rubber insulated soles with the appropriate safety rating.
- Remove all metal objects, such as rings, wristwatches and bracelets prior to working on energized equipment. Check clothing for exposed metal fasteners, zippers, buttons or other possible contacts.
- Use proper lock-out/tag-out procedures.

Working on De-energized Circuits

Some electrical equipment, such as capacitors and cathode ray tubes, retain a charge for a considerable length of time after they have been disconnected from a power source. Always assume that voltage is present when working with circuits having high capacitance. Consult the manufacturer's technical manual to determine the safe way of discharging this type of equipment.

When any electronic equipment is being repaired or overhauled follow an employer's safety program. This will normally include at least the following:

- Electrical and electronic circuits may have more than one source of power. Study the schematics and wiring diagrams of the entire system and ensure that all power sources have been disconnected.
- Use one hand when turning switches on or off, keeping the other hand ungrounded.
- Safety devices, such as interlocks, overload relays and fuses should never be altered or disconnected except for replacement.
- Fuses should be removed and replaced only after the circuit is de-energized. Replace with a fuse of the same type and with the same rating. Always use a fuse puller for cartridge-type fuses.
- All circuit breakers and switches that could energize the circuit should be secured in the open or off (safe) position and tagged. See Figure 12-1-3.
- After work has been completed, tags should only be removed by the individual who signed the tag when the work began.
- Keep clothing, hands and feet dry.
- Use properly insulated tools.

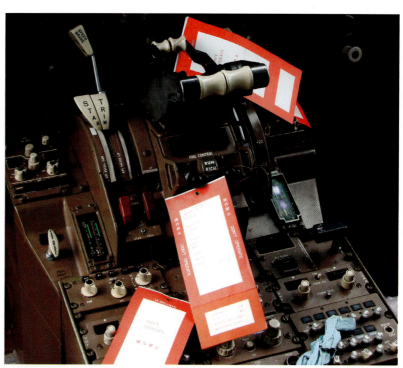

Figure 12-1-3. Cockpit controls secured in the open or off (safe) position and tagged.

First Aid for Electrical Shock

Avionics technicians install, maintain and repair electrical and electronic equipment in confined spaces where dangerously high electrical voltages may be present. This exposes the technician to the risk of injury caused by electric shock, electrical fires, harmful gases and through the improper use of tools.

It is important to develop safe and intelligent work habits to mitigate these risks. The technician should always be aware of the potential for dangerous conditions and work diligently to avoid unsafe acts. This includes knowing the methods authorized by his or her employer for dealing with electrical fires.

The technician should also have knowledge of basic first aid and know how to provide CPR (cardio-pulmonary resuscitation). This text does not provide CPR training. The standards change periodically. The best source for CPR and first aid training is a local fire department or Red Cross office. Both can provide CPR and first aid training resources that meet the current standards.

CPR is a critical life-saving skill to employ in the event of an electrical shock that causes heart stoppage. The first step in any emergency of this type is to dial 911 (or the appropriate local emergency services phone number for an area). If someone nearby is familiar with CPR, begin the procedure. If not, ask the emergency services dispatcher for instructions.

Electric Shock

Electric shock may cause burns of varying degree. It can also cause cardiac arrest, irregular heart rhythms, stoppage of breathing, unconsciousness and death.

A 60-Hz AC current passed through a person from hand to hand or from hand to foot causes the following effects:

- At about 1 mA (0.001 A) the shock is felt.
- At about 10 mA (0.01 A) the shock is severe enough to paralyze muscles and may prevent the individual from releasing the conductor.
- At about 100 mA (0.1 A) the shock is usually fatal if it lasts for more than one second.

Remember that current (amperage), rather than voltage, is the primary cause of shock intensity.

It is also important to understand the effects of resistance. Dry, unbroken skin provides a high resistance, normally between 300,000 to 500,000 Ω. However, when skin becomes moist or broken the resistance can drop dramatically to as low as 300 Ω. A 30-V potential can cause a fatal electrical flow at that resistance. Any current in excess of that is potentially life-threatening.

Care of Shock Victims

Electric shock is caused by contact with electric circuits or from the effects of lightning. The victim usually experiences a jarring, shaking sensation or what feels like a sudden blow. If the voltage is high enough, unconsciousness results. Severe burns may appear on the skin at the point of electrical contact.

Shock causes muscular spasms that in turn cause the victim to clasp the tool or wire that caused the shock. The victim is frequently unable to let go as a result. Electric shock can kill by stopping the victim's heart or their breathing. It can also damage nerve tissue resulting in wasting away of muscles. This type of damage may not be apparent until weeks or months after the shock.

The following procedures are recommended for rescue and care of electrical shock victims:

1. Call 911 (or a local equivalent) and activate the local emergency response system. If available, follow the 911 operator's instructions.
2. Remove the victim from electrical contact immediately without endangering the rescuer. Accomplish this by de-energizing the electric power causing the shock. DO NOT attempt to touch the victim while electrical power is present.
3. Determine if the victim is breathing. If so, keep the individual lying down in a comfortable position. Loosen the victim's clothing around the neck, chest and abdomen so that they can breathe freely. Protect the victim from exposure to cold and keep a constant watch on the victim.
4. Keep the victim from moving about. Shock can weaken the heart. Exertion, movement or other activities can result in a heart attack.
5. If the victim is not breathing, administer CPR or follow the instructions of the 911 operator.
6. Stay with the victim until trained rescue personnel arrive.

Section 2
Fire Protection

Fire Safety

Work on and around aircraft and their components requires the use of electrical tools and equipment, spark-producing tools and equipment, heat-producing tools and equipment, flammable and explosive liquids and gases. As a result, a high potential exists for fire to occur, and measures must be taken to prevent such an occurrence. Should one occur, extinguish it.

Spontaneous combustion. *Spontaneous combustion* occurs when a slow buildup of heat in flammable materials eventually erupts into a fire. It might occur in rags or waste that has been saturated with flammable materials. The following practices will aid in prevention of spontaneous combustion:

- Disposal of flammable wastes in closed, airtight metal containers, and empty the containers regularly.
- Keep flammable waste that can't be put in containers in a cool, dry, well-ventilated area. Dispose of them frequently.

Chemicals. Chemicals that are not a fire hazard by themselves may become flammable when mixed with an incompatible substance – air, water, heat or another chemical. This is known as *reactivity*.

The key to fire safety is knowledge of what causes fire, how to prevent it and how to put it out. This knowledge must be instilled in each technician, emphasized by his or her supervisors through sound safety programs, and occasionally practiced. Airport fire departments or local fire departments can normally be called upon to assist in training personnel and helping to establish fire safety programs for the hangar, shops and flightline.

Requirements of Fire

Three things are required for a fire:

- Fuel - Something that will, in the presence of heat, combine with oxygen, thereby releasing more heat and, as a result, reducing itself to other chemical compounds.
- Heat - Heat can be considered the catalyst that accelerates the combining of oxygen with fuel, in turn releasing more heat.
- Oxygen - The element that combines chemically with another substance through the process of oxidation.

Rapid oxidation, accompanied by a noticeable release of heat and light, is called *combustion, or burning*. See Figure 12-2-1. Remove any one of these things and the fire goes out.

Classification of Fire

The National Fire Protection Association (NFPA), for commercial purposes, has classified fires into four basic types: *Class A, Class B, Class C* and *Class D*.

- **Class A**. Class A fires are fires in ordinary combustible materials such as wood, cloth, paper, upholstery materials, etc.
- **Class B**. Class B fires are fires in flammable petroleum products or other flammable or combustible liquids, greases, solvents, paints, etc.
- **Class C**. Class C fires are fires involving energized electrical wiring and equipment.
- **Class D**. A fourth class of fire, with which the technician should be familiar, the Class D fire, is defined as *fire in flammable metal*. Class D fires are considered by the National Fire Protection Association to be a basic type or category of fire. Usually, Class D fires involve magnesium in the shop or in aircraft wheels and brakes, or are the result of improper or poorly conducted welding operations.

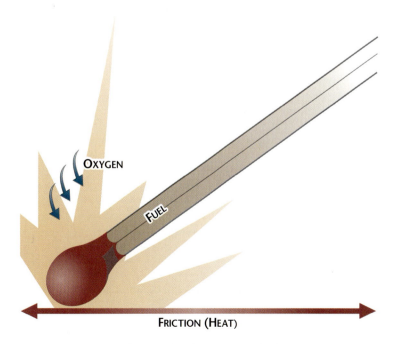

Figure 12-2-1. To start a fire, it takes three things: fuel, oxygen and heat

Any one of these types of fires can occur during maintenance of or operations on or around aircraft. There is a particular type of extinguisher that is most effective for each type of fire.

Types of Fire Extinguishers

Water extinguishers. These are the best type to use on Class A fires. The water has two effects on the fire, in that it can deprive the fire of oxygen, and at the same time cool the temperature of the material being burned. See Table 12-2-1.

Because they can only safely be used on one type of fire, water fire extinguishers have disappeared from any commercial establishment. When working with Class A material, having a firehose available is always a good idea. However, never use a water hose on the following types of fires:

- Since most petroleum products float on water, water-type fire extinguishers are not recommended for Class B fires.

- Extreme caution must be used when fighting Class C electrical fires with water-type extinguishers. Not only must all electrical power be removed or shut off to the burning area, but residual electricity in capacitors, coils, etc., must be considered to prevent severe injury and possibly death from electrical shock.

- Never use water-type fire extinguishers on Class D fires. Because metals burn at extremely high temperatures, the cooling effect of water causes an explosive expansion of the metal.

Carbon dioxide extinguishers. Carbon dioxide (CO_2) extinguishers can be used for Class A, Class B and Class C fires, extinguishing the fire by depriving it of oxygen. See Figure 12-2-2. Additionally, like water-type extinguishers, CO_2 cools the burning material. There are also some places not to use a CO_2 extinguisher.

- Never use CO_2 on Class D fires. As with water extinguishers, the cooling effect of CO_2 can cause an explosive expansion of the metal.

EXTINGUISHING MATERIALS	Class A Fire	Class B Fire	Class C Fire	Class D Fire	Self-generating	Self-expelling	Cartridge of N_2 cylinder	Stored pressure	Pump	Hand
Water and antifreeze	X						X	X	X	X
Soda-acid (water)	X				X					
Wetting agent	X							X		
Foam	X	X			X					
Loaded stream	X	X*					X	X		
Multipurpose dry chemical	X*	X	X				X	X		
Carbon dioxide		X*	X			X				
Dry chemical		X	X	X			X	X		
Bromotrifluoromethane- Halon 1301		X	X			X				
Bromochlorodifluormethane- Halon 1211		X	X					X		
Dry powder (metal fires)	X	X	X	X			X			X
*Smaller sizes of these extinguishers are not recognized for use on these classes of fires.										

Table 12-2-1. Extinguisher operations and methods of expelling

- When used, all parts of the CO_2 fire extinguisher can become extremely cold and will remain so for a short time after operation. Wear protective equipment or take other precautions to prevent cold injury (such as frostbite) from occurring.

- Extreme caution must be used when operating CO_2 fire extinguishers in closed or confined areas. Not only can the fire be deprived of oxygen, so too can the operators.

- CO_2 fire extinguishers generally use the self-expelling method of operation. This means that the CO_2 has sufficient pressure at normal operating pressure to expel itself. This pressure is held inside the container by some type of seal or frangible disk, which is broken or punctured by a firing mechanism, usually a pin. This means that once the seal or disk is broken, pressure in the container is released, and the fire extinguisher is spent, requiring replacement. See Table 12-2-1.

- Using CO_2 on Class A fires may disperse the burning materials and spread the fire.

Halogenated hydrocarbon extinguishers. While most effective on Class B and C fires, halogenated hydrocarbon (commonly called freon) extinguishers can be used on Class A and D fires. Halogenated hydrocarbon names start with the word *Halon* and end with a number.

- Carbon tetrachloride (Halon 104), chemical formula CCl_4, has an Underwriters' Laboratory (UL) toxicity rating of 3. As such, it is extremely toxic. See Table 12-2-2. Hydrochloric acid vapor, chlorine and phosgene gas are produced whenever carbon tetrachloride is used on ordinary fires. The amount of phosgene gas is increased whenever carbon tetrachloride is brought in direct contact with hot metal, certain chemicals or continuing electrical arcs. It is not approved for any fire extinguishing use. Old containers of Halon 104 found in or around shops or hangers should be disposed of in accordance with Environmental Protection Agency (EPA) regulations and local laws and ordinances.

Figure 12-2-2. CO_2 fire extinguishers can be used on Class A, B and C fires without creating contamination from the extinguishing medium.

GROUP	DEFINITION	EXAMPLES
6 (least toxic)	Gases or vapor which in concentrations up to at least 20% by volume for durations of exposure of the order of 2 hours do not appear to produce injury.	Bromotrifluoromethane (Halon 1301)
5a	Gases or vapors much less toxic than group 4 but more toxic than Group 6.	Carbon Dioxide, Bromochlorodifluoromethane (Halon 211)
4	Gases or vapors which in concentrations of the order of 2 to 2-1/2% for durations of exposure of the order of 1 hour are lethal or produce serious injury.	Dibromodifluoromethane (Halon 1202)
3	Gases or vapors which in concentrations of the order of 2 to 2-1/2% for durations of exposure of the order of 1 hour are lethal or produce serious injury.	Chlorobromomethane (Halon 1011), Carbon tetrachloride (Halon 104)
2	Gases or vapors which in concentrations of the order of 1/2 to 1% for durations of exposure of the order of 1/2 hour are lethal or produce serious injury.	Methyl bromide (Halon 1001)

Table 12-2-2 Toxicity table

Figure 12-2-3. Because dry chemical fire extinguishers may be used on Class B, C and D fires, they are commonly carried on mobile equipment.

- Methyl bromide (Halon 1001), chemical formula CH_3Br, is a liquefied gas with a UL toxicity rating of 2. Effective but very toxic, it is corrosive to aluminum alloys, magnesium and zinc. Halon 1001 is not recommended for aircraft use.

- Chlorobromomethane (Halon 1011), chemical formula CH_2ClBr, is a liquefied gas with a UL toxicity rating of 3. Like methyl bromide, Halon 1011 is not recommended for aircraft use. See Table 12-2-2.

- Dibromodifluoromethane (Halon 1202), chemical formula CBr_2F_2, has a UL toxicity rating of 4. Halon 1202 is not recommended for aircraft use. See Table 12-2-2.

- Bromochlorodifluoromethane (Halon 1211), chemical formula $CBrClF_2$, is a liquefied gas with a UL toxicity rating of 5. It is colorless, noncorrosive and evaporates rapidly, leaving no residue whatsoever. It does not freeze or cause cold burns and will not harm fabrics, metals or other materials it contacts. Halon 1211 acts rapidly on fires by producing a heavy blanketing mist that eliminates oxygen from the fire source. More importantly, it interferes chemically with the combustion process of the fire. It has outstanding properties in preventing reflash after the fire has been extinguished.

- Bromotrifluoromethane (Halon 1301), chemical formula CF_3Br, is a liquefied gas with a UL toxicity rating of 6. It has all the characteristics of Halon 1211. The significant difference between the two is that Halon 1211 forms a spray similar to CO_2, while Halon 1301 has a vapor spray that is more difficult to direct. See Table 12-2-2.

NOTE: *The Environmental Protection Agency (EPA) has restricted Halon to its 1986 production level because of its effect on the ozone layer.*

Figure 12-2-4. An airport fire crew undergoes training

Dry chemical extinguishers. These are most effective on Class B and Class C fires, and are the best for use on Class D fires. See Figure 12-2-3.

Dry powder extinguishers. Different from dry chemical extinguishers, dry powder units are best on class D fires of burning metals.

NOTE: Dry chemical is not recommended for internal aircraft use as a fire extinguisher, because chemical residues and dust left by their use is often difficult to clean up, and can cause damage to electronics or other delicate equipment. Use CO_2 instead.

Dry powder extinguishers are the best for extinguishing general shop fires, and especially for burning liquids.

Extinguisher operation. Before using the extinguisher, make sure your back is to an exit. Stand at least 6-8 ft. from the fire. Use the acronym P.A.S.S. (Pull, Aim, Squeeze, Sweep).

- PULL the pin: Hold the extinguisher with the nozzle pointing away from you and pull out the pin located below the handle. This unlocks the operating lever and allows you to discharge the extinguisher.
- AIM low: Aim the nozzle at the base of the fire.
- SQUEEZE the lever: Squeeze slowly and evenly to release the extinguisher.
- SWEEP back and forth over the burning material: Make certain the entire surface area is being targeted. Keep watching the fire to ensure that it does not reignite.

NOTE: Make sure you don't blow burning papers out of wastebasket fires. Don't attempt to fight a fire that is too big — call the fire department (Figure 12-2-4).

Checking Fire Extinguishers

Fire extinguishers should be checked periodically. OSHA and fire regulations require it.

Airport or local fire departments can usually help maintain fire extinguishers. In addition, they can be helpful in answering questions and assisting in repairs to or replacement of fire extinguishers. Most businesses buy or rent extinguishers from a company specializing in fire equipment. Most provide an annual inspection service that not only maintains the extinguishers themselves, but also provides documentation in the form of equipment tags which state a record of the service.

Identifying Fire Extinguishers

Classification of Portable Fire Extinguishers

Portable fire extinguishers are classified to indicate their ability to handle specific classes and sizes of fires. Labels on extinguishers indicate the class and relative size of fire that they can be expected to handle. The following symbols are illustrated in Figure 12-2-5.

Class A. Class A extinguishers are used on fires involving ordinary combustibles, such as wood, cloth and paper.

Class B. Class B extinguishers are used on fires involving liquids, greases and gases.

Class C. Class C extinguishers are used on fires involving energized electrical equipment.

Class D. Class D extinguishers are used on fires involving metals such as magnesium, titanium, zirconium, sodium and potassium.

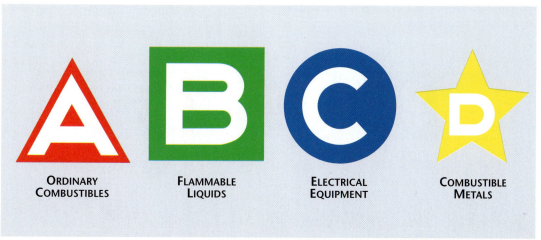

Figure 12-2-5. Fire extinguisher types are identified by standard symbols. The major symbol shows the fire class.

Fire Extinguisher Marking

The OSHA-recommended marking system that indicates the extinguisher suitability according to class of fire is a pictorial concept that combines the uses and non-uses of extinguishers on a single label. This system is illustrated in Figure 12-2-6.

- The first row of symbols illustrated is from a label for use on a Class A extinguisher. The symbol at the left (which depicts a Class A fire) is blue. Since the extinguisher is not recommended for use on Class B or C fires, the remaining two symbols (which depict Class B/C fires) are black with a red line through them.

- The second set (row) of symbols illustrated is from a label for use on a Class A/B extinguisher. The two left symbols are blue. Since the extinguisher is not recommended for use on Class C fires, the symbol on the far right (which depicts a Class C fire) is black with a red line through it.

- The third set of symbols is from a label for use on Class B/C extinguishers. The two right symbols are blue. Since the extinguisher is not recommended for use on Class A fires, this symbol is black with a red line through it.

- The fourth set of symbols is a label for use on Class A/B/C extinguishers. All symbols on this label are blue.

Letter-shaped symbol markings are also used to indicate extinguisher suitability according to class of fire. See Figure 12-2-5.

- Extinguishers suitable for Class A fires should be identified by a triangle containing the letter "A." If colored, the triangle should be green.

- Extinguishers suitable for Class B fires should be identified by a square containing the letter "B." If colored, the square will be colored red.

- Extinguishers suitable for Class C fires should be identified by a circle containing the letter "C." If colored, the circle should be colored blue.

- Extinguishers suitable for fires involving metals should be identified by a five-pointed star containing the letter "D." If colored, the star should be colored yellow.

Extinguishers suitable for more than one class of fire should be identified by multiple symbols placed in a horizontal sequence.

Numerical rating. Class A and Class B extinguishers carry a numerical rating to indicate how large a fire an experienced person can put out with the extinguisher. The ratings are based on reproducible physical tests conducted by Underwriters' Laboratories, Inc. Class C extinguishers have only a letter rating because there is no readily measurable quantity for Class C fires, which are essentially Class A or B fires involving energized electrical equipment. Class D extinguishers, likewise, do not have a numerical rating. Their effectiveness is described on the faceplate.

Class A ratings. An extinguisher for Class A fires could have any one of the following ratings: 1-A, 2-A, 3-A, 4-A, 6-A, 10-A, 20-A, 30-A and 40-A. A 4-A extinguisher should extinguish about twice as much fire as a 2-A extinguisher.

Class B ratings. An extinguisher for Class B fires could have any one of the following ratings: 1-B, 2-B, 5-B, 10-B, 20-B, 30-B, 40-B and on up to 640-B.

Class C ratings. Extinguishers rated for Class C fires are tested only for electrical conductivity. However, no extinguisher gets a Class C rating without a Class A and/or Class B rating.

Class D ratings. Class D extinguishers are tested on metal fires. The agent used depends on the metal for which the extinguisher was designed. Check the extinguisher faceplate for the unit's effectiveness on specific metals.

Figure 12-2-6. OSHA labels show how to define which extinguisher will work for what type of fire.

Section 3
Safety on the Flightline

The flightline is a place of dangerous activity. Technicians who work on the flightline must constantly be aware of what is going on around them.

Hearing Protection

The noise on a flightline comes from many places. The aircraft are only one source of noise. There are ground power units (GPUs), fuel trucks, baggage-handling equipment, etc. Each has its own frequency of sound.

All ramp or flightline noise can cause serious hearing loss. OSHA has established maximum sound exposure levels in the workplace. Sound in excess of 90 decibels over an eight hour period requires hearing protection. As sound levels increase, the permissible time period before hearing protection is required is reduced.

Types of protection available. There are many types of hearing protection available. Hearing protection can be external or internal. The external protection is the earmuff/headphone type. The internal type fits into the auditory canal. Both types will reduce the sound level reaching the eardrum and reduce the chances of hearing loss. See Figure 12-3-1.

External earmuffs are available with either passive or active features. Passive protection provides sound insulation to reduce noise levels at the ear. Active Noise Reduction (ANR) earmuffs and headsets are powered units containing electronics. These contain a set of microphones and speakers and produce sound out-of-phase with the external sound to cancel out the sound waves. ANR technology can be tailored to eliminate sounds over a certain threshold or to allow sounds within a specific frequency range such as audible speech. This can improve intelligibility and comfort, thus decreasing user fatigue.

Hearing protection should also be used when working with pneumatic drills, rivet guns or other loud or noisy tools or machinery. Because of their high frequency, even short duration exposure to these sounds can cause a hearing loss. And continued exposure WILL cause hearing loss.

Foreign Object Damage (FOD)

Foreign Object Damage (FOD) is any damage to aircraft, personnel or equipment caused by any loose object. These loose objects, also know as foreign object debris, can be anything, also know as from broken runway concrete to rags, safety wire and tools, and in rare instances, mechanics.

FOD can be controlled by good housekeeping practices, a tool-control program, and by providing convenient receptacles for used hardware, rags and other consumables.

The modern jet engine can create a low-pressure area in front of the engine that will cause any loose object to be drawn into the engine. The exhaust of these engines can propel loose objects great distances with enough force to damage anything hit.

The importance of an FOD program cannot be overstressed when considering the cost of engines, components or the cost of a human life.

While foreign object damage can be very expensive economically, it also includes physical damage that may not require costly repair. It may or may not degrade the safety or performance of the item damaged.

FOD programs start with the goal of foreign object elimination (FOE). This means eliminating or controlling foreign objects in the workplace. The easiest way to eliminate FOD is to prevent it from occurring in the first place. In practice this means both an operational mindset and a number of basic procedures.

A common operational method is to use the "clean as you go" philosophy. This includes the following:

- Clean the immediate area when work cannot continue.

Figure 12-3-1. Three of the most popular types of hearing protectors.

Figure 12-3-2. A standard set of aircraft hand signals

- Clean the immediate area when work debris has the potential to migrate to an out of sight or inaccessible area and cause damage and/or give the appearance of poor workmanship.
- Inspect and clean all tools after the completion of a job or the end of a shift.
- Clean the immediate area after work is completed and prior to inspection.
- Clean at the end of each shift.
- If you drop something or hear something drop - pick it up!

From a procedural standpoint, there are some simple workplace organizational methods that can have a big impact. Loose tools are a frequent source of FOD. Individual tool boards with outlines and tool drawers with inserts allow for rapid tool accountability. Shared tool

Figure 12-3-3. A standard set of helicopter hand signals

areas with inventory control sheets and sign-out/return procedures ensure all tools are returned to the storage area.

Parts can also become FOD. One way to reduce the potential is to "kit" the components for a job so that the technician has exactly the items needed with no leftover items to lose track of. Consumables, such as rags, gloves and safety glasses, can turn into FOD if left behind. Bring no more to the work area than required for the job.

Effective FOD prevention programs include training in FOD control, management and accountability, as well as support such as periodic screening of employees and facilities. Additionally, appropriate procedures need to be followed when FOD becomes hazardous or creates an emergency situation.

Safety Around Helicopters

Every type of helicopter has its own important differences. These differences must be learned to avoid damaging the helicopter or injuring the mechanic.

When approaching a helicopter while the blades are turning, observe the rotor head and blades to see if they are level. This will allow the maximum clearance while you approach the helicopter.

- Approach the helicopter in view of the pilot.

- Never approach a helicopter carrying anything with a vertical height that could be hit by the blades. This could cause damage to the blades or injury to you.

- Never approach a helicopter directly from the front. The blades/rotor head is designed for the greatest amount of "down traveler" in the front.

- Never approach a single-rotor helicopter from the rear. The tail rotor is invisible when operating.

- Never go from one side of the helicopter to the other by going around the tail. Always go around the nose of the helicopter.

When securing the rotor on some helicopters with elastomeric bearings, check the maintenance manual for the proper method. Using the wrong method could damage the bearings.

Hand Signals

Because of the difficulty in seeing from the cockpit and not being able to hear instructions from ground personnel, a standard set of hand signals has evolved. They are shown in Figure 12-3-2, Figure 12-3-3 and Figure 12-3-4. It will pay you to learn the most common ones and not freelance by making up your own. If you don't use the standard signals, no one else will know what you are doing. Some of the signals will be rarely used; the obvious ones will be used frequently.

Figure 12-3-4. Ground handling personnel directing a helicopter approach

13

Tools and Test Equipment

Section 1

Tool Procedures and Practices

The aircraft technician has a large variety of tools at his disposal. There are basic hand tools, measuring tools, power tools, special tools for aircraft and torque tools.

The efficiency of a technician and the tools he/she uses is determined to a great extent by the condition in which the tools are kept. Tools should be wiped clean and dry before being placed in a tool box. If their use is not anticipated in the near future, they should be lubricated to prevent rust. This is especially true if tools are stored under conditions of extremely humid or salty air.

Proper cleaning is of prime importance in the care of aircraft maintenance tools. Listed below are a few simple procedures which are the basis for their care.

Tool care. Wash grease and dirt from tools with Stoddard solvent, and wipe them dry with a clean, dry cloth. Clean serrated jaw faces of pliers, vises, etc., with a wire brush. Remove filings from between teeth of files with a file card.

When using air pressure, be extremely careful. Do not blow a stream of air toward yourself or any other person. Wear safety glasses, goggles or a face shield. Ear protection may be required. Use an OSHA-approved blow gun so pressure will not exceed 30 p.s.i.g. Do not horseplay with compressed air. Many permanent injuries have resulted from seemingly harmless fun.

Learning Objective

DESCRIBE
- how to perform measurements
- use of hand tools and power tools

EXPLAIN
- how to take care of tools
- safe tool usage

APPLY
- solder a connection
- check a circuit by measuring quantities like current, voltage, and resistance

Left. The proper handling of tools requires that the mechanic exercise a reasonable amount of skill.

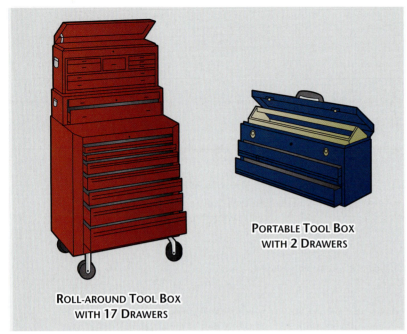

Figure 13-1-1. Typical tool boxes

Figure 13-1-2. Racks for tools are widely available and make orderly storage simple.
Photo courtesy of Snap-on Tools

Wipe excess lubricating oil or residue from taps and dies. Lightly coat non-working surfaces with a film of oil.

Tools should always be kept in their appropriate storage place when not in use. A tool box not only keeps the tool protected from dirt, it also ensures that the tool can be found, as long as it is returned to its place after use. The tool box should be locked and stored in a designated area, and an inventory list maintained for that box. Many shops have a tool control program to prevent items from being left in places that can cause damage to equipment. Following such a program is a proven way to prevent foreign object damage (FOD).

Tool selection. The selection of the proper tool or size of tool to fit the job is of prime importance. Using a tool not suited for the job or of incorrect size can result in damage to the tool, damage to equipment being maintained or injury to yourself or other workers. Proper choice of tools enables the technician to perform his work quickly, accurately and safely.

Tool use. Keep each tool in its proper storage place. Use each tool only for the purpose for which it was designed. For example, do not use a screwdriver as a chisel or pliers as a wrench. The tool and/or the aircraft component may be damaged beyond repair.

Keep tools within easy reach, where they cannot fall on the floor or on machinery. Avoid placing tools above machinery or electrical apparatus. Serious damage will result if the tool falls into the machinery after the equipment is turned on or running.

Damaged tools. Never use damaged tools. A faulty screwdriver may slip and damage the screw slot or cause injury to the user. A gauge stretched out of shape will result in inaccurate measurements.

Shop housekeeping. Housekeeping is the yardstick by which all shops are judged. A clean, well-arranged shop is safe and reflects credit on all personnel concerned with its operation. The following shop practices should be observed:

- Oil pans or drip pans should be used where leaking oil, grease and similar materials may cause hazardous accumulations on equipment or floors. All spills should be cleaned up immediately. Approved sweeping compound may be used to remove these materials from the floor.

- Floors should not be cleaned with volatile or flammable liquids. A flammable film may remain and cause a fire hazard.

- Floors should be maintained smooth and clean, free of all obstructions and slippery substances. Holes and irregularities in floors must be repaired to maintain a level surface free from tripping hazards.

- All unnecessary materials on walls should be removed and projections kept to a minimum. Aisles should be clearly defined and kept free of hazardous obstructions. Where possible, aisles should be suitably marked by painting or striping.

- All machines, work benches, aisles, etc., should be adequately illuminated.

- Machines should be located to provide operators with sufficient space to handle materials and perform job operations without interference.

- All machinery that can move or "walk" due to vibration (drill press, bench grinder, etc.) shall be bolted down.

- Shop machinery should be operated only

by qualified personnel. If you have not used a specific piece of machinery before, get checked out first.

- Safety devices, such as guards, interlocks, automatic releases and stops, should always be kept in operating condition. Suitable mechanical guards, such as enclosures or barricades, should be permanently installed on all machinery not already equipped with such to eliminate danger of injury from moving parts.
- Machinery should not be adjusted, repaired, oiled or cleaned while machine is in operation or power is on.
- Personnel operating machinery should wear protective clothing as prescribed. A protective face shield or goggles should be worn when operating a grinder, regardless of whether the grinder is equipped with attached shields.
- Jewelry should not be worn while performing any maintenance.

Fire safety. A constant vigilance must be maintained to seek out fire hazards. Fire hazards are constantly present in the shop where sparks, friction or careless handling can cause an explosion that may destroy equipment or buildings and injure people.

Most shops do not allow smoking on the premises.

Oily waste, rags and similar combustible materials shall be discarded in self-closing metal containers, which should be emptied daily.

Flammable materials should not be stored in the shop. They should be stored in an OSHA-approved area.

Use only approved cleaning solvents. Never freelance when choosing cleaning materials.

Tool boxes. Tool boxes come in a wide variety of sizes and styles. They are usually made of steel and not only provide storage and security, but are an important part of *tool control*. Tool control means that all tools are where they belong at all times. None are left in or on the airplane in such a manner as to turn into FOD. A stray wrench or pair of pliers can destroy a turbine engine in short order. Portable tool boxes are used for carrying and storing a variety of hand tools. Tool bags are usually made of canvas. Like the boxes, they are available in a variety of sizes and serve similar functions. Typical tool boxes are shown in Figure 13-1-1.

Tool storage inside tool boxes should be neat and orderly. This allows for instant recognition if a tool is missing. Many different types of

Figure 13-2-1. Typical tapes

racks and drawer organizers are available from tool suppliers and auto parts houses. A typical drawer organizer is shown in Figure 13-1-2.

Section 2
Measuring Tools

In the maintenance of aircraft, the fabrication of many parts may be required. During this process, accurate measurements must be made before and during the fabrication process. A partly finished or a finished part must also be checked for accuracy. This inspection includes comparing the dimensions of the part with the required dimensions shown on a drawing or sketch. These measurements are made using a variety of measuring tools. The accuracy of the measurements will depend upon the types of tools used and the ability of the aircraft technician to use them correctly.

Tapes and Rules

Tapes and rules are the measuring instruments most often used for all general measurements. They are graduated into fractions of an inch; 1/8, 1/16, 1/32 and 1/64.

Tapes. There are several kinds and lengths of tapes, but the one most often used is 6 to 12 feet long and made of flexible steel. It is coiled in a circular case and may or may not have one end fastened permanently to the case. It is graduated on one side only in 1/16-inch and 1/32-inch divisions. A small lip on the end prevents the tape from sliding completely inside the case and also easily lines up the end of the tape with the end of a piece of stock. Examples of typical tapes are shown in Figure 13-2-1. Tapes are generally

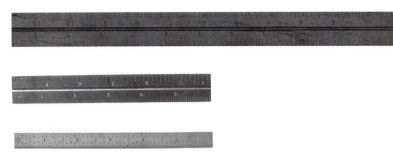

Figure 13-2-2. Rules come in various dimensions, from pocket sizes up to several feet in length.

Figure 13-2-4. A combination square has all of the components shown: a ruler, a square head, a protractor and a center head.

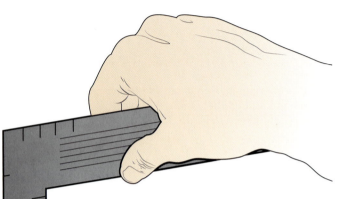

Figure 13-2-3. Carpenter's square

accurate, but some shops have established a specific brand and model of tape to be used, thus ensuring consistent measurement between individual technicians.

Rules. Rules are usually made of flexible or rigid steel and are 4, 6 or 12 inches long. They are graduated in 1/8ths, 1/16ths, 1/32nds and 1/64ths. There are special aircraft reading rules available that are graduated in 1/16-inch and 1/64-inch readings on one side and 1/50-inch and 1/100-inch readings on the other. When the total length of a measurement is not too great, the rule should be used. It is more accurate and easier to read than the tape. Typical rules are shown in Figure 13-2-2.

Squares

Squares are primarily used for testing and checking trueness of an angle or for laying out lines on materials. Most squares have a rule marked on the edge, so they may also be used for measuring. The common types of squares include the carpenter's, try, combination, sliding T-bevel and the bevel protractor squares.

Carpenter's square. The carpenter's square, shown in Figure 13-2-3, is made up of two parts: the blade (long side) and the tongue (short side). It has inches divided into 1/8ths, 1/10ths, 1/12ths and 1/16ths. If dropped on a corner, the square can be knocked out of square by the impact. To check for accuracy, lay the square on a flat surface and draw a line down both the blade and tongue. Raise the blade and rotate the square 180°, leaving the tongue on the surface. Draw lines as before. If the lines match, the square is accurate. If not, it is bent and should be replaced.

Combination square. A combination square is made of the components shown in Figure 13-2-4. It has a square head, a center head and an adjustable protractor with a built-in level. The protractor head can be used to check control-surface travel, as well as check or mark angled lines. A smaller 6-inch unit without the protractor head is also available.

Rule. The combination square has a slotted 12-inch steel rule which is graduated in 1/8ths, 1/16ths, 1/32nds and 1/64ths of an inch. It can be used as a measuring scale by itself or with any one of its components:

Center head. The center head, when attached to the rule, bisects a 90° angle. It is used for determining the center of cylindrical work.

Protractor. The protractor has a level and a revolving turret which is graduated in degrees from 0° to 180° or 0° to 90° in either direction. It is used to lay out and measure angles to within one degree.

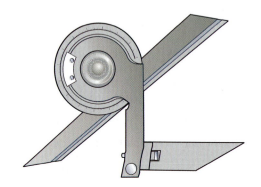

Figure 13-2-5. Bevel protractor

Square head. The square head has a level, a scribe, and 45° and 90° angles. It is used to lay out 45° and 90° angles and to check for levelness. It may also be used as a height or depth gauge.

Bevel protractor square. The bevel protractor is made up of an adjustable blade and a graduated dial which contains a scale. The bevel protractor is used to establish an angle and determine its relationship to other surfaces. The acute angle attachment is used for measuring acute angles accurately. This type of square is shown in Figure 13-2-5.

Uses of Squares

The various types of squares are used in the following manner:

Carpenter's square. In layout of sheet metal or other flat material, the carpenter's square is used to mark a square line. To mark a square line, proceed as follows:

Place the blade or tongue of the square against the side of the material, with the square tilted slightly so the blade or tongue of the square extends across the work.

> **NOTE:** *Do not mark on any metal surface with a graphite pencil. Graphite is cathodic and will establish the basis for galvanic corrosion.*

Mark a line across the work using a marking pencil.

Center head. The center head can be used to locate and mark the diameter of a cylinder, as shown in Figure 13-2-6.

Protractor head. The protractor head can be used to determine the angle of a previously marked line. Slide the protractor head on the rule, as shown in Figure 13-2-7, and tighten the setscrew. Loosen the protractor adjustment screws so the protractor may be pivoted about the rule, as shown in Figure 13-2-8.

Place the rule on the angle being measured, and pivot the protractor head against the edge. Tighten adjustment screws. Read the measured angle on the protractor (Figure 13-2-8).

Square head. The square head can be used to determine depth in the following manner:

1. Slide the square head on the rule.
2. Set the flat surface of the square head above the edge, and adjust the rule until it hits the bottom, as shown in Figure 13-2-9.
3. Tighten the setscrew.

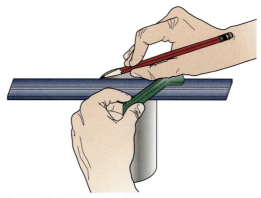

Figure 13-2-6. Setting the center head

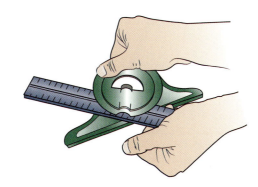

Figure 13-2-7. Installing protractor head on rule

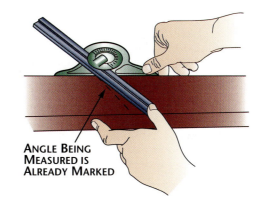

Figure 13-2-8. Checking angle

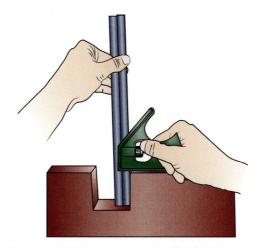

Figure 13-2-9. Determining depth with the square head

13-6 | Tools and Test Equipment

Figure 13-2-10. Spring divider

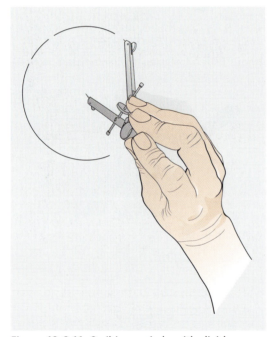

Figure 13-2-11. Scribing a circle with dividers

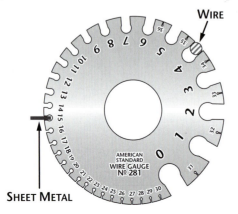

Figure 13-2-12. Measuring sheet metal and wire

4. Remove the square and read the depth indicated on the rule.

Bevel protractor. The bevel protractor is used much the same as the protractor head of the combination square.

Dividers

Dividers are tapered steel picks, hinged together on the blunt end. They are used to scribe arcs and circles and to transfer measurements when laying out work. They are also used to transfer or compare measurements directly from a rule. The most common types of dividers are the spring divider and the wing divider.

Spring divider. A spring divider, as shown in Figure 13-2-10, consists of two sharp points at the end of straight legs, held apart by a spring and adjusted by means of a screw and nut. The spring divider is available in sizes from 3 to 10 inches in length and is the most common model.

Use of Dividers

Dividers can be used to scribe a circle by using the following procedures (Figure 13-2-11):

1. Set the desired radius on the dividers using the appropriate graduations on a rule.
2. Place the point of one of the divider legs on the point to be used as the center.
3. Lean the dividers in the direction of movement and scribe the circle by revolving the dividers.
4. Scribe the circumference only if the line is to be removed by cutting. Otherwise use a compass with a small felt tip marker.
5. If the circle is to be saved rather than cut out, tape a small piece of sheet metal at the pivot point. Put a prick punch mark at the center point. This avoids marking the finished part.

Sheet Metal and Wire Gauge

The sheet metal and wire gauge, shown in Figure 13-2-12, is used for measuring the diameters of wires or the thickness of sheet metal.

Types. The type of sheet metal and wire gauge to be used depends on the type of material being measured. They are available as follows:

- English Standard Iron wire, hot-and cold rolled sheet steel

- American Standard Non-ferrous sheet metal and wire
- US Standard Sheet and plate iron and steel
- Steel wire gauge

Find the slot that refuses to pass the wire without forcing. Try the next larger slots until one is found that passes the wire. This is the correct size. Measurements are taken at the slot portion rather than the cutout portion of the gauge. The decimal equivalent of the gauge number is shown on the opposite side of the gauge.

Section 3

General Purpose Tools

Regardless of the type of work to be done, a technician must select and use the correct tools in order to do his work quickly, accurately and safely. Without the correct tools and the knowledge to use them, the avionics technician will waste time, reduce efficiency and may even injure himself. This section explains the purposes, correct use and proper care of the more common tools. Special tools are described in the individual sections to which they pertain.

Hammers

Hammers are striking tools which are composed of a head made of metal, plastic, leather or wood mounted on a handle. The handle is usually made of wood, although some modern hammers and mallets have handles made of fiberglass. The more common types of hammers are described in the following paragraphs.

Ball peen hammer. The ball peen hammer is the type most often used by mechanics. See Figure 13-3-1. It has a steel head and is usually available in 4, 6, 8 and 12 ounce sizes as well as 1, 1-1/2 and 2 pounds. As Figure 13-3-1 shows, this hammer is identified by the ball-shaped peen at the opposite end of the face.

Body hammer. A body hammer, shown in Figure 13-3-2, is used to straighten and form metal. The three most common types are shrinking, stretching and planishing.

Lead or copper hammers. These are used when it is necessary to avoid creating marks or sparks. The heads are generally one piece (Figure 13-3-3). They produce a heavy blow, but the head is malleable so any damage is relegated to the hammer, not the work.

Figure 13-3-1. Ball peen hammers *Photo courtesy of Snap-on Tools*

Figure 13-3-2. Body hammers are specialty tools used in the auto body trade. They are used principally for finishing hand-formed parts.

Soft-faced hammer. The soft-faced hammer, shown in Figure 13-3-4, is capable of delivering heavy blows to machined, highly polished or soft surfaces without damage to those surfaces. On some of these hammers, the faces can be removed and replaced when damaged or when a different hardness or toughness is required.

Figure 13-3-4. Soft-faced hammer *Photo courtesy of Snap-on Tools*

Figure 13-3-3. Lead or copper hammer *Photo courtesy of Snap-on Tools*

Figure 13-3-5. Rawhide mallets are used principally in sheet metal forming. They are not generally used for finishing.

Mallets

Mallets are generally made of softer substances for working items which would be damaged by metal hammers. The following paragraphs describe some of the more common types.

Rawhide mallet. The rawhide mallet has a cylindrical head which is made by tightly wrapping and staking a sheet of leather. It is used for forming and shaping sheet metal, as shown in Figure 13-3-5.

Rubber mallet. A rubber mallet has a cylindrical rubber head. It is used for forming sheet metal and driving dowels.

Hammer and Mallet Safety

The following precautions must be kept in mind when using hammers:

- Do not use a hammer handle for bumping parts in an assembly. Never use it as a pry bar. Such abuses will cause the handle to split, which can result in bad cuts or pinches to the hand. When a handle splits or cracks, do not try to repair it by binding with string or wire. Replace it.

- Ensure that the head fits tightly on the handle. If it is loose, it can fly off during use and cause serious injury to personnel.

- Do not strike a hardened steel surface with a steel hammer. Small pieces of steel may break off and injure someone in the eye or damage the work.

- When using metal hammers, always wear eye protection to prevent metal particles from entering the eyes.

- When using a hammer or mallet, ensure that the material will not be damaged by the tool. The hammer should be gripped near the end of the handle and should strike the surface evenly.

- Broken or chipped faces may be replaced. Remove damaged faces by turning in a counterclockwise direction. Use a pair of pliers or a rag on broken faces to prevent injury to the hands.

Screwdrivers

Screwdrivers are tools used for driving or removing screws. Generally, they consist of a steel blade and shank set in a handle of wood or plastic. They also come in various other shapes, some adapted for a particular usage. It is generally better to start out with a full set of screwdrivers. They can be obtained in sets stored in bolsters (tool rolls). These serve both as storage and as an inventory method for tool control.

Common screwdrivers. The common, or standard, screwdriver, shown in Figure 13-3-6, is suitable for driving or removing slotted screws. The blade must have sharp corners and fit the screw slot closely. The size is designated by the length of the shank and blade.

Cross-point screwdrivers. The most common cross point screwdrivers are *Reed & Prince* and *Phillips*. The Phillips screwdriver has a blunt cross tip. The tip is ground to a 30° angle, as shown in Figure 13-3-7. Phillips points come in four sizes: No. 1 through No. 4. The most common is No. 2. A Reed & Prince screwdriver is one of the early points designed for power drivers. It has a sharp point.

NOTE: *The Phillips screwdriver is* not *interchangeable with the Reed & Prince screwdriver. The use of the wrong type screwdriver*

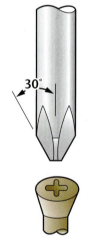

Figure 13-3-7. Phillips screwdriver with blunt point

Figure 13-3-6. Common screwdrivers   Photo courtesy of Snap-on Tools

results in mutilation of the screwdriver and the screw head.

Offset screwdrivers. The offset screwdriver shown in Figure 13-3-8 is composed of a shank with a blade on each end. The blades are bent at right angles to the shank. One is parallel to the shank, the other is set at 90°. This screwdriver is especially usefully in performing close work. Some offset screwdrivers are available as ratchet types, which allow the screw to be driven without having to remove the tip from the screw head (Figure 13-3-9).

Ratchet screwdrivers. The ratchet screwdriver shown in Figure 13-3-10 is fast acting in that it turns the screw without having to remove the tip from the screw head for repositioning after rotation. It can be set to turn the screw clockwise or counterclockwise, or it can be locked in position and used as a standard screwdriver. Many have extra tips stored in the handle. The ratchet screwdriver is not a heavy-duty tool and should be used only for light work.

> **NOTE:** *When using a ratchet screwdriver, extreme care must be used to maintain constant pressure and prevent the blade from slipping out from the slot in the screw head. If this occurs, the surrounding structure is subject to damage.*

Nonmagnetic screwdrivers. The nonmagnetic screwdriver is shaped like a common screwdriver, but the blade is made of brass so as to have no magnetic effect. It is used for compensating compasses.

Electric screwdrivers. There is an extremely large variety of electric and battery operated screwdrivers on the market. Most are good. Because of the large number of screws involved in servicing aircraft, they can be a real time saver when removing access panels. However, they can also do a large amount of damage if used incorrectly, especially during reassembly. If the wrong size screw (either diameter or length) is driven with an electric screwdriver, damage can be done before you recognize it. *Do not use electric screwdrivers around fuel tank access plates. They can present an explosion hazard.*

Screwdriver Safety

The following precautions may keep you from injuring yourself with a screwdriver:

- Ensure that the handle is clean.
- Do not use a screwdriver for prying, punching, chiseling, scoring or scraping.

Figure 13-3-9. Using an offset ratchet screwdriver

Figure 13-3-10. Ratchet screwdriver

- Do not use a screwdriver to check an electric circuit, since an electric arc will burn the tip and make it useless. In some cases, an electric arc may fuse the blade to the unit being checked.
- When using a screwdriver on a small part, always hold the part in a vise or rest it on a workbench. Do not hold the part in your hand, because the screwdriver may slip and cause serious personal injury.

Proper fit. Select a screwdriver large enough so the blade fits closely in the screw slot. A loose-fitting blade can slip and cause burring of the screw slot and damage to the blade. Proper and improper fits are shown in Figure 13-3-11. It is important that the screwdriver be held firmly against the screw to prevent it from slipping and possibly injuring the mechanic or scarring the work.

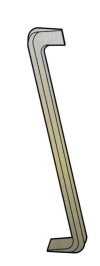

Figure 13-3-8. Offset screwdriver

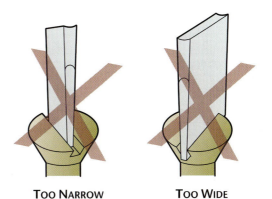

Too Narrow   **Too Wide**   **Proper Fit**

Figure 13-3-11. Proper fit of screwdrivers

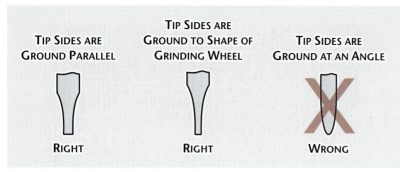

Figure 13-3-12. Screwdriver tip grinding

Screwdriver Repair

Battered or nicked blades may be repaired by grinding to the original shape.

Common screwdrivers. When grinding common screwdrivers, the tip should be squared and the sides parallel, as shown in Figure 13-3-12.

Cross-point screwdrivers. Phillips screwdrivers require special holding fixtures for grinding but can be shaped in an emergency by filing, as long as the original angles and bevels are maintained.

Removing Stubborn Screws

Special screwdrivers. There are special screwdrivers available that have a hexagonal section on the shank next to the handle. This allows a wrench to be used for additional leverage. Others are available that have a square drive fitting in the handle, for using a breaker bar or ratchet.

Hand-impact wrenches, designed to be struck with a hammer while under twisting pressure, sometimes work well when used with square-drive screwdriver bits. Sometimes light-duty impact wrenches can also be used to loosen (never to tighten) a stubborn screw. Aircraft tool suppliers also make drivers that use screwdriver bits and fit rivet guns. These work well because the air hammer blows while the screw is under rotational pressure.

Unfortunately, with all these special tools, sometimes nothing works, and the errant screw must

Figure 13-3-13. Open-end wrench

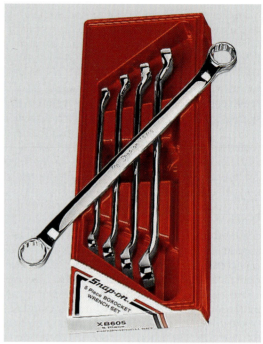

Figure 13-3-14. A set of five box-end wrenches offers 10 nut sizes. *Photo courtesy of Snap-on Tools*

be drilled out. Refer to the sheet metal section and read the part on rivet removal first.

Wrenches

Wrenches are used for tightening or removing nuts, bolts or cap screws and also for gripping round objects such as pipe. They are made of a relatively hard substance, such as chromemolybdenum steel, which enables them to withstand the rigors of normal use.

Types of wrenches. Wrenches used in aircraft maintenance can be generally categorized as open-end, box-end, combination, adjustable, socket, hexagonal and spanner wrenches.

Open-end wrenches. Open-end wrenches have two parallel jaws at each end of a bar, as shown in Figure 13-3-13. The jaws of an open-end wrench are usually machined 15° from parallel to the centerline of the wrench. The two ends of each wrench fit consecutively-sized nuts such as 3/8- and 7/16-inch, 1/2- and 9/16-inch, and so on.

Box-end wrenches. Box-end wrenches have a head on each end of a bar, as shown in Figure 13-3-14. The head completely surrounds the nut or bolt, which decreases the chances that the wrench will slip off the work. Box-end wrenches are available with 6-point and 12-point openings. These openings are offset from the shank at a 15° angle to allow clearance. A box-end wrench should be used whenever possible because it provides the best protection to both the user and the equipment. These wrenches are sized the same as open-end wrenches.

Combination wrenches. The combination wrench shown in Figure 13-3-15 combines the best features of the open-end and box wrench into a single wrench. The size opening on the wrench is the same on both ends, but one end has a box head and the other end has an open-end head. The length of the wrench varies with the size of the head. The box-end opening is offset from the shank by 15°.

Adjustable wrench. Adjustable wrenches include Crescent®, automobile and pipe wrenches, shown in Figure 13-3-16. These wrenches are generally intended for use on odd-sized nuts and bolts, and are adjusted by a knurled worm gear, which moves the movable jaw to fit the part. Adjustable wrenches are available in sizes ranging from 4 to 24 inches in length. The jaw capacity is proportional to the handle length.

Socket Wrenches

Sockets. Sockets are round metal sleeves with a square opening in one end for insertion of a handle, and a six-point or 12-point wrench opening in the other, as shown in Figure 13-3-17. They are available in common (short) and deep (long) lengths. The drive end can vary from 1/4 to 1 inch. Sockets are driven by a wide variety of handles.

Socket Wrench Handles

There are many types of handles used to drive sockets. The following paragraphs describe the more common types in use.

Ratchet handle. Ratchet handles may have either a straight head or a flex head. The flex head is used to go around objects. Both types have a selection lever on the top of the head to determine the direction of drive. A straight head type is shown in Figure 13-3-18.

Sliding T-bar handle. The sliding T-bar handle shown in Figure 13-3-19, has a single head which may be adjusted along a bar handle. It has two spring loaded balls, one for keeping the bar in the head and the other for keeping the socket on the head. The sliding T-bar is used for increased leverage or for working around other objects.

Hinged handle. A hinged handle has a hinged adapter on one end which may be rotated in 90° steps, used when additional leverage or torque

Figure 13-3-15. Combination wrench set in a molded plastic holder

Photo courtesy of Snap-on Tools

Figure 13-3-16. Adjustable wrenches

Figure 13-3-17. Sockets come in many sizes and lengths. *Photo courtesy of Snap-on Tools*

Figure 13-3-18. Straight-head ratchet handle

Photo courtesy of Snap-on Tools

Figure 13-3-19. Sliding T-bar handle

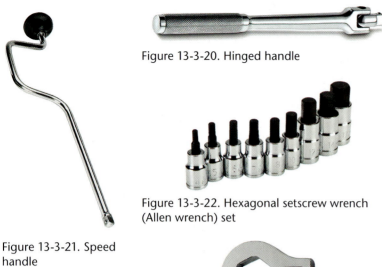

Figure 13-3-20. Hinged handle

Figure 13-3-22. Hexagonal setscrew wrench (Allen wrench) set

Figure 13-3-21. Speed handle

Figure 13-3-23. Crowfoot wrench

Photo courtesy of Snap-on Tools

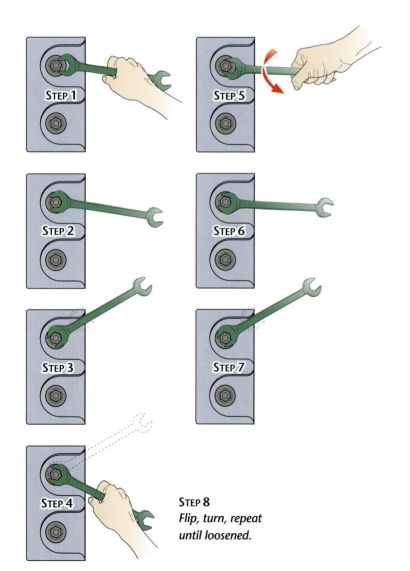

Step 8
Flip, turn, repeat until loosened.

Figure 13-3-24. Use of open-end wrench

is needed to loosen nuts or bolts. This type of handle is shown in Figure 13-3-20.

Speed handle. The speed handle, shown in Figure 13-3-21, has a brace-type shaft with a revolving grip on the top. It is used for rapid removal and/or installation of nuts or bolts, which are out in the open and have little or no torque.

Hexagonal Wrenches

Hexagonal setscrew wrenches (Allen wrenches) are L-shaped, headless, hexagonal bars that range in size from 3/64 to 1/2 inch.

A typical Allen wrench set is shown in Figure 13-3-22. They are used to tighten or remove screws that have hexagonal recesses.

Allen wrenches are also available to fit square-drive handles. They are frequently easier and faster to operate. They also have the advantage of fitting a torque wrench.

Crowfoot Wrench

Figure 13-3-23 shows a typical crowfoot wrench, to be used where a bolt is installed in a location where an obstruction does not allow the use of a socket or a wrench. The wrench is attached to an extension.

Ensure that the wrench being used is of the right size. Use of a wrench larger than the head of the bolt or nut will result in rounding of the faces.

Uses of Wrenches

When using any type wrench, special attention should be given to choosing the one best suited for the job. Selecting a wrench larger than the nut or bolt head will often result in rounded corners and additional maintenance time. Arrange work so a wrench is pulled, not pushed. Never use pipe or other extensions to increase leverage. The following paragraphs describe the various procedures involved with operating the previously described wrenches.

Use of open-end wrenches. The 15° offset of the jaws from the centerline of the wrench makes the open-end wrench appropriate for use in some applications where there is room to make only part of a complete turn of a nut or bolt. A typical procedure for this application is shown in Figure 13-3-24 and outlined in the following:

NOTE: *Where conditions prohibit use the use of a socket or box-end, an open-end wrench may be used. The open-end wrench has fewer*

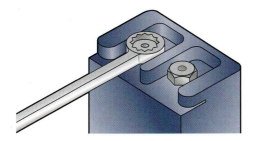

Figure 13-3-25. Use of box-end wrench

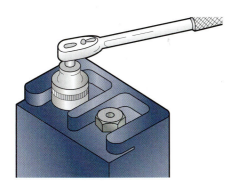

Figure 13-3-26. Use of socket wrench

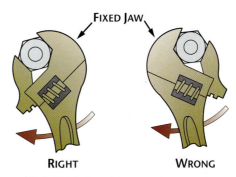

Figure 13-3-27. Adjustable wrench procedure

contact points than either a socket or box-end and is more likely to round off the corners of the nut.

1. Step 1 shows the wrench, with the opening sloping to the left, about to be placed on the nut.
2. Position the wrench on the nut (step 2). Note that space for swinging the wrench is limited.
3. Move the wrench counterclockwise to loosen the nut. The wrench will strike the casting which prevents further movement (step 3).
4. Remove the wrench from the nut and turn counterclockwise to place it on the next set of flats on the nut.

    NOTE: *The corner of the casting may prevent the wrench from fitting the nut (step 4).*

5. If this occurs, flip the wrench over so that the opening will slope to the right (step 5).
6. Position the wrench on the next two flats on the nut (step 6).
7. Turn the wrench counterclockwise to further loosen the nut (step 7).
8. Continue flipping the wrench as required until the nut is completely loose.

Use of box-end wrenches. Box-end wrenches are very good for final tightening of nuts. The following procedures describe the typical use of box-end wrenches:

1. Select the size of wrench that fits the nut or bolt.

2. Place the wrench on the nut or bolt and turn as required to loosen or tighten.
3. If there is insufficient room to swing the wrench in a full circle, as shown in Figure 13-3-25, lift it completely off the nut when it comes to the limit of the swing and place it in a new position, permitting another swing. A swing through a 15° arc is usually sufficient to continuously loosen or tighten a nut or bolt.

Use of socket wrenches. Where practical, a socket wrench is best for loosening or tightening nuts and bolts. Speed can be attained through the use of ratchets and speed handles. Length of the handle used is very important, as very little pressure is required to strip threads or twist off a small bolt using a long handle. Extension bars and universal joints enable a mechanic to get at nuts or bolts that would otherwise be out of reach or at a difficult angle. Figure 13-3-26 shows the typical use of a ratchet wrench. The procedure is outlined as follows:

1. Select the size of the socket that fits the nut or bolt to be turned. Push it onto the handle which is best suited for the job.
2. Turn the socket with the handle to tighten or loosen the nut or bolt.

Adjustable Wrenches

Use of adjustable wrenches. Adjustable wrenches should be used only when wrenches of the correct size are unavailable. They should be properly adjusted and pulled so the handle moves in the direction of the adjustable jaw, as shown in Figure 13-3-27. Place the wrench on the nut so that the force used to turn it is applied to the stationary jaw side of the wrench.

Spanner Wrenches

Many special nuts used in propeller systems are made with notches or holes cut into the outer edge (face) of the nut. These nuts are designed to be driven with spanner wrenches.

Figure 13-3-28. Hook spanner wrench

Figure 13-3-29. Pin spanner wrench

Figure 13-3-30. Face pin spanner wrench

Figure 13-3-31. Adjustable hook spanner wrench

Figure 13-3-32. Retaining ring pliers

Photo courtesy of Snap-on Tools

Figure 13-3-33. Slip-joint combination pliers

Figure 13-3-34. Diagonal cutting pliers

Photo courtesy of Snap-on Tools

Figure 13-3-35. Long-nose pliers

Spanner wrenches. Spanner wrenches can generally be classified as one of two types: solid and adjustable.

Solid spanner wrenches. The following paragraphs describe the various types of solid spanner wrenches.

Nuts with notches cut into the outer edge are driven with the *hook spanner*, as shown in Figure 13-3-28. This wrench has a curved arm with a lug or hook in the end. This lug fits into one of the notches of the nut, and the handle is pulled to tighten or loosen the nut.

The *pin spanner*, shown in Figure 13-3-29, has a pin in place of the hook. This pin fits into a hole on the outer edge of the nut.

Face pin spanners are designed so that the pins fit into holes in the face of the nut, as shown in Figure 13-3-30.

Adjustable spanner wrench. Solid spanner wrenches are sized for specific sizes of nuts. The adjustable spanner wrench, shown in Figure 13-3-31, has a pivoting end which allows the wrench to fit several nut sizes. The wrench shown is a hook spanner, used the same way as the solid hook spanner.

Pliers

Pliers are so constructed that a force or pressure applied to the handles is intensified through the pivot point to the jaws. This leverage enables the mechanic to hold materials which the hand alone is not strong enough to hold.

Types of pliers. Pliers are made in various types for various uses. The more common types are listed in the following paragraphs.

Retaining ring pliers. Retaining ring (snap ring) pliers (Figure 13-3-32) are used to remove internal and external retaining rings.

Slip-joint pliers. The slip-joint combination pliers, shown in Figure 13-3-33, have serrated (grooved) jaws, with a rod-gripping section, a cutting edge and a pivot. The serrated jaws and rod-gripping section are used to hold objects. The cutting edge permits the cutting of soft

Figure 13-3-36. Flat-nose pliers

Figure 13-3-37. Water pump pliers

Figure 13-3-38. Locking pliers *Photo courtesy of Snap-on Tools*

wire and nails. However, cutting hard materials or large gauge wire will spring the jaws, rendering the pliers useless. The pivot is used to adjust the jaw opening to handle large or small objects.

Diagonal-cutting pliers. The diagonal-cutting pliers, shown in Figure 13-3-34, have a fixed pivot. The jaws are offset by about 15° and are shaped to give enough knuckle clearance while making flush cuts. These pliers are used for cutting objects such as wire, cotter pins and similar items. These pliers are not to be used to hold or grip objects.

Long-nose pliers. Long-nose pliers (Figure 13-3-35) are used to reach places inaccessible to the fingers and perform tasks such as inserting cotter pins in close places. They are also used to bend small pieces of metal.

Flat-nose pliers. The flat-nose pliers (duckbills), shown in Figure 13-3-36, have flat serrated jaws, a fixed pivot and curved handles, which may have insulated sleeves. These pliers are used to bend light sheet metal and wire and install safety wire.

Water pump pliers. Water pump pliers, sometimes referred to as *Channel Lock® pliers* (Figure 13-3-37), are used for their powerful grip and ability to adjust to several different sizes. There are two adjustment methods used with this type of pliers. Water pump pliers should not be used to loosen/tighten cannon plugs and other electrical plugs. They will damage the connector.

Vise-grip® pliers. *Vise-grip®* pliers have a clamping action which allows them to be clamped onto an object. They will stay there and free the other hand for other work. These pliers, shown in Figure 13-3-38, are sometimes made with a clamp-type jaw which allows them to be used for clamping sheet metal. The pliers can be adjusted by turning the knurled adjustment screw until the desired jaw dimension is reached. They are made in many different sizes and shapes.

NOTE: *Vise-grip® pliers should be used with care since the teeth in the jaws tend to damage the object on which they are clamped. Do not use them on nuts, bolts, tube fittings or other objects which must be reused.*

Use of pliers. Pliers come in various sizes and should be selected according to the job being performed. They should never be used as a substitute for a wrench, because this practice batters nut and jaw serrations unnecessarily. Although there are several uses for pliers, they are not all-purpose tools and should not be used as pry bars or for hammering.

Section 4
Cutting Tools

Knives

Most knives are used to cut, pare and trim wood, leather, rubber and other soft materials. The types that the avionics technician will probably encounter are the shop knife, pocket knife and the putty knife.

Utility knife. The utility knife (Figure 13-4-1) can be used to cut cardboard and paper. It has an aluminum handle and is furnished with interchangeable blades which are stored in the handle. Different types of blades are available.

Figure 13-4-1. Utility knife

Figure 13-4-2. Putty knife

Figure 13-4-3. Prick punch

Figure 13-4-4. Center punch

Figure 13-4-5. Automatic center punch

Figure 13-4-6. Drive punch *Photo courtesy of Snap-on Tools*

Figure 13-4-7. Pin punch *Photo courtesy of Snap-on Tools*

Putty knife. A putty knife (Figure 13-4-2) is used for applying putty compound and sealant, as well as for scraping gasket material. The blade has a wide, square point and is available in different lengths and widths. The square edge can be restored by filing when worn or rounded.

Punches

Punches usually are made of carbon steel tempered on both ends. They generally are classified as either solid punches or hollow punches, and are designed according to their intended use. Hollow punches vary in size. Solid punches vary both in size and in point design.

Solid Punches

Solid punches are named according to their shape and are designed for various purposes. The following paragraphs describe the common types of punches used in aircraft maintenance.

Prick punch. A prick punch, shown in Figure 13-4-3, is used to place reference marks in metal. It is also often used to transfer dimensions from a paper pattern directly onto the metal. It is relatively slender and is tapered to a point of about 30°. The following precautions should be taken when using a prick punch:

- Never strike a prick punch heavily with the hammer, because it could bend the punch or cause excessive damage to the item being worked.
- Do not use a prick punch to remove objects from holes, because the point of the punch will spread the object and cause it to bind even tighter.
- A prick punch does not make a good center punch. The mark is not the correct angle.

Center punch. A center punch, shown in Figure 13-4-4, is used to make large indentations in metal of the kind needed to start a twist drill. This punch has a heavier body than the prick punch, and its point is ground to an angle of about 60°.

Never strike the center punch with enough force to excessively dimple the material around the indentation. The 60° angle causes a large amount of metal to displace (stretch). The stretch will cause a small buckle at each punch mark. When the hole is drilled, all of the stretched metal will not be removed, and the sheet will not lay flat.

Automatic center punch. The automatic center punch, shown in Figure 13-4-5, is used only to indent metal to make starting points for twist drills. It contains a mechanism that automatically strikes a blow of the required force when the user puts the punch in place and presses on it with his hand. This punch has an adjustable cap for regulating the stroke; the point can be removed for regrinding or replacement. Never strike an automatic center punch with a hammer.

NOTE: *If you have trouble with a drill "walking" after using a center punch, the trouble more than likely is not the center punch mark. Most likely the drill point is worn or uneven. Replace the drill.*

Drive punch. The drive punch, shown in Figure 13-4-6, is often called a *taper punch*. It is used to drive out damaged rivets, pins and bolts, which sometimes bind in holes. Therefore, the drive punch is made with a flat face instead of a point. The size of the punch is determined by the width of the face, usually 1/8 to 1/4 inch.

Pin punch. A pin punch, shown in Figure 13-4-7, is also often called a *drift punch*. It is similar to a drive punch and is used for the same purpose. The difference between the two is that the shank of a drive punch is tapered all the way to the face, while the pin punch has a straight shank. Pin punch points are sized in 1/32-inch increments and range from 1/16 to 3/8 inch in diameter. The usual method for driving out a pin or bolt is to start working it out with a drive punch, which is used until the shank of the punch is touching the sides of the hole. A pin punch is then used to drive the pin or bolt the rest of the way out of the hole.

Pins and bolts, or rivets that are hard to dislodge, may be started by placing a thin piece of scrap copper, brass, or aluminum directly against the pin and then striking it with a heavy hammer until it begins to move. A *backup bar* may be necessary to keep from bending thin sheet.

Transfer punch. The transfer punch, like the one shown in Figure 13-4-8, is used to transfer the holes through the template or patterns to the item beneath. This punch is usually about 4 inches long. Its point is tapered at the back and then turns straight for a short distance to fit the drill-locating hole in a template. The tip ends in a point similar to that of a prick punch.

Repairing the end of a punch. To a point, punches can be repaired by grinding. Pin, drive or other blunt end punches must be ground so that the end is perfectly flat and at right angles to the centerline of the punch. Center punches and prick punches are ground to conical points of 60° and 30°, respectively.

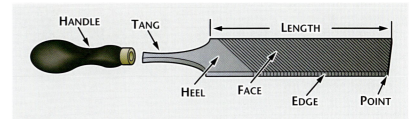
Figure 13-4-10. A typical file and its nomenclature

Figure 13-4-11. Single- and double-cut file teeth

Hollow Punches

Hollow punches, frequently called *gasket punches*, are used to cut holes in thin, soft metal or other items such as rubber, cork, leather or paper. Figure 13-4-9 shows a typical hollow punch. The edge of hollow punches should be protected by using a backup under the material being punched out. Plywood or masonite make good backup material.

Files

Files are hardened steel tools used for cutting, removing, smoothing or polishing metal. The cutting edges, or *teeth*, are made by diagonal rows of chisel cuts. The parts of a file are named and illustrated in Figure 13-4-10. Files can be classified by grade and shape, and they are graded according to whether they have single-cut or double-cut teeth and by their degree of fineness.

Single- and Double-cut Teeth

The difference between single- and double-cut teeth is apparent in Figure 13-4-11.

Single-cut. Single-cut files have rows of teeth cut parallel to each other. These teeth are set at an angle of about 65° from the centerline. These files are used for sharpening tools, finish filing

Figure 13-4-8. Transfer punch

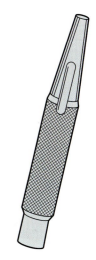
Figure 13-4-9. Hollow punch

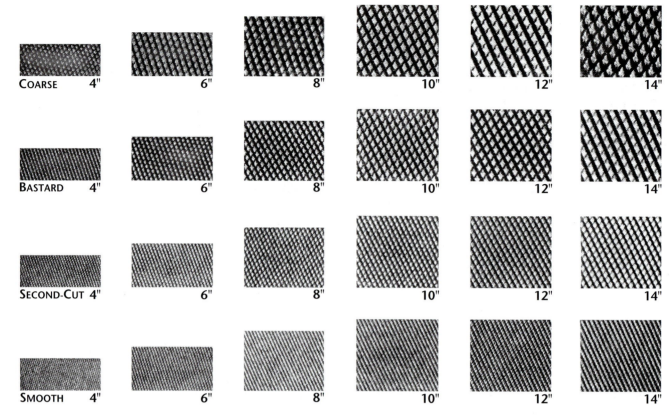

Figure 13-4-12. File teeth spacing and fineness

Figure 13-4-13. Mill file

Figure 13-4-14. Vixen curved-tooth file

and draw filing. They are also the best tools for smoothing the edges of sheet metal.

Double-cut. Double-cut files have crossed rows of teeth. The double-cut forms teeth that are diamond-shaped and fast cutting. These files are more abrasive than single-cut files, and they are used for quick removal of metal and for rough work.

Degree of fineness. Files are also graded according to the spacing and size of their teeth, or by their coarseness and fineness. Shown in Figure 13-4-12, the usual grades of fineness are called *coarse*, *bastard*, *second-cut* and *smooth*. The fineness or coarseness is influenced by the length of the file. Most round and half-round files are bastard cut and remove material quickly.

Shapes of Files

Files come in different shapes. When selecting a file for a job, the shape of the finished work must be considered. Common file shapes are described in the following paragraphs.

Triangular files. Triangular files are tapered toward the point on all three sides. They are used to file acute internal angles and to clear out square corners. Certain triangular files are used to file saw teeth.

Mill files. Mill files are tapered in both width and thickness. One edge has no teeth and is known as a safe edge. Mill files are used for smoothing lathe work, draw filing and other precision work. They are always single-cut. Mill files, Figure 13-4-13, are the most common files you will use.

Flat files. Flat files are general-purpose and may be either single or double-cut. They are tapered in width and thickness. Double-cut flat files are usually used for rough work, while single-cut, smooth files are used for finish work.

Square files. Square files are tapered on all four sides and are used to enlarge rectangular holes and slots.

Round files. Round files serve to enlarge or smooth round openings. Small round files are often called *rattail files*.

Half-round files. The half-round file is a general-purpose tool. The rounded side is used on curved surfaces, and the flat side is used on flat surfaces. When filing an inside curve, use a file whose curve most nearly matches the curve of the work.

Curved-tooth files. Curved-tooth files (also called *Vixen files* or *auto body files*) are generally used on aluminum and sheet steel, on both flat and curved surfaces. They are also used for smooth, rapid work on bronze, lead, babbitt, zinc and plastic. An example of this type of file is shown in Figure 13-4-14.

File Selection for the Job

Certain file grades are most effective and produce very specific finishes on certain metals. The following are some of the suggested grades of files to be used on the applicable metals.

- For heavy, rough cutting, use a large, coarse, double-cut file.
- For finishing cuts, use a second-cut or smooth-cut, single-cut file.

Cast iron. When working on cast iron, start with a bastard-cut file and finish with a second-cut file. A second-cut file is one grade finer than a bastard cut.

Soft metal. When filing soft metal, start with a second-cut file and finish with a smooth-cut file.

Hard steel. When filing hard steel, start with a smooth-cut file, and finish with a dead-smooth file.

Brass or bronze. When filing brass or bronze, start with a bastard-cut file and finish with a second- or smooth-cut file.

Aluminum, lead or babbitt. When filing aluminum, lead or babbitt metal, use a standard-cut curved tooth file.

Using a File Safely and Correctly

Using a file is an operation that is nearly indispensable when working with metal. Most filing operations can be classified as crossfiling and drawfiling. There are several basic precautions, however, that must be taken when using and maintaining a file.

- If the file is designed to be used with a handle, do not attempt to use it without the handle. *Holding the tang of the file in your hand while filing may result in serious injury* (Figure 13-4-15).
- Do not use a file for prying. The tang end is soft and bends easily, while the body of

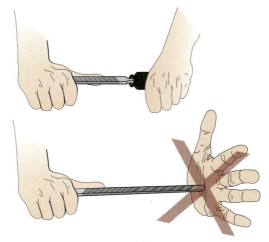

Figure 13-4-15. Correct use of file handle

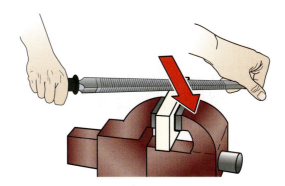

Figure 13-4-16. Crossfiling

the file is hard and brittle and will snap under a very light bending force.

- Do not hammer on a file. This may cause the file to shatter.
- The strokes with the file should be long and smooth and there should not be more than 40 strokes per minute to prevent overheating of the teeth.
- There should be no pressure on the file as it is being drawn back. The teeth slant forward and back stroke pressure will cause them to break more readily than on the forward stroke. However, when filing very soft metal such as aluminum, a slight back stroke pressure will aid in cleaning the teeth.
- For small work, use a short file. For medium- sized work, use an 8-inch file. For large work, use the file size that is most convenient.

Crossfiling. Crossfiling means that the file is moved across the surface of the work in an approximate crosswise direction, as shown in Figure 13-4-16. When an exceptionally flat surface is required, hold the file at an angle and file across the entire length of the stock. Then,

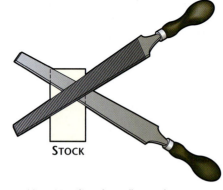

Figure 13-4-17. Filing for a flat surface

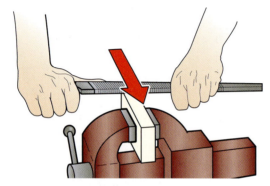

Figure 13-4-18. Drawfiling

Figure 13-4-19. File card

Figure 13-4-20. Hand drill

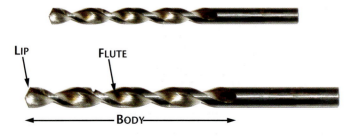

Figure 13-4-21. Typical drill bits

turn the file, as shown in Figure 13-4-17, and file across the entire length of the stock again. Because the teeth of the file pass over the stock in two directions, the high and low spots will be readily visible after filing in both positions.

Drawfiling. Drawfiling produces a finer surface finish and, usually, a flatter surface than crossfiling. Refer to Figure 13-4-18 and proceed as follows:

- Hold the file as shown. The cutting stroke is away from the body when the file handle is held in the right hand. If the handle is held in the left hand, the cutting stroke will be toward the body.

- Hold the file at right angles to the direction of the stroke, and keep hands relatively close together to prevent bending the file.

- Keep the pressure light. The pressure can remain the same for both the cutting stroke and the return stroke. The speed of filing is not important.

- When drawfiling no longer improves the surface texture, wrap a piece of abrasive cloth around the file and stroke in the same manner.

Cleaning a file. Keeping a file clean will make for smooth cuts. If metal filings are allowed to build up to the point that they stick together, they can end up marking the teeth, especially on a mill file. This will leave marks on the filed surface and may result in having to replace the file.

The brush used to clean a file is called a *file card* (Figure 13-4-19). File cards generally come with a small metal pick attached. Its purpose is to pick out any metal filings that will not brush out with the card's metal bristles. A clean file cuts better and lasts longer.

Hand Drills

A hand drill is used when electric or pneumatic power is not available. These drills provide a much slower drilling speed because they are hand-powered. The most common is the so-called *egg beater*.

Hand drill. The hand drill, shown in Figure 13-4-20, has a handle to provide pressure by hand. This drill is used to drill holes in wood and sheet metal, and is generally the most common.

Drills

A drill is a pointed tool that is rotated to cut holes in material. It is made of carbon steel or harder alloy steels, depending upon the type of work required. A typical drill bit and its parts are shown in Figure 13-4-21. Some of these parts are explained in the following paragraphs.

Lips. The lips are the parts which actually do the cutting.

Flutes. The flutes allow the chips to escape, give the correct rake to the lips or cutting edges and, when it is necessary to use a lubricant, they allow the lubricant to reach the cutting edges.

Body. The body of the drill is ground away slightly, except at the margin, to reduce the friction of the drill as it rotates.

Drill Sizes

The number, letter, fractional and decimal sizes of drill bits are shown in Table 13-4-1.

Laying out work. When laying out work to be drilled, mark the hole locations in the following manner:

DRILL	DECIMAL	DRILL	DECIMAL	DRILL	DECIMAL	DRILL	DECIMAL
80	0.0135	49	0.073	20	0.161	I	0.272
79	0.0145	48	0.076	19	0.166	J	0.277
78	0.016	5/64	0.078125	18	0.1695	K	0.281
1/64	0.0156	47	0.0785	11/64	0.171875	9/32	0.28125
77	0.018	46	0.081	17	0.173	L	0.29
76	0.02	45	0.082	16	0.177	M	0.295
75	0.021	44	0.086	15	0.18	19/64	0.296875
74	0.0225	43	0.089	14	0.182	N	0.302
73	0.024	42	0.0935	13	0.185	5/16	0.3125
72	0.025	3/32	0.09375	3/16	0.1875	O	0.316
71	0.026	41	0.096	12	0.189	P	0.323
70	0.028	40	0.098	11	0.191	21/64	0.328125
69	0.0292	39	0.0995	10	0.1935	Q	0.332
68	0.031	38	0.1015	9	0.196	R	0.339
1/32	0.03125	37	0.104	8	0.199	11/32	0.34375
67	0.032	36	0.1055	7	0.201	S	0.348
66	0.033	7/64	0.109375	13/64	0.203125	T	0.358
65	0.035	35	0.11	6	0.204	23/64	0.359375
64	0.036	34	0.111	5	0.2055	U	0.368
63	0.037	33	0.113	4	0.209	3/8	0.375
62	0.038	32	0.116	3	0.213	V	0.377
61	0.039	31	0.12	7/32	0.21875	W	0.386
60	0.04	1/8	0.125	2	0.221	25/64	0.390625
59	0.041	30	0.1285	1	0.228	X	0.397
58	0.042	29	0.136	A	0.234	Y	0.404
57	0.043	28	0.1405	15/64	0.234375	13/32	0.40625
56	0.0465	9/64	0.140625	B	0.238	Z	0.413
3/64	0.046875	27	0.144	C	0.242	27/64	0.421875
55	0.052	26	0.147	D	0.246	7/16	0.4375
54	0.055	25	0.1495	E	0.25	29/64	0.453125
53	0.0595	24	0.152	1/4	0.25	15/32	0.46875
1/16	0.0625	23	0.154	F	0.257	31/64	0.484375
52	0.0635	5/32	0.15625	G	0.261	1/2	0.5
51	0.067	22	0.157	17/64	0.265625		
50	0.07	21	0.159	H	0.266		

Table 13-4-1. Drill sizes

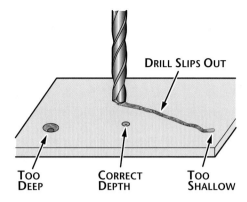

Figure 13-4-22. Correct depth of center punch for drilling

- Do not hit the center punch too hard, because it will dent the surrounding metal. Place a bucking bar behind the metal to prevent denting.
- Because it is hard to see around the 60° point of a center punch, locate the exact center of the hole to be drilled and mark the spot with a prick punch.
- Enlarge the prick punch mark with a center punch so that the point of the drill can seat properly. This is shown in Figure 13-4-22.

Drilling holes. To drill the material, proceed as follows:

- Use eye protection when drilling.
- Place the drill in the center-punched mark. When using a power drill manually, rotate the chuck a few turns before starting the motor.
- Hold the drill at a 90° angle to the work and apply pressure while drilling.

NOTE: *The amount of pressure to be applied while drilling depends on the size of the drill and the hardness of the metal being drilled. Stainless steel requires more pressure than steel, which requires more pressure than aluminum.*

- When the center punch mark has been cut away, lift the drill and examine the cut to ensure that it is in the required location. If it is not, the drill can be made to lead in the desired direction by cutting a groove in the side of the drilled portion with a cold chisel. The drill cannot be made to lead after the entire point has entered the item.
- As the drill begins to emerge from the stock, release pressure on the drill so that it does not catch on the chips in the hole. If it catches when drilling thin sheet metal, the drill will enlarge the hole.

Sharpening Drills

When drills are worn or need to be modified for certain metals, they can be reground. They can be reground by machine or by hand.

Machine grinding. The most accurate way to grind a drill is to use a machine designed specifically for this purpose. One is shown in Figure 13-4-23. There are many other types, some much better than others. A good drill grinding fixture must allow for heel clearance. It should also allow for 135° split-point drills.

Hand grinding. Drills may be ground by hand, but only if a drill-grinding machine is not available. It takes a lot of practice to learn to grind a drill by hand; not many people can do a good job. Drill sharpening is a skill that is best taught by someone that has the capability to do it correctly.

Holes are generally not drilled perfectly smooth, exactly straight and square. When an item needs a hole of an exact size, it must be reamed.

Reamers

A reamer is a cutting tool with one or more cutting surfaces used for enlarging or to size and contour a previously formed hole. A reamer functions by removing a small amount of stock from the walls of a hole. To ream effectively, the diameter of a reamer must be a greater diameter than the hole to be reamed.

NOTE: *Do not use the reamer to remove more than 0.002 to 0.003 inches of metal. If the hole is too small, enlarge it with a drill before reaming it.*

Figure 13-4-24 shows the parts of several types of reamers. The cutting face is the leading edge in

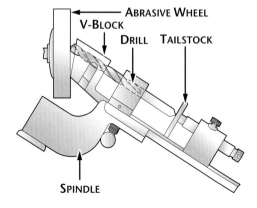

Figure 13-4-23. Machine grinding a drill

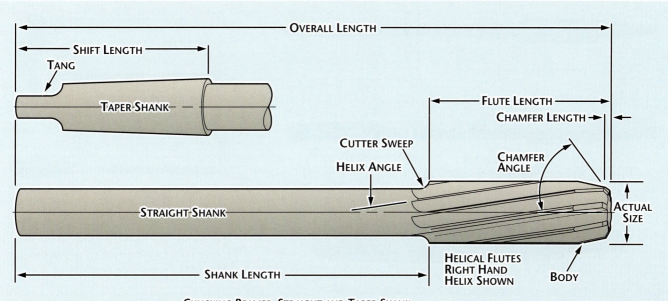
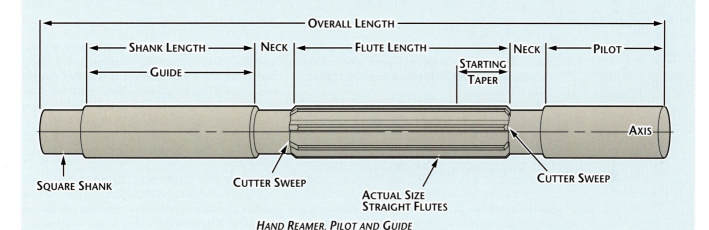
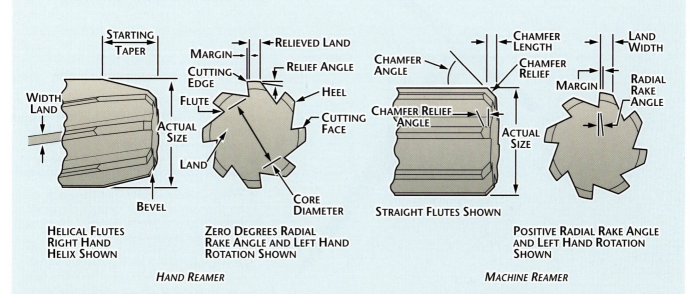

Figure 13-4-24. Identification of parts of reamers

Figure 13-4-25. Adjustable (hand) reamer

Figure 13-4-26. Jobber's (machine) reamer

Figure 13-4-27. Brown and Sharpe tapered (hand) socket reamer

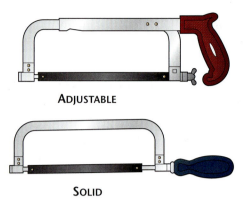

Figure 13-4-29. Hacksaws

the direction of rotation. Longitudinal channels (flutes) in the body of the reamer are used for the passage of lubricating fluid and chips.

Types of reamers. Reamers conform to types, classes and styles as specified by industry standards. Reamers are classified according to construction and/or method of holding and driving.

Adjustable, inserted blade, straight fluted (hand). These reamers are fitted with removable cutting blades, which are adjustable for reaming holes of any size within the range for which the reamer was designed. These reamers have straight, round shanks with square ends, and they contain slots for holding the blades. The reamer assembly is capable of reaming round, straight and smooth holes. This reamer is shown in Figure 13-4-25.

Jobber's (machine) reamer. These reamers are of grade-A, high-speed steel and have straight flutes and right-hand cut, as shown in Figure 13-4-26. The cutting section of these reamers is capable of cutting straight, round holes of specific diameters.

Brown and Sharpe taper socket (hand). These reamers have a fluted-type section and straight, round shank with squared ends. The cutting section of these reamers is tapered for reaming Brown and Sharpe (B&S) 1/2-inch-per-foot standard sockets. The B&S taper is used for tools with B&S taper shanks. It is also used for threaded taper pins. This type is shown in Figure 13-4-27.

Repairman's T-handle. These reamers have straight flutes and a solid handle. The cutting section tapers 1-1/4 inches per foot, as shown in Figure 13-4-28.

Selecting and Using Reamers

- The diameter of a reamer should be greater than the diameter of the hole to be reamed. All reamers, except for adjustable reamers, are marked with their nominal size.
- A reamer should enter a hole at right angles to the work surfaces to permit all teeth to simultaneously engage. On a curving surface, the rotating axis of the reamer is presumed to be at right angles to a plane tangent at the point of entrance.
- Where possible, provisions should be made for the reamer to pass through the workpiece. Line reaming is required for concentricity and alignment of holes.
- Work aids, which incorporate bushings to guide the reamers, are needed to produce holes that are in parallel alignment at exact distances from location points.

Figure 13-4-28. Repairman's T-handle (hand) reamer

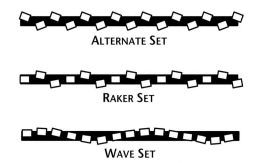

Figure 13-4-30. Hacksaw blade set

For long holes, it is preferable to guide the reamers at both ends. Work aids are locally fabricated.

- Reamers are operated at slower speeds and higher feed rates than drills of the corresponding diameter. Reamer feed rates will depend upon the type of metal and the size or strength of the reamer.
- Install the reamer shank into a tap wrench and tighten the handle to clamp the reamer in place.
- Turn the reamer in the cutting direction (direction of the cutting edges) only. *Do not ever turn reamer backwards. To do so will result in rapid wear, chipping and dulling of the cutting edges.*
- Turn the reamer very slowly in the cutting direction (clockwise) until the reamer is in the center of the hole.
- When reaming steel, use cutting oil or machine oil to lubricate the tool.
- Do not turn the reamer too quickly, or too slowly, because this will cause the reamer to chatter, producing an out-of-round hole.
- Turn the wrench in the cutting direction with steady, firm pressure until the reamer has been turned in the hole.
- Remove the reamer from the hole by continuing to turn the reamer in the cutting direction and raising the reamer at the same time.

Hacksaws

Hacksaws are used to cut metal that is too heavy for snips or bolt cutters. The two parts of the hacksaw are the frame and the blade.

Frame. The frame may be solid or adjustable, as shown in Figure 13-4-29. Adjustable frames can be made to hold blades from 8 to 16 inches long, while those with solid frames take only the length blade for which they are made. This length is the distance between the two pins that hold the blade in place. The blade is installed in the frame with the teeth pointing forward and is tightened by turning the handle or a wing nut.

Blades. Hacksaw blades are made of high-grade tool steel. They are about 1/2 inch wide, from 8 to 16 inches long, and have a pitch (number of teeth per inch) of 14, 18, 24 or 32.

Temper. Hacksaw blades come in two types: all-hard and flexible. The all-hard blades are hardened throughout, whereas only the teeth of the flexible blades are hardened.

Set. The set in a saw refers to how frequently the alternating teeth are set in opposite directions from the sides of the blade. The three different kinds of set are alternate set, raker set and wave set, as shown in Figure 13-4-30.

Stock thickness. Heavy stock is usually cut with the all-hard blade because it has less tendency to wander. The flexible blade is less likely to break and is used for thin stock.

Stock hardness. Generally speaking, the pitch of the blade depends on the hardness of the stock. Figure 13-4-31 shows the typical applications for the different saw blade pitches.

NOTE: *When cutting, there should always be at least two teeth working on the stock.*

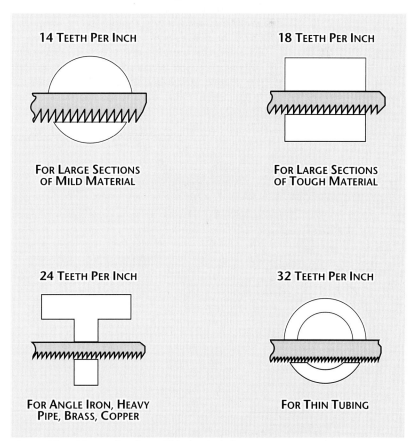

Figure 13-4-31. Application of blade pitch for certain materials

Figure 13-4-32. Proper way to hold a hacksaw

Therefore, for thin-walled stock, a finer blade than is ordinarily used may be necessary.

Using a Hacksaw Correctly

Install the blade in the hacksaw frame with the teeth pointing away from the handle. Tighten the wing nut so that the blade is taut.

Place the stock to be cut in a vise. Maintain a minimum of overhang to reduce vibration, give a better cut and lengthen the life of the blade. Ensure that the layout line on the stock is outside of the vise jaw and visible during sawing.

Hold the hacksaw as shown in Figure 13-4-32.

When cutting, apply pressure on the forward stroke, which is the cutting stroke. Do not apply pressure on the return stroke. Use long, smooth strokes.

Section 5
Power Tools

Pneumatic Tools

Pneumatic tools look much the same as electric tools, but they are driven by compressed air. These tools can be used for a vast variety of jobs that otherwise would be impossible to do.

Safety precautions. Air-driven tools do require additional safety precautions to prevent injury.

- Inspect the air hose for cracks or other defects.
- Before connecting an air hose to an air outlet, open the shutoff valve momentarily to expel any condensation.
- Stop the flow of air to a pneumatic tool by closing the shutoff valve before connecting, disconnecting, adjusting or repairing the tool.
- Always wear eye protection when using pneumatic tools.
- Always drain condensate drains daily. More often if the system is heavily used.

Cleaning Guns

Cleaning guns are used for applying air, a mixture of air and cleaning solution or solvent spray under pressure to parts which must be cleaned. There are two main types of cleaning guns: the *solvent cleaning gun* and the *air blow gun*.

Solvent cleaning gun. A solvent cleaning gun, shown in Figure 13-5-1, is used for applying a spray of solvent to engines and other structures which are cleaned with solvent. Before using

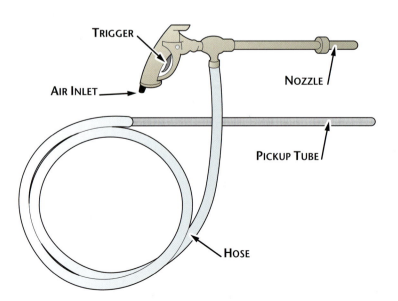

Figure 13-5-1. Cleaning solvent gun

Figure 13-5-2. Most blow guns have nozzles that limit discharge pressure to 30 p.s.i.

any chemical in a solvent gun, make sure it is approved for the project.

Air blow cleaning gun. The air blow cleaning gun, shown in Figure 13-5-2, is used for applying a direct blast of air to clear away dirt, dust and metal shavings, or to air dry parts cleaned with solvent. All blow guns should be of the pressure limiting OSHA-approved type.

Blow gun safety. Remember to never aim a blow gun at anyone. Debris flying from the hose could cause serious injury. Never horseplay with a blow gun. Air pressure can pierce the skin and inject air into a person's body, causing death and/or serious injury.

Vacuum Cleaner

The shop vacuum cleaner is used to clean up metal shavings which result from drilling and filing jobs on aircraft and in shops. The attachments give the vacuum cleaner versatility. These attachments include a round brush, a crevice tool, a fan-shaped end and tube extensions of varying lengths, which allow use in restricted areas. Smaller hoses can be attached to reducer fittings and threaded into very tight spaces. These attachments are available from hardware stores or home centers and come blister-packed.

Pneumatic Drill Motors

Pneumatic drill motors are used where sparks from an electric drill might pose a fire hazard. They also are somewhat more lightweight than electric drill motors. When working with aluminum, air drill motors tend to run at higher speeds (r.p.m.) closer to the desired speed and feed rates of the material.

Types. Pneumatic drills that are available are straight or set at 90°, like the drill shown in Figure 13-5-3. These different types allow a part to be drilled in just about any location.

Using air drill motors.

- Do not apply further pressure with pliers or wrenches after the chuck is hand-tight-ened with the chuck key.
- Always remove the key immediately after it is used. Otherwise, the key will fly loose when the drill motor is started and may cause serious injury to personnel.
- A drill bit that wobbles or is slightly bent should not be used because it will cause enlarged holes.
- Test the drill bit for trueness and vibration by running the drill freely.
- Wear eye protection when drilling. Failure to comply may result in serious injury to personnel.
- Always hold the drill at right angles to the work regardless of the position or curvatures. Tilting the drill at any time may cause elongation of the hole.

Pneumatic Grinders

A typical pneumatic grinder is shown in Figure 13-5-4. The grinders are rated by no-load speeds,

Figure 13-5-3. Pneumatic drills operate at higher r.p.m. than most electric models.
Photo courtesy of Snap-on Tools

Figure 13-5-4. Pneumatic die grinders are lightweight and powerful.
Photo courtesy of Snap-on Tools

Figure 13-5-5. A Ketts panel saw

Figure 13-5-6. Air-powered sabre saws are lightweight and reduce the fire/explosion hazard.
Photo courtesy of Snap-on Tools

which typically result in terms of light-, medium- and heavy-duty loads being used to describe the grinder. The grinding stones come in numerous shapes and give versatility to the grinder.

When changing stones, always make sure the replacement stone is of the correct rated speed. If the speed is too low for the machine, it will disintegrate, causing possible injury.

- A grinding stone that wobbles or has a bent shaft should not he used.
- Test the grinding stone for trueness and vibration by running the grinder freely. Grinding stones which are glazed, out-of-true or out-of-round may be reshaped with a dressing stick.
- Wear eye protection when grinding. Failure to comply may result in serious injury to personnel.
- Perform grinding operations by holding the grinder so that the proper edge of the grinding stone is against the work.
- Always protect surrounding parts and assemblies from grinding dust. Clean the area when completed.

Many additional air-powered tools are used in aircraft work, particularly in sheet metal and structural repair. They are discussed in the appropriate sections.

Air Ratchets & Impact Drivers

Normally, air-powered wrenches of any kind are not used in aircraft maintenance. The part of the impact wrench that actually does the impacting (hammering) on the drive square causes torque to spike with each hammer hit. The design makes it virtually impossible to control torque within the design limits specified by the manufacturer. Because of this difficulty in controlling the application of torque, they do not work well in a maintenance function.

Saws

Panel saws. The Keets saw panel saw (Figure 13-5-5) is an air-powered tool that has been a standard aircraft tool for many years. In essence, it is a drill-type air motor with a right-angle drive. On the shaft extension, there is a tool steel saw blade mounted with an appropriate guard. The blade is depth-adjustable and is used for cutting sheet metal either in place or before fabrication. It works well for material that would be difficult to cut with snips or a saber saw.

Sabre saw. An air-powered reciprocating sabre saw, Figure 13-5-6, is excellent for cutting heavier aluminum sheet or plate. They are lightweight, powerful and can cut curves easily. By drilling holes in each corner and then cutting to the holes, any opening can be sawed quickly. Because of marks left by the saw teeth, any sawn edges must be filed smooth. They need to be supported during filing so the sheet will not bend.

Electric Tools

The most common electrical power tool in most shops is the drill motor. It is a useful tool to have, but must be used properly to ensure the safety of personnel.

Safety

The following safety precautions should always be followed when operating electric power tools:

- Never operate power tools unless they are

Tools and Test Equipment | 13-29

Figure 13-5-8. Electric drills

The components of the drill are enclosed in a metal or plastic pistol grip case to permit ease of handling. Although it is specially designed for drilling holes, it can be adapted for different jobs by the addition of various accessories. It can be used for sanding, buffing, polishing, wire brushing and paint mixing. Typical electric drills are shown in Figure 13-5-8.

Sizes. The sizes of electric drills are classified by the largest straight shank drills that they will hold. Therefore, a 1/4-inch drill will hold straight-shank drills up to and including 1/4 inch, and a 3/8-inch drill will hold bits up to and including 3/8 inch.

Speed. The drill is made to run at speeds which will prevent the motor from burning out. For this reason, large drills run at slower speeds than smaller drills. This is because larger drills are designed to turn larger cutting tools or to drill heavy stock, both of which require a slower speed. Therefore, to drill in a metal such as steel, a 3/8-inch or 1/2-inch drill should be used; whereas for drilling holes in wood or sheet metal, a 1/4-inch drill will be sufficient.

Using an electric drill. The operation of an electric drill motor involves simply installing the drill bit, plugging in the cord and operating the drill.

Installing the drill bit. The drill bit is installed in the chuck on the drill. Nearly all electric drills are equipped with a three-jaw chuck, which is tightened and loosened by means of a chuck key, as shown in Figure 13-5-9.

Figure 13-5-7. Three-prong grounded plugs are used on most commercial electrical tools.

completely understood. If in doubt, consult the operator's manual.

- Inspect all power tools before use to ensure their serviceable condition.
- Prior to connecting the tool to its power source, ensure that the power switch is in the OFF position.
- Keep all safety guards in position and wear safety shields or goggles when necessary.
- Fasten all loose clothing and aprons. Watch out for neckties, chains, scarves or any other item that might be loose.
- Never try to clear jammed machinery before disconnecting the tool from its power source.
- Before plugging a tool into a power source, ensure that the power source provides the correct voltage required by the tool.
- If the power cord has a ground pin, as shown in Figure 13-5-7, do not attempt to use it with an adapter. The ground pin decreases the possibility of electric shock.
- Do not use sparking electric tools in places where flammable gases or liquids are present. Use pneumatic tools in these areas.
- Replace cords when they are damaged.
- Ensure that the power cord is of sufficient length so that it will not be pulled taut to reach the work location.
- Position power cords so that they will not be tripping hazards.

Electric Drill Motors

The electric drill motor is a hand tool driven by a small, high-speed electric motor. The motor is geared to the chuck through reduction gears.

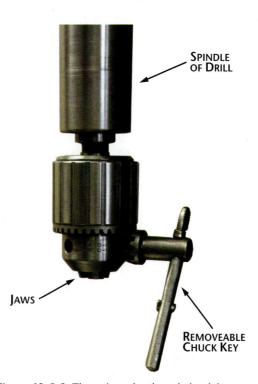

Figure 13-5-9. Three-jaw chuck and chuck key. Never leave the key in the chuck.

Section 6
Soldering Tools

Description and Identification

Soldered connections are used in aircraft electrical wiring to form a continuous and permanent metallic connection having a constant electrical value. The importance of establishing and maintaining a high standard of workmanship for soldering operations cannot be overemphasized.

This section describes the materials and equipment used in soldering aircraft interconnecting wiring. It also describes and illustrates preparation and care of equipment, procedures to be followed and the soldering techniques necessary to make a good soldered joint.

In addition, special materials, equipment and techniques used in soldering printed circuit assemblies are described where they differ from those used in general electrical soldering. In the repair of printed circuit assemblies, soldering is closely associated with repairs to the insulating base and conductor pattern, and with replacement of components. Therefore, typical procedures and techniques for making such repairs are included in this chapter.

Soldering. Soldering is the process of joining two (or more) metals together at a temperature lower than the melting points of the metals. In its molten state, solder chemically dissolves part of the metal surfaces to be joined. However, most metals exposed to the atmosphere acquire a thin film of tarnish or oxide; the longer the exposure the thicker the film will become. This film is present, even though it is not visible, and solder alone cannot dissolve it. A soldering flux with a melting point lower than the solder must be used to "wet" the metal and allow the solder to penetrate it and remove the film. The flux melts first, removing the tarnish or metallic oxide, and also prevents further oxide from forming while the metal is being heated to soldering temperature. The solder then melts, floating the lighter flux and the impurities suspended in it to the outer surface and edges of

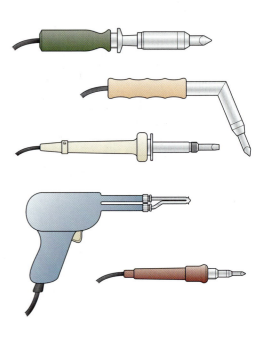

Figure 13-6-1. Types of hand soldering irons

the molten filler. The solder cools and forms an alloy with the metal. Most of the flux is burned away during the soldering process; any residue is removed by appropriate cleaning methods.

The soldering methods used for general aircraft wiring are essentially the same for both production soldering and for repair work. For printed circuit assemblies, production methods and repair methods are different. In production, a dip soldering method is used, where several connections are made at the same time. Soldering repairs, however, are made individually using techniques similar to those used for soldering general wiring, with special precautions to prevent thermal damage to the heat-sensitive, closely packed circuit elements.

Soft solder. Soft solder is an alloy consisting of various combinations of tin and lead with silver and other additives, which melts at temperatures below 700 degrees F. It may be in bar form to be melted for tinning, or in the form of rosin-cored solder for use with a soldering iron or other heating means.

Soft solder used in aircraft electrical wiring conforms to the requirements of Federal Specification QQ-S-571. For general applications at low temperatures (up to 248 degrees F max.), use composition Sn60 (60% tin, 40% lead) to solder tin-coated copper wire and coaxial cable. For silver-coated copper wire in high temperature applications (up to 375 degrees F max.) use a lead-silver mixture, composition Ag 2.5 or Ag 5.5. Do not confuse high temperature soft solder with the hard solder described in the following paragraph. For soldering printed circuit boards, use a eutectic solder (63% tin, 37% lead) with a silver additive of one to three percent. Rosin-cored solder, tubular type, 1/32 inch diameter is recommended for printed circuits.

Hard solder. Hard solder, often called brazing alloy, is a silver alloy, Federal Specification QQS-561, which melts at temperatures ranging from 700 to 1,600 degrees F. Hard solder is used when greater mechanical strength or exposure to higher temperatures is required. Hard solder is commonly used in the aircraft electrical system for soldering thermocouple connections. Hard solder is not used on printed circuits.

Flux. Flux is a chemical reducer used for surface conditioning before and during the soldering process. With soft solder, use only water-white rosin, dissolved to a paste-like consistency in denatured alcohol, (Mil-Spec MIL-F-20329). With hard solder, use borax, or similar material, mixed to a paste with water, (Federal Specification O-F-499).

Typical soldering operations. Following are examples of typical soft-soldering operations used in aircraft electrical wiring:

- **Tinning:** Wires or cables preparatory to joint soldering and to fuse ends; contact pins and inside surfaces of solder cups; shielded wire braid, after twisting, to fuse, terminate and connect.
- **Soldering:** Wires and cables, previously tinned, inserted into solder cups of terminals, or mechanically wrapped on shaped lugs and post or hooked terminals; twisted connections, or broken wire for emergency repair; printed circuit conductor pattern defects, or component leads and lugs to conductor pattern terminal areas.
- **De-soldering:** Soldered joints prior to remaking; printed circuit component connections to remove component for replacement.

Heat Application Methods

Soldering iron. The most commonly used method of heat application for soldering joints in aircraft electrical wiring is by means of an electrically heated hand-held soldering iron. In addition to the conventional iron, a pencil iron or a soldering gun are frequently used. See Figure 13-6-1. Pencil irons, except for their smaller size, are identical to conventional irons, and are used for precision soldering of small units and miniature assemblies. Soldering guns, because they heat quickly, are excellent for intermittent use.

Resistance soldering. See Figure 13-6-2. Resistance soldering is frequently used in large volume production, where the operation is standardized. In this method, a low voltage transformer is used and the metal to be soldered is heated by the resistance to a flow of electric current. The work is gripped between two electrodes, completing the circuit and heating the metal for soldering. In another application, a carbon pencil is used as one electrode, and the metal to be soldered forms the other electrode; when contact is established through the carbon pencil intense heat is generated at the point of contact. Resistance soldering is well adapted to the soldering of small parts, or for congested assemblies where it is desired to restrict heat to a small part of the assembly.

Torch soldering. Torch soldering is used where a high heat is required, as in silver soldering. This process is also suitable for soft-soldering large work which is not part of an assembly, or when the part to be soldered can be removed for soldering. For example, wires may be torch-soldered to large contacts which have been removed from MS connectors. Torch soldering is not suitable for soldering small parts.

Dip soldering. Dip soldering is the process of immersing connections in molten solder; one or more connections can be made in a single operation. This process is used on printed circuits, where the conductor pattern is one side of the board, and the components on the opposite side. Joints are mechanically secured, dipped first into liquid flux and then into molten solder.

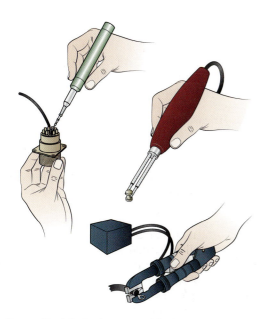

Figure 13-6-2. Resistance soldering

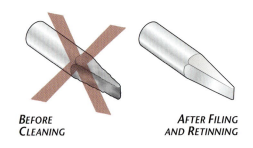

BEFORE CLEANING   AFTER FILING AND RETINNING

Figure 13-6-3. Soldering iron tip before and after cleaning

NOTE: Tin while iron is heating

Figure 13-6-4. Tinning soldering iron tip

Soldering Precautions and Procedures

For successful, effective soldering, the soldering iron tip must be tinned to provide a completely metallic surface through which the heat may flow readily from the iron to the metal being soldered. If no tinning is present, the iron will oxidize and the heat cannot flow through. Copper has a very high rate of heat conductivity, but copper tips oxidize quickly, and must be frequently cleaned and re-tinned. If a tip has become badly burned and pitted because of overheating, replace it.

Preparing the soldering iron. Before using the soldering iron, prepare it as follows:

1. With the iron shut off, file each working surface of the soldering iron tip with a double-cut mill file until it is smooth and of a bright copper color. See Figure 13-6-3. Remove copper fuzz from dressed edges with a file card.

2. Plug in the iron and apply cored solder just as the bright dressed copper color is turning to a pigeon-blue, bronze, oxide color. This will allow the flux to "wet" and clean the working area when the solder melts to form an even bright silver coating on the tip. (See Figure 13-6-4).

CAUTION: *Do not allow the iron to come up to full temperature before starting the tinning operation.*

3. Wipe off excess solder with a damp sponge or cloth.

Some copper soldering iron tips used in production soldering are coated with pure iron to help prevent oxidation. Follow manufacturer's instructions for cleaning such irons. A clean damp cloth may be used to wipe the iron.

NOTE: *Do not file soldering iron tips coated with pure iron. Filing will ruin the protective coating. If the tip is pitted, replace it.*

Soldering iron maintenance. During use, just before each application, pass the soldering iron tip with a rotary motion through the folds of a damp cleaning sponge, or wipe on an asbestos wiping pad. This will remove the surface dross and excess solder from the working surface.

CAUTION: *Never shake or "whip" an iron to get rid of dross or excess solder droplets.*

Once a day remove the tip from the iron and clean out the black scale from the inside of the iron and from the tip with fine steel wool. When the iron or tip is new, coat the inside of the shank with dry flake graphite or anti-seize material to prevent freezing, and to insure maximum heat transfer. When replacing the tip, make sure to insert the tip to the full depth of the casing, seated firmly against the heating element.

Soldering Operation - General Precautions and Procedures

Regardless of the heating method used in the soldering process, a good connection will result only if the proper soldering techniques are followed, and certain precautions observed. The following instructions apply generally to soldering operations.

NOTE: *A quality soldered joint can be accomplished only on a mechanical connection of approved geometry, dress and dimensions.*

Cleanliness. Cleanliness is of the utmost importance in the soldering operation. If possible, soldering should be done in an area that is reasonably clean and free from excessive dust. Drafty areas should be avoided so that the soldering iron will not cool.

Parts contaminated with dirt, oil, grime, grease, etc. cannot be successfully soldered. Make sure that the parts are mechanically "bright-clean", before soldering. Clean the parts with a cloth or brush dipped in alcohol, carbon tetrachloride, trichlorethylene or other approved solvent. Badly corroded parts may be cleaned carefully by mechanical means such as

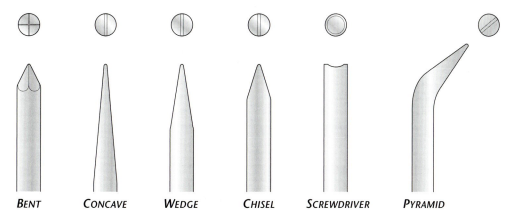

Figure 13-6-5. Soldering iron tip shapes

fine abrasive paper, a wire brush or by careful scraping with a knife blade.

Pre-tinning. Wires to be attached to most electrical connectors must be *pre-tinned*, or coated with solder or tin alloy prior to soldering or brazing.

Selection of flux and solder. Use only the solder and fluxes described earlier in this section.

> **CAUTION:** *Do not use any corrosive flux in aircraft electrical wiring.*

Heating capacity. Use a soldering iron or other heating method of sufficient capacity to heat the metal being soldered to solder melting temperature.

Selection of soldering iron. The sole purpose of the soldering iron is to heat the joint to a temperature high enough to melt the solder. Select a soldering iron with a thermal capacity high enough so that the heat transfer is fast and effective. An iron with excessive heat capacity will burn or melt wire insulation; an iron with too little heat capacity will make a cold joint in which the solder does not alloy with the work. Soldering irons are available in wattage ranges from 20 to 500 watts. Irons with wattage ratings of 60, 100 and 200 watts are recommended for general use in aircraft electrical wiring. Pencil irons with a rating of 20 to 60 watts are recommended for soldering small parts. The soldering iron recommended for printed circuit soldering is a lightweight 55 watt iron with a 600°F Curie point tip control. This iron has a three-wire cord to eliminate leakage currents that could damage the printed circuits.

A soldering iron should also be suited to the production rate. Do not select a small pencil iron where a high steady heat flow is required. A soldering gun is useful for intermittent work, but is not suitable for high speed production work because of the warm-up time required each time the trigger is depressed.

Choice of soldering tip. Select the tip best suited for the size and shape of the work being soldered. Some common tip shapes are shown in Figure 13-6-5. Soldering iron tips are available in sizes from 1/16 inch to 2 inches in diameter. For general use a tip of 1/4 inch to 3/8 inch diameter is recommended. For printed circuit soldering use a long shank tip of 1/16, 1/8, 3/32 or 3/16 inch diameter; Screwdriver, chisel and pyramid shapes are recommended.

Soldering iron. Before starting the soldering operation, make sure that the iron tip is clean, smooth and well-tinned. Instructions on preparation and maintenance of a soldering iron will be covered later in this section. When resistance soldering equipment is to be used make sure that probes are clean.

Securing the joint. Whenever possible make sure that the joint is mechanically secure before soldering. When this is not possible, as with MS connector contacts, make sure that the joint is held rigid during the cooling period.

Application of heat and solder. Apply flux-core solder at the exact point between the metal and the soldering iron, as shown in Figure 13-6-6 and hold the iron directly against the assembly. Melt the solder on the joint, not on the iron. Place the soldering iron firmly against the junction; if heavy "rocking" pressure is necessary, either the iron does not have sufficient heat capacity for the job, or it has not been properly prepared, or both.

Heat application time. Do not apply heat to the work any longer than the time necessary to melt the solder on all parts of the joint.

Amount of solder. Do not use any more solder than necessary. Do not pile up solder around

Figure 13-6-6. Position of soldering iron

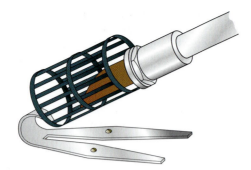

Figure 13-6-7. Soldering iron holder

the joint; this is wasteful, and results in joints difficult to inspect. Care should be exercised with silver coated wire to prevent wicking during solder application.

Soldering iron holder. When the soldering iron is not in actual use during operations, keep it in a holder such as is shown in Figure 13-6-7. This will protect the operator against burns, and the iron against damage.

Protection against overheating. Do not allow the iron to overheat. Disconnect the iron when it is not in use between operations, or use a heat dissipating stand, which will keep the iron at a constant temperature.

Cooling the solder joint. When the solder joint is made, hold the work firmly in place until the joint has set. Disturbing the finished work will result in a joint mechanically weak, and with high electrical resistance. Allow solder joints to cool naturally. Do not use liquids or air blasts.

Cleaning. If the correct amount of solder is used and procedure instructions followed carefully, there should be little or no excess flux remaining on the finished joint. If cleaning is necessary, remove excessive flux by brushing the joint with a stiff brush dipped in methyl alcohol, methyl isobutyl ketone or a similar approved solvent. Use alcohol sparingly, and avoid contact between alcohol and wire insulation. For cleaning printed circuit connections, use a cotton swab-stick for small areas, and a lint-free clean cloth for large areas and board edges.

Inspecting a Finished Solder Joint

Acceptable solder joint. See Figure 13-6-8. A good soldered joint will have a bright silvery appearance, with smooth fillets and feathered, not sharp edges. The entire joint will be covered with a smooth even coat of solder, and the contour of the joint will be visible.

Unacceptable solder joint. Any of the following indicate a poor solder joint, and are cause for rejection:

- Dull gray, chalky or granular appearance, evidence of a cold joint.
- Hair, cracks, or irregular surface, evidence of a disturbed joint.
- Grayish, wrinkled appearance, evidence of excessive heat.
- Partially exposed joint, evidence of insufficient solder.
- Scorched wire insulation or burned connector inserts.
- Globules, drips or tails of solder.

If any of the above are present in a finished solder joint, the joint should be taken apart, parts cleaned, and the entire soldering operation repeated, using fresh solder and flux.

Repair and Soldering of Printed Circuit Assemblies

Printed circuit assemblies are used in the aircraft electrical system to save space and weight, to increase reliability and to facilitate replacement. Typical locations are in equipment cases at area termination points of the interconnecting wiring, and in junction boxes at break-out points in the electrical system.

A printed circuit board consists of a conductor pattern bonded onto an insulating base. Components are mounted on the opposite side from the conductor, and are attached to it by leads through drilled holes or eyelets in the base. A printed circuit board may have conductor patterns on both sides. Each printed circuit board assembly is identi-

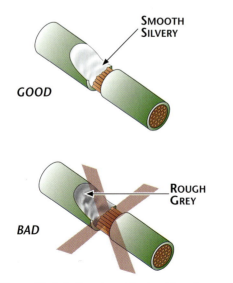

Figure 13-6-8. Good and bad soldered connections

fied by a number printed on the board, referencing the applicable circuit drawing or schematic.

Circuit Assembly Repair

Feasibility of repair. Many printed circuit assemblies are repaired and re-soldered to restore them to their original condition when they have been found to be defective or damaged. If the damage or defect is serious or extensive, it may not be practical to rework the board. It is not considered feasible to repair a printed circuit assembly if any of the following conditions could result:

- Repair is impractical because of the extent of the damage.
- The repair would decrease the life expectancy of any component.
- The repair could damage adjacent components or circuitry.
- The operation of the equipment would be changed by the repair.

In any of the above cases, replace the printed circuit assembly with a new identical assembly.

General Precautions and Procedures

Handling precautions. Printed circuit assemblies require very careful handling during repair and soldering operations, or when being installed as a replacement assembly. When handling assemblies withdrawn from cases and junction boxes or from replacement stores observe the following precautions:

- Keep the printed circuit assembly in a padded plastic or paper protective bag while awaiting use or repair. Keep in a cool dry place.
- Carry the assembly by its handle (if present) or by the edges.
- Do not handle or lift the assembly by any of its mounted components; this can result in broken leads.
- Do not stack one board on top of another. Always support the board on its long free edge.
- Never flex, bend or force the base during removal, repair or replacement.
- Avoid touching the face of the board with the hands, particularly the conductor or exposed contacts of plug-in assemblies and test points. Body acids produce corrosion and cause high resistivity that can affect the performance of the circuit.

- During repair, use an appropriate holding fixture to support the board by its edges, as shown in Figure 13-6-9. Provide adequate support underneath the board to offset the force of drilling, scraping and component removal or replacement.
- Make sure that all tools used for mechanical repairs are clean. Use only pliers with smooth jaws and radiused edges.
- Clean with short gentle puffs of low pressure, oil-free, dry air. Avoid violent bursts. Do not clean by ultrasonic methods this may affect the laminate.

De-soldering printed circuit components. When it is necessary to remove components from a printed circuit assembly, their leads or lugs must first be de-soldered, so that the leads or lugs can be readily withdrawn through the board to free the components. The procedures to be used and the precautions to be observed are as follows:

1. To melt the solder, apply the soldering iron tip to the fillet while slowly counting to four, then remove the iron.

CAUTION: *Do not exceed this time*.

Repeat as necessary, allowing the work to cool between applications. If it is desired to remove the component intact, as for testing, place a heat sink clamp on the lead, as close as possible to the component body before applying the iron.

Figure 13-6-9. Holding fixture for printed circuit assembly

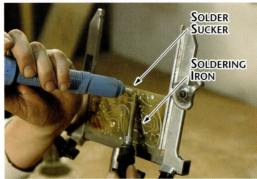

(A) Use of solder sucker in desoldering operation

(B) Removing solder with copper braid

Figure 13-6-10. Desoldering printed circuit components

2. Use a solder sucker to suck up the solder as it melts. See Figure 13-6-10A. Compress the bulb, place the tip directly on the liquid fillet, and release the bulb. Repeat as necessary.

3. In open areas, or to remove large terminal areas of soldering, a piece of 1/8 inch tubular electro-tinned braid may be used to remove the liquid solder as shown in Figure 13-6-10B. Flatten 1/4 inch of the braid end, dip sparingly into liquid flux, and place this end against the fillet. When the iron is applied, the solder will be drawn up into the braid as it melts. Cut off the solder-saturated part of the braid and repeat if necessary.

Soldering Procedures

Working space on printed circuit board assemblies is limited because of tightly packed components. The following special procedures will be helpful in soldering operations under these conditions:

1. Fix the board in the holder in such a way that gravity will aid in forming the fillet.

2. Select a tip shape to suit the angle of approach to the work. Use a screwdriver tip for an approach perpendicular to the board; use a pyramid shape when the approach is at an angle. See Figure 13-6-11.

3. Rest the elbow, arm or wrist against the bench top or holding fixture to assist in directing the iron to the work.

4. When soldering, coil the fine diameter cored solder into a small helix for easier handling, and feed from the center of the coil.

5. Apply the flat side of the iron against the work with a deliberate touch, not to exceed a slow count of four, until experience dictates the practical limit for the condition.

6. If the solder does not "take", allow the connection to cool, and reapply the iron tip, after adding a small amount of liquid flux. If this does not produce a satisfactory joint, remake the joint.

Soldering Precautions

When soldering printed circuits, the completed solder fillet must mechanically bond the component lead or lug to the foil terminal area, and electrically provide a low resistance path between the two. The soldering operation must be carried out without damage to the laminate, foil, and adjacent components. Observe the following precautions in addition to the general precautions listed earlier in this section.

- Make sure that leads are properly dressed and fixed in position before soldering.

- Use the smallest tip size and shortest heat application time possible to avoid damage to board, foil and components.

- Use only the solder and flux described at the start of this section.

- Use heat sinks to dissipate excessive heat. Excessive temperature will cause the base/foil laminate to discolor, delaminate, blister or burn; board components can be damaged or suffer a change in value from overheating.

- Protect areas adjacent to the soldering operation with lightweight solder shield, cut and shaped around components.

- Avoid excessive solder or splatter.

- Be careful not to accidentally touch the iron to the cored solder. This may cause the

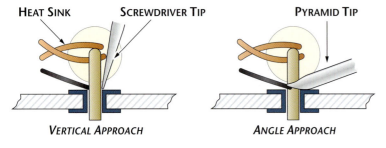

Figure 13-6-11. Soldering iron approach to work

Figure 13-6-12. Handheld magnifying glass

Figure 13-6-13. Head-mounted magnifying glass

solder to splatter, damaging the work and resulting in painful burns to the operator.

Magnifiers

Magnification tools increase the apparent size of an object. This is beneficial to the technician when working with small objects or close tolerances. The most common magnifying tool used by the avionics technician is the magnifying glass.

Key points for using magnifiers are the magnification rate and the ability to focus. The magnification rate is based on the combination of lens design and the way the lens is used. Every lens has an optical power, measured in diopters. This indicates the focal length. For instance a 3-diopter lens focuses at 1/3 m from the lens. This has a focus point approximately 1 foot from the lens and provides an enlargement ability of up to 1.75 time or 175 percent. A 5-diopter lens would focus at 8 inches and provide up to a 2.25 times or 225 percent magnification capability. Single-lens magnifiers do not have a fixed magnification amount. The useable magnification rate is a factor of the optical power of the lens and the focusing ability of the viewer's eye.

In practical terms, the closer the lens is held to the viewer's eye, the greater the magnification. Focus is obtained by moving the lens in relation to the object being viewed. When the viewer's eye, the lens and the object are at the correct distance from each other, than the object will be in focus. This may mean moving the lens away from or towards the object. Moving the lens closer to the viewer's eye increases magnification. Moving it away reduces it.

Single-lens magnifiers are found with magnification ranges of two to six. Multiple-lens magnifiers can provide up to 30 times magnification.

Three types of single-lens magnifiers are commonly used. The first is the handheld magnifying glass (Figure 13-6-12). The second is a head-mounted style (Figure 13-6-13). The third is a magnifying glass and lamp mounted on a flexible arm (Figure 13-6-14).

Each style has benefits, but all magnify in the same way. The handheld glass is light, inexpensive and

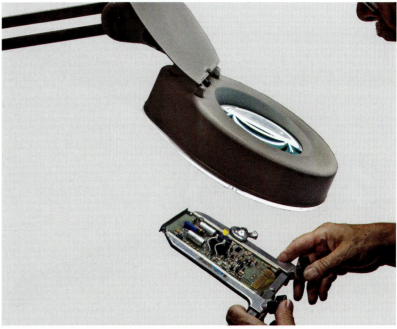

Figure 13-6-14. Magnifying glass mounted on flexible arm

simple to use. The head-mounted glass allows for hands-free use, enabling the technician to use both hands to perform a task. The magnifying glass with lamp not only allows hands-free use, but also provides additional illumination directly on the object. More light increases an individual's range of focus, allowing for higher, useable magnification ranges. It also reduces eye strain and fatigue.

Section 7
Conductor Termination

Aircraft wiring and cable must be cut to length in order to facilitate easier installation, maintenance and repair. To do this, wire and cable runs in aircraft are broken at specified locations by junctions, including connectors, terminal blocks or buses. All wires and cables should be cut to the lengths specified on aircraft manufacturer or equipment manufacturer drawings and wiring diagrams. Make the cut clean and square, using tools recommended by the wire manufacturer to avoid deformation of the wire or cable. It may be necessary to restore the shape of some large-diameter multi-stranded wires after cutting. Good cuts depend on cutting tool blades that are sharp and free from nicks. A dull blade will deform and extrude wire ends.

Stripping wire insulation. Preparing wire for assembly to connectors, terminals or splices requires that the insulation be removed from a short length of the conductor to expose the bare conductor. This procedure is known as stripping and is accomplished in a number of ways. Copper wire can be stripped with a variety of tools and according to the wire size and insulation type. Care must be exercised to avoid accidentally cutting or nicking the individual copper strands since this compromises the integrity of the connection. Aluminum wire, on the other hand, must be stripped very carefully, using extreme care because individual aluminum wire strands have a tendency to break very easily if they have been nicked or damaged in any way.

Follow these general precautions when stripping any type of wire:

- When using any type of wire stripper, hold the wire so that it is perpendicular to cutting blades.

- Adjust automatic stripping tools carefully and follow the manufacturer's instructions to avoid nicking, cutting or otherwise damaging strands. This is especially important for aluminum wires and for copper wires smaller than No. 10. Examine stripped wires for damage, then cut off and re-strip (if length is sufficient), or reject and replace any wires having more than the allowable number of nicked or broken strands listed in the manufacturer's instructions.

- Make sure insulation is clean-cut with no frayed or ragged edges and trim if necessary.

- Make sure all insulation is removed from stripped area. Some types of wires are supplied with a transparent layer of insulation between the conductor and the primary insulation. Any remaining insulation will cause a defective connection, so ensure all insulation has been removed. If necessary, examine the stripped wire with a magnifying glass.

- When using hand strippers to remove lengths of insulation longer than 3/4-inch, it is easier to accomplish in two or more operations.

- Re-twist copper strands by hand or with pliers, if necessary, to restore natural lay and tightness of strands. Ensure hands and any tools used are clean to avoid contaminating the wiring.

The majority of wire-stripping tasks will normally be done with a pair of hand wire strippers. The tool shown in Figure 13-7-1 is the wire stripping tool most commonly encountered, and may be used on most wiring types. The cutting blades are removable and are replaceable when they become dull. In addition, sev-

Figure 13-7-1. A common light duty hand operated wire stripper

Figure 13-7-2. Wire stripping with a hand operated tool

eral choices of cutting blades are available to handle a variety wire sizes.

Safely stripping wires with a hand stripper is a skill made easier by referring to the following suggestions and Figure 13-7-2.

- Insert the wire into exact center of correct cutting slot for wire size to be stripped. Each slot is marked with wire size. Move the wire until the length extending from the blade side of the stripping tool is the recommended length of bare wire required to complete the electrical connection.

- Slowly squeeze the stripper handles together until the clamp side of the tool securely holds the wire by its insulation and watch the blades bite into the insulation while continuing to squeeze the handles. When enough pressure has been applied, the stripping tool jaws will move apart, removing the insulation and revealing bare wire.

- Once the tool's jaws have moved as far apart as possible, quickly release pressure on the handles, allowing the clamping jaw and cutting jaw to fully open. Remove the stripped wire and proceed with the remaining steps to complete the connection.

- There are many different brands and types of commercial wire strippers and crimping pliers, including many that will do both (Figure 13-7-3). In almost all cases they will not be able to do a correct job, because they cannot be calibrated. In the case of commercial strippers, they will invariably nick the wire.

Wire splices and terminal connectors. Splicing of electrical conductors should be kept to a minimum and avoided entirely in locations subject to extreme vibrations. Individual wires within a group or bundle may be spliced,

Figure 13-7-3. A selection of commercial wiring tools

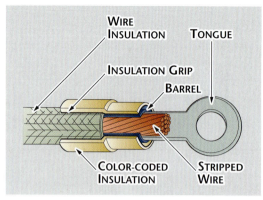

Figure 13-7-4. A wire terminal shown in a sectional view

as long as the completed splice is located where it can be visually inspected as needed. Splices should be staggered to prevent the bundle from becoming excessively enlarged or distorted in shape.

Many types of insulated and non-insulated aircraft splice connectors are manufactured by companies such as Amp, and are available for splicing individual wires. Self-insulated splice connectors such as the popular butt-splice are normally the preferred connector, however, a non-insulated splice connector may be specified for a certain application. You would normally cover non-insulated splice connectors with plastic sleeving, secured at both ends with lacing cord or a plastic tie. Solder splices have been used in the past, but they are particularly brittle and not usually recommended.

Whereas *solderless splices* are used to join electric wires to form permanent continuous runs, solderless terminal *lugs* permit easy and efficient connection to and disconnection from terminal blocks, bus bars or other electrical equipment. The great majority of solderless terminal lugs and splices are made of tin-coated copper or aluminum and are either pre-insulated or un-insulated, depending on the desired application. Most manufacturers color code the insulation on a splice or lug to indicate the wire size for which it is made.

Terminal lugs are generally available in three types for use in different space conditions. These are the flag, straight and right-angle lugs. The most commonly used terminal lug is a straight ring lug, designed to slide over the shank of a connecter stud. Terminal lugs are *crimped* (sometimes called *staked* or *swaged*) to the wires by means of hand or power crimping tools.

Copper wiring is terminated with solderless, pre-insulated straight copper terminal lugs. The insulation is part of the terminal lug and extends beyond its barrel so that it will cover a portion of the wire insulation, making the use of an insulation sleeve unnecessary.

The most popular pre-insulated terminal lugs contain an insulation grip (a metal reinforcing sleeve) beneath the insulation for extra gripping strength on the wire insulation. Color-coded insulation is used to identify the wire sizes that can be terminated with each of the terminal lug sizes. See Figure 13-7-4.

In addition to special wire stripping tools, special crimping tools are needed for installing splices and terminals on the ends of wire. While hand-held crimping tools are the most widely used in aircraft maintenance, aircraft manufacturing facilities may use portable power or stationary power tools for making thousands of crimped terminals quickly. These tools crimp the barrel of the typical terminal lug to the conductor and simultaneously crimp the insulation grip to the wire insulation for a very efficient and reliable electrical connection.

Better hand crimping tools all have a self-locking ratchet that prevents opening the tool until the crimp is complete. See Figure 13-7-5. Higher quality hand crimping tools are equipped with a "nest" of various size inserts to fit different size terminal lugs. All types of hand crimping tools need to be calibrated on a regular basis

Figure 13-7-5. Two sizes of ratcheting wire crimping tools

with gauges to ensure the proper adjustment of crimping jaws and a consistently reliable electrical connection.

A properly crimped terminal should provide a joint between the wire and the terminal that is as strong as the tensile strength of the wire itself.

Proper insertion of both the wire and the terminal in the crimping tool is essential for a good crimp. Figure 13-7-6 shows the correct placement of wire and lug in the hand tool. After stripping the wire insulation to proper length, insert the terminal lug tongue first into hand tool crimping jaws until the terminal lug barrel butts flush against the tool stop. Insert the stripped wire into the terminal lug barrel until the wire insulation butts flush against the end of the barrel, and then squeeze the tool handles until the ratchet releases. Remove the completed assembly and examine it for proper crimp. Figure 13-7-7 shows a good crimp on both the terminal and the insulation.

Un-insulated terminal lugs must be insulated after crimping. Before the days of shrink tubing, pieces of transparent flexible tubing called *sleeves* were used. The tubing was also called *spaghetti*. They are stilled used today. The sleeve provides electrical and mechanical protection at the connection. Certain types of pre-insulated lugs known as "hand-shakes" need this sleeve over the exposed portion of the two lugs where they "shake hands". When the size of the sleeving used is such that it will fit tightly over the terminal lug, the sleeving need not be tied; otherwise, it should be tied with lacing cord as illustrated in Figure 13-7-8.

Aluminum terminal lugs must be used with aluminum wire. You may recall that use of aluminum wire has both advantages and disadvantages. It has the advantage of being lighter in weight than copper, however, when aluminum is subjected to bending, it develops *work hardening*, making it brittle. This results in failure or breakage of strands much sooner than in a similar case with copper wire. Aluminum also forms a high-resistance oxide film immediately upon exposure to air. To counteract disadvantages, it is very important to use the most reliable installation procedures.

Use only aluminum terminal lugs to terminate aluminum wires. All aluminum terminal lugs incorporate an inspection hole that permits checking the depth of wire insertion. The barrel of aluminum terminal lugs is filled with a petrolatum-zinc dust compound. This compound removes the oxide film from the aluminum by a grinding process during the crimping operation. The compound will also minimize later oxidation of the completed

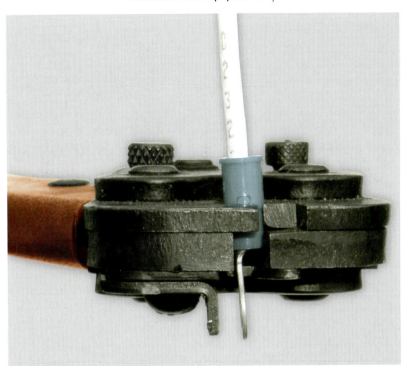

Figure 13-7-6. Using the terminal stop on an AMP ratcheting crimping tool

Figure 13-7-7. A properly crimped ring terminal

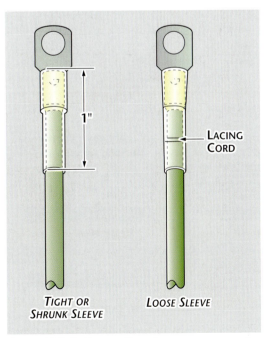

Figure 13-7-8. How to tie a sleeve on a connector

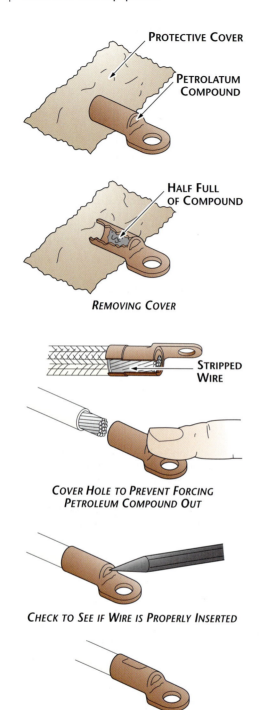

Figure 13-7-9. Although used very seldom today, this is the process for attaching terminals to aluminum wire

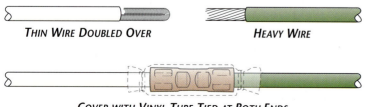

Figure 13-7-10. Using a crimp splice to join two different sizes of wire

connection by excluding moisture and air. The compound is retained inside the terminal lug barrel by a plastic or foil seal at the end of the barrel. See Figure 13-7-9.

As stated earlier, self or pre-insulated splice connectors such as the popular butt-splice are normally the preferred connector. These permanent copper splices join small wires of sizes 22 through 10 and each splice size can be used for more than one wire size. Splices are usually color-coded in the same manner as the pre-insulated small tin-coated copper ring-terminal lugs. Splices are also used to connect one wire size with another, as depicted in Figure 13-7-10. The same crimping tools used for the pre-insulated ring terminal may be used to crimp this type of splice. The crimping procedures are the same except that the crimping operation must be done twice, once for each end of the splice.

Section 8

Special Tools and Test Equipment

Proper use of specialized avionics tools includes knowing how to operate the tools and how to use them safely. This section covers the basic and safe operation of the most common tools.

Circuit Quantity Measurements

A number of instruments are used to measure quantities in a circuit—current, volts and resistance, for example. These instruments can also be used to check a circuit's function and continuity. If the electrical quantities in a circuit can be measured, it is easier to understand what is happening in that circuit. This is especially true when troubleshooting defective circuits. By measuring the voltage, current and resistance in a circuit, it is possible to determine why the circuit is not doing what it is supposed to do. An example of a digital multimeter is shown Figure 13-8-1 and an example of an analog multimeter is shown in Figure 13-8-2.

General Safety

When working on electrical or electronic circuits, always observe certain general precautions. The following is a listing of common sense safety precautions that must be observed at all times:

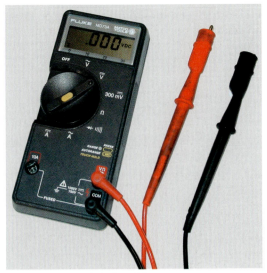

Figure 13-8-1. Digital multimeter

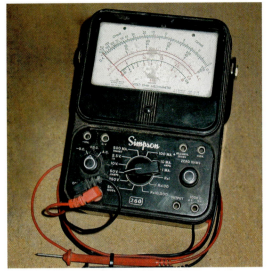

Figure 13-8-2. Analog multimeter

- Remember that circuits often have more than one source of power. Study the schematics or wiring diagrams of the entire system to ensure that all power sources are deactivated.
- All metal objects on the technician's body and clothing must be removed.
- Use one hand when turning switches on or off.
- Keep clothing, hands and feet dry if possible. When it is necessary to work in wet or damp locations, use a dry platform or wooden stool to sit or stand on, and place a rubber mat or other nonconductive material on top of the wood. Use insulated tools and molded insulated flashlights when you are required to work on exposed parts.
- When working on an energized circuit, keep one hand free at all times—behind the back or even in a pocket.
- Avoid reaching into enclosures, except when it is absolutely necessary. When reaching into an enclosure, use rubber blankets to prevent accidental contact with the enclosure.
- Make certain that equipment is properly grounded.
- Turn off the power before connecting alligator clips to any circuit.
- Never use a finger to test a "hot" line. Use approved voltmeters or other voltage-indicating devices.
- Remember that in equipment powered by alternating current, some voltage is present in switches, fuses and transformers even when the power switch is turned off.

Ammeters

Ammeters are used to measure current through a circuit. The earliest ammeter was developed by French scientist Jacques-Arséne d'Arsonval (1851–1940). This device used a permanent magnet and a moving coil that turned to a greater or lesser extent depending on the magnitude of the magnetic fields generated by a current. An indicator attached to the coil allows the user to read the magnitude of the current. Other ammeters work using double-magnet vane deflection, or thermocouples that heat up in proportion to the current that is present, or other means.

The basic mechanism is set up to measure a small, 0–1 milliammeter movement, but may be used to measure currents greater than 1 mA by connecting a resistor in parallel with the movement. The parallel resistor is called a shunt because it bypasses a portion of the current around the movement, extending the range of the ammeter. Often, the user can select the range of the current to be read on one of several scales on the face of the ammeter (Figure 13-8-3). The shunts protect the internal mechanism of the ammeter, but deliver the correct reading to the dial. Many ammeters today use a digital display, making

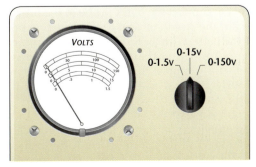

Figure 13-8-3. Multirange ammeter

Figure 13-8-4. An example of d'Arsonval meter movement

Here are some things to remember when using an ammeter:

- Set the range selector large enough to keep the deflection less than full scale. Before measuring a current, form some idea of its magnitude. Then switch to a large enough scale or start with the highest range and work down until the appropriate scale is reached. The most accurate readings are obtained at approximately half-scale deflection. Many milliammeters have been ruined by attempts to measure amperes. Therefore, be sure to read the lettering either on the dial or on the switch positions and choose the proper scale before connecting the meter into the circuit.

- Never connect an ammeter across a source of voltage, such as a battery or generator. Remember that the resistance of an ammeter, particularly on the higher ranges, is extremely low and that any voltage, even a volt or so, can cause very high current to flow through the meter, causing damage to it.

- Observe proper polarity when connecting the meter into the circuit. Current must flow through the coil in a definite direction in order to move the indicator needle up-scale. Current reversal because of incorrect connection in the circuit results in a reversed meter deflection and frequently causes bending of the meter needle. Avoid improper meter connections by observing the polarity markings on the meter.

the reading of the various scales immaterial. However, the internal workings of the digital ammeter are similar to those of an analog device.

Ammeters that measure alternating current use a rectifier to convert the AC to pulsating DC. Never use an AC ammeter to measure DC current, or vice versa.

Measuring current with an ammeter requires that the current being measured pass through the device via the probes. The original circuit must be broken and the meter inserted as part of the circuit, in series with the element through which the current flow is to be measured. It may be necessary to turn off and de-energize the circuit before disconnecting it, and then turn the power back on to perform the test. When the circuit has been physically broken, connect the black probe to the broken end of the circuit closest to the negative pole of the battery (in a DC circuit). Then connect the red probe to the other break in the circuit—for example, to the wire that was previously attached to the negative pole of the battery.

Sometimes, it is easier (or even physically necessary) to determine current by measuring the voltage across a known resistance and calculating the current using Ohm's law.

Voltmeters

The d'Arsonval meter movement (Figure 13-8-4) can also be used to measure voltage, in what is called a *voltmeter*. An ammeter becomes a voltmeter when a resistance is placed in series with the meter coil and the current is measured through it. In other words, a voltmeter is designed to indicate voltage by measuring current flow through a resistance of known value. The sensitivity of a voltmeter is therefore indicated in ohms per volt.

Various voltage ranges can be obtained by adding resistors in series with the meter coil. For low-range instruments, this resistance is mounted inside the case and usually consists of resistance wire having a low-temperature coefficient, which is wound either on spools or card frames. Multirange voltmeters, like multirange ammeters, are used frequently. They are physically very similar to ammeters, and their multipliers are usually located inside the meter with suitable switches or sets of terminals on the outside of the meter for selecting ranges. Like ammeters, many modern voltmeters use a digital display. An example of a digital multimeter operating as a voltmeter is shown in Figure 13-8-5.

When using a voltmeter:

- De-energize and discharge the circuit completely before connecting or disconnecting the voltmeter.
- Voltage-measuring instruments must be connected across (in parallel with) a circuit. Never connect the voltmeter in series with the circuit or device being tested. The voltage readings in this instance would be incorrect, and damage to the meter may occur.
- If the approximate value of the voltage to be measured is not known, it is best to start with the highest range of the voltmeter and progressively lower the range until a suitable reading is obtained.
- Observe the proper polarity when connecting a DC voltmeter instrument to the circuit. The positive terminal of the voltmeter is always connected to the positive terminal of the source and the negative terminal to the negative terminal of the source, when the source voltage is being measured. In any case, the voltmeter is connected so that electrons will flow into the negative terminal and out of the positive terminal of the meter. Never use a DC voltmeter to measure AC voltage.

Ohmmeter

The *ohmmeter* is used to measure resistance and to check the continuity of electrical circuits and devices. The range of a typical ohmmeter extends from a few ohms to a few megohms. When precision measurements are required, or when very low values of resistance must be measured, a milliohmmeter or resistance bridge circuit may be required. The megohmmeter, or megger, may have occasional application to measure extremely high resistance. Ohmmeters may be of the series, potentiometer or shunt type.

Most ohmmeters have more than one scale (Figure 13-8-6). Additional scales are made possible by using various values of limiting resistors and battery voltages. Some ohmmeters have a special low-ohm scale for reading low resistances.

Series ohmmeters can encounter difficulty reading high resistances; for those situations, a potentiometer is the better choice. The potentiometer-type ohmmeter design inserts a low-

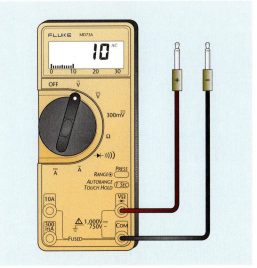

Figure 13-8-5. A voltage measurement displayed on a digital multimeter

value resistance, referred to as a standard resistor, in series with the unknown resistance being measured and the ohmmeter battery. The multiplier resistance, zero-adjustment variable resistance and meter movement are tapped off this circuit, forming a voltage divider. Therefore, the voltage across the standard resistor is proportional to the current flow through the resistance being measured.

Shunt-type ohmmeters are used to measure small values of resistance.

A megger (*megohmeter*) is a high-range ohmmeter used to test insulation resistance and other very high resistance values. In order to test resistance values in this range, it is necessary to use a much higher potential than could be furnished by an ordinary ohmmeter battery. This potential is provided by an internal hand-driven generator. Due to the high potential

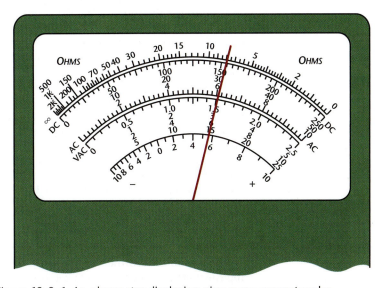

Figure 13-8-6. An ohmmeter displaying nine measurement scales

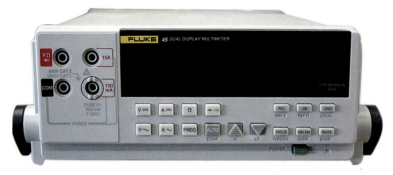

Figure 13-8-7. Bench-top digital multimeter

needed to perform very high resistance checks, the megger may have restrictions placed on its use by some maintenance agencies.

When using a megger, always observe the following safety precautions:

- Use meggers for high-resistance measurements only.
- Never touch the test leads while the generator is being cranked.
- De-energize the circuit completely before connecting a megger.
- Never use a megger on an aircraft if conditions do not absolutely require it.

The ohmmeter is not as accurate a measuring device as the ammeter or the voltmeter because of the associated circuitry. Thus, resistance values cannot be read with greater than 5 to 10 percent accuracy.

You can check the calibration on an analog ohmmeter by touching the probes together—the scale should read zero, or close to it. However, because this discharges the device's battery, you should disconnect the leads from the ohmmeter when not in use to avoid accidental contact.

In addition to measuring resistance, the ohmmeter is a very useful instrument for checking continuity in a circuit. Often, when troubleshooting electronic circuits or wiring a circuit, visual inspections of all parts of the current path cannot be readily accomplished.

It is not always apparent whether a circuit is complete or whether current might be flowing in the wrong part of the circuit because of contact with adjacent circuits. The best method of checking a circuit under these conditions is to send a current through the circuit. The ohmmeter is the ideal instrument for checking circuits in this manner. It provides the power and the meter to indicate whether the current is flowing.

CAUTION: *Never use an ohmmeter to check continuity of a circuit that includes explosive devices such as fire extinguisher cartridges, cable cutters, emergency jettison features, etc. The voltage and current flow caused by the ohmmeter battery, although small, may be enough to fire these devices.*

Always connect an ohmmeter in series with the circuit to be measured. The power switch for the circuit should be turned off. The ohmmeter provides its own test current, via a 3-volt battery, and uses it to measure resistance.

Multimeters

Multimeters are versatile tools that can measure resistance, voltage, and AC and DC current. If possible, use a multimeter rather than a more specialized tool. On most multimeters, you must turn a switch to indicate the circuit quantity you wish to measure, and also plug the probe leads into different ports depending on what the switch is set to. Follow the tool manufacturer's instructions on connecting the probes to the instrument. Connect the probes to the meter before you connect them to the circuit.

Digital multimeters allow for the largest *allowable error* that can occur under a specific condition. Figure 13-8-7 shows an example of a digital bench-top multimeter. Allowable error is an indication of how close a meter's displayed value is to the actual value of the signal being measured.

- Be sure the multimeter selection knob is set to the property you want to measure before connecting the probes to the circuit. Some devices emit a warning sound if the probes are configured for a voltage check but the selection knob is set to check current—but don't rely on that sound.
- Do not let the probes touch one another when connected to the circuit. This will result in a potentially dangerous short circuit.
- De-energize and discharge the circuit completely before connecting or disconnecting a multimeter. Never apply power to the circuit while measuring resistance with a multimeter.
- Connect the multimeter in series with the circuit for current measurements, and in parallel for voltage measurements. In other words, follow the instructions in previous sections that describe how to check with a specialized device for the quantity being measured.
- Be certain the multimeter is switched

to AC before attempting to measure AC circuits. When measuring DC, observe proper DC polarity.

Oscilloscopes

Oscilloscopes are another type of equipment used to measure voltages (AC peak-to-peak values) and frequencies. An oscilloscope (Figure 13-8-8) displays phase relationships (comparisons of waveforms in time) to identify equipment malfunctions. The waveform is usually displayed on a screen. Follow manufacturer's instructions to correctly and safely connect the probes required to make these readings.

Oscilloscopes can also be used to measure RF and microwaves. Analog oscilloscopes amplify the signal measured and display the signal at a specific sweep rate. Digital oscilloscopes use high-speed sampling to convert the signal measured into a series of "digital words" that are stored in the memory of the oscilloscope.

An oscilloscope can measure DC voltage if it has a direct-coupled deflection amplifier or terminals for connection directly to the deflection plates of the cathode-ray tube (CRT). Measuring a DC voltage with an oscilloscope is convenient only under certain circumstances; for example, when other measurements are being made on the same equipment with the oscilloscope or when a vacuum tube voltmeter is not available and a high-impedance measuring device is required.

Oscilloscopes have a high input impedance and normally will not load down the circuit under test. However, oscilloscopes are primarily designed for waveform observation and are typically less accurate than other pieces of test equipment used to measure DC voltages. A distinct advantage of the oscilloscope is its ability to monitor the level of AC ripple voltage riding the DC voltage. This feature makes the oscilloscope an indispensable aid in troubleshooting DC power supplies with excessive ripple caused by component failure.

Voltage measurements are most easily made when the deflection of the trace extends across the major portion of the oscilloscope screen; whenever possible, the trace should cover at least 60 percent of the vertical viewing area of the screen. If the amplitude of the measured voltage is very low, the trace dimensions may be small. If a voltage to be measured is large and cannot be attenuated to a usable value by attenuation circuits within the oscilloscope, an external resistive or capacitive voltage divider can be used. Such voltage dividers—known as high-voltage probes—are often furnished with oscilloscope test sets. When the voltage of pulses or other complete waveforms is being measured, the high-voltage probe selected must be so designed as not to distort the measured sig-

Figure 13-8-8. Oscilloscope

nal. Most probes have adjustable (compensating) capacitors that are used to adjust the symmetry of the displayed waveform. You adjust the probe by monitoring either the calibrator output of the oscilloscope or a known good signal and adjusting the probe for a symmetrical display.

Oscilloscopes are calibrated to display peak-to-peak values. To determine the root-mean-square (RMS) voltage of a sinusoidal signal, divide the number of graticule (scale) units from the positive to the negative peaks by two and multiply this value by 0.707. When using the oscilloscope for AC voltage measurements, ensure the upper frequency range of the oscilloscope is not exceeded; otherwise, inaccurate values will be displayed. Most commonly used oscilloscopes have a frequency response from DC up to 100 MHz.

Circuit Testing

Most of the time, a voltmeter or ohmmeter (or a multimeter configured as one of those) is used to test the continuity of a circuit. This is due in part to the fact that those devices do not require the circuit to be disconnected the way an ammeter does. Test at each terminal of the circuit to isolate the problem (Figure 13-8-9. For example,

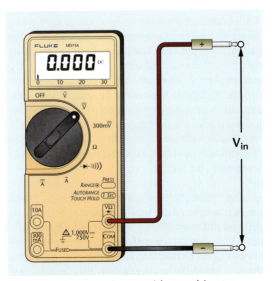

Figure 13-8-9. Circuit test with a multimeter

if there is zero output voltage, begin testing with a voltmeter at the input. A circuit diagram is your best ally in determining what components of a circuit to test.

The following subsections give further information on testing certain quantities of the circuit.

DC Voltage. When looking for a hazardous voltage condition, it is important to check between all possible points on the circuit, including between single wires and the ground. Regardless of the circuit expected, also check between points in both AC and DC modes. When checking a zero voltage situation, always check in the input first.

Voltages are usually measured by placing the measuring device in parallel with the component or circuit (load) to be measured. The measuring device should have an infinite internal resistance (input impedance) so that it will absorb no energy from the circuit under test and, therefore, measure the true voltage.

Digital multimeters typically have an accuracy of ±0.1 percent. A differential voltmeter, however, is accurate to approximately ±0.005 percent. However, differential voltmeters are less portable, heavier, and require greater skill and time when performing measurements than other types of voltmeters.

AC Voltage. When AC voltage measurements are performed, the input impedance of the selected test equipment determines the amount of energy removed from the circuit under test. If an AC meter is placed across a high-impedance circuit, the meter may load the circuit and disturb circuit conditions, possibly to the point of causing the circuit to cease functioning.

The frequency response of a piece of test equipment is just as important as its range limitations. If the circuit being measured is a relatively high-frequency circuit, the internal capacitance of an analog voltmeter rectifier could produce a disturbance by detuning the circuit. For high-frequency voltage measurements, a digital voltmeter or an oscilloscope should be used. The sensitivity of the meter (or oscilloscope) determines the lowest voltage it can measure accurately, and the shunt capacitance of its input determines the upper frequency limits.

Digital multimeters present a high input impedance to the circuit under test and are fairly accurate. The upper frequency limitations of digital multimeters generally vary from 20 kHz to over 300 kHz, depending on the model. Their upper frequency limitations can, however, be significantly extended by using optional RF probes. Remember that a digital multimeter is a "true rms" indicating devices, where the display is the square-root of the average of the square of the curve, and not to the average of the absolute value of the curve.

The differential voltmeter is the most accurate of the common ways of measuring AC voltage, with typical accuracies of ±0.05 percent.

Current. Unless an ammeter is already an integral part of the circuit under test, current measurements are rarely taken. In the case of a high-resistance circuit, it will contain such a small amount of current that it cannot be measured accurately with ordinary field test equipment. In lower resistance circuits, current measurements can be taken only if the ammeter is placed in series with the circuit under test. These measurements require that a circuit connection be unsoldered or otherwise opened to insert the meter in series with the circuit.

The accuracy of current measurements depends on the internal resistance of the meter as compared with the resistance of the external circuit. If the total circuit current is decreased by increasing the load, then the percentage of error will decrease. Therefore, greater accuracy is obtained if the meter resistance is considerably less than the load resistance. A method of obtaining greater accuracy of current measurement is to decrease the total internal meter resistance with respect to load resistance. This is accomplished by connecting two ammeters in parallel with each other and in series with the circuit in which the current is being measured.

Additional ammeters may be connected in parallel in the same manner for increased accuracy. This method also increases the range of measurements that can be taken. The arithmetical sum of the indications of all the parallel meters represents the total current flow in the circuit. Note that this is not a common test method and that your test equipment may be damaged if connected incorrectly.

Most analog multimeters cannot be used for measuring AC current and are only accurate to within ±2 percent on DC ranges. Digital multimeters will measure both AC and DC current (Figure 13-8-10), and if the work required to disconnect the circuit isn't too time-consuming, the results will be highly accurate: approximately ±0.3 percent for DC and ±1 percent for AC.

Another alternate is a current tracer. Current tracers do not actually measure current; rather, they indicate the presence of current and the relative magnitude of one source of current as compared to another.

Current probes, another alternative, are primarily designed to be used with an oscilloscope or milliammeter for measuring current. The primary advantage in using a current probe is that it does not need to be in series with the current being measured. Unsoldering wires or connections to terminals is not necessary, since current clamp on to insulated conductors. They are able to sense, through inductive action, the magnitude of the current flowing in the conductor. Current probes are designed for performing small AC current measurements. Also, when used in conjunction with current probe amplifiers, the capabilities of the current probe are extended to measurement of both AC and DC currents with large magnitudes. Current probes are extremely useful when you measure the current drain on a power supply, start-up current of a motor, or current flow in relays.

Resistance. Many aviation technical manuals contain point-to-point resistance charts that list correct resistance readings for major test points in circuits. These resistance charts are extremely useful when troubleshooting faulty equipment. Without them, equipment resistance measurements within a complicated circuit would not mean much. Many circuits contain other circuit elements, such as capacitors, coils, or other resistors in parallel with the resistances being measured. This, of course, is a possible source of measurement error that is eliminated when disconnecting or unsoldering one side of the resistor or a group of resistors under test.

Analog meters are typically more accurate and easier to read at midscale. With the exception of bridge circuits, a meter may provide only approximate resistance readings. However, these readings may be adequate when the wide tolerances of resistors themselves are also considered. An ohmmeter used in field testing should be portable, convenient and simple to operate—and these factors are often more important than extreme accuracy.

When an ohmmeter is used, completely de-energize the circuit under test and remove any current-sensitive elements before the resistance measurement is performed. Low-resistance measurements that require precision readings should be taken with a bridge type of instrument.

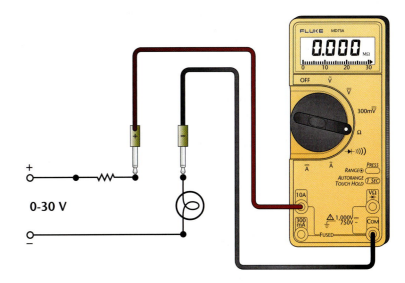

Figure 13-8-10. Multimeter connected to measure AC current.

Ohmmeter applications include resistance measurements; continuity checks; and inductor, capacitor and transformer checks. A transformer, for example, may be tested by checking whether there is an open or short, low-insulation resistance to ground, or improper continuity between transformer windings. A capacitor may be tested to determine whether it is open or shorted. Ensure that capacitors are properly discharged before testing them; otherwise, damage to the multimeter may occur. When an ohmmeter is placed in series with a capacitor, the changing current will cause a meter deflection that is proportional to the capacitance. The deflection obtained is compared with the deflection from a similar capacitor of known value. This deflection may be small or large, depending on the type and size of the capacitor and the voltage of the battery within the meter.

Digital multimeters also are ideally suited for measuring sensitive devices that might otherwise be damaged by the excessive current associated with analog multimeters. When measuring small values of resistances, remember to consider the resistance of the test leads. Most digital multimeters cannot be zeroed in the way analog multimeters can. With digital multimeters, short the leads, read the lead resistance displayed, and then subtract the reading from subsequent component measurements.

Index

A

absolute zero 9-2
acceleration 9-4
  negative 9-4
  positive 9-4
acceptor 5-10
acids 10-5
addend 8-4
adder 8-37
  full adder 8-38
  half adder 8-38
  parallel adder 8-39
  quarter adder 8-37
adjustable stabilizer 9-22
aerodynamic balance 9-22
aerodynamics 9-1
aerodynamic twist 9-25
  illustrated 9-25
Aerofiche 11-3
ailerons 9-13
  and spoilers 9-17
  balance cable 9-20
  differential travel 9-17
  illustrated 9-20
    bellcrank 9-20
  torque tube 9-20
air 9-1
aircraft drawings, purpose and function of 11-5
aircraft production drawings 11-16
airfoil 9-6
  angle of attack 9-7
  angle of incidence 9-7
  aspect ratio 9-7
  camber 9-7
  chord line 9-7
  lift-over-drag ratio 9-7
  planform 9-6
  shape 9-6
  skin friction 9-6
air pressure 9-6
Air Transport Association of America 11-3
alkalis 10-6
allowable error 13-46
alloy 1-10
alloy junction 5-12
alpha 5-33
alternating current 3-1
  resonance 3-49
    parallel 3-49
    series 3-49
alternator 4-16

American Standard for Tolerances, Allowances, and Gages for Metal Fits 11-16
Ammeters 13-43
ampere 1-23
amplification 5-26
amplifier 5-26, 7-2
  efficiency 5-31
  power amplifier 7-2
  voltage amplifier 7-2
amplifier class 7-3
  Class A amplifier 7-4
  Class AB amplifier 7-4
  Class B amplifier 7-4
  Class C amplifier 7-5
amplifier coupling capacitor 6-15
amplitude 3-7, 7-1
AND gate 8-27
angle of attack 9-7
  burble point 9-8
  chord 9-7
  critical angle 9-8
  stalling angle 9-8
angle of incidence 9-7
angles, measuring 13-5
anode 4-2
antistatic bag 5-45
antistatic caps 5-45
apparent power 3-43, 3-45
arc extinguisher 2-26
armature 4-9, 4-10
artificial magnet 1-11
  permanent 1-11
  temporary 1-11
aspect ratio 9-7
assembly drawing 11-7
asynchronous counter 8-42
ATA iSPEC 2200 11-5
ATA Spec 100 Manufacturers' Technical Data 11-5
ATA Spec 2100 Digital Data Standards for Aircraft Support 11-5
ATA Specification 100 11-3, 11-5
  replaced with 11-5
ATA Specification iSpec 2200 Information Standards for Aviation Maintenance 11-5
atmosphere 9-1
atmospheric pressure 9-2
  millibars 9-2
atom 1-2
augend 8-4
autotransformer 3-60
avalanche breakdown 6-3
avalanche effect 6-2
average value 3-8
avionics 1-1
axes 9-13
  lateral 9-13
  longitudinal 9-13
  vertical 9-13
  yawing 9-18
axial gear differential 4-21

B

backup bar 13-17
balance cable 9-20
balance tab 9-21
  illustrated 9-21
banking 9-16
barrier 5-13
base 8-2
base-current 5-29
battery 4-1
  lead-acid 4-2
  nickel-cadmium (NiCad) 4-3
battery cell 4-2
  primary cell 4-2
  secondary cell 4-2
Beechcraft Bonanza 9-19
  vee-tailed 9-19
    illustrated 9-18
bellcrank 9-19
Bernoulli's principle 9-5
beta 5-32
bias 5-13
  forward bias 5-13
  reverse bias 5-14
bill of material 11-18
binary 8-5
binary-coded hexadecimal 8-19
binary-coded octal 8-19
binary number system 8-5
bit 8-23
block diagrams 11-8
Bonanza 9-19
  vee-tailed 9-19
    illustrated 9-18
Boolean algebra 8-24, 8-27
Boolean expression 8-27
borrow 8-4
boundary layer 9-9, 9-23
  controlling 9-24
    using slats 9-24
  illustrated 9-24
branch 1-35
breakdown point 6-3
breakdown voltage 6-2
break lines 11-14
breakover point 6-10
bridge circuit 1-43
buffer amplifier 7-15
burble point 9-8
burning 12-9
buttock line stations 11-19

C

cabinet drawings 11-13
calipers
  hermaphrodite calipers 13-6
  spring-joint calipers 13-1
camber 9-7
canard 9-19
  illustrated 9-26
capacitance 3-22
capacitive reactance 3-39
capacitor
  troubleshooting 3-61
capacitor, fixed 3-32
  ceramic capacitor 3-33
  electrolytic capacitor 3-33
  mica capacitor 3-33
  paper capacitor 3-32
capacitor, variable 3-35
  rotor-stator type capacitor 3-35
  trimmer capacitor 3-35
carry 8-4
cathode 4-2
cavalier drawings 11-13
Celsius 9-2
center head 13-1, 13-5
center lines 11-14
Channel Lock pliers 13-15
chemical corrosion 10-1
chemical labels 12-3
chemicals 12-3, 12-9
chord 9-7
chord line 9-7
circles 11-14
circuit assembly 13-35
circuit breaker 2-18
  frame 2-26
circuit components 13-35
circuits
  parallel
    troubleshooting 1-47
  troubleshooting 1-44
    continuity 1-44
    discontinuity 1-44
    open circuit 1-44
      common causes 1-45
    short circuit 1-44, 1-46
      common causes 1-46
clamper 7-39
  common-base transistor 7-45
  negative-diode 7-43
  positive clamper 7-41
  positive-diode 7-40
  series RC 7-39
clamping. *See* **clamper**

clamping devices 13-16
cleaning materials
  methyl ethyl ketone (MEK) 12-4
  sodium bicarbonate 12-5
  sodium phosphate 12-5
cleaning solvents 12-4
clock 8-40
CO_2 fire extinguishers 12-11
combination circuit 1-41
combustion 12-9
commutator 4-9
complement 8-8, 8-25
complementary metal oxide semiconductor 5-43
complex wave 7-46
compound 5-5
conductance 1-24
conduction band 5-8, 6-2
conductor termination
  solderless splices 13-40
  stripping wire insulation 13-38
  terminal connectors 13-39
  wire splices 13-39
connection diagram 11-8
constant-speed drive 4-21
controllability 9-13
control surface
  primary 9-27
  secondary 9-27
conversion table 1-5
copper loss 3-19, 3-58
corrosion, inaccessible areas 10-8
  control cables 10-9
  engine-mount structures 10-9
  weld decay 10-9
corrosion inspection 10-5
corrosion-prone areas 10-7
corrosion, types of
  concentration cell 10-3
  exfoliation 10-4
  fatigue 10-4, 10-5
  filiform 10-3
  fretting 10-5
  galvanic 10-4
  intergranular 10-4
  oxygen concentration 10-3
  pitting 10-3
  stress 10-4
corrosive agents 10-5
  acid 10-5
  alkalis 10-6
  mercury 10-6
    amalgamation 10-6
  organic growth 10-7
  oxygen 10-6
  salts 10-6

  water 10-6
coulomb 1-17
counter 7-57, 8-40
  decade counter 8-43
  down counter 8-45
  increment counter 8-45
  negative-counter 7-59
  positive-diode counter 7-57
  ring counter 8-44
  ripple counter 8-41
  step-by-step counter 7-59
  synchronous counter 8-42
counter electromotive force 3-13
covalent bond 5-8
critical angle 9-8
crystal 5-9
crystal oscillator 7-7
current 1-22, 1-44, 1-45, 1-46, 1-47, 1-48, 1-49, 3-49, 3-61
current limiter 4-15
cutoff 5-29
cutting plane lines 11-14
cycle 3-7

D

damping 7-10
decimal number system 8-2
  number 8-2
  unit 8-2
decrement counter. *See* **down counter**
de-energized circuits 12-7
delay FF. *See* **D flip-flop**
delta winding 4-17
depletion region 5-13
detail drawing 11-5
diagonal-cutting pliers 13-15
diagrammatic 11-16
dielectric 3-23
dielectric hysteresis 3-25
dielectric leakage 3-25
difference 8-4
differential travel 9-17
differentiator 7-53
  medium time-constant differentiator 7-54
  short time-constant differentiator 7-54
dimensioning 11-16
  illustrated 11-16
dimension lines 11-14, 11-16
dimension, size 11-16
diode characteristics 5-17
diode rectifier 5-11
diode, semiconductor 5-17
dip soldering 13-31
direct short 2-17

distortion 5-28, 5-31
dividend 8-15
divisor 8-15
donor impurity 5-10
doping 5-10
dorsal fin 9-14
downwash 9-5
drag 9-6
  as relates to thrust 9-10
  induced 9-11
  parasite 9-11
  profile 9-11
drag component 9-8
drawing numbers 11-17
drawings, responsibility 11-18
drawings, types of 11-5
drills 13-20
  body 13-20
  electric 13-29
    and chuck keys 13-29
    installing a bit 13-29
    sizes 13-29
    speeds 13-29
    using an electric drill 13-29
  hand drills 13-20
  lips 13-20
  pneumatic drills 13-27
    safe use of 13-27
    types of 13-27
droop 9-28
dual-diode limiter 7-37
dual-path elevator 9-29
  artificial feel 9-29
  autopilot input 9-29
  stick nudger 9-29
Dutch roll 9-15
  illustrated 9-16

E

eddy current 3-58
  loss, eddy current 3-19
effective value 3-9
efficiency 1-29, 7-4
electrical power safety 12-7
electrical tools
  safety 13-29
electrical wiring diagram 11-8
electric power rate 1-27
electrochemical action 4-2
electrochemical corrosion 10-1
  electrode potential 10-2
electrode 1-21
electrolyte 1-21, 4-2

electromagnetic induction 3-5
electromagnetism 3-2
electromotive force 1-17
electron 1-3
electron current 1-22
electron-hole pairs 5-9
electrostatic discharge 5-43
electrostatic field 3-23
electrostatic force 1-8
electrostatic lines of force 3-23
element 1-2
elevator 9-13
  dual-path 9-29
  illustrated 9-17
  inboard 9-29
  outboard 9-29
emergency first aid procedures 12-3
EMF hazards 12-5
emitter current 5-23
empennages 9-18
  vee tail 9-19
energized circuits 12-7
energy band 5-7
energy conservation, law of 9-4
energy gap. See **forbidden band**
equivalent resistance 1-38
ESDS 5-43
exciter circuit 4-17
exciting current 3-53
exclusive NOR gate 8-32
exclusive OR gate 8-31
exploded views 11-7
explosion and fire data 12-3
exponent 8-3
extension lines 11-14
extinguisher operation 12-13
extrinsic 5-10

F

FAA regulations 11-3
Fahrenheit 9-2
farads 3-24
feedback 7-6
  negative feedback 7-7
  positive feedback 7-6
feeler gauge
  using a feeler gauge 13-6
ferromagnetic material 1-10
fidelity 5-31, 7-4
field effect transistor 5-1
field-effect transistor 6-18
field intensity 1-14
field of force 1-9
field winding 4-10

files
  cleaning 13-20
    file card 13-20
  crossfiling 13-20
  degree of fineness 13-17
    bastard 13-17
    coarse 13-17
    second-cut 13-17
    smooth 13-17
    double-cut 13-17
  drawfiling 13-20
  safety 13-18
  selection 13-18
    aluminum filing 13-18
    babbitt filing 13-18
    brass filing 13-18
    bronze filing 13-18
    cast iron filing 13-18
    hard steel filing 13-18
    lead filing 13-18
    soft metal filing 13-18
  shapes of files 13-17
    curved-tooth file 13-18
    flat file 13-17
    half-round file 13-18
    mill file 13-17
    round file 13-18
    square file 13-18
    triangular file 13-17
    Vixen curved-tooth file 13-18
  single-cut 13-17
  teeth 13-17
    spacing and fineness 13-20
filter 7-15
  capacitor filter 7-15, 7-18
  LC capacitor-input filter 7-15, 7-27
  LC choke-input filter 7-15, 7-21
  RC capacitor-input filter 7-15, 7-25
fineness ratio 9-6
fire extinguishers 12-10, 12-13
  carbon dioxide 12-10
  checking 12-13
  classification 12-13
  CO_2 12-10
  dry powder 12-13
  halogenated hydrocarbon 12-11
  identifying 12-13
  markings 12-14
  numerical rating 12-14
  symbols 12-13
  water 12-10
fire lanes 12-1
fire protection 12-9
fire, requirements of 12-9
fire safety 12-9
  spontaneous combustion 12-9

fire, types of 12-9
  chemical 12-9
  Class A 12-9
  Class B 12-9
  Class C 12-9
  Class D 12-9
fixed bias 5-29
flap 9-22
  blown 9-25
  Fowler 9-23
  illustrated 9-23
  Kruger 9-25
    illustrated 9-24
  leading-edge 9-25
    illustrated 9-24
  plain 9-23
  slotted 9-23
  split 9-23
  trailing edge 9-23
    illustrated 9-28
flashing the field 4-12
flight control surfaces 9-16
  ailerons 9-16
  elevators 9-16
  illustrated 9-17
  primary 9-16
    diagram of 9-27
  rudder 9-16
  secondary 9-27
flight, forces of 9-5
  drag 9-6, 9-10
  gravity 9-5, 9-10
  lift 9-5, 9-10
  thrust 9-6, 9-10
flightline safety 12-15
  hearing protection 12-15
flight, theory of 9-1
flip-flop 8-32
  D flip-flop 8-35
  J-K flip-flop 8-35
  R-S flip-flop 8-33
  toggle flip-flop 8-34
flow separation 9-25
flux 13-31
fly-by-wire system 9-27
flywheel effect 7-10
forbidden band 5-8
Foreign Object Damage (FOD) 12-15
fractional number 8-3
fractions 11-15
frequency 3-7, 4-19
frequency multiplication 7-14
full section view 11-7
fundamental frequency 7-46
fuse 2-18
  cartridge 2-19
    delay 2-20
    fast 2-20
    plug-type 2-19
    standard 2-20
fuse holder 2-21
fuselage stations 11-19

G

gamma 5-34
gas safety 12-5
gate 8-26
gauges
  sheet metal and wire gauges 13-6
  thickness gauges
    using a thickness gauge 13-6
generator 4-7
  AC generator 4-9
  DC generator 4-9
  generator, types 4-12
    compound-wound generators 4-12
    series-wound generators 4-12
    shunt-wound generators 4-12
generator control unit 4-16
generator faults 4-10
  armature loss 4-11
  armature reaction 4-11
  commutator-to-brush arcing 4-11
  copper loss 4-11
  eddy current 4-11
  hysteresis loss 4-11
  motor reaction 4-11
geometric dihedral 9-15
GPUs 12-15
gravity 9-5
gravity, center of 9-11
  stability 9-11
ground handling 12-1
ground potential 1-18
growler 4-11
grown junction 5-11

H

hacksaw 13-25
  blades 13-25
    pitch 13-25
    set 13-25
    stock hardness 13-25
    stock thickness 13-25
    temper 13-25
  frame
    adjustable 13-25
    solid 13-25
  using correctly 13-26

half section 11-7
halogenated hydrocarbon extinguisher, types of 12-11
  Halon 104 12-11
  Halon 1001 12-12
  Halon 1011 12-12
  Halon 1202 12-12
  Halon 1211 12-12
  Halon 1301 12-12
Halon 12-11
  carbon tetrachloride 12-11
  chlorobromomethane 12-12
  dibromodifluoromethane 12-12
  methyl bromide 12-12
hammer 13-7
  ball peen hammer 13-7
  body hammer 13-7
  copper hammer 13-7
  lead hammer 13-7
  soft-faced hammer 13-7
hand drill 13-20
hand signals 12-16, 12-17
  helicopter 12-17
hard failure 5-45
hard solder 13-31
harmonic 7-14
  even numbered 7-46
  odd numbered 7-46
hazard communication label 12-4
Hazard Communication Standard 12-3
hazardous liquids 12-4
hearing protection 12-15
  external 12-15
  internal 12-15
heating effect 3-9
helicopters 12-17
helicopter safety 12-17
hermaphrodite calipers
  Figure 3-18 13-6
hertz 3-7
hexadecimal number system 8-12
hidden lines 11-13
hole 5-9
horizontal stabilizer 9-14
  illustrated 9-18
horsepower rating 1-29
humidity 9-3
  absolute 9-4
  relative 9-4
hysteresis loss 3-5, 3-19, 3-58

I

illustrating objects, methods of 11-9
impedance 3-40
inductance 3-12

inductive reactance 3-36
inductor 3-15
  core type 3-15
    air-core 3-15
    iron-core 3-15
  troubleshooting 3-21
inertia 3-12
inspection, corrosion 10-5
inspection, visual 10-5
installation drawing 11-1, 11-7
instantaneous power rate 1-27
instantaneous value 3-8
insulated gate field-effect transistor 6-21
integrated circuit 5-1, 5-40, 5-41
  hybrid 5-42
  monolithic 5-42
integrated drive generator 4-21
integrator 7-46
  long time-constant integrator 7-53
  medium time-constant integrator 7-52
  RC integrator 7-49
  RL integrator 7-50
  short time-constant integrator 7-52
interconnect diagram 11-8
interpoles 4-11
intrinsic 5-10
inverter 4-15, 8-29
  rotary inverter 4-15
  static inverter 4-16
ionization 5-7
ionized 1-5
isometric drawings 11-12

J

jackscrew 9-22
jammed 8-33
joule 1-28
junction 1-36, 5-11
junction diode 5-1
junction gate field-effect transistor 6-18
junction recombination 5-13

K

Kelvin 9-2
kilovolt-amperes 4-17
kilowatt-hour 1-29
kinetic energy 1-3
Kirchhoff's law 1-32

L

laminar boundary layer 9-24
laminar flow 9-25
lateral axis 9-13
LC network 7-10
leakage flux 3-54
least significant digit 8-3
left-hand rule for a conductor 3-3
left-hand rule for generators 4-7
lettering 11-14
level 13-3
  using 13-3
lift 9-5
lift-over-drag (L/D) ratio 9-7
light-emitting diode 5-1, 6-12
limiter 7-31
  dual-diode 7-31, 7-37
  parallel-negative 7-31, 7-36
  parallel-positive 7-31, 7-35
  series-negative 7-31, 7-33
  series-positive 7-31
lineman 12-1
lines 11-5, 11-13
load 5-15
lockout 12-6
lockout devices 12-6
lockout/tagout 12-6
logic 8-24
logic flow charts 11-8
logic gate 8-26
logic level 8-25
logic polarity 8-25
  negative 8-25
  positive 8-25
logic states 8-25
longitudinal axis 9-13
long-nose pliers 13-15
long time constant 7-50
long time-constant differentiator 7-55

M

magnetic field 3-3
magnetic flux 1-14
magnetic induction 1-14
magnetic shielding 1-16
magnetism 1-10
magneto motive force 3-56
majority carrier 5-11
maneuverability 9-13
Material Safety Data Sheets 12-3
  emergency first aid procedures 12-3
  explosion data 12-3
  fire data 12-3
  handling precautions 12-3
  Hazard Communication Standard 12-3
  leak procedure 12-3
  physical data 12-3
  spill procedure 12-3
matter 1-2
  gas 1-2
  liquid 1-2
  solid 1-2
measuring tools
  bevel protractor 13-4
  carpenter's square 13-4
  combination square 13-4
  dividers 13-5
  rules 13-3
  square
    setting and using 13-5
    using a square 13-5
  tape 13-3
megohmeter 13-45
mercury 10-6
metal oxide semiconductor field-effect transistor 6-21
methyl ethyl ketone (MEK) 12-4
mho 1-25
mica 4-9
microelectronic devices 5-43
microelectronics 5-40
microfiche 11-2, 11-3
mil 1-24
millibars 9-2
minority carrier 5-11
minority current flow 5-14
minuend 8-4
mixed number 8-3
modular circuitry 5-41
modulo 8-41
modulus 8-41
molecule 1-2
momentary 2-9
most significant digit 8-3
motion 9-4
motion, Newton's laws of 9-5
  First 9-5
  Second 9-5
  Third 9-5
multimeter 13-46
mutual flux 3-56
mutual inductance 3-19, 3-56

N

NAND gate 8-30
National Fire Protection Association (NFPA) 12-9
  classification of fire 12-9
natural resonant frequency 7-11
negative alternation 3-7
negator 8-29
network 1-36

neutralization 5-44
neutron 1-3
Newton's First Law of Motion 9-5
Newton's Second Law of Motion 9-5
Newton's Third Law of Motion 9-5
  illustrated 9-9
noise 12-15
  GPUs 12-15
no-leak condition 12-6
nonsinusoidal 7-7
NOR gate 8-31
NOT gate 8-29
N-type material 5-12
N-type semiconductor 5-10
numerical rating 12-14
  Class A Ratings 12-14
  Class B Ratings 12-14
  Class C Ratings 12-14
  Class D Ratings 12-14

O

oblique drawings 11-13
Occupational Safety and Health Administration. *See* **OSHA**
octal number system 8-9
ohm 1-23
ohmmeter 1-45, 1-46, 1-47, 1-48, 1-49, 3-61, 3-61
Ohm's Law 1-25
operating mechanism 2-26
optical coupler 6-15
organic growth 10-7
OR gate 8-28
orthographic projection drawings 11-11
oscillator 7-7
  armstrong oscillator 7-11
  colpitts oscillator 7-12
  hartley oscillator 7-11
  LC oscillator 7-7
  RC oscillator 7-7
oscilloscope 13-47
OSHA 12-3, 12-13, 12-14
overdriven 5-31
oxygen 10-6

P

page 11-18
parallel circuit 1-35
parallel fed 7-13
peak-to-peak value 3-8
peak value 3-8
pedestrian walkways 12-1
pentavalent inpurity 5-10

period 3-7
perspective drawing 11-13
  illustrated 11-12
phantom lines 11-14
phase 4-18
  single-phase 4-18
  three-phase 4-18
  two-phase 4-18
photodiode 6-14
photoelectric voltage 1-20
photon 1-3
photosensitive 1-20
phototransistor 6-14
physical data 12-3
physiological safety 12-6
pictorial electrical diagrams 11-8
piezoelectric effect 1-19, 7-11
pig tail 4-10
pitch 9-13
planform 9-6
pliers
  diagonal-cutting pliers 13-14
  flat-nose pliers 13-14
  long-nose pliers 13-14
  retaining ring pliers 13-14
  slip-joint pliers 13-14
  water pump pliers 13-15
pneumatic tools
  air ratchets 13-28
  cleaning guns
    air blow cleaning gun 13-27
  drill 13-27
    90° 13-27
    Figure 3-141 13-27
    straight 13-27
    testing for trueness/vibration 13-27
    using air drill 13-27
  grinders 13-27
  impact drivers 13-28
  safety precautions 13-27
  saws 13-28
    panel saws 13-28
    sabre (reciprocating) saw 13-28
  vacuum cleaner 13-27
point-contact semiconductor diode construction 5-12
point-contact transistor 5-3
pole 2-4
pole shoe 4-10
portable fire extinguishers, classification of 12-13
  Class A 12-13
  Class B 12-13
  Class C 12-13
  Class D 12-13
positional notation 8-3

positive alternation 3-7
potential energy 1-3
potentiometer 2-31
power 1-27, 8-3
power consumption 1-29
power conversion 1-29
pressure 9-2
pressure, center of 9-13
primary cell 1-21
  dry cell 1-21
  wet cell 1-21
printed circuit assemblies 13-34
  desoldering components 13-35
printed circuit board 5-40
proton 1-3
protractor 13-1
P-type material 5-12
P-type semiconductor 5-10
punches 13-16
  hollow punches 13-17
  solid punches 13-16
    automatic center punch 13-16
    center punch 13-16
    drive punch 13-16
    pin punch 13-16
    prick punch 13-16
    transfer punch 13-17
pure 7-48
push-pull tube 9-20

Q

quanta 5-7
quiescent 5-27
quotient 8-15

R

radix 8-2
radix point 8-3
Rankine scale 9-2
  illustrated 9-3
RC network 7-9
reactance 3-40
reactive power 3-43, 3-44
reactivity 12-9
reamer 13-22
  adjustable 13-24
  Brown & Sharpe taper socket 13-24
  inserted blade 13-24
  Jobber's 13-24
  parts of 13-23
  repairman's T-handle 13-24
  selecting 13-24
  straight-fluted 13-24

rectifier 4-21
   three-phase 4-21
rectifier diode 5-15
relaxation oscillator 7-8
relay 2-2, 2-15
   control relay 2-15
   power relay 2-15
reluctance 1-11
remainder 8-4, 8-15
resistance 1-23
resistance soldering 13-31
resistivity 2-30
resistor 2-28
   fixed 2-30
   tapped 2-30
   variable 2-31
resonant frequency 3-49
restoring moment 9-13
resultant 7-46
retentivity 1-11
reverse current cut-out relay 4-15
revision block 11-18
rheostat 2-31, 4-13
Right to Know requirement 12-3
roll 9-13
rolling 9-16
rotor 4-17
R-S latch 8-33
rudder 9-13
ruddervator 9-19

S

safety
   chemical 12-9
   compressed gas 12-5
   electrical 12-6
   electrical fire 12-6
   fire 12-9
   flightline 12-15
   hearing protection 12-15
safety, chemical 12-9
safety, compressed gas 12-5
safety, electrical 12-6
   fire 12-6
safety, helicopter 12-17
safety lanes 12-1
safety solvent 12-4
salts 10-6
saturation 5-29
scale 11-18
schematic diagrams 11-8
sectional drawings 11-7
sectioning lines 11-14
selective tripping 2-28

self-bias 5-29
self-healing capacitor 3-35
self-induced emf 3-13
semiconductor diode 5-17
series aiding 1-34, 7-40
series circuit 1-30, 1-34
series fed 7-13
series limiter 7-31
series opposing 1-34, 7-40
servo tab 9-21
   illustrated 9-21
shop safety 12-1
short circuit 2-17
shunt fed 7-13
sideslip 9-14
side-slipping 9-18
siemens 1-25
signal 7-1
signal diode 5-15, 5-17
significant harmonics 7-49
silicon controlled rectifier 6-9
sine wave 3-2
   in phase 3-10
   lag 3-10
   lead 3-10
   out of phase 3-10
single-line diagram 11-8
sintering 4-3
sinusoidal 7-7
size, drawing 11-17
skid 9-18
skin friction 9-6
slats 9-24
slip ring 4-16
small-hole gauge 13-7
smoking rivet 10-5
sodium bicarbonate 12-5
sodium phosphate 12-5
soft failure 5-45
soft solder 13-30
soldering 13-30
   precautions 13-32, 13-36
     amount of solder 13-33
     choice of soldering tip 13-33
     cleanliness 13-32
     heat application time 13-33
     heating capacity 13-33
     pre-tinning 13-33
     selection of flux and solder 13-33
   procedures 13-32, 13-36
     application of heat and solder 13-33
     cleaning 13-34
   types of
     dip 13-31
     resistance 13-31
     torch 13-31

     typical operations 13-31
   soldering iron 13-31, 13-33
     holder 13-34
     maintenance 13-32
     preparing 13-32
     protection against overheating 13-34
     selection of 13-33
   solder joint 13-34
     cooling 13-34
     securing 13-33
solenoid 2-2, 2-13
solid state device 5-1
spanner wrench
   Adjustable spanner wrenches 13-13
   Solid spanner wrenches
     face pin spanner wrench 13-13
     hook spanner wrench 13-13
     pin spanner wrench 13-13
specific gravity 4-5
speed 9-4
speed brake 9-17
spillage 9-11
spill or leak procedure 12-3
spoilers 9-17
   as speed brake 9-17
   lateral control 9-17
spontaneous combustion 12-9
spring tabs 9-21
   illustrated 9-21
square
   bevel protractor square 13-4
   carpenter's square 13-4
   combination square 13-4, 13-6
stabilator 9-18
stability, aircraft 9-11
   directional 9-14
   dynamic 9-13
   illustrated 9-13
   lateral 9-14
   longitudinal 9-14
   moment 9-13
   negative static 9-13
   neutral static 9-13
   restoring moment 9-13
   rolling 9-16
   side-slipping 9-18
   skid 9-18
   spoilers 9-17
   sweepback 9-15
   vee tail 9-18
   ventral fin 9-14
   yaw damper 9-15
stability, directional 9-14
   dorsal fin 9-14
   sweepback wings 9-14
   vertical stabilizer 9-14

stability, dynamic 9-13
stability, lateral 9-14
stability, longitudinal 9-14
stalling angle 9-8
stall strip 9-25
   illustrated 9-25
standard day 9-4
standards, drawing 11-18
standard symbols 8-39
static balance 9-22
static electricity 1-8
static stability 9-13
static stability, types of 9-13
   negative 9-13
   neutral 9-13
   positive 9-13
station numbers 11-19
stator 4-17
subtrahend 8-4
sum 8-4
sweepback 9-15
   illustrated 9-15
sweepback wings 9-14
switch 2-2
   automatic switch 2-3
   manual switch 2-3
   microswitch 2-9
   multi-contact switch 2-4
   pushbutton switch 2-5
   snap-acting switch 2-9
   wafer switch 2-6
synchronous counter 8-42

T

tagout 12-6
tap 3-53
   center tap 3-53
telescoping gauge 13-7
temperature 9-2
   Celsius 9-2
   conversion 9-2
   Fahrenheit 9-2
   Kelvin, absolute 9-2
   Rankine scale 9-2
temperature coefficient 1-24
terminal connectors 2-26
thermal runaway 4-6
thermocouple 1-20
thermoelectric 1-20
theta 3-43
three-phase 3-50
throw 2-4
thrust 9-6
   as relates to drag 9-10

title block 11-17
tolerance, dimensioning 11-15
tool boxes 13-3
torch soldering 13-31
torque tube 9-20
total circuit resistance 1-30
total resistance 1-38
transformer 3-50
transformer, like-wound 3-54
transformer, step-down 3-56
transformer, step-up 3-56
transformer, unlike-wound 3-54
transistor 5-1
   NPN transistor 5-19
   PNP transistor 5-19
transistor configuration 7-12
   common base 7-12
   common collector 7-12
   common emitter 7-12
TRIAC 6-11
trim tabs 9-21
   illustrated 9-21
trip element 2-26
trivalent 5-10
true power 3-44
truth table 8-26
tungsten carbide 13-4
tunnel diode 5-3, 6-4
tunneling 6-3

U

unijunction transistor 6-16
unity coefficient of coupling 3-20
universal language, drawings 11-5

V

valence 1-4
valence band 5-8, 6-2
valence electron 5-7
valence shell 5-6
varactor 6-7
vee tail 9-19
   illustrated 9-18
velocity 9-4
ventral fin 9-14
venturi 9-5
vertical axis 9-13
vertical stabilizer 9-14
vinculum 8-25
visible lines 11-13
voltage 1-17
voltage regulator 4-13
   carbon pile voltage regulator 4-14

   three-unit regulator 4-14
   transistorized voltage regulator 4-20
   vibrating type voltage regulator 4-14
voltage source 1-19
voltage waveform 3-2
voltaic pile 4-2
volt-ampere 4-17
voltmeter 13-44
vortex 9-11

W

water 10-6
water pump pliers 13-15
watt 1-27
waveform 3-2
wavelength 3-7
wheatstone bridge circuit 1-44
whole number 8-3
windings 3-52
wind tunnel 9-1
wing fences 9-27
   illustrated 9-26
winglets 9-25
   illustrated 9-26
wing setting 9-7
wing stations 11-19
wire gauge
   types 13-6
word 8-23
wrench 13-10
   adjustable wrench 13-10
   box-end wrench 13-10
   combination wrench 13-10
   open-end wrench 13-10
   socket wrench 13-13
   spanner wrench 13-13
wye winding 4-17

X

x-axis 1-26

Y

yaw 9-13
yaw damper 9-15, 9-29
yawing 9-18
y-axis 1-26

Z

zener diode 4-20, 5-1, 6-1
zone numbers 11-18

Corrections, Suggestions for Improvement, Request for Additional Information

It is Avotek's goal to provide quality aviation maintenance resources to help you succeed in your career, and we appreciate your assistance in helping.

Please complete the following information to report a correction, suggestion for improvement, or to request additional information.

REFERENCE NUMBER (*To be assigned by Avotek*)		
CONTACT INFORMATION*		
Date		
Name		
Email		
Daytime Phone		
BOOK INFORMATION		
Title		
Edition		
Page number		
Figure/Table Number		
Discrepancy/Correction (*You may also attach a copy of the discrepancy/correction*)		
Suggestion(s) for Improvement (*Attach additional documentation as needed*)		
Request for Additional Information		
FOR AVOTEK USE ONLY	Date Received	
	Reference Number Issued By	
	Receipt Notification Sent	
	Action Taken/By	
	Completed Notification Sent	
*Contact information will only be used to provide updates to your submission or if there is a question regarding your submission.		

Send your corrections to:

- **Email:** comments@avotek.com
- **Fax:** 1-540-234-9399
- **Mail:** Corrections: Avotek Information Resources
  P.O. Box 219
  Weyers Cave, VA 24486 USA